INFAMOUS WOMAN

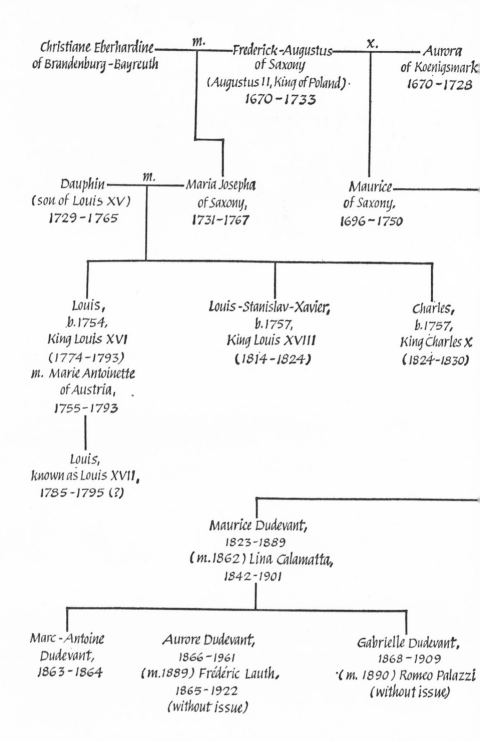

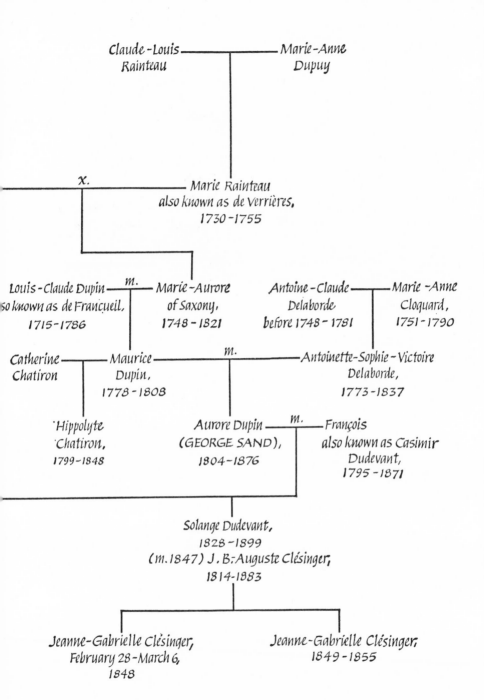

Books by *Joseph Barry*

LEFT BANK, RIGHT BANK
FRANCE
THE PEOPLE OF PARIS
PASSIONS AND POLITICS: A *Biography of Versailles*
INFAMOUS WOMAN: *The Life of George Sand*

INFAMOUS WOMAN

WOMAN

The Life of George Sand

JOSEPH BARRY

ANCHOR BOOKS

ANCHOR PRESS/DOUBLEDAY
GARDEN CITY, NEW YORK
1978

To Carine, Liliane, and Lola,
to all the women who spoke
when women were silent.

Originally published in hardcover
by Doubleday & Company, Inc. in 1977.

Anchor Books Edition: 1978

Recollections by Alexis de Tocqueville. Copyright © 1964 by Éditions Gallimard.
Reprinted by permission of Éditions Gallimard.

ISBN: 0-385-13366-9

Acknowledgments

Thanks would go if they could to Virginia Woolf and to Henry James for the insights of their androgynous sensibilities, as they go to less mortal institutions and their underpaid staffs. To the Bibliothèque Nationale and its Manuscript Division, where one turns the long, slim ledger pages of George Sand's diary and feels the *frisson* of death approaching, Manceau's and her own. To the most beautiful library I have known, the Bibliothèque Historique de la Ville de Paris, housed in the sixteenth-century Hôtel de Lamoignon with its high, painted-beam ceiling and tapestries, its superb lighting and formal garden, its priceless letters of George Sand and her intimates. To another great manor house north of Paris in Chantilly, the Lovenjoul library, with its manuscript treasures of the Romantic movement. To the women and men who care or have cared for all these treasures and open them to you.

To Georges Lubin, who reads proofs of his twelfth volume of George Sand's monumental *Correspondance* as he prepares the thirteenth and I write these lines. No one writing, talking or thinking about George Sand is not in debt to Georges Lubin, as kind and generous, scholarly and disarmingly honest a person as one might ever hope to meet. To Beverly Gordey for her warming encouragement. To Lisa Drew for her "virile," dry-point editing. To Robert Lescher for his professional guidance between the Charybdis of the market-place and the Scylla of, well, self-indulgence. To Evelyne Sullerot for her sociology of love and exquisite friendship. Above all to Liliane Lassen, whose collaboration made possible the indispensable man-woman dialogue underpinning and sustaining life, not to speak further of understanding George Sand.

Contents

List of Illustrations

Preface

"What will become of the world," Balzac once wondered, "when all women are like George Sand?" Henry James, more profoundly, extended the wonder to all people. It was not simply the new dimension Sand gave to "feminine nature," he observed in the gathering awareness of his own bisexuality, "but the richness that she adds to the masculine."

Wholeness is all. Men or women, we all seek it. "Only connect!" said E. M. Forster. Only connect the disparate parts of our alienated selves. "That was the whole of her sermon. Only connect the prose and the passion, and both will be exalted, and human love will be seen at its highest. Live in fragments no longer. Only connect . . ."

Forster was not talking of George Sand, but he might have been. To make whole the halves of her life in a land and time when women by law were lifetime minors was the achievement, the self-realization of that "infamous woman" who called herself George Sand. Beyond our own time, though she spoke out as a woman when women were silent, she transcended the male/female stereotypes. She was a lady who appropriated life exactly as if she were a man—and "exactly," said Henry James, "is not too much to say." Hers, moreover, was the creative, androgynous mind announced by Coleridge, the demonstration that one can be a gentle knight and no less "male," a strong woman and no less "female."

"This great man," said her great friend Flaubert. "The most womanly woman I have ever known," said her lover Musset. She was both father and mother, lover and nurse of another, the fragile, ailing, downy eaglet Frédéric Chopin.

George Sand's was completeness in another universal sense. "*Liebe und arbeit,*" said Freud, "love and work are the two pillars of man." George Sand was the author of some seventy novels and novellas, two dozen plays and several score essays. Collected, her work would total at least 150 volumes, twenty-five of which—with a thousand pages each— would contain her correspondence. She assured herself, by her work, not only a room of her own, but a room for her friends, in a château she sustained on her own, at Nohant.

It was not the flowing, expressional ease which alone forced the admiration of her contemporaries. Dostoievsky, when he first read George Sand—he tells us in his *Journal*—tossed that night in fevered excitement, and on her death in 1876, a month before her seventy-second birthday, he hailed the French writer as virtually mother of the Russian novel, an attitude warmly shared by Turgenev. Closer to home and our time, Henry James called George Sand "Goethe's sister"—a salute to the astonishing serenity of the later years. But George Sand was not Goethe's, nor Mozart's, nor Shakespeare's sister. She was George Sand.

Before James, Whitman listed Sand's *Consuelo* high among his few most precious books—but never acknowledged his full debt. Elizabeth Barrett wrote sonnets to the "large-brained woman and large-hearted man, self-called George Sand," and she and Robert paid her a visit in Paris, six years after Margaret Fuller's pilgrimage. The women of her time had no doubts about Sand's feminism, though a male biographer of our own, it seems, does. To be George Sand—to break the mold and become herself—was one of the most feminist actions of a century and a half. She was subject, not object, and in this sense was quintessentially the modern woman who goes beyond manifestoes to act out her life. George Sand is our existential contemporary.

Heinrich Heine placed her above Victor Hugo, and though Henrik Ibsen claimed he had never read her, his wife had read and reread her, and Nora is a very Sandian heroine, or rather hero, if not George Sand herself. She sent a shiver through John Stuart Mill, "like a symphony of Haydn or Mozart," but she also sent a "shudder" through Baudelaire ("she is heavy, she is garrulous"). And now we are prematurely in our own time and deep in the modern esthetic with its distaste for Romantic excess, its gusto, values and vitality. Or is there an eternal return?

Perhaps the superlatives defeat our purpose. The summoning of contemporary praise may bury George Sand rather than recall her to life, the cataloguing of achievements smother the very act of accomplishment—the earlier, struggling years, the slow self-creation of the woman who called herself George Sand. This biography attempts, ventures on, that voyage of discovery with the inevitable baggage of oneself, much of it to be discarded on the trip, for it is a voyage of self-discovery as well.

The rich complexity and ambiguities, the tangle of truths, insights and cover-ups emerge, particularly in Georges Lubin's continuing, devoted publication of George Sand's *Correspondance*, intact and complete. Biographers in the past have sought a single, esthetically satisfying key. André Maurois, for instance, however sympathetically, somewhat coyly suggested a "nymphomaniacal frigidity." He was followed more recently by another biographer who applied the more modish label of "nympholepsy" while also affirming a "basic frigidity." Both based themselves precariously on Sand's very early novel *Lélia* and the Comte de Grandsagne's summary conclusion in 1900 on reading the now missing letters to his father, Stéphane de Grandsagne, a very early lover.

The sexual passion in the resumed love affair with Musset is evidenced in Sand's *Journal Intime*. It smolders in the relationship with actress Marie Dorval and flames in the letters to Michel de Bourges, to whom George galloped one long, frosty night to spend "one instant" in his arms. Or is a *nymphomane*—and therefore a frigid woman?—for these gentlemen simply any woman who takes men as men for millennia have taken women?

But even this demonstration of George Sand's capacity for love can be overdrawn and overdone. As with Byron, a figure so comparable one would be tempted to call her a Lady Byron were it possible to define her through any man, the story of George Sand is not the story of her loves, unless they are expanded and extended to all her passions, of the mind as of the heart and body, from the political to the maternal, from self-fulfillment to *engagement* and commitment to the oppressed, men as well as women.

"For the aristocracy of the intellect she had always the deepest veneration," Oscar Wilde perceptively remarked, "but the democracy of suffering touched her more." From Paris to Moscow George Sand was a powerful and moving social force. Her novels alone passed through the czarist police border, smuggling in the heady, fragrant air of French socialism, feminism and republican revolt. In 1848 she was the Muse of the Revolution.

The very volume of her writing and the unfolding of her correspondence, published and unpublished, provide the crucial elements for understanding the phenomenon of George Sand and thereby that much more about her century—if not our own *fin de siècle*—and the condition of the creative woman, her relations with creative or commonplace men, with other women, with herself.

There are falsifications and untruths, as in the postdated letters to Musset. They also occur in Sand's memoirs, *Histoire de Ma Vie*. Here a minimum of sensibility seems called for. She was a mother as well as George Sand, a woman as well as a writer, and in her time—at least—no woman could be quite as frank as a man—as Musset, for instance, about his whoring in *Confession d'un Enfant du Siècle* or Byron of his bisexuality in his letters, because neither fact has ever greatly damaged or diminished either, but rather substantiated his "virility" or "universality." And neither has ever been dismissed for "satyriasis."

George Sand's "fidelity?" She was too faithful to herself to be faithful to the men of her time. Fidelity to oneself is the very theme of living an unfragmented life, a connection that must be made before any other can be made. The torsion of our culture, the tension of contrived and received differences, has torn men and women apart, despite another vision extending from Plato to Rilke and Virginia Woolf—the poet-philosopher's conception of the wholeness of a human being before the split at birth into man and woman, each half destined to search for and hopefully rejoin the other. It is a wholeness beyond sexuality, but as in George Sand's case always in the inclusive sense. "And perhaps," as Rilke wrote to a young poet,

> the sexes are more related than we think, and the great renewal of the world will perhaps consist in this, that man and maid, freed from all false feeling and aversion, will seek each other not as opposites, but as brother and sister, as neighbors, and will come together as human beings.

And perhaps it has required the hundred years since her death to appreciate the greatest of George Sand's achievements—her life. She did not simply indicate but in part courageously, even heroically, cleared the way.

INFAMOUS WOMAN

1

Past as Prologue

> The dead are alive in us.
> —*Correspondance*
> (1848) George Sand

George Sand, descendant of a Saxon king of Poland and of a French bird-seller, was born Aurore Dupin, July 1, 1804, in a poor quarter of Paris.

She was never certain of the day of her birth, but she knew, early enough in life, that had her father and mother not married a month before (twenty-six days, to be precise), she might have borne her mother's family name, Delaborde.[1]* Illegitimacy, however, was scarcely more of a moral concern in the immediate post-revolutionary years than it was during the pre-1789 *ancien régime* of the Bourbon monarchy.

She was conscious of her double "heritage," but there is no record of early snobbery, and George Sand would later write: "The royal blood in my veins was lost in mingling with the plebeian blood of my mother's womb."[2]

In her memoirs she began with her maternal grandfather, who sold birds on a Paris quai, and regrets her inability to take the maternal line back further ("nobles have captured the notion of ancestors"[3]). But ancestors, for a variety of reasons, capture the first *third* of George Sand's memoirs.[4]

The question of "blood lines" and "legacies" apart, however, there was George Sand's instructive novelist's sense of the past, of the passionate adventures and misadventures of her extraordinary forebears, which constitutes her *felt* heritage. "The dead," she wrote her publisher

---

* Notes, principally bibliographical, commence on p. 385. Exceptionally, the reader's attention is drawn to Note 1, which describes the two-volume Pléiade edition of George Sand's autobiographical writings and cites the source for the comment on the day of her birth and the wedding date of her parents.

as she probed her childhood, "are alive in us. That is certain. There is a mysterious link feeding our lives with theirs."[5]

And there was, too, her sense of history. In recounting the story of five generations—from Aurora von Königsmark to Aurore de Saxe to Aurore Dupin by way of sons, each named Maurice—George (Aurore Dupin) Sand led her reader to the historical situation into which she was thrust, to the conditioned societal relations of men with men, women with women, and each with the other, which she would challenge, and challenging, begin to change.

"All existences," she wrote in the middle of her journey into the past,

> are joined, one to the other, and the human being who presents his or her life as isolated, as unbound to that of his or her fellow-creature, offers naught but an enigma for unraveling. . . . I could not recount or explain my life without having recounted or explained that of my forebears. It is as necessary for the history of individuals as for the history of the human race. To read an isolated page on the Revolution or the Empire is to understand nothing about either, unless you know all antecedent history; and to understand the Revolution and the Empire, you will still have to know the history of humanity. Here I recount an intimate story. Humanity has its own intimate history in the story of its individuals. I must, then, embrace a period of about a hundred years to recount forty years of my own life.[6]

Maria Aurora von Königsmark was a Swedish countess described by Voltaire as having been "the most famous woman [of wit and beauty] of two centuries." Born in 1662, she entered the story of her great-great-granddaughter Aurore Dupin—George Sand—at the age of thirty-two by passage through Saxony in pursuit of a missing brother. In fact, Philipp von Königsmark had been murdered in ambush and buried in secrecy. He had fallen rashly in love with the wife of the Elector of Hanover (eventually George I of England). Jilted, jealous, middle-aged Countess Platen, whom he had been courting, had him assassinated in his beloved's castle, where she too was a guest, and "as he lay dying," she had "waddled down the Hall and stamped on his mouth with her foot."[7]

Aurora von Königsmark sought information in Dresden from her brother's friend, Frederick Augustus, Elector of adjacent Saxony. It is no proof of her beauty that she caught his eye. "While he is in the humour," wrote a chronicler, "the first woman that offers is sure of his caresses."[8] He was "the most extraordinarily debauched man of his time," says George Sand,[9] distant descendant of a debauchery that, by the end of Frederick Augustus' life, was estimated tentatively by his chancellor as having left behind three hundred and fifty-five bastards and one legitimate son.[10] By all accounts the most splendid among the illegitimate was the child born to the Swedish countess in 1696, Maurice, Comte de Saxe, future Marshal of France.

But it was Maurice's mother, Aurora von Königsmark, who held George Sand's attention. As she began her memoirs, she mused on her ancestor's portrait in her bedroom at Nohant—"the portrait of a lady still young and strikingly beautiful in tone."[11] The bright black eyes, the high, smooth forehead, the dark complexion and tresses, "as black as ink," foreshadow George Sand's own; and she engaged the first Aurore in a silent dialogue*:

> She seems to tell me, "What nonsense is cluttering your poor brain, degenerate sprout of my proud race? With what wild fantasy of equality are you filling your dreams? Love is not what you think. Men will never be what you hope. They are made to be deceived by kings, by women, by themselves."

Told that Maria Aurora had been unfaithful while he was off to war (the story of the Swedish countess continues), Frederick Augustus, who had meantime married, reproached his mistress on his return. Caesar's wife, he said, should be above suspicion. He was not Caesar, Maria Aurora coolly replied, and she was not his wife. She was shortly no longer his lover, though it was at this time she gave birth to their son Maurice. The following year (1697) Augustus was elected King of Poland. As the infant was fetched to Warsaw, Aurora was banished to the Protestant Abbey of Quedlinburg, where she soon won the worldly post of co-adjutrix.

Not long afterward, however, Augustus had need of her. Charles XII of Sweden had descended on Poland as its "liberator," and was at the door of success. Frederick sent for Aurora as someone "more capable than any minister of bringing off successful negotiations." The admiring phrase is Voltaire's. When Charles XII, whom Aurora had known at the Swedish court, refused to see her, she had waylaid him along a narrow path where he was accustomed to ride. "The king had saluted her without saying a word, turned his horse round and retreated on the spot. As a result, the Countess von Königsmark returned with the sole satisfaction of being able to say that the King of Sweden feared no one but herself."[12]

At the age of twelve Maurice was sent by his father to serve in Flanders during the War of the Spanish Succession. It was early in life, even for the period, but Maurice was an exceptionally robust boy and it was his ambition, virtually since he began to toddle, to become a sol-

---

* Throughout her writing, noted Henry James, George Sand interviews herself.

dier. War, after all, was the profession and opportunity for one of his high but illegitimate birth. His escort was told that the young lad must bear his own musket and "march on foot" with the infantry.[13] Thus legend has Maurice marching across Europe on foot to Flanders, though the retinue given him by his father included a campaigning coach, a dozen mules, four horses and a number of servants, among them, to his chagrin, a tutor.[14]

When fifteen, Maurice returned to Saxony, was acknowledged Augustus' son and given the title Count of Saxony (Comte de Saxe). There would never be a question of his bravery. At Mons he would lead his men into a freezing river and pistol down an enemy; in Pomerania he had a horse shot from under him. "You must learn the difference between foolhardiness and courage," Prince Eugène admonished.[15] When sixteen, he was made Commander of the King's Cuirassiers and married to the richest heiress of Saxony. He ran through her fortune and went off to war, now against the Swedes, now against the Turks. "A wife," he would explain years later to Madame de Pompadour, "is a useless bit of baggage for a soldier."[16] The remark is unquoted by George Sand, though she writes of her great-grandfather that he was "as brave as his father, but no less debauched."[17]

In the spring of 1720, Maurice de Saxe rode down to Paris to pursue his military career. He was quickly at home in the libertinism of the Regency and was named Field Marshal of the French Army, then the finest in Europe. His father bought him a regiment of German mercenaries which became the famous Saxe Regiment. He impressed Paris with his masterly drilling on the Champ de Mars, Parisians with his splendid uniform of a leopard skin slung across a black cuirass. He mastered tactics, siege strategy and France's leading actress, Adrienne Lecouvreur. She was thirty, he twenty-four. "It was said of the future victor of Fontenoy that his beautiful mistress taught him all he knew save the art of war (which he knew already) and the art of spelling (which he never learned)."[18]

But Maurice de Saxe wearied of peace, therefore of Adrienne and Paris, and when the vacant throne of Courland (Latvia) beckoned, he went off to Warsaw for support of his candidacy. His mistress and his mother pawned jewels, silver and carriages to send him money. While Maurice roved Europe trying to hire mercenaries, however, his mother died at Quedlinburg, exhausted by efforts in his behalf, leaving him all she possessed—fifty-two crowns.[19]

The Courland cause eventually lost, Maurice de Saxe nonetheless returned to Paris a hero. He whiled away his time designing new weapons of war, among them a hinged pontoon bridge, and putting together a compendium on military and other matters, *Mes Rêveries*, which would be carried by Wellington, scorned by Napoleon, and admired by his great-granddaughter. But oddly, George Sand does not cite a few remarkably pertinent reveries: "Marriage in the future should be for five years and renewable only by special dispensation, unless a child has been born during that period. . . . If women had the right to choose the husband they wished for as long as they wanted, everything would be more natural."[20] Rather, she refers to Maurice de Saxe's comparative humanitarianism—spies were to be put in chains and not summarily hung—and his advanced social views—"society is an assemblage of the oppressors and the oppressed," and it is from the latter that the former "make their soldiers." As for his "debaucheries, . . . they were of his time and his upbringing," and George Sand quotes an unidentifiable historian as saying, " 'the women of the time, too, contributed to them greatly.' "[21]

Poor, "contributing" Adrienne Lecouvreur died a sad, tubercular death, though poison by a rival was popularly suspected.[22] The French Regent died and Louis XV became king. Frederick Augustus died and France entered the War of the Polish Succession. For a few months Louis XV's father-in-law occupied the Polish throne. Maurice de Saxe now led the French against the Saxons, led by his half brother, who was his father's successor. The War of the Polish Succession dribbled to an end, the War of the Austrian Succession took its place and Maurice de Saxe, in the process, took Prague. At forty-seven he was named full Marshal of France's armies, though he was German, a bastard, and Protestant. At Fontenoy he masterminded a victory over British and Hanoverian troops that "gave the French monarchy," in Napoleon's expert judgment, "a forty-year reprieve."[23]

In gratitude the French monarch granted Maurice de Saxe the château of Chambord for the lifetime remaining him. Settling into the huge, turreted castle, second only to the Versailles palace in size (it had seventy-four staircases and four hundred and forty rooms), the Marshal created a small private kingdom behind a thirty-two-kilometer-long wall. He even arranged the marriage of his niece, Maria Josepha of Saxony (Marie-Josèphe de Saxe), as the Dauphin's second wife, thus securing himself more solidly in Catholic France. She would mother the last three French Bourbon kings—Louis XVI, Louis XVIII and Charles X—whom George Sand's grandmother, Marie-Aurore, would call cousins. And *she* was born to Maurice de Saxe the same memorable year (1748) as his last impressive gesture, the capture of Maastricht.

Brightening the Flemish campaign had been a theatrical company regularly entertaining Saxe and his men. (Once he had loaned his troupe to the opposing general.[24]) They would perform in the evening; as an epilogue, the leading actress would step forward prettily and announce the next day's program—if not a play, then a battle, to be put on by the Marshal. Prettiest and freshest of the actresses may have been seventeen-year-old Marie Rainteau, for she became Marshal de Saxe's official mistress and was established, together with her younger sister Geneviève, in a house in Paris. It was a happy twist of a nudged fortune's wheel, a social climb for the daughters of a pubkeeper soon permitting them the lofty sobriquet, les Demoiselles de Verrières.

Gently, mistakenly, George Sand refers to Marie Rainteau-Verrières as a "*dame de* l'Opéra,"[25] but so she might have heard from her grandmother, for Marie-Aurore was born from Marie Rainteau's liaison with Maurice de Saxe.

The baptismal certificate of October 19, 1748, reads, however: "Marie-Aurore, daughter of Jean-Baptiste de La Rivière, *bourgeois de Paris*, and Marie Rainteau, his wife."[26] La Rivière was a man of fiction, or straw, and George Sand would duly note it, remarking, "The story is a curious picture of the customs and morals of the time."[27]

A contemporary poet-playwright, Marmontel, filled in the picture, and colored it. Marie Rainteau "de Verrières," with ambitions as an actress, had sought lessons from Marmontel "in declamation," shortly after the birth of Marie-Aurore. Marmontel, his *Mémoires* unabashedly tell one, had just previously inherited another actress-mistress of the Marshal: "Monsieur de Saxe had found Mlle. Navarre too haughty, too lacking in abandon or desire to please. Mlle. Verrières, on the other hand, never tired him with tantrums about her rivals. Infinitely less artificial, she relied only on her beauty, adding nothing but good humor and the indolence of being easy to love. . . . This assiduity of my pupil made *me* assiduous, but my assiduity was maliciously misrepresented to the Maréchal [Marshal], who was then away in Prussia. His rage was not worthy of such a great man. He suppressed the fifty louis a month he allowed Mlle. Verrières and swore never to set eyes on her or her child again. He kept his word."[28]

With an irony that is as well lost, Marmontel recounted the furious Saxe telling everybody—"the Court, the King himself, that this insolent little poet was taking all his mistresses," blandly adding, "After all I had only those he no longer wanted."[29] Marie de Verrières, however, was not long Marmontel's. As, Saxe unknowing, she had been the mistress of Denis-Joseph d'Épinay, son of a rich tax collector, so more publicly, after Marmontel, she became mistress of Duc de Bouillon (their son would be Abbé, eventually Monseigneur, de Beaumont).*

Years later, Monsieur d'Épinay, inheriting his father's fortune and

---

* Madame d'Épinay, future benefactress of Jean-Jacques Rousseau, is worth more than a pause. After but three months of marriage, she had been scolded by her mother for reproaching her husband his spending the nights with a mistress (not yet Marie de Verrières). "My mother called me a child," Madame d'Épinay records, "she said I had conducted myself indecently . . . that my husband was quite properly offended . . . and I myself felt like a child."[30]

post, would return to Marie's life, setting her up with her sister in a house then in the Paris suburbs (now 45 Rue d'Auteuil) after having rented another for them in Paris. By then, too, Madame d'Épinay, resigned to the customs of the times, would be the mistress of the gifted, charming and wealthy Claude Dupin de Francueil, a frequenter of the Verrières sisters, a friend of Épinay and the future grandfather of George Sand.

By then, as well, Maurice de Saxe would have long disappeared.

Consistent to the end in his pursuit of a kingdom larger than a château park—was he not son of a king and half brother to another?—he petitioned Louis XV for the sovereignty of Madagascar. That refused, he formed a scheme for transporting the oppressed of the Old World to the New: he would be King of the Jews in America. But he had burned himself out in war and dissipation, and he died at Chambord in 1750 at the age of fifty-four. "I see now," he told his doctor as he lay dying, "that life is only a dream. Mine was beautiful, but it was short."[31] It may be significant only of a later period's Romanticism—and in no other sense revealing—that his great-granddaughter George Sand should reverse the last words of Saxe, "My life was short, but it was beautiful."[32]

As for the Verrières sisters: their houses flourished. They had a *salle de spectacles* installed in their Paris *hôtel* (town house) and a complete theater in the garden of their house at Auteuil. Marie was bright, accommodating and sufficiently cultivated to attract intelligent as well as "galant" men. Geneviève, too, had her patrons (particularly Dupin de Francueil). The two sisters, in the eyes of a contemporary, were "the Aspasias of the century."[33]

In fact, they were the fortunate and envied of their social class: they were free from poverty and the police—they had succeeded in the scramble to find rich protectors. Moreover, theirs were the luxuries, comforts and at least the outer trappings of the aristocracy, and "the respect they won from the world gave them a kind of self-respect"; they were the "flower," the incarnation, of the eighteenth-century's cynicism, "lending elegance to debauchery, even grandeur to vice," and men of the world pressed for admission to their spectacles and their presence.[34]

It was in this world, this "corrupt world," that Marie-Aurore spent her first years, but "without," continues George Sand, "losing a single feather of her wing."[35] Actually, Marie-Aurore's experience of her mother's and aunt's demimonde was interrupted when she was seven by a long interval at a choice convent school, and it was tempered by the fact that she was the daughter, albeit illegitimate, of Maréchal de Saxe. Indeed, the Marshal's nephew and heir, Count von Friesen, who had settled in France, paid her an annual *pension* (allowance), which the Dauphine, the Marshal's niece, supplemented.

Wherefore, when cousin Friesen died in 1755, seven-year-old Marie-Aurore's petition to cousin Marie-Josèph de Saxe:

"Madame, la demoiselle Aurore, natural and unique daughter of Monsieur le Maréchal de Saxe, throws herself at the feet of Madame la Dauphine. Abandoned since the death of Monsieur le Comte de Frise [Friesen], who had supported her until now, she has no resources other than the generosity of Madame la Dauphine. She humbly beseeches her to take pity on her childhood and poverty, and to deign ask for a *pension* for her, so that she might find refuge and a place to be educated."[36]

The Dauphine transmitted Aurore's petition through the Dauphin to the Minister of War—since it concerned a former marshal's daughter—who tendered it to the King. And on May 23, 1755, an approving note was appended to the petition:

"The King accords an annual *pension* of 800 francs for la demoiselle Aurore, so long as she remains in a convent chosen by Madame la Dauphine, who will supervise her education; and His Majesty further grants the sum of 600 francs for her trousseau for that convent."[37]*

A police note, found among the papers of the Bastille, records that Madame de Chalut, lady in waiting of the Dauphine, came "to the Verrières house" and took Aurore from her mother, "who could not be more surprised."[38] She was first taken to a convent at Saint-Cloud, where Madame de Chalut had a country house. Then "la demoiselle Aurore" was admitted to the convent school at Saint-Cyr, founded in 1686 by the pietistic Madame de Maintenon for the indigent but proud daughters of French nobility, which became "the best girls' school in France," its graduates "everywhere in demand."[39] Little wonder. The girls rose at six, went to Mass at eight, and woe to the one whose eye wandered or whose body slouched. Classrooms followed until midday, then from two to six. Bedtime was at 9 P.M. The routine was virtually the same for a century.

In 1766, when Aurore was almost eighteen and her time had arrived to leave Saint-Cyr, the Dauphine could hardly return her to her mother's household, so a suitable husband was sought. But what husband might be found for a *"fille naturelle de père et mère inconnus"* (a natural child of parents unknown)?[40] Again Aurore's recourse was a petition, on this occasion to the magistrates of the Paris Parlement, that "instead of the names of Jean-Baptiste de La Rivière, *bourgeois de Paris*, and Marie Rainteau, his wife, there should henceforth be written after the name of the petitioner—'natural daughter of Maurice, Comte de Saxe, Maréchal-Général of the Armies of France, and Marie Rain-

---

* For 1977 dollar equivalents, figure approximately $2.30 for the livre or franc.

teau.' "[41] Parlement approved, the birth certificate was correspondingly altered. Aurore was respectable and marriageable. She might even aid the career of a husband, because of her established relationship to the Dauphine.

Infantry Captain Antoine de Horne, forty-four, was found. His antecedents were sufficiently honorable, but it is more than doubtful that he was "Louis XV's bastard," as George Sand has written. For it to be true, he would have had to be fathered by an eleven-year-old Louis XV. Throughout the lively account in *Histoire de Ma Vie*, there are similar touches of fantasy, in part George Sand's, in major part, perhaps, her grandmother's. It is not true that the marriage was never consummated and ended with the death of Aurore's husband, "Count" de Horne, in a duel three weeks after.[42]

On the evening of the wedding, Marie de Verrières gave her daughter a splendid reception at the house in Auteuil, on which occasion Aurore first met her half brother, Abbé de Beaumont, George Sand's granduncle. As a royal wedding gift, Captain de Horne was named the King's Lieutenant, or Governor, at Sélestat in Alsace. *Five months* passed, however, before the couple reached the destined post, and there within a week Horne died, "despite repeated bleedings, of a congestion of the chest."[43]

Thus widowed at eighteen, again Aurore petitioned the King for aid, but the Dauphine, at the point of death, was no longer in a position to help, and royal aid was refused (as well as Aurore's request that she replace her husband as the King's Lieutenant at Sélestat!). And again, instead of returning to her mother's demimonde, Aurore betook herself to a Paris convent and sent off another petition, this time to the Minister of War, Duke de Choiseul:

"I am the daughter of the Maréchal de Saxe and have been recognized as such by the Parlement of Paris. . . . I am certain that the Minister who directs the War Ministry with so much wisdom, charity, and brilliance . . . will not permit the daughter of the Maréchal de Saxe to languish any longer in poverty."[44]

But the Duke would and did, and Aurore wrote to Voltaire for aid:

"It is to the poet of Fontenoy that the daughter of the Maréchal de Saxe addresses herself to obtain her bread. . . . I have been abandoned and I throw myself into your arms. You have a sense of humanity, you love the glory of your fatherland, you will be stricken to see the daughter of your hero in the most dreadful poverty."[45]

From his retreat at Ferney, near the Swiss border, Voltaire wrote Aurore, September 7, 1768:

"I shall shortly be joining the hero who is your father and I will tell him with indignation the condition of his daughter. . . . If I were in your place, I should present myself to Duchesse de Choiseul."[46]

With little hope and no success Aurore followed Voltaire's advice. Three years later she was petitioning Duke de Choiseul's successor:

"I am the daughter of the Maréchal de Saxe and have been recognized as such by the Parlement of Paris. . . . Finding it impossible to pay my board at the convent where I had sought shelter, I have been obliged to leave it."[47]

Indeed, Aurore had left for the household of her mother and aunt, her reluctance apparent in her petition. But her plea was successful; her allowance of eight hundred francs was doubled. Now at least Aurore had a modicum of independence in the Verrières twilight world.

The sisters "lived agreeably with the insouciance" of the promiscuous period, "cultivating the muses, as people then said." They put on their entertainments and Aurore participated. She "had an angelic beauty," her granddaughter continues, "a superior intelligence, a solid education equal to that of the most enlightened of her time; and this intelligence was cultivated and developed further by the commerce, conversation, and entourage of her mother. She had moreover a magnificent voice and I have never known a finer musician."[48]

Aurore sang the role of Colette in Rousseau's *Devin du Village*, appeared in the operas of Grétry and the plays of Sedaine, delighting the *galants* who crowded her mother's little theater. And during her own childhood, George Sand recalled her grandmother picking out her favorite airs from Porpora, Hasse or Pergolese with "two or three fingers of her paralyzed hands," and their singing together

> *Non mi dir, bel idol mio,*
> *Non mi dir ch' io son ingrato,*

from Mozart's *Don Giovanni*.

Among her mother's *habitués* Aurore's closest friends were the naturalist Buffon and increasingly Dupin de Francueil. But she moved among her courters unmoved by their courting, her coolness more a matter of temperament than religion, "knowing none other than the deism of Jean-Jacques Rousseau and Voltaire." However, "she was a woman of great strength of mind—clear-headed and imbued with a certain ideal of pride and self-respect. She disdained coquetry; she was too gifted to need it. Sly, provocative tricks offended her principles and accustomed dignity. She traversed a licentious period and a corrupt world without the loss of a single feather of her wing. Condemned by a strange destiny never to know love in marriage, she had resolved the problem of how to live without passion, beyond gossip and slander."[49]

Prudently Aurore petitioned again for an increase in her *pension*, and owing to a Saxon cousin who interceded in her behalf, it was again doubled; just in time, for her mother, at forty-five, died quietly in an armchair, "complaining only of cold feet."[50] And once again Aurore, now twenty-seven, retired to a convent, the eminent, respectable Dames du Calvaire, where she paid sixteen hundred francs a year, or her entire royal *pension*, for herself and her *femme de chambre*. Here Dupin de Francueil came frequently on visit and despite, or thanks to, his advanced age ("we at the convent called him *papa*," Aurore wrote an acquaintance[51]), she did not discourage his suit.[52] For some reason, possibly because of her aunt Geneviève (Dupin's all-too-recent mistress), the two were married discreetly at the French embassy in London, Dupin then sixty-one, Aurore twenty-nine. The ceremony was repeated religiously in Paris and almost to the day, a year after the London wedding, a son, Maurice—George Sand's future father—was born, January 13, 1778.

Her grandmother often spoke to George Sand of the grandfather Sand never knew. "She told me that for the ten years they lived together he and her son were the greatest attachments of her life. And though she never employed the word *love* (I never heard it from her lips about anyone), she smiled when she heard me say that it seemed impossible to love an old man.

'An old man loves more deeply than a young one,' she said, 'and it is impossible not to love one who loves you to perfection. I called him "papa" and "my old husband." He wanted it so and he always called me his daughter, even in public. Besides,' she added, 'was one ever old in those days? It is the Revolution that brought old age into the world. Your grandfather, my dear, was handsome, elegant, soigné, gracious, perfumed, lively, amiable, affectionate and good-humored until the hour of his death. When he was younger, he was too social to be satisfied with so quiet a life, and I should not have been as happy with him—I would have had too many rivals. I am convinced that I had the best time of his life and that never has a young man rendered a young woman as happy as I was. We never parted for a moment and never did I experience a moment of boredom with him. He was an encyclopedia of ideas, knowledge and talents, and it was inexhaustible for me. He had the gift of always knowing how to please others while he was pleasing himself.

During the day we made music together. He was an excellent violinist; he made his own instruments. But he was not only a violin-maker, he was also a watchmaker, architect, painter, locksmith, decorator, cook, poet, composer, woodworker and embroiderer! I do not know what he was not. He spent his fortune, it is true, satisfying his many tastes and indulging in so many experiments. But I saw only his brilliance and we ruined ourselves in the most pleasant ways imaginable. In the evenings, when we were not at a party, he would sketch at my side as I unraveled fabrics, and we would take turns reading to each other. Or sometimes charming friends would descend on us and exercise his fine, fertile mind with witty conversation. I had many young friends who had made more brilliant marriages, but they never tired of telling me how much they envied me my "old husband."

'In those days,' she continued, 'people knew how to live and how to die. There was no "demanding" illness. If one had the gout, one walked regardless, and one never pulled a face. We were taught to hide our pains. We did not have those commercial preoccupations of today which mar private life and muddy one's mind. We knew how to meet ruin without showing it, like gamblers who lose everything without a sign of disquiet or regret. We would rather have been carried half dead to a hunt than miss it. We thought it better to die while at a ball or a play than in one's bed between four candles and a few dreary men in black. We were philosophers. We did not play at austerity, though at times we experienced it. When one showed restraint, it was a matter of taste, not pedantry or prudery. We enjoyed life and when the time came to leave it, we did not want to spoil the pleasure of life for the living. And when my old husband took his last farewell, he made me promise to live as long and happily as possible. To show so generous a heart in dying was a sure way of being truly mourned.'

"To be sure," George Sand adds, "that philosophy of wealth, independence, tolerance and grace was pleasant and appealing, but one had to have an income of five or six hundred thousand francs a year to sustain it, and I can not see how the poor or the oppressed could ever have felt that philosophy as their own."[53]

In essence, relating her grandmother's story allowed George Sand to describe with some nostalgia the sweetness of life for the aristocrat before the Revolution. Her grandparents had spent, or squandered, most of their estate, but they had certainly not thought it misspent. They had patronized and enjoyed the arts, entertained their friends, and had even counted the fascinating, romantically agonizing Jean-Jacques Rousseau among them.

In the end, when Dupin de Francueil died on the eve of the Revolution, he left his wife and eight-year-old son a yearly income of seventy-five thousand francs, and his widow quite calmly called herself "ruined,"[54] as, in fact, as her world came to an end, she well might have.

2

Sons as Lovers

I am at times under a strange illusion. I think of myself as
the mother, rather than the daughter, of my father.
—Lines deleted by George Sand in her manuscript
for *Histoire de Ma Vie*[1]

The *ancien régime*, the old order itself, would be several years in its
dying.

Leaving the grand château overlooking the Indre River at
Châteauroux, where the late Monsieur Dupin had resided as tax collector, cloth manufacturer and *bon vivant*, Madame Dupin resumed
life with son Maurice in Paris—in the family apartment on the Rue du
Roi-de-Sicile, a thousand yards from the Bastille.[2]

The apartment was large, the income sufficient, so they managed,
particularly after the odd, devoted, remarkably Chekhovian François
Deschartres, tonsured and self-styled "Abbé," was taken on in 1787 as
Maurice's tutor. Twenty-six at the time, Deschartres was born the son of
a lime burner and haphazardly educated to the point of "bumptious
pedantry" and pretentious "omnicompetence," uniting "all the virtues
of a good soul with the insupportable character of one who has carried
self-satisfaction to the heights of delirium." But he would prove a "bargain package of lifetime savior, friend and tyrant" for three generations
of the Dupin family.[3]

Maurice was an indolent pupil of delicate health, sheltered from
Deschartres' tutorial tyranny by the protective adoration of an aging,
twice-widowed mother. "He was raised," says his daughter George
Sand, "quite literally in cotton . . . so that he would ring for his servant to pick up a fallen pen or pencil."[4] But he would change, she
rather hurriedly adds, to become a soldier and hero of the new revolutionary Republic.

As for the Revolution and Madame Dupin, George Sand describes
her grandmother as one of the "enlightened aristocrats of her time who

watched it approach without fear. She had been too nourished on Voltaire and Rousseau not to detest the abuses of the Court, and was one of those most ardently opposed to the Queen's coterie." At the age of twenty, George Sand reveals with regret, in a sudden "access of prudery," she had burned the more scurrilous pamphlets of her grandmother's collection (presumably those accusing Marie Antoinette of "*fureurs utérines*").[5] But there is her own mature attitude towards the Revolution as the "violent struggle to establish the principle of equality preached by Christ . . . against the old pagan world which has not yet been destroyed."[6]

But not a word about the part played by women, though it was the women of Paris who had marched in the rain by the thousands to fetch Louis XVI and Marie Antoinette back to the French capital in October 1789. They were the avant-garde. "Without women," said Mirabeau, "there would be no Revolution." In 1793, however, the National Convention banned women's clubs and Robespierre ruled that "assemblies of more than five women" were illegal. The few women's rights before the Revolution were abolished during it; the militants among them were disturbing the new order, as they had the old. Olympe de Gouges, who remarked that if women had a right to the guillotine, they had a right to the tribune, would "enjoy" both rights.[7]

Madame Dupin could hear, if she could not quite see from her windows, the taking of the Bastille on July 14, 1789, and "she joined her cheers with those of its victors among whom, with her approval, were several of her own domestics."[8] But as the violent disputes between opposing revolutionary factions increased and the Reign of Terror drew near, Madame Dupin discreetly moved her household to the more distant Rue de Bondy near the boulevards.

Disenchantment had preceded the move; so had indiscretion. Madame Dupin had contributed seventy-five thousand francs to a "secret" fund for the émigré Count d'Artois, future King Charles X. Perhaps, suggests George Sand, it was because her grandmother, after all, was "the cousin of Louis XVI and his brothers," the younger of whom was Count d'Artois.[9] Indeed, Madame Dupin might have emigrated, as did so many aristocrats, but instead she sought another refuge. On August 23, 1793, she purchased a country estate including a small château and two hundred and fifty hectares, among them three farms, for two hundred and thirty thousand francs.[10] Located in the province of Berry, twenty miles southeast of Châteauroux, where she had last known happiness, the estate was adjacent to the hamlet of Nohant and would assume its name.[11]

On the site once stood a fourteenth-century château, of which two small towers alone survived when Pierre-Philippe Péarron, Seigneur de Sérennes, had acquired it in 1767. But even as he completed a large manor house in the contemporary Louis XVI style, he saw something "so little reassuring in the faces of his peasants,"[12] he gladly sold it to Madame Dupin and departed for Paris, where he hoped to be less conspicuous. A southern garden wall blocking the horizon would be removed, the small moat filled in, a vegetable garden installed, but the limes and old shade elms were left intact, and several elms still stand like venerable sentinels in the square before the carriage entrance.

Before Madame Dupin could take possession of her country refuge at Nohant, however, events would overtake her.

The apartment to which she had moved on the Rue de Bondy was in the house of a Monsieur Amonnin, former valet of Count d'Artois. He easily persuaded Madame Dupin to hide her silver service and jewelry, together with his own valuables, in a hole between the wood paneling and masonry wall of one of the apartments. A decree aimed at such practices was implemented by a promise to any informer of a twentieth the value of whatever was found.[13] Citizen Villard, perhaps one of the workers who had dug the hiding place, disclosed it to the local Revolutionary Committee of the Bon Conseil Section.

On November 25, 1793, there was a descent on the Rue de Bondy house, the valuables were discovered, "Citizeness" Dupin was arrested.[14] She was taken to the Convent of the English Augustinians, which had been converted into a prison. Maurice, fifteen, and Deschartres, now "Citizen," not "Abbé," Deschartres, were permitted to remain in the apartment. Incompletely searched, the other apartments were put under seal.

More than prison threatened Madame Dupin, Deschartres well knew, if certain papers as yet unearthed, including acknowledgment of the contribution to Count d'Artois, were found. Deschartres that same night resolved to get the papers and destroy them. He was working on the wax seals. He heard a noise. It was young Maurice come to aid him. Together they continued, found some of the incriminating papers and burned them. There remained only time for resealing the doors before the morning guard arrived. They returned the next night and burned the rest of the papers, "putting the ashes in a box which they took away with them."[15]

And once again Madame Dupin put her hand to a petition. From her convent prison she addressed the Revolutionary Committee of Public Safety: "Citizens of the Republic, do not prove insensible to the sorrows of a mother torn from her son, from the child she has nourished from whom she has never been separated until this day, and whom she has raised to serve the fatherland. . . . Since the very first days of the Revolution, my conduct under every circumstance, my good will for the general welfare, must surely remove me from all suspicion. Moreover, not a single relative, either near or far, has emigrated. I myself might have fled to a foreign land with all my fortune, then entirely at my disposal, but my spirit of independence found it too repugnant to breathe the corrupt air abroad of slavery."[16]

And Madame Dupin, as further proof of her revolutionary sympathies, had witnesses testify in writing that "Citizen Antoine Baille, servant of Citizeness Dupin, had borne arms in the taking of the Bastille, as well as other servants of said citizeness."[17]

But nothing availed. A new decree exiled "ex-nobles" from Paris, sending Maurice to the Passy suburbs along with Deschartres. From here he could only communicate by letter, but letters of such passion to his mother that George Sand, reproducing them at length in her memoirs, with considerable rewriting, comments on the purity and intensity of a son's adolescent love for his mother, "a love minus the storms and mistakes of later loves . . . yes, the ideal love, which has but a moment in the life of a man."[18]

Release finally came for Madame Dupin after the fall of Robespierre, July 27, 1794, or the ninth of Thermidor in the new Revolutionary calendar. The "Incorruptible" had too long prevented the bourgeoisie from fully exploiting its revolution. So ended the Terror, though it was Terrorists who sent Robespierre to the guillotine—he who, in the words of George Sand, had been "the most humane" of them all—and the Thermidorian reaction which set in, she continues, "was the most dastardly history has ever produced." Ten days following Robespierre's fall, Madame Dupin had petitioned for her release. Fifteen days later it was accorded. Mother and son were reunited. They left for Nohant accompanied by Deschartres, Antoine and a housekeeper, but the remains of Dupin de Francueil's fortune had been further reduced by the Revolution's forced "loans" and canceled "bonds" to less than fifteen thousand francs a year.[19]

Madame Dupin put a good face on her bad fortune, often remarking that "she never had been as rich as when she was poor." It is either a demonstration of relativity or proof of the peaceful beauty of Nohant and the Berry countryside—the Black Valley of George Sand's novels, with Nohant at its center, the rolling hills and fields and "*grands horizons*," the "laughing perspectives," the hidden bed of the river Indre a quarter of a league from the Dupin manor, the peasant homes pressing to their very door and the peasants themselves, their "tact, reserve and natural courtesy. And thus my grandmother spent the next few years at Nohant, busying herself alongside Deschartres with the education of my father and straightening out her affairs."[20]

The education of Maurice consisted of music, "*déclamation*, drawing and literature, which impassioned him," as mathematics, Greek and Latin did not. "His violin would be his lifetime companion." He was "all instinct, all heart, all impulse, courage and trust," and Sand declares that had she been born a boy, she would have been all her father.[21] Contentedly Maurice played first violin with musical friends at Argenton or nearby La Châtre, or voyaged to Paris, now under the Directoire.

From Nohant to Paris then took eight to ten days by diligence, in George Sand's time ten hours. In Paris it was the Opéra that attracted Maurice and filled his letters home to his mother. But it was the choice of career, if choice there was, which filled her thoughts of him. Two lay open: the battlefield or Nohant's fireplace. The irony is George Sand's. She had no love for the Directoire; its corruption, intrigues and incompetence would lead to Napoleon.

When in Passy, Maurice had written his mother, he had passed his time reading the story of his grandfather, Maurice de Saxe, by Baron d'Espagnac, and poring over the maps of his ancestor's battles. "Perhaps one day," he added boyishly, "you will see maps of my own!" Madame Dupin, with less illusion, was not delighted with the prospect and discouraged the ambition. She would haved liked to see him at the head of a regiment, providing there was no war. But there was now war on every front: with the Jacobins and monarchists at home and the royalist coalition abroad. Only Bonaparte, hero of the Italian campaign and conqueror of Egypt, seemed to benefit.[22]

On September 5, 1798, the Directoire ordered general conscription. Maurice's choice narrowed to that of voluntary or involuntary service. From Paris he wrote his mother that an officer's commission was for some time impossible, despite the strings Madame Dupin was energetically pulling. Provocatively, the twenty-year-old reported an exchange with the "*brave* M. de La Tour d'Auvergne," to whom he had just been presented. " 'Is it possible,' said the famous soldier, 'that the grandson of the Maréchal de Saxe is afraid of battle?' 'Certainly not,' I replied, looking him full in the face."[23]

Maurice enlisted as a private in the light cavalry, bought a green dolman and a hussar's saber, and grew a mustache. He was small—too small to be an easy target, he reassured his mother—elegant and slim. His nose was slightly aquiline, his hair black, his eyes large, dark, "gentle and bright at the same time, the most beautiful," says his daughter, "you can imagine"—and one sees the link between the first Aurore and the third.[24]

There were well over three hundred pages of Maurice's letters to his mother, as he went from garrison to *opéra* to battlefield, in *Histoire de Ma Vie*—censored and embellished, rewritten and rearranged by George Sand.[25] The image is thus the work of the novelist as well as of the daughter, and the result is romantic biography: George Sand's story of her life is among the finest of historical fictions. The "touches of poetic feeling" noted by biographers[26] in Maurice's letters are generally

the retouches of his accomplished daughter, but there *are* historical
color and, occasionally, a hard truth. A striking, significant instance occurs early—significant, that is, not so much in the short life of her father as in George Sand's.

Suddenly among Maurice's letters from Germany, which talked of
his need for money (unfailingly sent him by his mother), his pursuit of
promotion, his conquest of a Cologne canoness (all according to the
aristocratic rules of the game accepted by Madame Dupin), there was,
on May 16, 1799, an abrupt mention of a little problem, a poor, "*faible
créature*" whom Maurice had left behind for his mother's care.

"The explanation of the letter you have just read," George Sand immediately followed, "is that a young woman attached to the service of
the house [at Nohant] had just given birth to a beautiful boy who
would later be the companion of my childhood and the friend of my
youth. This pretty woman was not the victim of seduction. She had
yielded, as my father, to the temptations of her age. My grandmother
sent her away without a reproach, provided for her, kept the child [in a
separate, "little house"] and raised it . . . with as much care as a legitimate son."[27]

In fact, the child would not know his father, nor would George Sand
know that he was her half brother, until well after their father's death.
The birth certificate at La Châtre identifies twenty-one-year-old Cath-
érine Chatiron as the mother, and a marginal note indicates he was
named Pierre Laverdure, adding, "natural son of the fatherland." He
would, however, be called Hippolyte Chatiron.

The grandson of Marshal de Saxe duly became a corporal, then a
general's aide-de-camp with a colorful yellow plume and gold-trimmed
sash, but Maurice also showed courage under fire and participated in the
rout of the Russians in Switzerland. Voluntarily he joined the attack on
the fortress of Bard, where a teen-age Stendhal first saw battle, went on
to Marengo, where the French under Bonaparte decisively defeated the
Austrians, and found himself, a first lieutenant, in Milan.

Here too, in 1800, Maurice found Sophie, gay, laughing, seductive
and beautiful. She was, he thought, the wife of the quartermaster adju-
tant general, Claude-Antoine Collin. He soon discovered his mistake.
She was the general's mistress. It made little difference. Maurice was
twenty-two, the general was forty-nine. Sophie was twenty-seven.

"For the first time the young man has been touched by an enduring
passion. . . . From this moment, this good, innocent soul . . . is torn
between two almost irreconcilable loves and the happy, proud mother,
who lived only from that love, was tormented and broken by a jealousy
natural for a woman . . . whose love for her son was the unique passion
of her life."

The other woman, George Sand continues, "was none other than my mother, Sophie-Victoire-Antoinette Delaborde. I give all three of her baptismal names, because during the agitated course of her life she bore them successively. . . . In her childhood they called her Antoinette, because Marie Antoinette was the name of the Queen of France. During the conquests of the Empire, the name of Victoire naturally prevailed. After their marriage, my father always called her Sophie."[28]

Sophie was born in 1773, five years before Maurice. Her father was Antoine Delaborde, a bird-seller on Paris' Quai de la Mégisserie; previously he had kept a billiard saloon. In 1789, according to police notes in Paris' Archives Nationales, sixteen-year-old Sophie was living with Claude-Denis Vantin Saint-Charles and had a child by him. Another child, Caroline, was born of another father in 1799. A year later, Sophie was with General Collin in Italy, where Maurice Dupin first saw her.

> My mother was of that vagabond, degraded race—the Bohemians of the world. She was a dancer, no, lower than a dancer, a *figurant*, in one of the lowest theaters of Paris, whom the rich removed from this abjection only to subject her to worse. My father met her when she was already thirty [sic] and in the midst of a wild life. But he had a generous heart. He realized that this beautiful creature could still love.[29]

Ambiguity and passion mark the relation of Maurice and Sophie from the start; it would be a long tortuous way to love. Initially there was Sophie's hesitation waltz between the general and the lieutenant, the security of the one and the insecurity of the other. For Maurice it meant deception of his mother. There was a touch of self-deception as well. For several months he made no mention of Sophie in his letters to Madame Dupin—a sign of its early seriousness, since he had not had similar qualms about his liaison with the Cologne canoness.

Rather, Maurice wrote of the Raphaels he had seen in Bologna, of the statues in Florence, of his friendship with Georges-Washington de Lafayette, the Marquis' son, and even of Deschartres' new honorific title, Mayor of Nohant. Finally, in December 1800, he wrote of Sophie, her "grave gentleness, shyness, sensibility and perfect deportment," their mutual affection, but he spoke of her as the quartermaster general's wife, though now his mistress. "How sweet it is to have a good mother," Madame Dupin read, "good friends, a pretty mistress, a bit of glory, fine horses and enemies to fight. All this I have, but best of all my good mother!"[30]

Without naming Sophie, Maurice adjured his mother to silence, lest there be harmful gossip about her. But Madame Dupin was too cautious, too zealously concerned about her precious son not to make inquiries, particularly as it became manifest that his infatuation was not a passing one.

The complexity of her grandmother's opposition to Sophie did not escape George Sand. "Without a doubt," she wrote, "my grandmother would have preferred a companion of his own social class for my father." But that, she continued, Madame Dupin would have more easily accepted than a daughter-in-law whose youth, "by force of circumstances," had been exposed to such "frightful hazards," that is, moral depravity. Moreover—and here George Sand placed the novelistic accent—there was Madame Dupin's passionately "jealous maternal love."[31] However, the first two reasons were sufficient for any eighteenth-century mother. They gave Maurice himself pause.

Early in May 1801, he returned to Nohant on leave. His reunion with his mother was warm and emotional, and she was content. She had regained her son. But Maurice had not left Sophie behind. He had installed her in La Châtre three miles away, in the Tête Noire Inn. He went there frequently, and he stayed late. Madame Dupin did not long remain dupe, and she informed Deschartres. With the delicacy and tact of a country bull, Deschartres took charge. He stormed into the Tête Noire, subjected Sophie, who was registered as Madame Collin, to a schoolmaster's catechism and a celibate's scorn, "ordering her to leave for Paris, else he would summon local officials." Sophie, "who was neither fearful, nor very patient, railed in turn and raged at the pedagogue." Deschartres went huffily off to fetch the mayor of La Châtre and "a friend of the family who had some municipal function," but when they arrived, instead of finding "the termagant described by Deschartres, they discovered a *toute petite femme*, pretty as an angel, sitting on the edge of her bed, crying." The officials shamefacedly departed, taking Deschartres with them.[32]

Maurice, however, consented to send Sophie away to Paris and went to a friend at Le Blanc in order to reflect. From there he wrote at length to Madame Dupin:

> I confess there is something in what has been told to you. This young woman whom I had known in Italy as the wife of Collin has admitted since she came to Berry that she was not Collin's wife, but finding herself abandoned by her first husband, who has since died, and on the point of falling into misery, she let Collin, whom she met, take her to Italy, where he always treated her as his wife. Then Collin indeed conducted himself too much as a mean, ugly husband. Not being bound to him, she left to follow me. That is the way it went. For one thing, she was afraid of falling into misery; for another, there was her love for me, because it certainly was not

money that attracted her, since she knew me when I looked like a man dying of hunger. . . . As for the debts I owe her, it is true that this woman loaned me money in Italy and when she told me how worried she was that I might abandon her to marry someone else, which she thought was the plot of everyone around me, I cheerfully wrote her a note saying I would pay her a hundred louis the day I did get married.

If that ever does happen to me, and since I would not marry for less than twenty or thirty thousand francs a year, it is only just that my future father-in-law should pay such a debt to one of my mistresses. . . . I am grieved, my dear mother, that I can not have a mistress without reducing you to despair. . . . I have done everything you have asked. I have sent away my mistress, separating myself from her only for you and to please you, because what else would keep me from following her?[33]

Maurice did in fact follow Sophie to Paris—where he also sought a very elusive promotion. His letter to his mother does not necessarily portray a true cynicism regarding Sophie, but rather a son's reassurance that he is a man of the world who knows how to treat a woman such as Sophie. He was still dependent on his mother (his horses, uniforms and expenses were paid by her); marriage and possibly even the thought of it were probably far from his mind (all the pressures were against it). But what is of more interest is the reaction of George Sand to this image of her father and its influence on her life, her attitudes, her relations to men.

"As I analyze and study the emotions and thoughts of my father," she wrote and then deleted in the manuscript of her memoirs, ". . . I am at times under a strange illusion. I think of myself as the mother, rather than the daughter, of my father, that he confides to me his troubles and thoughts and I console him. . . . Perhaps it is because I gave the name Maurice to my son, who has the same age as my father, alive before me in his letters, as is the other Maurice, my son, who is at my side. . . . *Eh bien*, my young father, my friend, my child! . . ."[34]

Thus the tangle of George Sand's feelings and motives as she recorded the story of her father and mother, and rewrote his letters. She wanted to tarnish his image neither in the eyes of her public nor in the eyes of her children. She was also writing a historical novel in the form of romanticized, personal memoirs; but the romanticism was authentic: it was of her time and of herself. The phrases and sentiments attributed to her father by George Sand in her version of the letter to Madame Dupin sent from Le Blanc are strikingly her own:

My dear mother [she has Maurice write], you suffer, and so
do I. . . . But love purifies all. Love ennobles the most abject
of beings, all the more those who have no other fault save the
misfortune of having been flung upon the world without help,
support or guidance. Why then should a woman thus abandoned be considered guilty if she looks for aid and consolation
from an honest man, whereas women of the world, who lack
for no pleasure or mark of respect, take lovers simply to distract themselves from their husbands?[35]

But even in the letters Maurice actually wrote from Paris one can
read his continuing infatuation, if not growing love, for a desperate,
drifting, uncertain Sophie (at one point she returned to General
Collin). And one can understand George Sand's sympathy for her
mother. In a letter to Madame Dupin, she has her granduncle, the Abbé
de Beaumont, then in Paris, say of Sophie: "She is charming, she has a
great deal of natural intelligence and sensibility."[36]

Maurice was soon with a General Dupont as aide-de-camp, playing
his violin, studying the piano, waiting for his promotion. Sophie had
been installed in a dress shop in Orléans; Maurice intermittently reassured his mother that, despite what she heard, they were not living
together—"it took too much money."[37] Briefly he returned on leave to
Nohant, then rejoined his general at Charleville, where Sophie joined
him.

"From this moment they virtually never quit each other and regarded
themselves as bound together by a tie that led to several children, of
which only one survived several years and died, I believe, two years before my birth."[38]

In his letters to his mother, Maurice made no mention of all this, but
rather spoke of his bitterness at being so long a lieutenant, of his dislike
for Bonaparte, the ambitious figure dominating all their destinies. For
three months in 1803 Maurice was on leave with Madame Dupin, who
was taking the waters at Vichy for kidney stones. Then orders came for
Maurice to depart immediately for Charleville: Bonaparte was planning
an invasion of Britain. The plan took General Dupont and his aide-de-
camp to the coastal town of Boulogne, where they awaited further orders.

And to Boulogne came Sophie, eight months pregnant. She did not
remain long. "Feeling her time drawing near," she left for Paris, and
Maurice shortly followed. They married: *this* child would be legitimate.
The marriage was, as well, an act of love.

It took place on June 5, 1805. The ceremony was held almost clan-
destinely, not only without the knowledge of Madame Dupin, but
without her required consent. Maurice was twenty-six, thus four years

short of the thirty releasing him from the requirement of parental consent, according to the new Code Civil (soon known as the Code Napoléon). Further, according to Article 1124, wives were limited to the rights of minors; their husbands were given charge of their wealth and property and even their salaries; and they could sign no contract or paper without their husband's consent. Article 213 stipulated: "The husband owes protection to his wife, the wife obedience to her husband."[39] Witnesses to the marriage also "testified" that Madame Dupin had disappeared during Thermidor, Year VIII of the Revolution, her husband in 1788, and *their* parents had been dead or missing for many years before.[40] Several months later, when Madame Dupin heard of the civil ceremony from someone other than Maurice, she wrote to Paris authorities seeking to have it annulled. Only a religious ceremony in her eyes would have consecrated her son's marriage.

Meantime, on July 1, 1804—six weeks after the French Senate yielded Napoleon Bonaparte the title of Emperor, launching him on imperial conquests which would take Maurice beyond domestic conflicts—the child of Maurice and Sophie Dupin was born in a room under the roof of a six-story house on Rue Meslée.[41] It was a "modest interior," says George Sand and she continues with the story of her birth:

> My good aunt Lucie [Sophie's younger sister] was on the eve of marriage with an officer who was a friend of my father, and they were all celebrating in the intimacy of the family. My mother was wearing a pretty dress the color of roses. They were dancing a quadrille composed by my father, as he played on his faithful Cremona violin. . . . My mother, feeling a slight malaise, left the dance and went to her bedroom. Since she showed no signs of indisposition and had left so quietly, the dancing continued. My aunt Lucie, as it was ending, went to my mother's bedroom, and almost immediately she was heard to cry, "Come, come quickly, Maurice, you have a daughter!"
>
> "She shall be called Aurore," said my father, "after my poor, dear mother, who is not here to bless her, but who *will* someday!" And he took me in his arms. . . .
>
> "She was born to the sound of music and in the color of roses," said my aunt. "She will know happiness."[42]

3

The Seedling Years

Seedling, *a tree not yet three feet high.*
—*The American College Dictionary*

. . . at no time in life are we more capable of impressions
and reproductions than during the years of childhood.
—Sigmund Freud, *Three Contributions to the
Theory of Sex*[1]

During the wars of the Empire, while husbands and
brothers were away in Germany, anxious mothers gave
birth to a pale, nervous and passionate generation.
—Alfred de Musset, *La Confession d'un
Enfant du Siècle*[2]

By the age of four, the die, if not cast, is, at the very least, loaded.
In the case of George Sand, born Amantine-Aurore-Lucile Dupin,
it is evidenced in her own account of her life—her memoirs' reproduction, in Freud's sense, of her earliest impressions, involving
concealment and repression, camouflage and transfer, is always revealing.

There is a determined optimism in *Histoire de Ma Vie*, though the
difficult first years are not passed over. Maurice had gone to Nohant
before and after the marriage, but neither time dared mention it to
Madame Dupin. He returned to Paris, had a bout with scarlatina, pursued his elusive captaincy and moved his family from its garret to a
rather better flat on Rue de la Grange-Batelière. Even as Madame
Dupin was writing to Paris, seeking ways to annul Maurice's marriage,
she and Maurice were writing to each other without either mentioning
"the principal object of their preoccupations."[3]

Soon, however, both mother and son were referring to Sophie's new
child. "My Aurore," wrote Maurice, "is very well and quite pretty"—
and he thanked his mother for inquiring about her. Meantime the

mayor of the Fifth Arrondissement had launched his own inquiry and sent Marshal de Saxe's daughter a reassuring letter. One of his men, he said, had investigated the young pair, whom he found in "an extremely modest but well-kept lodging . . . the young mother in the midst of her children, nursing the youngest herself."*

"I am convinced," the Paris official concluded, "that there is nothing which suggests your son will repent the union he has contracted."[4]

Madame Dupin nonetheless persisted. She arrived in Paris in the spring of 1805 without informing Maurice, firmly intending to end her son's marriage, if not union, with Sophie. Maurice learned of her arrival. With an infant Aurore in his arms, he drove in a fiacre to his mother's residence. Somehow he persuaded the doorkeeper's wife to take Aurore to Madame Dupin and present her, whatever the pretext, to his mother.[5]

The *portière* went upstairs and engaged in a conversation with the somewhat surprised Madame Dupin. "Look, madame," she said, "my pretty little granddaughter! Her nurse just brought her to me."

"Indeed," said Madame Dupin, "the child seems nice enough, and healthy, too." Distractedly she reached for a candy box as the *portière* put Aurore on her lap. She regarded the child more closely, then suspiciously. With a start she made a half-gesture of pushing Aurore away. Those dark, velvety eyes . . . "You are lying to me!" she cried. "This child is not yours! It is not you she resembles! I . . . I know who she is! . . ." Aurore wailed.

"Come, dearie," said the doorkeeper's wife, "you are not wanted here. Let us be off."

"Let her be," said Madame Dupin, defeated. "Poor little one, this is not your fault. . . . Who *did* bring you this child?"

"Your son, madame," said the *portière*. "He is waiting below. I will take her back to him. Forgive me! I did not know . . . I don't know anything! I thought it would give you pleasure. . . ."

"There, there, my dear," said Madame Dupin. "I am not vexed with you. Go, tell my son I wish to see him, but leave the child with me."

Maurice raced up the stairs, three at a time. He found Aurore in his mother's arms. Both were crying. He joined them in tears. When he finally left with Aurore, the child was clutching a great ruby ring in her little fist, the gift of Madame Dupin for her mother.[6]

It would be some time, however, before Madame Dupin would receive Sophie, and one can doubt it was ever very graciously. There is even more doubt that a religious ceremony shortly followed, though George Sand reported it as a fact.[7] No church record has been found,[8] and the absence of that all-important ritual helps explain Madame Dupin's continuing hostility to her son's wife.

* Caroline was now with Sophie; the "youngest" is Aurore.

There is a kind of splendid defiance in Sand's description of her mother at this time. "My mother never felt either humiliated or honored in finding herself among individuals who thought themselves above her socially. Feeling to her fingertips that she belonged to the people, she believed herself more noble than all the nobles, all the patricians of the earth." And she reflectively remarks that her mother and father enjoyed a compatibility and quiet domesticity which left her, "as my legacy, that deep sense of unsociability [*sauvagerie*] which has always made grand society insupportable for me and a *home* [in English in the text] a necessity."[9]

But the "legacy" is wistful hearsay. George Sand was, in reality, part of that French generation depicted by Musset in his *Confession of a Child of the Century*—"*ardente, pâle, nerveuse*":

> Conceived between two battles, raised at school to the sound of drums, thousands of children looked darkly at each other as they tested their puny muscles. From time to time their blood-stained fathers would appear, press them to their gold-braided uniforms and ride off once more to the [Napoleonic] wars.[10]

Told of young boys, it was as true of girls. The father of George Sand, or rather Aurore, returned the same spring of 1805 to his general, Dupont, and a camp near the Channel. Sophie joined him for a few months, leaving Caroline and Aurore with their aunt Lucie, who had married the retired officer, Maréchal, with whom she had danced at the time of Aurore's birth. Clotilde was *their* child, "my dear cousin," says George Sand, "perhaps the best friend I have ever known." The Maréchals lived in a small house at Chaillot, then open country not far from today's Arc de Triomphe. Aunt Lucie rented a gardener's donkey for her little charges and on Sundays they would ride to Paris, Caroline in one basket, Clotilde and Aurore in the other among the carrots and cabbages, on their way to the market. "At the same time, Emperor Napoleon, preoccupied with other cares, amused himself with other rides, going down to Italy to crown himself king."[11]

A third European coalition formed in defense against Napoleon and Maurice was off once again to the wars, as Sophie returned to Paris, to Caroline and Aurore. Through Flanders, Picardy, Champagne and Lorraine, to the Rhine and the Danube, Maurice rode with a division of the Sixth Corps, winning his captaincy at Austerlitz. Briefly he returned to Paris, pressed Caroline and Aurore to his gold-braided, if not blood-stained, uniform and rode off once again to battle—in the campaign of 1806, soon becoming aide-de-camp of Prince Murat, the handsome, swaggering "golden eagle" who was Napoleon's brother-in-law. There was thus little of the quiet domesticity enjoyed, says George Sand, by her parents and bequeathed her as her legacy, but there are Maurice's letters to her mother, showing a belated maturity on his part.

Maurice to Sophie, December 7, 1806:

> For the past two weeks, my dearest wife, on horseback from five in the morning, I have been crossing the deserts of Poland, and after riding until dark, I found but the smoking hut of some poor devil and a handful of straw to sleep on. . . . I love you a hundred times more than life. The thought of you follows me everywhere, consoling me, causing me despair. Sleeping, I see you; waking, I think of you; always you are with me. . . . Love me, love me, that alone will soften the hard life I lead.

On December 11, 1807, from Milan:

> The place I'm writing you from, dear friend, should tell you that I think of you twice as much as usually, if that is possible, for I am in a place so full of memories of our first love, of my sadness, torments and joys. Oh, what feelings I had in the gardens near the courtyard! They were not all pleasant, but above all I felt my love for you, my impatience to be again in your arms. We will most certainly be in Paris by the end of the month. . . . Adieu, a thousand tender kisses to you, to our Aurore and to my mother.[12]

By now Aurore was three and a half, her father but an intermittent presence. The reality of daily life was her mother, Caroline and Clotilde, her aunt Lucie, a young man named Pierret, and her own daydreams.

It was a happy infancy, says George Sand. Perhaps because she was the center of it, *since there was no brother* (the case of so many remarkable women) *to share it or automatically claim it,* and even halfsister Caroline was away most of the time in a boarding school.

Her earliest memory is at two. A maid given to drink had let Aurore fall and she had struck her forehead against a corner of the chimney piece. "I recall no pain . . . but I remember distinctly the fright, the suffering, the attitude of those around me."[13]

Memories of her third year involve the fourth-floor apartment on Paris' Rue de la Grange-Batelière, north of the *grands boulevards.* "Hours passed in my little bed, filled by the contemplation of a fold in the curtain or a flower in the wallpaper." And Aurore indulged in an easily evoked double vision, possibly doubling her personality, as her deliberately unfocused eyes rested on objects and the space just beyond them.

She walked at ten months, learned to talk rather late, then talked at

length, and read very well by four. Her mother and her aunt were
devoted to her. She and Clotilde were taught their prayers and La Fon-
taine's fables, which they recited by heart with that astonishing fluency
early inculcated in French children. Sophie sang to her, sweetly and
often, and Aurore had a belief and faith in Santa Claus which may
never have wholly abandoned George Sand. The first note of rebellion
was Aurore's refusal to say *B* after *A* when reciting the alphabet, because she didn't care for *B*. The first note of sadness was on hearing the
lyric,

> *Nous n'irons plus au bois,*
> *Les lauriers sont coupés.* . . .

She knew but vaguely what was meant by the woods of the song, and
of laurels nothing at all. But she mourned the woods and the laurels
cut down.

Commingling in the memory of George Sand were a book of Greek
mythology, a children's theater of Chinese shadow play near the Palais
Royal, the fairy tales of Perrault (*Cinderella, Little Red Riding Hood,
Tom Thumb*) which, exhausted, were reinvented by Sophie and
Caroline (when home) for Aurore's inexhaustible delight. With a
childishness of her own, Sophie regaled her "with all that was fresh and
lovely in Catholic legend, so that angels and lovers, the blessed Virgin
and the good fairy, punchinellos and magicians, little devils of the theater and saints of the Church were so mixed in my brain that they produced the most poetic mess you could imagine."[14]

It was by repeating the stories and making up her own that she
learned them—not by reading.

> I sought only images in books. What I took in by way of eye
> and ear entered the caldron of my little mind and I fashioned
> such vivid dreams from it that I lost all sense of what was real
> and where I was.

Standing on a cold foot warmer in a playpen improvised from four en-
circling chairs, she spun interminable stories for Sophie.

> It seems my stories when I was a child were a sort of pastiche
> of everything I had heard. They were invariably in the form of
> a fairy tale with a good fairy, a virtuous prince and a beautiful
> princess. There were few wicked people and no great misfor-
> tunes. . . . Most curious was their length, for I continued a
> story from the point I had left it the day before. . . . My aunt
> also remembers my stories and recalls them gaily. She remem-
> bers saying to me more than once, "*Eh bien*, Aurore, hasn't

your prince gotten out of the forest yet? Will your princess ever finish putting on her gown and her golden crown?"

"Let her be," my mother would say, "I cannot settle down to work until she begins her novels between the four chairs."

Thus, at four, George Sand had found an audience, the indispensable encouragement.[15]

She was a favored child. When Caroline came home from her boarding school, she would be given a couch next to Aurore's bed. Aurore's forebears were not forgotten, no less by her mother than by her grandmother, *née* Aurore de Saxe. But the apartment on Rue de la Grange-Batelière was far from a palace, and the daughters of the glazier on the ground floor would come up and play with Aurore and her sister. And then there was Pierret: when they went to see their aunt Lucie in Chaillot, several miles to the west, Aurore, as indolent as her father when a child, would often ride on his shoulders.

Heavy, ugly and hugely affectionate, Louis Pierret was twenty-two or -three when he had heard Aurore crying as a baby in her attic room on Rue Meslée. He had been visiting a relative on the same landing. Sophie was exhausted and Pierret came, perhaps to repay a similar kindness to his relative's child, to care for Aurore. Nightly, after working at the royal treasury, he would fetch Aurore and for several weeks kept her until morning. He had the tenderness of a father and the solicitude of a mother. He had tics, he liked his pipe, his wine, his beer, his dominoes and his billiards. He followed the family when it moved to Rue de la Grange-Batelière.

Pierret comforted Aurore when an old woman on the street played witch, and Sophie never frightened her into behaving. Fear was not among Aurore's experiences; it would never be a characteristic of George Sand's life. Her father, when he made his rare appearances, "spoiled [her] horribly." At home and at Chaillot, Aurore played at battle games as frequently as the French boys of her generation. Indeed, "we were reproached for our boyish games, and it is certain that Clotilde and I were avid for virile emotions." More than once Aurore adoped the hero's role, often that of Napoleon, among her companions, all little girls, and they would strew the rooms in Paris or the grounds at Chaillot with their dismembered dolls. "I beg you," Maurice would say to Sophie, when home from the wars, "sweep up the children's battlefield! It makes me ill to see all those arms and legs and red rags."[16]

The first sight of a pale, cold-eyed Napoleon reviewing his troops shared the equally haunting sound of a country flute at Chaillot in Sand's childhood memories, and if her father's appearances were rare, they were emotionally rich. "He would play with me all day long and carry me, unembarrassed in his grand uniform, in his arms in the streets and along the boulevards. Beyond doubt I was very happy, because I was very loved."

The ambiguity of Pierret's presence did not escape unremarked. "He was not sufficiently seductive to render my mother unfaithful, even in her thoughts," Sand replies to unnamed critics. But there is no confirmation of his having been married, as she asserted. The picture that remains of Aurore's earliest impressionable years is that of an atmosphere of relaxed, wartime amorality and warm, almost tribal communality, with Aurore feeling above all very happy at its center. "Take care of my wife and children," Maurice would say to Pierret when he left on yet another campaign, "and if I do not return, remember, it is for life."

Devotion can have its own satisfaction; it was Pierret who did everything in preparation for the trip to Madrid.

With the co-operation of a weak Spanish king and a corrupt minister, and as a counterplay to a threatened British landing in Portugal, Napoleon had dispatched one hundred thousand French troops to the Iberian Peninsula. On March 25, 1808, Prince Murat had arrived in Madrid to assume command. Maurice, as aide-de-camp, was with him. The stay in Madrid would be for some time; impulsively Sophie decided to make the long journey to him, taking Aurore with her.

Sophie was seven or eight months pregnant and Aurore was not yet four; she may not have been aware of the hazards. The wife of a purveyor to the French Army, Madame Fontanier, procured her two seats in a post *calèche* she and her groom were taking to Madrid, and soon all four were on their way.

The wild, craggy mountains of Asturias and a family of bears resembling brigands inspired some fear in Sophie, but Aurore would ever recall the first time she saw flowering bindweed. "Look, Aurore, how pretty!" her mother cried. "You must never forget it!" "My goodness, Madame Dupin," Madame Fontanier exclaimed, "how droll you are with your little girl!"

A pigeon killed for her meal in a Spanish inn was Aurore's first contact with death; the passage through villages, pillaged and still smoking, in the wake of the French Army was her first brush with war. It was early in May 1808. On the second day of the month the people of Madrid had revolted, briefly seizing Murat before being bloodily crushed, but the revolt went on, in the provinces. *Muera, muera!* [sic]. Aurore heard a caged magpie scream in the courtyard of an inn near Vitoria. It was crying, *Death, death!* for Godoy, the corrupt, collaborating Spanish minister, but she was told it was calling for the death of the French, of herself. Another event, however, distracted her.

A huge coach rolled into the courtyard and its horses were being changed in a panicky haste. "The Queen!" cried the villagers, "the

Queen!" "No," contradicted the innkeeper, "it is not the Queen," and he sent his servants to keep the crowd at a distance. Meanwhile a chambermaid led Aurore close to the coach. "Look, little one, the Queen!" It was among Aurore's first disenchantments. The queens of her rambling stories had always been resplendent. "But the poor Queen I saw wore a skimpy white dress yellowed with dust and her daughter of eight or nine was similarly dressed. Both were very dark, both quite ugly." The older woman was the Infanta, daughter of Charles IV, fleeing, as the rest of her family, from her own people to the protection of Napoleon at Bayonne, where, in fact, "he would seal their political fate."

It was the stuff of Alexandre Dumas' novels as it would be of George Sand's; Romanticism had *some* roots in reality.

Madrid, when they arrived, "Sophie carrying one child in her arms, another in her womb," offered them a palace which restored for Aurore her fairy-tale world. Prince Murat was installed in the lower, cooler apartments, the most luxurious of Madrid. The Dupins occupied an immense upper suite with damask hangings and massive gilded furniture which Aurore thought solid gold. A white rabbit with ruby-red eyes, at home in the palace, made friends with the little girl and slept in her lap to the singsong of her endless stories. The fled children of the palace had left their magnificent toys behind, but Aurore took little interest in them. "My own life had become a fable"—and the dashing Murat its Prince.

She was dressed by Sophie in an exact replica of her father's uniform: white cashmere dolman, fur-lined pelisse, gold buttons and braid, spurred, red Moroccan boots, dangling saber and her first handsome pants. Not yet four, not yet George Sand, she had found her costume, that of a male. "Seeing me dressed exactly as my father, either because he took me for a boy, or because it pleased him to pretend to, responding thus to the flattery of my mother, Murat presented me to his visitors as his aide-de-camp and admitted us to his intimacy."[17]

But Aurore discovered that the heavy uniform was too hot in the Spanish summer and was happy to put on another made by Sophie—"a Spanish gown of black silk like [Sophie's] own with a hem of net caught up at the knee and a mantilla bordered with velvet. In that fancy dress the child danced before the long mirror in her room, *marveling that she could be so many selves* and yet remain Aurore."[18]

She was on the palace terrace one day, calling *Weber!* (her father's orderly, her personal guard in hostile Madrid; her first words to him had been, "Weber, I like you, go away"). She heard her voice return. She called her mother's name. It came back. She called her own and heard it echoed.

Then a bizarre explanation occurred to me. I was double.
There was about me another *I* that I could not see, but which
always saw *me*, because it always replied to me. . . . I concluded that all things, all beings, had their reflection, their
double, their other *I*, and I wanted passionately to see mine. I
called it a hundred times, each time asking it to come to
me. . . . I was interrupted by the arrival of my mother. I cannot say why, but instead of asking her about it, I concealed
what was agitating me so much.[19]

The search for an explanation of "George Sand" does not lie in a single
key. A multiple key, a double identity, may not be the recipe for happiness, to mix the metaphor, but it can be the making of a novelist—
and of a rich, varied life of multiple fullness, experience and even
fulfillment: in a word, plenitude. To consider the most important characteristic of completeness—the androgynous mind: no less than Pierret,
George-Aurore Sand had been her father's surrogate vis-à-vis Sophie
when he was off to war, and her mother's rival on his returns. Would
she not later subconsciously identify herself first with the one, then
with the other? She has told us she thought of herself as her father's
mother. Would not the characters of her many novels be the search, if
not the expression, of her many selves? Add the thousands of letters
sent, as if cast upon the sea in so many bottles, in the search for understanding, for love; the desperate cry when she was twenty-four, "My
God, to whom can I write?" And two pages later, "Oh, anguish!"[20]

The stay in Madrid was a long two months. One night Aurore heard
her Prince Murat scream with stomach pains; he thought himself, and
may well have been, poisoned by a Spanish servant. One morning soon
afterward Murat brought her a tiny fawn from a hunt; it would disappear, it probably died, deprived of its mother. And one day in June
Aurore was sent out onto the palace terrace. Sophie was giving birth to
a child. She was long in labor. "I heard her cries, I entered [after the
birth of the child] to kiss my mother. She sent me away and I left crying."[21]

The child born was a boy, and he was born blind. Sophie in her bitterness thought she had seen the Spanish doctor blind him with his
thumbs and hear him mutter, "Here is one who will never see the light
of Spain!" It was more likely cataracts. Dread was generally in the air,
and the French would soon decamp. Maurice wrote his mother that he
had been granted leave and was acquiring a *calèche* to carry Sophie,
Aurore and the baby to Nohant; that hopefully Deschartres' acquaintance with medicine might help cure the baby of his blindness.
He himself would be astride the half-tamed stallion, Leopardo of
Andalusia, which had been given him by Ferdinand VII.

The ride was a nightmare for Aurore, Murat's passage of return through an insurgent Spain was half flight, half battle, and the Dupin *calèche* traveled in baking heat in its wake. "What I remember most is the suffering, the thirst, the devouring heat I endured throughout the journey." Sporadically, Maurice would join the beleaguered Murat, and one night, when they had found a room in an inn, her mother had taken her to a window, pointed at the cannon flashes in the dark sky and said, "Look, Aurore, a battle! Your father is probably in it."

Their *calèche* was requisitioned for the wounded. They found places on baggage wagons. Famine accompanied fever, and the jar Aurore felt, she was told, was caused by a corpse on the road. She was too sick to pay heed. Burned villages blurred with the memory of gutted towns and a soldier who had made a soup from candles. They regained their *calèche*, reached the border and the coast. Sophie insisted on a voyage by sloop to Bordeaux. They were shipwrecked. Maurice saved Leopardo and his saber. They went on. Aurore sank deeper into a fitful, then forgetful fever. When at last they traversed France and arrived at the green refuge of Nohant, she saw the small composed figure of her grandmother:

> She seemed very tall, though little over five feet, her face pink and white, her air imposing, her unvarying costume of a long brown silk dress of the *ancien régime*, her blond wig with crimped bangs, her little round bonnet with a cockade of lace . . . she was like nothing I had ever seen.

Aurore and the baby were wretched with lice and scabies.

" 'Scabies or not,' said my grandmother, taking me into her arms, 'I will take care of this one.' "[22]

Sophie was told to see to the other child.

4

The Apple of Discord

Art thou the topmost apple
The gatherers could not reach,
Reddening on the bough?
    —Sappho, who lived circa
      600 B.C. and "is said
      to have been small and
      dark."[1]

Keep me as the apple of an eye: hide me under the
shadow of thy wings.
        —*The Book of Common Prayer*, Psalms XVII

Madame Dupin carried Aurore into her own bedroom and placed her on her own bed. "Like a hearse," the great curtained bed sported huge feather plumes at each corner; the walls of the room were covered with flowered Indian linen. The wretched child shrank from the spotless lace-trimmed pillows and white sheets, then, reassured by her grandmother, relaxed and thought it "heaven." Dimly Aurore perceived a stout, awkward lad of nine draw near with a large bouquet of flowers. With heavy, "friendly" playfulness, he flung it at her head.

"'This is Hippolyte,' said Madame Dupin. 'Kiss each other, children.' We embraced without asking any questions and it was years before I knew he was my brother. He was the child of the 'little house.'" He was now staying in the big house.

Deschartres, too, in white stockings, yellow gaiters and nut-brown knee breeches, made his first appearance, "examined me solemnly" and pronounced, "good doctor that he was": *scabies*. Aurore was washed, cleaned and cured, and soon scampering in the garden with Hippolyte —"a bit humiliated that he considered me a little girl, but I quickly showed him I was really a very sturdy boy."

The sick, blind baby, however, worsened. In a few months he was dead, and he was buried on the morrow in the small cemetery in a corner of Nohant's park. Morbidly George Sand related how the child was exhumed, as she herself slept, in the secrecy of darkest night, because Sophie was hysterically convinced it still lived and persuaded Maurice to the act; and how it was reburied in the same secrecy the following night.

The following Friday—September 16, 1808—Maurice rode the half-wild stallion Leopardo to the neighboring town of La Châtre. He dined with the Duvernets; he stayed late. Ever jealous, Sophie fretted. Madame Dupin reprimanded her. Sophie retired to bed. Madame Dupin ascended to her room, but she did not sleep. At midnight she heard an unusual stirring in the house. She inquired the cause and learned that Deschartres had been sent for and had left in haste for La Châtre. She, "who never walked," stumbled and ran in slippers and nightgown through the rain and the night. She found Deschartres before her, bowing over the corpse of Maurice. Her son had been thrown by Leopardo at the foot of a poplar as he began his ride back to Nohant. His neck was broken. He was carried by his orderly Weber to the Lion d'Argent Inn, then Weber had ridden for Deschartres. By the time Deschartres had arrived, Maurice was dead—at the age of thirty.

At dawn the great Nohant carriage brought Madame Dupin, Deschartres and the corpse of Maurice home. It was Deschartres who informed Sophie of Maurice's death. She collapsed; the house went into mourning. A few days later Aurore was given black to wear. "They had to explain to me that it was for the death of my father." As for the grieving Madame Dupin, George Sand indelibly remembered:

> My voice, my looks, my ways recalled her son as a child, so that often as she watched me play, she would have a delusion and call to me, "Maurice!" And when she spoke of me to someone, she would say, "My son."

Hippolyte was upset, but less involved. "He did not yet know that my father was his." Nor is it ever clear when he or Aurore was made aware of it. Throughout her childhood, Aurore was raised as the only child of her father, and as such, on his death—she saw herself—his survivor, the protector of Sophie.

The niece of Madame Dupin's chambermaid was brought to Nohant from La Châtre to become Aurore's companion. Promptly Aurore sought to bend her to her will. Ursule resisted. The adults at Nohant, fearing she might allow Aurore to tyrannize over her, were relieved. The children fought, then embraced. "We were equals." But one was more equal than the other: it was not around the niece of a *femme de chambre*, even the formidable Mademoiselle Julie, that the Nohant household turned. "Compared with Ursule, I was a little princess and instinctively I abused my position."

Aurore was a princess on her father's side, but she was also the child of Sophie, a woman, for Madame Dupin, with a tarnished past and a dubious future. It was not the maternal legacy that concerned Madame Dupin so much as Sophie's influence. Ever mindful of her own mother's domestic looseness, from which she had fled to a convent, she deeply dreaded Aurore's being caught up in Sophie's Paris life, when she inevitably resumed it. The moral loss of Aurore now moved the grandmother to do battle for the grandchild, the daughter of her son.

And in this battle, too, the one was more equal than the other:

> Truly, they were the two extreme types of our sex—my grandmother, fair, blond, serious and dignified, a veritable Saxon of noble blood, with the ease and poise of her birth and the largess of her class; my mother, dark-haired, pale, hot-blooded, gauche and shy in company but ever ready to explode, Spanish by nature, passionate and prone to jealousy, quick-tempered and weak, bad and at the same time good.

The dramatic conflict at Nohant, with Aurore as "the apple of discord"* (torn, bruised but desired), endured six or seven months, but it was so emotionally replete—and lingeringly unresolved—that George Sand would recall it as having endured two or three years. Desperately Aurore clung to Sophie, and the desperation of her love is the more understandable when one realizes that at this turning point in her childhood Madame Dupin was a comparative stranger. For the four crucial years of her life, there had been Sophie ("she gave me my first notions of life."[2]). The lost paradise of infancy was the fourth-floor apartment on Rue de la Grange-Batelière.

In the days immediately following Maurice's death, mother and grandmother emerged from their sorrows only to indulge Aurore. The child had a thousand whims and rolled on the ground when they couldn't be satisfied. It was then Ursule had been sent for and Madame Dupin further stiffened in her resolve to oversee Aurore's upbringing. Maurice's child, a descendant of Marshal de Saxe, was growing up wild.

The initial truce of the "rival mothers" (Sand's phrase) was of short tenure; their "natural antipathy" soon asserted itself. When together in Aurore's presence, they managed a surface politeness. When alone with her, or, in the case of Madame Dupin, when among her aristocratic friends, they behaved differently. "She is a devil, a madwoman," Aurore heard Madame Dupin say of her mother. "She was never loved by my son. She dominated him, she made him unhappy, and she doesn't regret it." And she heard Sophie say of her grandmother that she was "a prude

* George Sand's metaphor.

and a hypocrite, a dried-up woman without any feelings," and Sophie would do a mimicry of Madame Dupin's friends—"the old countesses" —which invariably delighted Aurore.

On Sundays there were rides on a gentle donkey to Mass at the church of Saint-Chartier, a mile and a half distant, and a picnic lunch in the towered medieval castle adjoining it. There were the first serious lessons in writing. Bored, however, with the routine childish exercises, Aurore would pen long letters to Ursule, Hippolyte and her mother, without ever showing them. "My grandmother surprised me with one and found it very entertaining"—and she encouraged Aurore to continue. Aurore's feelings for Madame Dupin began to undergo a change.

But for a long time the child's sentiments were reserved for Sophie. Half child herself, Sophie had helped the children build a "magic" grotto, choosing the brightest-colored stones and pebbles they brought her from the nearby brook. It was lined with the finest moss to bed the Sleeping Beauty whose legendary name was Aurore, and inside was a little cascade and tiny pool. But when Grandmother was led to it proudly by Aurore, she responded very disappointingly by observing that the "pool" was in reality an old washbasin from the kitchen and the "cascade" was water pouring from a pot held by a partly hidden maid. Aurore's disenchantment was with her grandmother: "I really suffered when anyone tried to deprive me of my fantasies."

Uncle Beaumont, as Aurore called her granduncle Abbé de Beaumont, came that summer and stayed some time, exuding a jolly, relaxing presence. As pink and white as his half sister, Madame Dupin, he was rather fuller of the milk of human kindness—"and the handsomest old man I ever saw." He dressed in velvets, silks and black satin; he was an exigent gourmet and an excellent raconteur. Mourning was put aside—it was hardly proper to be more pious than the Abbé—and there was even an evening of theater—a playlet by the Abbé for the children to perform, a flageolet solo by Deschartres, a bolero danced by Aurore. Music was an early passion of Aurore's and brought her closer to her grandmother; she would sit beneath the harpsichord as Madame Dupin played.

Uncle Beaumont had come primarily in his capacity as senior family counselor. A decision had to be reached about Aurore's future. It was clear by the end of fall that Sophie's staying on at Nohant would intensify an already strained situation: there was no room at Nohant, however spacious the small château, for rival mothers. Nor was Sophie enamored with life at Nohant with Madame Dupin as its mistress. "Child of Paris," she felt at ease only in the capital. There was also Caroline, left behind in her boarding school. Madame Dupin would not harbor Caroline's coming to Nohant: she represented Sophie's past, one more source of contagion for Aurore. To be sure, Hippolyte was no less a bastard, but he was Maurice's.

Two thousand francs a year had been left to Sophie, along with Maurice's debts. "They could not provide a brilliant education for both her daughters"—an argument skillfully employed by Abbé de Beaumont, when he urged Sophie to leave Aurore completely in Madame Dupin's charge. Moreover, he had little difficulty impressing her with the other advantages of class and position, if Sophie had a brilliant marriage for Aurore in mind as well—facts of life which were hardly for the Abbé to impart to *her*.

The child listened attentively without letting on. When she was alone with her mother, she covered her with kisses, imploring her, "Don't give me away to Grandmother for money!"

There were few secrets at Nohant and less neutrality. "Do you really want to return to your garret in Paris and eat beans?" Madame Dupin's housekeeper Julie challenged the child.

George Sand: "Her words revolted me. The beans and the little garret seemed the ideal of happiness and dignity to me."[2]

Even Ursule took part. "With the common sense of the poor,"[3] she said to Aurore: "It is nice to have a big house and a big garden like this to play in, and carriages and dresses, and good things to eat every day. Where do you think they come from? From the *richness*. So you shouldn't cry, because if you stay with your grandmamma, you'll always have your *age of gold* and the *richness*."

Aurore was unconsoled; the day she dreaded finally came. There was even a formal agreement signed between her rival mothers on February 3, 1809: Madame Dupin would be the sole guardian of Aurore; in return she would redeem Maurice's debts and provide Sophie with an additional thousand francs a year. The departure of Sophie from Nohant followed. Aurore was promised that she too would soon go to Paris on a long visit and stay near her mother, whom she might see every day. There was a bustle of preparations for her benefit, but it would be almost two years before the Paris trip.

With all the warmth she could summon, Madame Dupin tried to compensate for Aurore's sense of terrible loneliness. She continued her ward's education with more indulgence than before—"no more reprimands, no more punishments." However, "she never treated me sufficiently as a child, so anxious was she to teach me *control*":

> I must no longer roll on the ground in play, laugh loudly, talk like the Berrichon peasants. I must stand erect, wear gloves, make no noise, talk in whispers to Ursule. . . . I must curtsy to the guests, no longer set foot in the kitchen, see to it that

the servants addressed me with a formal *vous*. . . . And I must even address my grandmother in the third person: "Would Grandmother permit me to go out into the garden?"

Madame Dupin avoided heat, cold, drafts and the sun. She kept Aurore by her side in her closed bedroom, as if in a quilted box. "Amuse yourself quietly," she would say to Aurore, giving her an album of engravings to leaf through. A dog's bark in the garden, the song of a bird, made the child start with pleasure. "I would gladly have been that dog or that bird." But when Aurore was in the garden with Madame Dupin, she had to be decorous and attentive, ready to pick up a dropped glove or snuffbox. Grandmother could scarcely walk and could no longer bend; and it seemed she had hardly any blood, for there was little drawn from her veins when she was bled. "I had a dreadful fear of becoming like her, and when she told me to be very quiet beside her, it seemed that she was commanding me to be dead."

Aurore was six when she made the promised trip to Paris. It was a grand voyage, for Madame Dupin traveled, when she traveled, in great style, rarely complaining during the three- or four-day journey (there were overnight stopovers). The voyage in the winter of 1810–11 was made in the huge berlin of Nohant, the large, closed carriage that was a "veritable house on wheels . . . its innumerable compartments packed with provisions, bonbons, perfumes, playing cards, books and money." On one seat sat Madame Dupin and her *femme de chambre*, wrapped in blankets and lap robes; on the other, Aurore.

Aurore was restless, but not bored, especially traversing the forest of Orléans towards sundown. Brigands were less frequent then, she heard her grandmother recount to Mademoiselle Julie, but before the Revolution, "holdups and murders occurred so often . . . that when the robbers were caught and condemned, they were hung from the trees at the very spot where they had committed their crimes." One could count the new ones each season, she said, if one traveled the roads often. "I remember one winter seeing a large woman who had hung for quite a while, her long black hair blowing in the wind and the ravens circling about her, quarreling for her flesh." The image would haunt Aurore for years every time she rode to Paris.

Madame Dupin's apartment in the French capital was on Rue Neuve-des-Mathurins (near today's Opera) and not far from Sophie's modest rooms. Sophie came every day for Aurore, and the two would walk the streets, enjoying the fairs, the dancing dogs, the bird markets, the toy shops. Aurore was dressed in the cut-down clothes of Madame Dupin, who lectured her on the simplicity of good taste. Sophie, who found her looking "like a little old lady," somehow persuaded Madame Dupin (who may have wisely counted on Aurore's reaction) to allow her to comb Aurore's long hair upward in the new "Chinese" fashion, so tightly that the eyes slanted.

But Sophie kept her side of the bargain. She told the child again of the better life she would have with Madame Dupin, and unfailingly she came without Caroline. The young girl had not seen Aurore since the trip to Spain and she constantly asked her mother to take her to Aurore on the days she was home from her boarding school. Sophie eluded her request. One evening, however, when Sophie was dining out, poor little Caroline walked to Rue Neuve-des-Mathurins and presented herself to the *portière*. She asked to see Aurore. She was taken to the door of Madame Dupin's apartment.

Madame Dupin was dozing in her armchair. Aurore's maid Rose went quietly to the door, opened it to Caroline, then beckoned to Aurore, who tiptoed towards them. Madame Dupin stirred awake and demanded to know what was going on. Reluctantly Rose told her. Harshly Madame Dupin ordered Rose to send Caroline away. Aurore heard Caroline sobbing as she left. Madame Dupin, regretting her loss of self-control, tried to coax Aurore to her lap. The child fled to a far corner and flung herself to the floor. "I want to go home to my mother!" she cried. "I don't want to stay here!"

Aurore had a feverish night. Shortly afterwards she had measles, from which she emerged in a delirium to hear the two maids talking in a low voice, unaware that she was awake and listening. Rose was a sturdy redhead who had served Sophie while Maurice was still alive. Mademoiselle Julie lacked Rose's forthrightness and had earned Aurore's suspicions as Madame Dupin's informer. She was a devourer of books, especially popular novels, "such as impassion chambermaids, so I often think of her when I write my own." She and Deschartres belonged to the camp of Madame Dupin; "Rose, Ursule and I belonged to my mother's."

Mademoiselle Julie: "See how foolish the little one is to love her mother, who does not love *her*. She did not come a single time while Aurore was ill."

Rose: "She came every day to have news of her, but she did not come up, because she is angry with Madame because of Caroline."

Mademoiselle Julie: "She could have come without seeing Madame. She told Monsieur de Beaumont that she was afraid of catching Aurore's measles. She's afraid for her complexion."

Rose: "Oh, no, it is because she does not want to give the measles to Caroline!"

"This explanation calmed my burning desire to embrace my mother. She came the next day to the door of my bedroom, and said *bonjour* from there. 'Go away, Mamma dear!' I cried, 'do not come in! I do not want to give my measles to Caroline!' 'You see,' said my mother, 'Aurore knows me. They cannot keep her from loving me!'"

Thus "was my poor child's heart buffeted by the rivalry of my two mothers. I was the object of their perpetual jealousy and conflict, the prey of prejudice, the victim of the sorrows I caused."

After Aurore had recovered, Madame Dupin unexpectedly bundled her into a carriage and took her to Rue Duphot. Caroline opened the door to them with a touching dignity. "Please be seated, Madame Dupin," she said politely. "I will call Mamma, who is with a neighbor." Prepared for rudeness, Madame Dupin was visibly disconcerted and uneasily took pinch after pinch of snuff. When Sophie arrived, she proceeded to make amends. She did not want to separate Aurore from Caroline, she said. Aurore might well see her—at Sophie's. She left Aurore with them for the afternoon. "As she rose to leave, Pierret arrived, just in time to help her into her carriage."

Gleefully Aurore explored the familiar objects—the alabaster clock, the vases of yellowed paper flowers, the old foot warmer from which she had spun her tales. Thus, Sundays were spent in Sophie's apartment (Caroline's day home from her *pension*). But at five in the afternoon Caroline would go to her aunt Lucie, and Sophie and Aurore would join Madam Dupin for one of Abbé de Beaumont's ritual Sunday dinners. The Abbé had a *cordon bleu* cook and a connoisseur's taste. Invariably around his fine table, or at his fire, were the *vieilles comtesses*—the old countesses—and their consorts, a number of them abbés.

"Tell me," said Aurore one day to the Abbé d'Andrezel (who wore a stylish spencer over his habit), "if you are not a priest, where is your wife? And if you are a priest, where is your Mass?"

It was a sally much appreciated in that company, and as Madame Dupin took Aurore on a round of visits to her "ancient" friends, Aurore further sharpened her "specialty of observing people and things." Madame de La Marlière was loud (permitted *old* women), gay and cynical. She cheated at cards and was a regular at the Abbé de Beaumont's gaming table. And there was the Chevalier de Vinci, whose wig traveled towards his nose with each convulsive jerk of a nervous tic.

While the Abbé and his guests played cards after dinner, Aurore wandered through her granduncle's apartment. Holding a candle, she examined the Italian and Flemish paintings, the Boulle furniture, the *objets d'art*. From doorknobs to ceiling moldings, the décor was meticulously *style Louis XIV*.

The long winter in Paris left Aurore more peaked and pale than ever, and Madame Dupin decided to return to Nohant. She conceded that Sophie might come for a time, since Aurore was so upset at the thought of separation. They traveled in two carriages (the berlin had been sold), Madame Dupin and Mademoiselle Julie in the one, Sophie, Rose and Aurore in the other. And Caroline returned, in tears, to her boarding school. Ursule was rediscovered, there was a second truce between mother and grandmother, and Madame de La Marlière, who came on a visit, brought a certain gaiety and breath of outside air to Nohant. Napoleon was at the summit of his power, all seemed well with France, and therefore the world. It would be six seasons before the icy retreat from Moscow.

Deschartres' tutorship of Aurore now began in earnest. He taught her French in the classic manner by teaching her Latin; resignedly Aurore accepted it. He exposed her to history and mathematics and later, best of all, to his library. The first years he was remarkably patient, remarkable in view of his irascible character and contrasting treatment of Hippolyte, whom he beat regularly. Hippolyte, however, was hugely to blame. He thought of little else but mischief and playing tricks on people. One day he threw flaming brands up the chimney, declaring them a sacrifice to the infernal gods, and set the house on fire. Another day he stuffed gunpowder into a fire log, which exploded, splattering the kitchen with the *pot-au-feu* on the stove. He called it a "study of the nature of volcanoes."

Mischievously, too, Ursule and Aurore mixed the sacks of experimental seeds carefully nurtured and noted by Deschartres for his quarrelsome papers to the Royal Society of Agriculture. To his astonishment, sorghum grew where he expected buckwheat, woad where he watched for colza. The sacks of seeds were ranged among the books of Deschartres' library, which offered their own fascination. Those out of reach on the top shelf dealt with medicines "for man and beast," but there were also tomes on sorcery and black magic, and that is what most interested the children.

Hippolyte, during one hurried search, said he had discovered the magical formula for invoking Satan. He and Aurore—Ursule was too frightened to join them—drew the prescribed circles, triangles and squares of Pythagoras and the signs of the zodiac, on the floor. When the devil appeared, Hippolyte planned to order him to carry off Deschartres, his flute and his old schoolbooks. But no devil appeared, there was not even the smallest flame of hell-fire.[4]

In the autumn, Sophie left Nohant for Paris, telling Aurore she could not abandon Caroline. Aurore followed at the first frost with Madame Dupin, Deschartres and Hippolyte. The latter was going to a boarding school in Paris and was in seventh heaven: he was wearing his first pair of boots. That winter of 1811–12, George Sand notes bleakly, "I saw a bit less of my mother"—not simply because of Madame Dupin, but because of Sophie's own decision.

When Hippolyte was not at his boarding school, he would join Aurore and a new friend, Pauline de Pontcarré, in dancing lessons. His *changements de pied* and *battements* shook the house, the dancing master despaired, and the lessons for Hippolyte were dropped. Three times weekly the girls received their writing master, dancing master and music master. (The writing master had devised special instruments of torture for keeping the head, neck and three fingers of the writing hand straight, and sold them profitably to the parents.) Drawing lessons were added for Aurore, taught by a Mademoiselle Greuze, who said she was the daughter of the famous painter. (There is no certainty.) Aurore did not like the lessons, but she learned to sketch very well, as so many of her class and generation. In effect, these were the finishing lessons for marriage, and Madame Dupin already dreamed of Aurore's betrothal to a Villeneuve—one of the rich, titled scions of Dupin de Francueil's first marriage. "Remarks of the chambermaids made me aware of this dream of my grandmother"—but the Villeneuves refused to receive Sophie, and that, for Aurore, made even the thought of it an impossibility.

There were more preoccupying thoughts in Paris that winter. "In every house we went we met officers leaving for the army, saying their farewells." They were almost gay, so accustomed were they to Napoleon's victories. One cavalry officer laughed when his aunt offered him her furs. "He would warm himself, he said, with his saber." And he rode off with his fellow officers, eventually to reach Moscow.

Meantime the Dupins, Hippolyte among them (the Paris school had not worked out), returned to Nohant, but without Sophie. Aurore found a changed Ursule. Left behind as always with her family at La Châtre (she called it "exile"), she was now embittered by the "*richness*" of Nohant which would never be hers. It was decided to send her back that fall to her family—"for her sake." Neither she nor Aurore, however, was told of the decision, and the summer passed as usual. Or almost as usual. Aurore too was changing.

The three sisters of Ursule would spend Sundays at Nohant. "The house, garden and woods would resound with our laughter. But at the end of the day, I would have enough. I had acquired the habit of study, and I suffered an indefinable ennui in the midst of my amusements. I would never have admitted it even to myself, but I missed my lessons in music and in history." Aurore also missed her mother and expressed it *maternally*. "From childhood," says George Sand, "I have loved little children with a maternal passion." For Aurore, that summer, it meant the pleasure of taking tender charge of the little children of the Fleury, Duvernet and Papet families, old friends of the Dupins.

Thus summer passed, or rather waned, for autumn brought news of the dramatic burning of Moscow and the beginning of the disastrous French retreat. "Until then I had regarded my nation as invincible, Napoleon's throne as that of God." Aurore had long, exhausting dreams (*pace* Freud) of flying through the air to the rescue of *La Grande Armée*, lost in the Russian snows, and virilely leading it back to France. Winter of 1812–13 was spent at Nohant; the following summer as well. War had twice resumed and columns of sad, famished German prisoners were seen in the Nohant countryside.

During this period there was one—and there may have been only one —visit of Sophie to Nohant, as Aurore approached the age of ten, which would remain sharp and unforgettable in her mind. Until then, whenever Sophie came to Nohant, Aurore would sleep on a divan in Sophie's bedroom and slip into her mother's bed during the night—"I lay there like a little bird nestling against its mother's breast. I slept beautifully and dreamed the most beautiful dreams." This time Madame Dupin sternly forbade Aurore's sleeping in Sophie's bedroom:

> Despite my grandmother's wishes, I managed to stay awake two or three nights until my mother retired, and barefoot I would tiptoe to her bedroom and snuggle deep in her arms. She did not have the heart to send me away, and she herself was happy to fall asleep with my head on her shoulder. However, my grandmother became suspicious, or was informed by Mademoiselle Julie, her *lieutenant de police*. She came up the stairs and surprised me tiptoeing from my room. Rose was severely scolded for my escapade. Hearing the noise, my mother emerged from her room. Sharp words were exchanged. My grandmother said it was neither healthy nor *chaste* for a girl of nine to sleep with her mother. . . . As for myself, I was so *chaste* that I did not even know what the word meant. . . . "If anyone lacks in *chasteté*," I heard my mother reply, "it is you for having such ideas! . . . My kisses are purer than your thoughts!"
>
> I cried all that night. I felt physically and morally bound to my mother, as if by a diamond chain, which my grandmother, vainly trying to break, tightened all the more around my chest so that I gasped for breath.

A reconciliation among the three generations of Dupins took place melodramatically over the tomb of Maurice, but the heart of little Aurore was torn by the struggle. Deprived of her father at the age of four, she had again lost her mother. There remained her grandmother, but Madame Dupin was failing and soon fell into a coma. Anxiously Deschartres, Rose and Julie hovered over her, and Aurore discovered her own triste concern for the old woman—who recovered almost simultaneously with the restoration of the Bourbons after the fall and exile of Napoleon. "Well, my dear," she said to Aurore, "it seems our cousins"—the two brothers of the beheaded Louis XVI—"are on the throne." The throne, for the tormented child, was as distant as her "cousins."

Sophie had left, and returned. Madame Dupin had sought her aid during a period of particular difficulty with Aurore. The month of her stay, however, had passed badly, and she repacked for Paris. Seeing the valises made ready, the poor child was seized with terror. "I thought my mother was leaving never to return. . . . I threw myself into her arms, at her feet. I rolled on the ground, I begged her to take me with her. I told her that if she did not, I would run away on foot to Paris to be with her."

She took me on her lap and tried to make me understand the situation. "Your grandmother," she said, "would reduce my allowance to 1500 francs if I carried you off with me to Paris."

"Fifteen hundred francs!" I cried. "But that's a lot of money! It is enough for the three of us!"

"No," she said, "it would not even be enough for Caroline and me. Her *pension* and upkeep consume half my allowance already, and I can hardly live and dress on what is left. . . . If I take you with me, we will be so poor you will never be able to endure it. You will ask me to take you back to Nohant and your 15,000 francs a year."

"Never, never!" I cried. "We will be poor, but we will be together. . . . We will be happy!"

"I am not thinking of myself," she said, "but of you. I am afraid that one day you would reproach me for having deprived you of a good education, a good marriage, and a fine fortune."

"Ha," I cried, "a good education! They want to make a wooden doll of me. A good marriage! With a man who would be ashamed of my mother. And a fortune that would cost me my happiness! . . . I would rather be poor with you!"

"Listen to me, my child," she said, "you do not know what being poor means for a young girl. I do, and I do not want you and Caroline to undergo what I went through—a poor orphan at fourteen.* Suppose I were to die and leave you orphans? Your grandmother might take *you* back, but never your sister. What would become of *her?*"

The argument was too coldly reasoned for a child of ten. Sophie felt obliged to hold out a larger measure of hope. She promised Aurore that

---

* In fact, Sophie's father had died when she was eight, her mother when she was seventeen.

she would open a dress shop in Orléans—with the help of Pierret and
Aunt Lucie—and they would all be together again, "as in the days on
Rue de la Grange-Batelière." Nor could Sophie resist adding a dig at
Madame Dupin: "And when your grandmother drives down the
grandest street in Orléans, she will see a sign in letters as big as your
arm, 'Madame-Widow Dupin, Dress Merchant'!"

Aurore jumped with joy and eagerly helped her mother to pack, believing it brought closer the day of their being together. That evening
she wrote Sophie a long letter which she hid behind a portrait of her
grandfather, telling her of it in a note tucked into Sophie's night bonnet. She beseeched Sophie to come to her during the night. At two in
the morning Aurore went to her mother's bedroom. Sophie had read
the letter, but had chosen not to go to Aurore. Sophie cried, she pressed
Aurore to her heart, and she confessed that "the dress shop" was to
gain time and win Aurore's patience, so that she might accustom herself to staying with her grandmother. The words were like knife thrusts
"as cold as death." Sophie, seeing the child's hysteria, promised to return for her in three months. Aurore pleaded for a reassuring letter
from her mother which she might keep. Sophie promised she would
write one that night and place it behind the portrait. It was a long day's
night of promises. Sophie left in the morning. Aurore ran to the portrait. There was no letter. "I told myself that my mother did not love
me as much as I loved her."

Sophie, says George Sand forgivingly, had suffered too much in her
life, and was now avoiding it. "As for myself, I was avid for suffering. I
had a great deal of energy for it." Aurore turned in her loneliness to
Liset, a peasant boy two years younger than herself whom her mother
had befriended. He was in tears on Sophie's departure, and Aurore comforted him, playing the mother both missed. When Madame Dupin un-
derwent another attack and was put to bed, Aurore shifted her maternalism to her grandmother, sitting for hours by her bedside.

Deschartres continued his lessons in Latin, in arithmetic and botany,
omitting "the mystery of generation and the function of the sexes."
Hippolyte was impossible, good only for madcap pranks. Rose proved
short-tempered and given to paroxysms of blind rage, "and she now
began to beat me," though she regretted it afterwards. By reporting it to
Madame Dupin, "I could have ended this state of affairs, but I did not
choose to." Rose, Aurore felt, truly loved her and her mother, and they
had struck an unspoken bargain never to carry tales to Madame Dupin.
That was for Mademoiselle Julie. In the meantime the Hundred Days
of Napoleon's return to power came and went, leading to Waterloo and
the Emperor's last exile on Saint Helena Island. But more pertinent
was the departure of Hippolyte for a cavalry regiment in 1816, leaving

Aurore alone at Nohant with her grandmother, Deschartres, Julie and Rose.

Two melancholic years of a turbulent puberty tempered only by music and reading followed each other. Passionately Aurore played the piano, and music might have been George Sand's profession had concert playing been open to women—or had Aurore's new music professor, the organist of La Châtre, not killed the musical impulse with his lifeless instruction. In any event, Aurore continued at the piano, composing and singing fragments of songs—"Oh, pretty butterflies, come light on my flowers"—"Mother mine, dost thou hear me? I cry, I sigh for thee!" And she continued to write, one metaphor remaining in her memory—"the moon in its silver *nacelle* ploughing the clouds." A composition of Aurore was sent to Sophie, who replied in one of her rare letters: "Your pretty phrases made me laugh. I hope you do not learn to talk that way." Aurore wrote back that she would never become "a pedant, never fear! When I want to say I love you, I adore you, I will say it as simply as that." But she ceased her compositions.

She stopped writing, but the necessity for "inventing," for "creating a world of fictions," had no respite, and never would ("all my life I have had a novel working in my mind"). Two books were of the greatest influence as Aurore reached twelve: Homer's *Iliad* and Tasso's *Jerusalem Delivered*. Homer, Aurore found grander, more heroic, the Italian Tasso, "more romantic, more of my time and my sex." Neither completely satisfied Aurore's religious hunger or filled the void left by the rationalist deism of her Voltairean grandmother. (Preparing for her first communion, she was taught the catechism by a La Châtre priest, "but I understood absolutely nothing of it.") "So I created a religion for myself."

Of this void and loneliness was born Aurore's private deity, "Corambé"—a name of her own invention. "He was as pure and charitable as Christ, as radiant and beautiful as Gabriel," and as personal as a pagan god. Indeed, more personal and familiar: "I completed him by dressing him on occasion as a woman, for what I had loved and understood most was a woman—my mother. . . . Thus he had no sex and assumed all forms." And Aurore loved him "as a friend and a sister."

In a thicket of Nohant's woods Aurore raised a secret altar and "temple" to Corambé. In conscious imitation of Sophie she chose the most beautifully colored stones and shells for it, the finest mosses and ferns, and she hung garlands and birds' nests and cockleshells as sacred lamps. She told no one of Corambé (whom she called her "novel"), and she came unobserved to his altar to commune with him. No sacrifice seemed proper. Instead, in his celebration, she liberated butterflies and caged birds—which first she had had to capture. One day, however, Liset, who had been looking for Aurore, found her before the altar of

Corambé. "Ah, mam'selle," he cried, "what a pretty little crib for the Infant Jesus!" The secrecy shattered, the spell was broken. Corambé came no more to their trysting place, though he continued to live "in my head." "I tore down the temple with all the care I had taken to build it"—and she buried the garlands and cockleshells under the ruins of the altar.

Paralleling the sense of loneliness and the communion with Corambé was the daily life, the seeming opposite. Young peasant children filled that more public part. Aurore ran and played with them in the fields and helped them with their chores, hunting eggs, harvesting fruits, vegetables and grains in season, caring for the farm animals, the cows and heavy-headed oxen and the sheep. It was to give her the strength that would make her capable throughout life of "a man's" efforts, "*des marches et des fatigues presque viriles.*" She particularly loved autumn and winter, when the flax-combers would spin their tales around the peasant fires, telling of specters and will-o'-the-wisps which they, as the peasants listening to them, had seen the week or the night before. Witchcraft and sorcery coexisted with the catechism for the Berrichon peasant, and Aurore herself as a child believed in the Great Beast of the Black Valley, though *she* had never seen it.[5]

But the interior life had the greater intensity. "The novel of Corambé continued to unfold," coinciding with Aurore's communion, an odd, half-hearted affair which she regarded as "an act of hypocrisy" on the part of herself and her grandmother. She went through it for her grandmother's sake, and Madame Dupin, for form's sake. There was some relief for Aurore in resigning herself to it, but soon after she was replunged in months of melancholy.

Brooding constantly within Aurore—whether half-disguised as, or semi-assuaged by, Corambé—was "the unhappy passion" for the absent Sophie, and at last it broke out, full and unrepressed. Aurore resolved to join her mother, to share her fate, "to be ignorant, hardworking and poor, but at her side." She now openly revolted by neglecting her studies, and was sternly scolded by her grandmother. One day, reprimanded more severely than ever, she burst from Madame Dupin's bedroom, hurled her books to the floor and shouted her exasperation to the walls. She was heard by Mademoiselle Julie, who flung the rebuke at her: "You should be sent back to your mother!"

"Send me back to my mother!" Aurore exploded. "That's just what I want, that's all I ask! . . . I don't want to stay here . . . I want to return to my mother. . . . It is she I love and will always love, no matter what you do. And now go make your report! I'll sign it!"

Mademoiselle Julie turned on her heel and went into Madame Dupin's bedroom. Aurore waited, hoping to be called by Julie and told, "Your grandmother is suffering, go to her and console her!" But a crueler strategy had been devised. Aurore was ordered to her room and directed to stay there. Her grandmother did not want to see her. Since Aurore "detested" her, she would let her go to her mother if the child persisted. Aurore accused Julie of having lied to Madame Dupin, because she did not detest her grandmother—she loved her, though "I love my mother more."

For three days Aurore was kept in her room, descending for her meals only after her grandmother had left the table. The servants were consternated, but could do nothing. At the end of the three days, Aurore went to her grandmother's bed chamber. Its door was closed to her. She went out into the garden and on to the woods. There she helped an old woman gather faggots and kindling. For hours she bent beside her, working all day. She listened to the blackbirds and purged her sadness in the labor. At the day's end, Aurore went with the old woman to her thatched cottage. Famished, she partook of her black bread. She exulted: she had done the work of the poor, she had eaten the bread of the poor. "Never had anything tasted so good!" She could work! She would work for her mother, "carrying her firewood, making her fire and her bed." They would "belong to each other at last."

Aurore was found by Rose and brought back to Nohant. The following morning Rose led her to her grandmother's bedroom. "Go to her," she said gently, "embrace her and ask her pardon." But in her grandmother's arms "there awaited the cruelest, most poignant and least merited punishment." For three days Madame Dupin had searched her mind for a way "to bind me to her."

I kneeled beside her bed and took her hands to kiss them. In a vibrant, bitter voice I could not recognize, she said, "Stay on your knees and pay close attention, for what I am about to tell you, you have never heard before and will never hear again from my lips. These are things that are said once in a lifetime, because they are never forgotten. But if they are not heard, you can lose your life, your very soul."

After this preamble, which made me shiver, she began to tell me about her own life and the life of my father . . . and then about the life of my mother, as she knew it, or thought she knew it. Here she was without pity, and without understanding, for there are temptations, misfortunes and a fatality in the life of the poor, which the rich can never understand, no more than a blind man can conceive colors. . . .

She should have told me how my mother had redeemed her past, how faithfully she had loved my father, how modestly and retiringly she had lived since his death. This I knew, or thought I knew. But my grandmother wanted me to know that if she had told me everything about my mother's past, at least she was sparing me the truth about her present—that there was something new and secretive in my mother's life which she did not want to tell me about, but which would make me tremble for myself, if I insisted on living with her.

Then my grandmother, exhausted from her long recital, her voice choked, her eyes moist and burning, let fall the harshest, most horrible accusation: my mother was a lost woman, and I was a blind child, seeking to throw myself into the abyss!

It came to me like a nightmare, seizing me by the throat. Each word brought death. I felt the sweat on my forehead. I wanted to interrupt, to jump to my feet, to fly away. But I could not. I was nailed to the floor on my knees. My brain was bursting. . . .

Aurore pushed the old woman's hands from her with horror. She ran from the room and fell into Rose's arms. Passionately she kissed her, "for Rose had never spoken this badly of my mother, though she must have known what I had just learned." She fled to her room. "Tears brought no relief. . . . I have never learned how to cry." She recovered her composure: she would show no signs of weakness, not even that of falling ill. She went down to dinner. She forced herself to eat. "When they gave me my lessons, I pretended to work." She resumed the surface of her life. She loved her mother still, but she no longer made any plans to steal away to her. "There was no more novel, no more sweet dreams. Corambé was mute. I lived mechanically." Then she went into the fields and found solace among the peasants, health and a restored strength as well. But it led to a renewed, more vigorous revolt. Aurore became an *"enfant terrible."*

Madame Dupin faced the dilemma, the impossible choice: either Nohant or Sophie for Aurore—the one which Aurore now hated, the other which might be fatal for her granddaughter. She concluded on a compromise. She called Aurore to her. "My child," she said, "you have lost all common sense. You are intelligent, but you are playing the fool. You could be nice to look at, but you are deliberately neglecting yourself. Your hands are impossible, your skin is black from the sun, you walk like a peasant. . . . You were a charming little girl. You must not become an absurd young lady." She had decided, she said, to send Aurore to a convent in Paris.

Aurore: "And I will be able to see my mother?"

Madame Dupin, icily: "Certainly, after which you will be separated from both of us, so that you can be educated."

Her grandmother took Aurore to Paris where she saw Sophie. She had hoped against hope that her mother would say no to the convent and take her to live with her but Sophie had not. On the contrary, "she extolled the advantages of money, surprising and hurting me by her manner . . . saying the convent would be useful to me." For there in the Convent of English Augustinians, where Madame Dupin had once been imprisoned, Aurore's classmates, as Sophie well knew, would be the daughters of the titled and the otherwise privileged.

At fourteen, Aurore entered the Paris convent, "without any apprehension, regret or repugnance." She thought to find there at last a neutral territory, "a resting place from the rivalry I had been suffering."[6]

5

From Deviltry to Piety and Back

> Life in common among people who love each other is the ideal of happiness. I felt it at the convent, I have never forgotten it.
>
> —George Sand, *Histoire de Ma Vie*[1]

During the Elizabethan Age, the revival of Protestant persecution drove English Catholics to the Continent, and the ladies among them into convents. The one of our concern was established in Flanders but moved to Paris in 1634.[2] Here on the eastern edge of the Latin Quarter the Convent of English Augustinians had flourished, and by the time Aurore entered its walls, it was as fashionable a finishing school as any in France. Two thirds of the nuns, lay sisters, boarders and visiting priests—perhaps one hundred and twenty in all—were English, Scottish or Irish. They spoke English, but taught some classes in French; the nuns took tea three times a day and invited the best-behaved of their students to sit with them.

Dressed in the purplish cotton serge that all wore at the convent, Aurore wandered through the grounds as Madame Dupin talked to the Mother Superior. She saw a veritable "village" of vine- and jasmin-covered buildings, a "labyrinth" of courtyards, corridors and cloister, Gothic chapel, workrooms, classrooms, dormitories and kitchens among which she "would feel lost for a month."[3]

It was recreation hour. Aurore joined the *petite* (lower) *classe* in a racing game, then said farewell to her grandmother. The leave-taking was cool and Madame Dupin reproached her for it, to Aurore's astonishment ("I thought I did well to control myself and that it would please her"[4]). From her Paris apartment, Madame Dupin sent Aurore a letter, admonishing her to hold herself upright, physically and morally, to take care of her cough, adding that she would be sent a piano (it would be a harp) once she had her own room. From Nohant came a longer letter of advice, including the counsel not to look at her feet when she was dancing, and not to fail to learn English, for which she would one day be grateful.[5]

Aurore was grateful, at this time in her life, for the convent itself ("I was tired of being an apple of discord"). But the beginning was not signally successful. Thirty of the *petite classe* were crowded into a joyless room, Aurore among them and Mademoiselle D———, "fat, dirty, bigoted, cruel, vindictive," over them. "She had delight in punishing, voluptuous pleasure in scolding." She made them kiss the ground in penance, and was enraged that she was so hated. She alternately petted and tormented a poor little English child of five or six, "pale, thin and sickly," whose hysterical shrieks could be heard from morning until night. The first day Mademoiselle D——— caught sight of Aurore, she remarked, "'You look to me like a very dissipated person,' and from that moment I was classified among her aversions."

And so, despite her initial eagerness to submit to convent discipline, Aurore was led to revolt, "resolutely enlisting in the camp of the *diables*"—the Devils. They were a handful of the disdainful ones, scornfully distinguishing themselves from the *sages*, or Sensible Ones, and above all from the *bêtes*, or Stupid Ones. They were led by Mary Gillibrand, an Irish tomboy. She had clapped Aurore strongly on the shoulder. Aurore had sturdily returned the same gesture. They became friends. At night the Devils engaged in their favorite adventure—"finding the victim," a woman who had somehow been imprisoned for two centuries somewhere in the labyrinthine cellars and hidden rooms of the convent. "Every condemned door, every obscure corner, every wall that sounded hollow" might hold her.

Devil at night, by day Aurore was a reserved "still water"—as the Mother Superior described her to Madame Dupin. Even in her moments of deviltry, she would withdraw into the private reflecting pool of herself. "I have always had my hours of dolorous reverie and somber thoughts. My English companions made fun of them. 'You are low-spirited today,' they would say [in English]. 'What is the matter with you?' And Isabelle would say, when I was sallow and downcast, 'She is in her low spirits, in her spiritual absences.'"

There were other nicknames for Aurore. One girl called her *Calepin*, or Notebook, "because I had a mania for little notebooks." A sister surnamed her Madcap and Mischievous, and when she entered the *grande* (upper) *classe*, she became Auntie and the Marquis de Sainte-Lucie (presumably because of her Christian name Lucile).[6] And Aurore had yet another for herself, which she penned on the flyleaf of an English book: "Generalissimo of the French Army of the Convent."[7]

There were schoolgirl crushes, inevitable in the essentially unhealthy, unisexual seclusion of a convent, and George Sand dwells on them: Valentine, a child of nine or ten, whom Aurore cared for, "as if she were my daughter"; Susanne, whom she nursed, "as she was continually ill"; Héléna, chosen victim of the Devils, whom Aurore took under her wing—and similarly, George Sand would nurse and care for Musset, Chopin and others. In the *grande classe* those loved would be Isabelle, Sophie, Fannelly and Anna, in that order of affection, and Aurore would inscribe on her books and notebooks as a cabalistic symbol joining them all, *Isfa*, in a simultaneity of infatuation. Each of the four gave Aurore something, and to each Aurore gave herself. "Anna liked to talk, so I listened. Sophie was a dreamer and melancholic, so I walked with her in silence. . . . Fannelly liked to run, laugh, rummage about, organize some deviltry, so I became all fire and joy and movement with her."

Even physically the *grande classe* was an improvement. The classroom had five or six large windows opening on the flowering garden of spring. The great chestnut trees were in candle, rivaling those of the Champs Elysées. The "*Comtesse*" who directed it—so called because of her grand airs—may have been dull and somewhat ridiculous, but she was good-natured and easy to get along with, and one sister was simplicity, sweetness and goodness itself.

Above all, for Aurore, there was Mary Alicia Spiring, not quite thirty, with gentle blue eyes and a soft manner. Aurore became one of her "daughters" and Mary Alicia her "mother," a form of special adoption in the convent.

The notebooks one day blossomed into a novelette of one hundred pages which Aurore was emboldened to show to her friends. Its hero was Fitz Gerald—whom Sophie and Anna found somewhat of a bore and its unnamed heroine no less so. Understandably, since hero and heroine spent their time praying in a tree-shaded chapel. Another fictional effort, "a pastoral novel," Aurore herself judged so bad it found its way into the stove "one winter day."[8]

Most satisfying for the young writer was finally having a cell of her own.[9] George Sand: "Life in common among people who love each other is the ideal of happiness. I felt it at the convent, I have never forgotten it. But every thinking being must have some hours of solitude and reflection. It is only thus one can savor the sweetness of communality."[10]

And a description of Aurore's cell written at this time allows one to savor George Sand's style years before she became George Sand:

My room is one floor down from the sky, next to the eaves and the nightly concert of the cats, neither round nor square and within which you *might* be able to take six steps, if they are short ones. My curtainless bed is in the widest part, next to the wall on one side and two feet from the window on the other. When I say "curtainless," I am wrong to complain, because I do not need curtains. The beams and sloping roof are just above my head, so that when I get up from bed in the morning I always bump my head against the beams, shaking the roof. My window, which has four small panes, looks out across an expanse of tiled roofs and chimney pots around which whirl the flights of sparrows who share my dry bread. The wallpaper of my cell once was yellow—or so I am told. But whatever its color, it is fascinating, for it is scribbled all over with names, sayings, verses, dates and all kinds of foolishness of everyone who has ever lived here. And whoever lives here after me will have something to amuse *her*, because I will cover the walls with complete novels and poems for her to decipher, and scratch intriguing drawings on the stone sill outside my window with a knife. My furniture is a harp, a wicker chair and a chest of drawers over which I have to jump to reach the door. . . . Sometimes [when it rains] I dream I have fallen into a river, and when I awake I find myself in it! . . .[11]

Aurore slept little, and would need little sleep the rest of her life. And she dreamt of Nohant, "which became paradise in my mind"—joining, if not replacing, the attic rooms on Rue de la Grange-Batelière. But she did not linger on thoughts of a return. Even her vacations, by preference, were spent at the convent with the accord of Madame Dupin, who believed it would shorten the time of her studies. Then: "I became *dévote!*"

Aurore's sudden conversion to fervent, devotional piety is recalled as taut, emotional drama. "The only violent love I had experienced—filial love—had left me exhausted and broken. I had made a sort of cult of Madame Alicia, but it was a tranquil love. I had need of an ardent passion. I was fifteen."

During afternoon Mass in the chapel, Aurore distractedly leafed through a book someone had given her, *Lives of the Saints*. Idly she read the story of Saint Simeon Stylites, the pillar-hermit. The following day at Mass, she read another life of a saint, the day after a number more. Then, lifting her eyes from her book, Aurore was struck by a painting in the chapel of Christ agonizing in the Garden of Olives. She was moved to study a second painting—of Saint Augustine under a fig tree—with its "miraculous ray of light on which was written the famous *Tolle, lege* [*take and read* the Holy Book], the mysterious words which the son of Saint Monica heard issuing from the foliage." Aurore read the life of Saint Augustine; she reread the Gospels. However, she had been too armed against the Scriptures by her grandmother and by "Voltaire's mockeries."

But that evening, as night was falling, Aurore walked disconsolately in the convent's cloister. From its shadows she observed "devout women come to lay their souls at the feet of the God of love and contrition." Out of "curiosity" she followed one into the chapel—and from deviltry, for it was an hour when permission had to be asked by a student to be there at all. In the dim light of a single, silver lamp, the curiosity faded, the deviltry disappeared, "the aspect of the chapel at night had seized and charmed me."

> The scents of honeysuckle and jasmin wafted in on a fresh breeze. A star lost in the immensity of the night sky seemed framed in a great window, and it regarded me fixedly. The birds sang, there was a calm, mystery, spell and enchantment such as I had never dreamed. . . . Time passed, the chapel was closing. . . . Suddenly I was shaken to the very core of my being, a dizziness overwhelmed me as if I were enveloped in a dazzling white light. I seemed to hear a voice murmur in my ear, *'Tolle, lege!'* I turned, thinking it was Mary Alicia who was talking to me. I was alone. . . .
>
> I felt faith taking possession of me by way of my heart, as I had longed. I was so grateful and moved that a torrent of tears poured from my eyes. I still loved God . . . that ideal of justice, tenderness and sanctity . . . a direct communication had suddenly been established with Him, an invincible obstacle between His infinite fire and my dormant flame had been melted away.

"Direct communication" with God would be George Sand's hallmark, and often He would be Herself, as personally self-expressive as Corambé.

The following morning Aurore slept through Mass, so exhausted was she. But the exhilaration persisted. "From that day all struggle ceased, my piety took on the character of a passion. My heart captured, I resolutely, and with a kind of fanatical joy, showed reason to the door."

Calmly Anna and Sophie accepted her conversion, but did not follow her into piety. Fannelly was most upset, but Aurore was too self-absorbed to comfort her, and when her confessor, Abbé de Prémord, came to the convent on his monthly visit, she eagerly brought him the "news," expecting hallelujahs and praise. Instead the sensible Abbé, a Jesuit of almost sixty years, gently sought to temper Aurore's *mysticisme* with his own more worldly common sense. But "Saint Aurore," as she was now called, was beyond reasonableness. Had she not "shown reason to the door"?

Impulsively Aurore befriended a poor, tubercular lay sister at the convent ("I saw in her a saint of old") and, with the enthusiasm of a teenager, helped her with her lowly tasks. She too would become a nun, Aurore told her, and they would work and serve God together. Aurore took this news to Sister Mary Alicia. The latter listened, then quietly remarked that there was no haste. Think about it, she said, and remember, "You do not yet really know yourself."

The good sense of Abbé de Prémord and Sister Alicia kept Aurore "from the imprudent vows young girls often make to God," but it did not markedly diminish her devotional passion or excesses. In lieu of a hair shirt, she wore a filigree chaplet that satisfyingly scratched her neck till it bled; and she wept for hours, as a form of prayer, in the chapel. "I literally burned like Saint Teresa. I could no longer sleep, no longer eat," and she worried sisters and classmates alike as she began to waste away. The exaggerated piety endured several months, but would soon come to a normal end. The excesses, after all, were not so very exceptional for a passionate girl on the threshold of young womanhood.

Once again, during his monthly visit, Aurore presented herself to Abbé de Prémord, confessed her sins, exposed her failings and awaited her penance. "My child," said the Abbé, "your parents are sorely concerned by your behavior. You mother believes that convent life is killing you. Your grandmother writes that you are being made into a religious fanatic. You, on the contrary, know very well that everyone is trying to bring you back to reason." He continued thus, and then said, "I therefore impose as your penance that you return to the games and innocent pastimes of your age. From this afternoon, instead of prostrating yourself in the chapel as your recreation, you will run and play with the other children in the garden."

In truth, the Abbé's words fell on fertile ground. Aurore was emerging on her own from the extremest forms of her sudden piety. She resumed play with the others, "at first passively, then with pleasure, then passion, for physical activity was a vital need of my age and my body, and I had been too long deprived of it." Fannelly, Anna and the others, "*diables* and *sages*," welcomed her back. A sense of calm returned to Aurore. Six months passed. Aurore was herself again. She even organized a little troupe, put on skits and a play for the convent, choosing the actors, ordering the costumes.

The play was Molière's *Le Malade Imaginaire*. Rather, it was what Aurore could recall of the comedy read at Nohant, since "Molière was forbidden in the convent." She wrote her own version from memory, delighting in the nuns' delight in its performance, in their laughter at lines forbidden them to read. There was even a moment during the same year when an epidemic of student rebellion swept all the lycées, *pensions* and even the girls' schools. For an hour a cry of "*Révolte, révolte!*" was heard in the *grande classe* of the convent, and soon after Aurore arranged another evening of theatricals.

Madame Dupin, however, remained uneasy, and she came to Paris. Aurore was still expressing a desire to become a nun, and her "quiet resolution" gave Madame Dupin more concern than her recent excesses. "When she saw me well again and gay . . . but nevertheless continuing to go nightly to the cloister with more pleasure than ever, she was afraid, and she resolved to take me back with her to Nohant."

Madame Dupin's decision struck Aurore "like a thunderbolt, in the midst of the greatest happiness I had ever known." The nuns, seeing her calmly persevere in the notion of eventually joining them, were becoming convinced of her sincerity. All but Sister Alicia and Abbé de Prémord, who knew her better than all the others and told her the same thing: "'Keep to the idea, if you find it good. But no imprudent vows, no secret promises to God, and above all not a word to your family until you are absolutely certain. . . . Your grandmother's intention is to have you married. If in two or three years you are still not married and have no desire to be, we will talk again of your future.'"[12]

It was April 12, 1820. In three months Aurore would be sixteen.

6

The View From the Saddle

If destiny had had me go directly from the domination of
my grandmother to that of a husband, it is possible . . . I
should never have been myself. . . . But fate decided that
from the age of seventeen there would be an interlude between the two exterior forces, that I would belong to myself for almost a year, to become, for better or worse, essentially what I would be the rest of my life.
—George Sand, *Histoire de Ma Vie*[1]

The specter of marriage haunted Aurore, that strange anomaly of
abrupt intimacy with a virtual stranger, attracted by her fortune before
he had even seen her face. And the haste of her grandmother was as apparent as her aging. "You must marry quickly, my child," she said to
Aurore, "for I will not be long on earth. . . . I would die in anxiety
and despair were I to feel I left you without a guide or support in life."

"And who is this husband, this master, this enemy of my dreams and
desires," Aurore asked herself—this man they would have her marry?[2]

Madame de Pontcarré, her grandmother's friend, proposed one; her
mother Sophie, through Uncle Beaumont, another. Aurore said she
found the first "quite ugly," though in truth she never really looked at
him, and quite forgot what happened to the other. She would need another six months or a year, Madame Dupin decided, and the bags were
packed for Nohant.

Aurore asked her mother whether she would join them. "Certainly
not!" Sophie exploded violently, "I will not go to Nohant before my
mother-in-law is dead!" Nor would Sophie have Aurore stay with her in
Paris. The "wildness in her dark, beautiful eyes," her erratic behavior,
struck Aurore for the first time "with a secret fright." Was her mother

half mad? Wisely that evening Madame Dupin took Aurore to the theater and hurried their return to Nohant.

They traveled in the swift blue calèche, and after they arrived Aurore slept in the bedroom once reserved for her mother. The air was fragrant with fruit trees in flower, the nightingales sang and in the morning she heard the distant chant of the peasants working the fields. But she woke with a mixture of "joy and sadness," in part because of the pleasure of Nohant in spring, in part because of the uncertainties after the easeful routines of the convent, but in largest measure because she was young and a child of her century, touched by its splenetic restlessness, by the brooding *mal du siècle*.

Late one afternoon Aurore wrote *in English* the Keats-like lines so expressive of her feelings, and, writer-born, she transcribed them in her dark-blue leather notebook.

> *Written at Nohant upon my window sill at setting sun, 1820:*
> Go, fading sun! Hide thy pale beams behind the distant trees.
> Nightly Vesperus is coming to announce the close of the day.
> Evening descends to bring melancholy on the landscape.
> With thy return, beautiful light, nature will find again mirth
> and beauty, but joy will never comfort my soul. Thy absence,
> radiant orb, may not increase the sorrows of my heart: they
> cannot be softened by thy return![3]

Letters went off to convent classmates, telling of "ailing, suffering and tears."[4] To provide the "melancholic" Aurore a companion, Madame Dupin invited Madame de Pontcarré and her daughter Pauline, who had also been at the convent. There were excursions into the country and piano duets in the salon, and in August Deschartres joined them in a pastoral sketch celebrating Madame Dupin's birthday. Aurore, brown as "Spanish tobacco," dressed boyishly as a shepherd, played opposite Pauline of the cream-and-honey complexion, who performed as the pretty villager. The contrast (Aurore noted) pained Madame Dupin, and Pontcarré mother and daughter departed not long afterwards.

However, Hippolyte now arrived on a three-month leave, dashingly dressed in the uniform of a sergeant of the hussars, and taught Aurore how to ride in a droll but effective fashion. "You see," he said, plumping Aurore on the back of the gangly, good-natured, four-year-old mare Colette, "it all comes down to this: to fall or not to fall. Everything else follows." Five or six times she half fell off, but each time she grabbed Colette's mane and held on. In an hour she was riding, and for a lifetime she would enjoy it. Hippolyte himself rode the grandson of the terrible Leopardo, whom Aurore named General Pépé after the leader of the Italian Carbonari, showing sympathy for revolutionaries at the age of sixteen. In a week they were jumping ditches and hedges and racing through the fields. But in December Aurore was plunged once more in melancholy. Hippolyte had left. She was alone with Deschartres and her grandmother.

She had become "an anchorite," she wrote Émilie de Wismes, deliberately shortening her day by rising late. "Then I lunch, chat with my grandmother for an hour or two, go back upstairs, play the harp and the guitar, read, warm myself, spit into the fire, as they say here, stir my memories, write in the ashes with the fire tongs, go down to dinner and while my grandmother plays cards with Deschartres, I go back upstairs and jot down a few ideas in my notebook."[5]

It was the time of winter thoughts and winter reading, particularly Chateaubriand's *Génie du Christianisme*, which Aurore read aloud to the fitfully dozing Madame Dupin. The pages disturbed Aurore: their humanism clashed in her mind with the more dogmatic *Imitation of Christ*, a gift of her beloved Sister Alicia. To be Christian, she read in Chateaubriand, meant above all to love man. "Of all religions that ever existed, the Christian religion is the most poetic and humane."[6] The austerity of the orthodox creed appealed to the lingering *dévote* in her, but Chateaubriand pointed to a reconciliation of humanity and religion, of human and God, that would prove permanent in the life of George Sand. "I would rather believe that God did not exist," she would write, "than believe that He was indifferent."[7] Her Christian socialism came out of that winter's struggle, however inchoate at the time.

"Read the poets," her old convent confessor advised her when she wrote to him for counsel, "they are always religious. Do not fear the philosophers, they are powerless before the true faith." And with the Abbé's tolerant permission, Aurore roamed freely among the books of her grandmother's library, even those forbidden by the Church: Locke, Bacon, Aristotle, Leibniz ("the greatest of them all" though she brushed by his theories of "Monads, Unities, Pre-Established Harmony,"[8]), Pascal, Montaigne, Pope, Milton, Shakespeare, Dante ("which I read in fragments but dreamt of all night"[9]), and Franklin (whose portrait would hang over her bed). But it was Rousseau, whose romantic salute to the heart's sensibilities evoked "the superb music of Mozart," who marked "a pause in my intellectual exercises."[10]

In the depth of the same winter and in the midst of such exhilarating, mind-expanding reading, Madame Dupin mentioned, as if it were a commonplace, the latest proposal of marriage. A general of the Empire, "a man immensely rich but fifty years old with a great saber-scar across his face," had formally asked her hand in marriage. He asked for no dowry—he had apparently remarked her in the parlor of the convent—but he had set one condition, said Madame Dupin: "You are no longer to see your mother."

"You refused him, did you not, Grandmother?" Aurore anxiously asked.

"Yes," said Madame Dupin, showing her a letter from Cousin René de Villeneuve. The letter, however, was not completely reassuring. It suggested their coming to Paris to discuss the proposal further. They would go to Paris, said Madame Dupin, but Aurore should have no dread. "I will not hear of *that* marriage."

They would not go to Paris. One morning soon after their talk, Deschartres woke Aurore at seven to tell her that her grandmother had had an attack of apoplexy and paralysis during the night. He had found her on the floor.

Madame Dupin partly recovered but now rarely left her bed. Aurore cared for her nightly, taking pinches of snuff to stay awake, and became more nurse than ever, breaking the routine only to tramp through the fields in her sabots or ride Colette across the slushy countryside of early spring.

Thus it was Cousin René de Villeneuve who came to Nohant, to aid Madame Dupin with her last will and testament. To prepare Aurore for it, Madame Dupin spoke to her of Sophie. "Your mother," she said, "is odder than you can imagine. You do not really know her. She is so primitive that she loves her children like a bird loves its young. . . . Once they can use their wings, she flies away to another tree and pecks at them with her beak to drive them off." The old woman spoke of her own relatives, the Count and Countess de Villeneuve, as the proper people for Aurore to live with after her death, and of their château at Chenonceaux as the place for her until marriage, or until her majority, when Nohant would be hers.

Aurore rode often with her cousin, a cultivated man in his forties, found his company amusing and regretted his leaving. But now began the long, determining interlude between "the domination of my grandmother" and the future reign "of a husband."

The care of Madame Dupin was largely at night; Aurore had the day to herself. Also Nohant. Increasingly an adoring Deschartres was turning over the estate to her, instructing her in its accounts, even its direction. Together they visited the peasants, supervised the plantings, discussed the crops. Aurore also helped Deschartres with his surgery, accustoming herself to the sight of blood and sickness, to the mending of broken heads and the amputation of smashed fingers and hands. She learned to accept the physical aspect of life; she discovered the satisfaction in helping life's wounded, in lending her strength to the weak.

Similarly enduring was Deschartres' encouragement of Aurore to dress as a young man, complete with cap, blue blouse, *redingote* (riding coat) and trousers. A neighboring count so clad his daughter, explaining to Deschartres its convenience for riding, climbing or jumping a horse. "Abounding in good sense," Deschartres did the same for Aurore, but unlike the count, he could not spend as much time with his boyish companion. Instead he had little André accompany her mounted on a pony, as her "page boy."

The male riding dress reminded Aurore of the time she wore an aide-de-camp's uniform in Spain, and it gave Madame Dupin such a wrench she wept, and cried, "You look too much like your father!"[11] There was a more amusing but no less pleasing occasion when a young girl mistook her for a young gentleman. She had ridden to a village, where she was unknown, to sketch an old Gothic castle of which she had heard. First the *dame* of the castle had emerged to propose to the "gentleman" sketching that "he" buy the castle. Then the *damoiselle* had appeared, had called Aurore *Monsieur* and had "cast meaningful sidelong glances" at her, as Aurore played along with "great effect."[12]

It was but one side of Aurore, as it would be of George Sand. She was at the same time bewitching Stéphane, her first young man.

Thin, elegant, consumptive, aristocratic and poor, Stéphane Ajasson de Grandsagne of La Châtre was two years older, the last of ten children, the oldest of whom had just died without a penny. As a student of medicine Stéphane had appealed to Deschartres, who was acquainted with his father, Count de Grandsagne. He had presented the young man to Aurore and engaged him to give her lessons in science, particularly anatomy and osteology to help him in setting bones. The lessons took place in Aurore's bedroom. The skeleton of a little girl served as their laboratory, text and pretext. Stéphane also brought other unfleshed bones—of arms, legs and skulls—for Deschartres and themselves, which were difficult to conceal, if indeed he made the effort, from the curious villagers. They rode together, Stéphane taught Aurore to shoot a pistol[13]; they were young and in love and scornful of public opinion. Their affair became a La Châtre scandal.

The good burgers were shocked by the freedom Aurore was boldly exercising, above all the Amazon-like dashes across the countryside on horseback, the eroticism and challenge of a woman astride a horse. Neither sensation may have been strictly in the eye of the beholder. "I felt alive and reborn," says George Sand, "dominating the landscape from the saddle," fixing eyes on the horizon and not, as the man on foot or the woman with "lady-like" modesty, on the ground. And lifting her eyes to the horizon, Aurore poetically merged with the vast blue spaces, greened with the distant verdure, and took wings, as in the dreams of her childhood. The hooves of Colette splashing through the Indre River lent rhythm to her thoughts, but it was in galloping through the wind that the most leaden and sometimes suicidal thoughts were left behind. "One breathed . . . one's body rediscovered joy," and in hurdling Colette over obstacles, "one reconquered life."[14]

On horseback a woman is the equal of a man, and Aurore found her companions among the young men of La Châtre, playmates of her childhood. Often they would clatter through the village, its windows shuttered against Aurore's passages through the streets with her companions.

The scandals were cumulative: Stéphane and their pistol practice (one story had them using a holy wafer as a target), Aurore's masculine dress and unfeminine studies (she disinterred graveyards with Deschartres, they said, looking for skeletons), her love of hunting and her hunting of men (little André was whispered to be her lover, and cousin René, though married, a suitor).

Aurore's confessor, the curé of La Châtre, had heard things, he told her. Was she perhaps beginning to fall in love with someone? Stéphane? It was one of a series of questions. Aurore was furious, then hurt, by his "indelicacy," so unlike Abbé de Prémord's gentleness during confession, *his* refusal to probe, to disturb with provocative inquiries the essential "innocence of his young charges."[15] She never returned to the curé or the parish church, though she was still concerned about the true meaning of Christianity.

It was a period of many things, a complex of activities and concerns: the rides, the young men, the reading, the music, the nursing of Madame Dupin, the surgical assistance of Deschartres, the love for Stéphane, which neither his father nor the cautious Madame Dupin encouraged. For the one, Aurore's mother was an impossibility; for the other, the Grandsagne instability and poverty made the thought of marriage impossible. And as fall approached, Madame Dupin's health so declined it was now *her* salvation that preoccupied Aurore.

Should not her grandmother be reconciled with the Church and be given absolution? Even as she herself left off going to Mass, Aurore wrestled with the dilemma, for at the same time she did not wish to worry her grandmother or urge her into a hypocritical action. Again she wrote Abbé de Prémord for advice, and again the old Jesuit responded with moderation. You do well, he replied, to do nothing. To torment your grandmother with thoughts of imminent death would be cruel and could be fatal. "You were well-inspired to keep your peace and allow God to work His own indirect way. Never be afraid of what your heart counsels: *the heart can never be wrong.*" The words were underscored in George Sand's memory.[16]

Late that summer, however, the Archbishop of Arles, yet another relative of illegitimate birth (he was the natural son of Dupin de Francueil and Madame d'Épinay), arrived on the family errand of converting Madame Dupin from her stubbornly Voltairean ways. He shocked

Aurore with his vulgarity and she quarreled with him. Resignedly Madame Dupin agreed to do what was necessary and told Aurore it was really for her sake. Aurore in her honesty pleaded with her grandmother not to do anything she disbelieved. But Madame Dupin had her old friend, the curé of Saint-Chartier, come to perform the sacraments, as Aurore knelt by her bedside and the servants and peasants of Nohant looked on.

In the fall Stéphane returned to Paris and his medical studies, forwarded Aurore the some hundred books she had requested of him and wrote her a dozen or so love letters. Distance cooled their relationship, but Stéphane seems to have gone to see Sophie in Paris, or so Sophie, scolding Aurore for her conduct, would write, perhaps to conceal her true informant at La Châtre, Dr. Joseph Decerfz, Madame Dupin's friend and physician. Aurore's reply is an insight into the burgeoning George Sand.

"My Dear Mother," it began,

> I have read the letter you had the goodness to write with respect and attention. I should not permit myself to reply to your reproaches, if you had not ordered me to do so immediately. . . . My grandmother being ill, you say, I leave her to run in the fields. I believe, my Dear Mother, that if I had not gone out during the past eight months of her illness, I would be as sick as she. . . . Monsieur de Grandsagne, you say, has told you that I have a belligerent character. To give credence to such an assertion, Dear Mother, is to believe that M. de Grandsagne has a profound knowledge of my character. I do not believe that I am sufficiently *intimately linked* to him for him to know either my good or bad qualities. He did tell you the truth when he said he gave me lessons in my bedroom. But where else should I receive people who come to see me? It seems to me that my grandmother is too ill to be disturbed by visitors. . . . You would prefer when I go walking that I take the arm of my *femme de chambre*, or of a maid. It would apparently keep me from falling, like the leading-strings when I was an infant and you were caring for me. But I am seventeen years old and I have learned how to walk by myself. . . . The man who would marry me, you say, would have to be a giant or a weakling. If so, I may never marry, because I no longer believe in giants and I do not like weaklings. . . . I will never look for a man who could be his wife's slave, for he would be a fool. But I do not think an intelligent man would want a wife who would feign shyness or fear. . . . Any man who liked such ridiculous behavior would be too ridiculous for me.[17]

A week later Sophie wrote Dr. Decerfz of Aurore's "harsh, stinging" letter.[18] A month later, Madame Dupin woke from a coma, called Aurore to her and said, "*You are losing your best friend.*" They were her last words. She died the day after Christmas.

Dressed in her finery—ribbons, rings and lace bonnet—tranquilly, even beautifully, Madame Dupin lay in state, and so Aurore would cherish the last memory. But during the night, Deschartres came to Aurore's bedroom. While overseeing the preparation of the small family vault for Madame Dupin's burial, he told Aurore, he had remarked that the lid of Maurice's coffin had become loose. He lifted it, he said, recalling that he had never embraced her father for the last time. "The head had become detached from the body. I raised it to my lips and kissed it." Deschartres thought Aurore, "who had also not embraced her father before he died," might show the same "sign of honor and respect." Thus they went in the icy night to Maurice's tomb and Aurore too raised her father's head and kissed it, "feeling no repugnance, no unnaturalness . . . so moved and exalted was I." And such was the accepted morbidity of the time.

After the funeral, Count and Countess de Villeneuve were the first to arrive for the reading of the will, followed shortly by Sophie, who brought Aurore's aunt Lucie and her husband. The occasion was important; Madame Dupin's will involved not only Aurore's immediate future, but the disposition of a considerable fortune and estate, which included the great Paris town house of Narbonne as well as Nohant, all of which Aurore would inherit. The reading itself caused little surprise in revealing that Comte de Villeneuve was named guardian of Aurore, since he himself had helped prepare the will. Nor did it surprise Sophie, since she had been informed of it beforehand, wherefore her bringing Lucie and her husband for support.

Sophie had come determined to contest Madame Dupin's testament, and even before it was read she upset Aurore with the violence of her invective against the dead woman. Characteristically, Aurore hid her agitated feelings behind a "cold, closed" façade which further maddened her mother. She would gladly have gone to Chenonceaux to live with the Villeneuves, but neither French law, custom, nor Sophie, who had arrived armed with both, would have it so. Aurore was to return to her mother's custody.

Again Aurore concealed her feelings and acquiesced with scarcely a word, despite the sharp letter she had just sent her mother, but it may have been shock at the sudden change from being mistress of Nohant to being a child once more in the charge of an increasingly irresponsible Sophie. Or was Aurore simply biding her time?

The spitefulness of Sophie's renewed authority swiftly became manifest. When packing her things for Paris (Sophie refused to countenance Aurore's staying on at Nohant with Deschartres), Aurore was told to take only a few of her books, since her mother "had a deep contempt for what she called my 'originality.' "[19]

It was a foretaste of what life would be like in Paris.

7

Marriage in Haste

Before going to war say a prayer; before going to sea say
two; before getting married say three.

—Polish proverb

Thus Aurore arrived in Paris with belongings "that could have been
wrapped in a pocket handkerchief and a single dress that had to do for
all occasions."[1] But even then she was capable of a *beau geste*.
Deschartres had been summoned almost immediately by her uncle
Maréchal on Sophie's behalf to render an accounting of his stew-
ardship of the Nohant estate. That poor "great man," as George Sand
affectionately called him, was in arrears for eighteen thousand francs of
Nohant's rents.

Sophie threatened Deschartres with prison, unless he turned over the
missing francs or satisfactorily explained them. The old man hesitated,
stammered . . . Aurore sprang to his defense. It was she, she said, who
had received them from Deschartres, and as the heiress of Nohant she
owed an accounting to no one. "*Dévote, philosophailleuse*, liar!"
Sophie cried in a crescendo of fury. On the staircase in departure, with
tears in his eyes, Deschartres said, "I will repay them, Aurore, surely
you do not doubt it?" "Of course not!" she replied. "In a year, in two
years, in three."[2]

And so life had resumed in Paris for Aurore with her mother. She
was allowed one visit to her old convent, but no more. Her maid was
brusquely sent away and even her little dog gotten rid of. When Cousin
René de Villeneuve came to invite Aurore to dinner, Sophie bitterly
turned *him* away, saying the Comtesse herself must come to make the
invitation. Never! said the Comte, "never would she set foot *chez*
Sophie," and it would be many years before Aurore would see him
again.

Auguste de Villeneuve, René's brother, also came—once. Before *he* left, he coldly explained the "impossibility" of Sophie and of Aurore's situation. "You are seen," he said, "on the street with those people—your mother, her daughter, her daughter's husband, and that M. Pierret." How could she expect the Villeneuves "to arrange a good marriage"?

There were times, Aurore replied, when she did think of leaving her mother, since they were both so unhappy together, and "I yearned to return to the convent or dreamed of a marriage which would remove me from her absolute domination." Then sadly—and defiantly—Aurore added that however much Sophie wronged her, she could not leave her mother.

So be it, said Cousin Auguste ("as coldly as ever"), "I advise you to marry as well as you can. What does it matter, for me, if you marry a man of the people? If he's a decent man . . . Well, I see your mother turning around us! I had better leave before she shows *me* the door! Adieu."[3]

The door that closed on the Villeneuves was, in fact, a door *they* closed, and Aurore now knew there was no exit via her father's family from life with Sophie. At the same time she felt freed, "by *la force des choses*, the force of circumstances . . . to marry according to my heart's desire, as had my father, the day I should feel like it." Under the circumstances, *la force des choses* and the heart's desire tended irresistibly to coincide. Sophie's paranoiac behavior, however understandable in terms of social injustice, was no less unbearable. "Suspicious to excess, carried away in a sick delirium, she damned whatever she could not understand, snatching books from my hand because, she said, she had tried to read them and couldn't: they were wicked books" and Aurore was a wicked, "perverse" creature. Then, exasperated by Aurore's impassivity, Sophie hurled the scandals of Nohant at her head, reading from Dr. Decerfz's letters, though she concealed the name—and Aurore spent the night, stunned, in her chair, "feeling body and soul dying together." But most maddening for Sophie, in the morning Aurore's manner did not show it.[4]

It was a bold front masking the final loss of a once-loved mother, protector and companion that would leave an emptiness to be filled the rest of George Sand's life. Concomitantly, however, she was moved by the powerful feeling of having replaced her father as her mother's protector, wherefore the reply to the Villeneuves that she could not abandon Sophie, an emotional dilemma pointing to one emotionally acceptable exit: marriage. But this confronted Aurore's strong-willed sense of independence: it would have to be a marriage of her own choice, or offer the illusion of it, and here free will and *la force des choses* would be happily confused.

Aunt Lucie and Pierret tried to jolly Aurore along, telling her not to take Sophie's moods too seriously. Uncle Beaumont, on the other hand, had sunk with age more than ever into himself and his own small concerns. Once, at least, he sided strongly with Sophie when Aurore sought to see Stéphane in Paris and was prevented by her mother.[5] The totality of Sophie's control, extending to Aurore's correspondence, indicates the depth of Aurore's desperation and sense of imprisonment.

Sophie's moods did change—as frequently as her wigs—and in her own moments of despair she "told me more about her life than I wished to know." Then she would push Aurore from her, saying, "I've told you too much, I see, and you despise and condemn me all the more. So much the better! I prefer tearing you from my heart and having no one left to love now that your father is gone—not even you!"[6]

As spring of 1822 approached, a season that always aggravated Sophie's sense of bitterness and *"aliénation,"* vexations increased and a particularly distasteful marriage was spitefully almost forced on Aurore:

> For some time I was even threatened with incarceration, to which I saw fit only to reply, "You could not be *that* cruel!" They tried to frighten me by taking me to the very threshold of the prison . . . putting me into a carriage, whispering instructions to the coachman. . . .
>
> Nuns came to open the gate and led us through dark devious passages to a cell. . . . "You asked for a convent," they said. "You hoped that returning to the one where you had been educated and where you had acquired such wicked ideas, you would have the freedom you want. Oh, they would have been happy to receive you, to overlook your faults, excuse your behavior and conceal your carryings on. But here you will be carefully watched. The Community has been warned about you and your pretty speeches. Accustom yourself to spending the three and a half years of your minority in *this* cell. . . . No one will listen to your complaints. Neither you nor your friends will know either the name or the place of your retreat."

Was it for that very night? Aurore asked. "Then send for my books tomorrow morning." She was brought back to the apartment in Paris. Whether Sophie regretted the act or was ashamed of it, or had meant only to frighten Aurore and had failed, she "renounced the scheme."[7]

Again it was a bold front on the part of Aurore, who was far from the impervious *"Sainte Tranquille"* Sophie furiously called her. "I succeeded in containing myself; that was all." The reaction was interiorized. She had lost her father as a child. Now her mother was dead to Aurore, or worse, rejecting her. Aurore's thoughts turned to suicide, as her stomach, ever the center of her violent emotions, rejected all food and she suffered intense pains. "Death, I told myself with a secret joy, will come by itself from starvation."[8]

Alarmed, fatigued, or simply trying to escape her own emotional dilemma, Sophie now took Aurore to the countryside, to spend a few days with friends at Plessis.

James du Plessis, forty-one, had known Maurice Dupin briefly as a cavalry officer and had met Aurore a few months before with Sophie in Paris. In five minutes, he told Aurore, he had understood the difficulty between mother and daughter and had spoken to Sophie about it. "She was tired, she said, of your sad face and wished you would get married. 'Nothing simpler,' I had said, 'than to marry off a daughter with a handsome dowry.'" He had then suggested Aurore's staying at Plessis, where he and his wife received many bachelor army friends. Sophie, accordingly, had brought Aurore to them. Then "bored after one day," she returned alone to Paris. Within a week Aurore was delightedly calling James "father" and Angèle "mother."[9]

James and Angèle Roëttiers du Plessis, were gay, hospitable, permissive parents of five girls, four of whom were with them at Plessis, an estate thirty miles south of Paris. It was a happy household and Aurore felt immediately at home—as if she were back in the green, spacious parkland of Nohant. She rode her own horse (Figaro), read in the large library, played with the young girls, and regained her own insouciant youth. But it was no longer that of childhood. As promised, several officers paid court, notably Garinet, thirty-three, son of a farm laborer and retired from active duty; and Tessier, thirty, son of a doctor and now a second lieutenant. Neither was appealing. Several were proposed by Uncle Maréchal, Uncle Beaumont and even Pierret. They too were rejected, "but not rudely." Each had come forward because marriage with heiress Aurore, "sight unseen," was a fine *affaire*. Aurore wished at least to see what she might be contracting—or contracted—for.

In April, when the Du Plessis went up to Paris, Aurore went with them, and though she stayed with Sophie, she spent most of her time with her new foster parents. One evening after the theater (curtains rose before dark), all three were having ices together on the sidewalk terrace of the Café Tortoni. "Look!" said Angèle du Plessis to her husband. "There is Casimir!"

A slim, rather elegant second lieutenant, his hair dark and thinning, his nose rather long and sharp, his age in the late twenties, came to their table and cheerfully joined them. The Du Plessis asked about his father, Colonel Jean-François Dudevant, a close friend of the Plessis family. Casimir replied, but had his own question to put. Seated next to Angèle, he asked in a low voice, but not so low as to be unheard, who Aurore might be. "My daughter!" said Angèle loudly. "Ah, then," said Casimir, "my wife! You know you promised me your first-born daughter. I thought it would be Winephride, but this one will do better. She is closer to my own age!"[10]

A few days later, Casimir Dudevant came down from Paris to stay with the Du Plessis. In the interim Aurore had made her own inquiries. Casimir, she easily discovered, was the illegitimate but acknowledged son of Baron Dudevant and a servant, Augustine Soulès. He had been born exactly nine years before herself (July 5, 1795) at Guillery, in the province of Gascony. Two years later, however, when the Baron had married a lady from Le Mans (acquiring sixty thousand francs a year from her estates), he had set his son aside to live with the servants. During the Baron's absence some years afterwards, Madame Dudevant chanced upon the boy eating in the kitchen. She asked who he was and, when told, insisted to the Baron on his return that the child join them as their own son, since they were childless.[11] It was a story, had Aurore heard it in all its detail, which could only have endeared Casimir to her, since it recalled her own father and Hippolyte.

In any event, Casimir's natural birth was a familiar one to Aurore, and recognition by his father was part of her own family history. Socially, then, Aurore and Casimir were fairly equal—with Aurore more equal than Casimir, since men then generally married upward socially, and women downward. Financially they were equal enough, though Casimir's inheritance, yet to be assured, was much longer in forthcoming. But that in any case meant, if they married, they would have to live at Nohant—by no means a displeasing thought to its mistress!

To speak so precipitously of their marriage is to anticipate neither Aurore Dupin nor Casimir Dudevant. Each frankly sought a mate, each quickly found the other superficially, at least, quite suitable. If Aurore was the more eager, because of Sophie, Casimir was no less loath to let such an opportunity pass: there were other suitors and Aurore would not wait long.

They played with the Du Plessis children and played children's games together. "I have a comrade here," Aurore wrote Hippolyte in May, "whom I like very much. I ride, jump and laugh with him just as I did with you!"[12] And undoubtedly flirted with him, as with the other officers. But with deadlier intent. Casimir was called "my husband" by Aurore, and Aurore "my wife" by Casimir. At the same time he did not pay Aurore open court. "That would have troubled our casualness." More directly, after he had briefly left for Paris and returned, Casimir proposed marriage to Aurore, asking her consent before he had his father broach Sophie—a brotherly regard Aurore considered a good omen. "He did not speak of love, in fact he confessed to be little disposed to passion. He spoke of an enduring friendship and of the tranquil domestic happiness of our hosts as the model of what he hoped he could promise me."[13]

Heartily their hosts approved, and the approval of the Du Plessis carried a decisive weight for Aurore, since their own contentment with each other was evident. Casimir greatly benefited from the happy communal atmosphere in which Aurore saw him at Plessis. It was the image of how graceful and carefree life could be at Nohant with the father-brother figure of a comradely Casimir. They too would read, ride, perhaps even love, and be happy.

Angèle du Plessis herself carefully arranged the meeting between Sophie and Casimir's father; and Sophie was agreeably impressed by the Baron's distinction, silver hair and gentle courtliness. "I said yes to the marriage," Sophie said to Aurore shortly afterwards,[14] "but in such a way that I could unsay it. I don't know yet if the son pleases me. He is not handsome, and I would like a handsome son-in-law to have on my arm!"[15]

Before settling on the wedding day, Sophie was to meet Baroness Dudevant on her return to Paris from Le Mans. In the meantime the parents were to discuss the marriage arrangements, particularly Casimir's income and inheritance, and the marital contract. Then, suddenly, two weeks later, Sophie descended "like a bomb" on Plessis. She had discovered, she said, that Casimir had led a wild life and had even been a café waiter! Her "discovery" was greeted with a laughter that infuriated her. James du Plessis tried to reassure her, and Casimir to persuade her, that his years at military school and studies at law provided little time for the leisure of being a waiter. But Sophie departed that evening unconvinced, declaring the marriage off.

In Paris Hippolyte, who had left the Army, intervened in favor of Casimir. The Baroness came in person to change Sophie's mind, flattering her pride. The wedding was on again. Then again it was broken off. And so on until late summer. Casimir's nose was too long, Sophie said to Aurore. But finally she consented, after insisting on one condition: the marriage contract must be that of *le régime dotal*, which meant Aurore could keep—but not control—her inheritance of five hundred thousand francs, with an additional clause stipulating that Casimir, though in charge of his wife's money and property, and receiving the interest and rents from them, must allow her three thousand francs a year for her personal needs.

Prudent, oft-bitten Sophie's last gesture was a protective one, despite Aurore's protest against it as demeaning Casimir. The marriage contract was signed on August 24, 1822. The marriage took place in Paris three weeks later.

Monsieur and Madame Casimir Dudevant—twenty-seven-year-old bridegroom, eighteen-year-old bride—lingered a few days at Plessis before going on, with Hippolyte, to Nohant, "where we were joyfully received by the good Deschartres."[16]

8

Ennui

. . . ennui—I use this word, though it is empty of mean-
ing, to express the secret sorrow that consumed me.
—Letter from Aurore to Casimir Dudevant,
November 9, 1825[1]

It is mind, not body, that makes marriage last.
—Publius Syrus, *Sententiae*, ca. 50 B.C.

In marriage, talk occupies most of the time.
—F. W. Nietzsche,
Human All Too Human, I, 1878

Aurore lay in the bed that had been her grandmother's, its corner
plumes replaced by pine branches, a green canopy spread overhead. It
was her winter garden. Outside was a deep frost. She was brought half-
frozen finches, linnets and sparrows, which she warmed with her body
and brought back to life. She fed them from her hand and released
them when they could fly. She lay listlessly, she read little, enjoying the
sentimental languor of her condition.

Pregnancy for Aurore had come quickly that winter, but she had had
a fall and the loss of some blood, and wisely Deschartres had ordered
her to bed. She dreamed, dozed and acquired the "fairy fingers" and
tranquilizing habit of needlework which would never desert her.

Casimir meantime indulged his passion for hunting, leaving Aurore
alone for long stretches of time. But he was generous, though they were
living on a modest seven thousand francs a year, and attentive as an ex-
pectant father was expected to be, sending to Paris for the music Aurore
demanded and the sweets she craved. "Woe to you," he wrote to
Nicolas Caron, his *commissionnaire*, "if a woman who is big with child
is not satisfied! . . . She will blame you for it, so I advise you to have
yourself candied like a lemon tree!!"[2]

Soon Aurore, like her half-frozen birds, was released from her bed. But the languor persisted. Needlework and preparing the baby's layette occupied her as managing the estate with Deschartres and hunting with Hippolyte preoccupied Casimir, who had resigned his army commission. "You can't imagine what pleasure it is to feel your child stirring in your womb," she wrote her convent friend, Émilie de Wismes, "and to make plans for its future!"

True, after four and a half months of marriage Aurore recognized the conflicts "born of different tastes and personalities" of which Émilie had written. However, Aurore continued:

> . . . you must also understand that it is *absolutely impossible* ever to meet someone whose temperament and tastes are exactly the same as yours. . . . So, I believe in marrying one of the two must renounce all thought of self, sacrificing not only will, but opinion, seeing through the eyes of the other, loving what the other loves, etc. . . . But what a source of inexhaustible joy when one obeys the one one loves! Every privation becomes a new pleasure. One sacrifices to both God and married love; one does one's duty and simultaneously assures one's own happiness.

The almost banal determination of a young bride to make her marriage a success, the conventionality of a young married woman writing to a young unmarried friend, then a sharp remark broke through the surface.

> There remains only to ask if it is the man or the woman who is to *remake* his or her self on the model of the other. And since it is "The Bearded One who is the All Powerful" and men are not capable of such an attachment, then it is necessarily we who must bend in obedience. . . . One must love one's husband enormously to achieve happiness and to make the honeymoon endure.[3]

There was the initial, if not enormous, love of the honeymoon. Nowhere in Aurore's confiding letters to Émilie is there a hint of horror of the marital bed, of the admonition she would write twenty years later to Hippolyte on the eve of his daughter Léontine's marriage: "Try, if you can, to prevent your son-in-law from brutalizing your daughter on the wedding night. . . . Men do not sufficiently understand that their pleasure is our martyrdom. Tell him, therefore, to restrain his pleasure and to wait until he has brought his wife to understanding and response. Nothing is more frightening than the terror, the suffering and the revulsion of a poor child ignorant of the facts of life who finds herself violated by a brute."[4]

Aurore had not been brought up as a saint either in the household of Sophie or in the freedom of her invalid grandmother's Nohant. Casimir was no more brute than the average man of his time. His great fault was simply that he *was* an average man, married to an uncommon young woman. There was the "normal" shock for Aurore in the lack of *tendresse*, but there was the greater shock of disappointment in her romantic expectations. Yet, as she indicated to Émilie, Aurore was determined to make the marriage, and if possible the honeymoon, endure.

As the birth of the baby approached, Aurore and Casimir thought it wiser to put it in the hands of a Paris doctor. With a stopover at Plessis, their touchstone of happiness, they went on to the capital, where they rented a furnished apartment from a former chef of Napoleon. Here on June 30, 1823, in the small pavilion of a tree-shaded court, Aurore gave birth to a son whom she would name Maurice. "It was the most beautiful moment of my life, when after the terrible pains I awoke from a deep sleep to find this little being asleep on my pillow."[5] And she would nurse Maurice herself.

From Nohant came Deschartres in his provincial coat with its gold buttons. Solemnly he unswaddled the child and critically inspected the minuscule descendant of Madame Dupin and another Maurice. Silently the old man held the infant on his knees, and finally said in a low voice, as if to himself, that the time had come for him to leave Nohant, to live for himself.

That summer, after Casimir returned to Nohant (Aurore to follow in the fall), Deschartres announced his intention. He felt superfluous, he said, and though Casimir did nothing to dissuade him from leaving, Deschartres, as he would write a friend, had nothing against "the young Baron."

On the contrary, Deschartres wrote, he found Casimir "very gentle, with a bit of Gascony liveliness but without its boastfulness." The old man continues his description of Casimir and renders this view of the young couple: "He loves his pretty wife, as he is loved by her, and between us, he can flatter himself on having found a very agreeable mistress for his household, one who will become even more so with experience. *Eh bien*, the spectacle of their happiness adds to my feeling of sadness."[6] After vainly looking for a place of his own in the vicinity of Nohant, Deschartres had left for the capital.

Aurore's letters to Casimir from Paris add to Deschartres' "spectacle of their happiness" and indicate her own eagerness to love, and to be loved. July 29, 1823: "How sad it is, my angel and dear love, to have to write to you . . . to know that you are no longer next to me, and to think that this is but the first day since you left. How long it already seems, how lonely I feel! . . . I cannot stop crying when I think of the moment of your departure, when you too cried. . . . Good night, my

love, my darling, I shall go lie and cry alone in my bed. . . . Write me
that you love me, that you will always love me the same way." August
1: "It is always some consolation to write to you and so to talk to
you. . . . Good night, my angel, good night, my dearest friend. I need
you."[7]

Physical revulsion, "basic frigidity," as Aurore-George Sand has several times been accused?[8] The usual nightly intimacy, if anything, com-
pensated for the lack of communion, the unshared interests, she was
discovering. It would be months before her full realization of the ultimately unsatisfying relationship of even intense sensuality.[9] But the
first elements of a changing attitude began to emerge with a changing
scene. Deschartres departed, Casimir Dudevant undertook the management of Nohant with gusto. He established discipline among the domestic servants and farm hands, and reduced the abuses. He
straightened out the walks and had the old trees burned down, the old
dogs shot, the old horses sold; and he disposed of the old peacock that
had eaten strawberries from the hand of Madame Dupin. Aurore understood the measures of efficiency and gave her approval, but sporadic
fits of melancholy fell upon her. The beloved Nohant of her childhood,
where she had rambled and roamed and so recently ruled, was being
transformed by its new master. She sought refuge in a return to reading, and she wrote long letters to Émilie, now married to a young viscount.

On November 9 (1823), Aurore reviewed her life since last she wrote
—the baby's first tooth, his gaiety, Casimir's adoration for him ("they
roll on the floor together for hours"), the trip to Plessis on the way
back from Paris, the ball at Melun, where she was called "the silent
one," because of the mood that often took her to a quiet corner.

> So now here I am [at Nohant], served beyond my desires,
> tucked away in my own desert. . . . I don't miss society, but I
> would like to have two or three friends come to sketch or sing
> with me. My dear Casimir is the most active of men, in and
> out of the house all the time, singing to himself, playing with
> his child; I can hardly manage an hour of reading in the eve-
> ning. But I did read somewhere that in order to love to perfec-
> tion, two people must have similar principles and souls, but
> different tastes and personalities. I am tempted to believe it.
> Besides, I really don't know whether I would love my husband
> more if he were a poet or a musician.

On November 28:

> I am still living in solitude, if one can think of oneself as
> alone when one is *tête-à-tête* with a husband one adores.

> While he hunts, I work, play with little Maurice, or read. At
> the moment I am rereading the *Essays* of Montaigne, my fa-
> vorite. You are too new a bride to know the author, but when
> you have the time, I advise you to read him.

"Too new a bride"? Aurore the romantic, in the second year of *her* marriage, was finding comfort, a sense of resignation in the classic lines of
Montaigne, and possibly a new direction for life with Casimir. "A good
marriage, if there be any," she read in the *Essays*, "refuses the company
and the conditions of love; it endeavors to achieve those of friendship."
And between the two letters to Émilie, she wrote to Caron, thanking
him for the marshmallows he had sent (for the teething Maurice),
signing her note, "The Two Casimirs."[10]

By this Aurore meant to signify her being at one with Casimir, and
she continued to go more than halfway to realize the unity, rereading
Montaigne to reinforce a sense of willing submission to the tastes and
habits of her husband, so different from her own. She had married him,
in her haste, because she had found him "a good man" and had valued
him for it.

> But I did not take the time to find out if you liked to study,
> to read, if your opinions, tastes and temperament were similar
> to mine.

So Aurore would write Casimir, explaining herself to him and her
husband to himself.

> I saw that you did not like music at all, so I stopped playing
> the piano, because it would drive you from the room. You
> would pick up a book to please me, but after reading a few
> lines, you would let it drop from your hands, because you were
> bored or falling to sleep. Most of all, when we talked together
> about literature, poetry or philosophy, either you didn't know
> any of the authors I talked to you about or you said my opin-
> ions were silly, sentimental or hopelessly romantic. I stopped
> mentioning them to you. . . . I resolved to accept your
> tastes.[11]

Events are telescoped in this extraordinary letter. All did not occur in
a single season. But it is evident that the winter of 1823–24 was painful
for Aurore and only slightly less so for Casimir, who had the male refuge of drinking and hunting with Hippolyte, now married somewhat
above himself and living in the nearby Château de Montgivray. As
much as love, friendship between two people has its requirement of
communion, but "conversations shrank," Casimir and Aurore discussed
only "daily affairs, simple things."

Years later, after meeting a considerably older Casimir, Heinrich Heine would remark on his "expressionless Philistine face," which seemed that of neither a bad nor a rude man. "But I readily understood," adds the German poet, "that his damp cold dailiness, those porcelain-blue eyes, those Chinese-pagoda movements, might have pleased the ordinary housewife, but would in time give shivers to a profounder woman and fill her, together with horror, with a desire to flee."[12]

Nineteen-year-old Aurore, however, was not yet George Sand. She was still trying to be the conventional housewife (to be ordinary was beyond her) and was passionately attached to her child. As for Casimir, he was still the "good, simple, open husband" she described in a letter to an old friend of Madame Dupin,[13] no worse than any other she knew. If there was little communion, there was no physical rupture, no horror (yet) of a husband to be fled. On the contrary, Aurore and Casimir soon decided to flee *together* from the vacuum forming around their lives—suddenly revealed in spring.

One morning, as they sat at breakfast, Aurore was "choked by a start of tears." Casimir was "thunderstruck." To his anxious inquiries, Aurore had no clear reply: she was subject to dark, inexplicable bursts of despair . . . she was too easily upset, perhaps even "unbalanced." Casimir seized on the explanation, attributing it to Nohant, to the too recent death there of her grandmother, "To the air of Berry itself, in short, to exterior causes, as he did the ennui he himself was experiencing, despite the hunting and shooting and the activity of managing the estate."[14]

They would go, they agreed, to Plessis for a time, and they would pay for their stay, so that they might feel more at ease. The Du Plessis were delighted to have them, and they spent spring and summer with their friends, their young daughters, their frequent visitors. To all appearances Aurore recovered her spirits as she joined in the balls and theatricals, the walks and rides in the woods; as she played with her own small group, chosen from the large company; and flirted with one of the officers, arousing Casimir's jealousy, provoking his own flirtation with one of the wives. But Aurore would also go alone into the park "to dream and cry."[15]

In June, Casimir left Plessis for a tour of inspection of Nohant. On June twenty-second Aurore wrote to him: "I am so sad! You know how I adore you. I dream only of you. The slightest sign of indifference, of your paying me no heed, makes me despair. . . . Eleven o'clock. I am in my bed, my angel, but I am without you. . . . I cannot wait until Friday to have a letter from you. . . . I kiss you a thousand times, I press you in my arms, to my heart. How I will kiss you on your return! But your lips will not be too bruised to return my kisses. . . . Write me about Nohant, about our people there, about our affairs. But write me above all about yourself, telling me everything, in detail. Rest, sleep well, but *sleep alone.*"

The signs are still those of sensuality rather than of physical horror, and the last admonition was underlined. Was it entirely in jest?

During a second trip to Nohant in August, Casimir received other letters charged with "a thousand kisses," with "loving bites." Written on August nineteenth: "Now that I do not have my angel to watch over the sleep of his little family and to protect it, everything worries me. When you are back, I shall sleep in your arms like a stump. . . . Good night, my angel, my dear love, my life. I love you, I adore you, I kiss you with all my heart, I press you in my arms a thousand times." When four days had passed without word, Aurore impulsively wrote to Caron, who ordinarily forwarded Casimir's letters to her from Paris: "I will wait until tomorrow, but if I don't have news, I will go to Paris on Wednesday. I don't know how that will help me, but I am too restless. My mind is running away with me."[16]

Distance lends emotional enchantment, and convention has its phrases for the letters of husbands and wives, but Aurore's are scarcely explained away by either truism. Nor is the converse any truer: that these letters prove the happy union of Casimir and Aurore. They simply disprove marital martyrdom and display an Aurore more passionately eager, or desperate, than ever to intensify physical contact in lieu of intellectual communion.

Casimir's own letters are quite as warm, if more awkward, in their protests of love: "I press you to my heart and kiss each pretty cheek a million times to recompense you for the little tears that stream from your adorable eyes. . . . I am touched by the sorrow you experience from my absence. Be persuaded that I share it most sincerely and on my return I will be so nice that it will make up for all you have suffered —yes, my angel."[17]

Distance was one thing; Casimir's "dailiness," on his returns, another. Friction and exasperation began to mark their relationship, and on one occasion in late summer it exploded unforgivably in public.

Aurore, gay again, was romping with the Du Plessis children and their young friends. They were throwing gravel at each other. Hardly the conduct for Madame Dudevant, whose twentieth birthday had just heralded "maturity." Angèle and James du Plessis were having coffee with Casimir on the veranda. A grain or two of sand fell into Papa James' cup. He called to them to cease their play, or to play elsewhere. They paid no heed. More sharply, Casimir ordered Aurore to stop. She did not. He rose from the table, strode to her and slapped her face. It was more gesture than blow, but the striking gesture of the commanding husband was blow enough to Aurore's pride. She ran to the park, and there she cried—"in anger."[18]

This symbolic incident marked the beginning of the end. "From that day I no longer loved him and everything went from bad to worse."[19] However, there is rarely a single point in the complexity of a couple's relations, and no less in Casimir's and Aurore's, where all might be said to have unraveled. Nevertheless, the time had come to leave the Du Plessis; the incident had hastened the departure.

A return to Nohant was mutually avoided. "We were afraid of it, afraid probably of finding ourselves face to face." A small house was found at Ormesson, just west of Paris. It had a large rambling garden, a suitably melancholic landscape of lawns, glades, gloom, tall trees and a shaded tomb. Here Aurore purged her own melancholy, inviting Aunt Lucie Maréchal and Cousin Clotilde to share it with her, as Casimir slipped off in the evenings to Paris. Sophie was uninvited; she did not hide her dislike for Casimir, who reciprocated it—for which she wildly reproached him. Time passed. "Cousin" Louis XVIII was buried in the basilica of Saint-Denis in October; Aurore attended. "Cousin" Charles X succeeded him.

That winter Aurore returned to Montaigne's essays in resignation; Casimir quarreled with the gardener; they took an apartment in Paris; and Aurore took her new onset of melancholy to her old Jesuit confessor, Abbé de Prémord. Gently, in an enfeebled voice, he warned Aurore not to surrender to her mood, and he counseled her to consider a retreat of a few days at her old English convent. Aurore asked Casimir's permission. He granted it gladly. "My husband was not at all religious, but he thought it a very good thing that I was."

But the return to the convent, Aurore discovered to her sorrow, was not like coming home again. She was no longer the schoolgirl she had been; the poor lay sister she had befriended was now robust and bigoted; her old companions envied her *her* freedom; and Mother Mary Alicia advised Aurore to rejoin her world outside. "You have a lovely child," she told her. "That is all you need for happiness in this short life." Indeed maternal love was the only love Aurore still felt. She asked Mother Alicia to permit Maurice to stay with her; and he was passed through the convent wall by way of a revolving cylinder used for packages. "Bunnies! Bunnies!" he cried happily, when he saw the nuns in their flopping white headdress. But Aurore found the nights too cold and damp for the child. She left the convent, returned to Casimir, and together they returned to Nohant.[20]

It was a black spring for Aurore, that spring of 1825. In her memory it would become the season of Deschartres' death—or suicide, as she darkly believed—in Paris, though in fact it would occur three years later. Hippolyte, too, she felt lost to her, as he sank fatly into the country life of drinking, hunting, shooting and wenching, Casimir accompanying him, though not yet openly to women. Casimir still tried—George Sand acknowledges it—to be "a good husband." He even had a piano brought to Nohant, though it cost more than they could then afford. He put on a brave show of suddenly liking Aurore's playing, but it was too much for his limited patience, and Aurore herself soon sickened of it. The sickness was literal. The interiorized conflict between dream and reality could no longer be contained. She began to have fits of coughing. She became feverish. Her heart fluttered, her pulse raced, she was certain she had tuberculosis.

Before the year's end, however, Aurore would realize, and write Casimir, that in truth she was being inwardly consumed by *ennui*—that "secret sorrow"—because her very self, her talents, knowledge and passionate intellectual interests,

> I felt were wasted, for you did not share them. I pressed you in my arms. I was loved by you, yet something I could not express was missing in my happiness.[21]

* * *

When two of Aurore's old convent friends, Jane and Aimée Bazouin, suggested that the Dudevants join them and their father at Cauterets in the Pyrenees, Casimir leaped at the opportunity. The spa would offer Aurore a change of air and perhaps of mood, and restore her to health. They would go on afterwards to Gascony, to spend the summer with his parents.

On July 5, 1825, a day Aurore still celebrated as her birthday, this time her twenty-first, the Dudevants—husband, wife and child with nurse and valet—drove south from Nohant. Before leaving, Aurore wrote in her journal:

> In ten minutes I shall have left Nohant. I leave nothing that I shall really miss, except perhaps my brother. But how cold our old friendship has become! He laughs, he is gay, at the very moment of my leaving! Ah well, adieu Nohant. Perhaps I shall never see you again.[22]

9

Half a Life
Plus Half a Life
Equals Half a Life

Less than all satisfies no man.
—William Blake[1]

Nor woman.

Aurore wept as she left Nohant for the Pyrenees, joined in her tears by the two servants. It would be a long, three-hundred-and-fifty-mile voyage by post chaise: she resolved to humor her husband. But Casimir was a weak man. Humoring him fed his ill-humor, as no doubt did her tears. In Périgueux he made a violent scene. Aurore walked in the old city, and wept again. But Aurore was not a weak woman. Bitterness edged her tears.

At the tiresome journey's end, the last drive up to Cauterets, ten miles from the Spanish border, the black, massed mountains and deep gorges, the rushing, plunging torrent accompanying their carriage lifted Aurore's spirits. Nature was ever her grand restorer. The warmth of her friends' welcome, the bustle of the fashionable spa in full season, the company again of gay, admiring men further stirred her blood. She was pensive, but never naturally melancholic.

The next morning she awoke with delight and raced to the window. There was no disappointment in the view: she felt suspended in space. Later that day a spa doctor prescribed the number of glasses of mineral water to be drunk, the hot baths to be taken, the long rests to follow. But Aurore quickly abandoned the rests for walks, rides and climbs in the mountains with Zoé Leroy, a somewhat older woman from Bordeaux with whom she rapidly became a close friend. Together they dashed off on excursions, with or without Casimir, to see grottoes, glaciers and gorges, braving a chance bear. Once as they skipped about, he shouted to Aurore that she was being "singular." She turned to her companion and echoed the accusation, "Zoé, you're being *singular!*" Zoé's mocking laughter infuriated Casimir, but the sound of a cataract drowned his reply. When alone, Aurore and Zoé talked fervently of love, friendship and marriage. (Aurore to her notebook: "Marriage is good for lovers and useful for saints. . . . It is the supreme goal of love. When there is no longer love in a marriage, sacrifice remains, which is all very well for those who understand sacrifice.") They relished their philosophical talks. "We have more intelligence," said Zoé exultingly, "and think more than most, who don't think at all!" Then, defiantly: "Too bad for us!"[2]

The two young women were often alone during the first days at Cauterets, for Casimir had his own crotchet. "Monsieur hunts with passion," Aurore recorded in her journal. "He kills chamois and eagles. He rises at two in the morning and returns at night. His wife complains. It does not seem to occur to him that a time might come when she will rejoice."[3]

Foresight, hindsight or coincidence, the timing is veiled in Aurore's recounting. *Qui va à la chasse*, says a French proverb, *perd sa place*—he who goes off to the chase loses his place. Casimir's was more than filled by Aurélien de Sèze. Rather, the noble, eloquent, slim and handsome— Casimir had become heavier and had never been handsome—young magistrate of twenty-five from Bordeaux would occupy a space left achingly empty in Aurore. Even their names—Aurélien and Aurore— spelled a kinship that seemed predestined, though the eagerness with which they came together needed no such nudging by fate. Zoé approved; Jane, Aimée and Casimir disapproved. But Casimir went on hunting; Aurore and Aurélien went walking, and Aurélien fell in love. "What of your fiancée?" asked Aurore teasingly of Mlle. Laure Le Hoult, also at Cauterets with her family. He no longer had a taste "for a woman who was pretty," replied Aurélien, "but who had no mind."[4]

"Even if you were ugly," Aurélien would write Aurore, "I would have loved you as much . . . for your qualities, your soul, your gifts, the perfection of simplicity joined with the superiority of your mind, the breadth of your knowledge . . ."[5] They shared the excitement of mutual discovery, these two parched intellectuals from the provinces, and their love, in most likelihood, was all talk. But let no one underestimate the passions of the mind, especially for Aurore. As for Aurélien, conservative, Catholic and traditional as his family lineage (Louis XVI's famous defense lawyer had been his uncle), platonic love would permit an honorable relationship with an enchanting, if married, woman. They were twin souls. Aurore to Aurélien: "No one talks like you, no one has your tone, your voice, your laugh, your turn of mind, your way of seeing things and expressing your thoughts. No one but I."[6]

Aurélien de Sèze was still a very young man, however, subject to impetuous moments. When early in their acquaintance they drifted together in a small boat on the Lac de Gaube, he took a penknife from his pocket and carved "AUR" in the gunwale. For the first time he declared his love as he spoke of the bond of their very name. Aurore feigned indifference, "though my heart beat with joy." He urged her to declare her own love in return; she pretended outrage, "but didn't you sense my hand running through your black hair?"[7]

For three days, in penitence or in pique, Aurélien did not speak to her. Then he left for an outing to the mountainous cirque of Gavarnie with the Le Hoult family. Aurore did not sleep that night. The next day she pressed Casimir to take her to Gavarnie. He offered objections and even pleaded with her not to insist. So did Jane. Aurore's pursuit of Aurélien was becoming an open scandal. Nevertheless Casimir yielded, and Aurore's dominion began. When they appeared unexpectedly, Aurélien was momentarily embarrassed. But this pursuit by a glowing young woman, whose bright, lively eyes and lithe, petite figure reduced Laure to a dull jade in comparison, overwhelmed his resolve to put her from his mind.

A night or two later at a ball, Aurore and Aurélien went for a stroll in the garden. He told her of his resolve. Provocatively perhaps, she urged him to maintain it, insofar as paying her court was concerned, but couldn't they be . . . friends? It was too much for any young man to resist. It was a warm, lovely night, the corner of the garden in which they happened to find themselves was invitingly dark. "He was no longer master of himself. He took me in his arms and pressed me warmly to his heart."[8]

Was it the satisfaction of conquest achieved or apprehension that she might be going too far? "I tore myself from his arms and begged him to let me return. . . . He swore his intentions were honorable." But on their way back from the garden, after she had told him that she did indeed return his love, he "pressed a burning kiss upon my neck."[9]

Aurore fled from him—and met Casimir. "You spoke harshly to me. No doubt I deserved it, but I suffered from it, too." She assured him that Aurélien considered her his "dear sister," who inspired him with her "purity." Casimir said little to this, but he hastened their departure. It was at the grotto of Lourdes that Aurélien said his fond farewell. " 'Here,' he told me, 'in bidding you adieu, I take the solemn oath to love you all my life as I love my mother and my sister, and to show you the same respect.' He pressed me to his heart, and that was the utmost liberty he ever took with me."[10]

The letters between Aurore and Aurélien out-Plato Plato in their protests of *pureté* and platonic love. In the remarkable "confessional" epistle to Casimir, Aurore would even reproach her husband for the lofty style of Aurélien's letters as contrasted with his own clumsier ones to her. They were by then in her father-in-law's place in Guillery, where Aurore had been hurriedly removed by Casimir, as Aurélien returned from the Gavarnie idyll to the law courts of Bordeaux.

Baron Dudevant's fairly modest, two-story manor house was isolated in the Gascon countryside; in the winter wolves howled outside its walls, and one night Aurore heard a wolf gnawing at the door of her ground-floor bedroom. It was fall, however, when she and Casimir had arrived, in full hunting season. Riding to hounds was the principal occupation for the men, and riding after them that of the women, Aurore astride Colette, who had been brought from Nohant for her.

Aurore liked the Baron, but disliked the Baroness, who returned it in kind. She was too fond of Casimir, too aware of what was happening, to be cordial to Aurore. There were other Gascon gentlemen as occasional guests, but even "the young men of the environs," Aurore wrote Zoé, "were *hunters*. By this I mean a leaden-spirited type who does nothing but eat at the table and sleep in the drawing room." A bit further: ". . . my husband hunts and I grow old."[11] Eagerly, in the same letter, Aurore accepted an invitation for Casimir and herself to spend a few days at La Brède, where Zoé's family had a country house. They would stop over at Bordeaux to meet Zoé—and Aurore to see Aurélien. "It seemed to me I might be seeing him for the last time."[12]

At Bordeaux, Aurélien came to their hotel to pay a courtesy call. Casimir was absent. Aurore spoke of her sadness, her remorse, her confusion. In a gesture of weakness, she put her head on Aurélien's shoulder, asking for "moral support."[13] Unexpectedly Casimir returned and found them thus. Aurore flung herself at her husband's feet, implored his forgiveness, and effectively fainted. She recovered; she repleaded her innocence. Aurélien had left, returned, and left again. Casimir, showing "more pain than anger," behaved as if more concerned about a public scandal than about Aurore's innocence—and was fairly easily relieved on that score by his wife.

The following day Aurore, Casimir, Zoé *and* Aurélien were en route to La Brède. Sitting between the two men—the one her husband, the other her dear friend—Aurore experienced "absolute bliss." The half life with Casimir would be made whole by the relationship with Aurélien. "I saw you press my hand in front of Aurélien," she wrote Casimir in her "confessional" a few weeks later, ". . . I dared to dream of a new kind of happiness." At La Brède, however, Aurélien spent a sleepless night writing Aurore a long, renunciatory letter. Blame him for everything, he begged Aurore, tell Casimir it was entirely his fault, but assure him of their "purity," so that so fine a man would not be hurt. To that end he would pledge never again to see her.

With dismay Aurore reread the words, while Casimir was hunting. When Zoé came, Aurore told of her misery. Zoé went to Aurélien, found him "in the same state," and brought him to Aurore. Their friendship, cried Aurélien, was "so pure, so unselfish," they should so inform "the good, the generous Casimir." They would be "brother and sister." Casimir himself would share their happiness and be their companion. Indeed, they would all join together "for the sake of *his* happiness!"[14]

That night, on Casimir's return, Aurore told him the noble news. Casimir made a gesture of irritation and annoyance, then excused himself for it—he was tired, he said, from the day's hunt. He believed in her purity, he trusted her not to deceive him. "But above all," he implored, "no one must know what has happened." Aurore to Aurélien, coolly later: "It seemed to me he was torn between the need to believe me and the shameful sense of being deceived."[15]

The trip back to Bordeaux was without incident. That evening all four good friends went to the Grand Théâtre. After the spectacle Aurore and Aurélien walked apart. Yes, they could be soulmates ("confidently, I permitted you a brotherly kiss"[16]). That coming winter they would make Casimir as "tranquil and happy" as themselves, rendering him *their* "peace of mind"—so Aurore assured Casimir.[17]

But the *ménage à trois* proved little more than an unfulfilling exchange of letters, not at all the whole life of two complementary halves. From October 11 to November 16 (1825), Aurore wrote almost daily to Aurélien de Sèze letters to be sent to him later. More urgent communications went immediately via Zoé. They began by exulting in the high-mindedness of their relationship: "We are pure. Our sentiments are . . . celestial." But frustration broke through the lines: "My husband dozes in the drawing room, and I? I wander over the countryside tasting its pleasures with *you*." They recalled the "burning kiss" even as they reassure Aurélien of "brotherly love." They spoke of devouring his letters, of observing husband and child tranquilly sleeping, then of the driving need to go out into the night, hoping that "the night wind will cool my burning brain." They recalled Aurore's childhood, her search for love, the failure of Sophie as a mother, of Casimir as a husband, of her search for someone to commune with, and so of her joy in finding Aurélien. Again and again they returned to the few physical gestures exchanged—but there is no hint of even one night of love.

Frustration alone was complete. Even the physical aspect of Aurore's life with her husband was at last affected. Casimir, she wrote Aurélien on October thirteenth, reproached her for repelling his "embraces." Although it is reasonable to assume that even a platonic lover would not like to be told otherwise, the fact is confirmed a month later in Aurore's "confession" to Casimir: "Your caresses made me feel ill. I was afraid to be false in returning them, and therefore you thought me cold."[18]

Only now might one speak of the martyrdom of the marital bed, and not only for Aurore. If Casimir did not know of the correspondence, he was too subject to Aurore's moods to enjoy that "peace of mind," not to speak of "happiness," which the two correspondents had sworn to "assure" him. To find Aurore repelling his embraces was evidence enough. He was losing her to a phantom lover. Then, shortly before leaving for a tour of Nohant on November sixth, Casimir discovered the letter-journal Aurore was writing to Aurélien.[19]

His first reaction was anger and outrage, soon afterwards hurt succeeded by humiliation, the crushing sense of inferiority and failure. Casimir, at the very least, is a figure for some compassion, certainly understanding.* At the same time one must see him as legal master of a young, unhappy wife with no recourse to divorce, but only to flight. Had Aurore thought of the latter, even fleetingly? When she wrote Aurélien of Casimir's discovery, and hurt reaction, Aurélien did not repy with an impassioned proposal that they defy convention and society and run off together, but rather with reassurances of how "noble" he considered Casimir, how Aurore must open her heart and their letters to show him how "pure" they were ("Aurore, show him this letter!"). Casimir had offered to bring her to Bordeaux? "Come! We will see little of each other, if he insists. Oh, but I am sure, once he sees us together, he will be reassured." Tell him everything. "I will be your friend, and his. . . . I love you, Aurore, but with a serenity love does not allow. I love you as my dearest sister."[21]

Aurore did not yet ask for more, so far as her letters reveal. She did not yet reject the convention of marriage; she was not yet up to it, perhaps because Aurélien never would be. She would tell Casimir all, or all enough. Meantime he journeyed to Nohant to inspect the estate.

Two letters cross, each dated November seventh. Aurore to Casimir: "I sorrow thinking of the sad days and nights you are undergoing." She understands his feelings, regrets her own "hard words" on his departure. But he should not ask for too many explanations: "you know how proud I am, my friend, spare me." However, all would be well: "if we like each other enough, we need not talk a great deal to understand each other. . . . You can return untroubled. . . . You have shown how good, honest and generous you are. You deserve the same. . . . Sleep at ease."[22] Casimir to Aurore, during his stopover at Périgueux: He recalled the scene he had made here on the way to Cauterets. "Oh, my

---

* He had thought he had married an ordinary French woman, "a nobody, approved and guaranteed, and he found on his hands . . . a sister of Goethe."— Henry James.[20]

good friend, how the memory of it pains me! . . . I sincerely curse my grouchy character . . . I beg your forgiveness. . . . How sad to be alone! . . . From now on I wish only to make you happy."[23]

Not a word, not a reproach concerning Aurélien de Sèze. The contriteness is Casimir's. Fragments from his Nohant letters of November eleventh, twelfth and thirteenth: "You are everything for me in this universe. . . . You are my divinity on earth. . . . Forgive me, my good angel, forgive me. I acknowledge my faults, I will do everything to make you forget them." "Love me a little, too. I so need it." He feels "abandoned." His head aches. He suffers nightmares involving Aurore and Stanislas de Grandsagne, Stéphane's brother. He took down Pascal's *Pensées* from the Nohant bookshelves. "We will read him together, dear friend, we will always read the same things so we can always have the same thoughts." He will bring back his English dictionary and several books. He will change, she will see. He thanked Aurore for her letter ("sleep well, poor soul," it says) and is grateful for it ("I am beside myself with joy"). He has talked to Hippolyte and confided his troubles; he is hastening his return to Guillery.[24]

There will be a long letter awaiting Casimir at Guillery—Aurore's "confession" of November fifteenth. Meantime she has received a communication from Hippolyte, scolding her for being a "bad wife." Stung, Aurore sent him a sharp reply: Who had told him this? "Certainly not Casimir." If someone had told *her* terrible things about her brother, *she* would have defended him. "The same father gave us life, the same blood flows in our veins." Besides, she was submitting a solution to Casimir for the situation in which they found themselves, a solution moreover "which he himself was the first to conceive."[25]

All through the night Aurore had written her "confession" to Casimir, filling more than twenty-one pages in her fine script. How sad Casimir sounded in his November seventh letter, Aurore began. She could "neither sleep nor eat" since reading it. However, Casimir himself had told her things on the eve of his departure which had hurt her deeply. "But I want to forget them, they were torn from you in a moment of anger." To prove that she no longer holds *his* hard words against him, she is going to write him "with an open heart." She will "confess *all.*" Her very humility should prove "the nobility of [her] sentiments," which, even as she writes, causes her to weep. Casimir had asked for explanations. She had hesitated—"not only because of my embarrassment, but also for fear of hurting you." However, he himself was involuntarily guilty, for he was "the *innocent cause* of my going astray."

Remember, Aurore continued, how unhappy she had been before going to Cauterets? "If you had conducted yourself differently," she might not perhaps have been subsequently "guilty." He had seen it for himself in the journal she showed him, though she knew it would give him pain. Aurore paused. "Read no further," she wrote, "if this letter redoubles your pain." It was intended only for his own good, to provide an explanation for her conduct so that he might again have peace of mind. "If you think otherwise, throw this letter into the fire now." Aurore continued: she reminded Casimir of their first days at Plessis, when he was her "protector," her "comrade." Unfortunately, however, she had failed to learn whether he liked to read, to study, whether they had the same "tastes," the same intellectual curiosity and "personality." Alas, she later discovered they did not. Even her piano playing had driven him from the drawing room. She felt wasted, "a secret sorrow consumed me." Then she had met "Monsieur de Sèze," and was struck by "his mind, his conversation . . . the rapport between us."

The days at Cauterets and the outing at Gavarnie are lingeringly dwelt upon, but the innocence of Aurélien and herself, their deep regard for Casimir's generosity and character, are underlined. The narrative resumed: "When you went hunting, I often found myself alone with him for hours. But his conduct quieted my fears. . . . In his wildest moments . . . he would say, 'Forgive me, Aurore, forgive me again my moments of weakness, when you are forced to restrain me. Continue to do so!'" When they met again at Bordeaux and La Brède, Casimir knows well what occurred—how, at the last, they had pledged each other brotherhood and sisterhood. Why, then, forego such a pure, precious love as Aurélien offered? Why should not Casimir himself take a warm part in it? Why, indeed, not a formal *pact* binding for all three?

To this has the long letter led! Of course, Aurore wrote, ordinary people, frozen "in their little world," could never conceive such a "great, splendid project," but for a person such as Casimir, who was above such "absurd" notions of how "men" should behave, all was possible. "Until today, I have undervalued you. But if I did not believe you capable of understanding me, I should never have dared write you such a letter. . . . Today I am opening my heart to you with delight. I am sure you will understand and approve me. Remember, my dear friend, how unhappy I have been for three years, to have all feelings pent up in me, to lower myself to trivial conversations, vulgar ideas and interests. . . . I needed a friend, you made it necessary, but you didn't understand it." Now Casimir knew Aurélien was that friend who understood her, as Casimir, too, at last. They would all three be friends together!

Should Casimir say *no* to the plan, she would acquiesce, Aurore wrote, "but any possibility of happiness in my life would be destroyed" —and Aurélien would remain forever a secret dream locked in her mind. How much better were everything in the open, were she and

Casimir of the "same mind," sharing the same thoughts. Therefore Aurore was confidently submitting to Casimir the conditions of conduct for their future married life, in fact, a bold new design for living. The "Articles" read, if only in parts, like a modern contract for an open marriage:

> *Article 1*—We will not go to Bordeaux this winter. The wounds are too fresh and I feel it would be too much of a burden on your confidence. . . .
>
> *Article 2*—I promise, I swear, never to write Aurélien in secret. But you will allow me to write him once a month, or less often if you wish. You will see all my letters and all his replies. I pledge before God not to conceal a line from you.
>
> *Article 3*—If we go to Paris, we shall take lessons in languages together. You want to instruct yourself and to share my interests. That will give me the utmost pleasure. While I sketch or work, you will read to me and our days will pass deliciously in this manner. N.B.: I do not insist on your liking music. I will bore you as little as possible, by playing the piano while you are out walking.
>
> *Article 4*—You will allow me to write often to Zoé, but I solemnly pledge to allow you to see all my letters and all her replies. . . .
>
> *Article 5*—If it is at Nohant that we spend the winter, we shall read many of the useful works in your library with which you are unacquainted. You will give me an accounting of them. We shall talk about them afterwards together. You will tell me your thoughts, and I mine. All our thoughts and pleasures will be shared in common.
>
> *Article 6*—There must be no quarrels, no outbursts on your part, no annoyances on mine. . . . When we speak of the past, it will be without bitterness, without sharpness, without distrust. . . . Has not what has happened brought us closer together, and made you more dear to me than ever? Without it, I would not have known your worth, and you would not have learned how to make me happy.
>
> *Article 7*—At last, having banished all regrets, all bitterness, we shall be happy and at peace. . . . You will permit me to speak to you at times of Aurélien and Zoé. . . . You will permit me to send him your regards in my letters. It will make him so happy!
>
> *Last Article*—We shall spend the winter in Bordeaux, if our affairs permit. . . . If not, we shall postpone it, but you will let me count on it for sometime or other.

"This is my plan," Aurore concluded. "Read it attentively, reflect on it well and give me a reply. I do not think it can wound you. I await your decision with anxiety. Until then I shall live in hope." Only Casimir's consent lacked for the "perfect happiness" dreamed of at La Brède. "Our great mistake was not daring to ask you for it then. Grant it now and all again will be well."[26]

Casimir, on all evidence, was simply overwhelmed by the frontality of Aurore's "project," the superb aplomb of its presentation. It was as if he had been handed a *chef d'oeuvre* and asked not only for a comment, but an improvement. (Countering with an open proposal of *mutual* freedom, which Aurore had certainly not foreclosed, was beyond him and his time.) Its effect was a dramatic declaration of independence, admittedly limited, in which Aurélien de Sèze was essentially incidental. These would be Aurore's articles of conduct for whatever remained of marital life with Casimir.

Pauvre Casimir? He felt damned if he accepted the fiat and damned if he did not. In neither case could he rise above himself or his time. Nor would Aurore, as she warned, lower herself much longer to either. At Guillery she continued her playful conquests of the local gentry, which she had earlier recounted in her journal to Aurélien, and treated Casimir with what can only be called condescension, albeit playful as well. One day, as the two generations of Dudevants were at the table with their guests, Casimir rather heavily essayed a pleasantry. Aurore bent towards him from across the table and in a voice not so low as not to be heard by everyone remarked, "My poor Casimir, how silly can you be? But never mind, I like you as you are!"[27]

Aurore was again in the saddle—but her range was still limited and her headaches continued.

In December Casimir journeyed to Bordeaux without Aurore, explaining her absence from his side as caused by illness. On Christmas Day he wrote with delight of everybody's regard for Aurore: "You enjoy a brilliant reputation here. People talk about nothing but your extraordinary intelligence. . . . Those who do not know you burn with desire to meet you—and it is to me they come to say this! Imagine how proud it makes me. I strut like a pigeon!"[28]

In February the Dudevants traveled to Bordeaux together. After the exchange of so many letters, Aurore eagerly looked forward to seeing Aurélien de Sèze again. But something seems to have happened, or rather *failed* to happen, on this occasion which Aurore, with her quick perception, understood before Aurélien, if ever, grasped it. He was, in short, too ready to play a role that Aurore already felt inadequate. A desultory platonic lover many kilometers distant was love twice, or thrice, removed. "He loved me as I feigned I wanted to be loved,"

George Sand would write in *Lélia*, "but as, in truth, I did not want to be. Then pain and anger awoke in me."

It was pleasant nonetheless to be surrounded by admirers in Bordeaux, to sense her power over Aurélien, one of its most eligible men. Then one day when she was with Zoé, Casimir rushed in with news that cut their visit short. He was very pale. "He is dead!" Casimir cried. Aurore, thinking it was her son Maurice, fell to her knees. Told it was her father-in-law, she rose with a fierce "maternal" joy, though she was fond of Casimir's father.

The Baron had been carried away by an attack of gout. When Aurore and Casimir arrived at Guillery, a widowed Madame Dudevant received them. She embraced Aurore, but with restraint, which was reciprocated. Neither savored the other, and Aurore soon had the additional excuse that Casimir had inherited little and would come into his full inheritance only on the death of his stepmother.

The time had come for their return.

In April 1826, Casimir and Aurore were back in Nohant.

10

Aurore's Aeolian Web

The artist is an instrument whose every chord must be
played before he plays any other.*
—George Sand, letter to Flaubert,
December 31, 1867[1]

Nohant spelled Nature, and a new beginning. But the eternal return to
Nohant for George Sand was never to the same point in the temporal
space of her life. For three years the small château, its woods and farms,
the neighboring town of La Châtre and its environs would be the am-
bient setting for the existential web, the veritable cat's cradle of divers
lives, she now began to weave. These would be the exploratory years
of a pattern, strikingly modern in its deliberate ramification, that would
be singularly hers.

* * *

The multiplicity was almost immediate. Three days after arriving at
Nohant, Aurore wrote Zoé Leroy of her delight in being under her
"own roof, among her own people, animals and furniture," each tree,
each stone, each wooded walk recalling a happy chapter of her past.[2]
The people on the farms were *her* peasants, the village poor were *her*
poor, and for a period even the management of Nohant was hers. It did
not last. Aurore spent four thousand francs beyond the allotted ten
thousand for the year and Casimir resumed the management with some
triumph. His triumphs would be few. Meantime Aurore was once again
the local doctor's assistant and became the popular apothecary, con-
cocting potions from her own herb garden, applying poultices and
bandages, leeches and cauterizing irons to the sick and hurt among her
peasants. She also frolicked with three-year-old Maurice in the garden
and conversed with nature, writing letters which passed from hand to

* "*L'artiste est un instrument dont tout doit jouer avant qu'il joue des autres.*"

hand, in Bordeaux and Paris, of frogs chorusing in the moonlight. *And* she entertained old and new friends who came flooding to Nohant, filling the spaces between Casimir and herself. There was the "absent one" as well, Aurélien de Sèze, "to whom I confided all my reflections, my dreams . . . my platonic enthusiasms."[3]

The old childhood friends of La Châtre were not to Casimir's liking, nor the new ones, and he often left them for Hippolyte, drinking bouts and heavy sleep. The *bande* of La Châtre was a fascinating lot: Charles Duvernet, fair-haired, a few years younger than Aurore's twenty-two, and given to melancholy; Alphonse Fleury, gigantic though five years younger, so blue-eyed, blondly mustached and boldly primitive Aurore called him "The Gaul"; Alexis Duteil, eight years older, married and pockmarked but eminently companionable, a witty, eloquent lawyer dependably good-humored at any hour of day or night; Jules Néraud, poet-naturalist, nine years older, as married as Duteil and no less enamored of Aurore, at his best at the twitter and chirp of dawn.

One wintry night, when Casimir had gone to bed at ten, Hippolyte and Aurore walked to La Châtre to wake Duteil, never-failing inventor of impromptu capers. Aurore, who loved doubling her personality, had dressed as a peasant lad, Hippolyte as a peasant woman. Hearing violins in the otherwise silent village, they insinuated their way into a workers' ball and danced the bourrée before going on to sing under Duteil's window. He woke, slipped away from his sleeping wife and joined them. They awakened the dogs, the town gendarme, the good burgers, who shouted angrily from their windows, demanding to know why they had been disturbed. "To make sure you weren't dead!" Hippolyte shouted back. They teased courting couples hugging the walls, "philosophized" in the empty streets and, as the night paled, the two returned to Nohant as Duteil went back to his wife.[4]

Dawns with Jules Néraud were another, deeper affair: the enchantment of butterfly wings, "the intoxicating scent of flowers," the pursuit of scarabeid beetles, those scuttling gems of emerald and sapphire; "the study of mushrooms one autumn, of mosses and lichen another." For the dawns often extended to dusk, and through the four seasons; and sometimes Aurore, sometimes Néraud, swung Maurice to their shoulders as the other carried "the magnifying glass, book and tin specimen box." They shared Chateaubriand's romanticism and reread Rousseau together; plants, insects and even minerals, deadened by Deschartres' lessons, were brought back to life by "The Madagascan"—Aurore's fond name for her friend, who had been to the island in the Indian Ocean a dozen years before.

"Naturally," Jules Néraud fell in love with Aurore. Gently she put him off, saying she "loved elsewhere." But he continued to slip love letters and poems among the "butterflies, bouquets and chickens" he presented to her.⁵ Aurore returned the billets-doux to Néraud, warning of his wife finding and reading them—as indeed she did. Furious, Madame Néraud wrote to Aurore, "accusing me of hypocrisy, coquetry and everything else ending in 'y.'" But most curious, this last was in a letter from Aurore to Casimir, written when she was in Paris, where she was again seeing Stéphane de Grandsagne.⁶

Cicerone and anatomy teacher of her teen-age years, Stéphane had re-entered Aurore's life the summer of her return to Nohant. "Half consumptive, half mad," she wrote Zoé with a compulsion to confide even in the friend of Aurélien, "he came to spend some of his convalescence here." The gaunt, El Greco face and figure, the intellectual daring and sharp, scholarly mind, the high scorn for the trivial, the tedious and the conventional had rekindled the fire Stéphane had been the first to strike in Aurore. In contrast to the "absent one," he offered an intense, consuming present, a bracing disregard for the social accident of marriage to Casimir, the recapture of a dream. His approach was direct and uninhibited, his ambitions were broad and stirring. He would shortly create a "People's Library" of two hundred volumes, driving his sick, ailing body towards the achievement. The drive, Stéphane's illness, his exalted purpose were immensely appealing to Aurore. Memories of childhood and Sophie evoked an unchanging sympathy for the people, and she was never more attached than to those, intimate and sick, who needed her. What then failed between them? Aurore's irresolution, the bleakness of the future? Stéphane's commitment to the scholar's penury, his premonition of an early death? When, in the fall of 1826, he returned to his studies and work in Paris, he had pressed Aurore's hand "in his emaciated one, as if fixing a rendezvous in another world."⁷

So Aurore wrote Zoé in the sad mood of Stéphane's departure. That winter his purpose hardened, but his condition worsened. With anxiety she asked Hippolyte, in a Paris apartment with his wife, to inquire after Stéphane, whom he knew and liked. "I have found him in a pitiable state," Hippolyte responded, "choking and feverish," living beyond his means, "but with his purse generously open to all his friends"; his brain burned with brilliance; "he works fifteen, twenty nights in succession, drinking liters of black coffee. . . . He has sublimity in his thoughts. . . . Volumes spring from his pen."⁸

Aurore to Hippolyte: "What you tell me of Stéphane gives me great pain"; he is difficult, "but one must love one's friends to the bitter end, no matter what they do." He has the faults of his brothers, and his family is looked down upon. "People will always hold it against me that I am so attached to him. Though no one dares say it to me directly, I can see the condemnation in their faces, forcing me all the more to defend him. . . . He will always find me beside him when others have turned their backs on him." Were she a man, she could help him more, but "differences of sex, social condition and a thousand other things" prevent it.[9]

Meantime the correspondence with Aurélien de Sèze sporadically continued. Aurore wrote of her plans for the education of Maurice, which Aurélien considered "perfect"; when he exposed his political and social views, Aurore called him "intolerant" and "Jesuitical."[10] The contrast with Stéphane was too acute; irresistibly Aurore spoke fondly of *his* philosophy in her letters to Aurélien. Their correspondence dwindled. "The absent one . . . was tiring of the superhuman aspiration towards a sublime love. . . . His passions needed a more substantial diet than devoted friendship and an epistolary relationship. He had religiously abided by his solemn oath of brotherly love . . . but it did not restrict him in regard to the joys and pleasures he might meet elsewhere." Writing thus of Aurélien, George Sand is retrospectively describing—the transposition is transparent—herself.[11]

Constant in the web of these days is the writer's strand. In August 1827, it took the form of disparate notes assembled two years later as *Voyage en Auvergne*. Traveling with Casimir and Maurice, Aurore had found herself for health's sake a hundred miles from Nohant, at the hot springs of Mont-Dore. The initial mood was melancholy. To whom could she write? To Sophie? " 'Oh mother, what have I done to you? Why do you not love me?' " No. "I will cry in silence." To Zoé? She would show the letter "to someone I would rather did not think of me." To Stéphane? No, she was in no mood for science or "pedantry." Should she kill herself? No. "There is Maurice." She would write to herself! She would write her *Memoirs* (at twenty-three). Two hours later the sound of the dinner bell interrupted a chapter-by-chapter draft of her life—the strong, incisive lines have the impact of Delacroix's sketch books—up to the time "I left for the Pyrénées."[12]

But if Aurore began her journal with thoughts of suicide, and continued it with an outline of her life, she ended it with stories of her flirtations at the spa. "Well!" she wrote of a Monsieur de F., "Another one in love! It is really worthwhile to grow older. But what an odd type! Of course, that is always my fate. 'Dear Sir, I like to be loved, but not to be adored.' " Monsieur de F. leaves Mont-Dore. "How silly of him!" He returns in forty-eight hours for another try. *"Transeuntibus . . ."* Aurore concluded with this salute "to those who pass"—the men in transit through her life.[13]

The permissiveness of Casimir, present at Mont-Dore, skirted complicity. But he would have his own fitful reaction, as a month later, on an excursion with others along the Creuse. Mounting his horse, which balked, he struck it across the muzzle; it backed into Aurore, who was on foot. She rebuked him. Hotly he retorted: "I do what I want! If you go on talking, I'll take the whip to *you!*" Without another word, Aurore withdrew.[14] It did not much matter. She was seeing Stéphane again that fall.

Yet they had things in common one might easily slight because of the dullness, the chasm yawning between them. Not simply an indissoluble marriage and a small son—George Sand's maternalism is never to be scanted—or even the understanding achieved by Aurore's "confessional," or more significantly, its contract for a freedom *unspokenly* mutual. There was the bind of daily life, its attachment as well as its frictions. Letters between the two at this time are disarmingly affecionate and have led to charges of hypocrisy on the part of Aurore, who "loved elsewhere." In part the accusation is true, but there was an honesty as well between them, an *entente* one might call fairly *cordiale* in their domestic relations.

The political phrase has a particular relevance. Politics in its largest sense would be among George Sand's passions. Here Casimir and Aurore had much more in common than Aurélien and Aurore, soulmates though they were. Husband and wife were liberal, the distant lover was monarchist. In the fall elections of 1827, liberals and Bonapartists joined in the growing opposition to the Bourbon monarchy under Charles X. In La Châtre that meant support by the Dudevants and their friends of the opposition candidate, Duris-Dufresne. Casimir was particularly active, presiding over meetings, renting a house in La Châtre where the Dudevants gave balls and held receptions for their candidate, a gentleman of Directoire elegance and doughty, "rock-like" republicanism. The parties were gay; Aurore sent to Sophie for the latest in hats, dresses and Paris fashions; and in November the Dudevant campaign was crowned with success.

Politics as passion, politics *and* passion—Aurore's lives continued in parallel and in tandem. During the campaign, while Casimir was on a quick trip to Paris, Aurore received Stéphane at Nohant. "The carriage," she wrote Stéphane, "will be at your door tomorrow. I await you for lunch at ten."[15]* And Aurore wrote to Casimir, in Paris: "I am very happy you are finding distractions. I am sure they will not keep you from thinking of your best friend, who loves you from the bottom of her soul." Several weeks after Casimir had returned to Nohant, and Stéphane to Paris, Aurore left for the capital—to see doctors about her tonsils.

From Paris Aurore wrote Casimir, *December 6, 1827:* She has just arrived, she is staying at their old hôtel, where she had given birth to Maurice; she is feeling much better . . . "Ah, here is Stéphane"—with advice as to what doctors to see.

---

* It is the only communication, almost in its entirety, that has come down to us. One hundred and twenty-three letters to Stéphane de Grandsagne have been suppressed by his descendants as too "revealing."[16] Those he wrote to Aurore have similarly disappeared, probably destroyed by her own hand.

Saturday, two days later: "At the end of the week, no matter what, I'm returning. . . . Stéphane says he will return [with me]. . . . Take care of yourselves, the two of you, and love me always. I need it badly." *Monday, December 10:* "Let her make a scandal, if it pleases her," Aurore wrote now of Madame Néraud's threat after discovering Jules Néraud's love letters. "Let her make it known that Monsieur Jules, toothless as he is, paid me court and was politely shown the door. . . . I've told you everything. . . . Adieu, my best friend." *Wednesday, December 12:* "I spend all my time seeing doctors or waiting to see them." *Thursday, December 13:* "I am to see [Dr.] Broussais, if Stéphane holds to his promise." *Saturday:* "Stéphane is coming this morning. If he can leave on Monday, I might let the rest of my appointments go hang. I'll let you know before I close. . . ." *Noon, same day, same letter:* "Stéphane and his brother have to spend Monday here and have begged me not to leave before Tuesday." *Monday:* "I sent for seats in the public coaches, but there is not one to be had in *any of them.* So we cannot leave before Wednesday, arriving on Friday."[17]

Exactly nine months after the Paris letter of December 13—on September 13, 1828—a girl was born to Aurore at Nohant, a child she would always insist was "premature,"[18] but which was in all probability hers and Stéphane de Grandsagne's.[19]

Aurore's Aeolian web was a continuum. Between the interlude in Paris with Stéphane and the child born to them named Solange were interwoven her lives with *la bande* of La Châtre, with Casimir and her son and the Nohant family of her peasants and her poor, with Aurélien by correspondence and with God, who was Herself, in an ongoing dialogue at her lowest moments.

She was almost two months pregnant, and now gloomily certain of it, when Aurore wrote to Zoé Leroy on February 2, 1828. She had heard from Aurélien about the death of Zoé's father and of Zoé's sadness on not hearing from Aurore. She tried to make amends, then her own feelings crept into Aurore's apology:

> I do not ask you to love me as once you did. I no longer deserve the friendship of anyone. I am like a wounded animal which has crawled into a corner to die. I cannot turn to my fellow creatures for either succor or comfort.[20]

Zoé was bewildered. Not until spring did she learn of Aurore's pregnancy, and then through a mutual friend. She reproached Aurélien for not having informed her, "but," she wrote Aurore, "he claims he had!"[21] Was it Aurélien's reluctance to seem the last to be enlightened?

The same day—May 10, 1828—he posted a letter to Aurore of controlled sadness, irony and resignation. Stéphane was his oblique target. He discussed him with hauteur as a "pseudo-philosopher," a man "who perhaps is simply trying to shine in your circle with a few brilliant paradoxes," but Aurélian never alluded to Aurore's pregnancy. Instead, he returned to Stéphane's "sharply defined ideas":

> You ask me, my dear, whether I too have come to such "arrested conclusions." I would think it quite useless to reply to such a question now, if it weren't best to overturn the pedestal on which you seem to want to place me. You have within you an ideal of reason, a model of wisdom. In your imagination you fashion a being who embodies this ideal, and when you have created him *from yourself*, you cry: "It is he!" No, no! I do not have fixed, rational explanations of everything. Dare I admit it? Must I smash the idol with one blow? . . . No one has reflected less than I. I scarcely know what such reflection really is.[22]

It was a letter of withdrawal, but in August Aurélien blandly announced his coming to Nohant in September. George Sand described his arrival:

> I remember the astonishment of one of our friends from Bordeaux who came to see us, when he found me early in the morning, alone in the drawing room, folding and arranging a baby's layette, still in my workbasket. "What in heaven are you doing?" he asked me. "Goodness, you can see for yourself," I said. "I am hurrying to prepare for someone who is arriving before I expected."[23]

Aurélien astonished? Hardly. Hurt? More likely. Though he had known in advance, there was the shock nonetheless of a nine-month pregnancy, as if of a plaster saint. The fallen, if not smashed, idol was Aurore. He stayed for the birth, he witnessed the birth certificate. In the next letter from Bordeaux there was no reproach, but there was little warmth. One would think him a reconciled, almost casual friend. But Zoé reported Aurélien as a "cortege of sadness, harrowing dismay and frightful loneliness." Two months afterwards he was still behaving "a bit madly . . . poking at the fire . . . picking at the piano with two fingers."[24] Aurore, in reply: "He could never play with five!"[25]

The same month of this correspondence (December) Casimir was finding consolation and pleasure with Pepita, the baby's maid—and Aurore was hearing the unambiguous sounds through the thin partition separating her bedroom from Solange's.[26] All lives, in short, resumed.

As the year 1829 began, Aurore persuaded the *sous-préfet* of La Châtre to mix the unmixable social circles of Berry at a ball, and to invite the music master and his wife as well. To top the evening, she and Duteil played a violin-piano duet and sang a song of their composition, whose provocative line was "vexing *la bourgeoisie!*" Hippolyte, his wife and their little girl Léontine were now living at Nohant. Baby Solange, Aurore wrote Sophie, was a "bundle of fat, pink and white," little Maurice was slimming nicely.[27] Mockingly, to a friend Aurore described herself as "*noble, libérale, canaille* [guttersnipe], *démocrate, hérétique, schismatique, quakress* [sic], *pamphlétaire, Jacobine, Émigrée, partisan du despotisme, de la république, Dévote, athée, etc. etc. etc. etc. etc. etc. etc.*"[28]—which fairly summarized the opinions of friends and foes at La Châtre. She left out a more damning observation: "Everyone knew who was the real father of Solange."[29]

Life with Casimir, who was no less knowing, went on. From May until the end of July, he and Aurore spent the months in the southwest —mostly at Bordeaux—about which Casimir had his cryptic say at a later date: "Departure of the couple for Bordeaux with the under-standing of spending three weeks there, a month at most. In fact, a stay of three months. Visits every morning by Madame Aurore D. to Monsieur Aurélien de S., using as her pretext being ill and going to the baths. Departure obtained thanks to Monsieur de S. in order to avoid public scandal."[30] Aurore had recaptured Aurélien.

Casimir's complaint, as noted, would come later. Meantime *both* carried on, Aurore not mentioning Pepita, though planning to dismiss her, and Casimir presenting the period's portrait of the grumbling, long-suffering country husband of a brilliant, eccentric and unbridled wife. There was the estate and there was Maurice, a bright six-year-old in need of education, whom Aurore had allowed to lag behind rather than "force" to learn his letters. In this connection, she engaged a young tutor who applied a new, simplified system of teaching children to read. Thus Jules Boucoiran, twenty-one, entered the Dudevant lives, and Madame Dudevant very soon was addressing him as "my dear little Jules" in letters from the region of Bordeaux, where she was once again seeing Aurélien—this time without Casimir.[31] Within two months Maurice was reading with fluency, La Châtre was gossiping about that "female Don Juan," who was inducting the young Protestant tutor of her son in the pleasures of life and her love, and Aurore gave young Boucoiran notice.[32] He returned to his former charge and remained her dear friend.

The freedom of Aurore's comings and goings—and doings—is an un-failing wonderment of some bewilderment. Perhaps because of one's as-sumptions about the first quarter of the French nineteenth century and Nohant country life in particular. In fact, if entirely fact, "there was a relaxing of morals among the bourgeoisie," according to a La Châtre friend of Aurore, Laisnel de la Salle. "The men, having nothing to do, spent their evenings and often their nights at the inn, getting drunk and indulging in every form of debauchery. The women, and the best of them at that, were incredibly loose. There were very few perfect marriages."[33] Though probably the hyperbole of a man who would soon flee La Châtre for a more hermitic life, it pictures a craggy moral landscape that reduces the otherwise unaccountable bold relief of Aurore's behavior. Likely it was her refusal of *complete* hypocrisy which offended even the most frivolous of the women and freebooting of the men among the bourgeoisie of La Châtre.

Casimir's own descents to Bordeaux had as one reason the small commercial house he had inherited from his father. It was not doing well and he did no better by it. Another reason was the mistress he shared with a scoundrel named Desgranges, a "business associate." From afar Aurore sniffed the swindle being prepared—part ownership of a nonexistent vessel—and wrote Casimir a scolding letter about it, after he had signed away twenty-five thousand francs:

> Don't ever do business after dinner, when you're not sober. . . . I say this now so we will never have to repeat it. The past is past. The future remains. I will take charge of it. . . . Do not be angry with what I say to you. The right to speak the truth is mutual, otherwise it is tyrannical. Besides, I am a mother above all and I can be strong when I have to be.[34]

Aurore took a firmer hand in Nohant's affairs and summarily discharged Pepita. Claire Mathelin, *femme de chambre* of Hippolyte's wife dwelling with them, became Casimir's mistress. Since the birth of Solange, Aurore slept apart from Casimir in a small ground-floor bedroom, formerly her grandmother's boudoir.[35] She put hooks in the wall (still in place) and arranged a hammock as a bed. The two children were installed in the large adjoining bedroom, insulating her from Casimir's.

Here Aurore created, or rather communed with, her interior life, recreating it with goose quill and ink in a writer's nook contrived from a tiny closet. A cricket accompanied her. When it was accidentally crushed by a servant, she thought its fate an omen and made it part of an unpublished novel, *La Marraine* (The Godmother). The great, enduring theme already emerged: "A woman who loves is the most courageous of beings."[36]

The work is a beginning writer's exercise—Aurore never submitted it for publication—but her mind was clearly turning to writing as the way to independence, to an income that alone insured that independence.

Friends fascinated by her letters were always asking for fragments of verse or prose, and even novels. "I came to realize that I wrote quickly, easily and at length without tiring, that ideas asleep in my mind awoke when I wrote, and flowed from my pen . . . that writing would be my breadwinner."[37]

Aurore had tentatively, but not secretly—though the goal remained hidden—tried her hand at the customary occupations of ladies on their own: portraits in watercolor and pastels ("lacked originality"), decoration of snuffboxes and cigar cases with painted flowers and birds; and she thought of needlework, but it was too eye-tiring and poorly paid— "ten sous a day." In May 1830, when in Paris alone with little Maurice, she found herself going to museums—the Louvre, the Luxembourg. It was not the first time, but she returned again and again, "as if drunk and nailed to the Titians, the Tintorettos, the Rubens." She suddenly responded to painting as she had long before to music. Whatever métier, whatever trade or profession she would choose, she knew she would be an artist—in letters, in life, in her very being.[38]

In truth, George Sand's literature and life were never discrete; they never slept in separate beds. From Paris, Aurore wrote Casimir: "I saw Stéphane today and yesterday. I don't know how he knew I was here [!] . . . We shall see how long the honeymoon will last." *Twelve days later:* "I am off, dear friend, on a little voyage," leaving Maurice with a friend "who is very good with him. I am telling no one here that I am going down to Bordeaux . . . simply that I am spending a few days in the country." Her husband had become her confidant. When she returned to Paris, Aurore wrote Casimir that she had found Aurélien "very changed, considerably older and quite sad."[39] There was *that* comfort for Casimir.

Scarcely a month after Aurore and Maurice were back in Nohant, the July Revolution broke out in Paris, driving Charles X into exile and bringing to an end a period in more lives than one.

11

Closing a Door
Opens a Door
Vive la Liberté!

Today he came to me in tears. Too bad! I shall prove to
him that marriage does not mean my being tolerated as a
burden, but sought and appealed to as a companion, who
will freely choose to live with him when he proves worthy
of it.

—George Sand, *Correspondance* (1830)[1]

Torvald. Nora—can I never be anything more than a
stranger to you?
Nora (taking her bag). Ah, Torvald, the most wonderful
thing of all would have to happen. . . . That our life together would be a real wedlock. Good-bye. (*She goes out
through the hall. . . . The sound of a door shutting
is heard from below.*)

—Henrik Ibsen, A Doll's House (1879)[2]

To live! how sweet, how wonderful! despite husbands, and
troubles, and debts and relatives and gossip, despite poignant despairs and wearisome pin-pricks! To live is intoxication, to love and be loved is happiness, heaven itself!
Ah by heavens, to live the life of the artist, whose banner
is freedom!

—George Sand, *Correspondance* (1831)[3]

Welcome, O life! I go to encounter for the millionth time
the reality of experience and to forge in the smithy of my
soul the uncreated conscience of my race.

—James Joyce, A Portrait of the Artist as a
Young Man (1916)[4]

Twice, thrice daily Aurore galloped to La Châtre for news of the Revolution. The intractable Chamber had been dissolved by the King, new elections ordered; an expedition had been launched against Algiers to regain abroad the prestige lost at home. By July 5, 1830, Algiers was taken, but the unpopular Charles X had recouped nothing. More than ever the liberal bourgeoisie felt robbed of their 1789 Revolution by the Bourbon Restoration, and reached for a second Republic. Four royal ordinances on July twenty-sixth sought to strengthen royal prerogatives. The Chamber re-elected in July, La Châtre's Duris-Dufresne among the returning deputies, was dissolved before ever meeting. Three days of barricades in the narrow, twisting streets of Paris followed, putting the white flag of the Bourbons to flight and the blue-white-and-red tricolor of 1789 in its place.

It was during these "Three Glorious Days," as history records them, that Aurore rode so hectically to La Châtre for news of friends in the fighting, for letters from Boucoiran, then with the Bertrand family in Paris. She felt a "fever in the blood . . . an energy I never knew I possessed," her spirit "expanding with the events." Casimir too was stirred to activity in "the great work of renovation." He, Hippolyte, Jules Néraud and a hundred others formed a National Guard unit with Casimir at its head and the tricolor cockade as its insignia. There were rumors of a royalist regiment preparing to march against La Châtre from Bourges. "If authority—overthrown authority—wants to fight on," Aurore wrote Jules Boucoiran on the last day of July, "it will find us confronting it!"[5]

The day before, Aurore had met Jules Sandeau.

He was part of the exciting, exhilarating days when everything was dramatically heightened. But there was beyond this the instant attraction for Aurore of a slight, nineteen-year-old lad with touseled, ash-blond locks curling around a Saint John the Baptist head, "something frail and charming which invites protection"—as Sandeau himself retrospectively described his appeal to stronger women—"and above all, the flower freshness of youth which hovered about him like a halo."[6]

Casimir was elsewhere, perhaps drilling his troops, when Aurore had ridden her horse Lyska to the Duvernet château at Coudray. Young Charles Duvernet had invited her together with Alphonse Fleury, the giant "Gaul," Gustave Papet, a richly pursed medical student who was "*milord*" of the Berrichon group, and Jules Sandeau, precocious son of a modest tax collector at La Châtre, on vacation, as the others, from studies in Paris. Aurore had never seen, or rather noticed, "little Jules" before, but it soon became evident that he knew of *her*. Immediately upon her arrival, he withdrew with a book to a grassy bank under an old pear tree, "by chance Madame Dudevant's favorite spot." Then, "slowly, bit by bit, talking all the time"—recounts Duvernet in his unpublished memoirs—"she drew us toward it, and thus discovered herself face to face with Sandeau, who seemed to be trying to avoid her." Talk turned around the revolutionary events in Paris, the obsessive topic. But when the group separated after dinner, Aurore, mounting Lyska, cried out: "Charles! You must bring all your friends to dinner tomorrow with you." Duvernet alone responded. "I expect *all* of you, gentlemen!" Aurore repeated, whipped her horse and disappeared in a gallop.[7]

Boucoiran's letter from Paris arrived the same day as the dinner party at Nohant. Aurore read it aloud to her guests. "To the whole town!" she wrote in reply at eleven that night, adding that she worried about her mother, her aunt Lucie Maréchal, whose husband was lately an *inspecteur* in Charles X's household. But "in moments such as these," the blood burned, the heart beat, the brain was too full for "sensibility."[8] Politics are never more passionate than when they are revolutionary; to be among the young men so recently from the churning capital and so soon to return was its own tantalizing heaven for Aurore. Revolution, republicanism with its new touch of socialism, the Romantic movement impulsively challenging the old order! Plays, such as Victor Hugo's *Hernani,* with an outlaw as its hero, were momentous events.

Performed in February on the eve of Hugo's twenty-eighth birthday (Aurore was twenty-six), the "battle of *Hernani*" anticipated the barricades of July in its triumphant assault on the academic past; and the group of friends at Nohant would sign their letters with *Hugolâtre* after their names. On opening night at the Comédie Française in Paris, the young playwright had replaced the official claque with his followers, for whom *Hernani* was the decisive engagement with the enemy. They came early—artists, sculptors, poets, teen-age dandy Théophile Gautier in a pink doublet, Honoré Balzac, famous at thirty—each leading his clan. Throughout the performance they battled with the classicists. Sticking paper was thrown from the balcony. Balzac was struck with a cabbage. "Madame," said a Hugo fan to a scornful lady, "you are wrong to laugh. You show your teeth!"[9]

Politically, however, Aurore and *her* clan shortly experienced a sharp letdown. The party they looked to, composed of republicans largely recruited among workingmen and students, seemed so embarrassed by its unexpectedly swift success it was at a loss as to how to consolidate it. The bourgeoisie, ever more concerned about social order than social justice, had second thoughts about the disturbances and their socialist directions. A vacillating, moribund Lafayette refused the leadership offered by the republicans and turned instead, as the bourgeoisie, to Orléanist Louis Philippe, duke of the rival, "*régicide*" branch of the royal family, to replace Charles X when he abdicated in August. It was

now a bourgeois monarchy with "rule by the bankers,"[10] and Aurore
told her friends of her own concern for those "despised, calumniated
lower classes who had done everything"—during the "Three Glorious
Days" which had put the upper fringe of the middle class into power—
and would as usual be rewarded with a new tyranny.[11]

But it was summer, and politics were not all. There were musical evenings at Nohant and dances in the village, walks, picnics and excursions
in the woods. Frequently the young men went hunting, Jules Sandeau
joining them. He started boldly enough in the morning, but by midday
he tired, slipping off with a book to the shade of a tree—and soon to
Nohant to see Aurore. He was drawn to this fascinating woman—"her
thick, black hair, the fire one felt burning under her fine, dark skin, the
slim, audacious figure, the incendiary, languorous, morbid eyes revealing
the incessant, unavowed interior struggles"[12]—even as she intimidated
him.

As for Aurore: "From the very first day, his expressive eyes, his frank,
youthfully blunt ways, his shy awkwardness with me, filled me with a
desire to see more of him, to explore him further. Each day my interest
grew livelier, and I did not think for a moment of resisting it."[13] The
resistance, in fact, was Jules'.

He arrived, as so often, straight from La Châtre, pale and breathless
from the heaviness of the stormy day, and he steered directly for their
rendezvous in a wooded corner of Nohant's park. Aurore's book and
scarf lying on the bench signaled her presence, but when he heard her
approach, he hid in a nearby copse, leaving his gray hat and cane next
to the book and scarf. "Even the red cord he wound around his gray
hat set me quivering with joy." The game over, Aurore took Sandeau's
hand and suddenly told him she loved him. "I myself did not know it
until I said it . . . and Jules learned of it the same moment as I."[14]

They made love, for Jules, too, learned *he* loved, in a small closed pavilion that opened on the road to Châteauroux and gave access to the
garden. Thus the lovers could meet without Sandeau appearing at the
main gate, attracting the curiosity of the servants and villagers. Or
Casimir's attention? There is a strange dwelling in Jules Sandeau's autobiographical *Marianna* on the *husband's* jealousy of the wife for having
won the love of the young hero. However unconscious the touch of homosexuality, it is probably revelatory of only Sandeau, who described
himself quite specifically as having "the supple, flexible waist of a
woman."[15] The appeal of this young man-woman to Aurore-George
Sand is striking.

Less complaisant than Casimir, however, or less willfully blind, were
the people of La Châtre. "Gossip here runs its course more strongly
than ever," Aurore acquainted the other Jules (Boucoiran) in the fall of
1830.

Those who do not like me very much say I *love* Sandot [sic]—
and you know what they mean by *love*. Those who do not like
me at all say I *love* Sandot and Fleury at the same time.
Those who detest me say that adding your name and that of
Duvernet would not displease me. So, I have four lovers simultaneously. That is not too many for a woman such as I with
such devouring passions. Ah, the wicked fools! How I pity
their being alive! Good night, my child. Write me. And by
the way, Sandot especially charges me to send you his
regards.[16]

There is more here than Aurore's reaching for a confidant and her
warning to a man who loves her, and might well think himself loved by
her, of the rumors that might reach *him*. There is the ingathering of intimates—"Sandeau likes you," the letter ends, "which doesn't surprise
me. Like him as well; he warrants it"—the communal binding of
friends around her with mutual love, likes and dislikes. Preceding the
defiant lines about the gossip of La Châtre, Aurore lifts a curtain on
her character: "I concentrate my existence upon the objects of my
affections. I surround myself with them as if by a devoted battalion
keeping black, discouraging thoughts at a distance. Absent or present,
my friends fill my soul entire."[17]

Fall that year was particularly a time for black thoughts. In a few
weeks Aurore's devoted battalion of friends would be returning to Paris,
their studies and work, leaving her alone at Nohant. "Alone" with
Casimir and the children, "alone" with Hippolyte and his family,
"alone" above all in her feeling of being alone. She sketched until her
eyes ached; she wrote until dawn at her tiny desk. She missed the exciting talk, the ever-fresh adventure of love, the quick, bright remarks
about the latest play, book, opera and poem. She missed "golden-haired
Charles . . . Fleury of the huge hands and terrifying beard . . . little
Sandeau, light and gay as a hummingbird," no longer darting about,
"hands in pockets, swift as an antelope." She yearned for Paris and
"chose to fall feverishly ill."[18]

Aurore was again cerebrally, psychosomatically ill, frequently mentioning it in her letters. Then she recovered. She had reached a decision. She had been searching for the right moment to put it into execution. Or, in blunter truth, for the proper *pretext*, and having looked for
it, found it? All supposition is based on an intriguing communication to
Boucoiran early in December. She has been ill, Aurore began, lying in
bed for almost two weeks with fever, but for the past three days she has
felt better.

Searching for something in my husband's desk, I came upon a
packet addressed to me. I was struck by its solemnity, for on it

was written: *Do not open until my death.* I did not have the
patience to wait until I was a widow. . . . . I imagined my husband dead and was happy to read what he thought of me
while he lived. . . . Good God! what a testament! Nothing
but maledictions! He had gathered in it all his petulant outbursts and feelings of anger against me, all his broodings about
my *perversity*, all his sentiments of contempt for my character,
and he left me *this* as the last token of his affection!

Poor Casimir had at last communicated. And in writing—leaving *his*
"confessional" where he clearly knew it would be found. But it was not
Casimir who was reading *this* "confessional."

Reading it woke me from my sleep. I told myself that to live
with a man who had neither respect for his wife nor
confidence in her would be like trying to bring life to the
dead. My decision was made immediately and *irrevocably*.[19]

That same day Aurore announced her decision to Casimir "with an
aplomb and *sang-froid*" which "petrified him." "I am leaving forever,"
she told him, "for Paris, and I am leaving the children at Nohant. I insist on an allowance."

Casimir recovered his speech, argued and pleaded, but Aurore
remained "unshakable." In fact, it was a tactical ultimatum. She had
no intention to leave her children "forever" or even, it soon followed,
Nohant. Her declaration reduced Casimir, as intended, to a "sheep-like
softness" and, a day or two later, "to tears" and an eagerness for any
compromise. Aurore would live six months a year in Paris (three months
at a time) and six months at Nohant. She would have three thousand
francs as her allowance—in fact the sum stipulated in the marriage contract. When Casimir proposed closing the house at Nohant—he could
not, he said, "live alone"—and taking Maurice to a boarding school in
Paris, Aurore was forcefully opposed. It might have meant Casimir in
Paris! Besides, Aurore wanted a life both in Paris *and* Nohant, trusting
her husband had been sufficiently taught a lesson, so that henceforth
she would be "sought and appealed to as a free companion," not as a
"burden to be tolerated."

But Aurore, as she wrote in closing to Boucoiran, would not feel free
in conscience if she did not know Maurice were well taken care of. "If
you are at Nohant, I can breathe and sleep peacefully. My son will be
in good hands, his education will advance, his health will be watched
over, his character will not be spoiled . . . and I would have news of
him every day."[20]

Thus appealed to, Boucoiran agreed to leave the Bertrand family in
Paris for the Dudevants at Nohant—though Aurore promised only six

months of herself at Nohant. It was a sacrifice, she told him, that she would repay with "thanks and *tendresse*—and you can give that word *any meaning you wish.*"[21] He would arrive January twentieth. Aurore could not wait. A new year, a new life beckoned in Paris. She would bring to the Berrichon "commune" already there, she exulted, "heart, head and pen!" She would even arrive with a novel, *Aimée,* "lacking only the beginning and the ending."[22]

Hippolyte had promised Aurore the loan of his apartment on Rue de Seine. There was the more alluring promise of life in Paris with Jules Sandeau—if only the lifetime of three months, and then three months more. However Hippolyte blew cold as well as hot, especially when Aurore disclosed her hope of having Solange with her.

"How can you dream of living in Paris with a child on two hundred and fifty francs a month!" Hippolyte exploded. "It's too ridiculous. Why, *you* don't even know the price of a chicken! You'll be back in a fortnight without a sou."

"That may be," Aurore replied, "but I am going to try."[23]

She brushed aside all objections, the tears of Casimir and Maurice as well. She had chosen Bohemia, the life and risks of the artist, to the comfort, security and deadliness of bourgeois existence. And she knew it was not simply "for a try."

"To the New Year!" Aurore wrote Félix Pyat, a yet unmet journalist friend of Jules Sandeau, "to a life of affection, hopes and happiness!"[24]

12

A Season in Paris

Paris still smelt of powder. . . . Revolt was in the air, riot-
ing in every quarter: in the streets, in books, in the theater. . . . Paris did not know very well what it wanted, but
it knew it did not want what there was. . . . Even the
sexes were indistinguishable. . . . Women had become
militant apostles . . . disputatious, proud, virile, joining in
our battles, fighting at our sides, astonishing us with their
fiery, male audacity. Everything was in question: social as
well as political and religious institutions, husbands as well
as kings and gods. From all sides came nothing but mockery for the laws, ridicule for marriage, unbridled aspirations for a better future.

—Jules Sandeau, *Marianna* (1839)[1]

The public carriage sped Aurore to Paris, to Jules Sandeau, who was
eagerly awaiting her at the coach yard with Félix Pyat.[2] She was too ex-
cited to be tired; and she had dozed with a sack of three stuffed turkeys
as her pillow on the way to Paris and the new life. Her companions
took her to Hippolyte's apartment at 31 Rue de Seine and carried her
few bags up the six flights to her rooms.[3] The quarters would be temporary, an address for her mail. In a week, in two at most, Aurore would
be living with Sandeau in a garret on the Quai des Grands-Augustins,
where one *did* see the Seine, Notre Dame's gray towers and the beautiful sixteenth-century bridge, Pont Neuf.

So much was done in those weeks: time itself was condensed and intensified, the Romantic movement was in both flower and harvest,
every day saw its esthetic or social manifesto, all was in ferment. As revolutionaries manned the barricades of July the previous year, Stendhal
sat writing the pages of *The Red and the Black*. Soon Aurore would be
reading Victor Hugo's *Notre Dame de Paris* even as she looked at its
towers, meet Balzac as his *La Peau de Chagrin* was appearing, applaud
actress Marie Dorval in Alexander Dumas' new play, *Anthony*, hear of

new verse by the wonder child, Alfred de Musset. The list of *chefs d'oeuvre* in the years 1830 and 1831 is staggering, the change of regime stirred all "to compete in distinction."[4] The July Revolution had liberated French literature, even though it had not liberated France.

What to do first? Meet new friends or divest herself of old ones? Perhaps both. Aurore paid a farewell visit to her old convent and to Mother Alicia, to Jane and Aimée Bazouin, now married to counts and conventionality. None of them realized it was Aurore's farewell. She saw her mother Sophie and her half sister Clotilde, and Casimir's mother. She would not see them often. She saw Stéphane, but it did not touch her life with Sandeau. She made a break—and it was conscious—with her former life most vividly associated with Casimir and her family—but it was not yet a clean break. In addition to Pyat, Jules introduced Aurore to Émile Regnault, medical student and intimate friend, and to Gabriel Planet, who had opened a Berrichon Club where one could leaf through newspapers or fill notebooks in some comfort and warmth. There were also the faithful giant Fleury and the others.

Aurore wanted to be one of them, not a man, but a writer among men, which meant dressing as one of them. The new style of male overcoat—long, square redingote—lent itself handsomely to her guise. She had one cut to her small, slim measure, made of strong, gray cloth— ideal for the winter weather—and ordered trousers and waistcoat to match. She tucked her long hair in the tall felt hat students were wearing and looked for all the world like a first-year Sorbonne *étudiant*. Boots, tipped at the heels with iron to cope with the slippery sidewalks, and a large, gray cravat completed Aurore's attire; and so costumed, so disguised, she tirelessly roamed Paris. No trailing skirts, no thin-soled, pointed shoes, no thin-souled, pointing fingers to hobble her. She was free, an "invisible woman," as anonymous as any man in the privacy that is the gift of Paris. "To be alone in the street," to decide for herself where to dine or where to go, to frequent the people she wished and not to have others forced upon her![5] To go and come at any hour, alone if she preferred, or join her comrades in the pit rather than be confined, as were women in women's clothing, to the boxes and balconies at the theater! But above all, Aurore could go her own way unnoticed, unremarked, uninhibited, "feet solid on the slippery ice, shoulders covered with snow, hands in pockets, stomach a bit empty at times, but the head all the more filled with songs and melodies, the new colors and forms, inspirations and fantasies . . . neither *dame*, nor *monsieur* . . . walking through the desert of men."[6]

She may have toyed with the idea of painting portraits or decorating snuffboxes for a living, or even of doing translations from English as she shivered in the reading room of the unheated Bibliothèque Mazarine. But Aurore's undoubted goal was to be a writer. Had she not brought a novel with her, and a letter from Charles Duvernet's mother to their cousin, the influential Berrichon man of letters, Henri de Latouche? Within five days of her arrival she arranged a rendezvous with him. He promised, in his note of reply, to be "severe" with her writings. "Is not benevolence," Latouche said, "simply the laziness of friendship?"[7]

Latouche's reputation had preceded him and prepared her. Born Hyacinthe Thabaud de Latouche, forty-five years before her in La Châtre, he had written verse, prose, journalism and criticism, eight or nine novels and several plays. His non-success—save for the *succès de scandale* of his novel *Fragoletta*, "the story of a hermaphrodite"—had soured him. He had nurtured the young Balzac, but their relations had already chilled by the time of Aurore's arrival. He was now director of *Figaro*, a new, waspishly satirical, four-page paper of the unconditional opposition.[8] Its office was the fireside of Latouche's apartment on Quai Malaquais. Here, in the evening, Aurore found a stoutish middle-aged man of "exquisite manners" and such "meticulous expression" that she thought his language at first was "an affectation," but soon discovered it to be Latouche's ordinary speech.[9] The voice was caressing, "too caressing," said his contemporary Sainte-Beuve, "even voluptuous,"[10] but there was always a sting at the end of the honeyed tongue. His face, lit with intelligence, was "by no means disfigured by the loss of an eye in childhood." On the contrary, "a kind of reddish gleam darted from its pupil and gave him, when his most animated, a fantastic éclat."[11]

Aurore read to Latouche from her manuscript of *Aimée*. He listened with remarkable patience. Finally, when she had finished, Latouche said:

"Do you have any children, Madame?"

"Alas, yes, Monsieur," said Aurore, "but I cannot have them with me, nor can I return to them."

"And you count on staying in Paris, making your livelihood by means of your pen?"

"I must."

Latouche: "It's a pity, because I see no elements that make for success. Believe me, madame, manage somehow to return to your husband's roof."[12]

Second version, from a letter of Aurore to Duvernet, following the encounter: "He said the novel was charming, but lacked common sense. 'That is true,' I replied. That it had to be entirely rewritten. 'That could be,' I replied. That I had best begin another. 'Enough,' I rejoined."[13]

Third version, two decades later: George Sand recalled that Latouche had "found the novel detestable, and rightly so. Nevertheless he said I could learn to do better and might even one day write a good one. 'But you must live in order to learn about life,' he added. 'A novel is life retold with art. You have the artist's nature, but you are ignorant of reality. You live too much in dreams. Be patient. Time and experience, those dreary counselors, will come to your aid soon enough.' "[14]

Latouche, in the meantime, offered to aid Aurore by paying seven francs a column for acceptable articles in *Figaro*.

Journalism, however, was not literature, and stubbornly Aurore persisted with her manuscript novel. Deputy Duris-Dufresne had called at the apartment on Rue de Seine, never finding her there, since she was living with Sandeau on Quai des Grands-Augustins. He had left his card, she had contacted him. He took her to a riotous session at the Chamber, but her interest remained elsewhere. "I needed a literary patron."[15] Duris-Dufresne proposed Lafayette. Aurore thought he was aiming too high. The La Châtre deputy obligingly lowered his sights and presented a colleague.

At eight in the morning, an hour fixed by her host, Aurore called on Monsieur de Kératry, a deputy from Brittany and author of *Le Dernier des Beaumanoir*. (She had read the story, involving a priest violating a dying woman, and pronounced it rambling and repugnant. "They want monsters?" she wrote Boucoiran. "Then let us give them monsters."[16] But she never would.) The white-haired gentleman received Aurore in his bedroom. His young wife, whom Aurore mistook for his ailing daughter, was still in bed, lying under a rose silk coverlet. She looked pityingly at Aurore's plain dress. "In two words," the old gentleman said, "a woman should not write." Aurore rose, asked why he had her—and his young wife—awakened so early in the morning to hear that, and prepared to leave. Kératry followed her to the door, developing his theory on the inferiority of women and the impossibility of the best of them writing anything printable. "Believe me," he said with a last word of advice, "don't make books, make children—*ne faîtes pas de livres, faîtes des enfants*." "Really, sir," said Aurore, departing, "you should follow your own advice, if you can."[17]

Again the truth is multiple. This was a second meeting with Kératry; the first was more polite. However, it acridly limns the outlook for a woman aspiring to be a writer in the 1830s of France, despite Mesdames de La Fayette, de Sévigné, de Staël. They were not, to be sure, "professional writers," if that means earning their living by writing, rather than winning acclaim and a public, even if posthumous, as in the case of Sévigné.

Perhaps it is one of her firsts as a precursor that George Sand should work as a professional *journalist* that winter season in Paris. It would not provide her living—Latouche offered at most forty or fifty francs a month—but it would provide the experience of writing for money under a man of sharp professional judgment and demands. Latouche, however, had little effect on the shaping of George Sand's early career as a novelist. He preached brevity, she never practiced it. But he launched her as a writer. Without a beginning—nothing, but in a larger sense George Sand *had* begun, as a child spinning stories to her mother, as an adolescent creating "Corambé," as a young woman penning letters that passed from hand to hand, continuing with notes, journals and finally manuscripts for a novel—rejected by the professionals. She had begun by beginning, but more important, by rejecting rejection. "I do not believe, my dear child," she wrote Boucoiran defiantly, "in the misfortunes predicted for me in a literary career."[18] It was the saving arrogance of the burgeoning writer, without which there is no beginning, or middle—only a self-aborted end.

Thus Aurore, in February 1831, joined Latouche's "nest of eaglets trying their wings" on *Figaro* at the fireside of his apartment.[19] She was the only woman among the young men, and she would not necessarily have had it otherwise. Latouche chose articles suitable for her story-telling talent and cut her exactly the size sheet for her to fill, but she would spoil ten sheets before even "beginning to begin" in the tight space.[20] She suffered, she laughed, she listened. "I did nothing worthwhile, but at the end of the month I earned twelve francs fifty centimes (or was it fifteen francs?) for my contributions."[21]

The first week of March Aurore turned out a short, stinging satire mocking the Government's neurotic fear of the opposition. A forthcoming decree of the Paris Prefect of Police, announced Aurore's article, would contain these provisions: "(1) All citizens capable of bearing arms shall assemble every day from seven in the morning until eleven at night so as to protect the Palais Royal, and from eleven at night until seven in the morning in order to defend churches and other public buildings. . . . (2) So that the tranquillity of the population shall be no longer disturbed, every morning before dawn, twenty-five cannon will be fired on the public squares. . . . (3) Every house owner must have a ditch, seven and a half feet wide, dug around his house and have his front door fortified. . . . Every Monday, Wednesday and Friday shall be devoted to preventing illegal gatherings, and every Tuesday, Thursday and Saturday to dispersing them. . . ."[22]

People laughed, but the "Citizen King"—Louis Philippe—was not amused. *Figaro* of that day was seized, suit would be brought. If she were lucky, Aurore wrote Duvernet, it would be brought against her. "Thank heavens! What a scandal at La Châtre! What horror and despair in my family! But my reputation will be made and I will find a publisher to buy my platitudes and fools to read them. I would give nine francs fifty centimes for the joy of being sentenced."[23] "Alas," the proceeding was dropped by the Prefect of Police. "Too bad! A political sentence would have made my fortune. . . ."[24]

Aurore acted as well in Sandeau's behalf, introducing him to Latouche after she had proved herself. He was received and put to work. Just previously, to Aurore's delight, the two lovers had successfully collaborated on a short story for the *Revue de Paris*, though it would be signed only by Jules. And that for two reasons. For one, the *Revue*'s editor "detested women and would have nothing to do with them."[25] For another, coupling her name publicly with Jules' would underline their liaison in Paris for the gossips of La Châtre.

Writing in concert with Jules presented Aurore little difficulty. His was the soft pliancy of character she demanded in a man: "Those delicate nuances which bend and twine with all my own oddities and asperities."[26] There was a tendency toward laziness, but the mothering and scolding of a sometimes ailing and always procrastinating "little Jules" was not, in the characteristic light of Aurore's love, entirely displeasing. They shared, above all, the intimate, communal life of the Berrichon group, the intoxication of ambitions on the road to achievement, the incomparable trip of comrades and mutual affection. At the end of the day at *Figaro*, they would all go to the theater, often on press tickets offered by Latouche. They would sit and talk in the cafés, "*milord*" Papet standing for the drinks, or in their garret rooms. They explored Paris and each other, walked its streets—no drama was livelier. They read aloud from their writings, went to concerts, museums, demonstrations, artists' studios. All was grist for their active minds and pens —half a dozen articles and novellas signed "J. Sandeau" poured from Jules and the indefatigable Aurore ("I have one goal, one task, *one passion . . .* writing"[27]).

More distantly, collaboration continued in Aurore's other life with Casimir. She had effectively separated herself from her husband, but not from the father of her children—nor from the titular proprietor of *her* Nohant. But Casimir too was demonstrating the soft pliancy, if not the "delicate nuances," of Jules. One has only to regard the picture of Aurore in Paris from the perspective of La Châtre to appreciate Casimir's astonishing tolerance. But then he also sought his own untroubled way of life.

"You have been told that *I wear the pants*," Aurore replied to a reproachful Sophie. "But you have not been told the whole truth. . . . I do not want my husband to wear my skirts. Each to his dress, each to his freedom. . . . My husband does what he wants: he has mistresses, or not, as he desires; he drinks muscat wine, or plain water, according to his thirst. . . . But it is also just that the freedom he enjoys should be mutual."[28]

"My dear friend," Aurore addressed Casimir in her letters from Paris —writing to ask about her allowance, inquiring about the children's health, acquainting him with her writing ventures, the state of her health, his mother's health—and closed conventionally, "I embrace you from the bottom of my heart." On March twentieth a short note announced Aurore's imminent return, as agreed, after three months in Paris:

> Please arrange for me to have money for stockings, shoes, etc. which the children and I will need for spring. . . . I have asked Maurice to write me what he and his sister need in the way of clothes for summer. . . . Good-bye, my friend. I have seen my mother and my sister, Charles Duvernet and Jules Grandsagne. I'm off now to hear Paganini. . . . *Je t'embrasse de tout mon coeur.*"[29]

No signs of a domestic drama. But several weeks before Aurore had received an unpleasant note from Hippolyte with an unconcealed warning: "The best thing you have ever produced is your son. He loves you more than anybody in the world. Take care you don't kill that feeling in him."[30]

Her season in Paris had come to a close. In early April Aurore returned to Nohant.

13

Between Identities

The return to Nohant after the season in Paris was not a return to Casimir, or even intrinsically to the children. It was Aurore's return to the soil, to childhood roots. Nohant was the essential center, and it was spring. The sweet smells of lilacs and lilies of the valley invaded her small boudoir-bedroom. Birds, butterflies and in the evening yellow-winged moths kept her company. Hippolyte's warning about killing Maurice's affections by her long stay in Paris had indeed sounded an alarm, but Maurice's warm smother of kisses and Solange's rosy sweetness reassured Aurore. April in Nohant was lovely.

But in May Aurore was already writing Émile Regnault, "I feel terribly lonely here where no one understands me and I cannot even trust my own shadow."[1]

Aurore wrote Jules Sandeau almost every night, but her letters have been lost; his as well. Consequently letters to Regnault, a young medical student, compose the record. Take care of "little Jules," Aurore wrote him, "see that he doesn't let himself starve to death, as is his wont." And she nostalgically recalled her Berrichon commune in the little bedroom on the Paris quai, "Jules in his dirty, torn, artist's coat, his tie under his behind, the shirt he has removed hung over three chairs," Fleury the Gaul in a corner "weaving a conspiracy," Émile in another singing his own praises. Ah, "curses on those who prevent us from living together at Nohant as we do in Paris!"[2]

Aurore yearned for Paris, but when there missed the countryside. She loved Nohant, but detested its provincialism. The people of La Châtre lacked the light touch of the Parisian; ennui entered her enjoyment of nature. Duteil tended to sympathize with Casimir, and the moodiness of Charles Duvernet did not help. However, Casimir went his way, Aurore went hers. The freedom *was* mutual. "I am completely independent. I go to bed when he rises. I go to La Châtre or Rome"—one can see Aurore's shrug—"as I wish. I return at midnight or at six in the morning. It is entirely my own affair."[3] There is defiance in this description of life at Nohant, as if Aurore were addressing the gossipers of La Châtre rather than Sophie.

In any event, with her young men in Paris, there was less for the good burgers to gossip about. Aurore sketched—it would always be her pleasure—and "scribbled"—it was her passion; she still hoped to implement her livelihood by doing portraits, and pressed Regnault to find her clients in Paris. A week later, however, she heard of Balzac's letter to Sandeau, praising him for their novelette, *La Prima Donna* (signed "J. Sand"), in the *Revue de Paris*. Balzac had added that Sandeau might lend him a hand with a play or two.[4] "The little one," Aurore exulted, "is on the way to earning his living—and mine!"[5]

Longing for Jules and Paris mounted, spurred by the Balzac letter—but unlikely influenced by Regnault's tale of Jules' flirtation with a young German girl ("the affections are free," Aurore replied). In five weeks, at the end of June, she would be back in the capital. Unfortunately Hippolyte and his wife were already there, occupying the apartment on Rue de Seine. Regnault must urgently find Aurore another "official" address, but with more than one room. Remember, she reminded her friend,

> I have a mother, an aunt, a sister, a brother, etc., who will certainly come and bother me. . . . With only one room, I run the risk of being unable to avoid them, of being caught in *flagrant délit* embracing *le petit* Jules. I should like to have a second door for him to use at any moment, because my husband might suddenly drop in, not from the blue sky, but from a diligence, at four in the morning, and not having a place to stay, do me the honor of disembarking *chez moi*. Imagine my state if I heard him ring and knew the charming gentleman was on the other side of the door! He might even break it down before I opened it.

The tone is mocking, but the letter evidences the constraints on Aurore's freedom, the scenes she might always face. She knew the outbursts Casimir was capable of displaying and did not at all relish provoking them. One does not wisely corner the weakest of men, and it would be Casimir, more than she, who would feel cornered if suddenly confronted by Aurore and Jules in *flagrant délit*.

Finally Regnault found a place at 25 Quai Saint-Michel, fifty meters from their former mansard. Aurore to Regnault: "Fine for Quai Saint-Michel! I adore the situation, the nearness of 'the Gaul,' who will take our old room and whom we will be able to see from our balcony. I adore the three rooms . . . but how about the second door? Well, if we

can't have one made, I'll manage to keep the back bedroom secret. . . .
It will be the black bedroom, the bedroom of mystery, the hiding place
of the ghost, the monster's lair!"

Does she talk too much of Jules in her letters? Aurore asks Regnault.
He should not mind. "Our common loves, our friendships bind us so
tightly together that to talk of one with special affection is not to alienate the other. There is not a thought we four"—Fleury, Regnault,
Aurore and Jules—"do not share in common, is it not so? . . . I leave
here on Friday, July 1st. I shall spend the night of Saturday and Sunday
at Étampes. Don't stay up waiting for me. I'll come and wake you with
a few blows!"

It was as well Regnault did not stay up. Aurore spent a week at
Étampes with Sandeau. Maurice had cried on her departure, she had
wept in the carriage on the way to Étampes, but as she drew near Sandeau, her "heart burned with impatience and leaped with joy." She
was happy, "too happy," she wrote Regnault.[6] More circumspectly she
penned another missile to Hippolyte in Paris: she was staying at
Étampes with the wife of a friend, she would be seeing Latouche in his
country place, she would arrive in four or five days, he should forward
her mail to General Delivery, Étampes.

Not the slightest fooled, Hippolyte wrote Casimir, July 6, 1831: "I
have this instant received a letter from Aurore. . . . We must stick together and help each other through a very troubled period. . . . Your
wife wants her freedom, a life of dissipation and movement. You have
not been a bad husband for her, and people here, as at home, recognize
it. Let her do as she wants. If she does badly, she cannot complain of
you, of me, or of her relatives. Since she is doing exactly what pleases
her, what should you do? Make the best of it, do not worry, swallow
your tongue, look after your affairs and your children. Your affairs are
solid, your children are being taught and cared for at Nohant."[7]

In Paris, Aurore's euphoria—"that perfect state of speechless im-
becility"—continued with Sandeau. They were now installed in the garret apartment six stories above the quai, with a balcony view of swal-
lows sweeping around the towers of Notre Dame and the golden
Gothic spire of Sainte-Chapelle, and across the Seine and the barges,
the morgue. They established the secret bedroom, but they also had "a
second mattress" for a friend, such as Charles Duvernet, should he
come to Paris on a visit. Two hundred francs borrowed from Sophie,
two hundred from Latouche, five hundred more from Duris-Dufresne
helped pay for the furniture, the rest was on credit from the merchants
—and too bad for them if she could not meet the payments, said
Aurore with bohemian scorn, though in fact she soon did.[8]

Boldly Aurore wrote Casimir about her money problems, suggesting it was to his interest as well that she have the apartment, since he too could use it when he was in Paris—and she was in Nohant. The same day Hippolyte reported to Casimir. He had gone to see her several times, he said, but she was grossly unjust to him and "keeps the family at a distance. She accuses me of selfishness and indifference. She told me she was hungry for three days, though my wife and I have invited her twenty times and she has not accepted once. What to do, I know not. She is astonished at the privations to which she has freely submitted herself. She thought she could make her living by writing, but now it seems she has been well disillusioned. . . . She even wrote me in her last letter that if I join with you in making her miserable and depriving her of the children . . . she will throw herself into the river. She told me to tell you this so that you won't have her death on *your* conscience!"—since it would be her brother's doing. On their last talk together, Aurore wept, said Hippolyte, "and I too. Despite that devilish mind of hers, you can't help liking her."[9]

It was high comedy. Aurore was far from being disillusioned about eventually living from her writing. She and Sandeau were even then literally ghost-writing a novel, *Commissionnaire*, since it was to be signed by a recently dead author. Such were the trials of the two neophytes. Yet they were encouraged to carry on by Balzac, who would climb the five flights of stairs to see them, heavily, pantingly, but enthusiastically —though often more full of his own projects than theirs, talking hugely "of himself, and of himself alone."[10] More exciting in its promise, as September approached and Aurore's trimestrial return to Nohant, was the contract for a novel of their own, *Rose et Blanche*, with their joint pen "J. Sand"—the invention of Latouche—attached. They would work on it together that fall, for when Aurore did go to Nohant, Jules Sandeau was not long in following.

While Jules was several weeks with his family, then at Niort, Aurore plunged feverishly into the novel, writing until six in the morning, finishing a volume—there would be five—in less than a week. As one ironic result, the people of La Châtre saw so little of Aurore the rumor spread that she had "gone off to Italy with Stéphane de Grandsagne," whom she hadn't seen, Aurore wrote Sophie, "for six months!" But if they wanted her in Rome, "so be it."[11] Aurore had been seeing Stéphane in Paris. Her scorn for public opinion, however, still had its bounds. When Jules arrived from Niort, he stayed—unknown to the townspeople, unknown to Casimir—with Gustave Papet at the latter's château near La Châtre. But one night, at least, he came to Nohant.[12]

Jules scaled the wall to Aurore's bedroom, momentarily on the second floor at Nohant, as Casimir slept and Papet stood guard. The following morning—September twentieth—Aurore, now twenty-seven, delightfully wrote Papet in thanks:

Dear Gustave, how good you are! How you love Jules and how I love you in return! You spent the night in a ditch, bivouacking like a wretched soldier, while we egoists of happiness could not tear ourselves from each other's arms. It is not as if we did not say at least thirty times, "We must . . . Gustave is down there, poor Gustave!" Surely Jules has told you how we blessed you in the midst of our wildest transports, mixing your name with our kisses, thinking only of you, because you were with us in our love, making it all the sweeter. . . . But all the while, my poor friend, we were giving you rheumatism! My God, how selfish love is compared to friendship. Forgive us, love me. A thousand kisses.

A letter to Émile Regnault, written in the fullness of the same aftermath, contains other elements, mingling concern and despair with delirious happiness:

Dear Émile, I am absolutely mad, but very happy! . . . In three days I have lived three years. . . . What will you think of it all? You won't scold me. That is impossible. You love me too much to reproach me such happiness. Gustave did not scold. Not he! He is devoted. He plunged up to his neck in our madness. He bivouacked in a ditch in my garden all the time that Jules was in my bedroom, because he came to me last night!—under the very nose of [my dog] Brave, my husband, my brother, my children, my maid, everybody. . . . I had foreseen and planned everything. The only risk Jules really ran was being "salted" with gunshot while he climbed to my window, which is only six feet above the ground, a risk no greater than being overturned in a diligence or breaking your leg dancing.

Three days previously (Aurore's letter continued) the two lovers had had a quarrel. She had fixed a place for a rendezvous, but Jules had failed to appear. Aurore despaired, thought Jules ill, scolded him "horribly" when next they met. Duvernet and Fleury also "scolded and lectured him and had even wanted to make him tipsy." Jules had said he was leaving without saying good-bye to Aurore, "because I had told him he should." Two hours later, Aurore had changed her mind and sent for Jules. He would not come. Then he did. Aurore showered him with "reproaches, foolish remarks, insults, mud, kicks." He became angry and told Aurore to go to the devil,

and last night he was here!—in my bedroom, in my arms, happy, beaten, kissed, bitten, scolding, crying, laughing. Never, I believe, have we experienced such wild joy. . . . Tonight, I hope, he will come again. Twice is not too much. More would not be wise. My husband cannot fail to learn that he is only three gunshots from Nohant. So far he knows nothing. He is busy with the wine harvest. At night he sleeps like a porker.

I am an idiot—a mass of bites and bruises! I can hardly stand on my feet. I'm in a state of ecstatic joy. If you were here, I would bite you until the blood ran, so you could participate a bit in our mad happiness.

But admire me! Lower your flag in salute! In the midst of all this delirium, these torments of impatience, these burning palpitations, the work goes on. Yesterday evening I made enormous changes in the second volume!

The work, the writing, went on. *Rose et Blanche* was reaching the halfway mark, and it merited equal time for Aurore. As for Jules, *there* was cause for another concern. He was always physically weak, easily ill. The nights at Nohant took their toll. Shortly before he left for Paris, Aurore was shocked by Jules' appearance. "Seeing him by day, I found him horribly changed." Whether from friendship, jealousy, pique or all three, Fleury and Duvernet had counseled "restraint" and had even found fault with Aurore. "You see," Aurore turned to Regnault, "I was right when I said you were worth more than all the others. . . . Their intentions are good, I know, but they do not understand me as well as you! They do not know what an hour of happiness can be, since it is so easy for them to tell me, 'Renounce it!' That is because they have always loved *badly*." Worse, "they always compare me to women they have known," who are careful about "their reputation" and beg them "to respect their secret." But how badly they know Aurore!

Nonetheless, Aurore fretted about Jules, addressing herself to Regnault, the practicing student of medicine, as a "fellow sawbones." He would see for himself, she said, how thin and pale Jules had become. "He is doing everything he can to kill himself. He doesn't sleep. During the day he is as lazy and idle as a dog, and at night he deprives himself of sleep to make up for lost time. . . . I am in despair. Everybody at La Châtre believes he has consumption. . . . I see him in a coffin every night, and I die from it."

"Burn my letter," Aurore admonished the unheeding Regnault. Another to him several days later has a third of a page cut from it, beyond much doubt by Regnault as too blunt for anyone else's reading. The censored paragraphs follow Aurore's speaking "more plainly," then the letter resumed: "How can I force him to sleep? Should I send him to sleep at your place?"

These details are wretched, and I ask your pardon for them. But you cannot know what horrible anxiety, what terrible remorse I feel to see the being for whom I would give my life, dying in my arms—to feel him growing thinner, more exhausted, killing himself day by day, and to tell myself that I am bringing him death, that my caresses are poison, my love a fire that consumes but does not warm, a fire that destroys, devours and leaves nothing but ashes. What a terrifying thought! Jules does not want to understand. He laughs at it. He dismisses my fear as that of a child, and when in the midst of his transports the thought seizes me and chills my blood, he says that such a death is what he hopes for. . . .

"But what a miserable creature I am," Aurore closed on a bantering tone, "bothering those I love with nothing but my troubles, fears and headaches. Forgive me! . . . Is Jules joking, or is it true that you are in love with a hospital nun? Is it Sister Raphaël, whom you mentioned to me one evening? So, you want to be the hero of my novel!"[13]

The work went on, the passion for writing, at least, has suffered no frustrating paradox. In mid-October Aurore left for Paris, taking her chapters and sections of the manuscript with her, such as the English convent scenes and descriptions of the Pyrenees. By the end of October most of *Rose et Blanche*—Rose is an actress, Blanche a nun—was on the press and Aurore was "running from magazine to newspaper, naïvely asking them to speak well of my book before it had even appeared."[14] Here Latouche's influence and her own contributions to *Figaro* and Paris revues were of immense aid. She had won the respect and friendship of fellow journalists and a few writers, of those who bring books to the favorable notice of the public.

Mistakenly Latouche thought Aurore had taken Balzac's advice in her writing and jealously scolded her for it. Balzac, in turn, on the brink of rupture with his former mentor, warned Aurore about Latouche: "Beware! You will see one fine morning, when you least expect it, that you have a mortal enemy."[15] Balzac's star was rising, that of Latouche, who talked better novels and plays than he wrote, was in decline, and on November fifth the curtain fell on his career: *La Reine d'Espagne*, Latouche's drama of an impotent king, a virgin queen and a lovesick monk, opened and closed at the Comédie Française. Aurore in her theater-going male attire was among the claque of Berrichon friends whose cheers were to no avail. The play's failure hastened Latouche's retirement to his country house at Aulnay, south of Paris.

Another drama, which Aurore found comic ("I died laughing"), was occurring on the domestic stage of Nohant. Aurore heard of it from one of its figurants, a worried Boucoiran. Madame Chatiron's *femme de chambre,* Claire, was pregnant; fingers were pointed at Boucoiran as the one responsible. "Poor child," Aurore wrote him, "don't torment yourself with it. Even if you had three children by her, her virtue would not suffer from it. A long time before coming to Nohant she had proved herself on that score. Whether my husband or my brother are the guilty ones, whether Duteil, Jules Grandsagne or Charles had a hand in it"—what a cool view of close friends!—"couldn't concern me less. They are all petty enough to balk at paying the violinist for their dance. Let them open a subscription. Even if you were one of them, you are poorer than they and should be passed by."

The worst of it, said Aurore, is that Madame Hippolyte, "bewailing the lost honor of her maid, may show her the door. She would be wrong. . . . When one is as little in love with one's husband as she and I, one should not be jealous. That would be tyranny."[16]

By a fascinating coincidence—or better, *conjunction*—within a few weeks Aurore received a letter from Casimir that was as generous in its way as hers to Boucoiran. "I am leaving Wednesday, or Thursday at the latest, for Paris," he wrote her. "I will be there most likely on Saturday morning. I will be staying in Hippolyte's apartment, but I do not at all want to bother you, nor *be* bothered, which is no more than right. Your children are fine, as are the rest of us. *Adieu, je t'embrasse de tout mon coeur.*"[17]

Casimir arrived, took Aurore to the theater and restaurant, and after ten days returned to Nohant. Aurore to her husband, December twenty-fourth: she hopes he had a pleasant trip, thanks him for the dinners, for the "lovely dress" which had just been delivered, reports a "*congestion cérébrale*" on the evening of his departure, sends kisses to the children via Casimir, and closes, "*Je t'embrasse de tout mon coeur.*"[18] Very civilized, no need at all for Jules' escape door at Quai Saint-Michel.

Four days before Casimir left, *Figaro* announced that "*Rose et Blanche*, by J. Sand" was on sale. Presumably Casimir took a copy with him. *L'Artiste*, of December 1831, deplored its ambivalence, "its equivocal, leering head so maladroitly grafted to a pure, decent body." One suspects that the reviewer was aware of its joint authorship. Belatedly Aurore's mother read *Rose et Blanche* and was "properly" shocked by it. Chambermaids, whose love life was more fantasy than reality, unlike Sophie, loved it.

"I agree completely with your criticisms," Aurore replied to her mother. "But I have already told you that the book is not mine alone. There are many farcical parts I disapprove, but which I accepted in order to satisfy my publisher, who wanted a *spicy* novel. . . . There is nothing like that *in the novel I am now writing*, and this time nothing of my collaborator will be attached to it, except his name."[19]

Aurore, at the time, was back at Nohant. She had returned earlier than anticipated, partly on Regnault's advice for her health, in greater part for the isolation and quiet she needed for her novel.

As for *Rose et Blanche* by J. Sand, its own ending best serves as the final comment:

"Sir, has life amused you greatly?"

"It is a bad book," replied the old man, "that I would not like to reread. I wish you a good evening."[20]

1. Aurore de Koenigsmark, George Sand's great-great grandmother, courtesy of Françoise Foliot

Maurice de Saxe, George Sand's -grandfather, courtesy of Fran- Foliot

3. Marie Aurore de Saxe, Madam Dupin de Francueil—Georg Sand's grandmother, courtesy Françoise Foliot

4. Madame Maurice Dupin, born Antoinette-Sophie-Victoire Delaborde—George Sand's mother, courtesy of Françoise Foliot

5. Maurice Dupin, George Sand's father, courtesy of Françoise Foliot

6. Stéphane Ajasson de Grandsagne, courtesy of Françoise Foliot

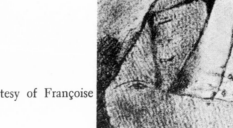

7. Jules Sandeau, courtesy of Françoise Foliot

8. Self-portrait of George Sand, courtesy of Françoise Foliot

9. Engraving of George Sand and escort by Gavarin, courtesy of Françoise Foliot

10. Marie Dorval by Jean Gigoux, courtesy of Françoise Foliot

11. Franz Liszt by A. Dev[...]
courtesy of Françoise Foli[...]

12. Alfred de Musset, a medallion by David d'Angers, cou[...]
of Françoise Foliot

14

Aurore Becomes George

Currer Bell, George Eliot, George Sand, all the victims of
inner strife, as their writings prove, sought ineffectively to
veil themselves by using the name of a man. Thus they
did homage to the convention, which if not implanted by
the other sex was liberally encouraged by them (the chief
glory of a woman is not to be talked of, said Pericles, himself a much-talked-of man) that publicity in women is
detestable.
  —Virginia Woolf, *A Room of One's Own* (1928)[1]

Aurore at Nohant was seized by creative cramps, the psychosomatic
agony of giving birth to herself. It began with the first stirrings of the
new *persona*, the conception of a novel of her own, which is part of the
writer's travail. She was morbidly ill, she was bled, it relieved her momentarily. "My illness advances swiftly, my poor, dear Émile," she
wrote Regnault. "I cannot hide its progress from myself. . . . I feel
constantly stifled, I cannot walk around my room without feeling
faint. . . . My stomach burns within me. . . . Don't let me die, my
dear Émile!"[2]

Regnault immediately offered to come, but Aurore reconsidered and
wrote back. "I cannot ask you to undertake the trip here. My brother
and my husband would show you a poor welcome. They are certain my
illness is imaginary . . . and would regard you as my lover."[3] Besides,
she reassures Regnault, "I am eating and sleeping now. I feel better, except for a few heart pains and stomach upsets. I play with my children,
I am fond of you, I think of you, I am writing a novel, and there you
are!"[4]

The writing had begun, and with it some relief. "Now that the first
steps have been taken, I can go on with more ease, with less torment of
the spirit. If sometimes I go at it with passion, it is because I cannot do
things by half."[5] Already Aurore is envisaging a new wholeness. Not

only would she bring the manuscript of her novel with her to Paris on her next long stay, but also her child Solange! She would gather the disparate parts of her life together.

There seems some mystery as to Casimir's attitude. Perhaps he raised no objection to Solange's going to Paris because a child, before the age of seven, belonged conventionally to her mother. Perhaps it meant greater freedom for himself. Tentatively Aurore mentioned the idea of having Solange with her to Regnault. Jules, she said, was wild with delight at the prospect. It was Regnault who took exception: there were limits even to bohemianism, and having a child of three and a half living with mother and lover was obviously one of them. He could scarcely believe it, even—or especially—of Aurore. Her long reply, February 23, 1832, is remarkably unapologetic:

> Yes, my friend, I am bringing Solange to you, and I see nothing to fear for her because of the inconveniences of my bachelor life. I will change that life to conform with hers. It will not be difficult or even meritorious. Jules will certainly not weep over it. . . . She will sleep on our sofa. We will rise in the morning at nine, when she normally awakes, and since she is only three and a half, she will make no remarks, no comments, ask no awkward questions, indulge in no gossip. . . . So you can put your moral scruples to rest. I have no more desire than the most *virtuous of mothers* to scandalize my daughter. . . . I am bringing Solange for Jules' sake and above all for her sake, for the sake of her character, which is just beginning to develop and which needs me. . . . If you knew how adorable she is with me, you would not worry about her under my care. She is as silly as a goose. . . . Jules will adore her and has promised me he will take care of her. They will play together all day and we will work from eight in the evening, when she always falls asleep like a log, until midnight, when I always go to bed. That, my friend, is our plan of conduct. . . . But please don't talk of my project to the others. I do not want their sermons. . . . Good night, I will talk literature to you tomorrow.[6]

On the morrow, the literature Aurore talked was her novel eventually titled *Indiana*. It was neither "romantic," she explained, nor "frenetic," but rather "everyday, bourgeois life." And it pleased Aurore, at this writing stage, to assert that "it would please few people," since she was making no concession to the popular taste for florid Gothic tales and costumed medieval romances. But, she asked herself, "would it be as boring as everyday life?" The question posed the problem of plunging into realism against the current.

Aurore's *hero* was a woman—to call her the novel's heroine is instantly to evoke, even today, the image of a man as the hero—"a typical woman, weak as well as strong, tired by as little as the weight of the air, but capable of holding up the sky, timid in mundane affairs and courageous in battle, adroitly disentangling the threads of communal life, but stupidly failing to see where her own happiness lay, laughing at the whole world, but letting herself be duped by a single man, taking no pride in herself, because she is too full of pride in the object of her choice, disdaining the vanities of the world, but letting herself be seduced by the man who epitomizes them."[7]

Would the reader, most likely a woman, accept this "typical woman" as a novel's hero? Aurore nervously asked herself.[8]

The novel did not "flow" (despite the later legend): it was painfully "reworked."[9] The pain was quite literal: the stomach pains resumed. Again Aurore was bled to bring relief. Finally, at the end of March, she could write Regnault, "Soon I will be in your arms." Comradely arms? Jules Sandeau, to his distress, was later to stumble on this letter.[10] In April, Aurore was in Paris—with *Indiana* and Solange.

The "plan" for Solange was put into operation. Jules did adore his "daughter" and daily took her to the Luxembourg gardens and the fascinating zoo at the Jardin des Plantes, where Solange saw her first giraffe and fed the Tibetan ponies. She played on the balcony with its hanging garden of flowerpots, made friends with the neighbors and became the child of the Berrichon commune, whose casualness was revealed to a startled Pierret, Sophie's old companion, when he unexpectedly arrived early one morning. He was stopped at the entry by one of the commune's members and saw another, through the half-open portal, stretched out in sleep on the floor. "I was ill, Dear Mamma," Aurore explained, ". . . with cholera"—the two were friends caring for her.[11]

Cholera may have served as an excuse for Aurore, but the epidemic sweeping Paris had a deadly reality. Before it passed, more than eighteen thousand of the city's six hundred and fifty thousand had died, eight hundred a day in the month of April. Aurore saw wagonloads of the dead from her balcony. Six people were stricken in the building on Quai Saint-Michel as the plague mounted "floor by floor," reaching the sixth landing before it was arrested.[12]

Cholera was also decimating the provinces, and from Paris Aurore sent word to Casimir, advising him to "wear woolen stockings," assuring him that Solange was not only well, but untouchable—"cholera almost never attacks children"—mentioning Paganini's playing to a full house at the Opera despite the plague, and asking for the length of Casimir's foot—"I am knitting you a pair of slippers."[13] Incredible wife, incredible husband, incredible times.

Jules Sandeau read the manuscript of *Indiana*; he was doubly troubled, embarrassed and impressed. He had written little if anything in the same period; he had had nothing to do with Aurore's novel, though the publisher wanted it signed by their joint signature, "J. Sand," because the name now had a public. Aurore and Jules took the problem to Latouche, begetter of the original *nom de plume*.

Aurore might have used her own name for her novel, but which was her "own name"—Dudevant or Dupin?

She had paid a courtesy visit to the old baroness, Madame Dudevant. Casimir's mother had expressed her astonishment that Aurore should spend such long periods in Paris without her husband. Casimir, Aurore replied, did not object.

Madame Dudevant (Casimir's mother): "Is it true that you have the intention of having books *published?*"

Madame Dudevant (Casimir's wife): "Yes, madame."

"What a droll idea!"

"Yes, madame."

"That is all very fine, but I trust you are not thinking of putting *my* name on *published books!*"

"Oh, certainly not, madame. There is no danger of that."[14]

Thus *Rose et Blanche*, articles and short stories, bore the pen name "J. Sand," Latouche's Solomon-like resolution.

Why not, then, "Aurore Dupin" as the author of *Indiana?* One can hazard a likely reason. Ladies did not like to be talked about. It was not done. In this respect, the attitude of Madame Dupin, Aurore's grandmother, did not differ from that of Madame Dudevant, Casimir's mother. Moreover, Aurore's mother, Madame Dupin, to which Sophie sometimes snobbishly added a gratuitous "de Nohant," was no less a "lady" in her pretensions. Her reaction to *Rose et Blanche* was violent; were *Indiana* signed "Dupin" it would be explosive. As for Aurore herself: "I had resolved to remain anonymous."[15] What young *man* of the period would not have been proud to see his name on the title page of his first novel, rather than mask it, as Aurore sought?

Again Latouche suggested a solution. Since the publisher, he said, wished to preserve the signature "J. Sand" for *Indiana*, because of the public it had acquired, why not keep "Sand" and simply prefix another Christian name or initial? (Jules, moreover, would thus recuperate his full name.) Spontaneously Aurore chose *George* Sand, because George "had a Berrichon sound to it."[16] Unconsciously she may have been echoing its source, *georgicus*—Latin for "agricultural," as in a georgic or pastoral poem—thus evoking the Berrichon peasant scene.[17] The English form of *George*—rather than the French *Georges*—might have been Aurore's homage to England, home of liberal thought, and to the

English convent of her youth.[18] The noblest character of *Indiana* is named Sir Ralph Brown; Indiana herself had an English mother.

In fact, "G. Sand" appeared on the title page of the novel when it first appeared in May 1832. Presumably the publisher welcomed the likely confusion with "J. Sand"—as occurred in the case of at least one critic. Perhaps it was Aurore's own choice: the name G. Sand was ideal for one who wanted to walk through life as "neither *dame*, nor *monsieur*"—neither man, nor woman—but rather as a writer among writers.

But if the initial G had to be spelled out, better George than Georgina. As in her wearing of male attire, calling herself George enabled Aurore to pass the more easily through a masculine world, although always herself—a woman—to herself and her companions. And if there seems to have been an insistence on Aurore's choice of name, it is because names—as authors especially insist—suggest, become, totemize, *are* the character, the essence of the *persona*. One's name becomes one. One also becomes one's name. The truth of it may strike immediately:

Henceforth, Aurore is George.

It was a long birth. Aurore was a long time creating herself. But *George Sand* was her greatest work.

By delightful coincidence—if there be coincidence in such a perfect instance—Henri de Latouche had climbed the stairs to George's apartment seconds after the first copy of *Indiana* had arrived from the publisher. He spied it immediately, picked it up, picked at it, leafed through the pages, "curious, uneasy, mocking." George was on the balcony. She tried to distract him from the book; let him read it when she was not with him. Latouche would not be deterred. He dipped into the novel. At each page he cried, "Come now, this is a *pastiche!* School of Balzac! *Pastiche!* What do you mean by it? Balzac!" He pursued George, book in hand, to the balcony, "proving" she had imitated Balzac, angrily declaring she had gained little "by copying," since *Indiana* was neither Balzac nor herself. George said nothing in self-defense. Muttering, Latouche departed, taking her novel with him.[19]

The morning following, George Sand woke to find a note from Latouche: "I cannot return to the country without kneeling at your feet in apology. Forget the nonsense I spoke yesterday. Your book is a masterpiece. I stayed up all night reading it. . . . Balzac and Mérimée lie dead under *Indiana*. Oh, my child, how happy I am!"[20]

How sweet the praise from so severe a critic and friend. Artists alone know how cutting friends can be. Nettled by George's rejection of his *Droll Stories* (they had quarreled, she had called him "an indecent fat man," he had called her a "prude"[21]), Balzac now told George Sand he liked her preface, but had no time to read the book. But Balzac too would make honorable amends—publicly. "I know nothing more simply written, more delightfully conceived," he wrote in *La Caricature*, May 31, 1832. "Incidents succeed and crowd upon each other without artifice, as in life, where everything collides with everything else and where chance heaps up more tragedies than Shakespeare could ever have written. In short, the success of this book is assured."

Nor did Latouche keep his praise to himself and George Sand. He let it be known on the front page of *Le Figaro*, May 24: "*Indiana* is the story of modern passion, the true story of a woman's heart." He compared the lover, Raymon de Ramière, to Lovelace, the rake of Richardson's highly regarded *Clarissa*. Uncannily anticipating the militant language of a later age, he summed up *Indiana*: "The second sex [*le petit sexe*] is crushed by the first sex [*le grand sexe*]—that is the whole of it."

Another friend (George Sand rarely lost one), Félix Pyat, in *L'Artiste*, May 27: "Every period has the novel which embodies its needs, morality and tastes. . . . The work of G. Sand . . . is a carbon of our own." A line of Pyat is particularly treasurable: "A woman of today [1832] loves either her husband, or her lover; formerly she loved neither the one, nor the other."

More gratifying was the expression of similar understanding, even more than praise, by others than friends, of her intention, which G. Sand boldly announced in her preface:

> Indiana is woman herself, that frail creature charged by the author to represent those passions which are compressed, or if you prefer, suppressed by social laws. She is free will butting her head against all the obstacles placed before her by civilization.[22]

She is thus Heathcliff as well as Antigone, the heroic protagonist carrying the burden of the author's purpose.

The social aspect was immediately grasped, the universality glimpsed. From *Le Cabinet de Lecture*, June 24: "*Indiana* is our story. . . . It is your story, it is the story of your neighbor. . . . *Indiana* is open war on the Napoleonic Code. . . . The ensemble of its four characters is all humanity. . . . I can find no fault. . . . It brings tears . . . and enriches the intelligence." The critic was a man.

From an article long attributed to Alfred de Musset, on the front page of the august *Temps*, June 14: "The particular merit of *Indiana* resides above all in its profoundly authentic feeling for the sorrows and moral turpitudes of our period." Its author, says the critic, has a "distinguished talent for observation and moral analysis," the story itself is "triste and touching."

A critic's cry of hurt may not have been as welcome to George Sand as the less restrained praise, but it reminds one that *Indiana* carried a sting that has since been lost. From the *Revue de Paris*, May 20: "*Indiana* by J. Sand" is a "profoundly true story of daily, bourgeois life, but sometimes it is unjust and often it is bitter." The critic, however, hailed the author's talent, placing "his" novel alongside Stendhal's recent *The Red and the Black*.

Yet another writer, in the *Revue des Deux Mondes*, June 1, remarked that he clearly distinguished two hands in the making of *Indiana*, "that of a young man responsible for the strong, sturdy fabric and that of a woman embroidering flowers of silk and gold." Obviously aware of the previous collaboration of Jules and Aurore, the critic was too clever by half, revealing more than he intended, namely, the general notion still abiding that strength in writing is "masculine," whereas delicacy, nuance and sensibility are "feminine." And here the comment of George Sand is still pertinent: such critics "all have a touch of Kératry."[23]

However, the crowning of George Sand, woman writer, would occur in the same *Revue des Deux Mondes*, December 15, by the "cruel" Gustave Planche, the writer's scourge, "who treated even Hugo and Balzac with contempt."[24] He devoted fifteen pages to an analysis and praise of *Indiana*'s "generative force, the struggle between love and law, the implacable duel between passion and society."

The condemnation of marriage did not escape any of the critics.[25] But the larger target of George Sand—the unhappiness, the non-fulfillment of women inside *or outside* marriage because of their frustrating relationship with men, husbands *and lovers*—was the larger, enduring theme sensed above all by women, though by no means restricted to them. The lives of men are limited by the lives they limit: all marriages in *Indiana* are unhappy, for the men as for the women.

Indiana, as the novel opens dramatically on a scene with her husband, is a comely, nineteen-year-old Creole. Her husband, retired Colonel Delmare, "once handsome, now heavy," the balding master "before whom all trembled—wife, servants, horses and dogs," is thirty or forty years older.[26] In the same scene before the fireside of a small provincial château is a third personnage, the blond, "phlegmatic," twenty-nine-year-old Sir Ralph Brown, Indiana's cousin (their English mothers had been sisters). With admirable dispatch, George Sand adds the fourth member of the novel's quartet, the aristocratic rake, twenty-five-year-old Raymon de Ramière, who had recently settled in the vicinity. Even as the novel opens he is climbing the garden wall of the Delmare estate on his way to a rendezvous with Indiana's Creole maid, Noun, "more beautiful" than her mistress. Alerted by a domestic, Colonel Delmare goes out into the garden with his gun, brings Raymon tumbling from the wall with a burst of salt and has him carried, bleeding from the hand, into the house. Raymon's identity is revealed, but not the purpose of his "prowling"; Indiana and Ralph care for him as Colonel Delmare looks jealously on. All this within the first few pages.

Hand bandaged, Raymon de Ramière departs. The Delmares meet him again in Paris, socially. Indiana falls in love with him; Raymon says he loves her; they see each other—chastely. Returned to his country place near the Delmare château, Raymon continues to see Noun, Indiana's *femme de chambre*, and spends a night and day with her in the bed of Indiana, during the latter's absence. The twenty-four hours are vividly described by George Sand—the two lovers in Indiana's bed, the doubling of the sexual pleasure for Raymon who *in his mind* was also seducing Indiana.

Colonel Delmare, bluff, coarse, "but not a bad man," is more recognizably Casimir than is Indiana, as a portrait of Aurore. Sir Ralph has a touch of Hippolyte and a great deal of Jules Néraud. Raymon is the most complex and roundly developed of the quartet, and as Milton's Lucifer, he fascinated the critics. No male author could have so thoroughly "exposed" such a man as Raymon de Ramière, noted Sainte-Beuve in *Le National*, October 5, "or would have dared to"—and he coyly speculates as to the true sex of "G. Sand" (though he already knew it). Ramon de Ramière is Aurélien de Sèze*; and he is Stéphane de Grandsagne—biting and cynical—and all Don Juans and Lovelaces who have drawn the resentment of women and their literary vengeance.

Realizing Raymon is simply toying with her while pursuing her mistress, Noun is driven to suicide. Though suicidally unhappy herself in her marriage, Indiana continues to resist Raymon's advances. If he really loves her, she says to him, then he must be "ready to sacrifice all—fortune, reputation, duty, career, principles, family." "Everything, sir," she says firmly, "for I am ready to put the same sacrifice onto the scales, and I would want them balanced."[27] But Raymon (as Aurélien) did not love so much he lost his head or even sight of his career. He marries elsewhere.

Colonel Delmare dies, Indiana discovers her true love has always been the faithful Sir Ralph. As the novel ends, they plunge together from a cliff on the primitive island of Bourbon, where they had been raised as children. Then, in an epilogue, George Sand rescues them virtually in midplunge, leaving the pair to live happily, if stoically, ever after in their "thatched, Indian cottage." The reader remembers them as having perished in their lovers' leap. Gustave Planche, in his review, would have the novel end with Raymon's unhappy marriage, as "the punishment to fit his crime." Sainte-Beuve agreed, and he who would

---

* Aurélien had a brother named Raymond and a sister named Indiana, whose sad story had moved Aurore.

be George Sand's confidant and the age's greatest critic ended his own review with a warning: "The success of *Indiana* will subject its author to a rude test. . . . He would do well not to force a precious talent," by responding too quickly to the demand of publishers, themselves bending to the cries of the public, for more novels by "G. Sand."[28]

A writer's second novel is ever the severest test. Within three months, at the end of the miraculous year, Sainte-Beuve would be praising *Valentine*.

15

Blood, Sand and Partings

The June 6th revolt . . . has thrust me brutally into real life.
—George Sand, *Correspondance* (1832)[1]

Boredom slipped into [our] intimacy.
—Jules Sandeau,
Marianna (1839)[2]

Between the first and second novels of George Sand's miraculous, metamorphic year were crowded months of near-revolution, personal success, beginning disillusion, new friends, more success, and the end of an affair. On the very heels of the cholera dead the June revolt broke out, shrouding her joy in reading *Indiana*'s reviews. The Paris riots had been anticipated the previous winter by the uprising of the Lyons silk workers against their condition—literal wage slavery, since wages were declining, poverty was growing against a background of increasing middle-class prosperity, and any workers' action, even forming a union, was condemned by the state as a criminal conspiracy ("working-class poverty should not disturb the bourgeois order"[3]). This France, still unfamiliar to the provincial young woman from Nohant, was as a pyramid rising uneasily to a point—two hundred thousand of the most privileged of a bourgeois class numbering three million, dominating a nation of thirty-five million.

In June 1832, the unfinished July Revolution of 1830 was resumed. Liberals and republicans, lesser bourgeoisie reaching for a share of the upper bourgeoisie's power, and workers with a crescendoing conscience of themselves as a class with its own interests, combined in opposition to the July monarchy of Louis-Philippe. On June fifth they joined in a funeral cortege behind the corpse of the popular liberal general, Lamarque. Massively they blackened the streets and boulevards, chanting slogans that rapidly changed from "Long live the Republic!" to more fiery cries of "Down with the Bourbons! Down with Louis-Philippe!" In a flash the new red flag of revolt was raised, and the troops charged. Arms were seized from gunshops and armories, paving stones were torn from the streets to make barricades. Paris was on the edge of revolution.

In the late afternoon George Sand was watching Solange at play in the sandpile of the Luxembourg gardens. She paid no attention to the sudden emptying of the park until she heard a roll of drums and saw a cordon of troops marching along the paths. She fled with Solange in her arms, picking her way through small streets to avoid the crowds. "Go back, go back!" people shouted to her. "The soldiers are shooting at everybody!" Solange whimpered with terror and George tried to comfort her. Finally they reached the river and raced up the stairs to the security of the apartment. George put the child to bed and placed her own mattress against the window to protect the room from a stray bullet.[4]

All night she heard the gunfire and at one moment the horrible, choked sound of strangled death cries. In the morning she discovered that a group of rebels had been slaughtered by a column of the National Guard on a nearby bridge, their bodies dismembered and thrown into the Seine. Two had been killed under her balcony. It was their death cries she had heard. Six hundred would perish in the two days of the military suppression, a hundred behind the barricade at the Cloister of Saint-Merri after a Calvary of twelve hours. Much of this George Sand witnessed, and for a long time the sight of a butcher shop, even of meat, sickened her because of the association.

Bourgeois order was restored, though blood still ran from the Morgue into the Seine, the scarlet rivulets visible from George's balcony. Brutally she had been "thrust into real life," the one-sided clash between power and the poor. But she was as innocent of the class struggle, of oppressor and oppressed, except for the sentiment of charity, as any lady from the provinces quilted by a château life. Her reaction to the June butchery was more humanist than partisan—"a soldier, a student, a worker, a National Guardsman, even a gendarme were living beings with a right to live." The horror of the spilled blood, pools of it still staining the streets, blotted out all distinctions. She confused victim with victor in the vague name of "the people." Yet the generous instincts of George Sand did not wholly betray her intelligence. She perceived in a police directive to all doctors and surgeons, ordering them to report any wounded who had managed to reach their homes, "a reopening of wounds barely closed," authority's move "to demoralize the most esteemed class in society, hoping to turn its members into police spies." She detested the ignobility, but she dreaded as much "the inevitable re-action to it," expressing her violent feeling of "abhorrence for the mon-archy, the republic, for all men!"[5]

Some have reproached George Sand, others praised her, for this blan-ket response to the events of June. But more damning and unfair is the explanation of it as the inevitable reaction of a woman. In fact, a failed, incompleted revolution, ruthlessly and brutally crushed, renders all spectators and most participants, save the truly revolutionary, violently antipolitical and pacifistic in the immediate aftermath, because of the bloodshed they have just witnessed.

However, if "June 6th had deadened the joy of *Indiana's* success" for George, it was not for long.[6] In July she was delighting in Victor Hugo's discomfiture on reading a critic declare that her novel was "the finest on the period published in France over the past two decades."[7] The next day Hugo had bearded the critic. How dare he, Hugo stormed, call *Indiana* "the best of books. Do you take *Notre Dame de Paris* to be nothing but a whore?"[8] And by the end of July, George was signing a contract for her second novel, *Valentine*, as she left for Nohant. (One clause ensured Jules sufficient money to buy his way out of military service, a common practice for those who could afford it.)

The quarrel the lovers had before parting—Jules for his family at Parthenay, George for the Berry—was surely about nothing as grubby as money, and Sand may well have awoke, the first morning at Nohant, "with a feeling of relief at the separation—a feeling which appalled her."[9] It was not the end of the idyll, but Jules for some time had irri-tated George with his spoiled-child caprices, his petulant moods. Poor Jules! He realized it, and worried about it, and wrote to Papet as soon as he arrived at Parthenay: "Dear friend, I shall not trouble your sleep this year by obliging you . . . to hide in a ditch at Nohant. So, sleep soundly . . . but see Aurore, see her often. . . . Tell her that I love her and have no life apart from hers."[10] To Émile Paultre Jules confided his sadness, how hopefully he looked forward to the fall, when they would all be together again at the fireside of the Paris attic apartment, where "I will smoke my cigar, you will stroke Solange's hair, and Aurore will make *plum pudding*." Meantime, he would set to work "tomorrow."[11]

George had set to work immediately, putting aside her own disquiet-ing thoughts and plunging into *Valentine*, fashioning a simpler, more realistic tale than *Indiana*, situated entirely in the "Black Valley" of the Berry. The writing went swiftly, in two months the novel was finished. The woman-hero, Valentine, was more George Sand than the hero's husband was Casimir. Her lover, a poor farmer's son, contrasts so sharply with Aurélien in his impulsive, all-for-love nature that Aurélien clearly inspired him. The condemnation of marriage is more explicit, the theme of free love would enchant the Saint-Simonians. The July Revolution had brought the followers of Count Claude Saint-Simon (1760–1825) to the fore with their proclamation demanding the community of goods, the abolition of inheritance and the enfranchisement of women. Soon after they pressed in popular meetings for complete equality between women and men and for freedom in love instead of "the tyranny of marriage." They would seek in George Sand the *Mother* of their movement. In vain.

As the writing drew to an end, however, the disturbing thoughts, the uncertainties, returned and with them an autumnal melancholy. Commingling, as always, was the period's romantic agony, the *mal du siècle*, intensified by the season. More personal was the writer's sadness after the birth of a novel, most poignant the sense of disappointment in Jules, in love. George was achieving half a dream, perhaps the greater part, the writer's free, independent life crowned by recognition and success, but the other half, the affective, passionate half was leaking away in the half-relationship with Sandeau. Would there ever be a full life with any man? She wrote Jules frequent letters, but her heart was not wholly in them. And when Jules read the lines, "he felt a cold chill streak across his heart."[12]

Disconsolately George revisited the scenes of her childhood, the trysting places she had known with Jules. "All has become quite ugly," she wrote him. "Where are the days of youth, the green fields, the poetry . . . ? The year's terrible drought has devastated everything. . . . I searched for the tree in which you had carved my name. It has disappeared. . . . Nothing lasts, it is folly to become attached to places where one has known happiness. Happiness passes, places change, and the heart grows older."[13] From a crack of the weathered, neglected bench in the park, where they used to meet, George plucked some moss and enclosed it in her letter to Sandeau.

As for the quarrel they had had before the summer separation, "for others," George wrote, "lazy, lukewarm, mutual forgiveness, but not for us. If the wound is deep, there can be no return. As much as one has loved another to whom one has given oneself without reserve, that much must one hate him, because the poison of ingratitude has penetrated the heart."[14]

Whatever its cause, the wound was not so deep it permitted no return, the one to the other. But when the time approached for the departure to Paris, George wrote forebodingly to Papet: "I leave with fever in my blood and despair in my heart—but you are not to involve yourself in that. Not you! The others have done me enough harm with their half-understanding. I shall see Jules. If we cannot come to an understanding by ourselves, no one else can hope to help us." Several days later, October twenty-fifth, George to Papet, from Paris: "My good, dear Gustave, I feel better, I sleep better, I am consoled. Jules is well, we love each other more than ever."[15]

George concealed the fact that she had returned from Nohant in anger, furious with the Berrichon commune, even with Regnault, for making common cause with Jules. Did they all feel that she was somehow slipping away from them? She was, indeed. They were too demanding, too critical, too "inexperienced," too "young." Rather, they made George feel "old."[16] The commune had become more exigent than Casimir himself, a collective husband that would, if it could, restrict her freedom, insisting on a fidelity no less binding because collective—though there seems to have been a laundress in Jules' life as there was a recognized mistress in Regnault's. Moreover, "the life of artists and bohemians which had once so appealed to her, the alternation of feast and famine which had at first seemed so poetic, now appeared to her as little more than a vulgar eccentricity, at best, a kind of childishness."[17]

Jules, for his part, returning to Paris from "exile" in Parthenay, "brought back a love exalted by the absence, irritated by the uncertainty, embittered by the jealous suspicions—a more impetuous and demanding love than he had known before."[18] The suspicions fastened on Latouche and soon on Gustave Planche—such already was the reputation of George Sand in the salons and cafés of Paris.

Latouche had given up direction of *Le Figaro* that spring and now spent most of his time at Aulnay, where George had gone more than once with Solange to see him early in the summer. "Later, people told me that Latouche loved me, that he was jealous without admitting it even to himself and hurt because I did not guess it. But it was not true."[19] A touching letter from Latouche to George, shortly before she left Nohant for Paris, indicates rather a sad recalling of what might have been, but what was not. "That you are changeable," he wrote, "I know too well, but then you have your share of humanity's faults, and its prizes as well. . . . Motherhood, pride, friends—you have everything and you have a right to it all! . . . Had I been successful, I should have loved you too much. Yesterday I reread Rousseau's four letters to Sara to re-enforce my feeling of having lived my life and of having been right in resigning from it."[20]

In the fall Latouche came into Paris and offered George, as a parting *beau geste*, the lease for his Quai Malaquais apartment, where she had scribbled—and rescribbled—her first professional lines among the other eaglets of *Le Figaro*. Though on the quai, the white-carpeted apartment turned its back on the Seine and looked south across the gardens of the Beaux Arts. A giant acacia reached the windows on the fourth floor, adding to George's pleasure. The spacious apartment became her refuge and workshop. During the day, publishers, journalists, would-be novelists, Saint-Simonians and complete strangers climbed the stairs to see her, asking for manuscripts, the story of her life, free copies of *Indiana*, her collaboration. Such was the ransom of success. "But in the evening, I shut myself up with my pens and my ink, Solange, my piano and my fire."[21] No mention of Jules in this letter to Boucoiran, December twentieth, though they shared the Malaquais apartment. "Come this evening to Madame Dudevant, 19 Quai Malaquais," Jules invited Balzac at this time. "We await you."[22]

After the reconciliation, reproaches. "Day by day, the air about them became stormier, heavier." Jules resorted to the insecure lover's device of tormenting George until she wept. "She loved him, then, since her eyes could fill with tears!" But George suffered more from the "young man's *tendresse*" and weakness, when she felt the dragging weight of his dependence, than from his outbursts. "She accused him of indolence and inertia." Jules replied with the ultimate reproach: "You have been a bad lover!" The liaison did not yet end—"they were both cowards, the one from love, the other from pity."[23] Early in winter, however, Jules moved out to a small apartment on Rue de l'Université, though they continued to see each other. But other men, new friends, entered George's life, and were received at the Malaquais apartment.

Valentine had appeared in November while George was briefly at Nohant. Gustave Planche had sent her an advance copy of his long, laudatory review. She thanked him. They met. Planche brought word that his editor, François Buloz, would like her to write regularly for *La Revue des Deux Mondes*. At the same time, *La Revue de Paris*, in which George's short story, "La Marquise," had just appeared, was bidding for her work. George hesitated; she had a cool business head. Tentatively she offered Buloz another short story. He rejected it, but offered her a contract she could not refuse: four thousand francs a year for thirty-two pages of manuscript every six weeks. Security and publication! The contract, brought by Planche and signed on December 11, completely took the edge off the rejection of her short story—which would, in any case, be part of a novel already gestating in George's mind.

Gustave Planche, the writer's scourge at the age of twenty-four, was so struck by George Sand that he was almost dumb in her presence—and apologized for it by means of the writer's resort, a fluent, witty letter. George, however, was not equally taken by Planche at first, nor did she attempt to hide it. Though tall and cameo-profiled—Balzac described him as "Raphaelite" in appearance—[24]Planche made a fetish of dirty, flamboyantly anti-dandy slovenry. He was morose and parricidal; he hated his father, an autocratic pharmacist who had tried to keep him from literature, but unconsciously he imitated his father's manner. Planche's mind, however, was clear and sharp, cutting like a diamond—especially the prose of his literary elders. But when he spoke, as he knew, he sounded pedantic. "I cannot say hello," he confessed to George, "without seeming to give a lecture."[25] Self-mockingly, Planche promised to spare her his "university, theological and metaphysical digressions."[26] He fell profoundly in love with George, and she learned to appreciate *him*.

Planche introduced George to Sainte-Beuve, a former schoolmate. And he cautioned George about Marie Dorval, the most famous actress of her generation, when the two women met, as the new year began and the affair with Sandeau was drawing to a close. George's interest was flamingly manifest.

Marie Dorval, Planche uneasily informed George, who shrugged away the warning "in a thoroughly virile manner," was known to have felt "the same passion for a sister-actress—Juliette Drouet—as Sappho for her young Lesbians." He had it firsthand, said Planche, from one of his friends, Juliette Drouet's lover.[27]

16

Women in Love

"Frankness, far from cleansing us in the eyes of men, would be yet another stain they would feel the right to inflict upon us."

So George Sand mused at 2 A.M., March 27, 1833, on "the secret of Byron," which was in fact no secret—his relations with his half-sister Augusta and their resulting child, which lent him, unlike ordinary mortals such as herself, a "magical aureole" in the eyes of the world. But no one, George wrote in her notebook, was without a "stain." The great difference was the stealth imposed on those not granted the license of "the great poet" to explore life without limits. Their secret "must be borne in silence and without false glory, for society reserves its most vulgar punishments and insulting proscriptions for those who brave its judgments." Openness for a woman, instead of being a virtue, "would be yet another stain."[1]

A more "open secret" of Byron was his bisexuality, his penchant for both women and young men, and on this too George Sand must have mused between night and morning in March 1833, when her own relations with Marie Dorval were at their most intense. It is a continuing irony that even Sandists would like to reduce the heat of that contact to a warm friendship, despite the passion in the letters between the two lovers.* It is as if anything else "would be yet another stain," though the Romantic convention itself was more permissive of passion, and not simply the language of passion. Openness was—is?—another matter. One wonders how many of the George Sand-Marie Dorval letters were destroyed, especially by George Sand. For George Sand was also Madame Dudevant, wife and mother, a woman, in other words; and in her time—and ours?—no woman, as we have earlier remarked, had the privileged frankness of a man.

Nevertheless there is an astonishing openness, for one with a key, in George Sand's novella *La Marquise*, published the previous December

---

* Witness Simone André-Maurois' long introduction to the *Correspondance Inédite* of George Sand and Marie Dorval (Paris, 1953). The burden of disproof remains.

(1832), when the liaison with actress Marie Dorval may well have been imaginatively forged.[2] The marquise of Sand's story, married at sixteen and widowed six months later, rendered frigid by her husband and unchanged by later men, is suddenly seized with infatuation for an actor, Lélio. Nightly she steals to the theater disguised as a man to see him perform. Chin resting (*à la* George Sand) on the chair before her, hands clasped on trousered knees, "forehead bathed with perspiration" from the fervor, she followed the actor's every movement, "every palpitation of his breast." When they met and kissed, the single kiss released the love pent in her; and when she bade him farewell, "Lélio wept like a woman."[3]

In Lélio, George Sand's marquise embraced all the heroes the actor portrayed. In Marie Dorval, splendid that winter in Hugo's *Marion Delorme* and Dumas' *Antony*, George Sand embraced all the heroines, all the roles Marie played. George's love for the theater and for its finest actress would become one; in Marie she found herself. "There is something cold and incomplete in my nature, " George Sand confesses, "a kind of paralysis preventing my feelings from taking an expressive form," inhibiting, sometimes blocking communication. Wherefore the compulsive writing? Simply and instinctively, Marie Dorval embodied what George sought. "So, when she appears on the stage with her drooping body, her listless walk, her sad, penetrating eyes . . ."—which spring suddenly to life, startling the audience with the emotion of her characterization—"I seem to see my own soul . . . recostumed to reveal itself to me, and to others."[4]

To the meeting of two souls, George Sand would never admit any impediment, or leave anything to chance. What she desired, she reached for. She wrote Marie Dorval, asking to see her. With similar directness, Marie responded. The day she received George's note, she was at the door of the Malaquais apartment. She threw it open without knocking, went straight to George without regard for Jules Sandeau—still frequently at Malaquais—and embraced her. "Here I am," she cried breathlessly, "*I!*" She stood, "swaying like a supple reed responding to her own mysterious breeze." "As light and soft," Sandeau later said, "as the feather adorning her hat," which seemed "to have dropped upon her from the wing of a fairy in passing." But it was by Marie's voice, the timbred stage voice, deep and penetrating, that George recognized her. More than pretty, Marie was a "charmer."[5]

Born illegitimately to a pair of touring performers in 1798, Marie had babbled her first words on stage, learning to please before she knew even a child's pleasure. (There was something of Sophie about the older Marie that stabbed at George Sand.) Married at fifteen to the ballet master of the troupe, who took Dorval as his name, Marie was a widow with two daughters when he died six years later. She had a third daughter by Piccini, the composer's nephew, in Paris, where she was engaged at the Porte Saint-Martin Theater—and where she won her great public. At thirty-three, Marie married Jean-Toussaint Merle, feuilletonist and minor playwright, who blinked at her liaisons and received her lovers. Less complaisant was her lover since 1831, Count Alfred de Vigny, moody poet (called the finest of the century by Benedetto Croce) and major playwright. "My Sappho," Vigny wrote of Marie in his journal, shortly before or after she met George Sand—of whom he would note the same.[6]

The day she came to the Malaquais apartment, Marie Dorval invited George and Jules Sandeau to dinner with her husband and "some old friends." George does not mention Count de Vigny among the guests. When George and Vigny did meet, he was cold and she cool. He describes "her black hair curling over her collar as in Raphael's paintings of angels, her large, dark eyes shaped like those of mystics and found in the most magnificent Italian faces." But he was taken aback by her manner and speech: "graceless in bearing, rude in address, a man in appearance, language, tone of voice and boldness of tongue."[7] George in turn admired Vigny's mind, but not "the person."

It was a spell of restlessness for George, of loose, frayed ends and tantalizing beginnings, including a contract for her third novel, significantly entitled *Lélia*; a defiant letter to Boucoiran about the "numerous liaisons" of which he accused her; a teasing on-and-off rendezvous with Prosper Mérimée, novelist, cynic and man about town, offered her by Gustave Planche even as he warned her of Marie Dorval's "perversity." And in the same month of January 1833, George wrote to the just-met Marie: "Do you think you can bear with me? You don't know yet, nor do I. I am such a boor, so stupid and slow to speak out what I have in my mind, so gauche and so dumb when my heart is most full! Don't judge me by that. Wait a bit before you decide how much pity and affection you can give me. As for myself, I feel that I love you with a heart made young again by you. If it is a dream, as everything else I have desired in life, do not wake me from it too quickly. It does me so much good! Good-bye, great and beautiful one, no matter what, I will see you this evening!"[8]

Two days later George canceled an evening with Mérimée and was soon writing Marie that she did not really live the day she did not see her—"but I am working like a horse" (on *Lélia*) and she sent Marie a copy of *La Marquise*. On February second, George offered to act as Marie's cavalier and escort her to a gala, closing, "I love you." On February fourth: "I wish someone loved me as I love you."[9] But on February tenth, Marie was writing Vigny, ill and sickly jealous of George

Sand (among others): "Oh, how miserable I am to love you . . . never to be at ease with you, or with myself. . . . I love you as you have never been loved."[10]

The letters and journals reflect the flight into love, poetry and fantasy, an escape from the bind of a vulgar, climbing bourgeoisie they refused and a fading aristocratic class they had abandoned. They were alone together in Bohemia—if only because they were bored or more alone elsewhere—and they rode the carrousel of their small circle with *a* pursuing *b* pursuing *c* pursuing *a*, or *a-b-c-z* forming a cartwheel, each thought free-wheeling. They expressed the contradictions of their period even as they tried to escape them. Romantics, they cultivated the cult of the new, but would have nothing to do with the crude upcoming class, the Balzacian *dévorants* clawing their way to great nineteenth-century fortunes. Creators of the new, they were often descendants, as Vigny and Sand and others of their circle, of a patrician past they regretted but could not live with, since it was dead.

But if they, the creative lights of the century, felt classless and superior, they were no less products—and prisoners—of their class culture, of the prejudices they absorbed with the milk of their mothers or wet nurses whose borrowed prejudices were fiercer, of the imprint above all of their parents' example of male-as-master, so deeply impressed upon them that they thought it the ineluctable way of men and women laid down by an unchangeable nature, which indeed they would not have changed. *They* were largely men, but the prejudices were buried deep in most women as well. Here George Sand was exceptional and exemplary, insofar as men and women—for it took two or more to play the game of living together—and her own broken, but trailing, chains permitted.

Born of a ruined noble family, "born," as he said bitterly, "without a fortune, which is the greatest misfortune . . . in this society based on money,"[11] Vigny was nonetheless cherished and spoiled as the last surviving son of four by his parents, particularly his mother. After twelve years as an officer, he changed his *épée* for a pen and wrote poetry. He had the aristocratic male's series of mistresses and illegitimate children, then married the daughter of an English lord, Lydia Bunbury. He called her "saint" and deceived her regularly. One's wife, as one's mother, in Vigny's world, was sacrosanct; one slept with other women for pleasure. Making love to Lydia, he said, was like "drawing a bow across stone"—a statue of the Virgin?—whereas Marie Dorval was "a beautiful harp" from which he drew "delicious sounds"—but morally uncomfortable, he abused Marie even as he loved and enjoyed her.[12] As for Marie, she loved Vigny, she loved easily, but she never felt "at ease" with either Vigny or herself: she was a lower-class prisoner of the same culture, as well as of the particular man, seeing herself as she was seen by society and her lover.

Again the figure of Sophie is shadowily superposed, blurring with that of Marie for George Sand.

There was, then, this impulse, this uneasiness with Vigny, driving Marie Dorval precipitously towards George Sand, herself suffering from the failure, the frustration of failed love, with her own man-child, Jules Sandeau. Did each feel that only with a woman could a woman be fully at ease, sexually, intellectually and emotionally? Or was there not the same conditioned sense of sin of two women in love, of a lesbianism which did not dare declare itself even to itself, and which *les précieux* of the period called Sapphism? This is reflected in George Sand's early-morning lines on "the secret of Byron," to which she was now returning nightly and daily and unintermittently in the writing of *Lélia*, painfully drawing her own bow across her own gut-strings.

It was a time of tangled lives, like skeins, and each of the characters has his or her own point in the web from the bias of which the story of each can be—and has been—spun. Vigny was not faithful to Marie, but he was jealous of Marie's husband and a man named Fontaney (actually courting Marie's oldest daughter), and of George Sand. Marie, unfaithful to Vigny, was jealous of Vigny's wife, Vigny's mother *and* of George Sand. She once reproached Vigny for having left her alone one evening (with her husband) while he went off with George on his arm. And early in the tangle, Vigny spoke to his journal of George Sand. "Yesterday," he wrote, "this monstrous woman suddenly told her new friend"—Marie, who patently retold it to Vigny: " 'Well, it's all over. I gave myself last night to [illegible, not likely Mérimée, as attributed].' So," continued Vigny, "she slept with that man who despises her and told her so. Thus without a qualm she deceives her lover [Sandeau] for whom she left her husband. She said further [to Marie], 'He treated me like a trollope. He said, "There is no point in pretending during the day in order to have you for the night. You have the ways of a prostitute without the advantages, and the pride of a marquise without the graces." ' "[13]

The male's dichotomy of women as mother/wife versus mistress/prostitute could not be more sharply drawn, though men have thought they sought both in one ideal woman. When they find it, as in George Sand, who overleapt the dividing line in a heroic reaching for wholeness, they are confounded. Vigny's anecdote, probably roughly true, demonstrates it. The torsion of their culture tears men—and women—apart.

Marie matched George in bravery and surpassed her in recklessness. In sad fact, an actress had less to lose having lost all: she was society's courtesan; her status as actress had not greatly changed from the time of the Verrières sisters—another echo for George's cavern of memories. In marrying her, Merle had known what he had undertaken, and he observed the rules of the game, not without profit.

George would meet Marie at the theater, in her loge after the spectacle, or "at the corner of the fire" in George's apartment, "living a great deal in a few hours."[14] They became known as "the inseparables" and the name of Marie Dorval was linked to those of Gustave Planche, Henri de Latouche and Jules Sandeau. "At this time," recounted Arsène Houssaye in his *Confessions*, "Sappho was reborn in Paris," uncertain whether she loved the men or the woman in her life. Each evening, "after sowing fire and flame in the hearts of her public," the actress would find in her blue-tapestried loge "the strange woman who awaited her prey as she smoked her cigarettes." At dawn, "the two *bacchantes* would finally take leave of each other, still reeling in the pale light of realized dreams."[15]

Houssaye, recording hearsay, was then himself eighteen, and later wrote more directly of the George Sand he met, of "her touching simplicity, her radiant personality," her capacity for friendship.[16] There is, however, George's own song of songs, such is its Biblical cadence, describing her feelings, their emotional truth, at this time. She originally titled it, "To the Angel Lélio," then struck it through, substituting, "To the Angel without a Name"—and further obscured the personal by pretending it was all a "translation."

Behold, the dawn is breaking. Come, for the dew will soon fall and you may catch cold. No, you do not fear the cold, nor the penetrating mist. But come! it is your hour, my window is open, my room full of flowers. I await you.

If you do not come soon, I shall fall asleep, for it is the hour of slumber. Ah, here you are at last! Blessed art thou, heavenly child! Give me thy forehead to kiss, let thy black hair fall across my breast, thy lovely hair a cubit long!

How beautiful is an angel with floating hair in the morning! Why do not men have such long hair?

Come, nameless one, sit by my bedside. You speak no language, you do not reveal yourself in words. How I love you thus, how well I understand you!

Angel of silence, place your cool hand on my shoulder, warm with love, but upon which no man has ever put his lips. Only your sweet breath, your damp hair, can freshen it.

What flowers are those on your forehead, in your hands? Flowers unknown, flowers more beautiful than any woman on earth. Their perfume is intoxicating, my angel, spread them over me, cover me with leaves from your dewy crown.

Enough, my angel! I am dying! I want to live for tomorrow to see you again. Adieu, the day grows bright. Go quickly, my treasure, so that none may see you, for they would steal you from me, and then I should have to give myself to men. Adieu, let me kiss thy snowy neck and thy forehead, where shines a star. Give me a feather from thy wing that I may keep it as proof of thy visit, a souvenir of my rapture.

Why do not men have wings so that they might come at night and fly away in the morning? I prefer thistledown to any man! You blow upon it, and it is lost in the wind. No man ever becomes lighter, evanescing into spirit.

Go then, morning angel! I am falling asleep. Kiss me on the forehead and make my soul as beautiful as thine.[17]

The "heavenly child" of the second stanza is textually "*fils du ciel*," son of heaven, which would correspond to the fictional Lélio. However, responding to George Sand's heavenly angel, one scarcely thinks of a man. Yet there is a sexlessness in the sensuality—or is it an ambiguous bisexuality?—a poetical straining towards spirituality, the ethereality of romantic yearning. "Hail to thee, blithe Spirit," sang George's kinsman Shelley to the skylark, "bird thou never wert!" There is in George's prose poem a sense of discontent with all mortals: the angel's flowers (phallic?) are more beautiful than any woman; the angel lies upon one more lightly than any man, and then flies away in the morning.

But if all were subsumed in sexuality, would there be any poetry? There would surely not have been George Sand.

Lightness is the motif, and the love of one unloved is never light. Scarcely had George Sand asked Marie Dorval for tickets to a ball for Planche, Sandeau and herself than the final rupture with Jules took place, and George canceled the tickets. It was not a single quarrel, but the end of a series; a bond had become a burden that even separate apartments could no longer attenuate. Her mind made up, George brought the affair to a complete break; half-relations would always be abhorrent to her. Jules' sympathizers, drawn by his weakness, called her ruthless, the men added "manlike," an adjective doubling back on its users. The account of Paul de Musset, Alfred's older brother, probably related to him by Jules and reshaped by him later, has survived not so much for its veracity as for its vividness. It was George Sand, he said, who told Sandeau he must leave for Italy and took care of all the arrangements, including passport, passage and travel money (more accurately, the royalties of *Rose et Blanche*, which George had turned over entirely to Jules). George, according to Paul de Musset's novelized version, had appeared, on the day of Jules' scheduled departure, in male attire—redingote, broad-brimmed hat and trousers; had found poor Jules staring helplessly at his empty trunk; and had proceeded to pack it and him off on the trip to Italy.[18]

The callousness is belied by George's letter to Émile Regnault. "Go to Jules," she urged the young doctor early in March, "and care for his health." Disconsolate, Jules had taken an overdose of "*acétate de morphine.*" "His heart is broken, but you can do nothing about that; do not try. I am not calling you to my own side; I would rather be alone today, I feel there is nothing left for me in life. See to it that Jules lives. He will suffer terribly for a long time, but he is very young after all. One day he will not regret having lived. . . . Go, my friend, go to him."[19]

George herself went to Marie for comfort, and turned to Mérimée for diversion. It was a melancholic spring that profoundly affected *Lélia*, or rather Lélia, its central Hamlet-like figure, as George Sand, in her inner writer's life, was now regarding herself. As for Jules Sandeau, he had his friends' sympathy.

Balzac to his beloved "stranger," Madame Hanska, end of March, 1833: "They are separating, and the real cause is a renewal of the affection of George Sand, or Madame Dudevant, for the most wicked of our contemporaries, Henri de Latouche. . . . Yesterday I met Sandeau, who was in despair." Balzac is several months behind in time and lovers, and maintains the lag in his letter of May 29–June 1: "Good God, the author of *Indiana*, Madame Dudevant, has thoroughly dishonored herself, and all Paris buzzes over the two lovers. Sandeau has just left for Italy, all despair. I thought him mad. Madame Dudevant has given herself to a man named Gustave Planche, a fellow universally despised, but who burned incense to her in the *Revue des Deux Mondes*. Pity Sandeau, a noble heart; forget Madame Dudevant."[20]

When Sandeau returned from Italy, Balzac commiseratingly took him into his own household, writing Mme. Hanska: "This poor, shipwrecked soul must be properly launched on the sea of literature." Then, several years later (March 8, 1836): "Jules Sandeau has been one of my mistakes. You can't imagine such laziness, such listlessness. He is without energy or will. The most beautiful sentiments in words, but nothing in deed or reality. . . . He has told me that it is impossible for him to follow up on any project. . . . In three years, he hasn't written half a volume. . . . He makes one despair of friendship, as he did of love."[21]

Balzac's disenchantment with Jules made him better understand

George Sand's. He resumed his friendship with her and would shortly stop over at Nohant.

* * *

From Balzac's atelier Jules Sandeau would go on to the French Academy via two dozen published novels and a half-dozen plays. A way station of more than passing concern was Rue du Bac. Here, at the age of twenty-seven he became the lover of an ailing Marie Dorval, forty and on the verge of abandonment by Alfred de Vigny. Marie and George Sand were still bosom friends, but when Jules wrote his autobiographical novel, *Marianna*, Marie was violently jealous of its heroine. "Jules still loves George Sand!" she cried to Arsène Houssaye. "When I talk of this woman, he never stops me to talk of *me!* If he loves me at all, it's because he knows I'm her intimate friend and he finds his mistress's kisses still warm on my cheek!" But did not Marie also find George's remembered kisses on Jules' cheeks, as well as, more obviously, the same virtues in Jules which George had found? "I love that woman," she essayed in endearing confusion to Houssaye, "because she loved Jules, or because Jules loved her. . . . To her, I speak only of him!"[22]

Things equal to the same thing are in love with each other. There are, in this episode of man and women in love, Jules Sandeau's own remarkable sensitivity and empathy, which enhance him in one's own memory. In 1840 he wrote in appreciation, rather than denigration, of his former lover (the word *mistress* does not apply easily to George Sand) "as the man, or woman, who lived on the border line of the two sexes." Sandeau paid this astonishing tribute: "Madame Sand [in her writing] was a sort of female Christ," carrying the cross of womanhood in her arms, "shielding the adultress from the world's stoning."[23] The title he gave George Sand was *marquise*, not baroness. He could have been thinking of *La Marquise*.

Of the two *"inséparables,"* Jules wrote in a closing, moving metaphor:

"Madame Dorval placed her friendship in Madame Sand. An instinctive feeling of sympathy drew the one woman to the other, both women stricken in their hearts, both bending before the storm, both incomparable in talent and unhappiness; the one an eagle, the other a dove, both swept away by the storm, they found that only in love could they find shelter for their poor, tired wings."[24]

Shadowed indeed was their love, and Sandeau had the sensitivity called "feminine" to sense and express it.

17

The Existential Spring of George Sand: Lélia Unlocks Her Heart

I am absolutely and completely Lélia.
—George Sand,
Correspondance (1833)[1]

I am not Lélia.
—George Sand,
Correspondance (1836)[2]

You will be the Lord Byron of France.
—Chateaubriand to George Sand,
after reading Lélia (1833)[3]

With 1833 a period of superlatives began that will last until the Revolution of 1848—from George Sand's thirtieth to her forty-fifth year.

The third of three works published within *fourteen* months, *Lélia* is one of the most remarkable, if marred, existential works ever written—the record of a life recording itself as it was being lived that black spring of 1833, when ten years of tension, mismarriage, lovers, illusions and despair uncoiled and snapped.[4] It is marred by George Sand's abandonment of her own language—a remarkable, necessary creation in itself, feminine, personal and realistic[5]—for a metaphysical form. To say it was Gustave Planche's influence is more to deplore than to explain it. Fortunately, there was another influence, or rather encouragement, she could turn to—Sainte-Beuve.

The same age as herself, Charles-Augustin Sainte-Beuve possessed a catlike delicacy and curiosity, a sensitive, subtle mind. An exquisite painter of literary portraits, he welcomed literary confidences; at the height of his cautious passion for Victor Hugo's wife, he was less pervious to George Sand. He was tempted, he says, then looked into the "abyss" and pulled back.[6] He was monkish in his plumpness and prudence, and made a good friend, helping George install nine-year-old Maurice, brought by Casimir, in a Paris school. He did not gain in being seen, Sainte-Beuve apologized to George, who suffered a similar lack of mundaneness, so the relationship between the two, who were within walking distance of each other, was largely epistolary—curious, but not uncommon for the literate time. Nevertheless, they enjoyed soirées together. Please come, George pleaded when the break with Sandeau was most painful, and talk to me. But the following day she wrote Marie Dorval, Come, "and spend the night."[7]

One evening George read from *Lélia* to Sainte-Beuve, and he quailed. Such despair! Such revelations! She frightened him, he said. George tried to reassure Sainte-Beuve. "Do not confuse the author too much with his account of his sufferings," she told him in a note.[8] Simultaneously Sainte-Beuve attempted to efface the impression he had left. He was all "admiration," he wrote. George's readers would indeed be surprised by her "philosophical novel," and perhaps even protest. But "to be a woman, to be less than thirty, and to have plumbed the depths without showing it, to bear such witness as would sear our [male] brow and whiten our hair, to support such knowledge with lightness and ease and sobriety—that is what I admire most of all."[9] In fact, Sainte-Beuve had not heard the most searing pages, in which the "sobriety" he approved was the last thing sought. "Go on with *Lélia*," he encouraged George—and proposed a number of men to distract her from her dark mood, and possibly from himself: Madame Hugo was jealous and fearful, knowing George Sand's reputation. "I would rather," George replied, "you did not bring me Alfred de Musset. He is very much of a dandy. We would not get along. . . . Instead, bring me Dumas . . . but come with him the first time. You know how bad I am on such occasions." ("She was always silent and embarrassed," Sainte-Beuve noted in the margin for future use.)[10] This too was the time of the March nights with Marie Dorval at the theater or in George's Malaquais apartment, the early-morning broodings over Byron's "secret"—all pouring into *Lélia*.

And in April there was Mérimée—an adventure of George Sand so publicly exposed and openly discussed one wonders suddenly about

Casimir, who so easily slips the mind. They had finally met, Prosper Mérimée and George, after a contretemps of canceled rendezvous. George had pleaded "neuralgia" and a newly arrived husband with Maurice in tow. Mérimée had replied, "Since you are not in the diplomatic service"—as was Mérimée—"I'll believe your neuralgia. . . . But I should appreciate knowing when you are better, and when your husband may be off by himself."[11] The letter is pure irony. Casimir did not stay at Malaquais, but rather in Hippolyte's apartment; he was a pretext for George's shyness, a shyness that soon became, as characteristically, boldness. One night at the Opera, Pontmartin relates, Mérimée and she were seen "at the top of the great staircase with little Solange, who had fallen asleep during the last act of *Robert le Diable*, on Mérimée's shoulders."[12] The two were together for seven days, though *all* Paris circulated the story, now become legend, of a single evening's sexual fiasco. The fault is Marie Dorval's. Miserable, George had confided her disappointment in the triste affair. Irresistibly, Marie had retold it to Dumas, who encapsulated it in a phrase, as if from George Sand herself: "I had Mérimée last night, and it wasn't much."[13]

George forgave Marie. "You say she has betrayed me. I know it well, but you, my good friends, who among you has not betrayed me? She has betrayed me once, but you have betrayed me every day." The bitter words were addressed to a notebook. She knew Marie's "faults," George wrote, "her vices," and loved her. As for the others, they were simply blind to their own.[14] She had been attracted initially to Mérimée, George related to Sainte-Beuve, because of his extraordinary "self-confidence" at a time of her greatest self-doubt. "For a week I thought he held the secret of happiness, that he would teach it to me, that his disdainful insouciance would cure me of my own puerile sensibilities." At her side, George said, she saw a woman—Marie Dorval—sublimely without inhibition, and envied her. She hoped Mérimée might teach her the same mindless pleasure. "I imagined that a few days' fascination would solve the secret of existence. So I conducted myself at thirty as no girl of fifteen would have done: I committed the most foolish act of my life: I became the mistress of Prosper Mérimée. . . . The experience was a complete failure. I wept from the suffering, the disgust and discouragement. . . . If only Mérimée had understood me. . . ."[15]

Men, whether Napoleon or Byron, Balzac or Stendhal, may go from woman to woman, adventure to experience, seeking that understanding which is self-understanding, and the future simply records it as their destined road to self-realization, their historical emergence as themselves. How many men, engrossed in their voyage, would understand George Sand's?

Henry James, while in no way "vouching for the truth of the anecdote," has drawn the essence, the existential essence, of the famous affair. He had heard the tale, he wrote, from someone who had heard it "direct" from Mérimée . . .

> Prosper Mérimée was said to have related—in a reprehensible spirit—that during a term of association with the author of *Lélia* he once opened his eyes, in the raw winter dawn, to see his companion, in a dressing gown, on her knees before the domestic hearth, a candlestick beside her and a red *madras* round her head, making bravely, with her own hands, the fire that was to enable her to sit down betimes to urgent pen and paper. The story represents him as having felt that the spectacle chilled his ardour and tried his taste; her appearance was unfortunate, her occupation an inconsequence and her industry a reproof—the result of all of which was a lively irritation and an early rupture.
>
> To the firm admirer of Madame Sand's prose the little sketch has a very different value, for it presents her in an attitude which is the very key to the enigma, the answer to most of the questions with which her character confronts us. She rose early because she was pressed to write, and she was pressed to write because she had the greatest instinct of expression ever conferred on a woman; a faculty that put a premium on all passion, on all pain, on all experience and all exposure. . . .[16]

The dawn scene James described is George Sand describing the scene, the situation, she is in, compulsively adding to the pages of *Lélia*. One best reads them by living them with her as she writes them, a doubling of all experience.

Prosper Mérimée himself was true to himself and equal to his time. In his novel touching on the affair, although he does give himself the grand, seductive role, he turns his habitual irony on himself, too. Indeed, Mérimée titled his short narrative *La Double Méprise*, The Two-Way Misunderstanding. Its hero is Darcy, "more eloquent in his suit than in his appreciation. But he was polite." He had met Julie de Cheverney, an unhappily married woman, at four one afternoon. "Nine hours later she was his mistress! . . . Nine hours had sufficed for her to be dishonored—in his own eyes." "Each word of Darcy," who had promised eternal love, "was now like a knife." But how could Julie de Cheverney reproach a man who, like all men, "was thinking only of how he might arrange a liaison for the summer in the most convenient manner?" Darcy drives home in his coupé, "whistling the air of a man satisfied with his day." Madame de Cheverney goes home—and "dies."[17] It is a small masterpiece of a double-take on the double standard: a mannered comedy, for the man.

One man's comedy, however, is another's . . . *Lélia?*

"I hope, I rest, I write. . . ."—George to Sainte-Beuve—". . . there is no secret in *Lélia*."[18] Published at the end of July 1833, its pages unlock George Sand's heart.

The opening burst is a lover's plaint. "Who are you, and why does your love cause so much harm? . . . Lélia, I am afraid of you!" The plaintive one is Sténio, a twenty-year-old poet, who is all George's young men—Sandeau, Boucoiran, Stéphane. Lélia is thirty, beautiful, black-haired, broad-browed, statuesque—and cold, Sténio complains, as marble. She is George Sand, spring 1833. There were, and will be, other springs and summers, but this is George Sand, spring 1833, who stands accused, and is still accused, of frigidity.

Trenmore, a mystical, stoical friend who purged a petty crime by five years' imprisonment—inspirer of Dostoievsky's noble-minded criminals —counsels Lélia to send Sténio away, or leave him, for otherwise she will destroy him. Lélia hesitates. She loves Sténio in her semimaternal fashion, stroking his curling hair, calling him "my child." They try separation for a month. Lélia withdraws to the desert to meditate, then returns "to the world." She is woman as Faust, Hamlet, Oberman, Manfred, clad in the language of their male creators. Then Lélia meets her long-absent sister Pulchérie, prostitute, courtesan, sensualist—and George Sand breaks through with pages of such intensity, revelation, intimacy and pain that no man could have written them, and no man should fail to read them.[19]

Pulchérie is Marie Dorval, and she is George Sand's *Doppelgänger*, for she makes love to Sténio, who mistakes her for Lélia. The two women rediscover each other at a lavish costume ball. "Oh, my sister," cries Lélia to Pulchérie, "save me!" Save her, she implores, from her marble coldness, her impotence in the face of life. Shocked by the despair of the once-gay sister she has not seen for years, Pulchérie replies lightly that Lélia's sin has always been pride. "Pride?" questions Lélia, stung, then admits it. "But I've tried everything." "Except pleasure!" laughs the "bacchanalian" Pulchérie. "Did you find happiness in it, my sister?" asks Lélia. "I did not seek it," Pulchérie answers. "Unlike you, I did not ask of life more than it can give. To keep myself from despair I've adopted the religion of pleasure." But the price of promiscuity! interrupts Lélia, "the contempt of men!" The price of marriage, responds Pulchérie, is higher: "The labors, sorrows and daily heroisms of the mother of a family are far greater than those of a prostitute. . . . Whether in the marketplace or by marriage contract, a woman is always selling herself."

Lélia is humbled. She evokes their youth, Pulchérie's cavalier treatment of her suitors, a hot, heavy summer day when they had slept together on the grass "and woke in each other's arms." Did Pulchérie recall that day? "It is the burning memory of my life," says Pulchérie. "I think of it often with a feeling of pleasure—and perhaps shame."

"Shame?" Lélia startles and withdraws her hand from Pulchérie's.

"You did not know," says Pulchérie, "I never dared to tell you, but now is the moment to tell each other all. Listen, my sister. . . . It was in your innocent arms, on your virginal breast, that God first revealed to me life's force. Don't draw away. Listen!"

During her adolescence, says Pulchérie, she greeted every day with joy. All life sparkled. "When I looked into a mirror, I wanted to embrace myself." But that summer day on the damp grass, it was as if an angel had descended to initiate her in the sacred secrets of life. She dreamed of a man, "bending to kiss me," and awoke "palpitating" to find Lélia lying beside her. "Oh, how beautiful you were!" At that instant, she says, she lost her narcissistic obsession with herself. She had run her fingers through Lélia's thick, black hair, admired her breasts, her skin, her feet. She had kissed her arm. "It was my first lesson in love, my first sensation of desire." Lélia had awakened. Pulchérie had taken her to the water to show her the reflected image. "See, my sister, how beautiful you are!" she had said to Lélia, who replied that she was less beautiful than Pulchérie. "No, you are more beautiful," Pulchérie had insisted. "You look like a man!"

And Lélia, Pulchérie reminds her, had shrugged her shoulders in distaste.*

Pulchérie's story concluded, Lélia began hers—the long passage preceded by a quotation of Musset's lines on an eagle, wounded and dying in the dust, lifting its eyes to the sky.

Mine, says Lélia, is an unhappy heart, "withered before it has fully lived," rendered impotent by the potency of her dreams. Mind and body were divorced. In her imagination she always made an idol of the man she loved, and "when I tired of prostrating myself before it, I pulled down the pedestal, reducing the idol to its true size." But during the period of idolatry, ecstasy—"I enjoyed to the fullest the full flight of sensation."

So much for Lélia's—that is, George Sand's—"frigidity." Or for her more esoteric "malady of nympholepsy," that frenzied, frustrated straining for the "unattainable."[20] The idol Lélia created in her mind was in fact the masculine equivalent of herself George Sand had thus far vainly sought. "You want me to take you as a woman, but also to talk to you as an equal," Sténio had reproached Lélia. The frustration came from that failure—no man could take her as a woman and accept her as an intellectual equal. So Lélia laughed in her heart, "when I hear men

---

* The alternating acceptance and rejection of the "male" elements of her character, of lesbianism itself, suggest a continuing identity crisis for George Sand at this time of her life.

reproach me for my insensibility." Love gone, the idol shrinks to its true size, diminished by the steady gaze, and the former idolatress is accused of *her* unfitness for love.[21]

Pulchérie felt otherwise. "You should experience in the arms of your lover," she told Lélia, "an even greater pleasure than his, because it is you who have given it to him." But even Pulchérie—who is also George Sand—sighed over the one-sidedness, the essential "crudity of men," the combat, "the mutual hate in the act of love," for the emotion which succeeded it was "disgust or sadness." Cruelest of all, echoed Lélia, was the egotism of a man who had called her shyness hypocrisy, laughed at her tears, brutally made love to her, "then fell asleep rudely and unfeelingly at my side, as I choked back my tears so as not to awake him." She had fled the bedroom—"the sanctuary, and coffin, of love."

Again Lélia withdrew in a semireligious retreat, and thus passed the winter. "But the odors and splendors of spring," of the earth's renewal, revived her own senses. "I became a woman again . . . frightened and overjoyed by what was stirring inside me." She had dreams of demon lovers and, Faust-like, called for preternatural pleasures, "even at the cost of eternal damnation." Desire alternated with fear, deviltry with piety, as during Aurore's adolescent years in the English convent. But this time the deviltry was adult sensuality and the sexual fantasies of the frustrated, brought on by the failure of her first lover.

She returned to society, she said to Pulchérie, "more miserable than ever," despairing to "find and share life with someone similar to myself. . . . But I am the cursed exception, that being does not exist." A platonic pact with another lover—perhaps Aurélien—also failed (the chronology of *Lélia* has its own arbitrariness). An adventurous seeking of happiness in a series or simultaneity of lovers ensued. "And if not happiness, then at least the emotion of a few days. In my imagination" —is it not rather in the *reality* of George Sand's life?—"I was unfaithful not only to the man I loved, but the day after to the man I had loved the night before."

"And so I now exist," Lélia concluded her long account, "possessed by the last caprice that crosses my sick mind, though the caprices, once so frequent and impetuous, have become rare and tepid. . . . Ennui desolates my life, ennui is killing me. . . . I withdraw within myself with a quiet, somber desperation and no one knows what I suffer. . . . No man has the breadth of intelligence to understand the abysmal misery of feeling incapable of attachment or desire."

Perhaps for the first time the feminine experience, examined by a woman who exhausted it, was at the center of a novel probing the inadequacies of life, where men and women find themselves in an impasse; where the writer, a woman, has faced herself—and exposed herself—at the cost of emotional agony and personal humiliation. "Filth and prostitution," protested a critic of *Lélia*.[22]

Lélia unlocked George Sand's heart, but its reception threatened to relock that heart, to end the great, frank, autobiographical novels when they had barely begun. However, there are limits to the autobiographical gloss. In *Lélia*, Sténio drowned himself. Lélia was strangled by a mad, improbable priest. George Sand, not yet thirty, lived on, dominating her life.

"Where are you?" she wrote Marie Dorval, who was away touring the provinces. "What is happening to you? . . . Your leaving without saying good-bye hurt me. I was in a dreadful mood. I felt you did not love me. I cried like a calf. . . . I look at the others, but no one is like you, so frank, true, strong, supple, good, generous, gentle, great, laugh-provoking, complete and perfect. . . . Where must I go to join you? . . . Answer me quickly with a simple 'Come!' and I'll set off for you immediately, whether I have cholera, or a lover."[23]

But Alfred de Musset, the golden boy of poetry, with a genius for literature, if not life, at least equal to George Sand's, has already intervened. It was no longer spring 1833. It was full summer.

18

The Cracked
Brilliance of Musset

The Muse of Comedy kissed him on the lips, and on the
heart, the Muse of Tragedy.
                                    —Heinrich Heine[1]

If we do not clearly perceive how and why the intelli-
gentsia then born reflects or *refracts* historical and social
reality, we shall understand nothing about Romanticism.
Particularly Musset wtih his multiple contradictions, his
inextricable mingling of debauchery and idealism, venal
and vainly-sought absolute love, his concern for purity and
perverse taste for smut, his sentimental exaltation of
women coupled with his execration of them.
                        —Henri Lefebvre, *Musset: essai* (1970)[2]

He dazzled at seventeen, he was celebrated at nineteen, he met George
Sand at twenty-two. Magnums of ink have been spilled over their affair,
Mussetists blackening the one, Sandists, a minority party, the other,
though to blacken the one is to blacken both, since they had loved each
other.

Alfred de Musset, Sainte-Beuve had marveled, "was Spring itself, the
very Spring of poetry, when he burst upon us, not yet eighteen, his forehead male and proud, his cheek with the bloom and pink of childhood,
his nostril assaying the air for pleasure. When he walked, his heel rang
on the pavement and his eye held the sky, so sure was he of his conquest, so full of an arrogant pride. No one at first sight had ever produced such an impression of adolescent genius."[3] He was the poet incar-
nate, a young Apollo.

Musset was not a provincial come to the capital. *Paris* was his province, where he exercised his seigneurial rights. He was born in a Latin Quarter mansion on December 11, 1810, second son of a family whose ancestors included Alexandre de Musset, companion-at-arms of Maurice de Saxe. He was born between two worlds, the one dead, the other struggling to be born. Born, he mourned, with the malady of his century, when "all that was is no longer and all that will be is not yet."[4] Born, as Alfred de Vigny, of an aristocracy mortally fractured by the bourgeoisie; born with a nostaliga for the grace of a dead past and the poet's drive to create the new; born with an urgency for living as if the sword of Damocles dangled over the short thread of his life.

When he was first taken to Mass, Alfred de Musset called it *"la comédie."* At three, he was brought his first pair of bright red shoes, and squirmed as his mother dressed him and brushed his long blond hair. "Hurry, *maman,*" he cried, impatient for the streets and their promenade, "or my new shoes will grow old!"[5] Alfred had a touch, a taint, a suspicion of epilepsy, and as Dostoievsky's prince, the precociousness, the sensibility, of *this* malady; and he was spoiled by his parents and his older brother Paul. His father was a War Ministry official who wrote cultivated, published essays, as had *his* father. Alfred's mother was loving and loved, not only by her sons but also by her husband. The income was small.

At school, the other boys laughed at Alfred's golden locks. He cried. They were cut. He wrote his compositions easily and they won prizes. When they didn't, he cried and refused to go to school. Vacations were spent with Paul, six years older, at the estate in the Sarthe of their uncle, the Marquis de Musset, a charming relic of the *ancien régime* whose son had killed himself. From his uncle's château, at the age of sixteen, Alfred first revealed his ambition to his friend Paul Foucher, whose sister Adèle had married Victor Hugo. He too would be a poet, he wrote. But he must be "Shakespeare or Schiller, or not write at all. So I do nothing." Love was the *sine qua non* of life, the supreme subject of poetry; and he fell in love, he wrote, "as easily as others catch cold." He desired women, "not to be happy, but to torment them." But if Alfred de Musset sought their misery, he would seek, as much, his own. Better to feel pain than nothing: feeling was all. And then the contrary: the drugs, the killing of sensation, the flirtation with death. The complexity, the tormenting and tormented contradictions of Musset appear early and, what is most remarkable, clearly and consciously to himself: they would be the motor, the genie, of his poetry. "If I found myself at this very moment in Paris," Alfred continued to Foucher, "I would extinguish what little of the noble is left in me in punch and beer, and I would feel relieved. Thus they put a sick man to sleep with opium, though they know the sleep might be fatal. I would act in the same way with my soul."[6]

In Paris, law studies bored Musset. He tried medicine. The sight and smell of post-mortems repelled him. He studied music, and painting, sketching mornings at the Louvre; and he wrote his first poems.

> Mes premiers vers sont d'un enfant
> Les seconds, d'un adolescent . . .[7]

The adult verses, one might say, began in 1828 when Musset was seventeen, "slept with his first woman"—as brother Paul surmised the day after by the cocky, rakish angle of Alfred's top hat when he came home —and saw his first poem published. "I too," he exulted to Sainte-Beuve, whom he awoke early one morning, "write verses!" And the alert Sainte-Beuve, whom Musset had just met through Foucher in the *cénacle* of Victor Hugo, along with Vigny, Mérimée and others, announced a few days later to the literary world of Paris, "There is a child of genius come among us."[8] The slim, golden-haired lad became the *cénacle's* brightest, but mocking, light. In four weeks he adapted De Quincey's *Confessions of an English Opium-Eater* so freely in French, it is virtually as much Alfred de Musset's as De Quincey's. He dressed like a dandy *à la* Byron—tight, light-blue trousers, turned, velvet-collared frock coat—and matched his richer companions in extravagance, riding his hired horses, gambling beyond his means, carousing and wenching —taking the "novice Sainte-Beuve" to his first bordello. With others of the *cénacle*, Musset climbed the towers of Notre Dame for its sunset view of Paris and at midnight partook of the ices at Tortoni's. Where else would a dandy go? He recited his verses in the salons and whirled in waltzes with the young ladies, very gallantly. But when he looked for "pleasure," he sought "prostitutes," whom "one caressed and insulted."[9]

"I must try everything," Alfred said to brother Paul. "Within me are two men, one who acts and another who looks on. If the first commits follies, the other profits from them."[10] No experience was declined. Poetry was a privileged madness. But there is always the forgiveness of posterity when, as in Alfred de Musset's *Contes d'Espagne et d'Italie*, the private passions and perversities are transmuted into the coin of poetry. Scarcely nineteen, he awoke to find himself hailed as France's Childe Harold. He immediately washed his hands of Febvrel & Co., military suppliers, with whom he had found a job, thanks to his father's War Ministry position. The bourgeois entrepreneurs had promised "more money" when Musset's "acquaintances" proved profitable.[11] The success of the *Contes d'Espagne* put an end to *that*. His Romanticism was, as it still is, exquisitely to the French taste—light, tart and controlled; as his father wrote delightedly to a friend, Alfred, at last, was "de-Hugoizing himself."[12] Students followed him in the streets and recited his verses to each other. There were parodies of his poem,

Ballade à la Lune, particularly its provocative imagery of the moon over a church steeple, "as a dot over an *i.*" But Musset's play, which soon followed, *Nuit Vénitienne,* was hooted and whistled off the stage. It mocked the Romantic hero without pleasing the classicists in the audience. Petulant as when a schoolchild, Musset would not write directly for the theater for almost two decades—he who is among France's most performed playwrights. He now wrote solely for "the spectator in his armchair," as he titled his next collection, publishing his poems and poetic dramas, on Buloz' solicitation, in the *Revue des Deux Mondes.* In May, 1833, appeared his *Les Caprices de Marianne,* whose two heroes are the vivid two sides of Musset: Octave, cynical, libertine, *nuancé,* and Coelio, sentimental, melancholy, in a word, Romantic; both, however, in pursuit of a certain purity and elusive integrity. . . . And in June Musset met George Sand.

19

The Pen-crossed Lovers

Since their first encounter, they knew that they had
dreamed of each other, that they might well fall in love,
separate and even betray each other, but that they would
never be indifferent one to the other.
                    —Paul de Musset, *Lui et Elle* (1860)[1]

George Sand and Alfred de Musset had met in the third week of June,
1833, at a dinner given by François Buloz for his staff and his favorite
contributors. The *Revue des Deux Mondes* was flourishing, and Buloz
was grateful. Gustave Planche was George's escort, but Buloz had playfully seated her next to his youngest, brightest acquisition. Alfred de
Musset was resplendent in his tight-fitting jacket and light-blue clinging
trousers, very much the dandy George had declined when Sainte-Beuve
had "offered" him to her in March. But Alfred was at his most brilliant
and on his best behavior—though he twitted his neighbor on the small,
jeweled dagger she wore at her waist (which she discreetly removed before the dinner was over). George was affected but characteristically reserved on the first meeting, as Alfred sparkled on the subject . . . of
Galileo. They talked "philosophy"—George's rather intimidating reputation had preceded her—and "literature"—that is, as two writers, of
their writing. Alfred promised a "fragment" of an unpublished poem,
and George a pre-publication copy of *Lélia*. They were sending probes
even then to each other's minds and souls. George sensed "a need for
love which gnawed at his heart."[2]

And Musset? "How did you find your dinner companion?" Paul
asked his brother. "Very beautiful," said Alfred, though "not on the
first impression." Physically she was the kind of woman who appealed to
him: "black-haired, olive-hued skin with highlights of bronze, and enormous eyes, like an Indian's."[3] Alfred's poetry often sang of Andalusian
women, not unlike George Sand, and the poetic "fragment" promised
was sent her the next day by courier.[4] He was intrigued; he would know

her better. He "reread a chapter of *Indiana*," Alfred wrote George a few days later, and was emboldened to address her "some verses" inspired by the scene of "Noun receiving Raimond [sic] in the bedroom of her mistress." He employed the intimacy of *tu*, though closed, "most respectfully yours." It was a sly performance of *personne interposée*, of courtship and lovemaking by literary proxy. Had George, he asked, experienced "those pleasures without happiness" she described, or had she imagined them? Unlike Raymon, Alfred implied, he could offer the understanding to fill the vast emptiness of her previous love life.[5]

> Sand, when you wrote it, where had you witnessed it,
> That terrible scene in which Noun, half-naked,
> Reels in passion on the bed of Indiana with Raimond?
> Who had dictated it to you, that burning page
> Where love seeks in vain with a quivering hand
> The beloved phantom of its illusion?
>
> Does your heart contain that sad experience?
> What Raimond felt, did you recall?
> And all those feelings of a vague suffering,
> Those pleasures without happiness, so full of a vast emptiness,
> Did you dream it, George, or had you known it?

Musset closed with a couplet:

> And the vain heart that failed to understand her
> Will love *the other* in vain. Is it not so, Lélia?[6]

George Sand responded the same evening, delicately but forthrightly. She was a nineteenth-century lady with the directness of a man, a disconcerting combination for her male contemporaries, who thought the one categorically excluded the other. George praised Alfred's poetry, found a "sad, secret fraternity" between his heroes and her own, and chose not to reply to the personal questions for fear of depressing "the poet of twenty"—actually twenty-two—by recounting the "sad secrets" of her past. But George invited Musset, if its "soberness" would not bore him, to her "cell of a recluse"—a clear signal that she was now living alone, save, of course, for Solange.[7]

As suggestive were George's attire and manner when she received Musset in a silk dressing gown and Moroccan slippers. "She offered him some fine Egyptian tobacco and sat at his feet on a cushion, smoking from her long pipe of Bosnian cherry wood." Alfred, in turn, feigned an avid interest in the embroidered slippers, dropping to one knee "to examine them more closely." He admired their shape with his hand and lightly traced their design with a finger, remarking on the "orientalism in the embroidery." The slippers, he said, softened the effect of the dagger at dinner. The conversation eased, both relaxed, but Planche and a Berrichon friend of George dropped in.[8]

For all Paris—and Musset—Planche was George Sand's lover, and Alfred was given to jealousy. George was not an innocent cause: she was not then exclusively any man's. She was the pasha of her group, receiving whom she wished, though generally with less than a pasha's openness.* Even as she ritually climbed to the towers of Notre Dame with Musset and vaguely talked of a trip together, she was congratulating Mérimée in a note on his appointment to the Madrid embassy, accepting a rendezvous with a handsome Italian stranger passing through Paris, Alessandro Poerio, on the condition that when meeting in her apartment the attraction be mutual or he depart,[10] arranging another with Musset shortly afterwards, and writing Marie Dorval, "Where are you?" All in the month of July 1833.

By the end of July, however, despite the "cholera or lover" declaration to Marie, George was choosing Musset. Either the complications were too much for both women or Musset was fulfilling the male-female needs of George Sand. Significantly, no other woman would appeal so strongly in her life as Marie Dorval. Nevertheless, there was a remarkable restraint for George in her relations with the younger man. Was it his youth itself that gave her caution, his moodiness, his fits of jealousy, his already manifest streak of sadomasochism? She sent him the first proofs of *Lélia*, perhaps as forewarning. Alfred responded with warmth, while still addressing her as Madame. "There are twenty or more pages in *Lélia*," he enthused, "that strike straight at the heart, frank, vigorous pages as beautiful as any in [Chateaubriand's] *René* or [Byron's] *Lara*. Here indeed you are George Sand and not Madame So-and-So, who happens to write books." Twenty pages out of two volumes! But George knew Musset was a perfectionist, and she was pleased with the compliment. Musset, however, continued, and what followed had his own peculiar tone:

"You know me well enough by now to be sure that the ridiculous words—'Will you?' or 'Won't you?'—will never cross my lips. There is the whole Baltic Sea between us in this respect. You can offer only *l'amour moral*, which I could offer to no one. . . . But I could be . . . not your friend, for even that sounds too platonic for me, but a comrade claiming no rights who is consequently neither jealous nor quarrelsome, but simply smokes your tobacco, musses up your dressing-gowns and catches head-colds philosophizing with you under all the chestnut trees of modern Europe."[11]

---

* Here five-year-old Solange was unfortunately placed. She developed a horror of these "men of letters" she saw come and go, George Sand herself wrote to Charles Duvernet, July 5, 1833, calling them " 'rascals and scoundrels,' " and becoming "fat as a little royal elephant."[9]

The rather adolescent mixture of comradeship, Platonism, crumpled dressing-gowns and head-colds was hardly in keeping with either Musset or George Sand, as both were well aware. This was courtly fencing with all Paris and eventually the world as witness. These were pen-crossed lovers over whom the acrid smell of printer's ink hovered from the beginning. Each letter of the début was addressed to posterity. They engaged each other warily and with mutual respect. "I do not believe any more in the possibility of friendship between a man and a woman," Alfred told George, "than of love." "And I," replied George disarmingly, "have a feeling of interest and affection for you." She readily acknowledged his genius and hoped he also had a heart. He talked of the "canker worm" devouring him. He could not write without suffering, so he sought in debauchery the "appeasement" of his frantic nervousness. "I work well only when I am collapsing with fatigue." It was a cry for nights of love, and George recognized it. But Musset coupled his overture with a warning, as if to cover himself in advance. "I love all women," he said, "and despise all of them." For several days they would not see each other: "he would return to his debauchery." But George had begun to love "this unhappy child. . . . She was devoted to her own cult, which she called 'what could have been' . . . and had a genuine respect for this suffering, straying genius."[12]

And Musset was so haunted by her "beautiful velvet-black eyes" one night in July, perhaps because of their reproaches (he had been rather wild the evening before), that he rose from bed to do a sketch from memory.[13] But George would not be so easily exorcised. A day or two later, Musset fully declared himself: "My dear George, I have something foolish and ridiculous to tell you. . . . You will laugh in my face and accuse me of making literary phrases out of our relationship. You will show me the door and think me lying. I am in love with you. I have loved you since the day I came to see you. I thought I could cure myself by seeing you simply as a friend . . . but I pay too high a price for the moments I spend with you."[14]

George did not laugh, nor did she show Musset the door. Instead she gave him something to indicate her own apprehensions and mixed feelings, a profile she had penned of him. He read it, and replied, "You must learn to know me better. . . . Do you remember that once you told me that someone had asked you whether I was Octave or Coelio, and you had answered, 'Both, I think'? I was a fool to show only [the Octave] side. . . . 'What a prison wall,' you said to me yesterday, 'everything would smash against it!' Yes, George, what a wall! But you forgot one thing: there is a prisoner behind it." But Musset the poet also appears, typically in a mood of self-mockery. He will scrawl his life's story, he wrote, in verses on that wall. What he cannot bring himself to say in person to the one he loved, he will have printed, "at six francs a copy! Ugh! . . . I can kiss a mangy, drunken slut, but I cannot kiss my mother. You should love only those who know how to love. I know only how to suffer. . . . Adieu, George, I love you like a child."[15]

It was not the male's dichotomy of slut versus mother that caught George's eye, but the last appeal that clutched her heart, and twenty-six years later held her mind. " 'Like a child,' she repeated, clasping the letter tightly in her trembling hands. 'He loves me like a child! My God, what is he saying! Does he know what he is doing to me?' "[16] Did they know what they were doing to each other? George invited Musset to come to her that midnight. Still trembling, she met him at the top of the staircase, rushed into his arms, took him into the apartment, and shortly "the bolts were drawn on the bedroom door."[17] July twenty-ninth they were lovers. In two days George was inscribing the freshly printed volumes of *Lélia* to Musset. In the first she wrote, "To my street-urchin, Alfred"; in the second, "To Monsieur le Vicomte Alfred de Musset, with the respectful homage of his devoted servant, George Sand." The first was signed, "George." Thus the urchin and the viscount were in love with and loved by George and George Sand. The multiple relationship was marked out from the beginning. Two lovers, two writer-observers. In the lover Alfred: Octave and Coelio. They made life poetry and they made it hell.

George saw both during the week of August fifth to the thirteenth in Fontainebleau, to which she and Alfred slipped away on the seventh day of their love.

They walked by moonlight in the Franchard woods, the loveliest of France, clambering the rocks climbed by the young Louis XIV with his first mistress. Nature for George was Nohant and her youth, for Alfred "the most powerful of aphrodisiacs."[18] Their hotel was two leagues from the forest. They would ride to the rocks, often leaving their mounts with the guide, and walk back to their rooms at dawn. They were happy. Alfred had his sketchbook, George her notebook. She was already at work on her next novel for Buloz. They read to each other. It was a dream recaptured. The nightmare came later. They were again among the great rocks one evening. For no apparent reason other than an impulse for self-laceration and -destruction, Musset talked of another young woman he had brought to the same spot in Fontainebleau, then moodily went off for a climb by himself.

Suddenly George heard a terrible cry of "inexpressible distress." She ran towards the cry and found Alfred, "shivering convulsively," staring wildly into space. She soothed him and they walked aimlessly until they came to a cemetery. Here Alfred finally told George what had occurred. He had had a hallucinatory vision of a pale ghost running across the heath towards him, clothes torn, hair flying. He had seen the specter plainly as it passed, its face hideous with hate and loathing. "I became terrified and threw myself to the ground, my face to the earth. For that man was . . . myself!"[19]

The next day Musset thought no more of it and behaved as if nothing had happened. He had recovered, but not George—not that quickly. The night of their return to Paris, when he drew a caricature of the nocturnal scene, George was not amused. Musset added to the mockery by writing under the sketch of himself, "Lost in the forest and in the mind of his mistress." He wrote under the drawing of George, "Her heart as torn as her dress." Morbidly he titled the composition, *Honeymoon in a Cemetery.*[20]

It is difficult to imagine a return to gaiety on their return to Paris, but it took place. Alfred had previously moved his affairs into the Malaquais apartment. His recently widowed mother was aware of it and made no complaint. The mature George Sand was preferable to the *filles* Alfred pursued and the debauchery he practiced; moreover, an older married woman as mistress was the classic fashion of keeping a young Frenchman from the gravest of mistakes—a mismarriage. To Malaquais Alfred now brought his friends—poor Planche had to make the best of it—and a "mad gaiety reigned there," says Alfred's brother. "Never did I see a happier group, so insouciant about the rest of the world, idly talking, sketching, making music," and playing pranks on an occasional, stuffy visitor.[21] Once Alfred dressed as a pretty Breton maid and "clumsily" emptied a water pitcher on the head of philosopher Lerminier. And during the day, Alfred wrote:

> George est dans sa chambrette
> Entre deux pots de fleurs,
> Fumant sa cigarette,
> Les yeux beignés de pleurs.[22]

One pauses not at the "cigarette," but at "the eyes bathed in tears." Was it from "laughing so hard she cried"?[23] One doubts it; torment and suffering were the trademark of Musset, and not only in his poetry.

The reviews of *Lélia* began to appear. George's novel was creating a sensation. *Figaro's* entire front page on August eighteenth, and half the second (of a four-page paper), were devoted to it. "*Lélia,*" said *Figaro,* "is desire deprived of satisfaction. . . . It makes us blush to our knees." The accusation of "filth and prostitution" unequaled since an "unmentionable book by the Marquis de Sade" came from a Capo de Feuillide in *Europe Littéraire.* "The day you open *Lélia,*" he wrote, "lock your *cabinet* door so you contaminate no one."[24]

George Sand to her notebook: "Learn caution. . . . Men do not like to be exposed or made to laugh at the mask they wear. If you no longer love, then lie, or draw the veil so close about you no eye can penetrate it."[25]

Planche sprang to *Lélia's* defense in the *Revue des Deux Mondes*. "Women above all," he wrote, "will underline those passages in which they find the expression of their own lives, the tableau of their own sufferings." Had Planche stopped there, he would have won George's eternal gratitude. Foolishly, however, he undertook to challenge Capo de Feuillide to a duel, blunderingly establishing himself as George's official champion, infuriating Musset, who had intended, he told Buloz, to challenge the critic himself. Exposed to a buzz of ridicule which she did not relish, George decided to put an end to Planche's championship by making her liaison with Musset public. How better than by letter to Sainte-Beuve, critic, midwife and concierge of the literary world? "I have fallen in love, and this time very seriously, with Alfred de Musset," she announced to him. "It is no longer a caprice, but a deeply felt attachment. . . . Planche has passed as my lover. It was unimportant, so I did not deny it. . . . Now it is important that all know he is not." She has determined to part with Planche. In fact, it has already taken place, amiably. Perhaps Sainte-Beuve will be shocked by her behavior and the public avowal of love for Musset. "But I beg you to understand my exceptional situation and my being obliged from now on to expose my private life to the light of day."

It was not concern for public opinion, said George Sand. "People will continue to say that I am unconstant and whimsical, that I go from Planche to Musset while waiting to go from Musset to a third. It doesn't matter, so long as no one can claim that I receive two men in my bed the same day." Wherefore this letter to Sainte-Beuve about the "distancing" of Planche, so all will know there is only Musset.[26]

Perhaps there were not two men in George's bed the same day, but on different days, almost certainly. August third, George Sand wrote to Alessandro Poerio asking why she was no longer seeing him. "Have I displeased or bored you? It's possible, but since it's not the way I feel, I protest your abandoning me." Would Poerio dine with her the following Monday? The next day, G.S. wrote to postpone the dinner, because something had arisen requiring her leaving Paris.[27] That "something" was the trip to Fontainebleau with Musset. As for her statement about never having "two men in my bed the same day," what else could a woman of 1833 be expected to declare?

Planche went ahead with his challenge to Capo de Feuillide, sending his seconds, Buloz and Émile Regnault. The duel was held in the Bois de Boulogne, but not even a cow was hit by either man. Musset alone scored with a long satirical poem on the affair—which George Sand carefully transcribed and preserved with the writer's full appreciation of another's mastery.

Paul de Musset was no blinder than the rest of Paris and additionally possessed the older brother's tender concern. If Alfred did indeed fill

George Sand's immediate present, which no one could safely affirm, there was her immediate, notorious past, which might well point to the no less distant future. "Remember," Paul said to his brother, "when we took that boat trip together to Le Havre, the dangerous bar at Quilleboeuf, where you could see the black flags above the waves signaling sunken ships? There is a black flag"—the singular is a tribute to Sandeau—"in that woman's life. It warns of a hidden reef."[28] But living and loving dangerously, Paul also recognized, was his brother Alfred's poetic lot.

As with Sandeau, George set for Musset the example of her own assiduous work. Little more than Sandeau did he take to it. He was not a spring, he said, responding automatically to the press of a button. In another image he spoke of tearing verses from himself with forceps. In any event he was salting away memories, the bittersweet of their life together. He tormented George with questions about her past and tortured himself with thoughts about her former lovers. Pages of her new novel, *Le Secrétaire Intime*, were written directly to him, demonstrating that whatever the amorous dalliances of its woman hero, she had never been really touched by them. George was also addressing the legion of her readers and reacting to her critics, recovering from her wounds. "The world," she wrote, "will know and understand me someday. But if that day does not arrive [in my lifetime], it does not greatly matter. I shall have opened the way for other women."[29]

It was George Sand's rapidity of recovery, the seeming ease of her tranquil arrival at emotional equilibrium, that has most exasperated her critics and lovers. Lélia she was, but Lélia she did not remain. From her old friend Jules Néraud came a note of reminder. "What the devil is it?" he asked in amazement after reading *Lélia*. "Where did you get it all? Why did you write this novel? Where does it come from, where is it going? . . . They are making fun of me because I love the book so much. Perhaps I am wrong to love it, but it has taken hold of me and keeps me awake. Bless you for shaking me up like that." The Madagascan was man enough to admit the *Lélia*-shock on any man. "But who is the author of *Lélia*? Is it really you? No. This fellow is fantasy. He does not resemble you at all, not you who are gay, the person I know who dances the *bourrée*, appreciates lepidoptera, who likes puns, who doesn't sew too badly and makes excellent preserves!"[30]

In need of money—a trip to Italy with Musset was now uppermost in her mind—George quickly wrote and sold a short story about a student, *Garnier*, "a Narcissus who thought himself somewhat of a Byron."[31] It is the very image of the poet, the essence of the artist—Musset as Narcissus. The mirrored doubling of herself, the self-justifying reflections of George Sand, are a continuing, fascinating display of the same phenomenon. They loved themselves in each other. She was "very, very happy," George reassured Sainte-Beuve. "Every day I become more attached to him, every day I see those little things in him, which made me suffer, disappear."[32] It was almost true.

At seven in the morning of October second, George wrote the last sixty pages of yet another short story, *Métella*. "Come for the manuscript this evening," she said in a note to Buloz. But not before. "Alfred is sleeping like a stout fellow at this hour, and I want to read it to him first."[33] The story enchanted Sainte-Beuve. In several weeks he would be shown the manuscript of *Le Secrétaire Intime*.

Money was the matter of discussion with Buloz, a goodly advance on the *next* novel to be written during the Italian journey, promised for spring. With Casimir letters were exchanged about the children. She had arranged with Papet, George informed her husband, to care for Maurice on his days off from school, but if Casimir preferred, she would talk about it to his mother, the baroness, "who would certainly be bored with the whole business."[34] Finally, it was George's mother, Sophie—with whom a quarrel of long standing had just ended—who would look after Maurice. As for Solange, George's maid would be bringing her to Casimir at Nohant. The Italian trip itself, said George, was for her rheumatic pains. Casimir, no less knowing than all Paris (Hippolyte kept him posted), hoped it would be instructive and pleasurable.

There remained the young man's mother.

Much has been made of George Sand's going to Madame de Musset for her consent to take Alfred to Italy, and "wringing" it from her. But it was most likely the conversation between an old, concerned woman and one no longer young about a particular prodigal son, soon twenty-three. Had Madame de Musset objected to their intimacy, it would have been months earlier, when Alfred had left home for George's apartment. In any event, Italy was preferable to Paris for such things. The elaboration is Paul de Musset's—the story of their mother's protests and tears when approached by a very nervous Alfred, his solemn renunciation of the journey with George ("If anyone must cry," he promised Madame de Musset, "it will not be *you*"), his departure to inform his "mistress" of his decision, and the arrival of a veiled, incognita George Sand in a carriage that evening.

> The unknown lady [Paul de Musset continues] disclosed who she was, begging the desolate mother to confide her son to her, vowing to show him the affection and care of a mother . . . employing all her eloquence, which must have been remarkable, since she succeeded. In a moment of emotion, the consent was wrung from reluctant lips, and no matter what Alfred had promised, it was his mother who cried.[35]

There is a good deal of motherhood in the passage and most probably in George Sand, who rather overly insisted on it herself, yet the grounds are as solid for remarking that, "once again, she was the man of the couple."[36] More accurately, and repeatedly, she was once again exercising the male elements of her character by fathering as well as mothering Musset, as she had Sandeau, without minimizing the sexual companionship. That, too, counted.

20

"Is Love of Life a Crime?"

The lovers set off for Italy on the twelfth of December 1833, with the artist's thirst for southern climes and the glamorous peninsula, and the illusion that life there would be gentler, sunnier and at the same time more intense. George wore pearl-gray trousers, Russian leather boots and a visored velvet cap. Her spirits were on the same high plateau as Alfred's. Paul de Musset saw them off from the courtyard of the Hôtel des Postes. The thirteenth coach for Lyons was theirs; Alfred brushed aside Paul's forebodings. But the coach, as it rolled out onto the street, careened against a post and almost knocked down a water carrier. Leaning from a window, Alfred and George laughed at Paul's alarm.[1]

At Lyons the lovers took the Rhone River steamboat for Avignon and discovered Stendhal, the novelist, among the passengers. George enjoyed his company—to a point. His irony, his scoffing at her Italian illusions clashed with her mood and she was glad when they parted, Stendhal to continue his journey to Italy by land, Alfred and George by sea from Marseilles. Here, before embarking for Genoa, George wrote Boucoiran—as obliging as ever, he was now tutoring in Paris—to lock away her papers at the Malaquais apartment, lest "Mr. le baron," Casimir, rummaging among them, find letters of mutual embarrassment.[2]

On the boat to Italy, the discomfiture was Alfred's. While George smoked a cigarette sturdily on deck, the more queasy Musset lay seasick below. His humor, irritable and mocking, breaks to the surface in the jingle he wrote:

> George est sur le tillac
> Fumant sa cigarette;
> Musset, comme une bête,
> A mal à l'estomac.

A situation scarcely flattering to a man's ego. In Genoa the situation was reversed: George was ill and Alfred restored his virility among the street-women of the city. Similarly in Florence on their way to Venice, to which a toss of the coin—"ten times"—directed them, as if by inexorable destiny. Through the haze of illness George viewed Cellini's Perseus and Michelangelo's statues for the Medici tomb, "until I, at times, felt like a statue myself."[3] It might well have been Musset's reproach. The weeks of confinement to each other wore on him badly; George did not make love in the manner prostitutes had accustomed him, and the reproaches further chilled, then fevered, her. She had loved him, Musset told a friend, Pierre-Jules Hetzel, years later, "with her head and her heart," but refused him the *"griserie* [intoxications] offered by any whore." George had replied in despair that he wasn't fit for an ordinary woman. "I agreed, and we would both cry about me."[4]

The sight of George sick, but manfully toiling on her commissioned novel for Buloz, was additional irritation. Her urging him to work on his play, *Lorenzaccio,* whose story she had suggested, did not help. Alfred was roaming Florence, he protested, studying its setting for his drama, but he rarely put pen to paper, writing three lines to George's twenty pages. (But what admirable lines.)

Their arrival in Venice after dark was ill-omened: the gondola with its black, drawn curtains looked like a coffin; and the debut of the famous "lovers of Venice" began with George Sand's fitfully dozing to the rhythmic lilt-and-lap of the gliding boat. She half-woke for a first glimpse at the Piazza San Marco in the magical light of an immense rising moon, the domes of the Doges' Palace glowing like alabaster, the Gothic starkness of the piazza's tower silhouetted in the great white circle of the moon. But, alas, when the lovers finally settled in their suite—No. 13—at the Hotel Danieli, overlooking the Grand Canal, it was, for George, to sink into the horrors of diarrhea, that ignoble killer of the romantic dream. Rage, outrage and physical distaste—and perhaps a measure of shame for being so self-centeredly possessed—convulsed Musset. He cursed his fate and caressed his faults. He left George to the care of the hotel keep and a young doctor of twenty-six, Pietro Pagello. Together with the French consul, flattered by the company of the young poet whose fame had spread, as had George's, to

Italy, Alfred plunged into the available pleasures of Venice—its actresses, its ballet dancers, its brothels—as George lay in her room, listening to the noises of the Venetian night. And one evening, before going out, Alfred came to her bed and told her, as George Sand retold it: "'George, I was mistaken. I ask you to forgive me, but I do not love you.'" Had she been well, says George Sand, and had she lacked a sense of responsibility for the "child" entrusted to her, she would have immediately left Venice and Musset. Instead (she recalled) "the door was closed between our two rooms, and we tried to recommence our lives as good friends. But that was no longer possible. *You* were bored."[5]

By the end of January 1834, however, George had recovered and Alfred was suddenly stricken. Typhoid, delirium tremens? George sent for the young Italian who had treated her. His patient this time, she told Dr. Pagello, would be a "very celebrated poet," enfevered by his "intellectual activity, drinking, dining, carousing and gambling." George thought to help the young doctor by describing Musset's behavior at Fontainebleau. "Once before, three months ago [?], he had carried on as a madman all one night following a period of great anxiety. He saw phantoms all about him and screamed with horror and fright. . . . He is the person I love more than anybody else in the world, and it is agony for me to see him in this state."[6]

It was a strange, bold statement. She loved Musset "more than anybody in the world," George informed Pagello in both appeal and challenge, for she was already attracted by the handsome, healthy, well-built Italian. And Pagello had been struck by George even before he had treated her, when he had caught sight of her sitting on the balcony of her room at the Hotel Danielli, "her face melancholy," her black hair held by a red scarf tied like a turban, "the expression of her eyes determined and virile." She wore a flowing tie, he recalled, a Byronic white collar, smoked a small cigar and talked casually to a young blond man sitting beside her. The following day he had bled her. Now he was to watch over the young blond man, her companion and lover, a poet whose work he had read and admired.[7]

They watched over Musset together, restraining him in his most violent seizures, talking quietly to each other during the long nights of their vigil, touching each other when they thought he slept. But dimly through the mist of his sickness, Musset saw George and Pagello having tea with *a single cup* between them, and his tormented mind imagined the rest.[8] He questioned George, she denied it. To have told him the truth would have been doubling the injury to one dangerously ill. She lied. She would eventually tell him so. But he who had abandoned her for the women of Genoa, Florence and Venice, he who had told her he no longer loved her, was it his right to accuse her? Was it a crime to reach for the simple, generous man beside her? "Is love of life then a crime?"[9]

One night Musset had requested George and the doctor to withdraw from his bedside. He felt better, he wished to sleep. They moved to a table by the fire, and talked in low voices—of Venice, of Italian literature. "Is Madame planning a novel about our beautiful city?" Pagello inquired. "Perhaps," she replied, then impatiently took a sheet of paper and began to write furiously. "Respectfully" Pagello opened a volume of Victor Hugo and read from it, so as not to disturb the famous novelist at her work. An hour passed. Finally George put down her pen, held her head in her hands for a moment, then folded the letter she had written into an envelope and gave it to Pagello.[10]

"For whom is it?" the young doctor asked. George snatched the envelope from his hands and wrote on it: "To the stupid Pagello." The young man took the letter home and read it three times. One can understand his astonishment. It was a striking declaration of searching love. "Born under different skies," George's letter began, "we have neither the same thoughts, nor the same language. Have we at least the same hearts? . . . The sun that has bronzed your forehead, what passions has it created *in* you? I know how to love and suffer, and you? How do you love?

"Your burning looks, the rough strength of your arms, the boldness of your desires tempt and frighten me. . . . In my country men do not love like that. . . . I cannot know whether you really love me. I will never know. . . ." The questions tumble and still trouble: "Will you be my support or my master? . . . Do you have patience, compassion, a capacity for friendship? Have you been raised in the belief that women have no soul? Do you realize that they do? . . .

"Will I be your companion or your slave? Do you desire me or do you love me? When your passion is satisfied, will you know how to appreciate me? When I make you happy, will you know how to tell me so?

"Do you know what I am? Does it bother you not to know? Am I something of a mystery which makes you search and dream, or am I nothing in your eyes but a woman, like those who grow fat in harems? . . . Do you know the soul's desire, which the senses cannot slake and no caresses put to sleep or tire? When your mistress falls asleep in your arms, do you stay awake to gaze upon her, praying to God and weeping? . . ."

Perhaps it was fortunate, the long letter continued, that she and Pagello did not speak the same language. If they did, Pagello would then find the right words to deceive her. Better that they remained strangers; ignorance of each other may be wiser, and silence better than lying. "I will be able to give my own interpretation to your reverie and

eloquence to your silence. . . . So let us stay as we are. Do not learn
my language. . . . I would like not to know your name."[11]

The sheer passion of wordless love, the anonymity, indeed the
animality, of sex between passing strangers was George's bold proposal.
There was, too, her impassioned reaction, her pendulum swing, away
from the tortuous complexity of Musset's needling mind and needless
teasing of emotions. It is ironic that George Sand should ask of Pagello
the sheer physicality reproached her by Musset as lacking. For despite
the earlier, searching questions about Pagello's ability to communicate
his love, whether he viewed women as possessors of souls or simply as
harem sex-objects, there is an unprepared switch to the "masculine" impulse for love in silence (in part explaining the appeal of prostitutes)—
no questions, no past, no future. A present. *Masculine*, because possibly
no woman before George Sand felt free enough to so express herself—
and few since.

Pagello, reading and rereading the extraordinary letter, turned to his
late mother's portrait, as if there at least were something solid to which
he might still anchor his suddenly shaken world, then, reassured, he
went to bed and to sleep. In the morning, the tremors resumed as
Pagello thought of his father, his practice, his several mistresses, his
duty to his patient, and of his patient's mistress. He found that attractive foreigner from Paris awaiting him as he made his morning call on
his patient. The turban had been replaced by a chic hat with an ostrich
plume, the casual attire by a satin dress, a cashmere shawl and white
gloves. "Signor Pagello," said George Sand to the stunned Italian, "I
have shopping to do. If it's not too much trouble, would you accompany me?"

"Alfred," Pagello noted, "gave us leave, and we left together."[12] They
became lovers. Musset in his fever "saw the single cup," observed the
lovers kiss and in a nightmarish moment imagined they planned to
have him shut up in an asylum to prevent his return to Paris with the
tale.[13] Throughout her life George Sand would protest that she had
never offered a "dying Musset" the "spectacle of a new love."[14] Tokens
of it unwittingly, but not the certainty. Indeed it was the doubt—had
she given herself completely to Pagello?—that plagued Musset, and he
tormented George and himself with his catch questions about it,
hurling the epithet "whore" in his more provocative moods, the irony
of the term escaping him.[15] Musset's jealous insistence on knowing
whether she had actually slept with Pagello or maintained platonic relations is an unintended tribute to George, to the woman's less trivial
view of sexual relations. A woman gives herself, he was in effect saying,
a man takes. Without commitment. As Musset took the women of
Venice. It was true, but not always true, for George Sand: her lovers
are not easily counted, but one cannot see her going to a brothel. In

truth, too, her love for Musset had *not* vanished, even as she reached for Pagello. "I deceived you, I was there between two men. . . . Ah, poor woman, poor woman! It is then *I* should have died!"[16]

Besides her worry about Musset's illness and Madame de Musset's concern, reaction of her friends and of *tout Paris*, there was their staggering hotel bill and other expenses. George borrowed money, set to work on *several* novels for Buloz and was frankly happy when Musset's close friend, Alfred Tattet, arrived in Venice on a visit. *He* would satisfy Madame de Musset and the Paris world that everything possible was being done for Alfred (as he would do, praising George's devotion, describing her fatigue). And then after Tattet left, the three—George, Musset and Pagello—became virtually a *ménage à trois*, a most odd, morbidly affectionate trio, as Alfred regained enough strength to plan his return to Paris. Without George. He loved George; he loved as much the nobility of his self-sacrifice, his leaving her with Pagello, whom he regarded as a brother: did they not love the same woman, the same woman love them? On March twenty-ninth Musset departed. George accompanied him to Mestre by gondola. They embraced. George cried. Considerately, Pagello waited for George's return at the Piazzetta, and quickly spoke to her when she came back.

"'Courage,' he said to me. 'Yes,' I replied, 'it is what you said the night he lay dying in our arms. . . . Yet, think what you will of me, I yearn for that dreadful night when his poor head leaned against your shoulder and his cold hand lay in mine. He was there between us, and he is here no more. You too weep, even as you shrug your shoulders.'"[17]

"Write me!" Alfred pleaded from Padua, where he spent the first night. From Geneva, several days later: "George, I love you still."[18] And before she had received either letter, George wrote to Musset, *poste restante*, Milan: "Surely we will see each other at vacation time, and with what happiness! How we will love each other, no, my little brother, my child? Ah, who will take care of you, of whom shall I take care? Who will have need of me and of whom shall I want to take care? How can I do without the good and the ill you caused me? May you forget the sufferings I caused *you* and recall only the good days! Especially the last. . . ."[19]

For a week George and Pagello went on a walking tour of the Alps, to change the scene, to relieve the tension of Musset's departure. When they returned to Venice, George counted "seven centimes" in her purse. She must resume work. She asked Buloz to advance her money and to address his letters to "Mr. Pagello, Pharmacia Ancillo, Piazza San Luca, to be forwarded to Mme. Sand."[20] She settled down to life with the gentle doctor, writing with her usual energy, fulfilling a neglected domestic urge by "sewing curtains, driving nails, covering chairs"—all this in a letter of love to Musset.[21] Meantime Pagello continued his practice, fended off the fiercest of his former mistresses, at the cost of his beautiful waistcoat, championed "La Sand" before his criticial family and "would rise at dawn, walk two leagues on foot to pick flowers in the outskirts of the city, not having the money to buy her a bouquet." This, too, in a letter to Musset.[22]

The resumption of their love by correspondence has become literary history and heritage, and if one thinks of the letters of Abélard and Héloïse it is not by chance: Musset and Sand were as conscious of it. In Geneva, before going on to Paris, Alfred roamed the streets, looked into shopwindows and wrote to George, "Though I know you are beside a man you love, I am calm. . . . I saw my reflection in a window and recognized the boy I had been. . . . the man you had wanted to love." He was awakening from his nightmare, Alfred said, thinking of "that pale face watching over my bed for eighteen nights," musing about their relationship. "You thought you were my mistress. You were my mother. . . . We committed incest. Oh, my only friend, I was almost your executioner."[23]

"Whether I was your mistress or your mother," George replied, "what does it matter? . . . I know I love you, and that is all." She loved him, she said, "with a strength that is wholly virile but also with the *tendresse* that is a woman's." Again: George's extraordinary self-awareness, the androgynous mother-father image. Their love was both "incestuous" and "innocent," she wrote Musset. "Our mordant, passionate temperament does not permit us to accept the life of ordinary lovers." The hurt they had foreseen they would inflict upon each other was their destiny, and if the world would never understand their relationship, "so be it." Then calmly George wrote of Pagello, the starling he had given her which sat on the stem of her long pipe, stole her tobacco and drank her ink. She was deep in her *Lettre d'un Voyageur*, addressed: "To a poet," and Paris would know who the poet was. She would send it to him for his decision as to whether it should go on to Buloz. Alfred was free to change it or cut it, "or throw it into the fire." (Musset thought the *Lettre* "sublime." It was published that May in the *Revue des Deux Mondes*.) They were fellow writers, George's letter continued, and in Venice publishers were pressing her for the Italian rights to *both* their works.[24]

Back in Paris, Musset wrote, he had replunged into his former life. From Venice, "on bended knee," George beseeched him, "no more wine, no more women! It is too soon. . . . Do not seek in such pleasure the cure for boredom or unhappiness. It is the worst of all pleasures, when it is not the best."[25] "Tell me," Musset replied, "about *your* pleasures," then scratched out a phrase and wrote, "No, not that!" He went on to other things: Planche, Regnault and even "Monsieur Sandeau, according to Buloz, are vomiting everything they hold against me," accusing Musset of having mistreated George Sand. Musset was shouldering all the blame, telling Sainte-Beuve, et al, that George was guiltless. As for Madame de Musset, "it was enough to recount the nights you spent caring for me." And on May first: "So it is not a dream, dear Brother, this friendship which survived love. . . . You love me! Be proud, my great, my good George, you have made a man of a child."[26] George to Alfred, May twelfth: Love in such a fashion that someday you can say, as I: "I have suffered often, I have been sometimes mistaken, but I have loved. It is I who have lived, not some factitious being created by false pride."[27] The passage would go entire into Musset's play, *On ne badine pas avec l'amour.*

They vibrated through the space between them. George asked for all the poems Alfred had written her. He went to the apartment to fetch them. "I came across some cigarettes you had made before we left," he wrote her. "I smoked them sadly and with a strange happiness. I also stole a little broken comb from your dressing table, and I carry it everywhere in my pocket." Gallantly he was launching on a defense of his lady, carrying her comb as if it were her scarf. "I am going to write a novel. I want to write our story." Two months later: "I have begun the novel I wrote you about. If you happen to have kept the letters I've sent to you since I left, I'd be very pleased to see them."[28] The novel would be *La Confession d'un Enfant du Siècle*, as gentlemanly a performance by a former lover as any lady might wish.

George's own performance was an awesome prodigy of fluency. In less than a month she produced *Leone Leoni*, whose fictional, seductive, amoral hero is modeled on Alfred, for whom the beautiful Juliette convincingly sacrifices all. Another short novel, *André*, was completed, and the more durable *Jacques*, in which it is the hero who is sacrificed, saw its last chapters going to Buloz in July. To this were added several *Lettres d'un Voyageur*, whose lyrical pages are among the finest in Romantic literature. The hammering of emotions while still warm into a metal which miraculously retains its liquidity would always be the gift and genius of George Sand. Little wonder Henry James called her Goethe's sister, and Charles Maurras, Tolstoyan, well before Tolstoy's time.

George Sand was the woman who spoke when women were silent. In *Jacques*, in 1834, she scorned the wife's marital vow of eternal fidelity and obedience as an "absurdity" in the first part and a "baseness" in the second. "I have not changed my mind," she wrote, "I am not reconciled to society, and marriage is still, to my way of thinking, one of the most barbarous institutions it has ever roughed out. I do not doubt it will be abolished if the human species makes some progress towards justice and reason. A more human and no less sacred bond will replace it, assuring the existence of children who will be born of a man and a woman without forever enchaining the freedom of the one and the other."[29]

"Love and write," George wrote Musset, "that is your vocation, my friend."[30] It was the signature, and might serve as the epitaph, of their passionate affair, though *that* was yet to be written.

To Papet, and Buloz, and Boucoiran, to Casimir and Musset, George sent letters mentioning a possible return to France before fall. It was as if she were testing for their reaction. She lacked money, she missed her children, she longed for Nohant. On July 24, 1834, George left Venice for Paris—with Pagello.

21

Journeys End

Journeys end in lovers meeting,
Every wise man's son doth know.
—William Shakespeare,
Twelfth Night,
Act II, Scene 3

I am embarking on the last stage of my madness.
—Pietro Pagello to his father,
on leaving Venice for Paris[1]

At this journey's end was Alfred de Musset, as Pagello was aware; and it was by a lingering, dallying route, as if with some presentimental dread, that George Sand and her Italian companion made their way to Paris. They paused in Verona and Milan, Brigue, Chamonix and Geneva—three weeks in reaching the French capital. "As we drew nearer," Pagello would recall unhappily, "our relations became cooler and more circumspect. . . . George Sand was somewhat melancholic and much more withdrawing . . . and I began to see more clearly through the mist in my eyes."[2]

George had begun to see more clearly before she left Venice. "Are you happy?" Émile Paultre had asked in a letter. "Yes," she had replied, "when I love. . . . Love is all." But that, George continued, was not as simple or naïve a reply as it seemed. "True, complete love is when two hearts, two minds, two bodies meet in understanding and embrace." That meeting, that many-sided embrace or *sympathie* "occurs once in a thousand years. So long as but two elements concord—mind and body without heart, or body and heart without mind—one believes the third somehow exists, until its absence becomes so strongly felt it kills the *sympathie* of the other two."[3] George missed Musset's mind; the communion with Pagello's heart and body was ending, and *her* body was withdrawing along with her heart.

In Paris they were met by Boucoiran, who escorted George to the Malaquais apartment and Pietro to a small room on the fourth floor of a nearby hotel ("1 fr. 50 per day," noted Pagello[4]). George and Alfred were not to see each other until August seventeenth—three days later. The hesitation was mutual. They had burned for each other at a distance. What would happen when they met? The Venetian experience and Pagello still hung over them.

George had brought Pagello along with her to Paris as a gentleman would his mistress, telling him, nonetheless, that she planned to return with him to Venice, though his memoirs express his doubts. Unlike a man, however, she could not simply tuck him away in his hotel room for her convenience. She had to create a public figure of Pagello, for whom, after all, she had left Musset—and *le tout Paris* wanted a look at the poet's successor. He was a doctor, but that gave him little status—Molière's scornful attitude still lingered in France. Was he also a count, as Buloz was saying, an irresistible Don Giovanni? Buloz arranged a grand dinner immediately on George's arrival (delicately omitting Musset from the guests). George spoke vaguely of her Italian companion as a learned archeologist. With Parisian maliciousness the conversation turned, to Pagello's bewilderment, to excavations and historic discoveries. When he understood what was happening, he said to the company "with dignity and a touching simplicity, 'You are wrong to laugh at me. I am not a *savant* and do not pretend to be one. I am among you simply as the *cavalier sirvente* of the illustrious signora.' "[5]

One can imagine George Sand's reaction and almost see the blazing, then darkening eyes as she listened to Pagello. "Those who have been alternately caressed and cursed by those eyes," Musset told Louise Colet, "at once so tender and so terrible, are haunted by them until they die."[6]

Those eyes were veiled when George and Alfred met for the first time since Venice. They were not alone. George had invited Pagello to the apartment, as if in need of a third person. The conversation was awkward; the strains of a waltz they had heard in their intimacy drifted through the open window. Tears came to George's eyes, as Musset remarked, but she told him what she had resolved: they must never meet again except as friends among friends.

Musset left in desolation, determined to quit France forever for Spain. He asked his mother for money; she gave him what she had. He wrote Buloz for more as an advance. He also wrote to his beloved "Georgette," announcing his departure in four days. He asked for "an hour alone, one last kiss," she should not fear the voice of their destiny.

"Take me to your heart. We will speak neither of the past, nor the present, nor the future. Let it not be the farewell of Mr. So-and-So and Madame So-and-So. Let it be two souls that have suffered, two minds that are suffering, two wounded eagles that meet in the sky and exchange a cry of agony before they part for eternity."[7]

They met alone for two hours of tears and last kisses, perhaps chaste. On August twenty-fourth they parted once again. George Sand for Nohant, Musset for Baden-Baden, Germany. He had changed his destination, but remained certain of his imminent death. "But I shall not die," he wrote in farewell, "before I have done my book on me and thee. . . . I swear by my youth and my genius that only stainless lilies shall grow on your grave. . . . Posterity shall speak our names as it does those of the immortal lovers—Romeo and Juliet, Abélard and Héloïse. Never shall the one be spoken without the other."[8]

* * *

Nohant and renewal, and a rallying of George's friends on her arrival —Papet, Fleury, Duvernet, Dutheil, Néraud—comforts and supports in the confrontation with Casimir after the Venetian fiasco. She had also brought her mother Sophie for the same purpose. All quite needless. "Amiably" Casimir even agreed to invite Pagello to Nohant "for a week or ten days." Sensibly Pagello declined; he stayed on in Paris and visited hospitals. With a *beau geste* George sent him fifteen hundred francs, saying they were from the sale of paintings he had brought with that in mind.[9] Thus, without complaint, would George pay not only for her own independence, but also for that of her lovers.

George felt terribly old, however, as she turned thirty—and suicidal. She sat down and reviewed her life in another *Lettre* from the spiritual voyager, addressed this time to her dear friend Jules Néraud, "the Madagascan." The exposure of the writer's private thoughts is a fortunate paradox, a missile, as George Sand would say on the publication of the *Lettres,* dispatched "to unknown friends." On the edge of the loss of faith, she recalled for Néraud the innocent man, guillotined in La Châtre, who had cried out, "There is no God!" Was the Madagascan happy in *his* life? Was there not a demon in the shape of an angel who cried to him during a sleepless night, "Love, happiness, life, youth!" Did he not desolately reply, "It is too late! It might have been, but it is not!" She, too, contemplated another world in a butterfly's wing, intoxicated herself with the scent of a flower, but there was also the dust on the road of return, the stench of the public coach. Reading Madame de Staël's *Reflections on Suicide*—"from curiosity, wanting to know what this man-woman understood by 'life' "—had finally bored her. Instead of persuading George to live, it had re-enforced the contrary impulse.

She would have infinitely preferred "the conversation of Madame Dorval."[10]

Other impulses were reaching George Sand from Baden-Baden. Far from the suicide he had intended, distant again from George, Musset was rekindled with passion for her. "I am lost, I sink, I drown in love . . ." he wrote wildly from Germany. "They tell me you have another lover. It kills me, but I love you, love you, *love you!* . . . Send me your lips, your teeth, your hair, the face I held. Everything! Tell me that you are embracing me! Oh God, when I think of it I choke, I go blind, my knees tremble. . . . Oh George, my beautiful mistress, my first, my last love!"[11]

"You still love me too much," wrote George in reply.[12] "We must never see each other again." Pagello, she said, was no longer the brother, but rather the jealous lover. His accusations proved he no longer loved her (the line would reappear in a Musset play). "He was leaving, he may already have left for Venice."

In fact Pagello had not, and between letters from Pagello and Musset, George walked until dawn in the woods of Nohant with the most platonic of her friends, François Rollinat, pouring out her heart. Néraud's wife, as in George's youth, had jealously forbidden her husband to see George as frequently as they both wished. On September fifteenth, Musset announced his return to Paris. When he arrived a month later, he found a letter from George Sand, who had arrived a week before. Did he wish to see her? Musset: "Wish to see you! . . . Write me but a line saying when. If tonight, so much the better."[13]

To Pagello, George brought what solace she could and another five hundred francs, telling him they represented the balance of what she had received for his paintings. The money would pay for Pagello's return to Venice—to his father and his mistresses, to medicine, marriage and many children. He would die at ninety-one, wearing well the legend of his affair with "La Sand." The description of their parting is his: "Our farewell was in silence. I shook her hand without being able to look into her eyes. She seemed perplexed. I do not know whether she was suffering. My presence embarrassed her. He was a bother for her, this Italian. . . ."[14]

In the loneliness of his stay in Paris, however, Pagello had made a confidant of Musset's friend, Alfred Tattet, all too intent on harvesting the "true story" of the Venetian lovers directly from the lips of one of them. Yes, Pagello had told Tattet, he and George had been lovers before Musset's departure. When George and the poet resumed their intimacy in October, coming together like a clap of thunder, Tattet was not long in retailing to Musset what he had learned from Pagello. Scenes of delirious lovemaking at Malaquais were interspersed with violent scenes of jealousy on the part of Musset. Exactly when had George and Pietro become lovers? Had it been when he lay sick and dying? Had he dreamed the single cup, their embrace? "Dear God, a hand other than mine on that fine, transparent skin, another mouth on those lips!"[15] Musset relished in his exquisite agony, demanding more details, as if it were he who felt the press of Pagello's mouth. Enough questions! cried George. Did not Alfred recall those dreadful Italian days when he had disclaimed her and gone off to the brothels? What right had he now to raise doubts? Had she not foretold that he would view their love "as a beautiful poem," so long as it was from a distance, but that he would think of it "as a nightmare," once they were together and he had repossessed her? What was now left to them? "Neither love, nor friendship."[16]

Desperately George sought stability and normalcy in her work, in new friends, in the companionship of fellow artists. Musset had invited Franz Liszt, the young Hungarian pianist then dazzling Paris, to sup with them at Malaquais. George asked him to come with composer Berlioz and bring the German poet Heinrich Heine. Liszt was clearly attracted, and Heine would find George "as beautiful as Venus de Milo."[17] But Musset was jealous of the handsome, twenty-three-year-old Liszt and displayed it on the occasion of yet another rupture with George.

Sainte-Beuve to an acquaintance, November 18, 1834: "The greatest storms I've known are the breaks between Lélia and Rolla, who have spent the entire month cursing and rediscovering each other, tearing each other apart and suffering."[18] Musset to Tattet, six days previously: "My friend, it is all over."[19] Tattet was delighted; he urged Alfred to hold firm. It was like telling the tides to cease their ebb and flow, the moon its compulsive attraction.

By some miracle, however, Alfred did hold firm, perhaps perversely because the moon refused to stand still. It was George who now surrendered herself completely, hopelessly, shamelessly to the power of fully awakened passion. As with Aurélien, she confided her feelings in a *journal intime* which she would send to Musset, since he was not responding to her imploring notes. "Why cannot you love me? . . . Oh mad one, you left me at the most beautiful time of my life, when my love was never deeper, truer, more intense!" Never had her senses been so satisfied, her pleasure more replete. The Musset she had found on her return from Venice had fully roused the woman in the benumbed Lélia. Why had she let him awaken her flesh, "why, since I was so resigned to my glacial couch? Angel of death, fatal love in the form of a blond and delicate child! oh my destiny! oh how I love you, assassin! May your kisses burn me alive, so that I might die consumed!"

But Musset had closed his door to her, their bodies might never again meet in the ecstasy of love. The lines are lyrical and scarcely bearable:

> Dear, blue eyes, you will never more look down up me! dear, blond head I shall never again see bending over me in sweet languor! Small, warm, lissome body, you will no longer lie upon me, as Elija upon the dead child, to bring me back to life. . . . Farewell, fair hair, farewell, white shoulders, farewell, everything that I have loved, all that once was mine. Henceforth, in the burning of my nights, I shall clasp the trunk of pine trees and the rocks of the forest, crying out your name, and when I have dreamed the ultimate delight, I shall fall exhausted to the damp earth.[20]

In sacrificial mood and silent plea, George cut the long locks of her black hair and sent them, together with his last letter, to Musset. He wept. They came together. They quarreled, they fought, they were separated by Sainte-Beuve, they parted once more.

With her hair shorn as if in mourning, George sat for Delacroix's portrait of her, commissioned by Buloz for the *Revue*, exposing her wistful, terribly vulnerable face like an open, wounded heart, her eyes gazing darkly into the distance. During the sittings, sometimes postponed because of emotional upset, George showed Delacroix an album she cherished of Musset's sketches. Delacroix praised them, remarking that Musset could have been a "great painter," if he had put his mind to it. As she posed, George talked to Delacroix of her sadness, asking his counsel, beginning a friendship which would end only with the death of the age's finest painter. He offered George the advice she secretly sought: "Not to be brave!"

" 'Let yourself go,' Delacroix continued. 'Whenever I am in that state, I don't pretend to any pride. I was not born a Roman. I abandon myself to Despair. It crushes and almost kills me. After it has had enough, it is as tired as I and leaves me in peace.' "[21]

But George Sand's despair increased. She dreaded isolation, separation, loneliness, the denial of love. "What if I were to run to him, when love overwhelms me! What if I were to ring his bell until he opened his door to me, or lay across his threshold until he came home? . . . It is cruel to beset him, to ask the impossible, but what if I were to throw myself into his arms and say, 'You love me still. . . . Don't speak, kiss me . . . caress me, since you find me pretty still, though my hair is cut short and two lines have formed around my mouth since the other night. And when you feel yourself tiring of me and your irritability returning, send me away, maltreat me, but let me never hear that horrible phrase, *This is the last time!*' "[22]

But pride, too, stirred in George Sand, almost as strongly as her passion. "I am still able to make a man happy"—a man as proud as herself. But perhaps he had to be a stronger man than Musset—and without his vanity. "If I had ever found a man like that, I should not be where I am. But," George paused, "such men are gnarled oaks whose bark repels. . . . And then, too, strong men lie, and are brutal . . ." How unlike her "Poet" with his "dewy fragrance."[23]

There was no escape. Neither in long conversations with Sainte-Beuve, who simply said, "If you weep, you love." Nor in the long evenings with Marie Dorval in her loge at the theater. Worst of all, George could no longer work: for the first time, the words refused to flow.

On December seventh, George fled to Nohant.

On January second, she was back in Paris. Her respite had lasted less than a month. While she was in Nohant, Musset had sent her a lock of *his* hair; in return he had received a leaf from George's garden. With the New Year—1835—they were back together again in the Malaquais apartment, and with a note of triumph George announced to Tattet: "Alfred has again become my lover."[24]

The reunion was short-lived; their love, in truth, was in its terminal agony. Alfred's desire had been rekindled, but not his trust. He wished to possess not only George's present but her past. What she had done before, he said without cease, she would do again. Regretfully but firmly, to strengthen his trust, George withdrew from her new friends, telling Franz Liszt that she could no longer receive him. Perhaps coincidentally, she began discussions with Casimir which led to an agreement to separate legally. When Alfred fell ill and went to his mother, he begged George to come and care for him. Without hesitation she responded. She would borrow a bonnet and apron from her maid. "Your mother will pretend she does not recognize me, and I will pass as the night nurse."[25] But there were wilder moments when Musset brandished a knife, George spoke of suicide and both talked of going to Fontainebleau to blow their brains out together.

Finally the stronger of the two, the "man of the couple," put an end to their exhausted wrestling. She could fight no longer, George said. Even her tears irritated Alfred. To remain together would only mean more shame for her and further torment for him. Better, dear God, to part. This time forever. On March 6, 1835, George had Boucoiran buy a coach seat for Nohant without Alfred's knowledge. "You will come at five," she told Boucoiran nervously, "and with an urgent, preoccupied air, you will tell me that my mother has just arrived and is very tired and seriously ill . . . that she needs me immediately and I must go to her at once. I will put on my hat, say [to Alfred] that I will be right back and you will put me in a fiacre."[26] She would take it to the coach station, and leave.

There was always a touch of self-conscious theater, of tragicomedy, in their love, their literary outpourings and confessions. ("It is all rapture and all rage and all literature"—Henry James.[27]) There was also a final dignity. On being told of George's departure, Musset wrote a short note to Boucoiran. Had she reasons for not wanting to see him before she left? "I need not add that if such is the case, I shall respect her wishes."[28]

Epilogue

Musset went on almost immediately—therapeutically—to Aimée d'Alton and other mistresses. But he also wrote to Alfred Tattet, in the summer of 1835: "If you see Madame Sand, tell her that I love her with all my heart, that she is still the most womanly woman I have ever known."[29] And he went on, also, after *Camille et Perdican* and *Les Nuits* to *La Confession d'un Enfant du Siècle*, the "hymn of love" he had promised George Sand. It was published in 1836, when Musset was twenty-five. It was his last important work, and if more memorable for its evocation of the imperial Bonaparte past than its portrait of a too spotless George Sand, it remains a classic of the Romantic literature which was their love.

"That love was the great event in his life," said Sainte-Beuve of Musset, "and I speak only of his life as a poet. His youthful talent was suddenly purified and ennobled." The dross had disappeared, the lines had hardened, enabling him to write the four *Nuits*, "which mark the highest reaches of his lyrical gift."[30]

Alfred wrote the first—*La Nuit de Mai* (The Night of May)—two months after George had journeyed to Nohant, leaving him for the last time. "Poet," his Muse called to him that night in May, "take down thy lute and embrace me." "Love and write," George had told him. Such was the fertility of their union, fatal as it proved, that Musset could fashion these lines:

> Rien ne nous rend si grands qu'une grande douleur.
> Mais, pour en être atteint, ne crois pas, ô poète,
> Que ta voix ici-bas doive rester muette.
> Les plus désespérés sont les chants les plus beaux,
> Et j'en sais d'immortels qui sont de purs sanglots.

> Nothing renders us so great as great sorrow.
> But, though touched by it, do not think, o poet,
> That your voice here below should remain mute.
> The most despairing songs are the most beautiful,
> And I know immortal songs that are pure sobs.

In *La Nuit d'Octobre* the lover's calumny and curses in the heat of jealousy and passion have been alchemized into poetry—Musset emerges:

> Honte à toi, femme à l'oeil sombre,
> Dont les funestes amours
> Ont enseveli dans l'ombre
> Mon printemps et mes beaux jours!

Even as Musset writes these verses in a poem of love addressed to Aimée d'Alton, it is clear that the "woman of the somber eye" who wrapped his youthful springtime in the shroud of "her fatal love" continues to haunt him, and will continue to do so.

One evening, three years after, Musset chanced on George Sand in the lobby of a theater. "Yes, young and still beautiful—more beautiful!" he wrote in his poem *Souvenir*. He had seen her lips part in a smile, he had heard her voice, but they were not for him. He had wanted to take her in his arms, and cry out:

> "Qu'as-tu fait, infidèle,
> Qu'as-tu fait du passé?"

What have you done, unfaithful one? What have you done with our past? Not long before Musset had walked in the woods of Fontainebleau and warmly remembered his "Lady of Franchard." Now he had come upon her at the theater—a stranger who had somehow borrowed "that voice, those eyes." He had lost. Nevertheless, he had loved. No one, not even she, could rob him of the memory of a certain spot in Fontainebleau's woods.

> Je me dis seulement: "A cette heure, en ce lieu,
> Un jour, je fus aimé, j'aimais, elle était belle.
> J'enfuis ce trésor dans mon âme immortelle,
> Et je l'emporte à Dieu!"

> I tell myself only: "At this time, in this place,
> One day, I was loved, I loved, she was beautiful.
> I tuck this treasure into my immortal soul
> And take it to God!"

For the remaining two decades of his life, the lute of Musset hung virtually mute. Memories were not enough, though neither drink nor debauchery could ever drown them. If the poet must live and love, he must also write. So it was with George Sand, now at Nohant, and so it would be for the many years of her life. Much of the bitterness of the Mussetists and their animus toward George Sand reside in that unforgivable fact.

22

The Republic
of Comrades

It is for *us* to tear down, for *you* to rebuild.
—George Sand,
Correspondance (1836)[1]

Arriving at Nohant after the flight from Musset, George sent three lines to Liszt and a longer letter to Boucoiran. She had already seen "all our La Châtre friends. . . . I dined with Rollinat at Duteil's. I shall start to write for Buloz. I am very calm. I have done what I had to do." Would Boucoiran send on her hookah (oriental water pipe) and its attachments, her sixteen volumes of Greek plays and thirteen volumes of Shakespeare? And would he buy her the Koran and Plato? Buloz would repay him.[2]

The calm was more Coué than reality: George shortly suffered from an embarrassing, body-covering, nervous rash. However, she did set to work for Buloz, nightly filling pages of manuscript for *Mauprat,* begun as a popular, swashbuckling novel with a dash of social consciousness. Buloz in the meantime feared that his prize author was turning to mysticism, what with her request for the Koran and Plato. His confidant was Sainte-Beuve, to whom George Sand confessed, "I should have stayed with [the common-sensical Ben] Franklin . . . whose picture over my bed makes me want to weep, as if that of a friend I had betrayed."[3] It was Musset, not mysticism, for whom Poor Richard's creator was the polar opposite.

George was in low spirits, but she was a professional writer. Her publisher was soon reassured by the first packet of the new novel. It was frankly escape literature in which George herself found refuge; while all slept, she lived in a world of her own making where she was master.

The real world was never distant—the readers recognized it—but she refashioned it closer to their heart's desire. Could she do the same in her daily life? George was never keen on the divided self, which she never confused with multiple selves.

The agreement of separation *à l'amiable*, signed by Casimir in February, was to take effect in November. George was to regain Nohant and Solange, Casimir was to have the Paris town house, Hôtel de Narbonne, with its annual income of 6,750 francs, and Maurice. "You surely do not think I'd let my husband starve, miserable creature that he is," George told Hippolyte, "though he would let me go to the morgue for a matter of twenty francs?"[4] So few months to endure, after so many years, but they seemed insupportable, precisely because the end *was* in view.

How make the time pass? By a trip to Switzerland? To Constantinople? Neither was convenient. What to do about the prickly situation at Nohant and the petulance of an uneasy Casimir, who saw his little duchy slipping away from him? Possibly with a male humor to which George willfully was blind, Duteil suggested that she could easily become mistress of the interim situation by becoming the mistress of her husband. George recoiled. "To make love without loving," she retorted, "was loathsome in the very thought. A wife who toys with her husband in order to dominate him is no better than the prostitute who does what she does for her daily bread, or the courtesan for her luxury." More seriously, Duteil mentioned the children's interests and future, which called for the temporary sacrifice.

Physical repugnance, George replied, was sufficient reason for refusing, though Casimir, for her, was no more repugnant than most men. It went beyond that. A young woman, freshly married, might sacrifice herself unwittingly from a sense of marital duty, because she "takes for love what is not really love. But at thirty, a wife can no longer delude herself. . . . She knows the price, not of the physical person—which can be humbly resigned to giving itself as if it were a thing—but of her very being, one and indivisible. . . . Love is not a matter of cold calculation and will. Marriages of convenience are a pitfall, a lie one tells oneself. We are not wholly body or wholly mind, but body and mind together. . . . If the body has its functions with which the soul has nothing to do, such as eating and digesting, can the union of two beings in love be so considered? The very thought is revolting."

"Fortunately," said Duteil wryly, "the human race has no need of such 'sublime aspirations' in order to find the function of reproduction very agreeable and quite simple."

"*Unfortunately!*" responded an unyielding George. "In any event, once a human being, man or woman, has learned what complete love can be, he or she can never—and never should—fall back to the level of pure animality."[5]

There is the stiffness of the *public* George Sand in this conversation from her memoirs, but no betrayal of what she deeply felt. The wholeness of being is consistently her attitude and conviction. She is speaking as well from the carnal knowledge of contrasting experiences —of a Pagello and a Musset, a Casimir and an Aurélien, a Mérimée, Planche, Sandeau and Grandsagne. She had sought the experience and was undeterred by the failures. Those who descend into the den of lions, she reflected to Sainte-Beuve, may well emerge "half-devoured, but are they condemned to remain mutilated the rest of their lives? . . . Long live love, despite everything!"[6]

Curiosity took George to Bourges to see the celebrated lawyer and leader of the radical opposition, Louis-Chrysostome Michel, known throughout France as Michel de Bourges. Curiosity and concern about her marital affairs.

On April 9, 1835, Fleury and Planet, an admirer and follower of Michel, brought the famous firebrand to her inn at Bourges. It was at seven in the evening of her arrival. She was immediately struck by the immense expanse of the bald, exposed brow of Michel de Bourges. (She had recently taken up phrenology and kept a skull on her writing table at Nohant, terrifying the gardener's wife.) "It was as if he had two skulls welded together," George observed. "The signs of the highest faculties of the soul were as prominent on the prow of this powerful ship as those of the most generous instincts were at its stern."[7] She knew Michel was under forty, but he looked middle-aged, until he began to speak, when he became, as all orators in even muffled flight, a vigorous and almost handsome man. It is possible that she knew Michel had married a rich widow with several children some years before. It did not matter. It was the legend of his peasant youth that fascinated her, the story of his father bayoneted to a tavern table by a gang of murdering royalists, seven months before Michel was born. Iron had then entered Michel's soul, and revolutionary republicanism had become part of his earliest life—all grist for George's next novel, *Simon*.

Shortly before they met, Michel had read *Lélia* and was as impressed and curious about its author as she was about him. From seven in the evening of her arrival until four in the morning, Michel held forth eloquently for Planet, Fleury and especially George Sand, as they walked from the inn to his home, then back to the inn, to and fro nine times, through "the austere, silent streets of the beautiful city of Bourges . . . in the light of the moon."[8] His elocution was like music, modulating from pianissimo to fortissimo, raising his listeners to the heavens, then returning them to the earth. But it pleased him to startle, stun, *épater* the intellectual innocents before him with forebodings of violence, revolution and the guillotine. George's marital problems were lost, if ever mentioned, in the political flow.

"Never have I seen him like this," Planet told her. "For a year I have been at his side, but I have never known him until tonight. He delivered himself to you entirely. He summoned all his intelligence and sensibility to impress you." George spent a restless remaining night. Three days later she wrote Gustave Papet from Nohant: "I have met Michel. He has promised to have me guillotined at the first opportunity."[9]

But she had already received a passionate letter from Michel de Bourges, continuing his political courtship, and had begun her own to him—the sixth *Lettre d'un Voyageur*, addressed to a mythical "Éverard."[10] Extending over the first two weeks of their acquaintanceship and lovemaking, the open letter to Michel-Éverard is an extraordinary, dexterous performance, putting on bold display his disturbing appeal and George's own political and emotional response.

Provocatively, teasingly, George tells Michel he is a "magnificent hypocrite"; his devotion to revolution and reform is not simply out of a sense of social obligation. "You misread yourself when you see as duty the rigorous, predestined drive of your natural power. I know you are not of those who are obedient to duty, but rather one who imposes it. You do not love men; you are not their brother, for you are not their equal. You are an exception among men, you were born a *king*."

There is flattery and a puzzle in these lines. George bowed to the "king" and was opposed to him out of principle. Had she found her "strong man" and already recognized in him her future "tyrant"? Had she been able to submit to a man, she had written to Sainte-Beuve apropos Mérimée, she would have been "saved." Saved from the destiny of being George Sand, a being in process of self-creation? It would seem, rather, that she was bowing to the societal archetype of the subordinate woman in this open letter—she who had already become the prototype of the self-liberated woman for the women of her time. The ambiguity was in George herself, the imprint from childhood of expected attitudes and the struggle to emerge from them.

Characteristically, however, George Sand gave herself fully in the fresh burst of love, each time as if for the first time. "It is you I have loved from the day I was born," she would cry to Michel—even as the end was visible.[11] Thus it was lovingly she teased Michel. Of all causes, his was "the most beautiful and noble," the only one the poet, writer and artist could espouse. She saw in him all the public virtues and no private vice, a man in the service of humanity. She felt drawn from her own private grief back to her abiding sense of people and the social injustices so bleakly obvious about her. In any factory were found children of six working sixteen hours a day. Strikes and collective protests were illegal, unions a criminal conspiracy, crushing the Lyons silk workers was the premeditated event of but the past year. Simply to be republican, as was always George Sand's egalitarian impulse and conviction, was already to be halfway, in the age of Louis-Philippe and the monarchy, towards the advocacy of revolution. Michel furthered the impulse and politicalized the conviction. George responded to the power of his mind and stirred to his purpose.

"From the first day we belonged to each other by our thinking. . . . No other man had ever exercised such intellectual influence upon me." Then the red light blinks again: "I was mentally a virgin, waiting for a good man to come and teach me. You came and taught me."[12] This was in a later, *personal* letter to Michel, all the more striking for its privacy. Again, the expected pose: even intellectual virginity was assumed to appeal to the nineteenth-century man, however liberal or radical. In truth, Michel *had* expanded George's mind and extended her experience. There were no greater grounds, no more gripping reason, for her opening to love; and this small, gritty, bent, bald, prematurely old and quite ugly man of peasant birth may have been George Sand's most satisfying lover.

But it was the mating of minds that preceded, if only by days, the profound agreement on principles, such as "the great law of equality—inapplicable as it seems today to those who are afraid of it and uncertain as its rule on earth seems to be in the future." It was the only just and wholly moral goal, the *Lettre* to "Éverard" resumed, and had been all George's life, though she now felt guilty for not having more actively pursued it, instead of engaging in "fated loves." As for Michel, on occasion she found him discouraged, "beaten down, trembling" before the colossal task. "You find it long in coming, that accomplishment of a great destiny! Time drags, your hair recedes, your spirit is consumed and the human race refuses to advance." She herself laughed at the men who looked at her frail, woman's arms and scornfully proclaimed the "right of the stronger" when she talked to them of "justice." Nevertheless, small as she might be,* she could still serve, "if only by raising a barricade the height of a corpse," or marching with her comrades, a "foot soldier" on the roads to the future, "in the name of Jesus . . . Washington and Franklin . . . of Saint-Simon." (Marx at this moment was sixteen.)

The impression that George Sand was uncritical of Michel de Bourges would be as mistaken as the general assumption that he had "created" her republicanism, if not her social conscience; that her political views and writings were but a reflection of his own in the mirror of

---

* Five feet one and a half inches (1.58 m.), according to her passport of the same year.

her own unreflecting love. George contributed to the assumption: the conventional poses and attitudes at times, the acceptance, however fleeting and more often opposed, of the contemporary idea of the "truly feminine." In their discussions, Michel overdid the rhetorical "startling" of intellectuals in the drawing room with his apostrophes to the flowing of blood and his scorn for the hypersensitivity of the poet and artist. Like Plato, he would expel them from his republic, accusing them of weakening the revolutionary will and even of corrupting public morals—striking indirectly at Musset and Liszt and others of Sand's intimate, or once intimate, friends.

On these occasions, George admirably flashed back, usually in writing, since, she said (overplaying the *"femmelette"* role), she felt overpowered in their conversations. Michel, she pointedly remarked in her *Lettre*, would permit the poets "to say what they wanted to say, so long as it was what *he* wanted them to say!" When a follower of Michel told her one day, half seriously, that she "merited death," she was shocked, puzzled, then delighted, George wrote. "I confidentially tell all my friends that I am a literary and political personnage of such immense importance, I give umbrage to people of my own party. . . . The Madagascan asked for my patronage, so that he might have the honor of being hung on my right, and Planet on my left." She maintained the same mocking, but deeply stinging tone, when she recounted the dialogue with Michel to a young Saint-Simonian, Adolphe Guéroult: "I swore to him that if the extreme left were ever to win, my head would fall like many another, because I would not be silent."[13]

It was Guéroult who had brought George Sand the proposal of Saint-Simonian leader Father Barthélémy Enfantin, that she formally become "Mother" of "the family." She had refused the offer, though she sympathized with the movement's socialism and its equal-rights stand for women. However, she remained on her own, leading by her example. The Sandist hero(ine) especially was widely imitated in dress and attitude and domestic stance, some women to the extent of leaving their husbands in the provinces to live in Paris *à la* George Sand.

Money was still the key to such freedom, however, and there were very few who did not simply become mistresses of other men. The cost of her own independence, George related to Michel, had its price. "Pressed, obliged to make money, I forced my imagination to produce, envying those who could carefully reread their pages, correct them, polish them meticulously." She, on the other hand, had to rush her manuscripts, "the ink barely dry," to her publisher. So George concluded her *Lettre d'un Voyageur*, VI—rushing it to her publisher.[14] She lived well, spent generously, entertained and took care of a number of people: she more than paid her own way. With Nohant, Solange and Sophie soon at her charge, it was more pressing than ever to increase her income.

Ironically, it was the halving of George's money—the revenues of the estates left her by her grandmother—which now loomed before Casimir and made him conspicuously unhappy and growingly difficult. He regretted the February agreement.

Disgusted, George tore up their contract and sent the fragments to Duteil, who was acting as her lawyer. She didn't want Casimir, she said, "to strike the pose of a victim, especially in the eyes of the children." Moreover, she sought "no favor from anyone, even when the charity is my own money."[15] Abashed, or recontemplating his own freer life as a bachelor in Paris, Casimir returned virtually the same contract, ceding to Aurore, he wrote, his "little empire."[16]

George in the meantime had gone to Paris for the *procès monstre*, the "monster trial" in which Michel took a prominent part. One hundred and twenty-one workers and opposition leaders were collectively accused of conspiracy in the past year's uprising in Lyons and the accompanying outbursts in other cities of France. They were prosecuted *en masse* and public sympathy was on their side. The tactic of the defense counsels—Michel, Garnier-Pagès, Ledru-Rollin, Barbès, among other notable republicans—was to turn the courtroom of royal judges into a people's tribune in which the accused would become the accusers and the monarchy would be on trial. Moreover, as George Sand perceived, "the historical moment was beginning to crystallize when purely political ideas and purely socialist ideas were jointly commencing to fill the gaps between the partisans of democracy."[17]

Women were not admitted to the monster trial, but at least one accused man's wife was discreetly advised by a guard to put on a pair of trousers, and he would let her pass. Dressed as a man—no disguise in her case; people nudged each other in recognition of the famous novelist—George Sand came to the sessions not so much to hear Michel's pleadings as to "show her support and give heart to the accused, her political friends."[18] She collected money for the prisoners, and her apartment on Quai Malaquais became a republican center. The government police noted the comings and goings.

Nightly, fatigued to the point of nausea and illness, Michel would climb the stairs to George's rooms after the long day's hearing in court. (He was lodged, for public purposes, further along the quai.) The crowded salon would revive him and he would resume his political oratory, though he was addressing political friends—Sand, Planet, Fleury, Arago, the men he had brought with him, and the ever-serious, ever-searching Franz Liszt, who sometimes joined them. The walls resounded with arguments about the means to the agreed socialist ends. Then, well after midnight, when all had left, Michel would collapse, George would comfort and restore him—"passion took possession of us both." The minds had met, the bodies united. So strong was the union that Michel talked of their life together, and even set a date for it—in a year or two, presumably after he had arranged his domestic affairs in some manner for his wife and her children. George wholly believed it: she loved Michel, he loved her—"when every fiber of my being was laid bare and vibrating under your touch, my attachment to you became so strong and deep that I could imagine no other goal in my life but to live with you."[19]

Thus would George *reproach* Michel as the second anniversary of their meeting neared and the emotion she felt was no less strong and deep. But emotions recollected in the difference of two elapsed decades, political passions as well, are neither poetry nor entirely trustworthy memory. In this retrospect, George recalled in her memoirs of twenty years later a night scene in Paris during the great trial. They were returning, the three comrades—Planet, Michel and George—from an evening at the Comédie-Française, crossing the bridge leading to the Left Bank quais and George's apartment. It was another splendid night of spring. Lights from the Tuileries palace and gardens shimmered in the Seine. George fell into a reverie—there were always such moments of withdrawal—which clearly upset the discoursing Michel. He raised his voice and the temperature of his politics. Timorously Planet questioned the politics of terror and a bestirred George spoke of the requirements of a "civilized society."

"Civilization!" cried Michel, rapping his cane sharply against the bridge railing. "Ha! the big word of the artist! I tell you that your corrupt society will never be made over until this river flows red with blood, that cursed palace is reduced to ashes and the whole of Paris has become a bare stretch of land upon which the poor man's family can drive its plough and build its thatched cottage!"[20]

It was the provocative rhetoric of the political orator, grossly out of place, and the gratuitousness of Michel's exhibition crudely ruptured the intimacy of the evening. In view of the later course of Michel's life, his greater concern for money and political honors than for principle, it was particularly obnoxious. As George Sand would remark, when she "had become a socialist, Michel no longer was."[21]

Another incident recalled by George was more significant, revealing Michel, as many a "friend of mankind," to be an autocrat at home.

They were alone at the Malaquais apartment. Michel talked feelingly and effectively of individualism versus social conscience. "You dream of the freedom of the individual," he remarked to George. "You have worked hard to achieve it for yourself. But it cannot be reconciled with collective social action." People, too, wanted to be masters of their destiny, but it would take a revolutionary transformation of society for *them* to achieve it. They must act jointly for their individual sakes. She must join them. Truths applicable to a more just society in process of birth emerged in collective, not solitary, thinking. "They are to be sought in the company of others."

So saying, Michel left for a political meeting—and *he locked the door of the apartment.* George thought he had done it absent-mindedly, but he returned three hours later—laughing. He had locked her in, Michel said, because he had remarked that she was "not quite convinced," and he wanted to ensure her "reflection." It was playfully meant, and so George chose to accept it.[22] But the gesture was heavy with the barracks humor of a sergeant playing a joke on a private. The roles are never reversible. To conceive George conducting herself similarly with Michel is scarcely imaginable, though "equality" was the political password between them.

The socially and politically agitated year, however, was not monopolized by Michel de Bourges for George. He was also quite taken up with his own trial for contempt of court, for which he was condemned to a delayed sentence of a month in prison. During that hectic spring, Franz Liszt had brought the famed radical priest, Abbé Félicité de Lamennais, to the Malaquais apartment. A slight, austere man in his mid-fifties, the Abbé had early dropped the *de* of nobility, undertaken to reform the irredeemably royalist Church and incurred the censure of the Vatican. The Christian socialism preached in his *Paroles d'un Croyant* (Words of a Believer)—"a small book," said Pope Gregory XVI in a damning encyclical, "but immense in its perversity"[23]—had become the liberal layman's creed throughout Europe.

George had read and admired the work, and had eagerly looked forward to the meeting. She was not disappointed, though she did not, as did Franz Liszt, become Lamennais' disciple. Profoundly religious—he would spend nights on his knees in prayer—and seeking instruction with a passion that was almost pathetic—as a performing child prodigy, his only school had been the piano—Liszt acquired in the Abbé a teacher and father.* He had dedicated his composition honoring the Lyons workers to Lamennais, inscribing it with the strikers' insurrectionist slogan: "To live working or to die fighting." The Abbé, too, was very taken by Liszt, whom he saw straining towards his own conception of the artist as "prophet of the new order."[25]

There was much about Liszt that appealed to George Sand, although they seem never to have become lovers, despite the opinion of Musset and *tout Paris.* "If I could have loved Monsieur Liszt," she told Musset, "I would have, if only out of anger with you. But I could not. . . . I should hate to like spinach, because if I did, I would eat it, and in fact I cannot stand it." For George Sand, Franz Liszt was simply spinach. Moreover, she said, "Monsieur Liszt thought only of God and the

---

* "Liszt," said Heine, "likes to poke his nose in all the pots in which God is cooking the future of the world."[24]

Holy Virgin, who resembles me not in the slightest."[26] Yet the whole truth about George's feelings for Liszt could not be told in a letter to Musset. She was more fond of Liszt than she revealed. He was among the century's greatest pianists—only Chopin rivaled him in Paris—and one of its most gifted composers. George Sand's love for music was second to no one's. As in her childhood, when her grandmother stiffly performed at the piano, she would curl under Liszt's piano to become part of his playing—and perhaps that was physical enough.

There was also Countess Marie d'Agoult.

The relations of the two women—George Sand and Marie d'Agoult, granddaughter of a rich German banker, daughter of Count de Flavigny, wife of Count d'Agoult—would be long, affectionate, competitive and curious. As brilliant and almost as talented as George, a year younger and more beautiful, Marie, writing as Daniel Stern, would become almost as famous. The story of her life with Liszt was as exemplary in courage, and as legendary—their daughter Cosima would become the wife of Richard Wagner.

Marie d'Agoult, mother of two children, had met Franz Liszt at a musical soirée in the winter of 1833. She was struck by his fiery piano playing, his tall, thin, sloping figure, his pale face and striking, sea-green eyes. After she left Paris for the country with her husband, she exchanged letters with Liszt. He was invited to their estate (the much older Count d'Agoult proved polite and complaisant). The attachment grew. A few months after Franz met George Sand, he declared his love for Marie. In fact, George was both their inspiration and spur. Franz and Marie fondly disputed who had first read and adored *Leone Leoni*, the story of all for love. *Lélia* was one of Liszt's passions, less so for Marie. But they both pointed to George's bold way of life as the model for their own, and it shaped their decision to do likewise. Besides, Marie was pregnant with Liszt's child.

By June 1835, the decision was taken: Marie would leave for Switzerland, Liszt would join her later. Before she left, Franz brought her to the Malaquais apartment. She appeared to George "like one of those marvelous princesses in the tales of Hoffmann . . . a golden-haired fairy in a long, blue robe" who had descended from the heavens "to the garret of a poet."[27] Marie, on first seeing George, asked herself: "Is she a man, a woman, an angel, a demon? Does she come, as her Lélia, from heaven or hell?"[28] After Marie and Franz had settled in Geneva, both wrote George, urging her to visit them. She would, she replied, and to Marie she wrote: "I believe I can say . . . that I love you, that I regard you as the only beautiful, estimable and truly noble object of the patrician world. You had to be striking for me to forget you were a countess." George had also found Marie d'Agoult formidably intelligent. "You say you want to write? Write, then! . . . Write quickly, before reflecting too much," write out of the present, "not out of memory."[29] Write about women, George later advised.

She longed to see them, George said, and "caressed" the project of seeing them soon. But a problem arose to prevent it.

The great trial had ended, sentences of exile and prison for the accused were blanketly laid down as expected. The radicalization of George Sand meanwhile had proceeded at a remarkably accelerated pace. In July 1835, she bravely defended regicide in the aftermath of Fieschi's attempted assassination of Louis-Philippe by a bomb which killed several people around the monarch. Further, to Buloz' dismay, she made it part of her seventh *Lettre d'un Voyageur*, addressed to Franz Liszt. To Adolphe Guéroult and the Saint-Simonians she expanded on her political beliefs and convictions: she advocated the abolition of private property and predicted that its day would come. George spoke also of a future "race of fierce, proud proletarians, prepared to win back by force all the human rights it had lost."[30]

Only a day or two before she had expressed this, George had experienced her own personal explosion, microcosmic in comparison, but involving the critical problem of the married couple: its uncoupling.

23

Trials and Interludes

Free at last!
—George Sand,
Correspondance
(1836)[1]

Casimir suffered his own ambiguous, embarrassing, "unmanning" situation, particularly when Madame Dudevant was at home in Nohant receiving friends. He knew—and the friends knew—it was her Nohant, her money, talent, intelligence and literary success which brought them and provided him with his own ease and comfort. The inner conflict had to burst forth periodically.

So it was on October 19, 1835. Family and friends—Fleury, Papet, Duteil, Monsieur and Madame Bourgoing—were having after-dinner coffee in the salon. Casimir had hunted during the day and at dinner drank too much champagne. His irritation with Aurore—she was never George for him—and the situation showed through the usual cover. Twelve-year-old Maurice, sensing the storm, moved restlessly about the drawing room. His father told him to settle down. His mother called the boy to her side. He remained there for a moment, then squirmed away. Casimir scolded him, then George, loudly accusing her of having spoiled their son. He ordered Maurice from the room. The boy hesitated. George advised him to obey, since his father did not know what he was . . . She didn't complete the phrase. After Maurice withdrew, Casimir finished it for her: he didn't know what he was *saying*, because he was "stupid." No, said George, "a bit drunk." Casimir ordered his wife from the drawing room. Composed, George refused. "You forget," she said, "I am as much in my home as in yours." Casimir lunged toward her, hand raised. Fleury and Papet intervened. He cried out that *he* was the master of *this* house, and would show them! He rushed from the room and returned with a gun, brandishing it with more bluster

than real menace. Eventually Duteil restored calm and a modicum of
sociability in the drawing room, and soon George went to her room.

It was not the scene—there had been others, though of less violence;
there would be more, perhaps of more violence—but the situation itself
which struck George most sharply: the humiliation to which she was always legally subject. Casimir *was* the master of Nohant. The freedom
he "allowed" of a separate life, she saw clearly, was the freedom he
gained for himself. It even extended to writing George friendly letters
when she was openly in Italy with Musset, "because," she said with
some bitterness to Hippolyte, "he was content to find me elsewhere—
and himself absolute lord of a château and estate. The ill-tempered
treatment recommenced the moment I returned."[2]

The witnessed scene was too good an occasion—we should be as honest about it as George Sand herself[3]—to let go by. While Casimir accompanied the two children to Paris, Solange to her boarding school
and Maurice to his *collège*, George drove in haste to Châteauroux with
Papet to confer with Rollinat, then all three went on to Bourges to consult with Michel. The conference was in the fortress prison where he
was finishing his sentence. As Rollinat, Michel advised an immediate
suit for separation in the court of La Châtre. In view of what had just
taken place at Nohant, it was doubtful Casimir would contest it. In the
meantime, George was not to return to Nohant—in the eyes of the law
it would mean she and Casimir had resumed cohabitation. She therefore took up residence with Duteil and his wife.

From La Châtre, George cautioned her mother Sophie to be extremely careful with Casimir, should he pay her a visit in Paris, pleading his cause. To Maurice, she wrote with equal care—of education, republicanism and his father: "In time you will freely choose between his
ideas and mine."[4] To the people of La Châtre, whose opinion she now
courted because of the coming trial, George presented as demure an appearance as she could contrive. "I am living a monastic life," she wrote
Marie d'Agoult, "outrageously respectable, so as to win the admiration
of three imbeciles"—her future judges. "I am emulating Sixtus
V"—who pretended to be dying, then, elected Pope, threw away his
crutches and ruled actively. "So, at this very hour a league away, four
thousand fools believe I am on my knees in sackcloth and ashes, weeping for my sins like Mary Magdalene.

"They will have a terrible awakening. The day after my victory, I will
throw away my crutches, gallop through town over the bodies of my
judges and set fire to the four corners of the village. If you should hear
that I have been converted to good sense, public morality, love of the
law, Louis-Philippe, the All-Powerful Father, and Poulot-Rosolin, his
son, and to the Holy Catholic Chamber, do not be surprised. I am capable of writing an ode to the King, or a sonnet to Monsieur

Jacqueminot"—Commanding General of the National Guard—"in order to win my suit."[5]

Finally, in February 1836, the separation suit was heard at La Châtre. The plea, prepared by George for Michel de Bourges, is the long, dreary record of a failed marriage, unastonishingly one-sided in its recounting of Casimir's mismanagement of his wife's dowry, estates and monies; his "blows" at Plessis because of a few grains of sand in his coffee; his emotional explosions and public insults; his drinking and "orgies" at Nohant; his "concubinage with Claire" and their child; his acceptance of his wife's living apart six months of the year; his amiable letters when she was in Italy, his "brutal" reception on her return; the gun scene at Nohant.[6]

It would be another century—but not yet even in France—before a less demeaning plea of incompatibility would be sufficient, instead of this display of dirty linen in open court.

Casimir made no defense. He had agreed to default beforehand in return for a stipulated income. The court at La Châtre consequently decided in Madame Dudevant's favor. She was to have Nohant and custody of the two children.

With a burst of joy, George hurried to a Nohant which was now hers, cleaned house of all but the old gardener and his wife, and awaited Casimir and Duteil in order to clear up all the odds and ends of the final settlement. "I savored for the first time since the death of my grandmother the sweetness of composure undisturbed by a single note of discord."[7]

It was a short idyll. Within a few days she was told by Hippolyte that Casimir had decided to appeal the La Châtre ruling. All was to recommence! Deeply hurt when she heard of Hippolyte's own hypocrisy—he had encouraged Casimir in his action—George was determined nevertheless to go ahead with her suit. "Nothing is going to stop me from doing what I should do, and shall do," she wrote Sophie. "I am my father's daughter. . . . If he had listened to the fools and idiots of this world, I would never have borne his name." For he would not have married Sophie, George ungently reminds her mother. "The world can go to the devil. All I care about are Maurice and Solange."[8] This was not the occasion to speak of herself.

George Sand was indeed betrayed by her brother, wherefore her bitterness. Hippolyte was shortly writing Casimir, "Duteil had to be blind to think you wouldn't appeal such a decision. . . . Aurore is furious. . . . As for me, I don't want you to have me appear in any connection involving her. You have enough proof without me. I will help you with my advice and some important information. . . . There are people close to you who could, with one stroke, ensure the winning of your appeal. You have only to loosen their tongues. I'll tell you how, when we see each other."[9]

Meanwhile George had left Nohant, repossessed by Casimir, and returned to Paris via Bourges and Michel. Her depression is part explanation of a strange, transient interlude between trials.

* * *

Many a man who prides himself on his fidelity has simply never had a beautiful woman offer herself freely to him. Such a beautiful creature for George Sand was Charles Didier. A year younger, he had been born in Geneva, from which he fled in his twenties to become a writer in Paris. Hugo had taken him into his *cénacle,* and Hortense Allart, feminist, novelist and pamphleteer, into her arms.[10] Rather foolishly, Hortense Allart had presented her tall, well-built, very attractive lover to George Sand on February 2, 1833 (the pre-Musset, *Lélia* period; the definitive break with Sandeau would be a month later).

Charles Didier kept a diary* and that night crisply wrote in it: "Hortense presents me to Madame Dudevant. Like I imagined her and expected, rather dry and stand-offish. Has a striking face. Don't think she is capable of passion any more." George invited Didier to return two days later. Didier to his *Diary:* "As before, stand-offish. Is she capable of passion? Think she has crossed the Rubicon. Visit to Princess Belgiojoso, who receives me with grace and courtesy. Saw Musset, who passes for her lover."

Days elapsed with no mention of George Sand, then on March 15, 1833: "Long visit with Madame Dudevant. Chat with much more intimacy, but still with a certain reserve." March twenty-first: "Visit with Madame Dudevant—sick. She is beautiful and gentle. Her beautiful face framed in black hair creates a gracious effect. Some grimy provincials come and go. One is her brother. Planche comes by. She chats with him." March twenty-eighth: "Letter from Madame Dudevant, who asks for letters of recommendation for Jules Sandeau, who's leaving for Italy." March thirtieth: "At Madame Dudevant's. She keeps me for dinner with Hortense Allart and Planche. Find her sad. Think that Planche, with whom she is very close, has a bad influence on her. . . . We remain together, alone, the lady and I. We read a page aloud from [Senancour's] *Obermann,* which strikes me straight to the heart. Madame Dudevant, charming and abandoned. She breathes love. I'm afraid for her liaison with Planche—a man not made for her."

Desire, jealousy, romantic impulses and Calvinistic scruples warred within Didier. His next reference to George Sand was several months

---

* Providing an extraordinary, if sketchy, view of George Sand from a man's closeup—intimate, personal, prejudiced and priceless—a veritable Pepys' Diary for our purposes.

later. June ninth: "Sainte-Beuve tells me about the turpitudes of Madame Dudevant. She has given herself to Mérimée. Duration twenty days. Her affair. She was insulted during a dinner by Dumas. Planche challenged him to a duel. Dumas retracted his insulting remark only on condition that Planche declare he was not Madame Dudevant's lover. [Which Planche did.] Pretty dirty business!" August ninth: "Read *Lélia* fervently and steadily, very late." Next day: "*Lélia* finished. . . . Find my own novel stupid in comparison. Won't tell this to Madame Dudevant, who doesn't think much of people who admire her." August twelfth: "Feel effect of *Lélia* more than ever. Not jealous . . . but feel a poor, weak writer, a petty artist in comparison with such powers of construction and passion. Why then write? To eat."

On August 14, 1833, Didier was astonished to receive a note from George Sand asking for the loan of a hundred francs. He managed to borrow the money for her and took it to Quai Malaquais. "Discovered she had just come back from the forest of Fontainebleau." He saw her again on the twentieth: "Very friendly, very gay. Told me she felt like fifteen. . . . Is it still possible for her to love? Hortense very jealous . . ." August twenty-seventh: "Musset said to be her lover. He was with her at Fontainebleau. . . . She told me she had been alone, riding in the woods. . . . I feel great pity for this unhappy woman, who goes about wasting her wonderful gifts, degrading her sublime genius." September, undated: "Sainte-Beuve talks to me about Madame Dudevant and Musset. She just wrote Sainte-Beuve she was really in love: 'I yielded out of friendship, love came afterward.' Planche dismissed. O *contradiction! O vanité!*" O Sainte-Beuve, concierge of literary Paris.

Throughout 1834, Charles Didier mentioned George Sand only twice and saw her once. November of that year he left for Spain, not to return to Paris before September 1835. A post-Musset George Sand welcomed him back, helped him with Buloz, offered him money and wrote letters from La Châtre, telling him of the trial, Casimir's appeal and her arrival in Paris.

Didier to his *Diary*, March 22, 1836: "Evening chez Madame Dudevant, who arrived this morning. There were Emmanuel Arago [son of the famous astronomer, close friend of G.S.] and Guéroult. She is keeping bad company, as always. It's deplorable."

March twenty-sixth: "At the Salon exhibition, where I found George Sand. Returned to her place with Emmanuel Arago. Stayed there all day, mooning about. . . . Charles d'Aragon, Arago and I remain for supper, drink tea, talk all night. Fantastic night. We didn't leave until five. When it was daylight. Arago was drunk. . . . They are both in love with her. I lay on the divan, my head on a cushion, observing, and she, melancholy and not too imperious, ran her fingers through my hair, calling me her 'old philosopher.' " Didier was handsomely, prematurely white-haired.

March twenty-seventh: "To George Sand's with three bottles of champagne, 11:30 P.M. Supper as yesterday. D'Aragon not there. . . . We were all drunk, I less than the others. George was laughing and gay. I don't like her vulgar side, but forgive it. She was tipsily affectionate. I too. She kissed me. I kissed her. Left at eight. Terrible storm outside. She exchanged her cashmere shawl for my white silk scarf."

March twenty-ninth: "At George Sand's. Dine. I'm afraid something is going on between her and that ass d'Aragon"—a count of twenty-three.

March thirty-first: "At Quai Malaquais. Fortoul [journalist] there with Arago. George Sand supposed to read to us from *Engelwald,** but did not. She felt a bit ill. . . . She goes too far with Arago. Treats him with a scorn that is too insulting. . . . Episode of the garters. . . . Back home at six."

April first (1836): "Up at 3 P.M. To George Sand, who receives me in bed. She rises, but I do not stay long. I was silent, cold, tired. . . . She kissed me on the forehead twice, once long and lingeringly, which surprised me. . . . At Carnot's, Fortoul talks about last night. . . . He is convinced George Sand wants me as a lover. I think he's mistaken and doesn't understand her. . . . I would not want to become attached, because I would be quite unhappy, what with our different characters."

April twelfth: "At George Sand's, just for a moment, from midnight to one. Bores there. I only like her when she is alone. All the faults of her vulgar side appear only when she is in company."

April thirteenth: "At George Sand's, where we sup, Artaud [brother-in-law of Baron Haussmann], Martineau [young baron], Calamatta [artist], Arago and d'Aragon. We all get drunk, especially d'Aragon and I. Fantastic, delirious night."

April fifteenth: "At George Sand's, 1:00 P.M. Good-humored tête-à-tête for five hours. Dine with her. Stay up all night. We do not part."

April sixteenth: "Still alone with her. At eight I take her to the Jardin des Plantes. . . . At eleven to my place, where we lunch. She is a bit ill. Take care of her. Cure her by mesmerizing her. Return with her [to Malaquais] at six. Thirty hours without separating, twelve tête-à-tête. We are binding ourselves intimately together."

April eighteenth: "Leave George Sand at eight in the morning. Sleep until almost three, then return and bring her to my place, where we

---

* *Engelwald the Bald,* a never-published novel based on Michel de Bourges. George had worked long and nightly on it at La Châtre and Nohant, but held up publication so as not to alienate her judges with its radical republicanism. Then, in 1864, she burned the manuscript, since she was no longer of the same mind.

dine and stay until midnight. I was happy, but spoke little. She was serious—ravishingly beautiful."

April nineteenth: "Together, as much as yesterday. Bring her to my place for dinner. David Richard [fellow lodger] gives her a lesson in phrenology. He's falling a little in love with her and I'm a bit jealous. . . . Richard goes off to bed. I'm alone with George Sand. I make her bed in my study and go to my room. What a life! If only people knew!"

April twentieth: "Up at eleven. Helped her with her dressing. We lunch, then I take her to the Collège Henri IV to see Maurice. She talks a great deal to me about Michel de Bourges, and tells me that their relations are purely intellectual. She swears to me that she has had no lover since her rupture with Musset. . . . She is beautiful and charming."

April twenty-fifth: "George Sand moves today to my place. I have turned over my apartment to her." Fearing Casimir's legal seizure of her affairs, since he was still lord and master of all she possessed and earned, George had closed up the Malaquais apartment, sending its furniture to Buloz for safekeeping. "We read *Engelwald* in the evening, then spend the rest of the night tête-à-tête. . . . Her settling into my place has provoked much gossip, here in the house and outside it. Rest of month do nothing else but keep her company and talk to her. Long hours of intimacy. . . . I study her and observe her—anxious, troubled, wondering. This complicated being is unintelligible to me in more ways than one. I fear her impetuous changeableness. I study her and do not understand her. Is she being honest? Is she play-acting? Is her heart dead inside of her? Problems without solution."

May second (1836): "She goes out in the evening and does not return until midnight. She finishes the heading for her sixth *Lettre d'un Voyageur* [addressed to Éverard-Michel]. Afterwards she becomes tender and loving. She sits at my feet, her head on my knees, her hands in mine. . . . Oh, Siren, what do you want of me?"[11]

The following day George left directly from Didier's apartment for Bourges and La Châtre, where Casimir's appeal was to be heard within a week.

* * *

Casimir meanwhile had been uncommonly busy, leaving no stone unturned in hope of gathering the dirt beneath. To his Paris agent Caron he dispatched an urgent note: could Caron dig up letters Aurore had written to Marie Dorval? "These letters, they say, and I myself heard in Paris, are very compromising. Couldn't you, through Dumont or somebody else, use your wits and pinch a few?"[12] (Caron could not or would not.) For his lawyer, Casimir drew up a bill of plaints, appropriately titled, *Griefs contre A.D.* (Aurore Dudevant).

Casimir's plaints went back to March 1825, with Aurore's "withdrawal to the English convent," then continued:

August (1825)—Trip to Pyrenees. Meeting and correspondence with A. Desèze [sic]. Surprise A. Desèze and A. Dudevant together.

1827—Intimate correspondence between A. Dudevant and Stéphane Ajasson [de Grandsagne]. November: Trip to Paris with Stéphane, pretending for her health's sake. . . .

1829—Letter written by A.D. to Stéphane A. in Paris, month of March, asking for poison, claiming she wanted to end her life. April: Departure of two spouses for Bordeaux. . . . Visits every morning of A.D. to Monsieur Desèze, claiming ill health and going to baths. . . .

1830—September: Meets Jules Sandeau. . . . November: Arrival in Paris of Madame A. Dud. Stays in brother's apartment on Rue de Seine, where she scandalizes entire house, according to concierge. Monsieur Jules Sandeau. She writes novels.

1831— . . . lively quarrel with Jules Sandeau, followed by blows, etc., etc.

1832—Monsieur Gustave Planche. Julie Dorville [maid] says Madame A.D. slept with him and had her daughter, age four years, come into same bed. Dislike of Solange for Monsieur Planche.

1833—Departure for Italy with Monsieur Alfred de Musset for stay of eight months. Public remarks of Monsieur Alfred de Musset about conduct of Madame A.D. . . . Quarrel. Reconciliation.

1834—August: Return to Nohant with her mother, fearing bad reception. . . . October: Return to Paris with children Maurice and Solange. Boarding school for Solange, mother and daughter, age six years, not being able to live together.

1835—Mutual dislike between two spouses. Madame Dud. affecting manners of young man, smoking, swearing, dressing like a man, having lost all graces of the feminine sex. Does not know value of money. Author of *Lélia*. Political testament in *Revue des Deux Mondes*, letters of June 1835 [to Éverard-Michel].[13]

To his *Griefs*, Casimir added a special *Note on Michel and A.D.*:

June 1835—Monsieur Michel came for first time to Nohant, spent two or three days. Monsieur Dudevant was at La Châtre attending burial of Monsieur Duvernet *père*, became sick, returned to Nohant with fever and took to bed on arrival.

Monsieur Michel and Mme. Dudevant had remained at Nohant and left next day for La Châtre and then Bourges, Madame caring very little about the condition of her husband.

August 1835— . . . Monsieur Dudevant left to fetch his son in Paris. Without his knowledge, Monsieur Michel came and installed himself at Nohant during his absence. Monsieur Dudevant learned this after suit for separation. . . .

January 1836—Monsieur Michel came to Nohant with Madame Dud. about seven or eight in morning, went to bed on arrival in upper bedroom, Madame went to bed in her study below. . . .

April 1836—Monsieur Michel installed in Paris . . . and spent a week there. It was while he was at Madame D.'s [Casimir seems completely unaware of Didier] that Monsieur Dudevant was told that they had prepared a trap for him. [The "trap" remains a mystery.] Madame Dud. had changed name of occupant of her apartment to Monsieur Gustave Papet or some other person. [When she stayed *chez* Didier?][14]

If it were Casimir who was suing for separation, he would certainly have established his case. However, he was appealing the separation decision, and that made no sense to the La Châtre court. On May eleventh, the judges ruled in George's favor; the very facts cited by the defense were actually an "attack," they decided, and of such a "defamatory nature as to leave no hope for the re-establishment of harmonious relations between husband and wife."[15]

Again George Sand was awarded "separation of bed, board and property," as well as custody of Solange and even Maurice. But again Casimir, who saw himself losing virtually all, appealed the La Châtre decision, this time to the higher court of Bourges, the regional capital.

Maurice was George Sand's pet and caution. He was affectionate, pliant and precocious. Solange was petulant, difficult and jealous of her older brother. She was more resentful of the men she saw at the Malaquais apartment, if only because she was there—before going to a boarding school—whereas Maurice was not, though he was often with one or the other on his day out from school. George's letters to her twelve-year-old son are long, tender and educational, a veritable catechism of republicanism, and they reveal the struggle with Casimir for his love and approval. When, for instance, Maurice had been entertained by young Prince Montpensier, son of Louis-Philippe and fellow student at the *collège*, George wrote him: "However nice the son of a king, remember that he is destined to be a tyrant, and we are destined to be demeaned, repulsed and persecuted by him." Knowing it would please his mother, the lad stoutly replied: "Never fear . . . the blood that flows in my veins and yours, my dear old Georges, forbids my liking aristocrats. . . . But my father was happy when I went [to the prince's ball], and said it would help me when I was grown and wanted employ in the government. I did not say anything, but inside me I said, 'NO, NO! . . . long live *la République, la justice, l'égalité,* long live my dear old George, my dear old Michel!'"[16]

The unpleasantness of the public hearings, the notoriety suffered by George Sand, painfully emerge from the correspondence between mother and son. Immediately after the La Châtre decision in May and shortly before his thirteenth birthday, Maurice wrote to her: "The other day at school a boy said that D'Arago, he meant Arago, was my father and your husband. They said all kinds of things, because you are a woman who writes and because you are not an old mare like the other mothers. . . . I can't tell you the word they used. P——— [*putain,* whore]. There, I said it. But you have to know what goes on in my heart. It's the heart of a good son and a real friend." He would also be "a true friend and a true son" for his father, the boy touchingly added, then closed: "I am at Didier's now. He will send you the letter."[17] It was Maurice's day out from school.

* * *

Waiting for the final hearing at Bourges, George Sand worked on an edition of her *Collected Works,* reworked the "infamous" *Lélia,* eliminating personal passages and changing the ending, and wrote to her friends—to Liszt, Marie d'Agoult and Charles Didier.

Too frequent appearances with Michel may have been thought by George Sand too prejudicial for her approaching trial at Bourges. On the other hand, there may well have been an emotional lull in their liaison. The second interlude, like the first, was largely filled by Didier, though he had received few letters from George in May, and noted in his *Diary* on the twenty-eighth: "I think all is over between us."

June 1836: "Letter from her. Harsh answer from me, more in form than substance. . . . Her reply the 15th. Terrible! I'm thunderstruck. . . . She is breaking with me, in tears. I do not reply, but leave for La Châtre."

The "terrible" letter George wrote Didier has never been found. The letter she addressed him the same evening, he never received—he had already left. For Didier, George had written, intimate friendship was "a contract with clauses." For George, it was "an embracing and an identity." Didier claimed he was very fond of her, then attributed to her "calculation . . . a kind of prostitution of the heart." As for the handsome Swiss, George arrowed this remark: "The *beautiful* is not always the *good*." His jealousy was intolerable. She had no need of such friends. "I ask the support of no one, neither to kill someone for me, gather a bouquet, correct a proof, nor to go with me to the theater. I go there on my own, as a man, by choice; and when I want flowers, I go on foot, by myself, to the Alps. . . . If ever I have a name, it will be entirely of my own making."[18]

Meantime, Didier had been on his way to George. His *Diary* resumed (June 1836): "Miserable trip, inner struggles, perplexities. I arrive the 18th. She is asleep. I wake her and throw myself into her arms without speaking. She clasps me in her arms and the reconciliation is achieved in that long, silent embrace. No words of explanation between us until evening at Nohant, where she took me. I spend five days with her, which are the most pleasant of my life. . . . riding in the woods . . . the world forgotten, country solitude, evenings under the trees . . . moonlight. Alone, alone together, fifteen, twenty hours. Nights on the terrace, chats in starlight, my arm around her, her head on my chest. I would have been very happy if the name of Michel had never been pronounced. But it was, and a shadow fell. . . . I see all her friends of the Black Valley—Duteil, the Madagascan, etc., etc. . . . Intoxicated, charmed, happy, I am lost in delicious intimacy. . . . We love each other a thousand times more than before. Michel is very jealous of me. He says so in all his letters."[19]

An interlude of five days. On June twenty-third, Didier departed for Paris. A few letters from George. Then silence.

* * *

Alone now, George walked during the warm nights, chased butterflies at noon. One hot day she plunged into the river Indre fully clothed, emerged, walked on, plunged in again, this time stripping herself to her petticoat. Three, four times, three, four leagues, always on foot. "Such are my secrets of happiness," she wrote Marie d'Agoult. "If one day you find yourself alone, which I neither wish nor believe possible for you, remember them." She was about to leave for Bourges, for the trial, for Michel. Was not Michel on her mind, when she continued to Marie?—

"Those devoted to the noblest principles are often the rudest and most bitter, because of their sickening disappointments. We esteem and admire them, but we can no longer love them. . . . I've had my belly-full of *great men* (if you'll forgive the expression). I would like to see them all in Plutarch, where their personal side can do no harm. Let them be carved in marble and cast in bronze, and let us hear no more of them. While they live, they are wicked, persecuting, moody, despotic, bitter and suspicious. In their arrogant scorn, they confound sheep and goats. They behave worse with friends than with enemies. God keep us from them!"[20]

And George left for Bourges.

People arrived early at court to ensure themselves a seat, or a place to stand, on July 25, 1836. By the time George reached the scene, the courtroom was packed tight, especially with women. She observed the public's surprise at her dress, its expectation of someone "in red pants and pistols in her belt."[21] Carefully she had appareled herself, a reporter noted, "with a great deal of simplicity in a white dress, white hood, flowing white lace collar and flowered shawl."[22] And modestly lowered veil. All her friends had come in her support—the Duteils, the Rollinats, Planet, Papet, Regnault, her "dear Berrichon group." There was a parade of seventeen witnesses, only four for Casimir. Boucoiran's testimony concerning Claire was most telling, Michel's summing up most eloquent.

Casimir's lawyer, Thiot-Varennes, pleaded along the lines of his La Châtre performance, then dramatically addressed George Sand for the court's—and the public's—benefit. Return to the conjugal home, he adjured her. Only there would she find refuge and salvation for her torment and errors. "The pages you have written show the bitterness and regrets which are devouring your soul. . . . You have searched for happiness and found it nowhere. Now I would like to indicate the right road: return to your husband, return to the roof of those first peaceful years, become again a wife and mother, return to the path of duty and virtue. Submit to the gentle laws of Nature, for outside them all is error and disappointment, and there alone will you find peace and happiness."[23]

To this nineteenth-century rhetoric and moralizing, and to Casimir's preceding bill of plaints about his wife's loose behavior, Michel de Bourges replied with high scorn and his own rhetoric. If indeed Madame Dudevant were "no better than the prostitute painted by Monsieur Dudevant," how could he possibly want her back? And if she was not as her husband represented her, then why the absurd gesture of forgiveness? In truth, Madame Dudevant had bravely left the conjugal "roof of debauchery" to make her living in the world by writing, "while Monsieur Dudevant enjoyed the wealth of his wife"—a fortune he had gained simply by marrying her. The defense counsel had said that George Sand would be a bad mother, because of her libertarian novels and well-known views? What then of Diderot, "glory of the past," author, it is true, of a few licentious pages, but famous for having been a fine example of a father?[24]

The judges withdrew. On July twenty-sixth, they announced their indecision—they were evenly divided. The public, now demonstratively for George Sand, expressed its indignation. The case was adjourned for further consideration.

The following day, however, Casimir withdrew his appeal, discountenanced by the public reaction. Two days afterwards he signed a final agreement with a weary Aurore. George Sand to her mother Sophie: "I abandon to him the revenue of Hôtel de Narbonne, on the condition that he pays for the education of Maurice [in Casimir's custody]. . . . I keep Nohant [and its revenues] and my daughter. . . . I will see my son whenever I wish. . . .

"So, here I am—free at last!"[25]

With Solange, George returned to Nohant, now indisputably hers. It was Sunday. The villagers were celebrating the feast of Sainte-Anne, their patron saint, and were dancing under the great elms in the little square before Nohant's gate when she arrived.

24

Arrivals and Departures

Deliberately, women are given a deplorable education—
and *that* is the crime inflicted upon them by men.
—George Sand, *Third Letter to Marcie* (1837)[1]

To Charles Didier, George Sand wrote of a trip she was about to take
with Michel de Bourges. She was free at last for the open life together
he had promised. The trip, however, was never taken, the promise at
best was postponed. In sharp disappointment George mentioned her
chagrin to Charles d'Aragon, who had announced his own plans for
marriage. "I, too," she said, "had a dream of similar happiness, but no
longer believe in it, and have the good sense not to hope for it." The
last is less true. Michel was not a lost hope.

As she wrote to d'Aragon, she listened with compensatory content to
Maurice and Solange "snoring" in bed beside her. At school the boys
had continued ragging Maurice about his mother, retailing what they—
or their parents—had read in the *Gazette des Tribunaux* about the testimony at the separation trial. The poor lad had written his mother:
"The *Gazette* said that one day in Bordeaux you had met some young
men and did what a good wife should never do, and when you came
back, you told your husband, who forgave you, and lately you did the
same thing in Italy. . . ." Tartly she replied that she was very vexed
that he should gossip about his mother with his schoolmates. He
should treat them with "contemptuous silence," and read the *Gazette
du Berri*, which she was enclosing, for a truer account. The letter to
Maurice was opened by the headmaster, who confiscated the periodical
as not fit for youthful reading.[2]

Now, with Casimir's consent, Maurice had joined Solange and his mother for the summer. But only the first days were spent at Nohant. On August 28, 1836, George, the two children and Ursule, the peasant girl of George's youth with them as the children's maid, set out for Switzerland on the long-delayed visit to Franz Liszt and Countess d'Agoult. By the time the entourage reached Geneva, however, Franz and Marie had already left for Chamonix. But they had left behind a picturesque Genevese friend, Adolphe Pictet, savant, philologist and gentleman artillery officer, to bring them to the new destination. Here at the Hôtel de l'Union of Chamonix, George opened the registry and fell upon the entry of a "Mr. Fellows," who had filled out the required information in a most Franz Liszt fashion:

Occupation: Musician-philosopher

Home: Parnassus

Arrived: From Doubt

Destination: Truth

In the same playful spirit, but with the disadvantage of all imitations, George registered herself and her brood as "Piffoël and family," coining the name from the French slang word for a rather large nose, *pif*—the mark of herself and Maurice—and added:

Occupation: Loafers

Home: Nature

Arrived: From God

Destination: Heaven

Date of Passport: Eternity

Issued by: Public Opinion[3]

The Piffoëls rushed to the suite of the Fellows, and when the chambermaid saw Mr. Fellows warmly embrace "Mr." Piffoël, she thought she had lost her senses. Then when Liszt's young pupil, "Puzzi" Cohen, who looked like a young lady, revealed himself as a boy to Solange, who was dressed as a boy, and all whirled from embrace to embrace, screaming with delight, even the elegant countess, the chambermaid fled, spreading word through the hotel that No. 13 was occupied by a strange tribe of men indistinguishable from women. Only the Swiss major kept his aplomb, and Marie shortly recovered hers.[4]

In this wild manner the "tribe" went on a week's excursion among the mountains of Switzerland, walking and talking, riding and talking, ever talking—of Schelling, Hegel and God. More precisely, so Major Pictet, nicknamed "The Universal One" by the Genevese, carried on, heavily, pedantically, trying to impress the famous lady novelist and his titled French friend the *comtesse*. And as Marie played the *belle dame de Paris*, George played guttersnipe and gamin in counterpoint, a cigar eternally in her mouth. Philosophy in the open air never overly pleased her, and pedantry not at all. The major's preoccupation with Schelling's phrase, "The absolute is identical only with itself"—"What can it mean?" he endlessly asked—provoked only a cruel drawing from George, which Pictet with Germanic thoroughness reproduced in his little book on the Swiss excursion, *Une Course à Chamonix*.[5] Once, standing before a mountain, the major extolled its magnificence and George responded: "Can you conceive anything more stupid than a mountain?"—and challenged him to a race up its side. At another time, the major typically intoned—out of Aristotle—"Art is imitation," and George cuttingly replied: "Art is creation."[6]

When they reached Fribourg and its celebrated cathedral organ, Franz Liszt came into his own. Each had his or her turn: in the major's book Marie is all "grace" versus George's "strength," "reflective intelligence" versus the latter's "spontaneity and genius."[7] Liszt was the "spirit of music" as he filled the cathedral with Mozart's *Dies Irae*. George noted the Dantesque, "Florentine profile" of the performer and mused on the music: the Day of Wrath would strike down the grandees of the earth, but she would be among the common people, who alone would pass on Judgment Day.[8] God was invariably on George's side.

On the return of Fellows and Piffoëls to Geneva, a more stately round of theaters and concerts and salons followed. The curiosity about these Bohemians was intense and the local gazettes were full of the event of George Sand's arrival. On the whole it was a happy visit. One evening at home, Liszt played a *Rondo Fantastique* he had just composed, based on a Spanish song made popular by Malibran, a contralto George admired. That night, as all slept, she wrote a counterpart in poetic prose, *Le Contrebandier*, and read it to the group the next day. Neither Liszt's nor George's composition (it pleased Marie to note) was up to the best work of its authors.[9] Nor did Liszt's dedication of his piece to George Sand aid in Marie's appreciation. Franz had long since twitted his companion for her burgeoning sense of rivalry, saying the "laurels" of George Sand kept her "from sleeping."[10]

Marie's self-perception and understanding win respect, however, since it was she who quoted this remark to George Sand—and George who had generously replied: "Write, by all means, write!"[11] Before the Chamonix excursion, Marie had asked herself whether she would please or displease her Nohant friend. The anxiety, Marie wrote in her memoirs, "made me cold and awkward when she did come. Then her childish pranks put me off. I felt ill at ease and consequently was not very friendly. It made me sad, because I passionately desired her friendship.[12]

The parting of the Piffoëls and Fellows nevertheless was quite amiable, if not as enthusiastic as arrival day at the Hôtel de l'Union. They would see each other very soon in Paris, each promised. George had another preoccupation. She had written Michel several times, asking him to come to Geneva, but for one reason or another, never specified, he did not. She wrote again as she was leaving Switzerland, arranging for their meeting in Lyons en route. With the two children—and a new admirer, twenty-two-year-old Gustave de Gévaudan, who had trailed along from Geneva—George awaited Michel in Lyons. He never arrived. In sadness and anger she left for Nohant. There she found a letter from Michel—"the kind of letter an old banker might have written to his kept woman." After so many weeks of "hoping and yearning" for him in Geneva, she had eagerly waited for him in Lyons, to which she had come "filled with poetry and fire." But no Michel. No, "according to your Pasha views, I was supposed to go to you with the obedience of an odalisque." Michel had heard of her young companion, Gévaudan, and accused her of gross infidelity. "That child of twenty [sic]—shy, good, insouciant, loving to hunt but above all to sleep! . . ." How could Michel?

George's long, impassioned letter to Michel, mid-October 1836, contains passages of astonishing, if self-justifying, frankness:

> I have told you once and for all that if ever I had the misfortune of being unfaithful to you—out of weariness, physical weakness or morbid desire—I would confess my failing and leave you master of your decision to punish me by putting me out of your mind forever. . . . [But] rancor to that extent would be punishment out of all proportion to the crime, admittedly vulgar but also forgivable, since you yourself have committed it regularly with your wife ever since we have belonged to each other.

George would be sorry if it meant the end, but she was no more prepared to wear sackcloth and ashes than Michel and a "good many other 'respectable' men" who have done the same thing "a thousand times." She protested her own innocence, but continued:

> I do not hide from you, however, that I suffered a great deal from my chastity. I have had very exhausting dreams. The blood has rushed to my head a hundred times. In the midst of the mountains when the sun was high and I listened to the song of the birds and smelled the perfumes of the valley, I often sat apart from my companions—my soul full of love, my knees trembling with voluptuous desire. I am still young, though I tell other men that I have attained the tranquillity of age. There is still fire in my blood. In the presence of an intoxicatingly beautiful nature, love [desire] stirs in me like the sap of life in the universe.

I can still walk ten leagues in a day, and at night, when I
fall into bed at an inn, still dream of a loved man's body as
the only pillow for the repose of body and soul.

The occasion, said George, never lacked. There were always many men
about her, "younger than you," whom a single inviting look would have
brought running. But . . .

It is of you I dream when I wake drenched with sweat, you
whom I call upon when nature sings her hymnals of passion in
my ear, when the mountain air pricks my flesh with a thousand needles of desire.[13]
Is this the language of a 'frigid' woman?

Michel, with his "Pasha views" of her going humbly to him, might
consider joining her in Paris next week. She would be staying, George
said blandly, with Didier, since she no longer possessed the Malaquais
apartment. Was the frankness to allay all suspicion and remove jealousy
on the part of Michel, or frankness for its own sake? In fact, it was more
than the truth, and the "frankness" may have been to *provoke* jealousy.
For Didier waited in vain for George's arrival at his place.

On October twenty-fourth he had a note from her. She had indeed
arrived in Paris, but she was staying at the Hôtel de France, where Liszt
and Marie d'Agoult had taken a suite. George Sand had installed herself on the floor below; they shared the large salon. Didier saw her the
morning after her arrival. "Her Bohemian side," he deplored, "always
wins."[14]

It was Bohemianism on the highest level Marie d'Agoult could hope
to aspire. Rejected by the aristocratic Faubourg Saint-Germain society
of her pre-Swiss flight, the countess was determined, on her return to
Paris, to create another salon of literary and artistic lights. The invitation to George Sand to preside alongside her in the shared drawing
room was part of the plan. They already enjoyed in common a number
of notable friends—Meyerbeer, Lamennais, Heine, Eugène Sue, Pierre
Leroux. The few faithful of her former world followed Marie to the
new salon—Countess Charlotte Marliani, colorful French wife of the
Spanish consul, eminent among them. Liszt, too, attracted his literary
and musical circle, particularly the Polish group—Count Albert
Grzymala, poet Adam Mickiewicz and the reclusive, sought-after pianist-
composer, young Frédéric Chopin.

The initiative had come from George Sand. She had asked Liszt soon
after her arrival to ensure Chopin's presence. Chopin had at first refused. He did not, he said, like "bluestockings." He was frail, fastidious
and snobbish. Liszt bided his time. He chose a day when Chopin, in an
exceptionally social mood, invited Franz and Marie for a musical soirée

in his apartment. They brought George with them. Chopin played. George listened, silently, intensely. "From that day Chopin became a familiar figure in the salon of the Hôtel de France."[15] There were musical soirées *chez* Marie and Chopin, where he and Liszt played together, George in her Turkish costume and slippers, smoking her long pipe, listening. But Chopin, if not George, shrank from any intimacy, and again it is Didier's *Diary* which adds the poignant note.

November 21, 1836: "She was cold and indifferent. . . . Liszt plays his Swiss pieces. My heart was so heavy I burst into tears in the middle of the drawing room." George received Didier four nights later at midnight. "The night ended with horrible accountings and appalling confessions. What she told me froze my blood, instead of giving me new life, so that I lay beside her as one dead." George Sand, Didier decided, had no heart. She had no heart for him. Thus no heart. She was cruel, because he loved her and she not him.[16] "He who loves less," George in turn would write Michel, "is always master of the other."[17] There are those who love, said Thackeray, and those who tolerate being loved. When the forbearance wears thin, the heart hardens. Thus Didier accused George Sand, thus George Sand would accuse Michel de Bourges.

The remainder of the year was passed in Paris. There was an evening with Musset about the exchange of their letters. George felt quite "cured" of her love for Alfred, she told Didier. (So much, he noted in his diary, for the great passions.) And there was an earlier, perhaps more moving, evening at a joint concert of Berlioz and Liszt, who played the piano part of the exuberant *Grande Fantaisie Symphonique*, based on a Berlioz theme. George sat with Meyerbeer, who squeezed her hand sympathetically as she felt slightly ill. Franz had his usual success with the Parisian audience, as always responsive to virtuoso playing. George was not unaware of Liszt's faults, though less perhaps than his sharper critics who wrote of his *"grimaces," "contorsions grotesques"* and even of his *"charlatanisme musical."* Liszt himself would later confess to having been too easily seduced by his audience in his younger years.[18]

Of more personal concern for George Sand was Maurice's chronic, feverish ill health, which affected his heart. The boy still suffered the torments of his schoolmates and reacted sensitively to them. His mother thought it better to remove him from the Paris school and have him tutored at Nohant. Casimir, at first opposed, finally agreed. Before he might change his mind again, George engaged a tutor, adding to her heavy expenses. Money more than ever was the subject of quarrels with her publisher Buloz, all the more surprising when one considers the productivity and success of her work. As 1836 came to an end, the first of twenty-four volumes of George Sand's *Collected Works* began to appear—this exactly five years after she had begun her first independent novel, *Indiana!* Yet, other than to her publisher, the event was scarcely mentioned. Modesty about her work would always be her trademark.

Life was the pressing concern. "Could you accord me but a quarter hour?" George wrote Michel as the new year of 1837 began. She would be stopping off at Bourges on her way to Nohant. She knew, George said, Michel was involved in yet another affair. He could be frank with her, but surely they should meet. "I cannot believe you are as frightened of me as you are of your wife."[19]

They met several times during the two days at Bourges with the usual passion followed by the customary reproaches. Michel again accused George of infidelities with her companion of Geneva, Gévaudan, skating over his own peccadilloes. In reply George gave Michel two letters she had just received from Gévaudan to prove their innocence. Had she, she asked, reproached Michel for anything? Rather, she had told him, "be happy!"[20] She and Maurice went on to Nohant. From there George wrote, "There is only one reality, one certainty: I love you, Michel."[21]

The tutor for Maurice arrived, Eugène Pelletan, whom George dubbed "the Pelican." He was solemn and somewhat sluggish, though in his early twenties. He would prove unsatisfactory, but for several months George could devote herself to *Mauprat*, a novel that increasingly gripped her. It went beyond the original concept and grew in length and importance. Published, it became a striking forerunner of Emily Brontë's *Wuthering Heights*, which appeared ten years later. It might have been read by Emily, as it undoubtedly had been by her older sister Charlotte, who regularly read the *Revue des Deux Mondes*. No woman aspiring to writing would have missed reading George Sand. The similarities of the two novels are remarkable; so are the differences. There is the same principal theme of the transformation of a man by a woman, a form of the legendary Beauty and the Beast.[22] As Brontë's Heathcliff, Sand's earlier hero, Mauprat, is described in literal, animal metaphors—"wounded wolf," "bear," "wild falcon," "slumbering lion . . . transformed by a fairy."[23] The terms are gentler than Emily Brontë's "fierce, pitiless, wolfish man," a mad dog who prowls about like "an evil beast."[24] The differences were personal and social. George Sand had loved, made love and been loved by an Aurélien de Sèze, an Alfred de Musset. Emily Brontë had not. In Sand's novel, Mauprat's "transforming fairy" is his cousin Edmée; they marry and live long and happily together. Brontë's *Wuthering Heights* is a tragedy, for both man and woman. George had known French society, particularly the Paris salon with its civilized discourse between men and women, even though the inferiority of women was sometimes the subject. Emily had not. There was violence in the suffragette movement of England, whereas in France *féminisme* has been largely literary protest rather

13. Portrait of Countess Marie d'Agoult, courtesy of Bulloz

14. George Sand by Auguste Charpentier, courtesy of Françoise Foliot

15. George Sand by Alfred de Musset, courtesy of Françoise Foliot

16. George Sand by Alfred de Musset, courtesy of Françoise Foliot

17. Pietro Pagello by Bevila
courtesy of Françoise Foliot

18. Michel de Bourges, courtesy
of Françoise Foliot

19. Pierre Leroux by Marin Lavigne, courtesy of Françoise Foliot

20. Casimir Dudevant by Maurice Sand, courtesy of Françoise Foliot

21. Frédéric Chopin by Delacroix, courtesy of Bulloz

22. Maurice Sand, George Sand's son, by Josephine Calamatta, courtesy of Françoise Foliot

than confrontation politics, the latter inevitable where incommunicability between the sexes is so marked.

George was writing *Mauprat* even as she sent despairing letters to Michel. Her life was still both Aeolian web and harp. If the description of Mauprat's happily married life occurs briefly at the end of the novel, as in a fairy tale, it is nonetheless moving. It had been the ideal George and Michel had envisioned in the passion of the previous spring. And George refused to abandon it without a final, determined effort. She did not believe in leaving anything vital to chance. The arrival of Marie d'Agoult early in February at Nohant was no interruption.

Franz Liszt, nursing a career threatened by the newly popular Austrian pianist Thalberg, was busy with concerts in Paris and joined them at Nohant three weeks later. He and Marie were experiencing their own problem of clashing temperaments. For Marie there was "forgetfulness and peace" in the long rides she took with George along the banks of the Indre River and across "the flowering meadows of forget-me-nots."[25] When the way was difficult, George would descend and lead Marie's horse by hand. There was kindness and coquettishness in the act, a Sandian mélange to which were added Michel and a new figure. "Tell Chopin," George wrote Liszt, "that I beg, I supplicate him to come with you, that Marie cannot live without him and I adore him."[26] Michel in the meantime was ill or "sulking," in any case, not writing.[27]

It was a full February—fullness always finds room for more, emptiness never. When last in Paris, George had been easily persuaded by Abbé Lamennais to contribute to *Le Monde*, a journal he had just taken over. In Nohant she immediately began a series of *Lettres à Marcie*, the correspondence of a man counseling a young woman without fortune on love, marriage and much else "feminine." The first fictional letter appeared in mid-February, two quickly followed. They aroused the ecclesiastic's abiding suspicion of women in Lamennais and an uneasiness about the "indelicate" problems discussed. When George Sand proposed as her seventh *Lettre à Marcie* the bold advocacy of divorce—"I see no other solution but freedom to dissolve and remake marriages"[28]—the good Abbé balked. Unknown to George, he had already censored passages of the third letter—and the discovery of it greatly upset her.

"She had written him a very proper, very affectionate letter," Marie informed Franz Liszt, "saying she could not continue writing for him in the dark. . . . To this he replied quite coldly. He wanted nothing to do with divorce. All he asked from her were flowery little things, such as tales and other amusing items. . . . George is very annoyed."[29]

The Abbé suspended the Sand series with the sixth *Lettre à Marcie*, though they had proved very successful. It's somewhat of a miracle that they had appeared at all in his paper. The sixth spoke out sharply against the male plot to stifle women's intellectual growth in order the more easily to dominate them. "Deliberately," it read, "women are given a deplorable education—and *that* is the crime inflicted upon them by men. . . . The only recourse left a woman has been religion. While man frees himself from constraining civil and religious bonds, he is only too glad to have women hold tightly to the Christian principle of suffering and keeping her silence."[30]

The third *Letter to Marcie*, mutilated by Lamennais' excisions, though longer than the others, was left distorted and deformed.[31] Nevertheless, it disclosed the larger view of a George Sand less interested in promoting women's rights than humanity's, believing mankind's necessarily preceded women's. "How," she asked, "could any woman, in our time, achieve such rights on her own?" And were there not even greater concerns? "The people are hungry: let our bright spirits allow us to dream of bread for the people before dreaming of building them temples. Women cry out against slavery: let them wait until mankind is free, for slavery cannot give birth to freedom." Only art—literature, music, painting—remained open to women; and she who chose the free life of the artist closed her *Letter to Marcie* counseling wedlock and motherhood.[32]

As February ended, Liszt arrived. Without Chopin. The week of his stay he was nervous, preoccupied and capricious, brooding over his return to Paris for the resumed piano duel with Thalberg. When George invited her Berrichon friends to hear him play, as he said he would, it was fairly certain he would not, and when it was announced he would not play, "he took it into his head to sit down and improvise."[33] Charles Duvernet thought Liszt a poseur and described an evening at Nohant: Liszt sits at the piano, his flowing hair like a ruffled lion's mane; he looks at the ceiling for inspiration, then drops his hands nonchalantly on the keys; discords precede a prelude that never takes place; "suddenly he rises, closes the piano noisily and declares, 'The bear will not dance this evening!' "[34]

After Liszt left for Paris, Marie followed to be with him for a few weeks. George was alone at Nohant with Maurice—and she wrote Michel. She was in torment, she said, not only because of the young woman in his household with whom he was having an affair ("tell me it is only fatherly love, tell me that and I will believe it!") But because of something else she had heard when she had passed through Bourges: that Michel had become infatuated with a "repulsively fat" woman. "Does she satisfy your physical needs as any streetwalker might? Alas, I am younger than you and with hotter blood." When desire seized her, she had herself bled. "The doctor tells me it is a crime, a form of suicide and, besides, no relief for me. What I need is a lover. . . . If only you swore to me that you prefer me to all the others, that no one else can give you the pleasures you say you find in my arms! . . . It is odious for me to think of your body, so beautiful, so adored, so deeply impregnated with my kisses, so often brought close to death by my love and revived by my lips, so often bruised and crushed in our lovemaking. . . . Oh, where are my memories taking me!"

To love, said George, was her destiny. "It is God's will and Nature's wish—one and the same necessity." It is Michel she loves, without the reservations she has always known. And he, knowing this? "You will continue to abuse me, because you are a man, and however righteous you may be, you will sacrifice me for a passing passion, the claim of society, the fraudulent goods of life."[35]

The letter was barely dispatched when George sent another, begging Michel's pardon, pleading for a moment with him—"a day, an hour." "Since you are unfaithful to me, you can certainly be unfaithful to the other one. . . . I'll go anywhere you wish." Anywhere, she implored, but Bourges. "There for some devilish caprice, you took me into the house of your wife and showed me your nuptial bed." It was an example, George said bitterly, of Michel's desire to impose an "absolute, brutal dominium" reminiscent of a "barbarian age." But the next day she was writing: "I want to bring you happiness . . . also pleasure, because I know you like pleasure, and I know how to give it to you!"[36] George's surrender of identity seems complete in her confusion of sex and love: she would do as Michel wished, she would go humbly to him in Bourges.

However, to Marie d'Agoult, George sent a note saying she must see the Fellows and their friends, Mickiewicz, Grzymala, Chopin. "Tell him I idolize him!" Marie was expected to bring them all with her on her return to Nohant.[37] "Chopin," Marie replied, "coughs with infinite grace," but would come.[38] He would not; he went instead to London.[39]

Michel and George met in Bourges, under the acacias of Nohant, and at points in between. But Michel was a much-married man, and each meeting with George, he told her, cost him two weeks of discomfort. Besides, he complained jealously, Gévaudan was now a guest at Nohant. He was awaiting Franz and Marie, George replied. At least the jealousy between the two was equal, the one as justified as the other. Had Michel chosen to venture on the life together he had promised, however, it might have been different; although he obviously thought otherwise, either because it would compromise his career, or because the submissiveness he demanded, he was aware, could never be assured, no matter what George in all sincerity wrote. She would be a Biblical wife, she often told him. But there was—he knew—the irrepressible George Sand of the feminist novels and strong statements. In a letter to a mutual friend at this time, George spoke almost stoically of Michel's having a new mistress and her acceptance of it, but lines later there is her solemn "pledge": "I will raise women from their abjection, both by my example and by my writings. . . . [I will be] the Spartacus of women's slavery."[40]

Yet. . . . In a week or two, George was addressing the "dear angel of my life"—Michel—on the joy of just having seen him, on having galloped seven leagues in two hours returning to Nohant, still delirious from the night with him.[41] In an existential sense there is no contradiction. It is the behavior of a Romantic, a Byron, even if in the same letter to Michel there is the expected language of a submissive, nineteenth-century woman—a language *not* characteristic of the novels, where George Sand found her true identity, if not sex or love. However, Michel, too, was cognizant of the real George Sand—from her past and his own experience. Between the days and nights "stolen" from his work, however delirious ("my body still bears the stigmata!" exults George), there were Michel's recriminations and "punishing" silences.[42] George Sand was simply too much for a man who wanted no change in the comfortable pattern he had set for himself, who was more loved than loving, though that made him, as George now remarked, "the master of the other."

"Damnation!" Michel wrote George irately, as May, 1837, drew to an end.

> Because of you, and on your account, I am at war at home every hour of the day and night. Well, that's the way life is. Nothing on earth is ever given a man without a struggle and a fight. If only I could at least find a refuge in your arms from this wretched situation, an asylum. But, no! You are always demanding something from me, so that I have to fight against you, too.
>
> An enemy to the right of me, an enemy to the left of me. The position can't be held.
>
> I would have joined the Trappist monks a long time ago, if I believed in those———.
>
> I must live in peace and quiet. Any fight with a woman is unspeakable. It was not given me to fight with enemies of my own stature—tyrants. Well then, let me at least know absolute, profound tranquillity. . . .
>
> I am going to settle down in a cabin on the side of a hill under figs, pines and almonds within sight of the Mediterranean.[43]

The reply of George Sand was swift and sharp:

> Whenever I tell you the truth, whenever I ask for the reciprocity of feeling without which love is as unbearable a yoke

as marriage, you flare up and insult me in the most wounding words you can find. You are really saying that loving a woman is unworthy of you! . . .

Then the attitude and tone changed:

> You threaten to go off and live in a hut. God would be good to me if He granted your wish. I would soon join you. You would find in me the devoted black slave to care for your poor, tired body, the faithful dog happy at least to be useful and appreciated. Soon you would learn that the love of a woman is not something "unspeakable," and that the men of clay with whom you regret not being able to measure yourself, are not, and never will be, equal to you.[44]

Would that this had been written in irony, rather than in the humbling, humiliating courtship of a man by a woman. George's state was observed and described by Marie, again at Nohant, in her diary. "June 5th: all evening George has been as if numbed, in a state of leaden non-being. Poor, great woman! The sacred flame which God has lighted in her no longer finds anything outside herself to feed upon and now consumes all that remains of faith, hope and youth within her. Charity, love, voluptuous desire, those three aspirations of the soul, heart and senses, all of them too ardent in this gifted, destined nature, have encountered doubt, disappointment and satiety, and driven deep into the depths of her being, are making her life a martrydom. . . ." A *man* of comparable genius, such as Goethe, Marie d'Agoult perceptively observed, "could embrace all in the immensity of his love," and the countess closes: "Dear God, grant to George Goethe's serenity!"[45] It was a good deal to ask, even of God, for a woman in the fire and prime of her life. George was thirty-two. It would be many years before Nohant would become her Weimar.

On the evening described by Marie, George was writing Michel: "Man wants to possess in order to destroy. . . . My heart overflows with love, but my mind is full of memories and past experience. Never have I felt so intensely the need to be loved as I love. Never have I felt more irrevocably that it is impossible.

"Come to me! You, at least, will be happy, for *you* are loved as much as any man might wish. If I see you happy, I will forget that I am not."[46]

A rendezvous was arranged some distance from Nohant. After a night's reflection, George canceled it. "I am too ill," she wrote Michel in a brief note—and so she was. "I cannot travel in the heat of tomorrow and do not have the strength to set off tonight. I would arrive exhausted. I don't believe you would find much pleasure in having me thus in your arms at the inn."[47]

It was the last letter, though it was not quite the end. George left a few days later to see Michel in Bourges, and this time the testimony of her resolution in the aftermath is in the pages she wrote *for herself*—the imaginary dialogues with "Dr. Piffoël," published after her death. The contrast between the woman writing Michel and the woman addressing herself is striking. The forced humbleness completely disappears: she is herself.

"Piffoël, Piffoël!" George wrote at dawn on June eleventh. "What a frightening calm is yours! Has the torch indeed been extinguished? Hail, Piffoël, full of grace, wisdom has become yours! . . . Holy weariness, mother of rest, descend upon us poor dreamers, now and in the hour of our death. Amen." And on June 13, 1837:

> Must one be, for one's beloved, as blind, as devoted, as tireless as a solicitous mother for her first-born? No, Piffoël, there is no need for all that, and all that is to no avail if love is lacking.
>
> You believe, Piffoël, that one can say to the object of one's love, "You are a being like myself. I chose you from among all humans because I thought you were the greatest and the best. Today I no longer know what you are. It seems to me you have dark spots in your character like other men, for you often make me suffer and perfection is in no man. But I love your flaws, I love my sufferings, I prefer your faults to the virtues of others. I accept you. I *have* you, and you have me, for I hold nothing back. . . ."
>
> No, Piffoël, no! Doctor of Psychology you may be, but you are a fool. That is not the language a man wants to hear. He completely despises devotion, because he believes it his natural right by the simple fact of having emerged from the womb of Madame, His Mother. . . . To dominate, to possess, to absorb, these are the conditions he accepts for himself—to be adored as a God. . . .
>
> Woman has only one way of lightening her yoke, of holding on to her tyrant, when that tyrant is necessary to her. That is to flatter him basely. Her submission, her faithfulness, her devotion, her care, have no value in his eyes. Without that, he tells us, he would not burden himself with a woman at all. . . .
>
> No, my dear Piffoël, learn the scientific truth about life, and when you write your novels, try to read the human heart a little better. Never take as your ideal woman someone who is strong-minded, disinterested, courageous and frank. The pub-

lic will whistle derisively at you and call you by the odious name of *Lélia the Impotent!*

Impotent? Yes, by God! Impotent when it comes to servility, impotent in adulation, impotent in baseness, impotent when it comes to fearing you [man]—stupid beast, who would not have the courage to kill, if there were no laws punishing murder by murder,* who find your strength and vengeance only in calumny and defamation! But when you find a female who knows how to do without you, then your vain power turns to fury, and your fury is punished by a smile, a farewell, an eternal forgetfulness.[48]

Farewell, Lélia. Farewell, Michel! They would meet again, they would make love, but it *was* farewell.

* George Sand strongly opposed capital punishment.

25

The Odds and Ends of Art and Life

The same weeks of farewell in June 1837, George Sand was finding solace in the music of Franz Liszt and the companionship of young, admiring men. From the bedroom on the ground floor, which she had redecorated for Marie and Franz, she often heard the music in her bedroom just above as she communed with "Dr. Piffoël." The notes silenced the "jealous" nightingales and set the linden leaves dancing and vibrating. "When Franz plays the piano, I am comforted. All pain is transformed into poetry." As herself, Liszt was transcribing to paper with the artist's resource the final, captured phrase, containing, calming, resolving the interior storm.[1]

George noted Liszt's own "melancholy," his "secret wound," the artist's lot. In the case of Franz, a restless twenty-five, and Marie d'Agoult, thirty-one, the wound opening between them was personal as well. It was not the gap in age, though it played its part. It was more the exigent, severely critical turn of Marie's mind. She was conscious of it and the self-awareness, as she wrote a friend, Louis de Ronchaud, when at Nohant without Liszt, was like a "serpent's poisonous fang ever slumbering in my heart. . . . Believe me, never throw yourself into the arms of a woman, asking her for anything you do not find in yourself. You will dream of heaven, as you lie next to her, and hear the angels . . . and then you will realize it is all an elusive, passing shadow, and you will be left alone to cry like a child, or blaspheme like an old man."[2]

There is an acerbity here that has an appeal, a realism verging on modern cynicism, but also a lack of generosity, a dryness of spirit in striking contrast to George Sand's. Love is dead? "Then, long live love!" cried George. That capacity for love was essentially her capacity for life, her openness to all experience. "Your penchant towards severity," Liszt would remark to Marie shortly before they parted, "grows by leaps and bounds."[3]

Scarcely a word from George Sand revealed her knowledge of *that* wound appearing in the relations of Franz and Marie during the spring and summer of 1837. Rather, she scolded Liszt for his ingratitude: "Happy man to be loved by a beautiful, generous, intelligent, chaste woman. What more could you ask for, ungrateful wretch! Ah, if only *I* were loved!"[4] A proof of George's generosity was her calling Marie, Comtesse d'Agoult, generous.

However, these were the soft, spring evenings at Nohant, warm with friendship and George's hospitality. Actor Pierre Bocage had arrived from Paris; Charles Didier was expected. It was the very eve of George's farewell to Michel, though her guests could not have suspected it from her manner. "That evening, while Franz was playing one of Schubert's most fairylike songs"—based on Goethe's haunting *Der Erlkönig*—Marie d'Agoult, still "the Princess" for George, floated about the group on the terrace, dressed in a pale-white gown, her head draped in a long white veil falling to her feet. She well knew the effect and all eyes were upon her as the music swelled and the moon set, outlining the linden trees and Marie's shadowy figure. It was a stately dance to Schubert's music, ending on the hushed note of the child's death and Marie, looking like a "medieval Lady," disappeared in the salon of the Nohant manor house.[5]

The flattering description is entirely George Sand's, yet there was an entente between Franz and herself which Marie resented. More than once, when they were tête-à-tête, Marie would interrupt with a cry to Franz Liszt, "Time to work, lazy one!"[6] In fact, when the others had retired for the night, that was often what they did together, facing each other across the same table. One such night, George finished *Mauprat* and immediately began a new novel, *Les Maîtres Mosaïstes*. Venice was its scene, the city's mosaic masters its subject. It was written, said George, for Maurice's pleasure. The performance of ending one novel and promptly beginning another was awesome. Meantime that summer Liszt was working hard on his transcriptions—virtual orchestral scores for two pianos—of Beethoven's symphonies, completing the First, Second, Fifth and Sixth.[7]

The visit of Bocage to Nohant was brief, as if to clear the stage of the handsome actor for the arrival of Charles Didier on June fifteenth. However, George's welcome was at the least "embarrassed." She had not expected him quite so soon. Didier was only somewhat assuaged by the sympathy and friendship of Franz and especially Marie. Didier's *Diary*, June seventeenth: "Bad day. George talks to me in that unpleasant, teasing way which irritated me so much in Paris. She is cold and reserved." Two days later: "I made an enormous mistake coming here. She is ice."[8] The Swiss gentleman went riding with Marie, and almost wept from the memory of an earlier ride with George. Marie herself rather coolly noted in *her* diary, with the eye of the future novelist, the behavior of the rejected lover: the forehead flushing at the "slightest word" of George, the withdrawal behind the "gold-rimmed glasses," the darting looks at his fellow guests to check fearfully on their "facial expressions," the smile that would suddenly freeze on his lips "in doubt and mistrust."[9] Didier had nightmares, when he did manage to fall asleep, and morbidly fantasied killing George. Appalled, he left for a week, but things were no better when he returned.

Didier arrived at ten in the morning of July fourteenth to find all sleeping at Nohant, among them additional guests: George's old friend, François Rollinat; a new friend, Félicien Mallefille, aspiring young playwright; and a returned friend, Pierre Bocage. Didier's *Diary*: "The greeting is warm . . . but I have no illusion—she is occupied with Bocage. This rivalry with an actor wounds and disgusts me. Liszt agrees I should leave." July fifteenth: "In Marie's room. Long conversation about George Sand, whom she thinks about to embark on gallant affairs. I almost left without seeing [G.S.]. . . . 'You are not leaving, I hope?' she said. 'Yes, at once.' So our conversation went. . . . She embraced me. I kissed those great, dry, impenetrable eyes."[10]

And so Didier departed.

Neither Franz nor Marie could resist bantering George about Bocage and, more annoyingly, provoking the actor, a rather stupid fellow, to go beyond the bounds in his behavior. George, late one night, left a note for Marie, adjuring her to tell Franz to drop his "pleasantries" about Bocage and herself. "It vexes me to the extreme. . . . Does Bocage have the wit to take them lightly?" He did not. He was pressing more heavily than George cared, and they were, thanks to Franz and Marie (nettled by the spectacle of so many men paying court to George), on the edge of a quarrel. In such cases as a casual affair with a man like Bocage, "all goes well," George wrote Marie, "so long as everything remains in the realm of gaiety, a handshake and comradeship."[11] Otherwise, adieu Bocage. A love affair was something else; appearances became secondary. As for the *grandes passions*, all was permitted.

It was soon adieu to Franz Liszt and Marie d'Agoult. The summer flowers of friendship had faded, though the falling out was for another season. With Rollinat and Mallefille, George made a jolly excursion of their departure, accompanying them on horseback to La Châtre, where

Franz and Marie took the coach to Paris. One would like to follow them on their own destiny, to their own parting from each other, young Liszt to the fulfillment of his long career and Marie to hers, as "Daniel Stern." However, it is Marie d'Agoult's reflection on her stay at Nohant which here concerns us, for the light, though faintly green, it bears on George Sand.

"It was not useless," the countess' diary revealed, "to see George, the great poet, cheek and jowl with George the intrepid child, George the feeble woman even in her audacity, inconstant in her emotions and opinions, illogical in her life, ever influenced by the haphazard of circumstance, rarely guided by reason or past experience. I finally realized how puerile it had been of me to believe (and the thought had often flooded me with sadness) that she alone could have given Franz's life its full development, that I had been an impediment between two destinies made to merge and complete each other."[12]

Marie d'Agoult was eerily prophetic of another pair of destinies, George Sand's and Frédéric Chopin's, towards the merging of which each, the one far more warily than the other, seemed already wending. And in the same prophetic mood that issues from the penetrating intelligence of Marie d'Agoult, one plucks her observations on George Sand's two children for later recall:

"Passionate and undisciplinable, Solange is destined for the absolute, whether of good or evil. Her life will be full of struggle and battles. She will not bend to the rules of society; there will be a kind of grandeur in her errors, a sublimity in her virtues. Maurice seems to me a living antithesis of his sister. He will be a man of good sense, of social conformity, of accommodating virtues."[13]

The tutors of Maurice were of more than passing import to George Sand: they were substitute fathers who became her sons. How often she called them, *"mon enfant"*![14] But since in reality the tutors were neither, George could the more freely take them as lovers. So it was with Boucoiran; so Pelletan would claim. He did not last long enough to lend him credibility. Having quickly proved unsatisfactory, he had to be replaced. His successor was ready at hand—Félicien Mallefille. Twenty-four, author of two performed plays, he had been the protégé of Marie d'Agoult, who had presented him to George, then resented Mallefille's falling in love with her. That they did become lovers is a certainty, though it probably occurred later than Marie assumed. There was the intervening affair with Bocage, though a simultaneity is not to be excluded. Confiding Maurice to Gustave Papet, George went off with Bocage to Fontainebleau, registering as "Monsieur and Madame Gratiot" at the Hôtel Britannique, where she had stayed with Musset four years before. One lover to exorcise the ghost of another, the novelist returning to the scene for more, refreshed material? Or was it the callousness of the surgeon after many operations? The stay at Fontainebleau was intermittent: George received word from old Pierret that her mother was very ill, and she went frequently to Paris to see her.

Sophie had wasted away in a long, lingering illness, most likely cancer. George found her looking as if she were a century old. "You bring me life!" she cried to her daughter. But death was near and, sensing its approach, she said to George, "I don't want to see a priest, do you hear me? If I must go, I want gaiety around me. After all, why should I fear to face God? I've always loved him." There were days, however, of false recovery, and Sophie told George, "The next time you come, you will find me cured!" On the last day she called to George's half-sister Caroline: "Come, comb my hair! I want to look well!" She regarded herself in the mirror, she smiled, the mirror dropped from her hand, she was cured at last—"cured," says George Sand, "of the terrible weariness of living."[15] A week later, when George visited Sophie's grave and saw the butterflies fluttering among its flowers, she was "so struck by the gaiety of the Montmartre cemetery," she wondered why the tears sprang to her eyes, and flowed.[16]

It was a harrowing month, August. As Sophie lay dying, George had heard that Casimir was on his way to Nohant to carry off Maurice. Horrified, she had Mallefille bring her son to her posthaste at Fontainebleau, then discovered it had been a false alarm. However, in September Casimir came unannounced to Nohant and foolishly kidnaped *Solange*, carrying her away, crying, to his family home at Guillery, which he had just acquired on the death of Madame Dudevant. Furious, George ran around Paris from ministry to ministry, finally securing a court order for Solange's return. Leaving Maurice with Charlotte Marliani, she departed immediately for Guillery with Mallefille, arriving after a carriage ride of three days and nights. Losing no time, she hastened to the *sous-préfet* of Nérac with the court order, and then went with a police escort to Guillery, "like a Spanish Queen on Heaven knows what revolution." The people of Nérac were agog at the spectacle and followed the small parade to Casimir's house. He had been alerted and was on the point of packing off. However, the police surrounded the house and he "surrendered." "Dudevant," George recounts whimsically, "suddenly became all politeness and meekness, leading Solange to us by the hand, to the threshold of his royal residence, after having invited me to enter—which I 'graciously' refused. Solange was ceremoniously turned over to me, like a princess at the frontier between two states. The baron and I exchanged a few agreeable words, such as his threats to regain his son by a court order of his own, and so we separated, the one more charming than the other. . . . The day after, the mad impulse seized me of going on to the Pyrenees."[17]

And thus George Sand, traveling with Solange and Mallefille, went to the nearby mountains—to the Marboré *massif* and Gavarnie, to the sites she had seen with Aurélien de Sèze, this time with Mallefille. A week or two before she had been in Fontainebleau's Franchard woods with Bocage. But on her return to Nohant, she reflected that fall in her journal, and the hard, whipping lines remind one that George Sand was also the pensive, self-probing, self-critical "Dr. Piffoël":

> Recapitulate a bit what has happened to you the past three months. . . . Do you even remember? Or have you already forgotten the facts? Your mother dead, your son saved, your daughter carried off and recovered—and the rest! You have seen Franchard again, but with whom? You have seen the Marboré again, but with what? You have come back here, but what are you going to do now? What fate awaits you? Whom will you love? What sufferings will you endure? Whom will you hate next month or next year—or tomorrow? Here you are as tranquil as if your life were another's, and you sleep in your bed as soundly as Buloz in his. . . . Oh, what a beautiful soul you have, my great Piffoël! You could drink the blood of your children from the skull of your best friend and not even have a cramp. The sun could fall on your great nose and you wouldn't even sneeze. . . .[18]

Into this mood, by invitation, came Pierre Leroux, forty, messianic philosopher, one of those influential figures of his time forgotten in our own.[19] For George he was a protean resource, a natural hero for a Sandian novel, or two, and she saw in him all the rich, operatic possibilities of Mozart's Papageno, a reborn Corambé, though she was also recklessly given to calling Pierre Leroux "a new Plato, a new Christ"—this last, years later to another Leroux admirer, Charlotte Marliani.[20]

George had first met Leroux in 1835 on Sainte-Beuve's unusually warm recommendation. Leroux had come to dinner at Quai Malaquais and fed George, at her hungry request, a veritable smörgasbord of pantheism, optimism, utopian socialism and a neo-Pythagorean theory of the transmigration of souls reappearing on earth in a neat upward spiral of inevitable progress. Leroux himself was a brilliant child born of the lower orders, who had spiraled intellectually upward only to arrest his academic career to support the family thrust upon him by the death of his father. It became the pattern of his life: this fall of his visit to Nohant, in 1837, he was supporting four or five children and a half-mad wife. Both George and Charlotte Marliani, who was also staying with her, played with the idea of dividing the children between them and installing Leroux at Nohant as its spiritual father.

Briefly on the staff of the Saint-Simonian *Globe*, Leroux and his friend Jean Reynaud had broken away to undertake a universal *Encyclopédie Nouvelle* with Leroux, *à la* Diderot, writing the vast majority of the articles. Before he had met George, he had been struck by her *Lélia*, whom he called "a soul crying for sustenance" in his article on *Conscience*.[21] George knew his writing before she met the man; the conceptual mind, the attempt to encompass all knowledge for social ends, always impressed her. Though Leroux's first visit was but for a few days, their relationship would endure unstrained for decades. As a house present, Leroux sent George the first two volumes of his encyclopedia—from A to an incompleted C, which was as far as he had gone—"for Maurice, since it is for our children we are working." For George, there is a word of appreciation for her own gift of evocative listening: "You made me open myself to myself, giving me a flash of understanding of myself."[22]

Leroux had greatly helped George recover her usual equilibrium, and she resumed her nightly quota of twenty pages of manuscript, quickly completing two short novels set in the same colorful, romantic Venice of the mosaic masters—*La Dernière Aldini* and *L'Orco*. A play for Bocage never reached the stage. There was a constant pressure for money. Nohant's needs—guests, gardeners, household help including a maid and governess for Solange, as well as a tutor for Maurice—required "twenty-five to thirty thousand francs a year," and it was George's pen that had to provide the income.[23] Also there were generous "loans" to friends in need, such as Stéphane de Grandsagne's brother Jules, in prison for debts. Several years later, Pierre Leroux would become a costly dependent.

The pressure was relieved by the devoted, loving Mallefille. Life at Nohant in December, 1837, was "peaceful and hardworking." Sand was "piling" novel upon novel, Mallefille "play upon novel," Maurice "caricature upon drawing" and Solange "chicken legs on false notes from the piano."[24] Mallefille had succeeded Bocage and replaced Michel. George had made perhaps her last "gallop through a frosty night to be an instant with Michel," as she wrote a mutual friend, Frédéric Girerd. "At last," she said, "I have slain the dragon. That tenacious, ruinous passion has been cured by another affection—more gentle, less rapturous, but less bitter, too, and, I hope, more enduring."[25]

Mallefille, however, was not a model of intelligence—or tact. He enclosed a note to Marie d'Agoult along with a letter from George, and the countess took umbrage at his "impolite" tone, holding George responsible for her former protégé's discourtesy. Decidedly the relationship between George and Marie was becoming scratchy. George Sand to Franz Liszt, January 28, 1838: She hadn't read Mallefille's note. "I have enough stupid letters to read every day! . . . When one

allows Mallefille to write to one, what the devil does one have to complain about? When one knows Mallefille and his style, one should be
prepared for anything! Good God, it's all I need—teaching Mallefille
how to write a letter! I know for my part I shall always find his letters
irreprochable, because I hope I shall never have to read one. I love him
with all my heart. He could ask me for half my blood, and get it—so
long as he never asks me to read one of his letters."[26]

The derogation of Mallefille is not to be taken literally. George was
not at the point of announcing to Marie that he was the lover-in-
residence—not by correspondence. Such letters often circulated in
many copies, each recipient copying it for a few friends, each sworn to
secrecy. Moreover, most memorably with Musset, all experience, all outpourings, however personal, were considered grist for the writer and became thinly disguised fiction, *romans à clef*. The remark is particularly
apt at this season of George Sand's life, involving as it does Franz,
Marie, George and Honoré de Balzac, especially Balzac's novel about all
three—*Béatrix*.

Since his disillusionment with Jules Sandeau, Balzac and George
Sand had become reconciled. In February 1838, he found himself staying with friends eight leagues from Nohant. He had always wanted to
make a "pilgrimage to Nohant," Balzac wrote Sand, and now he was
actually in the vicinity. "I would not like to return to Paris without
having seen the lioness of Berry in her den, the nightingale in her nest,
for you have a strength and grace appreciated by no one more than

Yr dev'ted serv'nt,
H. de Balzac"

It was a gracious note and George, as much novelist as Balzac, was as irresistibly curious. "I'll always be here for you," she replied.[27]

In Balzac's long account to Madame Hanska—"*l'Etrangère*" who
would become his wife but a few months before his death—there is
more mention of the lioness, rather, *lion*, than of the nightingale, as
one might expect of a lover writing his beloved after a three-day stay
with a rather notorious lady. Madame Hanska, a collector of autographs, had asked for George Sand's, and Balzac procured it for her.

> I boarded the château of Nohant [writes Balzac] towards
> seven-thirty in the evening and found comrade George Sand
> in her dressing gown, smoking a cigar by the fire after dinner
> in a huge deserted room. She was wearing pretty yellow
> slippers with a fringe, coquettish stockings and red trou-
> sers. . . . Physically, she has developed a double, canonical
> chin. Despite all her frightful experiences, she hasn't a single
> white hair. Her swarthy complexion hasn't changed, her beau-
> tiful eyes are as brilliant as ever, she still has the same stupid

look when deep in thought, because, as I told her after I had
studied her, her entire physiognomy is in her eyes. She has
been at Nohant for a year, very sad and working enormously.
She conducts her life as I. She goes to bed at six in the morning and rises at noon. I go to bed at six in the evening and rise
at midnight. Naturally I conformed to her habits, and for
three days we have talked after dinner from five in the evening
until five in the morning. . . .

So there she is, living in deep seclusion, damning both marriage and love, because she has had only disappointments in
both. Her kind of male is rare—that's the whole of it. And he
will continue to be, because she is not lovable and consequently will be loved with difficulty. She is a *garçon* [bachelor,
young man], she is an artist, she is great, large-hearted,
devoted, pure. She has the best qualities of a man; ergo, she is
no woman. During the three days we talked so openly together, side by side, I was no more stirred by her physically
than I had been before, never felt what a man should for any
woman, whether in France or in Poland [where Polish Countess Hanska was staying]. I was talking to a comrade.

"Our writings," George had told Balzac, "are preparing a revolution in
tomorrow's morals, but I am bothered by the problems of both marriage and freedom." They talked of this all one night, Balzac proclaiming his favorite thesis of sexual freedom for a young woman *before*
marriage—so she'll know what she's contracting for when she promises
fidelity—but not after: "I'm all for the freedom of the young woman
and the slavery of the wife." Balzac prided himself in his letter on having obliged George to admit the necessity of marriage in any event.

She is an excellent mother, adored by her children, but she
dresses Solange as a little boy and that is not good. She has allowed her son Maurice to taste the dissipations of Paris too
early. Since twelve he's been listless and has trouble with his
back. *Morally* he is like a young man of twenty, because she
[sic] is inherently *chaste* and *prudish*, an artist only in appearance. She smokes without measure and plays, perhaps
overly, the role of Princess.

When they talked métier—shop, the business of writing—George said
frankly she felt weak in the conception and construction of a novel.
"But without knowing the French language," said Balzac, "she has
style." Moreover, "like myself, she wears her fame lightly."

She works hard to pay off the debts of so many—friends and
lovers. . . . Right now she is in love with a man who is her in-

ferior. In such a relationship, there can only be disenchantment and disappointment for a woman of a lofty nature. A woman must love a man who is her superior, or be so completely infatuated that she thinks he is.[28]

There is as much Balzac in this long letter as George Sand, that is, Balzac's conception of "man" and "woman," their relationship, their roles, their "nature." He returns again to the charge that George "is a man, and all the more because she wants to be. Women attract, she repels; and as I am very much a man, if she affects me that way, she will produce the same effect on men like me, and she will always be unhappy." George Sand was not that repulsive, nor most likely Balzac that repelled. Nevertheless, this is fairly straight nineteenth century in its attitude, in its definition of the sexes; nor did it end with the century.[29]*

Balzac touched on the subject in the novel George Sand had suggested at Nohant, which he wrote several years later and titled *Béatrix* (Beatrice). George herself, he had mentioned in his letter to Madame Hanska, felt she was in no position to write it, because it dealt so directly with Franz Liszt and Marie d'Agoult. Balzac's title uncannily preceded Franz Liszt's explosion in his last days with Marie, who frequently posed as Beatrice to his Dante (in view of his Florentine profile): "Dante! Beatrice! It is the Dantes who create the Beatrices, and the real ones die at eighteen!"[30] Not quite as cruel is Balzac's portrayal of the couple as a pair of lovers dragging the ball-and-chain of their public affair, when pride and no longer passion alone held them together (the original title was *The Galley Slaves*).

Unfortunately, George Sand appears as an important, but "secondary personnage," Félicité des Touches, who writes under the pen name of Camille Dupin. As we, Balzac regrets he cannot go more fully into the mystery of this "monumental" figure, "the masculine incarnation of a young woman," who had recreated herself as "a man and a writer."[31] (The first name of the *nom de plume*, Camille Dupin, recalls that of Latouche's hermaphroditic *Fragoletta*; the last, Gautier's lesbian *Mademoiselle de Maupin*.) Balzac described Félicité des Touches as strikingly, femininely beautiful. This is possibly his true view of George Sand as compared to the attitude struck in his letter to Madame Hanska, or perhaps simply the novelist's improvement on life. She is olive-skinned, black-haired, bright-eyed, full-breasted—but he lingers on Félicité's carriage as "more Bacchus than Callipygenos Venus," an androgynous characteristic, he said, common to the handful of "famous women." Her male, too, would be rare, but for intellectual as well as sexual reasons: "What man could ever fill the two precipices of her

* For Henry James' long comment on Balzac's letter see p. 411.

eyes?" At twenty-one, "she was the equal of a man of thirty." As the
novel begins, Félicité-George Sand is single, forty, famous and still desirable, but "with an awesome clarity about herself." What explained
this phenomenon, so full of "anomalies?", asked Balzac rhetorically,
and replied with an extraordinary précis remarkable for its perception
of the cultural rather than the anatomical forces bending a woman's
destiny:

> Félicité knew neither father nor mother, and was her own mis-
> tress from childhood. . . . Chance thrust her into the fields of
> science and the imagination and the world of literature, in-
> stead of leaving her in the small, tight circle of frivolous edu-
> cation traced for women—a mother's instruction in how to
> dress, in the hypocritical proprieties of society, in the arts of
> hunting a man.[32]

The two principals of *Béatrix* ended alone in their disillusionment.
Balzac, for want of a better solution, dispatched Félicité-George Sand
to a convent, but so George terminated her own revised *Lélia* at this
time.

For George Sand herself, however, an end was but a beginning. Balzac was oddly prophetic in the end he chose for his fictional George
Sand. For the coming decade with Frédéric Chopin could be called the
convent years, in the rich, medieval sense of devotion, music and fine,
illuminated manuscripts.

26

Frédéric Chopin— Fragile Genius

I can play a pyrotechnical Liszt sonata, requiring forty
minutes for its performance, and get up from the piano
without feeling tired, while even the shortest étude of
Chopin compels me to an intense expenditure of effort.

—Arthur Rubinstein[1]

The enduring legend has Frédéric Chopin, twenty-six, murmuring to a
fellow pianist after meeting George Sand, thirty-two: "Is she indeed a
woman? I rather doubt it." And George Sand saying to Charlotte
Marliani: "*Ce Monsieur* Chopin, is he not rather a *jeune fille?*" There
is one reason at least for a legend's durability: it recreates history as it
should have been—in view of what happened.

Chopin did indeed write to his family that he had just met a "great
celebrity—Madame Dudevant, known by the name of George Sand,"
but had not found her face "sympathetic" and had felt "put off."[2]
However, subject as she was to the appeal of weakness to her strength,
the frail, young girl aspect of Chopin did not put off George Sand. She
herself was too self-knowing for that. "The love of weakness for
strength," she wrote at this time, "is a sacred law of nature, but holier
still is the love of strength for weakness."[3] She was aware of her own
maternal—we would add paternal—reflexes. How well did Chopin understand his own—the initial aversion, the later attraction, his own invitation to his fate?

The word *fate* has an ominous ring, according with another legend—
that of Chopin as the doomed, Romantic artist destined to die young,
"victim of love and tuberculosis." But the metallic strength of his
music is the real victim of that legend at the hands of sentimental

scores of limp-wristed pianists. A second victim has been George Sand as his *dea ex machina*, for she must somehow be fitted into the machinery of Chopin's predestined doom. But *what* is popularly known of Chopin, except that he is, along with Mozart, the most loved of composers? That he was as secretive as his music is accessible? That as tensily tough as his genius was the fragility of his sexuality, that if he is universal, transcending divisions East and West, Near and Far, *his* universe was his piano?

He was born in Poland, his father was French, he would spend the last half of his life in Paris. He was Frédéric Chopin, and not, as Maria Wodzinska would one day wish, Chopinski. He was born March 1, 1810, in the village of Zelazowa Wola, twenty-eight miles from Warsaw. Of a Polish mother of a lower class—he who would be meticulously aristocratic. He may have improvised on the piano at three. We know he composed and played a Polonaise in public before he was eight. The child prodigy was petted by princes and countesses. He always would be. His piano teacher was a Czech whose musical gods were German and Austrian—Bach and Mozart. They would be Chopin's. He had his last piano lesson at twelve? In a profound sense it is truer than fact. Chopin was essentially his own teacher with the capacity of genius —self-learning, sudden, inexplicable development. The teen-age Chopin of the Nocturnes, Preludes and Mazurkas is substantially the late Chopin.

At school he had a boyhood crush on Titus Woyiechowski. Here too the early Chopin is the mature Chopin, though later at the Warsaw Conservatoire he thought he loved a young student singer, Constance Gladkowska. At sixteen he suffered acutely from a sore throat and swollen lymphatic glands. They were treated by application of leeches to his throat. At seventeen he saw his younger sister Emilia die of tuberculosis, witnessed with horror the successive bleedings, purges and blisterings, her withering away until he found her unrecognizable.

At eighteen Chopin went to Berlin and Prague for applause—he played his Variations (Op. 2) and Rondo (Op. 14)—and received it. At nineteen he was in Vienna, and he was there again at twenty with Titus, when the Poles rose against the occupying Russians. Titus left immediately to join the insurrectionists. Chopin did not. He felt remorse, but it was the composition of his Concerto in E minor and his first Études that seems most to have preoccupied him. He was in Stuttgart when the Polish revolt was crushed. "Oh, Titus! Titus!" he cried— but he also bewailed Constance.[4] A week later, in 1831, at the age of twenty-one, he was in Paris.

By the time Chopin had arrived in the French Capital, he had composed most of the twelve Études (Op. 10), a number of his Nocturnes, two piano Concertos, the first two sets of Mazurkas, his Trio and various other pieces. His musical features were definitively Chopin. What was to follow would be refinement and reproductivity. Here George Sand would play her role, but since one lives with a person as well as a composer insofar as they are distinguishable, the life of George Sand with Frédéric Chopin requires a more personal, perhaps private, possibly awkward, exploration.

The warmth of Chopin's feelings for his friend Titus Woyciechowski —a robust, athletic youth who admired Chopin's genius, played the piano surpassingly well and became an efficient gentleman farmer and devoted husband—continued into Chopin's twenties. His letters to Titus, asking for his "lips," his "mouth," though Titus neither liked nor encouraged it, go beyond even Romantic convention and we have Chopin's own recognition of his *outrance*. "I kiss you cordially," he wrote Titus on October 29, 1829. "That is how people habitually end their letters, but they do not know what they are writing. Believe me, I know what I just wrote you, because I love you. . . ." Chopin was twenty when he closed another letter, "Give me your mouth. . . . I don't know why, but I am afraid of you. You alone have power over me, you and no one else." They are long letters. Those he received from Titus he kept close to him, "like the ribbon of a loved woman." And he now confided to the piano, Chopin wrote to the distant Titus, "what I used to be able to say to you."[5] The intimacy, the tenderness, the *tension* (including the halted breath of the famous *tempo rubato*) confided to Chopin's piano is the transfigured, unmistakable music. It would not be stretching Freudian analysis too far to suggest that the dissonances which make Chopin our contemporary derive in some measure from the same tension.

Fairly quickly Paris was intrigued by the slight, youthful Chopin of the gray-blue eyes, fair hair and downy-eaglet look; and he was fascinated by the city that would be his home half his life. Quite naturally he fell in with the clan of Polish patriot exiles, Count Grzymala among them, all the more patriotic for being in Paris. To this circle were joined Liszt, Berlioz and the singer Nourrit. Inevitably Chopin met the patron of his youth on the boulevards of Paris, Prince Radziwill, who took him the same evening to a soirée *chez* Baron de Rothschild. There he met the duchesses, countesses and ladies who wilted at his playing and would, on the morrow, queue up for piano lessons in his apartment at twenty gold francs an hour. But at least they relieved Chopin of the concert performances he detested and dreaded, and helped him to live as a white-gloved, black-caped, daintily booted dandy-prince with a cabriolet and coachman waiting at the door for his sorties in the late afternoon. Money from his family and friends was of greater help, until George Sand and Nohant entered his life. Chopin was sought in the salons, and he received in his apartment, playing for himself and a few friends. To the question titillating Paris, "Who is the finer pianist, Liszt or Thalberg?", Ernest Legouvé replied, "Chopin." For Berlioz, whose own music jarred on Chopin's ear, he was the "Trilby of pianists."[6]

When, several years later, Constance Gladkowska married, it evoked scarcely a comment from Chopin to his family or to Titus. She was easily replaced in his sentiments by Maria Wodzinska, sister of schoolboy friends, whom he remet in 1835 in Dresden, when Maria was sixteen and he twenty-five. They considered themselves "engaged" and Countess Wodzinska, Maria's mother, was vaguely sympathetic. The Wodzinskis, however, possessed fifty thousand acres of Polish soil, which might sufficiently indicate the social distance between Frédéric and his fiancée, and cast doubt on the seriousness of their engagement. The same year, moreover, Chopin was struck by his first attack of tuberculosis, though it was diagnosed as influenza. He coughed blood. Warsaw papers announced his death. Not only was Chopin poor, as compared to the Wodzinskis; he was conspicuously of poor health. Scarcely a husband for Maria. But the break was gently prolonged. Not until early 1837 did Chopin receive the last letter from Maria. "Adieu," she wrote, "Mamma embraces you tenderly. Adieu, remember the two of us, you and me."[7] Accepting it as final, Chopin did not reply. As with Constance, he chose a passive role. A few of Maria's letters and a dried rose were found on Chopin's death in an envelope, upon which he had written in Polish: *"Moja Bieda"*—My Sorrow.

But also found among his things after Chopin's death was this note, carefully folded and preserved in a cherished album:

You are adored.
George
By me too! By me too! By me too!
Marie Dorval

The note is undated, but it was most likely written late in April 1838.[8]

27

The Dominant Note of George Sand

[George Sand's] was a method that may be summed up indeed in a fairly simple, if comprehensive, statement: it
consisted in her dealing with life exactly as if she had
been a man—exactly not being too much to say.
　　　　—Henry James, *Notes on Novelists* (1914)[1]

George had arrived in Paris mid-April 1838, and was staying with
Charlotte Marliani and her husband, the Spanish consul. She had also
taken a small hotel room in which to work undisturbed, and no portrait
of her is ever complete without a pen, preferably moving, in her hand.
What wins one's admiration, however, is not only the freely flowing
"expressional ease" of George Sand, but "the force of her ability to act
herself out, given the astounding quantities in this self."[2] It may help,
too, to think of her as a man, if the image of a woman on deliberate
conquest is too disconcerting even today, although ideally the mind's
eye should be broadened for a more sweeping view of a woman master-
fully ahead of her time. There was, for instance, a caution in George's
courtship of Chopin which might simply be called intelligent rather
than either feminine or masculine. She offered her strength to his weakness, but she did not want to frighten him with it. Chopin was an ab-
normally sensitive young gentleman of the old school, accustomed to
the niceties of well-brought-up young ladies. The *"On vous adore"* of
George's treasured note was probably written in the aftermath of a musical evening at the Marlianis, where Marie Dorval was present.[3]
George's tone and phrasing—"You are adored"—are passive, discreet,
softly enveloping. She was surely aware of Chopin's initial flinching
from her and was sufficiently sensitive herself to adjust in response.

Moreover—and more important—there was a tenderness, a motherliness in George which drew Chopin, despite himself, to her at this moment of disorder, disappointment and sorrow in his life. As others of the small circle, George knew of Maria Wodzinska and the engagement, but not, as closer friends, such as Count Crzymala, of the rupture that had ensued.

With growing frequency George and Chopin found themselves together—at Chopin's apartment or at more mundane affairs, such as the Marquis de Custine's, where one memorable evening Chopin had improvised, Duprez had sung, and a duchess, a countess, a baroness, George Sand and the Victor Hugos, *La Presse's* society page breathlessly noted, had been present. But Chopin preferred a smaller, intimate group clustered around his piano; he played with a light, melodic touch and a nuance of tone—"too light," said the critics of his few concerts. "Come at midnight," George invited Delacroix, shortly before returning to Nohant. Chopin would play. There would be but a few, "our elbows on the piano—and that's when he's really sublime."[4]

And there were evenings when they were alone. They had kissed. They were heaven-borne—"for a few instants."[5] They had touched, as if in a hesitation waltz. Chopin was fleeting, virginal, evanescent. *Jeune fille?* Or was it inhibiting thoughts of his "fiancée," Maria Wodzinska? Not knowing how to answer, not content with her own confusion, George Sand wrote from Nohant in May, 1838, to Chopin's closest friend, Count Grzymala.

It was another astounding, controversial letter—four thousand words long. The frankness, the honesty, is so unmasked as to appear stark naked, leaving the reader a bit chilled by the exposure. It's as if George Sand were asking about a son she considered marrying off, or a child she thought of adopting. "Our child," she said of Chopin to Grzymala. But he was not a child; he was a man of twenty-eight. And as if man to man—rather, not *quite* man to man, for Grzymala expected the conduct of a lady and George had a delicate, difficult path to trace, even as she determined to trace it—George wrote to Chopin's friend. It was perhaps a circuitous road she was taking to reach Chopin (who would have been shocked by a frontal approach, as if by an assault), writing a letter which Grzymala might *not*, in the name of a higher friendship, conceal from Chopin. There are twists and turns in it, frankness and self-justification and room for a turnaround, should Grzymala so counsel. She solicited his advice: let his reply be "clear, categorical and to the point."

Was "this person"—Maria Wodzinska—whom Chopin wanted to love, thought he loved or thought he ought to love, really for him? Would she make him happy, or simply "add to his pains and sufferings"? George asked the Polish count. "I do not ask if he loves her, if he is loved by her, whether he loves her more than me, etc. I know approximately by what I am experiencing what he must be feeling. I only want to know which of the *two of us* he must forget or give up for his peace of mind, his happiness, his very life, which appears to me too frail, too fragile, for great sorrows."

She herself, said George, did not welcome a great passion. Besides, there were her children to care for. And there was "an excellent being" —the unnamed Mallefille, "malleable as wax"—from whom she would "never part," because of his flawless devotion. "Engaged, chained as I am, perhaps for years, I would not want our little one"—Chopin—"to cut his own ties."

This was not, for George Sand, an unsolvable dilemma. She knew that the only way to have one's cake is by eating it. Offered alternatives, she reached for both. Mallefille would be the anchor for her ship when in its home harbor. She and Chopin would love, as they had begun to, when a "good wind from time to time brings us together" for a "trip to the stars." But if the "person" in Chopin's life could give him—as George implied she herself alone could—happiness, tender care, order and calm in his life, or if Chopin, with his "excessive, perhaps foolish, perhaps wise scrupulousness," refused to love "two different people in two different ways," would find that spending a week, a "few hours of chaste passion and sweet poetry," made the rest of his year with the other "person" miserable, then, George promised, she would withdraw and try to forget him.

But if that "person" was to become the "grave of his artistic soul"— and it was for Grzymala to decide—then she (Maria) must be cast aside and Chopin himself weaned from his "religious scruples." George would nurse his genius, in no manner weigh heavily upon him, demanding no accounts and having none demanded of her. Their loving would be at sublime moments and Chopin, George assured Grzymala, would be preserved whole and intact.

George was not seriously contemplating another fateful "half a life plus half a life" to fill an emotionally empty one, as had failed so long ago with Aurélien, though she doesn't face it in this letter. Rather, the remarkable woman broached another problem of more interest to Grzymala. She was the notorious George Sand now asking, as it were, for the hand of his friend Chopin, a woman coupled in the public's mind with many loves, several of them simultaneous. George took the offensive: she had always believed in fidelity. She had preached it, practiced it, insisted upon it. People had not been up to it, but "neither," she said unexpectedly, "have I. And yet"—George retreated from a too exposed position—"I have never felt remorse, because in my very infidelities I have always submitted to a kind of fatality, an instinct for the ideal which impelled me to leave the imperfect for what appeared to me to come closer to perfection." She had always been faithful to those she loved "except for very good reasons, when their faults killed my love." Like Caesar, George Sand could do no wrong save for righteous cause. She was not unconstant by nature, but she could be swept away by her feelings and "forced to lie, like others."

As, surely, she was now lying to Mallefille, the faultless one. "Alas," George no longer felt the same *tendresse* for "poor M." since her return from Paris and Chopin. "If I thought seeing Chopin frequently would increase the coolness, I think I should feel duty-bound to abstain." George perhaps believed *this* for the time it took to write the sentence —with its cautious "I *think* I should feel duty-bound"—because two sentences later she was writing, "One can be more or less faithful, but once one has allowed even a simple kiss to invade one's soul, infidelity has been consummated and the rest is less grave." The words might be addressed directly to Chopin. "When the heart is lost, all is lost." The act of love follows, despite one's best intentions of fidelity. George has bent to her purposes of self-justification the Romantic, Rousseauian primacy of the emotions, but at least she did not plead the "feebleness" of women. There was *that* honesty which shocked her contemporaries and Chopinists of our day, particularly those who protectively view their "doomed, stalked" hero as if they were vestal virgins guarding the sacred flame.

They are not entirely wrong! George Sand herself squarely confronted Chopin's sexual fastidiousness, though there was no reason for her knowing its likely cause—an unconscious, certainly unacknowledged, homosexuality emerging from its repression as simple prudery. The night before her departure from Paris, George told Grzymala, she had experienced it. Chopin had expressed his revulsion, "in the manner of a bigot," for certain "human vulgarities . . . fearful of soiling our love" by the consummation of it.

"I have always been repelled by this manner of viewing the ultimate embrace of love," George flatly continued. "If this last act is not as sacred, as pure, as devoted as all the rest, there is no virtue in abstaining." Was there ever "purely physical love" or "purely intellectual love"? "Was there ever love without a kiss, or a kiss of love without desire?" *Despising the flesh* is only for those for whom flesh is all. Chopin had said to her that "certain acts" would spoil everything. "Tell me," pleaded George, "that what he said was stupid, was it not, and he does not mean it. Who is the dreadful woman who has left him with such impressions of physical love? Did he have a mistress unworthy of him? Poor angel!" The separation of soul and body, she said, has inevitably led to "convents and brothels."

George was confident she understood Chopin. She could make him happy, she assured Grzymala. Only his feeling for Maria Wodzinska might prevent it. "If he can be happy with me without ceasing to be happy with her, I can do the same on my side." If not—and it was for Grzymala to tell her—she would gracefully withdraw. George invited the count to Nohant. "As for the little one, he may come if he wishes. But in that case I should like some advance notice, so that I might send Mallefille to Paris or to Geneva."[6]

Grzymala's reply to the extraordinary letter may have indicated that George's concern about Maria was groundless. Chopin, possibly *self-protectively*, concealed the rupture from George Sand. In any event, the reply must not have been bluntly discouraging, for within a few days of receiving it, George left Nohant for Paris. "Try to keep the little one from knowing," she wrote Grzymala on the eve of her departure.[7]

But Chopin heard from Charlotte Marliani, with whom George Sand was again to stay. He felt panicky and slightly ill. "God only knows what is going to happen," he moaned to Grzymala. "I really don't feel very well."[8] With infinite tact, however, George conducted her courtship. The two met, they walked and talked one evening in the twilight mist.[9] As if he were a lyre, George drew music from Chopin "without touching the strings." She played him "with her eyes." He "trembled," he "suffered," he "cried." She put her hand to the strings. "They vibrated strongly." The two embraced, and loved. "Your embrace consumes me," said George. "I faint!" In the sleep that followed, she held him "as if he were her child."

These lines are plucked unapologetically from a play George wrote that summer, *Les Sept Cordes de la Lyre* (The Seven Strings of the Lyre), an otherwise fatal imitation of Goethe's *Faust*, complete with a Mephistopheles.[10] Chopin is the bewitched spirit of the Lyre, released by the "immaculate purity"—overly insisted upon by George—of the play's heroine. However, George did sound her theme of wholeness— "the soul is a lyre whose every string must be made to vibrate" and sing the song of the earth, the grandeur as well as the man-made miseries of man.[11] It is a bad play, but a beautiful love letter.

Few, the pair thought, were privy to their liaison, but among them were Grzymala and Delacroix. In July the latter painted the lovers with Chopin at the piano, specially brought to the studio, and an enraptured George Sand musing behind him. The famous canvas, after Delacroix's death, was cut into two, George Sand's shadowy figure separated from Frédéric Chopin's, so that a dealer might profit from the sale of two paintings. That summer the lovers were inseparable, if discreet— Chopin wanted no word to reach his family in Poland. To Delacroix, George confided her happiness, "the delicious fatigue of love" which was hers, not for the first time, but once again. Would it last? she asked. When she dipped into her memory and consulted her past, it didn't seem so. But her heart unfailingly told her it didn't matter. "Three intoxicated months" were a lifetime. "That is where we artists have it over the grocer," she exulted to Delacroix.[12] Art and love were all. Love and work, for the writing of *Les Sept Cordes* went on to its completion, while a Pierre Leroux-inspired novel, *Spiridion*, was put aside, though a first part was published.

Less artist perhaps, less easily set aside, Mallefille proved far from "malleable." He became terribly jealous, fighting a duel with one of Maurice's teachers, because he believed him flirting with Nohant's mistress. "We have been nothing more than friends for the past three months," George assured Leroux, to whom she sent Mallefille. As always, she protested her own innocence. Had she not told Mallefille their affair was over? He seemed to be controlling himself at the moment, but what if his jealousy were rekindled and he threatened "another"—the frail, vulnerable Chopin? Leroux must do his best to exorcise Mallefille's madness. He must lecture him "that women do not belong to men by right of brute force, that cutting one's throat is hardly the way to make amends."[13]

Mallefille had taken to haunting the apartment house of Chopin when in Paris, hoping to catch the lovers together. One evening *tout Paris* had been made aware of it. Seeing his successor with George, Mallefille had gone berserk. "He shouted, he screamed, he became ferocious, he cried for blood. Friend Grzymala threw himself between the illustrious rivals. Finally Mallefille was calmed down."

"And now," a delighted Marie d'Agoult continued this tardy account to Major Pictet, "George has decamped with Chopin to pursue a perfect love in the shade of the myrtle trees of Palma"—Majorca.[14]

28

That Winter in Majorca

No one with a feeling of tenderness for Chopin or George
Sand should make a sentimental pilgrimage to Majorca.
— Anonymous (1976)

For some time George Sand had planned a trip to Italy as a climatic
treatment for Maurice's rheumatism of the previous winter. Now there
was Chopin's worrisome cough and his doctor's advice that he too go
south for a spell. Thus Mallefille's wild jealousy was not sole cause for
the famous departure for Majorca. The Marlianis had sung the praises
of the Spanish isle as a Balearic island paradise. It would be cheaper,
George was told, than Italy—and the expenses, as usual, would be hers.

The departure itself was as discreet as they could make it, but less
discreet than Chopin, who dreaded his private life made public and his
liaison with George Sand precipitously disclosed to his family in
Poland, had hoped. Nothing that touched the celebrated pair could
have been kept secret: Palma papers would be full of their arrival. However, the adieus were not quite as brazen as those on the eve of the departure for Venice with Musset—and there in itself is a marked
difference between the two lovers, so similar in frailty, dependence and
younger age (though the one, Chopin, was vastly more dependent than
the other). The Sand ménage, including fifteen-year-old Maurice, ten-
year-old Solange and a maidservant, left first, traveling by short laps to
Perpignan, where the party was joined by a "rosy" Chopin.[1] They all
embarked for Barcelona. There in the late afternoon of November 7,
1838, they boarded the steamer *El Mallorquin* for the island of
Majorca.

The night was warm, the sea was calm and glowed phosphorescently
in the wake of the ship. All night in their own rapture George and
Chopin listened to the helmsman softly singing to himself in a kind of
unfamiliar flamenco, his voice drifting through the air "like smoke from

the ship's funnel." In the morning they arrived in the Bay of Palma, bemused by the beauty of it all, and disembarked shortly before noon. The enemy—Paris winter—was behind them, the unknown before them. They felt blessed by the Spanish sun.[2]

George took her brood in charge. Less typically, she had not arranged for their lodgings beforehand and unpleasantly discovered that Palma was overcrowded with Spanish refugees from the mainland's civil war, and no decent hotel was to be had. For a week they had to put up in a boardinghouse above a noisy barrel shop in a quarter George considered "disreputable." Promptly and energetically she went househunting, finally falling on Señor Gomez and his villa called *So'n Vent*, or House of the Wind. They moved to it in the village of Establiments, five miles north of Palma.

Chopin was enchanted. "Here I am in the midst of palms, cedars, cactus, olive trees, aloes, orange and lemon trees, fig trees and pomegranates," he exulted to Jules Fontana, his friend and music-copier. "The sky is turquoise, the sea lapis lazuli, the mountains emerald, the air heavenly. Sunshine all day, at night long hours of song and the sound of guitars. Enormous balconies with hanging vines. . . . In short, an admirable life!" However, his Pleyel piano, shipped via Marseilles, had not yet arrived. He would have to make do with a local, rented instrument whose very sound upset him. "Go to Pleyel . . ." Chopin pleaded, then cautioned, "but say little of me to our acquaintances."[3]

For George, their love nest secured, *So'n Vent* was also enchantment restored. And six miles further north, she rented a group of three cells and a garden in a charming, abandoned monastery—the Charterhouse of Valldemosa. "It is the most poetic residence on earth!" she announced to Charlotte Marliani.[4] Even Chopin may have ventured to it, partway on foot, with George and the two children in a not too tiring excursion. It was foresight itself, but for the moment all was almost blissful. The people seemed friendly, both Maurice and, at first, Chopin seemed to be flourishing, and Solange and George shamelessly put on weight, despite the detested olive oil in the cooking. Chopin was particularly affected by it, and George had to prepare special meals for him.

However, the myrtles and lemon trees were still in flower, though it was now December, and George, after a night's work, would watch the dawn from the terrace, listening to the distant donkey bells and the faint, far-off sighing of the sea. At last, she felt, she had reached "the promised land."[5]

Then came the Deluge. The rainy season was upon them, beating down the flowers, moving rocks in its gushing torrents. The villa they had rented became truly a House of the Wind, providing no more shelter than a summer cottage. The thin, plaster walls soaked up moisture "like a sponge." The damp, clammy house settled "like a cloak of ice on our shoulders." There were no fireplaces. They burned charcoal in open braziers for heat, and were suffocated by the smell. Chopin especially suffered, and he coughed incessantly and terribly, spitting bright blood. "From that moment, we became the objects of horror and dread for the Majorcans."[6]

Actually the turning point in Chopin's health had occurred earlier, as he wrote Fontana, December third: "Three doctors—the most celebrated of the island—have examined me. One sniffed my spit, the second tapped to see where the spit had come from, the third palpated me while listening to me spit. The first said I was going to croak"—*crever* —"the second that I was in the act of croaking, the third that I had already croaked. . . . I had great difficulty escaping their bleedings and blisterings . . . [and] my illness has been no help with the Preludes."[7]

The Spanish doctors, who diagnosed Chopin's illness as a very contagious consumption, were unfeelingly right. So, when it became known, were the local peasants, whom George Sand regarded with French scorn as ignorant and superstitious. And she too was partially justified, for the people now turned against the foreigners as if the threatening contagion were a medieval plague. Señor Gomez ordered them from his house in writing. Their contagion, he said, threatened his own family. Furthermore, according to the local law, they were to pay for the furniture that must be burned and for the disinfection of his house. Expelled, George, Chopin, the children and the maid returned provisionally to Palma, staying a few days with the French consul, then made their way with difficulty—no one wanted to rent them a carriage —across the rough country in a springless coach to the mountain refuge George had prepared: the Carthusian monastery at Valldemosa, eleven miles to the north.

They had been in Majorca—the promised land—less than six weeks.

Almost fourteen hundred feet above the sea, the Charterhouse of Valldemosa had harbored thirteen monks but three years before. *They* had been expelled by government decree when their order had been dissolved. Now the great building was virtually deserted, when George arrived with Chopin and the children—"my family," she referred to them[8]—and the overwhelmed maidservant, all climbing on foot up to the monastery the last part of the way. Better perhaps had it been completely deserted. An old ex-monk had remained as the monastery's apothecary; he would sell the new arrivals badly needed drugs and herbs at a robber's prices. The keeper-of-the-keys was the village seducer acting as sacristan. And at night, another ex-monk would haunt the corridors, drunkenly knocking on the cell doors, a knife in one hand, a rosary in the other, calling for a long-gone Father Nicolas. But the plague of George and her family would be Maria Antonia, who occupied a cell near their own and piously offered the newcomers her services as an act of Christian charity but, George soon discovered, was stealing them blind, pinching her best outfits and their food.

The stark beauty of the site, however, wrung from George another cry of admiration: "The Charterhouse is the most romantic spot on earth!"[9] Eagles soared overhead, cypresses marked the path twisting to the bottom of the gorge at their mountain's feet. The children dashed about exploring the twelve chapels and their Moorish mosaics, the roofs and upper galleries. Maurice, his rheumatism forgotten, endlessly sketched. Décor and mood entered as well the religious novel, *Spiridion*, George was bringing to completion. Chopin too was hard at work on his Preludes.

"Imagine me," he wrote Fontana on December 28, "between rocks and sea, in a cell of an immense, abandoned Chartreuse with doors taller than any carriage entry in Paris. Here I am, with neither curled hair nor white gloves, and pale as usual." The image of death appears. Though his cell has a "little window opening onto the orange trees, palms and cypresses of the garden," its enormous, dusty vault and general shape suggest to Chopin "a huge coffin." But he was stoically composing. On the same music stand were Bach's *Well-Tempered Clavichord*, which he was preparing for publication, and his own "scribblings." The Pleyel piano had been traced to Palma, where it was in the hands of the Spanish customs officials, "who are demanding a mountain of gold."[10]

It would be several weeks before George rescued the piano by paying a princely ransom, and the vaults of Chopin's cell "rejoiced" at the new, melodic sound. All payments, all tasks, burdens and errands devolved upon George Sand, and she performed them with the same competence as her own flowing pages. Her "handling power" was never more evidenced, the successful meeting of all tasks "never an instant in doubt." She was father and mother of her family of three children, one of them morbidly ill. And it was not so much the "extension" she gave to her "feminine nature" which would so impress James, as the "richness" she added to the "masculine," a hymning of wholeness, the union of Plato's two halves in one person, man as well as woman. That was the "moral"—and the beauty—"of her tale."[11] It both included and was beyond, because including, sexuality.

George cooked and wrote. She nursed Chopin and instructed Solange in participles and read Thucydides with Maurice. She wrestled with the Spanish authorities, walked with the children, shopped in Palma for provisions, stood watch over Chopin's food and fought off the stealing servants. And she, the notorious George Sand scandalously living with her consumptive lover and her husband's children, and refusing to go to Mass, was operating in this hostile, Spanish, patriarchal, medievally pious land! "They called us pagans, Mohammedans and Jews, which for them was the worst of all."[12] Priest and peasants looked blackly at Solange's boyish dress. The French foreigners became pariahs in the land, "because of Chopin's cough," and the children were stoned in the fields. Thus those stricken with tuberculosis, and those close to them, were treated—as if they were lepers.[13]

And so, as the winter weather worsened, did Chopin's health. He became visibly weaker, wasting away to less than a hundred pounds. Wind and dampness penetrated the monastery. The family huddled around a single stove. Sadness sometimes paralyzed even George Sand. And yet, from these depths, by January 22, 1839, Chopin produced some of his finest music, sending off the set of twenty-four Preludes (Op. 28) he had promised to Fontana for copying, and announcing a new Ballade, Scherzo and several Polonaises. The lilting "Raindrop Prelude" in D-flat Major was one of the set, perhaps the "wonderful Prelude" George wrote about, whose drip-drip rhythm established by the left hand rises to a stormy crescendo, then subsides in "quiet desperation." The descriptive account, as romantic as the music, delivers a precious scene of the family one evening at Valldemosa—and reveals some of the emotional, musical and slightly hysterical elements in the relations of the two lovers.

George had gone with Maurice and Solange to Palma and returned in a torrent of rain late at night. They had hurried back, because they knew Chopin would be anxious. And so he had been. "Very anxious, but the anxiety had become frozen into a kind of quiet desperation"—*désespérance tranquille*—"and he played us his wonderful Prelude as he wept." Chopin had sat at the piano waiting for them, seeing as if in a vision their dying in the storm. Then he had become calm, he recounted, and played, as if disembodied, convinced that he too was dead, drowned in a lake, "icy, heavy drops of water falling in musical measures on his chest." When George attempted to relieve the lingering nightmare by having Chopin listen to the rain, still falling rhythmically on the roof, he furiously denied it was that he had heard. And when George referred to the "imitative harmony" of his Prelude, he protested violently against the "childishness" of such musical interpretations. "And he was right," George acknowledges. "His genius was full of the strange harmonies of nature, but they were transposed into the sublime equivalents of his musical thought and were never slavishly imitated from exterior sounds. . . . He has made a single instrument speak the language of infinity. . . . Only Mozart is his superior."[14]

Almost nerveless in the face of his sickness, Chopin was almost maniacal when it came to irritating trifles. None of this ever showed in society, where he was impeccably self-controlled. But in the privacy of his Majorcan martyrdom, Chopin's "ordeal" became George's "torment."

Hypersensibility was his illness as much as his tuberculosis. "His very soul was flayed raw," George observed sadly. "The wrinkle in a rose petal, the shadow of a fly, made him bleed." Save for herself and the children, everything about him repelled and revolted him. "He was dying with impatience to be gone."[15]

The time had come to put finis to the Majorcan misadventure. One cannot call it a fiasco, as in the Venetian affair: George and Chopin emerged more tightly bound than before, the latter because he had learned he could depend on the former, and the former because she was depended upon. Once again a carriage to Palma was impossible to procure—such was the dread of contagion. Finally they made it to the port city in a public coach, as if in a tumbrel, but the jolting trip brought on a hemorrhage for Chopin, and he was deadly sick when they boarded the *El Mallorquin* for Barcelona.

On board as well were a hundred pigs, filling the air with their stench and their anguished squeals, as the sailors beat them systematically "to prevent their becoming seasick." The captain himself wanted to give Chopin the worst bunk in the cabin, so he would not have to burn a better one on his departure, but George sent him off to see to his pigs. When they reached Barcelona, Chopin, who was spitting "basins of blood," was transferred immediately to a French naval vessel and cared for by the medical officer. Ten days later, February 24, 1839, they arrived in Marseilles, stayed initially with a Dr. Cauvière, whom George had met in Paris, then went to a series of hotels.

"Another month in Spain," George wrote Charlotte Marliani, "and we would have died, Chopin of melancholy and disgust, and I of anger and indignation. They have wounded me in my most sensitive spot. They have pierced a suffering being before my eyes with their pinpricks. I shall never forgive them that. If ever I write of them, it will be with gall." Chopin, she reported, was no longer spitting blood. "Best of all, he is in France! He can sleep in a bed which will not be burned because he has lain in it. He sees no one who recoils when he stretches out his hand in greeting." They would stay, as Dr. Cauvière counseled, in the south, rather than return directly to the winter of Paris, or Nohant. After having tapped and palpated his patient, the doctor had pronounced him nontubercular and lesion-free, and simply in need of sun and repose.[16] There was, in fact, little else he could prescribe.

Stoutly George spoke in her letters only of Chopin's "angelic" behavior during his—which were her—most trying moments, but Chopin, knowing better, wrote to Grzymala gratefully of *his* "angel's" care and patience. "Unceasingly I see her hovering anxiously over me . . . nursing me by herself, for God preserve us from the local doctors! . . . making my bed, cleaning the room . . . depriving herself of everything for me . . . watching over the children as well. . . . Add to this, she continues to write."[17]

Chopin requested that he be addressed at their hotel (Beauvau), George directed her correspondence be sent care of Dr. Cauvière. To this extent they maintained their discretion. As in Paris, however, every literary or musical hopeful, every celebrity seeker, sought out the famous pair, assailing them by letter or in person, trailing them in the streets. George received no one and replied to no notes, finally giving out that Chopin was dead. "Don't be alarmed," she wrote Charlotte humorously, "if news reaches you from here that I am dying. . . . If this sort of thing continues, we're going to send out invitations to our joint funeral, so that people will mourn us and leave us in peace."[18]

Leave them in peace, so they might work—particularly George. She now found herself burdened with a staggering debt of seventy thousand francs—the result not only of the heavy expenses of the Majorcan trip, but of the even more costly repairs to her Hôtel de Narbonne in Paris. To help meet them, she instructed Hippolyte to sell off one of her estates in the Black Valley. In addition, she was in constant, complaining correspondence with Buloz about advances and payments, sometimes rightly, sometimes wrongly; her book income for the past four years had been an average of twenty-five thousand to thirty thousand francs per year. Buloz, in turn, spoke of his unhappiness with her last manuscripts —*Les Sept Cordes*, for which he paid the usual five thousand francs, but vainly begged off publishing, and *Spiridion*, which had already begun to appear in the *Revue*. Buloz found them too mystical, too philosophical, and Sainte-Beuve, too confusing. Buloz said he much preferred *Uscoque*, an earlier pirate tale, to the all-male *Spiridion*. Interestingly, *Uscoque* was also a favorite of Dostoievsky, if only because it had been the first of George Sand's novels he had read in his youth. Buloz did not mention the revolutionary allusions which embarrassed him vis-à-vis the Louis Philippe regime.

Dedicated to Pierre Leroux, *Spiridion* reflects his philosophy and George Sand's own religious evolution from convent Catholicism to Christian socialism. The story traces the life of Abbé Spiridion—in the words of the Benedictine monk Alexis to the novice Angel—as if it were the travails of humanity itself. Born a Jew, he became Protestant, Catholic and Christian Deist. Spiridion's spiritual journey was taken further by Alexis to a "free faith," complete with violence and martyrdom to advance the cause of a more humane society. The ending alone is worth recording, if only to explain Buloz's qualms and George's attitude ten years before the great upheaval of 1848:

The *sans-culotte* revolutionaries of 1789 have invaded the Benedictine monastery as symbol of the oppressive *ancien régime*. They overthrow statue of Christ. One bayonets the old monk Alexis, shouting: "Down with the Inquisition!" Dying, Alexis addresses the novice Angel with the novel's last words: "This is the work of Providence and the mission of our murderers is sacred, even if they themselves do not understand it! For they proclaimed—and you yourself have heard it—that it was in the name of a revolutionary"—*sans-culotte*—"Christ that they profane the sanctuary of the Church. This is the beginning of God's reign on earth, as prophesied by our Fathers."[19]

This, complained Buloz, was not exactly what George Sand's public expected. Her readers, George replied, could and would be elevated to a higher level than offered by her more sentimental works. However, to Charlotte she confided her own doubts about her public, which she recognized as ranging from "ladies to their chambermaids," but not about her determination to aspire to a higher form of writing.[20]

Neither good intentions nor noble sentiments have ever assured good novels. The literary superiority of *Gabriel* as compared to *Spiridion* is a case in point. Written swiftly at this time in Marseilles as a slighter "*fantaisie*," clearly meant as a Buloz- and public-satisfying potboiler, *Gabriel* would also bring praise from Balzac for its psychological insights. Even the circumstances of its writing did not seem propitious. The children were noisy and demanding, Chopin no less so. "Though doing much better, my poor Chopin cannot be left alone. He becomes bored when the children are not playing, or I not reading, near him."[21] But it was precisely out of these essentially *domestic* circumstances, and George's self-analysis, that *Gabriel* was born.

"My angels," Chopin informed Grzymala, "are finishing a new novel, *Gabriel*. Today she is going to spend all day in bed writing it. You would love her even more, if you knew her as I have come to know her." The book, George added in a postscript, was being delivered by "forceps."[22]

Who were these multiple "angels" of Chopin? Gabriel-Gabrielle, we might now reply, or George-Aurore (Chopin insisted on "Aurore"; calling Sand "George" was probably too discomfiting).[23] The hero of the new novel is in fact a woman raised and dressed as a man until the age of twenty-five, when, by her choice, she dresses three months a year (*pace* Casimir) as a woman to please her love, the dissolute Astolphe, who is in more than one way like Musset. The complications are as delightfully ambiguous as those of the boy actor in Shakespeare's company who pretended he was Rosalind disguising herself as a page boy. George's novel is in the form of armchair drama, heightening the similarity. Gabriel-Gabrielle would be "brother, friend, companion and lover" of Astolphe, but he proves jealous and unworthy of her, turning to a prostitute-mistress in his pique. The hero dies as a man, but with the word "*liberté*" on her lips. "I have always," she said earlier, "felt more than a woman."[24] If read as the *conventionally defined* woman, it becomes clear. Her soul, says Gabriel-Gabrielle, has no sex. Rather, it contains both sexes. Is this not depictive of the situation with Chopin, who has found a mother and a man—his guardian "angels"—in George-Aurore, though it would have been completely out of his life-character for him to have even wished to recognize it?

Musset himself could not have missed the inferences ("I get drunk," says Astolphe to his prostitute-mistress, "in order to persuade myself that I love you."[25]) He chose, however, to strike somewhat later in *un merle blanc* at a point in George where he thought she would feel most vulnerable. Not at her own infidelity, but at her *writing*.[26] George might have felt more wounded had it been the first. "While I was composing my poems," said Musset's allegorical white blackbird, the *merle blanc*, who has fallen in love with a literary white female blackbird, "she filled reams of paper with her scribbling. I would recite my verses aloud to her, but that did not inhibit her scribbling in the least. She would hatch her novels with a facility almost equal to my own, choosing always the most dramatic subjects—parricides, rapes, murders, swindles—and always taking care, in passing, to attack the government and preach the emancipation of all little blackbirds." She never blotted a line, nor needed a plan. "She was the very model of the little literary blackbird"—*la merlette lettrée*. But, Musset's pure white blackbird discovers, the little litr'y female blackbird was secretly dyeing her russet feathers white, presumably to hold him.[27]

Most likely George's love for Musset was the most intense, if not, save for a brief period, the most physically satisfying (here Michel de Bourges might lay better claim) of her life, and once again, still troubled about its failure, she returned to it in *Gabriel*. Chopin and Musset, supreme expressions of the Romantic spirit, each in his own medium, identical in age, sufficiently similar physically, each recalled the other in George Sand's existential writer's mind. While in Marseilles, she did what came to her naturally: she took Chopin and the children on a week's stay in Genoa. And this too was a kind of wholeness—the integration of experiences.

While in Italy, George refused Marie d'Agoult's invitation to Lucca, in Tuscany, where she and Liszt were staying. Charlotte Marliani had previously written Sand about Marie's gratuitously biting letters concerning her liaison with Chopin. Drawing too much on her own souring relation with Liszt and her resentment at George's snatching Chopin from her circle, Marie was predicting the liaison would soon end with the pair "at daggers drawn."[28] But more important for George during her trip to Genoa was news of the Paris insurrection of May twelfth. Led by Blanqui, Barbès and the printer Bernard (but unfollowed by the masses of Paris), the uprising had failed, giving Louis Philippe's monarchy another lease on life. "The regime's shipwreck," George remarked, "is inevitable, but too long delayed."[29]

Two weeks later, George, Chopin and the children were on their way to Nohant by short, restful stages. "I no longer love travel," Sand had written Charlotte before leaving Marseilles. "Rather, I'm no longer in a position to enjoy it. I am not a *bachelor* any more."[30] Indeed the four were truly a family. And perhaps the mysterious date penciled by George Sand on the windowsill of her bedroom at Nohant—June 19, 1839—marked the new domesticity.

29

Beyond Sexuality

But always in the inclusive sense.

George Sand's real history, the more interesting one, is the history of her mind. [It] is of course closely connected with her personal history.

—Henry James, *French Poets and Novelists*[1]

A new spaciousness must enter consideration of George Sand as she enters her middle years, marked as they are by their new domesticity. Each day, month or year does not count so separately—or intensely—as before. The nine years with Chopin, however, are not an interlude: they constitute the length of a marriage. New powers would enter his compositions and George Sand's novels.[2] Within a few years they would create their masterpieces. George would reach and deeply influence the young Dostoievsky in Russia, Thackeray, the Brontë sisters and the future George Eliot in Britain, Whitman and Margaret Fuller in America. By 1843, Arnold Ruge would be advising twenty-five-year-old Karl Marx, who had just arrived in Paris, above all to see George Sand, as one "more radical than Louis Blanc or Lamartine."[3] By 1845, Elizabeth Barrett (Browning) would be addressing sonnets to "that large-brained woman and large-hearted man, self-called George Sand," imploring her, encouraging her: "Beat purer, heart, and higher!"[4]

George and Chopin were much like the married, mutually enriching Brownings, though it was Elizabeth who was six years older and sickly, Robert who was robust and solicitous. So the friends of Chopin and especially George regarded them, delicately and appreciatively viewing the group newly installed at Nohant as a family of four with Chopin both foster father and child—"another Maurice," said George.[5] Had it been otherwise, the hypersensitive Chopin would have long since withdrawn.

Gustave Papet, as the family's doctor-friend, palpated and examined Chopin and pronounced him free of any lung infection; but rest and unceasing care were counseled. Fleury, Duteil, Duvernet and their families, Planet, Rollinat and Hippolyte, too, welcomed Chopin as warmly as he permitted. Tranquillity and happiness were the note of life at Nohant that summer of 1839. Chopin walked with George in the park and the neighboring woods—but soon returned to his piano. To Grzymala he wrote of the "lovely countryside, the larks and the nightingales," meticulously referring to George as "my hostess"; to Fontana he wrote of the music he was composing—the Sonata in B-flat minor (incorporating an older "funeral march"), the Nocturne in G major and four new Mazurkas. He also asked for a four-handed arrangement of Weber, so that he might play it with George.[6]

Thus the pattern was early set for Chopin: winters were reserved for lessons and a very rare concert in Paris, summers spent composing at Nohant. "His seven summers there were the most productive of his life."[7]

Movingly, one evening George spoke to Chopin of the wondrous peacefulness of meadows and woods. "How beautiful it sounds when you say it!" he exclaimed. "Do you think so?" she asked quietly. "Then put it into music." He began to improvise on the piano. George stood by him, her hand lightly on his shoulder. It could have been the scene Delacroix painted. "Courage," she murmured, "courage, fingers of velvet."[8]

She was a "fine listener," Heine observed. And she offered Chopin the fine example of her own steady working habits, an artist's understanding of a fellow artist's ways, organizing life at Nohant to accommodate them both, unobtrusively, fully cognizant of Chopin's frailty and chronic invalidism—and of his incomparable genius. The piano has known no greater composer.

As chronic, as perennial, was the need for money. Buloz, now Royal Commissioner of the state's Comédie Française, encouraged George Sand to try her hand at drama. Successful, a play's returns could be counted in thousands of francs. While Chopin slept—he retired early— George wrote *Cosima*. It was accepted that fall by a committee of the Comédie for production the following spring.

It was always with a burdened heart that George left the countryside, but expenses at Nohant, with so many house guests, were almost equally heavy—twice those of Paris. "A dozen mouths to feed before I even awake!" While two little houses were being readied at the end of a garden at 16 Rue Pigalle, the family *sans* Chopin stayed in Paris with Charlotte and her husband. Chopin had a place on Rue Tronchet. Here he gave lessons until four, then carriaged to Pigalle, when George was finally installed there.

Steep stairs led to George's rooms above the coach house. Balzac has climbed and described them for us—the dining room of carved-oak furniture, the little salon in café-au-lait, the large drawing room, "where she receives," full of superb Chinese vases ever "full of flowers." The upholstery was green. Delacroix paintings hung on the walls, also a portrait of George by Luigi Calamatta. Prominent was a "magnificent, upright piano of rosewood," since "Chopin is always there." The bedroom was brown, George's bed, "two mattresses laid on the floor, in Turkish fashion."[9]

Eventually Chopin moved from his cold, damp apartment to the second of the two little houses at the end of the garden, sharing it with Maurice. George was with Solange in the other.

Winter of 1839 was a busy one for George, charged with work on her play for Buloz as well as a short novel for his *Revue*, evenings with Marie Dorval, who was to perform as Cosima, dinners with good friend Delacroix, in whose atelier Maurice was now a student, unremitting care of a frequently ill Chopin, and a despairing relationship with an increasingly difficult, coquettish Solange. Finally, in March, rehearsals of *Cosima*, last, frenzied rewritings and the premiere on April twenty-ninth. Failure! Perhaps wrongly, George had disdained the customary claque of paid applauders. The jeers and whistles at the opening— Heine thought them organized by George's enemies, though the play is indeed inadequate—upset the actors, especially Marie Dorval. Quite calmly George put an end to the production after seven performances. "Let us laugh," she said to Marie. "That is the best remedy for everything human."[10]

In larger truth, she was already launched on the most expansive, humanity-embracing venture of her life—a political *engagement*, a socialism she would be calling communism before the mid-1840s, culminating in the explosion of 1848 with herself as Muse of the Revolution.

The ideological journey had not begun with George Sand's reading of *Le Livre du Compagnonnage* by Agricol Perdiguier, a former carpenter devoted to the union of workingmen's brotherhoods. Nor did it begin with their meeting in May when George invited Perdiguier, a man in his thirties, to dinner at Rue Pigalle and listened to his life story. Her populist faith had predated Michel de Bourges' influence and would outlast Michel's own. It now sharpened politically as the political crisis itself quickened into street clashes between Louis Philippe's forces of order and the opposition. When Perdiguier undertook yet another tour of France to proselytize among the *compagnons*, or journeymen, George supported him with funds and solicited money from her friends, even Chopin. As urgently, a new novel, *Le Compagnon du Tour de France*, its carpenter-hero Pierre Huguenin modeled upon Perdiguier, germinated in her mind and flowed from her pen.

That summer of 1840—largely for reasons of economy—George and her family remained in Paris rather than leave for Nohant. Part of the summer, however, George spent in Cambrai with a new but instantly close friend, Pauline Viardot, a singer of as great promise as her late sister, Maria (La) Malibran. With them too for the concerts in Cambrai was Pauline's husband, Louis Viardot, who had given up direction of a Paris theater to further his young wife's career, a male reversal of the usual role, which George fruitfully noted. From Cambrai George sent "Chip-Chip" (Chopin) news of Pauline's performance, and her love to the "other two children."[11] By the time she returned to Paris, her novel *Le Compagnon*, as she informed Perdiguier, who was on his tour of France, was half completed.

"The future of the world," George wrote him, "resides in the people, especially the working class. . . . In time the masses will emerge from the blinding ignorance in which the so-called enlightened classes have kept them . . . [and finally united] will become the masters of the world, the initiators of a new civilization."[12]

Le Compagnon was brought out as a popularly priced novel. It never appeared in Buloz's *Revue*, despite his contract with George. He was further alarmed by Italian revolutionary Mazzini's introduction, saluting George Sand for her unmasking of a corrupt society. Worse, from Buloz's royalist view, was to come the following year with George's *Horace*. Meanwhile—it is a measure of the Louis Philippe repression—Abbé de Lamennais was condemned to a year in prison for a pamphlet denouncing such practices of the monarchy as clubbing down workers for simply demonstrating their discontent. "Slowly," George noted, "the revolution is building."[13]

Meanwhile, too, winter passed as George wrote, cared for Chopin, worried about Solange, now in a boarding school, petted Maurice and rode twice a week in the Bois. In spring Chopin nervously girded himself for the nightmare of a public concert. To jolly him out of his mood, George lightly suggested he "play without candles or a public and on a silent keyboard."[14] Was it taken as lightly by Chopin? It has not been by George's critics. In June the family *sans* Solange, left in her boarding school, went to Nohant, where George continued work on *Horace*, begun in May.

When Buloz received installments of the new novel, the radicalism of the proletarian hero Paul Arsène, contrasted to the dilettantism of Horace Dumontet; the vividness of the massacre of students and workers in 1832, whose death cries George had heard beneath her balcony; the boldness of her hero's exhortation to the proletariat to unite and create a new social order—brought on the long-brewing break with Buloz. He refused to publish *Horace*. Further, he commissioned an article in his *Revue* denouncing the new "communism" of men like

Proudhon ("Property is theft") and Louis Blanc ("Towards a socialist organization of labor"). Buloz's own vagueness about the new scare-word is indicated by a note on the manuscript of *Horace*: "She is trying to transform me into an old-fashioned democrat."[15]

More contemporary light is thrown by a letter of Pierre Leroux to George Sand. It is deplorable, he wrote, for Buloz to be "the arbiter of your publications." Has she read the *Revue*'s attack on the ideas known as "communism," for which she and he were considered responsible—and rightly so? "For you *are* a communist and I am a communist. Only Lamennais, wrongly, does not want to be one." The word, Leroux explained in his heavy manner, "is the analogue in France of the Chartist movement in England." He himself would prefer *communionism*, "which expresses a social doctrine based on fraternity. But the people, who always go straight to the practical goal, have preferred *communism* to express a republic based on equality."[16]

A new *Revue Indépendante*, named by George, was now begun by Leroux in collaboration with Louis Viardot, who contributed money to it as well. Returning the advance for *Horace* she had received from Buloz, she let Leroux have the novel without payment—a trifle in comparison with the sums she would give him. The *Revue*'s first issues were not a howling success. "Leroux," Sainte-Beuve, who had his own commitment to Buloz, remarked acidly to a friend, "writes on philosophy like a water buffalo floundering in a marsh."[17] But with *Horace* and *Le Compagnon*, George Sand became the recognized spokesperson not only for women, but for all the underprivileged—for nine tenths of humanity—now not only in France, but throughout Europe, and beyond. "For the aristocracy of the intellect," Oscar Wilde would write in appreciation, "she had always the deepest veneration, but the democracy of suffering touched her more."[18]

Back in Paris after a summer at Nohant, George Sand explained her growing *engagement* in her own words. Many, she said to Duvernet, speak of "charity" and "brotherhood," but the bourgeoisie mouth the sentiments hypocritically. "There is no profit in it for them—and their institutions demonstrate it." Her own yearning for a "moral revolution" was based not so much on class against class as on a "religious and philosophical feeling for equality." When the communist revolution came —and it would, she thought—it might come "too quickly," before the people were prepared. George continues: men like Michel de Bourges say, " 'Let's make a revolution, we'll see what happens afterward.' We say, 'Let's make a revolution, but let's see beforehand what we'll see afterward.' " People in revolt will inspire the great, necessary change, but on the condition that they are enlightened—"about truth, justice . . . equality, freedom and brotherhood, in a word, about their rights and their duties." George Sand did not want "vague formulas." "What," she asked, "would be the precise freedom for the individual, what authority for the state, for society?" "What would be the form of property"—the means of production? Private, with all that implies in the way of exploitation of the worker, or collective—socialist?[19]

It was, as has been remarked, a period before Karl Marx's *Communist Manifesto* defined an unsentimental—he would say scientific instead of utopian—socialism, "when a slogan like 'Property Is Theft' did duty as a political platform."[20] But it spoke of the new social vision, of the narrowing down of the social problem to that of property—the factory—and of class relations, of profits and privileges and those who provided them, but of which they were deprived. George Sand's and Leroux's was a Christian communism, thus to the left of Christian socialism, more militant, more class conscious, but still utopian and ultimately classless in its hope: all would come together in a brotherhood of common humanity.

There was a mutual discovery of George Sand and the new wave of French proletarian poets: twenty-one-year-old Charles Poncy, stonecutter; Reboul, a baker; Magu, a weaver; Gilland, a locksmith. They sent her their poetry for advice. She wrote generously in their praise. They came to Rue Pigalle and sat at her feet. Some fell in love. Gently she rebuffed Poncy. "Like the moon," said Heine, "she looked upon them from her great height and with gentleness."[21] "No individual," George herself noted in her Piffoël journal, "is isolated from humanity."[22]

The worker-poets, for Chopin, were the great unwashed. He winced in their presence and flinched away from their exuberance. Their poetry was no more his than their manners. Their opinions, expressed heatedly, offended his own, their radicalism clashed with his aristocratic conservatism. The miracle was George's winning and holding the affection of both, though it was this spring of 1842 that Mickiewicz, Chopin's friend, confided to Madame Olivier, Sainte-Beuve's, that he considered Chopin, the morbidly sensitive invalid, George Sand's "evil genius, her moral vampire and her cross," who "tormented and might one day end by killing her." Madame Olivier had agreed. She doubted Chopin would ever bring George happiness: "He is a man of intelligence, talent and charm, but I do not think he has a heart."[23] He did, but he did not easily display it.

Mother, mistress and nurse, George Sand was the great consoler of Chopin and all the young men. "*You* are Consuelo!" burst from Pierre Leroux as he read the first chapters of the novel which was appearing even before *Horace* came to a close in the *Revue Indépendante*.[24] The vastly inventive novel *Consuelo* and its sequel *La Comtesse de Rudolstadt* constitute the major work of George, often compared to Goethe's *Wilhelm Meister*. Tracing the Europe-wide *wanderjahre*, adventures and evolution of a singer, in part inspired by the remarkable Pauline

Viardot, it would fill the next several years, though not exclusively. No novel, no single activity ever did. A veritable duffel bag of mid-nineteenth-century liberal ideals—virtually alone G.S.'s novels passed the censor of czarist Russia, smuggling in the new socialist ideas to the young revolutionaries—it was packed with Leroux's influences. Only half-jokingly, George ironically rebuked him for it.

"What a labyrinth of Freemasonry and secret worker societies you have led me into!" she wrote Leroux.[25] There was, too, a burgeoning reproachfulness for Leroux's bumbling inefficiency as an editor, for the incessant financial demands of his new piano-style linotype machine, which would never quite reach the operational stage.

Never would the novel satisfy more needs, combining as it did the functions of the following century's cinema, radio, television and shelfful of cassettes. *Consuelo*, including its continuation, *La Comtesse de Rudolstadt* (Consuelo's title and name upon marriage), has the flowing style of the *roman fleuve*, the cliff-hanging suspense of the serial novel spinning the endless tale of a free-spirited, wandering artist, a woman-troubador, a female Don Juan not so much in search of an impossibly perfect man as a perfectly possible life impossible without love. "That beautiful book," Elizabeth Browning called it; almost annually would Ibsen's wife read it.[26] Ideas abound, experiences multiply, bold statements fly like hot sparks: "Charity degrades those who receive it and hardens those who dispense it. All that is not a true exchange will disappear in the future society. We, I and my mate, practice that exchange now and so enter the ideal." "Preach to princes" as well as to the poor. "Life is a voyage with life as its goal." "We"—revolutionaries —"are marching to victory, or to martyrdom."[27]

A man no longer young read these lines in an American translation which he had found among his mother's books. At twenty-eight in 1847, he had reviewed George Sand's *The Journeyman-Joiner* (*Le Compagnon du Tour de France*) in the Brooklyn *Daily Eagle*—favorably but cautiously, since George Sand was viewed in puritan America as the seductive, seditious devil herself. Thus, a half-dozen years later, Walt Whitman came upon *Consuelo*, "his mother's copy." The epilogue and last pages changed his life, his language, his life-style. The pursuit of that story, hidden from the world by Whitman himself, by an American woman, Esther Shephard, is fascinating and instructive. That George Sand, in Dostoievsky's and Turgenev's eyes, should have been virtually the sainted, if maculate, mother of the Russian novel has become a commonplace. That she had seeded the first flowering of authentic American poetry, Whitman's "barbaric yawp," is still to enter not simply "women's studies," but world literary histories.

From *Le Compagnon*, and especially its illustrations, the conventionally dressed Whitman had taken his carpenter's garb and posed for his "carpenter portrait" in the first edition of *Leaves of Grass*. But what, Esther Shephard asked herself, "had turned Whitman, the conventional editor, writer of conventional and undistinguished, though flamboyant and patriotic prose and puerile poetry of conventional pattern, into the author of that strange poem *Leaves of Grass*, strange and wild in both its matter and manner? And what had turned the irascible newspaper editor, often angry and sometimes vituperative . . . into the [publicly] serene and happy and all-embracing expounder of love?" Her reply, with thesis-length proof: the epilogue of *The Countess of Rudolstadt*.

"My name is *man*," sings George Sand's poet-musician in those last pages. Whitman echoed it. "Man," he read, "is a trinity like God." He repeated it. "Man is free, equal and brother," said George. "No more masters, no more slaves. . . . France is the predestined among the nations." Whitman substituted America. George spoke of her period's "heaping up of scientific materials" as at most "the work of a stone-cutter," but found "neither edifice nor architect." Whitman hailed the "well-beloved stone-cutters" and prophesied, "When the materials are all prepared and ready, the architects shall appear." Whitman's "O Hymen! O Hymenee!" derived from lines of Sand. So did his concept of the all-encompassing lover, flinging "his arms, drawing men and women with undeniable love to his close embrace."[28] This was not only in the lines, it was in the lives, of George Sand.

Would Walt Whitman have arrived at himself without George Sand? Most likely. One chooses one's influences. However, his self-discovery came rather late and he did *not*, we know, come to it *without* her.

How many of George Sand's some seventy novels and novellas, so many like bullets expended in a battle, are still read with passion? Perhaps a dozen. Even six are a great deal, but it doesn't really matter. To be forever part of the living chain that is literature is immortality enough.

30

George and
Solange and Chopin

"Chopin," George Sand wrote happily to Delacroix from Nohant, "has composed two Mazurkas that are worth more than forty novels and say more than all the literature of our time."[1]

It was spring, 1842.

There were the good years with the bad days. After 1845 there would be the bad years with the good days. It may be the banal description of any marriage that sours. There were many good days of the good years, when the lovers went on gay excursions into the Nohant woods, Chopin astride the velvet-saddled little donkey reserved for him, George alongside on foot prodding it with her parasol; when Delacroix, who would soon have his own studio at Nohant, would listen as he painted to the bursts of music coming from Chopin's open window, "mingling with the song of birds and the scent of roses."[2]

In Paris that fall of 1842, the pair of lovers had moved to the romantic, enclosed Square d'Orléans, which still stuns visitors with the sudden, unexpected splendor of its vast, hidden garden, courtyard and lovely fountain. Chopin occupied the ground-floor apartment at No. 9 of the Square. From his small salon, across fountain and garden, he could lift his eyes to the larger apartment of George Sand above the vaulted passageway at No. 5. Maurice had a studio above his mother, Solange a small adjacent bedroom. At No. 7 were Charlotte Marliani and her husband. In the same cluster around the great courtyard were sculptor Dantan the younger, pianist and composer Kalkbrenner, dancer Marie-Sophie Taglioni. Nearby lived Louis and Pauline Viardot. No wonder

George called the commune at Square d'Orléans her Fourierist phalanstery. Meals were taken with the Marlianis, leaving George and Chopin free to retire when they wished, to work or to "dream."³ They had a rich mix of friends—artists and Polish patriots, writers and social philosophers, princesses and social snobs. Heinrich Heine enjoyed their company, and they his wit. Delacroix was the most intimate. The quintessential Romantic painter, he appreciated the same values in Chopin's music, though not uncharacteristically deplored them in George's writing. Chopin, Delacroix declared, was the "truest artist" he had ever met,⁴ a sentiment unreciprocated. Chopin, the musical innovator, preferred the conventional in painting, as he did in literature and life. He remained silent when Delacroix showed him and George the frescoes in progress at the Luxembourg palace, withholding his objections to their violent movement and explosive color; he was, as always, fastidiously polite.

"Delacroix," George observed, "understands Chopin and worships him. Chopin does not understand Delacroix. He esteems, cherishes and respects the man, but detests the painter. . . . He is a musician, and only a musician. . . . Michelangelo makes him uneasy, Rubens exasperates him. Everything that seems eccentric scandalizes him. . . . Strange anomaly!"⁵

It was one of the good days of the good years, glowingly described by George in her journal. She had spent half the day with Delacroix, talking—"he talks better than I write"—of Ingres' classic line and Delacroix's turbulent color. Ingres' personages, Delacroix had objected, were like the stiff figures of a Chinese fan, "figures of ivory, one glued upon the other." Ingres, he declared (anticipating the Impressionism of which he was a forerunner), "forgets one thing—reflections. . . . All is reflection in nature, all color is an exchange of reflected light."

They had talked as they walked to Delacroix's studio, where he changed for the evening, and went on to George's place, where they met Chopin at the door, and went up together. Maurice joined them. He listened as Delacroix continued to expound to Chopin on his theory of "reflections," comparing tones in painting to musical tones.

"How about the reflection of reflections?" asked Maurice.

"The devil!" exploded Delacroix. "Enough for today!" But restlessly he resumed. A chair, he insisted, his arm, he gesticulated, "drink insatiably of light," of color. Chopin was no longer listening. He had sat down to the piano and begun to improvise. He stopped.

"Go on," urged Delacroix. "You haven't come to the end."

"I haven't even begun," said Chopin. "But nothing is coming . . . nothing but reflections, shadows, shapes that have no form. I'm looking for the right color. I don't even find the right form."

"You won't find the one without the other," said Delacroix. "You'll find them both together."

"But what if it's only moonlight?"

"Then you will find the reflection of a reflection," said Maurice.

Chopin, continued George, "seemed pleased by this idea" and resumed his playing. "Slowly we began to see the quiet colors of the suave modulations sounding in our ears. Suddenly the note of blue appeared and we were in the deep azure of the translucent night." The music came to an end. Chopin rose. He accompanied Delacroix back to his studio. They talked . . . about their tailors.[6]

Chopin's "exquisite delicacy of *savoir vivre*," his canon of perfect manners, made him an excellent companion. But his very perfectionism, his sensitivity to a crossed look, a crumpled rose leaf, made him a difficult one.[7] In the first years, however, everything about the Venetian-glass Chopin had its endearing enchantment for George, "his fine face, his voice, his piano, his little sadnesses, even his cough."[8] When he went to Paris without her, Sand wrote in detail to Charlotte and Marie de Rozières about his care—to be sure he was greeted on arrival with hot water for his bath, that he have a cup of chocolate or broth when he rose, that he not be told she was writing.[9] Chopin fretted at the care, but appreciated it; when George was ill and in bed, he in turn became the zealous nurse.

They were mother and child—"the perfect incest," as was said of George's later novel, *François le Champi*, the story of a foundling raised by a woman who eventually married her charge and lived happily ever after, incidentally inspiring Thackeray's own *Henry Esmond*. Remarkably, George was not unconscious of it. Rather on the contrary, she consciously acted out her nature. As characteristically, she would spell it out clearly in a "splendid" novel, *Lucrezia Floriani*, scandal of the time.[10] Chopin's friends would find it cruel, but George was scarcely less lucid and cold-eyed vis-à-vis herself. Her Lucrezia Floriani is George Sand, faintly disguised as a thirty-year-old retired actress (and occasional writer for the theater) who has four children of three different fathers, none of them husbands by marriage. She falls in love with twenty-four-year-old Prince Karol, who is transparently Chopin— with his soft, adolescent beauty, his finely modeled face that showed "neither age nor sex" and was as hauntingly beautiful as that of a "sad and wonderful woman." The incestuous and the androgynous are never left in doubt. Nor are the sexual ambivalence and ambiguity of the conventional man in love. Prince Karol, says George, had probably loved only his mother before loving Lucrezia, and sought in his mistress, *à la* Musset, the licentious and virginal in the same person. As for Lucrezia, "Karol had become something like her son." They even discussed it (did George and Chopin as well?).

"'You are my mother, then?' Karol asked.

"'Yes, I am your mother,' she said, without reflecting that he might think it profane . . . which at such moments it indeed was."

Neurotic jealousy on Karol's part, straining quarrels with Lucrezia's children, led to the fatal break between the two lovers. Only the surface quarrels are recounted, particularly with Lucrezia's older son, mirroring the real-life coldness growing between Maurice, twenty-two in 1845, and Chopin. The year previous, Maurice and Pauline Viardot had become brief, clandestine lovers, but such was the closeness of mother and son, George had become Maurice's confidant. His now adult awareness and Oedipal resentment of Chopin as his mother's lover were inevitable. However, George was surprisingly insensitive to the similar, if more complex, feelings of Solange, seventeen in the fall of 1845, and the form they would take.

Solange had a wildness unblessed by genius which is unpardoned by posterity. She was George's daughter, George's product; she paid the price of her mother's moral freedom. If it was difficult to be George Sand's husband (to add to the complexity, Solange rather doubted Casimir was her father), it was as difficult to be Sand's daughter. (But does one ever ask, even if one should, Whatever became of George Byron's daughter?) Solange had seen her mother's lovers in an intimacy her brother had not. It was too much for any child. She had both resented and envied the lovers and her mother, and when she became a young woman, she *knowingly* became her mother's rival, flirting with the young men of Berry, as did the young Aurore Dupin. It is in the knowingness that one tends to find wickedness. She coquettishly teased the intrigued, delighted, then infatuated Chopin, deeply shaken by the boyish, if buxom, beauty of Solange. In turn, an aging George Sand was affected with envy and jealousy, troubling, unconscious, understandable and sad. And culpable.

Solange had experienced her own sadness in the love-hate relationship with her mother, but George Sand had failed to respond to it. For instance, at fourteen Solange had read *Mauprat* and had movingly written her mother about it. "Edmonde," she said sadly, "is the most beautiful of your daughters. I am the ugliest."[11] George replied with a scolding letter about Solange's behavior at the boarding school and unfeelingly remarked that it was Edmée, and not Edmonde, who is the heroine of *Mauprat*. George's letters were almost always hectoring, concealing from herself any sense of guilt. Two years later she expressed a concern that is virtually prurient in her letter to Marie de Rozières, a former pupil of Chopin who had become Solange's chaperone and piano teacher, and along the way the unhappy, discarded mistress of Comte Wodzinski (Maria's brother, to Chopin's chagrin). "There comes a time when little girls are no longer little girls," George wrote

Marie in June 1845, "when you must carefully watch what you and others are saying in their presence. So, not a word, *however casual,* about the masculine sex."

Marie de Rozières, George sharply instructed, was no longer to take Solange with her on Solange's days off from school. Solange was too advanced in womanhood and Marie had become too forward since her affair with Wodzinski. "True love and marriage," wrote George Sand the mother, "are equally sacred to me. Formerly you were not a coquette, but now, my little pussycat, your eyes have taken on a terribly voluptuous expression . . . and men have noticed it." It is Marie's business, of course, George remarked, but until she has resolved her "little nervous crisis by taking a lover or a husband," George preferred her seeing a bit less of Solange.[12]

The particular vulnerability of young women—surely George often thought of her mother Sophie in her youth—in the male-contoured society of her time was never far from her mind. Count Wodzinski emerged unscathed from his having had and abandoned a mistress, but Marie de Rozières was forever marked by it. It makes the courage—and achievement—of the young George Sand all the more remarkable. At this mid-moment in her life, however, she exercised more caution and care, perhaps because with middle age there was less passion, perhaps because Maurice and Solange were no longer children, perhaps because of Chopin's jealousy, so often referred to in the letters and *Lucrezia*. At the end of 1844, slim, slight, thirty-three-year-old Louis Blanc, the leading socialist of his day—"from each according to his abilities, to each according to his needs," he had written in his *Organisation du Travail* eight years before Karl Marx—was briefly George's lover, but so carefully managed that it was unknown at the time.[13] George may well have been faithful to Chopin during the five or six good years; afterwards there was the young Victor Borie, twenty-seven in 1845, whom George chose as the editor of the liberal revue, *l'Éclaireur,* which she and her La Châtre friends had founded.

"There are some infidelities," George had remarked shortly before to Pierre Leroux, "which do not destroy love."[14] It is one of her wisest observations. We cannot look to Louis Blanc or Victor Borie for the beginning of the end of the long liaison with Frédéric Chopin, but rather to the accumulation of frictions between two sensibilities exasperated by the intrusions of Maurice and Solange. Indeed, had George and Chopin been only two, their love might well have endured until Chopin's death—from tuberculosis—several years later.

In the fall of 1845, however, George compounded the fractured scene when she introduced and eventually adopted a daughter at Nohant, Augustine Brault, a distant cousin on Sophie's side. The similarity of her story to Sophie's, in fact, induced George to become the poor girl's protectress, saving her from the youthful Sophie's fate, paying her grubby, avaricious parents for the privilege and burden. The pretty young woman soon drove thoughts of Pauline Viardot from Maurice's mind as George looked fondly on. Predictably, however, Solange became livid with jealousy when George foolishly displayed her partiality for Augustine. She found constant fault with her comely cousin, took on airs and lorded it over the poor girl as the true daughter of the household. She easily enlisted Chopin, equally resentful of the plebian intruder and by now helplessly ensnared by Solange.[15] The enlarged Nohant family found itself divided into two hostile camps with Augustine as the occasion, or the pretext—George and Maurice versus Solange and Chopin. Meantime, for distraction and money, *in four days* of November 1845 George wrote one of her small, enduring masterpieces, *La Mare au Diable*, a novel of the idealized Berry countryside. In the midst of personal storms, George always managed thus to assure herself a restoring serenity. It was the source of her strength; it could also be the cause of her companion's further distancing.

Chopin's father had died; George had written to his widowed mother in consolation and received a reply in French, expressing gratitude for George's *"solicitude maternelle"* for her *"dear child,"* Frédéric.[16] Chopin's sister Louise and her husband then visited Nohant for several weeks in the summer; and George and Chopin talked of going to Italy together. It was an interlude of happiness which did not last. Chopin's letters home began to express his extreme distaste for "the young man" —Maurice—and "the cousin"—Augustine.[17] He was both fascinated and irritated by his feelings for Solange. He commenced uncommonly to criticize George's treatment of her, breaking his own code of sacrosanct privacy. He translated his jealousy of the young men around the flirting Solange into a redoubled jealousy directed at George Sand. Too late she understood it.[18] At the time it simply brought a bewildered, redoubled irritation on her own part.

It was the following spring that George began to write *Lucrezia Floriani*. The same spring Solange met a suitor in Fernand de Preaulx, a young man of lesser, land-poor nobility, who initially was more attracted to Augustine, piquing and infuriating Solange. By summer the exchanges were irascible, the irritations undisguised. During a hot spell George wrote Marie de Rozières with rough humor, "Chopin is astonished that he *sweats*. He's desolated. He says despite all his bathing, he *stinks!* We laugh until the tears run to see that *ethereal* being refuse to sweat like everybody else. But don't speak of it to him. He would die if he discovered people knew he sweated." More gravely, George and a justly shocked Chopin quarreled when she sent away an old gardener who had been with her forty years, because, she said, he had been robbing her for twenty.[19] She fired a warning shot at Chopin as well—and wrote about this, too, to Marie do Rozières: "It was a good thing to get a little angry with him. It gave me courage to tell him a few truths and to warn him that my patience might wear thin. Since then, he has recovered his good sense, and you know how good, admirable and even excellent he can be when he's not mad."[20]*

Either Chopin from a blinding narcissism failed to recognize himself in Prince Karol, when George Sand, one evening, read the manuscript of *Lucrezia* aloud to him and Delacroix, or he refused to acknowledge it. Delacroix was not in doubt, and he spent an uncomfortable evening as he listened. "Executioner and victim astonished me equally," he later confided to Madame Jaubert. "Madame Sand seemed to be completely at ease, Chopin throughout expressed his admiration for the story. At midnight we retired. Chopin walked with me and I seized the opportunity to sound out his true feelings. Was he playing a role for me? No, he simply did not understand. Not for a moment did he cease his praise for the novel."[22] Others, such as Heine, Charlotte Marliani, Balzac, Liszt and Hortense Allart, on the other hand, instantly recognized Chopin in Prince Karol and George Sand in Lucrezia when the novel was published. They were as indignant as Delacroix and sharply criticized George for writing it. George, of course, stoutly denied any resemblances.

In the fall Solange's engagement to Fernand de Preaulx was formally announced. George was neither opposed to the marriage, nor warmly in favor of it. Rather, she was somewhat bemused by the prospect of a "son-in-law who was an aristocrat, a monarchist and a hunter of wild boars."[23] She and her guests, among whom was Emmanuel Arago, went on several excursions, twice salmon fishing in the Creuse. Chopin did not accompany them. "These things," he wrote his family, "fatigue me more than they are worth, and when I am tired, I am not very gay, and the young people resent it. . . ."[24] He would remain at Nohant instead and work on his Sonata for piano and violoncello; it would be his last major composition. However, when all were together again at Nohant, Chopin would often improvise on the piano as the young people performed in little ballets or skits on the stage of the ingenious theater he had devised for the château. In the appropriate mood, Chopin was a magnificent mime and incomparable entertainer, though his imitations, particularly of old Polish Jews, could be cruel.

Darker moods became the more prevalent. As Solange flaunted her engagement to Fernand de Preaulx, she simultaneously set about destroying any possibility of marriage between Maurice and Augustine by

---

* When a twenty-three-year-old British admirer of George Sand's writing, Matthew Arnold, visited Nohant at this time, he found nothing untoward. The "striking" George Sand, he noted, received him with "frank, cordial simplicity" and he remarked on Chopin's "wonderful eyes."[21]

telling Chopin and others that they were already lovers. She thus rendered Maurice ridiculous for marrying someone who had so easily become his mistress. They probably *were* lovers: Maurice was puerilely indecisive and irresponsible, and George sometimes scolded him for it. Tantalized and troubled by the emotions tearing at him, Chopin was exceptionally beside himself and interfered. He behaved badly with Augustine and spoke sharply to Maurice. Solange alone was untouched by his cold anger as he struck, exasperated with himself, at those around him. Maurice told his mother he was leaving Nohant. "That," said George Sand firmly, "could not be considered." She so informed Chopin, who resented what appeared to him as her "choice." "He hung his head and declared I no longer loved him. What blasphemy after eight years of maternal devotion! But the poor irritated soul was in a state of delirium. I thought a few months of separation and silence would heal the hurt he felt."[25]

In November 1846, Chopin left Nohant for Paris. It was not the first time he had gone on alone, George following shortly afterwards. But this time, though neither knew it, it was for the last time. And this time, the most wretched months of George Sand's life were to follow.

In February 1847, Solange and her mother went to Paris with Maurice and Fernand de Preaulx, George to arrange her publishing affairs and Solange her trousseau and marriage contract. Chopin was seen, cordially enough, but George was already determined to give up her residence at the Square d'Orléans and live the year round at Nohant. "All Paris" was aware that all was not well between the lovers, but since it had been predicted from the beginning—eight years before —not much was made of it now.

The American feminist writer Margaret Fuller, bearing a letter of introduction from Mazzini, visited George at this time. "I never liked a woman better," she wrote a friend, passing on the current Paris gossip: "Her daughter is just about to be married. It is said there is no congeniality between her and her mother; but for her son she seems to have much love, and he loves and admires her extremely." Shortly afterwards Margaret Fuller met Chopin, but not, she says, with George Sand, "although he lives with her, and has for the last twelve [sic] years. . . . He is always ill, and as frail as a snow-drop, but an exquisite genius. . . . It is said here that Madame S. has long had only friendship with Chopin, who, perhaps, on his side prefers to be a lover, and a jealous lover; but she does not leave him, because he needs her care so much, when sick and suffering. About all this, I do not know; you cannot know much about anything in France, except what you see with your two eyes. Lying is ingrained in 'la grande nation.'"[26] Actually, it is somewhat startling to learn that so much *was* known about George

Sand's intimate life—and talked about in Paris' salons with a cutting truth Margaret Fuller, with American innocence, mistook for lying.

At this point a brash, thirty-one-year-old bohemian sculptor, Auguste Clésinger, entered George's life. Rather, he re-entered it: the year previously Clésinger had written Sand a wildly enthusiastic—and calculating—letter, begging permission to carve the name of Consuelo on one of his bolder sculptures. George had readily granted her accord. Hearing of her arrival in Paris with Solange, Clésinger now hastened to them, imploring the "glorious" opportunity of immortalizing them both in marble. Again George was agreeable. Separately mother and daughter sat for their busts in Clésinger's studio. Between poses, the sculptor paid court to Solange, and they may well have become lovers. On the very eve of signing her marriage contract, Solange announced to poor Preaulx that the marriage was off, and she sent him back to the Berry. George pitied the jilted fiancé, but was more impressed by the impassioned Clésinger. Was he not an artist, one of their own kind, "all flame and fire"?[27] And was not Solange imitating the young George Sand, neither mother nor daughter seemingly realizing that *all* copies are bad copies?

Charlotte Marliani, Delacroix, Emmanuel Arago and Chopin united in warning George about Clésinger, his drunkenness, dissoluteness, indebtedness, his brutality concerning women. George went directly to the sculptor with the stories. He denied them; she believed him. She left with Solange for Nohant in April. From there she wrote Clésinger, suggesting he come, but not mention to anyone that she had written him. He arrived, exuberant and compelling, "winning" George's consent to his marriage with Solange. George (duplicitly) to Maurice (who had remained behind in Paris): Clésinger had stormed Nohant, like a "Caesar," demanding a *yes* or *no* reply in twenty-four hours. Solange had said *yes*. Clésinger was leaving that very night for Paris to see Maurice, then to Besançon to see his father, whom he would take to Guillery to get Casimir's consent to the marriage, returning with them both to Paris, where George and Solange would meet them for the publishing of the banns and the signing of the marriage contract, etc., etc. "You see," George continued, "that's the way it will be, because that's the way he wants it and does things, immediately, going without sleep or food. . . . I am astonished and pleased by such strength and untiring will . . . it will be the saving of your restless sister. She will go straight with him and be happy, too, because he loves passionately whatever he wins by conquest." As for Chopin, "not a word to him. It is none of his business. Once the Rubicon has been passed, his *ifs* and *buts* can do only harm."[28]

The Rubicon *had* been crossed when Clésinger and Solange had become lovers, and George was aware of it. She was both anxious that they marry and half-fearful of it. She slept badly or not at all and was in a state of nerves. She was desperately in need of money for Solange's dowry and equally desperate for assurance that she was doing no wrong in pressing for the marriage. She sought advice which she did not heed. She wrote *Célio Floriani* as if in a dream, in twelve days, suffering painful migraine headaches. It was George Sand's thirty-third novel. And when Chopin finally heard of Solange's imminent marriage, he fell seriously ill. George was struck with remorse. "Take care of him!" she cried to Marie de Rozières.[29] She herself, she explained, could not leave Nohant, because of Solange and Clésinger. She worried, she fretted, she alternately accused and defended herself, and thought fitfully of suicide. A week before the wedding, on May 12, 1847, she wrote a long letter, an *apologia pro vita sua*, to Count Grzymala; it was accusation and excuse, attack and self-defense; it would be shown to Chopin.

She would go to Paris, George wrote, "and if Chopin is up to it, I shall bring him back with me to Nohant." But he must not interfere again, because of his dislike for Clésinger or his differences with Maurice. It would mean the loss of everything for herself as well as for Chopin.

> It's all so difficult and delicate. I do not know any way to calm and reassure the poor, sick soul [Chopin], who is irritated even by my efforts to restore him to health. . . .
>
> For seven years I have lived the life of a virgin with him— *and with others.* I have grown old before my time, though it was no sacrifice or effort for me, since I had become tired of passion and disillusioned beyond remedy. If any woman on earth should have inspired him with absolute confidence, it was I. But he has never understood. I know many people blame me, some for having exhausted him by my sensual demands, others for having driven him to despair by my indiscretions. I think *you* understand! But *he,* he complains that I have half-killed him by my restraint, whereas I know for a certainty that I should have really killed him had I acted differently.

If only, said George despairingly, Chopin would allow one to enter his heart and cure him, "but, no, he closes himself off hermetically even from his best friends."[30]

At least Solange, George hoped, was settled at last and would find some measure of happiness with Clésinger. But this, too, was not to be. While they were away, a marriage had been arranged for Augustine with Théodore Rousseau, a fine landscape painter who was a friend of Maurice. On their return, the Clésingers found plans for *that* wedding well advanced and blessed by George Sand, who, moreover, had promised Rousseau one hundred thousand francs as Augustine's dowry. That may have rankled most. Solange promptly wrote Rousseau an anonymous letter, retailing Augustine's "scandalous" behavior with Maurice and accusing her of deceitfulness in concealing it. Rousseau was so thoroughly discountenanced he unceremoniously took off. George wrote him denying the accusation, then, disheartened, told him to go to blazes. Disillusionment with Clésinger was a harder blow. Discovery of the extent of his debts—over twenty-four thousand francs spent in fantasies for himself and Solange: jewels, carriage, a tailor bill of over five thousand francs—was not nearly so disenchanting as his demand on George that she mortgage Nohant—*Nohant!*—to repay them. George indignantly refused. Solange insolently insisted. There was a bitter quarrel and George asked the couple to leave.

The following day Solange packed, stripping the room George had furnished for them of almost all its belongings. Clésinger meanwhile blustered about the house, picking a quarrel with Augustine. George kept to herself upstairs, hoping to wait out the storm until the pair had departed. The village priest, having heard through Hippolyte of the trouble brewing, saw to it that he was nearby should it occur. This wretched scene took place:

Clésinger accused a house guest, Maurice's painter friend Lambert, of rudely failing to "salute" Solange when she came into the drawing room. He aimed a blow at Lambert, and missed. Maurice stepped between them. He was menaced by Clésinger's mallet. George, who had hurried downstairs, intervened. She was hit in the chest by the hammer. Pistols were brandished. A male servant pinned Clésinger to the wall. The priest rushed in. Solange, who had been cheering her husband on, now changed sides. How, she asked, could he have struck her mother? The couple left, bag and baggage, for an inn at La Châtre. There they told all and sundry of their ill-treatment. "Three hundred" were in the streets when they departed several days later for Paris, Solange crying from the carriage taking them away, "This is the happiest day of my life!"[31]

George Sand to Marie de Rozières, mid-July 1847: "The diabolical couple left yesterday evening, crippled with debts, triumphant in their impudence and leaving behind them a scandal they'll never be rid of. For three days I was threatened with *murder* in my own house. I never want to see either of them again. They shall never again set a foot in my home. They have gone too far. Dear God, what have I done to deserve such a daughter!"[32]

Sleepless, nerve-torn, racked with headaches, George wrote to Chopin (and was both worried and irritated by his not answering), to Delacroix and other friends. A letter of seventy-one pages went to Emmanuel Arago, an outpouring that recapitulated everything that happened from the time of Solange's courtship by Fernand de Preaulx to the harrowing scene at Nohant. Once again George tried to prove too much, persuading herself and the world that she had been entirely in the right, that although she may have been "the worst of women," she had been "the best of mothers," that only now had she become aware of Chopin's feelings for Solange and his betrayal, however platonic, of herself. The anger rose as she wrote, and George Sand scrawled the ugliest line she ever penned: "And I? . . . For nine years, bursting with life, I have been bound to a corpse, chained by pity and fear of seeing him die of chagrin," because she refrained from making love for Chopin's own sake. The letter had taken a week in its writing. By its end she had recovered her composure. "Since this morning," she closed, "I have begun to regain control of myself once more."[33]

Entering her forty-fourth year, George Sand now set calmly to taking stock of herself, examining her past so as to see where she was going: she commenced writing *Histoire de Ma Vie*, the story of her life, as history itself was swelling to a full tide, bearing her with it.

31

Muse of the Revolution

Should one be surprised that a society based on the opposition of classes ends with a brutal clash between them?
. . . As George Sand has written, "Combat or death, a
bloody battle or nothingness. That is the way the question
is inescapably posed."
> —Karl Marx, closing lines of *Misère de la Philo-
> sophie*, written in the winter of 1846–47[1]

Strike and strike hard! . . . Fight as I never have. Leave
behind those who fall. Dig a trench. After victory it will
be time enough to bury the dead.
> —George Sand, letter to Louis Blanc, early
> November, 1847[2]

Life in France, Alexis de Tocqueville observed as he looked about him,
was peaceful, flat and enervating.

"France is bored," remarked poet-politician Alphonse de Lamartine
on the eve of the February, 1848, revolution.[3] Diplomat before he was a
poet, eloquent, romantic, fifty-seven-year-old Lamartine had slowly
evolved under the "enervating" Louis Philippe into a liberal republican
and leader of the opposition to the monarchy. As such he had met and
corresponded with George Sand.

The street riots in Milan on January 2, 1848, seemed distant from
the perspective of Paris. How much more so from provincial Nohant.
The revolt shortly following in Sicily and Naples would bring Giuseppe
Mazzini hurrying back to Italy from exile in London. But on January
twenty-fifth George Sand wrote simply to thank him for the gift of his
mother's ring which he had left when visiting her. Two weeks later she
took up the revolutions in his Austria-occupied homeland. "They
were," she said, "a big step—perhaps. But it merely meant despotism
replaced by a constitutional régime," brutality by bourgeois corruption,

as in France. A real, that is, socialist, change was remote, certainly in France.[4]

George Sand was right, but only in the historic long run, for she did not anticipate—despite her fiery letters to Louis Blanc—what was to occur a fortnight later in Paris and thereafter throughout Europe. In six weeks a dozen rulers would fall, though eventually they or their equivalents—it is here George Sand was prophetically right—would return to power. On the eve of their downfall events everywhere seemed under control. Prince von Metternich, the Austrian foreign minister, dominated the Holy Alliance of Russia, Prussia and Austria, as the Holy Alliance dominated Europe. Since the Congress of Vienna in 1815 he had stamped the Age of Metternich on the Continent with his image of the ideal State: autocratic absolutism tempered by salon wit and supported by a loyal army, a submissive bureaucracy, a grateful Church and a mounted police. The first signs of republicanism were a sickness to be cured, if in an acute stage of contagion, by bleeding—with the Austrian Army as the Continent's medical corps.

True, France had been feverish with revolt in July 1830, but in that crisis the *grande bourgeoisie*—financiers and bankers—had simply supplanted an anachronistic Bourbon king with the perfect bourgeois monarch, Louis Philippe, Duc d'Orléans.

More than bordeom, however, shook his régime in 1848. As Lamartine had also remarked, the Revolution of 1789 had multiplied the discontent by substituting the "domination of a king by that of wealth . . . instead of one tyrant, there were now several thousand." Lamartine overlooked the feudal overlords of the *ancien régime*, but his description of the post-revolutionary scene is effective and accurate enough. "Two or three hundred families," estimated Adolphe Thiers, Louis Philippe's one-time Minister of Interior, in a work bluntly titled *The Right of Property*. Indeed it was the propertied who constituted the *pays légal*, the legal country—the less than two hundred and fifty thousand who were privileged to vote and hold office in a land of thirty-five million. "Get rich," advised François Guizot, the Prime Minister, "if you want to vote."

As production increased, "society" became richer, but as competition increased, the workers became poorer: wages were lowered as profits went into machines. Factories became the dark, satanic mills which were Blake's vision of hell. In Lyons of 1848, Adolphe Blanqui, brother of the more radical Auguste, observed working girls "laboring fourteen hours a day at looms, where they were hung from a strap, in order to be able to use both their hands and their feet, whose continuous, simultaneous movement was indispensable for the weaving." In the Haut-Rhin in 1847, thirteen thousand of sixty-one thousand workers were children.

In Rouen, they were so stunted, said Blanqui, that they looked like little old men; in Lille, they were "skeletal, hunchbacked, deformed."[5] From the age of six to eight, they stood in front of their machines up to sixteen hours a day. But when child labor was protested in the Chamber of Deputies, it was replied: if children were not allowed to work, how would their families live?

Strikes were illegal, unions a criminal conspiracy, but in Paris alone at the end of 1847 thousands of workers were members of hundreds of secret societies and political clubs. "In the silence," Heine had written of Paris, "one can hear a soft, monotonous dripping. It is the dividends of the capitalist continually trickling in, continually mounting up. One can literally hear them multiply—the profits of the rich. And one can hear too, in between, the low sobs of the destitute; and now and then a harsher sound, like a knife being sharpened."[6]

The sound was heard throughout Europe; Paris was the center of the socialist "conspiracy." On the request of the Prussian Government, Marx was expelled from the French capital. So was a new friend of George Sand, the Russian aristocrat and anarchist, Mikhail Bakunin. He was less familiar than Mazzini, but scarcely less warm. "I have just received an order to leave France. . . ." he wrote on December 14, 1847. "Please think occasionally of a man who venerated you, even before he met you, for often in the darkest days of his life you were a consolation and a light."[7]

For six months Louis Philippe's opposition had been holding a series of huge political banquets at which criticism of his prime minister was the principal entertainment. The opposition consisted of a handful of deputies, mostly constitutional monarchists, but some, such as Lamartine, republicans; the bulk of it was the petty bourgeoisie clamoring for entrance into the *pays légal*.

Criticism of François Guizot's government, which ran France as if it were a private industry, was again the announced entertainment for the affair of February 22. Nine hundred subscribed to it. But this time the government banned the banquet. The opposition persisted; the government threatened to send troops; the opposition retreated.

From Nohant it all looked like a political charade. "I don't see anything coming out of the banquet affair," George wrote Maurice, then in Paris. "It's no more than an intrigue between ministers on their way out and ministers on their way up, they hope. . . . I don't believe the people will take sides in a quarrel between Monsieur Thiers and Monsieur Guizot. Thiers is the better, but he won't give more to the poor than any of the others. So don't get involved and have your head beaten for no good cause."[8]

In fact the people of Paris with their particular genius—one is tempted to call it—for transforming a crowd into a political force did take sides, believing it their own. Summoned to demonstrate at the Place de la Madeleine by radical newspapers, leaflets and club leaders, they turned out on February twenty-second, banquet or no. From nine to eleven that morning women and men stood in the intermittent rain. There were a few cries, a few slogans, some rough humor. Then, at eleven, a great column of students arrived from the Latin Quarter singing the "Marseillaise"—"To arms, citizens!"—their ranks swelled on the way by young workers and artisans.

The crowd became a multitude. It pressed on to the Place de la Concorde and across the Seine to the Chamber of Deputies. Finally persuaded to leave by a company of the National Guard, it returned to the Place de la Concorde. Then, trotting from the Quai d'Orsay, came a platoon of horse troops. The rain was heavy now, and as darkness fell, barricades went up. There was some firing—the first in Paris since a long time—and two women were killed.

The next day Louis Philippe thought it preferable to call for the National Guard rather than the Army, fearing civil war. The National Guard, however, was composed of citizens paying for their own uniforms and fed up with the government, and led by officers who wanted the vote Guizot refused them. In a dozen places that morning, the Guard came between the demonstrating crowds and the charging horse troops—and the Guard, too, cried, "Long live reform!" as well as "Down with Guizot!"

Disheartened by this 'betrayal,' essentially a retiring man, Louis Philippe offered to sacrifice Guizot and replace him by another conservative. Opposition deputies rejoiced in the Chamber and officers of the Guard galloped with the news through Paris. A bit more pressure on their part, they felt, and they would have their perfectly reasonable reforms from a chastened monarch. The Parisian mob having played its role, it could be thanked and sent home. But students again marched through the streets singing the "Marseillaise." The massed crowds cheered them, the National Guardsmen protected them, and the news that one conservative might replace another did not send many people home. On the contrary, the crowds sensed their strength—and the barricades that had gone up the day before remained standing. More men and women than ever stood behind them, but they continued to raise the limited cry, "*Vive la Réforme!*"

That evening of February twenty-third, along the Boulevard des Capucines, came a cheerful enough crowd from the Place de la Bastille, carrying torches and flags, but no arms. They were stopped by a cordon of troops. A sergeant, believing his colonel menaced by a brandished

torch, nervously pulled the trigger of his rifle. Hundreds of other soldiers fired, and fifty-two demonstrators were dead. The crowd fled one
way, the soldiers another. But revolutionaries—or simply angry men—
returned, seized passing tumbrels, piled them with the dead and
solemnly paraded through Paris under torchlight. Now barricades
sprang up everywhere, across broad boulevards and narrow working-
class streets, some with red flags raised above them. Few of the barricades, however, were razed by the demoralized troops. During the
night, the secret workers societies and clubs under their leaders formed
hard, organized cores among the people; a riot had become a revolution. The cry now was "Long live the Republic!" And at noon the next
day Louis Philippe abdicated in favor of his nine-year-old grandson,
packed his bags, and fled to London as Mr. Smith.

In three days, at a total cost of two hundred and seventy-five men
and fourteen women dead among the people, and seventy-two among
the forces of order, France had overthrown a monarchy. Before the
third day was over, it would be a republic.

The grandchild of Louis Philippe was rejected that afternoon in the
Chamber of Deputies. The people of Paris had taken possession.
Names for the provisional government of the Second French Republic
were shouted and written down, such as Lamartine, who became chief
of the government, Étienne Arago, brother of George Sand's close
friend Emmanuel, and Ledru-Rollin, a socialist and another friend.
Through massed, cheering streets the new leaders then marched in a
body to the Hôtel de Ville. There they added Louis Blanc and three
other radicals as secretaries of the government. It was on Blanc's insistence that Albert "the Worker"—he was known by no other name—was
among the three. A gas worker, he was probably the first workingman
ever to be a cabinet minister.

There was now a government, but no program. Revolutions rarely
come into power with five-year plans. On February twenty-fifth, the
Right to Work, thanks to Blanc, was proclaimed. On the twenty-sixth,
National Workshops were established for the thousands of unemployed. The idea had long been Louis Blanc's, but the workshops were
entrusted to Alexandre Marie, a right-wing minister. On the twenty-
eighth, in compensation, a Commission for Labor was created to be
headed by Blanc, but it had no power.*

On March first, George Sand arrived in a festive Paris, bright with illusions about the future, to join her friends in the government—Arago,
Ledru-Rollin, Lamartine, Blanc. She installed herself on Rue Condé

---

* On the twenty-eighth, too, Marx's *Communist Manifesto* was published in London and copies of it, in German, reached Paris. Little, if any, note was then taken
of it, however.

with Maurice, a step from Louis Blanc's headquarters in the Luxembourg palace. She set up her own "office" in the nearby Pinson restaurant. "You can find me here," she joyfully scribbled to Delacroix, "from eleven to one in the morning and six to eight in the evening. Be happy and calm about the future, so long, at least, as God wills it that my friends remain in power."[9] Life was exciting, too full of revolution's promise to waste time in sleep. "It was not in the tower of art that George Sand ever shut herself up."[10] Certainly not in these lively days.

The men in the government, George found, were on the whole "honest and good men." The bourgeoisie was frightened, but pretended "enchantment."[11] As for the people of Paris: four days after her arrival, from a window of Guizot's former offices, George watched with Lamartine a great cortege as it followed the dead of February. "It was a beautiful sight, simple and touching—four hundred thousand people shoulder to shoulder from the Madeleine to the Column of July. Not a gendarme, not a police officer, yet such order, such decency, such composure, such mutual consideration that not a foot was stepped on, not a hat crushed. . . . The people of Paris are the greatest in the world!"[12]

And that evening, amidst the moving events of a day when a new and better world, it seemed, was being born, George met Chopin. They met at the door of Charlotte Marliani's foyer. In a letter to Solange, to whom he was writing frequently, Chopin told the story of their last meeting on March 4, 1848:

> Yesterday I went to see Madame Marliani and, on leaving, found myself in the doorway of the anteroom facing your mother, who was arriving with Lambert. I said *bonjour* to Madame your mother and my second words were to ask whether she had heard from you recently. "A week ago," she replied. "Nothing yesterday, or the day before?" "No." "Then let me inform you that you are a grandmother. Solange has a little girl, and I am pleased to be the first to inform you." I bowed and descended the staircase. Combes was with me, and since I had forgotten to say that you were doing well, an important thing above all for a mother (as you yourself now understand, Mother Solange), I asked Combes to go back up the stairs, not being able to make the climb myself, and tell her that you were well, and the child also.* I waited for Combes below. Your mother descended with him and asked me with a great deal of interest a number of questions about your health. I replied that you had written me *with your own hand* the day after your child's birth; that you had suffered a great deal; but that the sight of your little girl had made you forget your suf-

---

* Solange's child died the next day, March 6, at Guillery, having lived a week.

fering. She asked me how I was. I said I was well, and told the concierge to open the door. I bowed and went on foot to Square d'Orléans.[13]

Chopin thought George "looked well," adding with a touch of sad irony, "I daresay she's happy at the republican triumphs." George, too, recalled their meeting in her memoirs. "I saw him for a moment in March. I shook his hand. It was icy cold and trembling. I wanted to talk to him, but he fled."[14] In April Chopin would leave the republican scene for London.

As soon as she heard of the child, George wrote a letter of felicitation to Solange, then sorrowfully shortly afterwards, on hearing of its death, one of condolences, both arriving almost together. She would do all she could for Clésinger, George consoled her daughter, in the way of government commissions. A good friend now was Ledru-Rollin, Minister of Interior—and it was at this time that George effectively changed his mind about appointing Michel de Bourges as *Commissaire* of Bourges, on the grounds that Michel was no longer the same man politically.

Commissaires were the Republic's Commissioners, generally sent from Paris to the provinces with the mission of promoting the Republic, directing its propaganda, supervising its affairs. The government needed friends wherever it could find them: the countryside was largely royalist. Duvernet became *Sous-Commissaire* at La Châtre, because of George's influence, as well as others in the departments of Indre and Nièvre. On March eighth she returned to Nohant to install Maurice as Mayor and oversee the beginnings of the Republic in the Berry. Nohant celebrated her arrival and Maurice's assumption of office, but in La Châtre the bourgeoisie mobilized demonstrations against Duvernet. "If only all the communes were like Nohant!" George cried.[15]

Before leaving Paris, she and Ledru-Rollin had discussed her writing the leading articles for the government's *Bulletin de la République*, which was distributed officially throughout France. While in Nohant, George set to it with a will. Articles seemed to flow from her pen: she became the Muse of the Revolution. In monarchist Europe republicanism meant revolution. Her impassioned *Lettre au Peuple*, her appealing *Mot à la Classe Moyenne* (A Word to the Lower Middle Class) were reprinted in the *Bulletin*. In No. 4 she boldly extended the idea of republicanism—which to George Sand was essentially equality —to the extreme of utopian socialism. "The Republic," she wrote, "is the rule of the people."

> Citizens, France at this moment is trying to achieve . . . the greatest work of modern times: the foundation of a government of all the people, the organization of democracy, the Re-

public of all rights, all interests, all spirits, all virtues! . . .
The new idea may well take over in Europe.

George added a few paragraphs addressed *To the Rich:*

> The great fear—or pretext—of the aristocracy [sic] at this
> hour is communism [*l'idée communiste*]* . . . By the word
> *communism* they really mean the people, their needs, their
> hopes. Let us not be confused—the people are the people,
> communism is the calumniated, misunderstood *future* of the
> people. The ruse is useless: it is the people who upset and
> worry you.[16]

Later George Sand would write that *immediate* communism, imposed
by force, would be the negation of communism itself, because destruc-
tive of the principle of fraternity.

Bulletin No. 4 appeared on March nineteenth; the day following
George was back in Paris, plunged into work. "Here I am," she exulted
to Maurice, "already as busy as a statesman. Today so far I've written
two government circulars, one for the Ministry of Public Instruction,
the other for the Ministry of the Interior. What amuses me is that all
go to the mayors, and you'll be getting your *mother's* instructions
through official channels! Ha, ha, Mr. Mayor, you'd better watch your
step and to begin, you must read aloud every Sunday the *Bulletins* you
received to your assembled National Guard. And after you've read and
explained them, you must post them on the door of the Church. The
couriers have instructions to report all mayors who don't."[17]

From all sides, George wrote, she was being solicited, and couldn't be
more pleased. This was the life she loved: planning a new magazine, *La
Cause du Peuple*, with Louis Viardot, wringing a commission for
Pauline Viardot to compose a new "Marseillaise," writing a prologue
for a play—and meantime trying to earn money, since she received
none from the government.

Politically there was less to be pleased with. The momentum of February had become the inertia of March. Decrees were not a program.
The National Workshops, instead of being models of co-operative productivity (designed to slowly force capitalism out of existence), were
demonstrations in absurdity—and so their director, Marie, intended. A
hundred thousand workers in Paris were marshaled, like an army dangerously idle, for such futile projects as digging holes in the Champ de
Mars and then refilling them.

Under pressure from moderates and radicals, and playing for time,
Lamartine announced elections early in April by universal—manhood—
suffrage. Louis Blanc and Ledru-Rollin said the nation was unprepared

---

* "A specter is haunting Europe," Marx's *Manifesto* began, "the specter of Communism." George Sand's own phrase is strikingly coincidental.

to vote; George Sand thought likewise: the voice of the Republic was only beginning to be heard against a background of too many years of lies. The *Bulletins* were going everywhere, but seven of the nine million eligible to vote were illiterate.

Pressure on the left came from such club leaders as Auguste Blanqui, a radical released from prison by the February revolution. He both terrified and horrified Tocqueville, for whom he was a scruffy workers' spokesman whose demands anticipate a later century's cry for worker power. Pressure on the right came from the bourgeoisie, now an enlarged united force since the petty bourgeoisie had won its right to vote and a share of the government.

The inertia of March extended into April. Each faction maneuvered for position in the forthcoming elections—postponed until April twenty-third as a concession to the left. Paris had spoken; the provinces were soon to be heard from. George Sand went to meetings of the *Club de la Révolution*, but preferred the provisional government, vacillating as it was, to a coup by Blanqui. More serious and troubling were the secret meetings at Ledru-Rollin's home with Louis Blanc and other socialists in the government. Should *they* seize power before the elections? It was neither in their character nor in their politics. "There will be no Reign of Terror under the Republic," George in effect promised in one of her weekly *Bulletins*.[18] They would travel the election route, though not without misgivings.

George Sand, in her articles, ranged over the problems of the underprivileged. On April sixth she touched on those of women, as "suffering the heaviest load of oppression." The new Republic, she said, would change that.[19] Ernest Legouvé of the *Club de l'Émancipation des Peuples* had proposed her candidacy in the coming elections. *La Voix des Femmes* (The Voice of Women), founded in March by feminist Eugénie Niboyet, took up the proposal. Her candidacy would point up the irony of the situation, the revue said: she would be elected by men, who alone could vote, and speak for women in the new Assembly. George Sand was appalled. Disdaining to reply directly to the feminist journal, she addressed a letter to *La Réforme*. She would not, she wrote, be the representative of a "*cénacle féminin*," a coterie of women, whom, moreover, she did not know.[20]

It was unfair; it was gratuitously scornful (though George had been stung by the use of her initials G. S. to sign an article in *La Voix*). It was men, Madame Niboyet reminded George Sand, who had first put forward her name, soon seconded by the *Club des Jacobins*. And it is tempting, but inadequate, to quickly explain George's impulsive reaction as that of one who had never wanted to be a woman writer among men, but rather a writer among writers; or more classically that of the woman who had crashed through the barriers and did not want to return to the company of those who had not; though there is truth in both instant observations.

The inadequacy, if not the injustice, of her own reply via *La Réforme* seems to have worked on George Sand. She drafted a longer letter to the Central Committee of the Left, requesting that its members, too, withdraw her name as a candidate, and she explained herself, addressing women as well as men. The letter was never finished, for some reason, or sent, but it is indispensable to understanding George Sand's feminism—for it is not a case of feminism versus anti-feminism, but the enduring debate, often the posing of false alternatives, of which way to sexual equality.

"Should women participate one day in the political life?" George Sand asked. "Yes, one day. Here I agree with you. But is that day near? No, I do not think so. In order for the condition of women to be changed politically, society must be changed radically. . . . But some women ask: In order for society to be changed, must not women intervene politically in public affairs? I risk replying that they must not, because social conditions are such that they couldn't honorably and honestly exercise a political mandate." They are too much dependent upon marriage and under the dominance of men; to be truly independent politically, they must break that mold cast by society. Those "of my sex" who hold otherwise, "are beginning where they should end, and ending where they should begin."

What then should be done about emancipating women? "I believe it easily done and immediately realizable," continued George Sand. "It consists simply in rendering to women the civil rights that marriage alone deprives them of . . . the detestable error of our laws that makes a married woman an eternal minor. . . . Yes, civil equality, equality in marriage, equality in the family, that is what you can and should ask for, indeed demand." If today, however, women sat as deputies, they would represent but "half a person; the other half would be their husbands."[21]

There was reason as well as sophism in the argument. George Sand as a deputy would certainly not have represented *her* husband. Nor would Madame Niboyet and the other militant feminists have represented theirs. Moreover, Sand did not consider a two-road approach, a two-front attack on sexual inequality—civil *and* political—as indeed did her feminist contemporaries. However, she did uncase a deeper meaning for equality than the right to vote and sit as a deputy. Over a century of time has since brought a certain political equality, but it has yet to bring that equality in life, in marriage, in the family, in the one-to-one relationship of a man and a woman, which, essentially, is what George Sand's life and work are all about.

There was yet another factor in Sand's refusal to join a *"cénacle féminin.*" She may have loved Marie Dorval, but "with few exceptions" she did not like women as companions. Alcibiades held Socrates, other than sexually, as Xanthippe did not: *he* could talk philosophy. Slaves—though husbands should be the last to complain about it—don't make intellectual companions. George found that quality in Marie d'Agoult, but it didn't last, perhaps because they were socially different, because Marie was jealous of George's success, because they were rivals for men's attentions—all underlining the difficulty of even a woman-to-woman relationship down to our own time; and here one thinks of the deprecating attitude towards their own sex with which virtually *all* women are early and deeply impressed. Should one then, *can* one historically, take George Sand completely to task for not having risen supremely above her century to a high, full consciousness of these factors? I think not.

This said, however, her reply to the feminists of her time, who risked the ridicule George Sand's remarks in *La Réforme* immediately exposed them to, was less than admirable. Fighting as they were—at meetings, in street demonstrations—for divorce, for women's rights, seems obviously to have appealed to George as somewhat unseemly, if not ignoble, compared to the "larger" campaign she was engaged in for "the people." Madame Niboyet had chosen *La Voix des Femmes* as the title of her publication; George had called hers *La Cause du Peuple.* Half humanity was not enough. Even that must be qualified. *Le peuple* were the ordinary men and women, the underprivileged, and Sand clearly stated that women carried the "heaviest load of oppression." But, as a socialist, she also believed, with an illusion which lasted a long time, that a socialist revolution would automatically care for that. George Sand was not alone in this belief, but as a woman she might have injected a skepticism wrung from experience.

Yet . . . George Sand *did* speak for women, though she would not be their spokesman or spokeswoman.

As for "the people," a more realistic pessimism had begun to temper and tarnish that cult for her. It was the people of La Châtre, George now feared, rather than the people, i.e., proletariat, of Paris who more accurately represented the people of France. The elections shortly to be held threatened to bring to the capital men who would efface republican gains, if not the Republic itself. George moved on to another concept of "popular democracy," but never sharply defined or clearly understood, as Marx attempted, pitting one class against another in the struggle for power. Was there not, George would ask in the last issue of *Cause du Peuple,* a "unanimity" of the people (citing the February revolution as an example, though it was largely a Paris affair) beyond that of an electoral "majority"?[22] In *Bulletin No. 16* the question was strongly put, and the role of Paris underlined. Never did George Sand draw closer to the Marxist sense of revolution:

> Citizens, we could not go from a régime of corruption to a régime of law in a day or an hour. One hour of inspiration and heroism sufficed for the people to establish the principle of truth, but eighteen years of falsehood oppose obstacles to truth, which human breath cannot dispel. If the elections do not assure the triumph of social truth, if they are only the expression of the interests of a caste torn from a trusting people, then these elections, which should be the salvation of the Republic, will be its end. In that event, there is only one road to salvation for the people who raised the barricades, that is to show their will a second time and put aside the decisions of a false National representation. Does France wish to force Paris to this extreme, this deplorable remedy? Please God, No![23]

It was more a warning of violence, which Sand ultimately could not stomach, should the vote go wrong, than an appeal to it, though in the reactionary aftermath, so the words would be read—and it would not be wholly mistaken.

Louis Blanc and the socialists continued to press for social reforms, but were told to wait for the elections. Factories closed, unemployment rose. A mass demonstration was called for Sunday, April sixteenth, the day after George's *Bulletin No. 16* had appeared. But leaders of the left pulled in several different directions, taking their factions with them; one consisted of the Paris clubs led by Blanqui, Cabet, Raspail and possibly Blanc. The demonstration failed. The revived bourgeoisie had mounted a counterdemonstration with a new, reorganized National Guard—"the personification of society defended and refound," Lamartine would write—and a hundred thousand from the conservative Paris suburbs.

"They shouted, 'Long live the Republic!'" George reported to Maurice the night of the march, "but they also cried, 'Death to the Communists!' . . . Today Paris conducted itself like La Châtre." She recounted the day's misadventures and miscarried coups. Had that of Ledru-Rollin and Blanc succeeded, she said, "it might have saved the Republic by proclaiming an immediate reduction in the taxes of the poor, by taking measures which, without ruining men of honest fortunes, would have saved France from its financial crisis, and by changing the electoral law, which is bad and can only have bad results; in brief, by doing everything possible now to rally the people to the Republic—which the bourgeoisie have succeeded throughout the country to disgust them with—and so win a National Assembly we would not be forced to overthrow."

She was terribly saddened by it all, George said in closing. "If it continues like this and there's nothing that can be done that should be done, I shall return to Nohant to write and console myself in your company. I want to see what kind of a National Assembly we will have. Afterward, I'm afraid, there'll be nothing left for me to do here."[24]

George Sand would work until past midnight in Ledru-Rollin's ministry, then walk home alone from the Rue de Grenelle. Now armed government patrols were stopping people and questioning them; the Paris clubs had stationed their own armed guards, and their leaders were spending the nights in the club headquarters rather than risk the streets. An "unnameable fear," George noted, gripped the city, as it had the French countryside in 1789 before the fall of the Bastille.

Then on April twentieth, in response, there was an immense outpouring of people for the *Fête de la Fraternité*—the Feast of Brotherhood. Up to four hundred thousand massed and marched, a singing, chanting line of five leagues, along the boulevards, reassuring, recomforting itself with the body-to-body warmth of their numbers— "the most gigantic human scene that ever happened!" George Sand exulted from the government tribune at the Arc de Triomphe.[25]

It was the last great expression of fraternity in Paris for twenty-three years, and it was swiftly smothered by the "hatreds, slogans and ruptures" of the election campaign.[26] More quickly and far more effectively than the socialists, the bourgeoisie and landowners had learned the tricks and uses of universal suffrage. "The elections," Lamartine confidently told a friend, "will go against them"—the left. In the country "they" were called "Communists"—"a name," said Proudhon, "contrived to stir the passions."[27] A name, wrote George Sand, summoning up for the peasants "pillage, theft, destruction of the family," nationalization of their land.[28]

And so, on Sunday, April twenty-third, the newly enfranchised voted. On Tocqueville's estate, he tells us, "all the voters met before the Church in the morning," to be advised to stay together until they had voted. " 'Let no one,' I said, 'enter a house to eat or to dry himself [it had rained that day] before accomplishing his duty.' They shouted that they would do this, and so they did."[29]

In Paris, outside the Hôtel de Ville, three hundred thousand, mostly workers and their wives, George Sand among them, waited five days later to hear the final results. The workers talked to George about the future and their lot. There was a lingering hope and a larger measure of defiance. "If the new Assembly pockets the question of the proletariat," George wrote Maurice, "they will pick up their guns again."[30] Maurice, Mayor of Nohant, had his wind up and was about to desert his constituents and join his mother in Paris. It was midnight when George learned the election results at the ministry. The left had lost.

Lamartine's middle-class moderates won some five hundred seats; the royalists divided three hundred between the Orléanists, who wanted to restore Louis Philippe or his descendants (two hundred), and the Legitimists, who supported a Bourbon restoration (one hundred). Louis Blanc and his socialist followers polled approximately the same number as the Legitimists. Conservatives, such as Thiers, declared they were now converted to universal suffrage. Tocqueville noted, without discontent, that the new Assembly, meeting on May fourth, himself among the deputies, contained more great landowners than any under Louis Philippe; the "reds" had been crushed "by the weight of their own dogma—the sovereignty of the people." The political revolution of the middle class was consolidated; the social revolution had been blocked. The Monarchy was dead; long live the "Republic of Privilege." The phrase is George Sand's. She also foresaw "a furious battle yet to be waged—against the bourgeoisie."[31]

"Personally," Tocqueville agreed, "I had no doubt that we were on the eve of a terrible struggle. Nevertheless I did not fully understand all the dangers of that time until a conversation with the famous Madame Sand."

Mistakenly Tocqueville dated the remarkable conversation in June. In fact it took place at a fairly large luncheon on May fourth, when the new Assembly first met. A mutual friend, a member of the British Parliament and a man of letters who was stopping at his Paris house at the time—Richard Monckton Milnes—had arranged it. Milnes, says Tocqueville, was always "infatuated about somebody or something. This time he was dazzled by Madame Sand and, despite the seriousness of the situation, wanted to give a literary luncheon for her."

"The company was anything but homogeneous . . ." continues Tocqueville. "There were some fairly obscure writers"—Alfred de Vigny was one of them!—"and Mérimée. Some of the guests did not know each other, and others knew one another too well. That was the case, if I am not mistaken, between Madame Sand and Mérimée. . . . There was great embarrassment on both sides, but they soon pulled themselves together, and for the rest of the day there was nothing to notice."

Mérimée remarked a woman "neither old nor young, rather pretty with magnificent black eyes, which she lowered whenever I looked at her. . . . Twelve years ago [fifteen had passed] she looked much less well, it seemed to me." After luncheon he sent George a cigar via a colonel, which she accepted "graciously." But they never said a word to each other.[32]

The conversation was largely with Tocqueville. "I had never spoken to her," he says, "and I don't think I had even seen her before (for I have not lived much in the world of literary adventurers which she in-

LA GIGOGNE POLITIQUE DE 1848

23. Cartoon of George Sand by Gaucher(?), courtesy of Françoise Foliot

Alexandre Manceau, courtesy
. Lalance

Août

21. LUNDI. — S. Privat, év. (N.-L.) 233—132

22. MARDI. — S. Symphorien. 234—131

25. Page of George Sand's *Diary*, August 21, 1865, commenting on the death of Alexandre Manceau that morning, courtesy of the Bibliothèque Nationale, Paris

26. George Sand by Manceau, in the manner of Thomas Couture, courtesy of Françoise Foliot

27. Solange Dudevant Clésinger, George Sand's daughter, courtesy of R. Lalance

Château de Nohant (Berry).

George Sand

28. Nohant, George Sand's estate, by George Sand, courtesy of Françoise Foliot

29. Gustave Flaubert by Carjat, courtesy of Françoise Foliot

30. George Sand and her works by Nadar, courtesy of Françoise Foliot

31. George Sand by Delacroix, courtesy of the Hansen Collection, Copen-
hagen

habited)." Tocqueville belonged to an old Norman aristocracy, and despite his own appreciation for the inevitability of an ascendant democracy he obviously viewed writers, such as novelists and playwrights (*pace* Vigny), as mere entertainers who moved in lower circles. Moreover: "I had a strong prejudice against Madame Sand, for I detest women who write, especially those who systematically disguise the weaknesses of their sex, instead of interesting us by displaying them in their true colors."

But despite that, Tocqueville admits, displaying his own quality, George Sand "charmed me. I found her features rather massive, but her expression wonderful; all her intelligence seemed to have retreated into her eyes, abandoning the rest of her face to raw matter. I was most struck at finding her with something of that naturalness of manner characteristic of great spirits. She really did have a genuine simplicity of manner and language, which was perhaps mingled with a certain affectation of simplicity in her clothes."

Tocqueville preferred, he says, "more adornment." But they talked and he was impressed. "We spoke for a whole hour about public affairs, for at that time one could not talk about anything else. Besides, Madame Sand was then in a way a politician; I was much struck by what she told me on that subject; it was the first time that I had found myself in direct and familiar conversation with somebody able and willing to tell me part of what was taking place in our adversaries' camp. Political parties never know each other; they come close, jostle and grip one another, but they never see. Madame Sand gave me a detailed and very vivacious picture of the state of the Parisian workers: their organization, numbers, arms, preparations, thoughts, passions and terrible resolves. I thought the picture overloaded, but it was not so, as subsequent events clearly proved. She seemed to be herself frightened by the [coming] popular triumph, and there was a touch of solemnity in her pity for our anticipated fate.

" 'Try to persuade your friends, sir,' she said to me, 'not to drive the people into the streets by rousing or offending them, just as on my side I want to instill patience into our people; for if it comes to a fight, believe me, you will all perish.' "[33]

Privately George Sand was not that confident of final victory, but publicly she was still the revolution's muse and propagandist. The revolution? One might date its end shortly after its beginning, certainly in its sense of broad social change. To Lamartine, liberal republican, who maintained a temporary, transitional balance of power, was entrusted the formation of a new government, including Ledru-Rollin but no longer Louis Blanc or such token figures as Albert the Worker. The balance had shifted to the right—the right, reaffirmed, of the propertied.

"Beware the party of misery," Blanc warned the new Assembly, "beware the revolution of hunger!" But in two minutes, by raised hands, the deputies dismissed his motion for a Ministry of Labor, and sent the hungry and miserable once more into the streets. There was no other place to press for reforms: George Sand's *Bulletin No. 16* was more prophetic than provocative. The mass demonstration called by Paris club leaders for May fifteenth was in support of a "free Poland" against its Russian occupier—a stand refused by Lamartine's new government. The Poles were popular in Paris; defending freedom beyond the borders of France was part of the revolutionary tradition. Above all, demonstrating for a free Poland was the occasion for mobilizing a huge crowd, and a Paris crowd was always a potentially powerful political force.

Fifty thousand in number, the demonstrators reached the bridge crossing from Place de la Concorde to the Chamber of Deputies. Here they found a few troops with a rather foolish general in charge. "*Vive la Pologne!*" he cried, waving a Polish flag. He told them they could not cross, then left the center of the bridge open. Was it a deliberate invitation to disaster? Blanqui seemed to think so, but he went along when a red-bearded leather-worker named Huber shouted, "Forward!" and the crowd swept across the Seine and into the Chamber of Deputies. There, amid the shouting, Blanqui called for work and the end of poverty. Barbès called for war in defense of Poland and a billion-franc tax on the rich; he then led a march to the Hôtel de Ville, followed by no more than five hundred.

At the Hôtel de Ville, Barbès proclaimed a new revolutionary government, as well as war against Russia. At this point a National Guard officer burst into the room where Barbès was at work.

"Who are *you?*" the officer demanded.

"Member of the Provisional Government," Barbès replied.

"Yesterday's or today's?"

"Today's."

"Then you are under arrest."

More arrests were made. By nightfall the left was decapitated. "Everything," says an objective witness, Maxime du Camp, "seems to have been carefully prearranged."[34]

For three hours George Sand had been among the crowd. Among the leaders? She would deny it, asserting that she had known nothing beforehand nor had seen anything during the events; that she had stopped with most of the crowd in the Rue de Bourgogne, *outside* the Assembly; that she had even seen a woman haranguing the people from a café window, had asked who she was and had been told it was George Sand; and that that was all.[35] Is it true? At the Hôtel de Ville, Barbès was about to name her as a minister of his new revolutionary government. Would he have done so without Sand's knowledge? Possibly, since he too was overtaken by events, but more likely George Sand was at least Barbès' confidant and was aware of what he had hoped for from the demonstration.[36]

Barbès jailed, Blanqui and Leroux would be shortly, and Louis Blanc would flee to England to avoid prosecution. George Sand feared prison; the night of the demonstration she decided to return to Nohant. Two days passed, however, before she left. She would say it was *because* she had been told she was about to be arrested, and chose to face it. In truth nothing did happen; it is very likely she was protected by Ledru-Rollin, who was still with the government. On May eighteenth she was in Nohant. Fleury and Arago advised her to go to Italy until things cooled down. She preferred, she said, to "suffer a little in France than to live in security elsewhere. But they wouldn't do such a ridiculous and odious thing as to persecute a *woman* [George's emphasis], who had never abandoned her role as a woman, any more in politics than in literature."[37]

One wonders what Eugénie Niboyet and the *"cénacle féminin"*—of which George Sand had wanted no part—might have thought of that. Perhaps they might have been more generous than a man, because more understanding. Prison for a woman was a particular hell; so, to a far lesser degree, was political exile for a woman alone. George wrote to Barbès in his fortress jail—courageous enough, since her sympathetic letters were opened and read by the authorities—telling him of her fear, "as a woman, . . . of the insults worse than blows, the dirty invectives," such as she had heard the day of the routed demonstration, the humiliations worse than anything inflicted on a man.[38] George Sand was not a Flora Tristan; life had not hardened her for *that* role.* The *cénacle* of women would not have condemned her for it; martyrdom was too much to ask (and they had not asked it). Perhaps it was disillusionment with revolution, having seen it fail. Was there complete sincerity in George Sand's asserting, after May fifteenth, that social revolution was one thing, class war another? Formerly she had made a distinction between the daily violence of oppression and that of revolt against it. Were, then, the words she had penned to Louis Blanc—"Strike hard! . . . Leave behind those who fall. . . . After victory it will be time enough to bury the dead"—little more than verbal, literary violence? The answer to the latter, finally, must be, Yes.

---

* Flora Tristan (1803–44) was born in poverty of a Peruvian father and a French mother. She married her employer at seventeen to escape poverty, had three children (one would be Paul Gauguin's grandmother) and a miserable life, and left her husband, who shot her and went to prison for a while. She met Fourier and began to write on the condition of women and workers. Before Karl Marx, she urged an international of the proletariat. Her book, *Union Ouvrière* (Workers Union)—to whose publication George Sand, Blanqui and others subscribed—made her well-known. She toured France, trying to organize its workers, and died in 1844 during her tour. Flora Tristan, at her death, was forty-one.

32

Aftermath

Nohant was no sinecure. Reaction was everywhere, and nowhere more strongly than in the countryside. Leaving the craggy threat of Paris meant falling into the whirlpool of Charybdis.[1] The peasants of Berry were provoked by the bourgeois merchants of La Châtre to demonstrate outside the walls of the Nohant château, where they came to chant, "Down with Madame Dudevant, down with the communisks!" George Sand, they were told, had been promised their land by Monsieur le duc [Ledru-]Rollin and was part of a sinister communist plot "to kill all children below the age of three and all the old above sixty."[2]

George's pessimism deepened. Uneasily she continued contributing to Théophile Thoré's *La Vraie République* (but would cease as quickly, and as nearly decently, as she might). She wrote of Louis Blanc and Armand Barbès as heroic, but mistaken, saints with too much of the saint's irrationality. The most wildly dogmatic of the left, she privately remarked to Thoré, "wished to impose by surprise, by audacity (by force, if they could have), an idea which the people had not yet accepted. They would have established a rule of fraternity, not like Christ, but like Mahomet. Instead of a religion, we would have a fanaticism. . . . At the end of three months . . . we would not have been republicans, but Cossacks."[3] The words have a striking, contemporary ring.

Sand did not renounce her own socialism; she even accepted the epithet of "communist." Communism was the ideal for the future, she reaffirmed to Mazzini, once again in exile, this time in Switzerland; and she stoutly held to it in her correspondence with her royalist cousin, René de Villeneuve. But the future was far off, and George turned to her memoirs, "waiting for the flood to carry me elsewhere."[4] So she philosophically wrote to Pauline Viardot, who was in London to sing alongside Jenny Lind. In the same note, George inquired about the health of Chopin, whom Pauline was frequently seeing. It was steadily worsening, replied Pauline; inevitably in the damp climate. George tried to put politics out of her mind, but she could not resist musing about Louis Bonaparte, whom she recalled as being "a personable prince."[5]

Suddenly as May, 1848, drew to its dreary close, the profile of Prince Louis Napoleon Bonaparte, "the Nephew," had begun to appear on countless medallions and matchboxes, in throwaway newspapers and pamphlets (in an astutely planned campaign financed by French bankers). Twice—in 1836 and 1840—Napoleon's nephew had conspired to have himself declared Emperor of France, and twice he had failed. The first time he was exiled by Louis Philippe to New York, but made his way back. The second time he was sentenced to life imprisonment, but escaped to London.

It was during his imprisonment that George Sand distantly made his acquaintance. The occasion was Louis Napoleon's prison-written, Louis Blanc-inspired pamphlet, *On the Extinction of Pauperism*, which he had sent to her. Sand was favorably impressed. So was Louis Blanc, who visited the prisoner-prince. George, invited, had not, but she corresponded with "the young man" (thirty-six at the time), stressing her own credo of republicanism ("impossible in a monarchical Europe," replied Louis Napoleon), but saluting him for his proletarian sympathies.[6]

In 1846, Louis Napoleon had escaped to London. The February revolution of 1848 found him again in France, offering his services to Lamartine, who sent him back to London. Now, just turned forty, Louis Napoleon presented himself as a "working-class candidate"—on the strength of his pauperism pamphlet—for a seat in the Assembly. He was elected in the partial elections of June fourth by four separate constituencies! However, as the Chamber debated seating him, he shrewdly resigned, declaring that he reserved himself for whatever duties "the people choose to impose on me."[7]

On June twenty-first the new government ordered the National Workshops closed. The Commission for Labor had already been suspended and the Right to Work annulled. Two days later, thousands of dismissed workers met near the Panthéon and walked to the Place de la Bastille, chanting "Bread or death!" Slowly the barricades went up. With them rose, not "a certain number of conspirators," Tocqueville testifies, "but one whole section of the population," an entire class of workers "trying to escape their condition. . . ."[8]

The new Minister of War, General Cavaignac, now took charge.

Strangely, it first seemed, Cavaignac made no attempt to storm the barricades before they were solidly established. (For several days in the confused situation George Sand's friend and publisher, socialist republican Pierre Jules Hetzel, was secretary-general at the War Ministry.) In fact, Cavaignac had other plans: he sought a crisis forcing the government to resign and turn over power to him. All day Friday he held his hand and was unavailable to Lamartine and Ledru-Rollin as they despairingly sent for him.

Fatalistically, the workers waited behind their barricades; but during the night they cast bullets, and on Saturday they used them. That morning, convinced nothing else would save them, the deputies forced Lamartine to resign and gave full powers to General Cavaignac. Carefully he now directed attacks; but he was in no hurry. The morale of his troops was good; even the ladies of western Paris came to entertain them.

The attacks reached full savagery on Sunday. By now the barricades in some streets were the height of three men, and the men and women behind them fought with the bravery of the hopeless. On Monday evening, June twenty-sixth, Tocqueville went to the Hôtel de Ville to get the day's "results." As he walked along the Seine, he met National Guardsmen carrying their wounded. "I observed in talking to them," he writes, "with what terrible rapidity, even in so civilized a century as our own, the most peaceful minds enter, as it were, into the spirit of civil war, and how quick they are, in these unhappy times, to acquire a taste for violence and a contempt for human life. . . ."[9] His own bloodthirstiness surprised him.

In four days it was over and the barricades crushed. But an estimated three thousand "insurrectionists" were killed *after* the fighting had stopped. They were flung into the Seine, shot or hanged in the streets, in the cemeteries, in their cellar-prisons as they asked for water or bread. The four June days shook Europe. But from Moscow the Czar sent congratulations to Cavaignac for having saved France from communism.

"I no longer believe in a republic which begins by killing its proletarians," George Sand wrote to Charlotte Marliani in distress. Waves of reaction had again reached Nohant. "A considerable band of imbeciles from La Châtre talk daily of coming and burning down my house." If for that reason only, she said, she must stay at Nohant, since in her presence "they doff their hats" and go off to mutter, " 'Down with the communisks!' " in the distance.[10]

There is a moving exchange with Abbé de Lamennais, whose *Le Peuple Constituant* had come to an end with its last, black-bordered issue condemning the butchery of June. "You alone," wrote George Sand, "have had the courage in the midst of the greatest danger to proclaim the truth."[11] George confided her own protest to her correspondence, often asking that the letters be burned. The public silence was not entirely her choice. *La Vraie République* had also been suppressed and its editor Thoré was being sought by the police. George herself was under police surveillance, and would remain so for several years. There was a renewal of the charge that her *Bulletin No. 16* had brought on the "insurrection" of May, if not the events of June. And again she had the grace to accept full responsibility for it—to Ledru-Rollin's immense relief.

If there was one consolation during these harrowing days, it was the smothering of Brault's sleazy, blackmailing pamphlet, which had just appeared, in matters of obviously greater public concern. Joseph Brault was the father of Augustine—whom George had finally succeeded in marrying to a penniless drawing teacher and Polish émigré, Charles de Bertholdi, the past spring, though her activities in Paris had kept her from the wedding in Nohant. In mid-June Brault's eight-page, ghost-written flimsy had found a publisher, and George had moved speedily to have it suppressed (sequels were promised). The pamphlet was ordered seized, but the June horrors intervened. Entitled *A Contemporary: the Biography and Intrigues of George Sand*, the tract narrates the ensnaring and seduction at Nohant of innocent Augustine, daughter of poor, hard-working parents, by the infamous George Sand and her son, and then, tainted, being married off to another. As an extra plum, Maurice is described as being in love with P.V. (Pauline Viardot) and George, in effect, with M.D. (Marie Dorval).[12]

The apparent public knowledge of the affair between Maurice and Pauline is somewhat more surprising than the last allusion to George as a lesbian. But most unpleasant is the discovery of Chopin's reaction. On reading or hearing of Brault's pamphlet, he wrote his family from London, "It is an infamy on the part of the father, but it is the truth. So much for the 'good deed' she thought she could accomplish, and against which I had fought with all my strength, ever since that girl entered the house! She should have been left with her parents. . . ."[13] The last, at least, is quite true: Augustine and her husband would prove an endless drain. However, Chopin's petulant assertion of the truth of Brault's lurid account tells us more about his own sad sinking into bitterness, as his health drastically declined, than about his last days at Nohant. According to Pauline Viardot, Chopin did not speak publicly of George Sand in this manner, and one might charitably attribute the letter to his family as an attempt to reassure himself, as well as they, of how much better off he was to be no longer with George Sand. How easily the happiness of love is wiped from the memory in its aftermath.

Returning, this strained summer, to the field of pastoral romances in the form of a novel to be titled *La Petite Fadette* was not wholly a form of escape for George Sand as well as for her public. The first volumes of her memoirs were ready for the printer, but the parlous state of the book world indefinitely postponed their appearance. The publishing of so formidable a work was too risky, George was told. Meanwhile she received an allowance of a thousand francs a month from the publisher. It was time for another pastoral idyll, such as *La Mare au Diable* and *François le Champi*.

Little Fadette, the teen-age heroine of Sand's tale, is a female Mauprat, a Rousseauian noble savage, wild and proud (too proud for a peasant girl, said Sainte-Beuve), tamed before the novel's end by love. It was the third of her pastoral series, said George Sand, "dedicated to our prisoner friends. Since it is forbidden to talk politics to them, we can only write tales to distract them or lull them to sleep. This one in particular is for Armand [Barbès]. . . ." She herself, George continued in the preface, was gently led to writing *La Petite Fadette* by good friend François Rollinat, "as we talked of the Republic of which we had dreamed—and of that to which we are now subjected."[14] The little idyll has since lulled and distracted millions, but at the time even this romantic rustic novel had difficulty finding a publisher, and George had to accept two thousand francs, less than half her usual fee, for its serialization.

Sand's need for money was endemic, and now more so than ordinarily. There were her own long-standing debts, sums to be sent to the prisoners' families, new debts incurred by the Bertholdis and the tiresome, clangorous demands of the Clésingers. In vain she dispatched twenty-six hundred francs to Solange—and Victor Borie, lover in residence at Nohant, to Paris—in order to save the debt-laden Hôtel de Narbonne from its creditors. Several months later, first the furniture, then the town house, were sold off "for a song." But only George seems to have been affected by it; the Clésingers simply piled up more debts.

Try as she might, George Sand could not put the social realities very far from her mind. She might not write about them publicly, but she brooded over them in her letters. To a prisoner, she reduced the struggle of June to a terrible simplicity: "a question of bread, of whether the poor have as much right to work as the rich to be idle."[15] To Charles Poncy she exposed her new thinking about property, dividing it into two categories, that which is personal and thus belonging to the individual, and that which is the riches of all, which should belong to all, such as the earth's mineral treasure, now the "preserve of the privileged."[16] Writing to Hetzel, George Sand added "the tools of work"— the means of production—to the social category.[17]

In the fall of 1848 she explained her public silence to an inquiring young journalist, Edmond Plauchut:

> You ask which paper I am writing for. For none, at the moment. I cannot speak out my thoughts under siege conditions. It would mean making concessions . . . of which I am incapable. Besides, my spirit has been broken and discouraged for some time. It is still sick, and I must wait until it is cured.[18]

There would be no quick cure, no quick political cure, at least.

As George found some refreshment—and sought a new source of income—in adapting *François le Champi* for the theater, Louis Napoleon Bonaparte had made his reappearance on a larger stage: in September he was elected to the National Assembly in *five* French departments, and this time took his seat.

Consistently, Sand and her political friends underestimated Louis Napoleon. Though a poor speaker, he proved to be hardly the "brainless" person George now described.[19] His campaign for power demonstrated his own shrewd capacity for stage management, though some of the strategy and all of the financing came from others. Above all, the circumstances were propitious. Wretchedness, division and disillusionment after the June massacre accounted for most of his appeal and the revived magic of his uncle's name. It was particularly effective, George daily discovered, in the countryside, where "all the peasants are for the royal pretender."[20] The unknown was at least preferable to the known. For workers the latter now meant socialist fumbling and failure and a discredited socialist leadership, most of it, moreover, in prison or exile. The workday had risen by decree from ten hours to twelve—except where the "nature of the industry" demanded more; unemployed from the closed workshops had been conveyed by the thousands far from Paris, their families left behind literally to forage in the streets.

On November fourth a new constitution, modeled on America's, was passed by the Assembly. As America's, it provided for a president elected by universal manhood suffrage. Tocqueville had helped write it; Lamartine's eloquence had ensured its passage. The presidential campaign opened, and it quickly became apparent that the electoral conflict was between Cavaignac ("the bloody saber") and Louis Napoleon ("the rusted imperial sword").[21]

Astutely the self-styled "pauper-prince" established himself above all parties, though his was the Party of Order. He was, he said, a man for all the people, a unifier of a divided nation. His program was a sweeping promise of stability and progress, order, glory and the egalitarianism of 1789. Louis Napoleon's may have been the first campaign to blur nationalism and socialism, and it was remarkably effective. In late November, typically, one of his posters suddenly flowered overnight on the

walls of Paris and the provinces. Surrounding his portrait were reproductions of letters of praise addressed to him—from Louis Blanc,
Béranger, George Sand. In protest, Sand sent a disclaimer to three
Paris publications: the prisoner of 1844 was not the presidential candidate of 1848. Think of the danger, the absurdity of his pretentions, she
warned. "Mr. Louis Bonaparte, *convinced, systematic enemy of the republican form of government,* has no right to be a candidate to its pres-
idency. Let him have the frankness to admit he is a claimant to the
crown. Then France can decide whether or not it wants to re-establish
the monarchy for the profit of the Bonaparte family."[22] The damage
had been done, however.

Elections were held on December 10. Almost seven and a half mil-
lion Frenchmen voted, with these results: Lamartine—17,910; Ledru-
Rollin—370,719; Cavaignac—1,488,107; and Prince Louis Napoleon
Bonaparte—5,434,226.

The workers had voted for the new Napoleon out of hatred for
Cavaignac, as George Sand remarked. The petty bourgeois, Marx would
add, in voting for Napoleon were voting against the bankers, the
bankers, monarchists and *grande bourgeoisie* against the Republic, and
the peasants against everybody. It added up to a crushing victory, the
popular election of a Prince-President. A new surge of republicanism,
George thought, would put an end to Louis Napoleon. Instead, it
would be its president who would put an end to the Republic.

The deaths which followed in the wake of that turning-point year
seem anticlimactic. Two days before Christmas, 1848, it was Hippolyte's premature turn; he had drunk himself to death at fifty. But in a
sense, said George, her half brother was already dead to her; she had
not seen him since the marriage of Solange. Less than five months later
Marie Dorval died; she had never recovered from the death of her little
girl, whom she had named Georges. "She spoke to me of you," Marie's
son-in-law wrote to George Sand of Marie's last days, "of your heart.
Oh, dear Madame Sand, how you loved Marie, how you alone knew
how to reach her soul!"[23]

Then five months after Marie Dorval, Chopin died.

Mortally ill, he had returned the previous fall from England. He had
not sought George Sand, nor she him, though in the summer of 1849
she had been told by a relative stranger, Madame Grille de Beuzelin,
that Chopin "painfully" missed her.[24] The last time they had met,
George replied, Chopin had fled her half in anger, half in hate. Had he
changed? She doubted it. She had heard of too many cruel things he
had said of her. As for herself, she maintained in his regard "a silence of
the dead."[25]

The silence was sealed on October 17, 1849, when Chopin expired. Though recalling "his jealousies, his capriciousness," and her own "greater suffering," George Sand was ill, she says, for days thereafter.[26]

A month later, *François le Champi* opened at the Odéon theater in Paris with "immense success,"[27] ending the decade for George Sand, forty-five.

33

Come, Twilight

Nothing perhaps gives more relief to her masculine stamp
than the rare art and success with which she cultivated an
equilibrium. She made from beginning to end a masterly
study of composure, absolutely refusing to be upset, closing her door at last against the very approach of irritation
and surprise.

—Henry James, *Notes on Novelists* (1914)[1]

After the tensions, the storm and stress of George Sand's younger years,
the very mundane fact of being forty-five suggests tamer dramas, paler
reading. The seeking for equilibrium, however, the finding of tranquillity, the closing of her door against the very approach of irritation
and surprise, slowly reveals itself as the igneous keystone, the fire into
rock, of her long life, whose great arc vaulted three quarters of a century.

A fragment of George Sand's manuscript describing her mood at this
time is particularly appropriate, if only because she chose to leave it
out of the published version of her *Histoire de Ma Vie*. Most likely it
was written in a post-Chopin mood of self-examination—and self-justification.

Invariably, Sand began the long passage, she had "badly invested"
her affections:

But perhaps I bear within myself the great misfortune of loving someone too much and seeking too much to be loved.
Time has taught me not to be too demanding, not to make
useless reproaches, to hide my private suffering, and to blame
myself for the loneliness I so often feel left with, even in the
finest affections.

She had always been the first to love, the last to be unfaithful, George
protested—once again. But she also recognized for the first time,

"There is something in me that wounds or bores others." She searched her mind and conscience, and, as too often, found them flawless. However,

> When I search for it in my character, in my way of being, I don't know which of my faults to select as fatal. I must be vexing in a thousand ways at the same time. I am the kind that is dead on the surface, and I have always been so. Liking gaiety, I am nonetheless listless if I am not shaken up. Sensitive to the core, I am cold to all appearances. What I feel most deeply I find always the most difficult to express; all is concentrated in me as in still waters in which all goes to the bottom.

It was Lélia again, the woman whose soul had been untouched and unmoved. But George Sand has moved on.

> Since, with all this, I am never bored with myself, I have difficulty in seeing that others are bored with me. But when it does happen, I recover, after a period of private sorrowing, by beginning to be bored with them, and it is this which keeps me from importuning them with the sense of persecution of a wounded heart. Mine, fortunately, is quickly discouraged. If it were not for that, what with the [*wounds received* is struck through] disappointments I have undergone, I would not have been able to carry on.[2]

George carried on, as the new decade opened, surrounded once again by young men, "artists who loved fun," as she wrote Mazzini, and all was well so long as no one went too deep. The surface was gay, she said, as it must be in France, "where gaiety, the appearance of light-heartedness, is the very law of *savoir-vivre*. You must always laugh with those laughing."[3]

The young men were Maurice, Eugène Lambert, Émile Aucante, and two newcomers, Hermann Müller-Strübing, a German refugee, musician and classics scholar, and Alexandre Manceau, an engraver Maurice had met in Delacroix's studio and had brought home. Victor Borie, who had warmed the two previous years for George Sand but had proved less successful as her business manager, was no longer at Nohant. Briefly he edited a working-class weekly in the Berry, *Le Travailleur de l'Indre*, and was now himself a refugee in Brussels. Almost as briefly, Müller-Strübing replaced him as George's lover. ("I cannot, I will not, live without love," she wrote Hetzel.[4]) His "wholesome" strength appealed to her. Within a month, his halting French and slow spirit appalled her. ("He bores me too often," Sand wrote Hetzel.[5] Müller was *not* the first bored.) However, the tall German stayed on for a while at Nohant, then remained as a tutor in the neighborhood.

The person for George Sand as she traversed this midpoint in her life was decidedly not a Musset, nor a Chopin, but rather an Alexandre Manceau. With him she found love, not at last—how often one says it—but once again, though it would last his lifetime.

Manceau had come to Nohant at the very end of 1849 for at most a few months; he remained for fifteen years. He was, to record a last statistic, thirteen years younger than George Sand.

Müller-Strübing to Manceau was not the too glibly described eternal Sandian swing from strength to weakness, as from Michel de Bourges to Chopin. The strength of Müller did not include the strongest of bonds, that "mysterious entente of minds" George quite rightly insisted upon and found wanting.[6] Thin, consumption-prone Manceau, in fact, had the same tensile strength as Chopin.

From the beginning of his arrival Manceau quietly took over at Nohant—to Maurice's increasing annoyance. "He came, he saw, he criticized," said George contentedly of Manceau's transformation of Nohant's theater and amateur performers.[7] He directed Lambert in the repainting of the décors, the local carpenter in his redoing of the stage, the entire little troupe in a tightening of its rehearsals and discipline. The former billiard room became a professionally important tryout theater for George Sand's plays, now the focus of her writing and the principal source of Nohant's income. She immediately appreciated its uses. There was a run-through of a new play—eventually *Molière*—for Bocage, lines were changed, scenes revised. "You see," George wrote Augustine in March 1850, "the family theater is a really serious business."[8]

In April George was writing Hetzel about her love for Manceau. From childhood she had a need to *write* to someone, and Hetzel had shown himself to be a trustworthy confidant. It was not simply that she expressed herself best in writing. She explored her mind, she *thought*, with a pen, which helps explain its expressional ease, the sense of discovery in its flow. Writing of her love of Manceau in the letter to Hetzel, George Sand probed for herself the *why* of that love. The result is another astonishing analysis of herself and the *other*, a prescription of the person she could enduringly love in her maturity, the combination of traits she now required for her tranquillity.

Manceau, George Sand began, had a speck of jealousy, "which he promises to control." (It made the aging one of the two feel still desired, still desirable, while unharassed by *uncontrollable* jealousy.) He was secretly proud to be loved by her, but feared he would prove himself unequal to it. (Thus he will keep trying; the nicety of attention will continue.) He was born in poverty and had worked for his bread all his life, but was "incredibly artist in spirit"—since youth his engravings have been hung in the annual Paris Salon. (Like George, but unlike Musset, he was a *hard-working* artist.) He had an "extraordinary intelligence," but it was not on exhibition; "it serves only him, and consequently myself. He knows nothing, but intuits everything; forever questioning, he proves to me how much his mind works internally." The entente of two minds was alive and well.

Manceau, George continued, was a kind of primitive poet, with no "ambition for money or renown." He merely wanted to ennoble himself "in the eyes of God and himself"—that is, of George. (Was this not the master key—Manceau's noncompetitiveness? It would be a large ingredient in George's contentment with Manceau. The acceptance of her dominance—must there be one who happily submits in every enduring couple?—was a new, but would be a lasting, experience for Sand.) "He loves, he loves, you see," followed closely—and logically, "as I have seen no one to love." His faults disappeared in the intimacy of a *tête-à-tête*. He became "a caressing cat and a faithful dog; all his calculations and intrigue have but one goal—to win the approval of the one he loves." The cat-dog is the androgynous image of the woman-man. The metaphor will recur. He was "as ardent and chaste"—delicate—"in love as the senses, heart and mind can ever have dreamed," or George have hoped. He was delicately cat-pawed in his movements through a room (like Chopin), "never breaking anything," unlike most men, who clumsily shatter the porcelain soul. "Do not take that as a pleasantry," Sand admonished Hetzel. A man's clumsiness was the external sign of his internal attitude. "He"—Manceau—"puts himself entirely into the glass he brings to me, the cigarette he lights for me. He never gets on my nerves! He is punctual. . . . I have never had to *wait* a minute for him."

And when sometimes Manceau was in the wrong, George continued, "I have never *waited* a minute for the look and the word that repair everything" (unlike the grievance-hoarding Chopin). "He has the attentiveness, the nursing care of a woman, of a skilled, active, ingenious woman. When I am sick, I am cured by merely seeing him prepare my pillow and bring my slippers." (Manceau was part man, part woman, and sometimes entirely "man" or "woman.") "In short, I love him with all my soul and with all his faults. . . . I love him for all he is, and there is an astonishing peace in my love, despite my age and his . . . despite that terrible distrust which has always tormented me deep down in all my loves. . . . I am as if transformed, my health restored, I am tranquil. I am *happy*, I can endure everything, *even his absence*, and that's to say everything, for I could never endure that."[9]

The miracle of April was confirmed in July. "Yes, I am very happy," George reported to a skeptical Hetzel, "very happy. I really think this is the first time I have known it"—each time was the first time in the freshet of George's love—"and I have been able to abandon myself to it selfishly"—man's millennial experience with the "good wife." "I am forty-six, I have gray hairs. I have learned that old women are more loved"—better loved?—"than young women."[10] The emphasis on being an old woman at forty-six is a bit heavy, but the happiness is evident, down to the perimeter of the soul.

Two deaths marred August—those of Charlotte Marliani and Balzac —but run-throughs and revisions of a new play, *Claudie* (*Molière* was put aside), left less room for morbid thoughts, if indeed any penetrated the closed door. Mazzini met the same impasse when he asked for an article on politics for his new revue. She could not write it, George replied. The situation was too "sickening." Besides, why encourage workers to a new militancy, to expose them to inevitable massacre?[11] She was still a socialist, if not communist, George told Mazzini in other letters, but she now feared a tyranny of the left. So long as it was an insufficiently persuasive *minority*, it would necessarily resort to force to maintain any power it managed to achieve. She herself was abstaining from politics.

The personal life, coupled with theatrics both domestic and professional, absorbed George Sand. She regarded herself "entering old age with a rare serenity," attributing it to "the featherless bird I have taken under my wing"—Manceau.[12] On this score, however, her son Maurice, now twenty-seven, was becoming a problem. Rather, his mother was beginning to recognize the problem of Maurice, man-child. Provocatively or foolishly, he told George he thought of marrying an actress he was seeing so as to fill a gap in the almost all-male Nohant troupe. He was scolded by his mother for this disconcerting immaturity and lectured conventionally on the seriousness of marriage. Manceau, who was closer to Maurice's own age than to his mother's, but was now closer to Maurice's mother than Maurice himself, was clearly the irritating element and eventual target. The story of Chopin threatened to repeat itself.

When George was about to go to Paris in connection with her new play, Maurice, who was in the capital, protested her planning to stay in Manceau's apartment. George replied appeasingly, "I will put up wherever you wish, but I'd really be better off in Manceau's place than in yours, because of the toilet facilities. . . . You know what that means for people constipated from birth. . . . It's awkward to mention it, but in Paris that's my greatest problem." In Maurice's tiny apartment, one had to go out and up to a cold water-closet. So George, she wrote, had leaped at Manceau's offer. As for the wagging tongues Maurice feared, "there would be no talk if you stayed with me and slept in the studio. There wouldn't be any, even if you didn't. . . . No one but the porter would even know I was there. . . . Every day a young man lends his apartment to a lady from the country, especially when she is forty-six. . . . Besides, the bedroom is independent of the studio, should anyone come."[13]

The overconcern for Maurice, if one might call it that (it hardly inhibited Sand's remarkably free life at Nohant, which housed both incoming and outgoing lovers—Müller and Manceau—for a time), was as always partly in compensation for her relations, more precisely her rejection, of Solange, who recently committed the ultimate in lese majesty. Wildly calling attention to herself at any cost, she had told Charlotte and others that George Sand had written her husband, saying, "Your wife is illegitimate. She is not the daughter of Mr. Dudevant."[14] Hearing of it, Sand had been horrified. Solange's giving birth some months earlier to another child now meant very little. "Don't break bread with them," George cautioned Maurice when he came upon the Clésingers in Paris. "Clésinger is a madman and Solange is without the bowels of affection."[15] She did not want to receive either one at Nohant. Nothing was to disturb the restored equilibrium, George was determined.

However, she weakened slightly. With her infant daughter Nini and a nurse, but without her husband, Solange appeared at Nohant for the first time in more than three years. "My daughter," George wrote Hetzel, "dropped in out of the blue last Friday, and left this morning"—February 5, 1851. "Coldly" George had let her know that there was no question of the Clésingers living with her, as Solange intimated.[16] Solange and her child might visit Nohant, but "not her husband, servants, friends, horses or dogs."[17]

1851 was an odd, dramatic year with a strange interlude—when even the dead, it seemed, returned to be reburied—and a numbing end. In January, George Sand's play *Claudie*, with Borage as director and leading man, proved to be another "immense success."[18] It was followed by *Molière*, which opened—and closed—in May, but led to a strange coincidence. Healing a breach dating back to the Mérimée fiasco of 1833, George had dedicated her play in printed form to the elder Alexandre Dumas. They dined in reconciliation. The elder Dumas mentioned it in a letter to his son, who was in Myslowice, on the Russian-Polish border, where he was waiting for a visa. (His married lady-love was in Russia and an alerted police kept the younger Dumas dangling his heels.) When Dumas received a letter of reply from his son, he forwarded it to George Sand.

"While you were dining with Madame Sand," George read, "I was also occupied with her. Let no one laugh at strange affinities! Just think, I have her ten years' correspondence with Chopin!"[19]

In Myslowice the younger Dumas had just met a Polish gentleman with whom Chopin's sister had left the packet of George's letters, because she had dreaded their being read by the border officials. The Polish gentlemen thought they might amuse the young Frenchman, as they did indeed—he meticulously copied them in a notebook. George Sand, reading the younger Dumas' letter, was not at all entertained. She was terribly upset and told the elder Dumas, who promised to bring them personally to her at Nohant when the younger Dumas returned. The latter, when George urgently wrote to him, was equally obliging. He would bring back the letters, if at all possible, and send her his copy as well.

George Sand's letters to Chopin finally arrived in Nohant in October. They have never been seen again. George undoubtedly destroyed them, reinterring the past. And it seems the younger Dumas gallantly destroyed *his* copy, as George requested, since it, too, has disappeared from sight.

In November, George Sand was in Paris for the last rehearsals of yet another play, *Le Mariage de Victorine*. It opened on Wednesday the twenty-first. "Success," George noted laconically in her journal.[20] She had gone backstage to congratulate the cast. So had Solange, her husband and her current lover, Count Alfred d'Orsay, such was the new state of affairs with the Clésingers. George supped with them at the Pinson restaurant, drank coffee and slept badly. For three nights the actors played to a full theater. "Complete success," noted George. On Sunday she "played dominoes with Manceau before the fireplace." On Monday, December first, the two went shopping. At noon George lunched with Emmanuel Arago and was taken with surprise by his conversation. Talk of a *coup d'état* by President Louis Napoleon came from Arago's lips as if nothing else was Paris table talk.

"If the President doesn't mount his *coup* soon," Arago said, "he will miss his opportunity, because nothing at the moment would be easier."

Delacroix, on the other hand, did not even mention the subject when George saw him in the afternoon. That evening she went to the circus with Manceau and Solange. Returning home at one in the morning, they passed by the President's Elysée Palace. Its massive carriage door was shut as usual at night. A single sentry stood guard. No light shone from the palace; the streets were silent. "Well," said George Sand with a laugh, "it's not for tomorrow, anyway!" For the first time since she came to Paris, she slept soundly the entire night.

At ten the next morning, Manceau woke her. He told her Generals Cavaignac and Lamoricière had been arrested, the National Assembly dissolved, and universal suffrage re-established in anticipation of new elections. (The previous May a reactionary parliamentary majority had disenfranchised three million workers.) George Sand, too long withdrawn from political activity, shared the general confusion about Louis Napoleon's purposes. They would shortly be enlightened.

Tactfully Louis Napoleon had played his role as President according to a constitution both presidential and parliamentary. He gave the conservative majority all the rope it wanted, meanwhile consolidating his popular appeal.[21] The squabbles, the antidemocratic actions, the parliamentary *disorder* had led, as Louis Napoleon had gambled, to a general discrediting of the National Assembly not only in the eyes of the people, but of the financial and industrial bourgeoisie as well, for whom social stability was the essential condition. On November 29, 1851, the London *Economist* declared editorially to its conservative readership, "The President [of France] is the guardian of order, and is now recognised as such on every Stock Exchange of Europe."[22] Three days later, December second, he struck.

That day, George saw several of her friends as unsure as herself about the popular reaction. Would there be an uprising? The Paris streets and boulevards, she observed, were placarded with Louis Napoleon's decrees, including announcement of a "people's referendum." There were no signs of abnormal activity. "No outcries, no demonstrations," George noted. But that evening at the theater, only three hundred showed up to see her play. She comforted the leading actress, who was in tears, and talked to her "violently anti-Red" husband, restraining her own radical comments. "I am so in control of myself these days, nothing makes me indignant." She spent the rest of the evening by her fireside reading Quinet's *Révolutions d'Italie,* while listening for the sounds of a Paris stirring to revolt. "Nothing! A silence of the dead, of imbecilic stupor or of terror. You do not stir, do you, good old Jacques" —the French common man. "How right you are, your time has not come!" The Assembly which had ordered his massacre in June 1848, and disenfranchisement in May 1851, was not *his* to defend.

The next day, however, George saw "an army of policemen on the streets." In the Latin Quarter, demonstrating students were clubbed down. In the evening Delacroix told her he had slept all day. "It was all the same to him." Others told George of barricades, cavalry charges, shootings. Token resistance seemed encouraged, so that the new regime might start with a display of overwhelming force ensuring the stability it promised. Hundreds died on December fourth, when George ("with death in my soul"), Manceau, Solange and little Nini boarded an evening train leaving Paris. "Ah, if I were a man, I would not leave. . . . But then what would I do here? Simply be killed." The train to Châteauroux was full of soldiers. The tired group arrived at Nohant by carriage in the fog of a cold dawn.

Roundups in the Berry had begun. Friends not already in flight faced arrest and deportation to Algeria or French Guiana. Ledru-Rollin, like

Louis Blanc, was now in London; Müller-Strübing fled France; Pierre Leroux was safely abroad, but his son-in-law, Luc Desages, was not— prison was his fate and deportation his sentence. George advised Alphonse Fleury to avoid the same fate by leaving France.

Discreetly Hetzel left Paris before the "referendum" of December twenty-first, then went on to Brussels, where he joined Victor Borie and Luigi Calamatta. The results of Louis Napoleon's "consultation" of the people were foregone; George was not alone in predicting them. In the *Yes* or *No* plebiscite, seven and a half million voted *Yes* to the Napoleonic *coup*, slightly over half a million voted *No*. It foreshadowed the proclamation of an Empire exactly a year later with Louis Napo- leon as Napoleon III, Emperor of all the French; "consulted" a second time, almost eight million Frenchmen approved, a lonely quarter of a million did not. In the interim, immediately in the wake of the first plebiscite, Louis Napoleon reinforced his new powers with massive ar- rests and deportations. On January 9, 1852, sixty-six former deputies of the opposition, Victor Hugo, Perdiguier and Raspail among them, were expelled from France; many others were forbidden residence in Paris. A friend of George Sand, whom she had Ledru-Rollin appoint as *commis- saire* of the Indre, Marc Dufraisse, was on the list for French Guiana (home of Devil's Island). She herself, she heard, was threatened with arrest and possible deportation.

This time, however, George Sand did not shelter herself at Nohant to wait out the storm. Nor was it her personal situation which moved her to action. Dozens of people she knew, friends and their friends, were imprisoned in the Berry, in exile or about to be deported. Personal pride, sensitivity to public exposure, were set apart; so was a cooler esti- mate of the political consequences. Friendship—that inviolate part of love—was affected, and that was sufficient. There was a generous exten- sion of that feeling to the downtrodden, the underprivileged, and now to the imprisoned, whom George impulsively from childhood, from memories of her mother, from personal identification over the years, now befriended. Her unhesitating response was passionately human; the po- litical implications, if weighed at all, weighed little. She determined to appeal directly to Louis Napoleon, to be as humble and suppliant and Machiavellian as she must be.

"Prince," George Sand wrote to the French President on January twentieth, "I am not a Madame de Staël"—Napoleon I's enemy No. 1. "I have neither her genius nor the pride with which she fought the twin force of genius and power. . . . Nevertheless I venture to approach you. . . . My family—the friends of my childhood and old age, those who have been my brothers and my adopted children—are in prisons or in exile. Your hand lies heavy on all who have taken, accepted or been labeled with the title of socialist republican." She would not attempt to defend socialism, George said, or play its advocate with him, though she had always regarded him as a kind of "socialist guardian spirit," now "accepted by the people" as the guardian of the nation.

Sand reminded Louis Napoleon of his own prison days and pointed out the political uses of benevolence and mercy while protesting that she was but a mere woman, too "ignorant" to discuss politics with him. Liberate the prisoners, return the exiled; in them, she says, he would find the "forces vital for France." Having assumed the burden of the nation, he had the responsibility for it. "An amnesty, my Prince," George pleaded, "an amnesty—and soon!" Personally, she, too, who knew of a mandate for her arrest, might have fled. She chose not to. "In asking you for a private audience . . . I have burned my bridges behind me, putting myself entirely at your mercy and good will."[23] The bridge burned behind her was that to her socialist friends, who would censure her, she knew, for this approach.

It was a long letter. Louis Napoleon sent a short but cordial reply in his own hand. He would see her whenever she wished. The audience was held on January 29. Louis Napoleon listened to George Sand at length, took both her hands in his and with "a tear, a real tear in that cold eye, he cried, 'Ah, it is true what you say, but it is not my fault! . . . Ask whatever you wish, for whomever you want!' "

So wrote George Sand the next day to Hetzel. Defensively. Fleury, who was also in Brussels, had opposed her project of going to Louis Napoleon and had rejected beforehand any favor she might win for him. Napoleon Bonaparte, Fleury had objected, would use her pleading for his own political advantage—as indeed proved the case. The Bonapartist press would play it up joyfully. She had asked only for a *general* amnesty, George insisted to Hetzel, not favors for particular individuals. In any case, she knew before she went to the Élysée Palace what would be said of her action by many socialists. But "if others go to prison or into exile for political reasons, I can well risk my honor for friendship, since it is I alone who undertake that risk." She would "walk through horse dung" for her friends, and that has not been the worse "muck" she has known.[24] To her aristocratic cousin René de Villeneuve, George wrote that Louis Napoleon "showed the greatest esteem for my character, though I told him I was as republican, as communist, as he had known me to be, and I would never change."[25]

Immediately after the interview, most likely with Louis Napoleon's personal recommendation, George Sand went to the Minister of the Interior and asked for the release of some of her Berry friends, meanwhile "pressing him for more than that."[26] Specifically mentioned were two in prison—Ernest Perigois, son-in-law of Jules ("the Madagascan") Néraud, and Émile Aucante, one of the Nohant young men—as well as Fleury, for whom, despite himself, George asked that all charges be dropped. But it was still an amnesty for all the department of the Indre, she repeated in a follow-up letter, that she sought. And George reminded the Minister that she herself had sat in his very office in 1848, pleading mercy and justice for political opponents—"not that they be liberated, for the prisons were empty," but that they be allowed the freedom of their opinions.[27]

George Sand had a second audience with Louis Napoleon; she would never seek one again. She solicited the help of his more liberal cousin, Prince Jérôme Bonaparte—presented to her by Count d'Orsay—who would remain her friend the rest of her life. From ministry to ministry, justice officials to police and army chiefs, with lists of names in her hand, George went that winter on her personal mission. Hundreds benefited from her doggedness—the Berry prisoners, who wrote her in gratitude; four condemned soldiers saved from a firing squad; families of men who themselves spurned her help. Luc Desages was sent to Corsica instead of North Africa; Fleury himself was permitted to return to France. It had meant, for George Sand, running the gauntlet of opposition from the left, even from Louis Blanc, to the unwelcome salutes of the right. But men on both sides of the political barricades recognized her actions for what they were. "You are 'Our Lady of Succour,'" wrote Marc Dufraisse from Brussels. Saved from deportation to French Guiana, he had been most skeptical of George Sand's efforts. "You are a much-loved woman," said Count d'Orsay, an intimate of Louis Napoleon since the latter's days in London, "besides being the outstanding man of our time."[28]

Together with her husband Robert, Elizabeth Barrett Browning had seen George Sand several times in these arduous months. The Brownings had sought the meeting since December. ("I won't die," said the invalid Elizabeth, "without seeing George Sand.") Finally a letter of introduction by Mazzini made it possible. On February 15, 1852, they called on the French writer at Manceau's Rue Racine apartment:

> She received us very kindly [wrote Elizabeth Browning in a letter home] with hand stretched out, which I, with a natural emotion (I assure you my heart beat), stooped and kissed, when she said quickly, "Mais non, je ne veux pas," and kissed my lips. She is somewhat large for her height—not tall—and was dressed with great nicety in a sort of grey serge gown and jacket, made after the ruling fashion just now, and fastened up to the throat, plain linen collarette and sleeves. Her hair was uncovered, divided on the forehead in black, glossy bandeaux, and twisted up behind. The eyes and brow are noble, and the nose is of a somewhat Jewish character; the chin a little recedes, and the mouth is not good, though mobile,

flashing out a sudden smile with its white projecting teeth. There is no sweetness in the face, but great moral as well as intellectual capacities—only it never *could* have been a beautiful face, which a good deal surprised me. . . . Her complexion is of a deep olive. I observed that her hands were small and well-shaped.

We sate with her perhaps three-quarters of an hour or more —in which time she gave advice and various directions to two or three young men who were there, showing her confidence in us by the freest use of names and allusion to facts. She seemed to be, in fact, the *man* in that company, and the profound respect with which she was listened to a great deal impressed me. . . .

And we may be impressed by the fact that a woman, such as George Sand, even viewed by another woman, is invariably called a "man" because she dominated, though effortlessly, an entire drawing room, including men.

What is peculiar in her manners and conversation is the absolute simplicity of both. Her voice is low and rapid, without emphasis or variety of modulation. Except one brilliant smile, she was grave—indeed she was speaking of grave matters, and many of her friends are in adversity.

But you could not help seeing (both Robert and I saw it) that in all she said, even in her kindness and pity, there was an under-current of scorn. A scorn of pleasing she evidently had; there never could have been a colour of coquetry in that woman. Her very freedom from affectation and consciousness had a touch of disdain. But I liked her. I did not love her, but I felt the burning soul through all that quietness, and was not disappointed in George Sand. When we rose to go I could not help saying, "C'est pour la dernière fois," and then she asked us to repeat our visit next Sunday. . . . She kissed me again when we went away, and Robert kissed her hand.

Of the Sunday meeting, Elizabeth Browning wrote to the same friend, "She sate, like a priestess, the other morning in a circle of eight or nine men, giving no oracles, except with her splendid eyes." In all, she says in a third letter, "I think Robert saw her six times. Once he met her near the Tuileries, offered her his arm, and walked with her the whole length of the gardens." Robert Browning did not find George Sand "looking as well as usual, being a little too much 'endimanchée'" —Sunday-dressed—"in terrestrial lavenders and supercelestial blues—

not, in fact, dressed with the remarkable taste which he has seen in her at other times."

More interesting are Elizabeth Browning's own direct observations, as are the insights we get into the man-woman relationship of even the Brownings, one of the most rightly famous pair of lovers in history.

> Her usual costume [E.B. resumed] is both pretty and quiet, and the fashionable waistcoat and jacket . . . make the only approach to masculine *wearings* to be observed in her. She has great nicety and refinement in her personal ways, I think, and the cigarette is really a feminine weapon if properly understood. Ah, but I didn't see her smoke. I was unfortunate. I could only go with Robert three times to her house, and once she was out. He was really very good and kind to let me go at all, after he found the sort of society rampant around her. He didn't like it extremely, but, being the prince of husbands, he was lenient to my desires and yielded the point.
>
> She seems to live in the abomination of desolation, as far as regards society—crowds of ill-bred men who adore her à genoux bas [on bended knee], betwixt a puff of smoke and an ejection of saliva. Society of the ragged Red diluted with the lower theatrical. She herself so different, so apart, as alone in her melancholy disdain! I was deeply interested in that poor woman, I felt a profound compassion for her. I did not mind much the Greek in Greek costume who tutoyéd her [used the intimate *tu*], and kissed her, I believe, so Robert said; or the other vulgar man of the theatre who went down on his knees and called her "sublime." "Caprice d'amitié," said she, with her quiet, gentle scorn. A noble woman under the mud, be certain.
>
> *I* would kneel down to her, too, if she would leave it all, throw it off, and be herself as God made her. But she would not care for my kneeling; she does not care for me. Perhaps she doesn't care for anybody by this time—who knows? She wrote one, or two, or three kind notes to me, and promised to "venir m'embrasser" [come and embrace me] before she left Paris; but she did not come. We both tried hard to please her, and she told a friend of ours that she "liked us"; only we always felt that we couldn't penetrate—couldn't really *touch* her—it was all vain.[29]

Was it the impasse of language or George's "closed door," the non-dialogue of two different cultures or of two women differing in their attitudes towards what a woman could, or should, be? Likely everything played its part, but more likely the second half of the two alternatives played the greater role.

And Manceau, who was unmentioned? Was he never present, or was he so unobtrusive he was unobserved—the "good wife" to George's "man"?

Through the closed door, however (nothing in life is that opaque: the poet in Elizabeth Browning penetrates), we catch a glimpse of George Sand at twilight, the twilight of her dream of the ideal republic, the twilight of spent passions and consumed years—her "kindness and pity" with its "under-current of scorn"; her "burning soul through all that quietness," "alone in her melancholy disdain." Not all was in the eye of the beholder.

34

Last Passions

There are the truths of youth and the truths of age: each has its decade as it has its own life-style. Marriage for George Sand, when it meant confinement with Casimir during her early, vaulting years, was one thing. She compared it, at its worst, to prostitution, and out of this came the passion of revolt that produced *Indiana* and *Valentine*. With the advance of age marriage meant Maurice and Solange, and that was another matter.[1] After Maurice turned thirty in 1853, finding him a wife became increasingly a major concern for his mother, all the more so because of the special case of Solange.

The Clésingers, mutually unfaithful but no less incriminatory, indulged in one of their chronic separations in 1852. Solange, for her part, went for a short stay at a convent, then a kind of women's club where unhappily married women frequently sheltered. From here Solange wrote her mother in a plaint as much a portrait of her period as of herself. "I have been boarding here since yesterday," George Sand read. "Is this the way I am to spend the best years of my life? Without parents, without friends, without my child, without even a dog to fill the emptiness? . . . To live alone amidst the sound and movement of others—people enjoying themselves, horses galoping, children playing in the sun, men and women happily in love—is not boredom, but despair. And there are those who wonder how poor girls without any special talent or education can let themselves be drawn into a life of pleasure and vice!"[2]

The reply of Solange's mother was stiff. Solange invariably evoked a sense of remorse, if not guilt, in George Sand. She did not warmly invite her daughter to Nohant. Rather, she read her a lecture, rewriting her own youthful experience in the process. George Sand was supremely a *now* person, permitting her the more easily to survive earlier disorder and sorrows. She, too, said George, spent the best years of her youth "working *alone* between four *dirty walls*"—she underlined the words—and did not regret them. Solange's isolation was her own choice. "Your husband, insupportable as he may be in character, does not deserve such dislike or such an impetuous departure. . . . Your *child* should have made you more patient." The only consolation for Solange, it seemed, would be "money, a great deal of money." The "emptiness" of her heart would not be filled, but at best forgotten, by a life of "luxury, idleness and giddiness." Solange, George said, might come to Nohant, so long as she did not upset everyone and drive them as usual to despair with her "caprices and malice." George would take in her child and raise it, but Solange should expect no sympathy for her "hard life in Paris." Solange's very remarks about "pleasure and vice" made her mother feel that Clésinger was not always lying about "certain threats" he had heard from Solange. "He may be mad, but you are diabolically insane."

As for a life of vice, George Sand exploded, "Try it, try prostitution! I defy you!" Solange could not pass through that door without recoiling. "Besides, it is not as easy as you seem to believe. . . . Men with money want women who know how to earn it." Solange, said George, had been brought up differently. "I have seen young women who struggled against the passions of heart and body, and dreaded any domestic unhappiness for fear of being drawn into unfaithfulness by sudden impulses. But I have never known a single person brought up like you, in an atmosphere of dignity and moral freedom, who dreaded deprivation and isolation for reasons of . . . cupidity."[3]

Solange replied simply to say she was sending her child Nini to George at Nohant. It was a provisional arrangement subject to the whims and moods of Solange and her husband and their spasmodic reconciliations. Kidnapings were not excluded, and for three years the possibility haunted both women, Solange scarcely less than George Sand, though Solange was away much of the time with one or another lover. Effective defense against a Clésinger incursion was entrusted, as so much else, to Manceau and his "fire brigade," as George called it, composed of the young men at Nohant.

Nevertheless, these were the comparatively peaceful years of puppet plays, playwriting, long walks and gardening, the eventful along with the trivial recorded daily by Manceau or George Sand in the long, slim, annual ledgers they kept together as a diary. June 23, 1852, in Manceau's small, careful handwriting: "It's raining; can't go out. Conversations. Work. Dinner. Embroidery. Maurice is writing a play. Lambert has gone to bed, Mme. Solange too. We go upstairs at midnight; Madame has letters to write."[4] George was always "Madame" or "My Lady" for Manceau.

Three-year-old Nini's mornings were spent with Manceau, her afternoons with her grandmother, generally in the garden. Briefly that summer Solange and her sculptor husband, the "monumental mason," came together and took Nini. George objected: if the reconciliation failed (as it did) it would be very hard on the child to be bundled back and forth. She needed "one person to be exclusively concerned about her." But in the fall George could report with relief to Solange that Nini, who was back at Nohant, had quite recovered. "No little girl could possibly be nicer."[5]

Through Nini, George Sand relived her own childhood, recreating a doll's garden in the park for her granddaughter, complete with miniature mountains and fountains, a chalet, a "Bacchus" grove, a "Trianon" grotto. Together they tended the garden, trundling stones in their wheelbarrows, large and small, weeding and planting, cutting and pressing flowers. Until nine in the evening they were inseparable, both embroidering at the great oval table as Manceau read aloud from a novel by Balzac or Walter Scott, or from verses sent to George Sand by Victor Hugo; as Borie, back from Brussels, dozed, Émile Aucante sententiously expounded and Maurice carved puppets from lime-tree roots. There was a "monastic regularity" about the days at Nohant—with George both Mother and Father Superior—and one could almost set one's watch by the activities from early lunch to midnight, when George went upstairs to resume her writing, Manceau before her to prepare the quills and the paper, the blue ink and the tobacco, the glass of sugared water George would sip at six in the morning when her labors were finished.[6] Manceau was the parfit companion. Once, when his "Lady" rose from bed with a headache which lasted all day, he noted in their ledger-diary, "I did everything possible to distract her: I took her into the garden to plant flowers; I was witty, stupid, gay—but nothing worked . . ."[7]

There is a curiously coincidental abandonment of the novel for playwriting in this stage of George Sand's retirement from Paris life and political thinking. In five years she would write ten plays. There would be a total of twenty-four in all, many of them adapted from her novels; only six would be successful. She thought the theater offered a larger, life-size form of art. In fact her plays are generally lifeless and diffuse—the rambling *interior* life and flow of her fiction are missing, the worst features are exposed on the stage. Delacroix remarked this "lack of dramatic talent" in his *Journal*, apropos the première of *Mauprat* at the Odéon theater, November 28, 1853: "Absence of structure: the beginning is always piquant and promising, but the middle drags . . . phrases full of charm—there lies her talent. Her ever-virtuous peasants are deadly . . ."[8] The month previous George Sand had written to Augustine (Titine), "The Emperor and Empress went to see *Le Pressoir*"—another of Sand's plays. "The Emperor applauded many times, the Empress wept many tears."⁹ Too often in her writing for the theater George Sand was trying to please the wrong public.

She had to be taken out of herself, shaken from the intellectual dullness and emotional ease of Nohant. Left to herself, George Sand gardened, collected butterflies and classified plants, watched Maurice play with his elaborate puppets and wrote too many pages each night, as if piling so many logs.

Clésinger proved to be the *deus*, rather *diabolus, ex machina*.

In January 1854, George "never felt better."¹⁰ Though winter, the days were sunny and she could spend long hours with Nini digging in the garden. The Crimean War was at a distance and she herself was plunged in the past, preparing the multivolume *Histoire de Ma Vie* for serialization in the fall, and writing yet another play. Clésinger intervened with a tawdry domestic drama. Told in May of an affair Solange was conducting, he burst into her bedroom, made a terrible row and seized her lover's letters. The scene was not wholly spontaneous, for Clésinger turned over the letters he had long sought to his lawyer: this time a legal separation would be on his terms, and they would include his custody of Nini. Joyfully anticipating the court's decision, he sped to Nohant and demanded the child. George, despite Manceau's "fire brigade," was defenseless. Thus, three days before her fifth birthday, Nini was taken away by her father and kept first in his place, then in boarding school. Solange herself hied once again to a convent to undergo an hysterical conversion.

Summer passed; autumn passed; Sand's memoirs began to appear; her play was performed. In December 1854, the court granted the Clésingers a separation of body and property, but it gave custody of Nini to her grandmother. George Sand rejoiced: perhaps there *was* something to Solange's conversion and prayers. Before the decree could be enforced, however, Clésinger intervened again. Clumsily and fatally. On a particularly cold day in January he fetched Nini from her boarding school and returned her that evening shivering and ill: he had not noticed she was thinly clad. For several days the child tossed with fever; too late Solange was allowed to care for her. Her poor body swollen from scarlatina, Nini died in her mother's arms.

A telegram informed George Sand. She was in despair. Three days later Nini was buried in the Nohant family cemetery. George cried herself to sleep. Manceau in the diary of January 23, 1855: "Madame somewhat better. Thaw . . . Madame, together with Mme. Solange, is making notes about poor Nini's life. Dinner. Discussion about life after death. Embroidery. Reading from [James Fenimore] Cooper. Mme. Solange has a cold; she's covered with compresses. Madame is to go on with Nini's story tonight, using our diary."

George Sand was purging her grief with her pen, releasing her feelings in the outpouring of her sorrow. But she was too distraught to do other writing; too many things at Nohant reminded her of Nini—the doll's garden, the little wheelbarrow. It was not that life had stopped for her: George Sand was too much Goethe's sister for that. But there was a block to the usual flow, and the ever-sensitive, ministering Manceau suggested the cure—a trip to Italy. Moreover, he offered some of the money for it from his small purse—a new experience for George Sand.

On February twenty-eighth the two set off from Nohant, stopping in Paris to pick up Maurice. By train they went to Lyons, from there by riverboat to Marseilles, where they embarked for Genoa. The sea voyage was pleasant and bracing, the subsequent stopover in Leghorn and Pisa diverting. But Rome was their destination, fortunately, for here George Sand rediscovered and renewed her passion. She viewed the Eternal City through political eyes and found it foul. "Do not believe a word about the grandeur and sublimity of Rome and its environs," she wrote back home to Lambert with refreshed force. "In many ways Rome is pure *hoax*. . . . It is curious, beautiful, interesting, astounding —and dead. . . . It is ugliness and muck; it is La Châtre enlarged a hundredfold!"[11] To Luigi Calamatta, who would mildly scold her for this jaundiced view, George replied that the "martyred radicals" of Italy "were mute, paralyzed and invisible," that Rome must be ripped open for this to be seen. "Rome is the kingdom of Satan . . . of people kneeling in servitude to its Cardinals. . . . The story must be told of what happens to those subjected to the tyranny of the priesthood."[12]

All the thwarted, strangled feeling for Mazzini's heroically led revolt; for the fatal role of France under Louis Napoleon, who had sent troops against a liberated, newly republican Rome and handed it back to a pope who had bluntly declared war "on liberalism, progress and modern civilization"[13]; for the restored power of France's own Catholic Church under the Second Empire—all this boiled up in George Sand as she viewed Rome, its rulers and ruled.

After her return to Paris, after the failure of several indifferent plays, Sand poured this still-burning emotion into a novel, *La Daniella*. The travels and love affair of a young French painter in Italy are incidental to the passionate anticlericalism. Priests are everywhere in the fabric of the novel, as in the Italian society she had seen. Pope Pius IX is depicted as the devil's own emissary on earth, his Roman realm pullulating with thieves, beggars, paupers and police spies. The ancient ruins themselves seem to say, "Look at us, and shiver!"[14]

Both Romantics and nationalists were outraged when George's novel began to appear serially in *La Presse*. The nationalists clearly saw that her fictional Italy was largely a transposed France; the Romantics were shocked by the denigration of their precious Roman ruins. The imperial government stirred: the smothering of French thought and expression by officially encouraged clericalism was obviously George Sand's target. A violent controversy ensued in the pages of *La Presse* and its conservative rivals. Twice *La Presse* was warned of government action. Finally it was suspended. Taken aback, George wrote directly to Empress Eugénie, requesting that the action be reconsidered. Four thousand workers, she pleaded with forgivable exaggeration, were affected. *La Presse* was allowed to resume publication, but *La Daniella* was published as a book in a milder version.

That year, 1857, there is another sense of withdrawal after a rousing entr'acte. Not a return to the theater. George seems to have realized that her strength lay in her novels. But rather a retreat from a new hecticness in her life. She needed a refuge from Nohant, as formerly she needed Nohant as a sanctuary from Paris. Too many knew of her influence with the imperial family through Prince Jérôme Bonaparte; too many knocked, unbidden, on Nohant's door, knowing there was some chance for a hearing. Too often the intimate commune of friends gave way to a crowd of guests, less accustomed to George Sand's habits of work. In June she ventured into the valley of the Creuse, thirty miles from Nohant, with Manceau, as she had a dozen years before with Chopin. The previous spring she had taken Manceau to Musset's Fontainebleau for three days, as she had Mallefille and Bocage. For George Sand there was a continuity of love identified with place and independent of lovers. On this excursion to the Creuse she rediscovered the lovely sunken village of Gargilesse and its Swiss-like environs of mountains and gorges and foaming streams, of "paradise and chaos." Gargilesse was a veritable sun-pocket in which rare Algerian butterflies were warmly at home. As much as the sunny, sheltered site, the openness of the villagers, their natural freedom—"even women go swimming" and all live "the communal life"—delighted George Sand. Here, she decided, was the artist's dream of a pastoral retreat "from the foolish fatigues of civilization."[15]

It was Manceau, responsive to Madame, who bought the little cottage in which they were staying. That made it theirs, as Nohant was not. Manceau had it repainted and refurnished, refitting it snugly as a "ship's cabin." But George thought it best to write Maurice, "It is really more for us than for himself." Each would have "his nail, his pot, a place for his boots, etc., etc."[16] Never had George found a place more congenial for her labors. Here she would come to work, usually alone with Manceau, writing the greater part of thirteen novels, two volumes of essays and three plays between 1857 and 1862.[17] Typical is the entry in their diary, May 29, 1858: "Magnificent weather, warm and bright. Manceau left after lunch to net butterflies. . . . I stayed home to finish my novel, *Elle et Lui* [She and He], begun on May 4. 620 pages in 25 days! I have never worked with so much pleasure as in Gargilesse."[18]

Alfred de Musset having died the previous year, George Sand, giving herself the more noble role, told the story of their tormented love in *Elle et Lui*. Musset had been more generous in his *Confession d'un Enfant du Siècle*. However, twenty-five years had passed and, as in her memoirs, George Sand was rewriting her past as if for the reading of her grandchildren. When her novel appeared it provoked the angry rebuttal of *Lui et Elle* by Alfred's older brother, Paul de Musset. And as if that were not sufficient, Louise Colet, mistress of Gustave Flaubert before turning to Alfred de Musset, entered the fray with a tasteless, talentless *Lui*.

The three novels titillated *le tout Paris*. George thought publication of the letters exchanged with Musset, which she possessed, would vindicate her version and establish her innocence in Venice. She consulted her old confidant Sainte-Beuve; he counseled against it. She thanked him for his advice. "The letters," she agreed, "will be published after my death." They would not, however, be published exactly as she and Musset had written them.[19] Nevertheless, as George's epistle to Sainte-Beuve continued, "the letters"—even as eventually published—"prove one thing":

> that underlying the two novels—*Elle et Lui* and *Confession d'un Enfant du Siècle*—is a true story, marked by the folly of the one and the affection of the other, or if one wishes, the folly of both, but never anything odious or cowardly in either heart, nor anything that stains their souls' sincerity.[20]

A fitting epitaph for the pen-crossed lovers.

Another last word further involved Sainte-Beuve. Hot and cold as had been their relationship, his was an abiding respect for George Sand's literary achievement. In 1861 he attempted to persuade his fellow "immortals" of the French Academy, among whom no woman has ever had a seat, to award Sand their prize of twenty thousand francs. Vigny, Mérimée and three others joined Sainte-Beuve in the balloting that took place. Eighteen voted against George Sand, Guizot justifying his negative vote by citing her "outrageous" writings on property and marriage. Jules Sandeau, elected to the immortals two years before, was not even present. In recompense the Emperor, who still courted George Sand's allegiance, offered her twenty thousand francs from his own purse. George refused them. The Empress "suggested" that the Academy "at least" elect one of France's greatest living novelists as a member. An anonymous pamphlet, *Les Femmes à l'Académie*, imaginatively described her installation. George replied with a wittier pamphlet of her own, *Pourquoi les Femmes à l'Académie?* (Why

Women in the French Academy?). She was sure, she remarked, they were a respectable, able body of men quite happy in their own company, but she was equally happy not to be part of it. They were, in short, old fogies long out of tune with the time. As for those who might call her refusal to join them *sour grapes*, she could only reply, "Not at all, those grapes are not sour—they are merely over-ripe."[21]

Wit in trenchant abundance best describes George Sand's new, close friend, Alexandre Dumas the younger. She had been grateful to him for his handling of the Chopin letters; she would be even more indebted to him for his doctoring of her plays. They had met finally in 1852 at a performance of his *La Dame aux Camélias*—which has been steadily performed since as *Camille*, in the English-speaking world, by rising young actresses. As a dramatist, Dumas *fils* knew his business thoroughly—the art of situation, repartee, climax and character. It was not until 1861, however, that George succeeded in persuading the twenty-year-younger Dumas to visit Nohant. In accepting, he asked permission—quickly accorded—to bring along not only his green-eyed Russian inamorata (and future wife), Princess Naryshkin, and her daughter Olga, but also a friend—"a big friend," he explained, "who rather resembles one of your Newfoundland dogs. He is named Marchal, he weighs 182 pounds and has enough esprit for four. He can sleep anywhere—with the chickens, under a tree or a fountain."[22]

Eventually the jolly giant, the "Mastodon" Charles Marchal, a painter two years younger than Maurice, "slept" with George Sand. It may have occurred one evening that fall in her bedroom, while the others (says George's diary) "were rehearsing downstairs" in the little Nohant theater; it certainly took place several years later at Gargilesse. Very quickly Marchal, who stayed on for several months after Dumas' departure, became George's "big baby" and amusing friend, "collaborating with Maurice in puppet plays" and generally entertaining the Nohant commune with his rapid, lifelike sketches and ebullient chatter.[23]

More interesting, however, is the professional—deep and platonic—friendship between George Sand and the younger Alexandre Dumas; he called her *mamma* and she, *dear son*. She helped him face up to the phenomenon who was his father, a man with as prodigious a number of mistresses as novels. Dumas *fils*, a natural son, was obsessed by the paternal example and overpowered by the inevitable comparison. He brooded over it. He was as moral as his father was not; it was a bond between him and George Sand. But he must realize, she told him, "that father Dumas owed the great abundance of his faculties to his expenditure of them. . . . He needed all the excesses of life in order incessantly to renew his enormous capacity for life."[24] In part, it is a description of the younger George Sand.

It was the older woman now, however, who was addressing herself to the younger writer, offering him a tranquilizing, releasing wisdom. "I have spent many an hour of my life watching the grass grow, or contemplating the serenity of great stones in the moonlight.* . . . I have identified myself so much with this way of being of tranquil things, called inert, that I have come to share their calm beatitude. . . . When I was your age, I was more troubled, more sick in mind and body, than you." But "one fine morning," she had asked herself, "What does it matter? The universe is grand and beautiful. Everything we believe full of importance is so fugitive that we need not even think about it."[25]

Theirs, too, was a working relationship. George Sand's *François le Champi* inspired the younger Dumas' *Le Fils Naturel*. He greatly helped her fashion a successful play from a slight novel, *Le Marquis de Villemer*—Dumas drafted the first act. But the story of that play's success is not one of dramatic technique. Rather, it is the chronicling of another episode, a last station, in the most moving passion of George Sand's later years—anticlericalism, the passion firing *La Daniella*. It makes the matter of whether or not she bedded for a few hours with Marchal in the fall of 1861 trivial in comparison. Hers, throughout her life, were the passions of the mind as much as of the body: the triptych of heart-body-and-mind alone representing for her the totality of love.

This time it was not the view of Rome that freshly stirred George Sand, but the vision of France under Napoleon III, the paradox of economic liberalism creating an industrially expanding nation as well as a growingly influential Church restraining literary expression, as exemplified by the government's earlier prosecution of Baudelaire's *Flowers of Evil* and Flaubert's *Madame Bovary* for offending religious morality. George's own feelings were eloquently stated in her letter to Prince Jérôme Bonaparte, February 26, 1862:

> The Emperor fears socialism. From his point of view, he is quite right to fear it. By hitting it too hard and too soon, however, he has raised on the ruins of that party another, fully as clever and dangerous in quite a different way, a party *united* by the sentiment of class and clan, a party of nobles and priests, and unfortunately I can see no counterweight in the middle class.
>
> With all its faults, the bourgeoisie once possessed its useful, ponderous effect. Skeptical or Voltairean, it nevertheless had

---

* Compare Walt Whitman in his *Song of Myself*:
  > I loafe and invite my soul,
  > I lean and loafe at my ease observing a spear
  > of summer grass.

its own clannishness, its own vanity of the newly rich. It resisted the priests, it flouted the nobles, whom it envied. Today it flatters them. Their titles have been restored. The legitimists [pressing for a Bourbon restoration], who are all around us, are shown the greatest deference. And you think they have been defeated! The middle class is eager to be on good terms with the nobles, whose influence is growing. The priests are acting as intermediaries. People have become churchgoers in order to have entry to legitimist drawing rooms. Civil servants are showing the way, and one sees them, all smirks and obsequious bows, at Mass; and middle-class wives have plunged ardently into the legitimist cause, for women never do things by half.[26]

Against this background, Octave Feuillet published in George Sand's "own" *Revue des Deux Mondes*—she had renewed ties with Buloz—a novel entitled *Sibylle*, a sentimental hymn to the virtues of the priesthood and the Church. George responded with the fury and fluent speed of her best days. She reversed the situation in *Sibylle*—that of a young woman refusing to marry a young man because he does not share her Catholic faith—and makes it, in her novel *Mademoiselle La Quintinie*, that of a young freethinker who will not marry a young woman so long as she does *not* renounce her Catholicism. Vehemently the young man denounces the Church's doctrine of Hell and eternal damnation, its denial of the flesh and the possibility of earthly progress, its demand of full, intimate confession, which no husband could possibly wish to share with a priest. At one point he cries, "Show me a single Catholic precept other than that of a wife's passive obedience to her spouse!"[27] The young woman is shown the way to the true religion—Christian humanism, the creed of *Spiridion*—and weds the young man.

In her Preface, George Sand warned that the greater danger was not clerical doctrine, but a clerical party that might one day explode "in a vast plot against social and individual freedom."[28] Once again—in her sixtieth year—she became the political clarion of a rising generation. The youth of France, particularly the university students of Paris, responded to *Mademoiselle La Quintinie* and its bold attacks with an enthusiasm rarely enjoyed even by the younger George Sand: in the stifling atmosphere of the Second Empire she still represented intellectual revolt. When they heard there would be a new play by George Sand and an organized demonstration against it at the Odéon theater, so close to their own Latin Quarter, they had the occasion they sought to salute their new hero en masse.

Despite the rain and the "river of mud" on the day of the opening of Sand's *Villemer*, "students in bunches of four, their student cards stuck

in their hats, climbed the stairs to my apartment to ask for seats!"
From ten that morning they stood in line before the Odéon theater,
"shouting and singing" in the square (George Sand's diary continues,
February 29, 1864). Throughout the performance, those who could not
get in crowded the streets from the square to Sand's apartment on Rue
Racine. There was almost a riot when six hundred students led six
thousand on a march to the Catholic Club and the neighboring Jesuit
House, where they put on their own anticlerical show.

Inside the theater, the Emperor and Empress sat uneasily in the imperial box. George Sand was in another with Prince Jérôme and his
young wife. Catcalls and stampings greeted every scene, but they were
drowned by louder cries of applause. Even the Emperor carefully
clapped. At the fall of the final curtain there was an ovation. "Incredible, unheard-of success." In the foyer at intermission two hundred,
many of them titled, had come one by one to kiss Madame Sand's
cheek. Among those with George Sand on opening night was Gustave
Flaubert, "who wept," she wrote Maurice, "like a woman." He wept,
surely, for George's success, and she thanked him warmly for it. But the
greatest triumph awaited her outside. Thousands escorted her home to
cries of "Long live George Sand! Long live *La Quintinie!* Down with
the clericalists!" Students were barely persuaded by the police not to
unhitch the horses and pull the carriage themselves to her apartment.[29]

The second night witnessed a similar success, and for weeks there
were queues of carriages stretching from the Odéon to the Left Bank
boulevards. Thus even at "twilight" George Sand won the applause of
her contemporaries, particularly among the young, for whom her older,
militantly socialist novels were available in a cheap, popular edition and
for whom the later, more moderate work simply did not count. Compare Sainte-Beuve's reaction: When *Mademoiselle La Quintinie* appeared and aroused its controversy, Sainte-Beuve had called Sand a
"powerful, irritated eagle" who had "pounced on the white dove" of
Sibylle and soared away with it, presumably to dash her pious prey on
the rocks below. The whole affair, concluded Sainte-Beuve, was "a bit
uncivilized."[30]

Meantime a man who as the *poète maudit* is more our contemporary
than he is George Sand's, the somber, sin-obsessed Charles Baudelaire,
had been brooding about that serene colossus straddling his age; and he
who had said, "I cultivate my hysteria with joy and terror," could not
have been more antipodal. Baudelaire's comments are private notes to
himself, published after his death:

> *On George Sand.* The woman Sand is the Prudhomme [smug,
> banal personification] of immorality. She was always a moral-
> ist, though once it took an antimoral form. Besides, she's

never been an artist. She has that famous *flowing style*, so dear
to the bourgeoisie. She is stupid, she is heavy, she is garrulous;
she has as much depth of judgment, as much delicacy of feeling in her moral judgments, as a concierge or a kept woman.
The things she has said of her mother [in *Story of My Life*].
The things she has said of poetry. Her love for workers. That
some people can become enamoured with such a latrine is
proof enough of how low the people of our time have sunk.
Take her preface to *Mademoiselle La Quintinie*, where she
maintains that true Christians cannot believe in Hell. La Sand
is for the *God of the good folk*, the god of concierges and
thieving domestics. She has good reasons for wanting to suppress Hell.
The Devil and George Sand. You must not believe that the
Devil tempts only people of genius. No doubt he despises
fools, but he does not disdain their aid. On the contrary, he
bases his great hopes on them.
Take George Sand. She is above all, and beyond anything
else, a *great fool*; but she is *possessed*. It is the Devil who has
persuaded her to trust in her *good heart* and her *good sense*,
so that she may persuade all the other great fools to trust in
their good hearts and their good sense.
I cannot think of this stupid creature without a shudder of
horror. If I were to meet her, I could not refrain from throwing a basin of holy water at her head.
George Sand is one of those aging ingénues who will never
leave the stage.

Baudelaire burns with impatience and frustration. He immediately follows his pillorying of George Sand (whom he had qualifiedly praised
ten years before) with a stoning of Voltaire, "whom all France resembles"—Voltaire, "the anti-poet, . . . the anti-artist, the concierge's
preacher."[31] It puts Baudelaire's perceptions into better perspective,
without removing their sting. Voltaire *was* too rational, George Sand
was too commonsensical, for the tortured sensibility of a poet of the
damned. And both, for Baudelaire, were lingering too long on the
French stage, that is, in the French mind.

Son Versus Lover
"Let Us Go, My Friend"

"He was raised quite literally in cotton," said George Sand of her father, Maurice Dupin.[1] There is not the same sharp perception of it in the raising of her son. Maurice Sand had become an indolent illustrator who left the drudgery of engraving his work to Manceau; who dabbled in literature, leaving the dénouement of a novel, for instance, to his mother; who played with puppets like an arrested child. His Oedipal fix was transparent, but he had successfully come between his mother and Chopin. In 1862 he was a year short of forty. His marrying became of more concern to George Sand, more for the sake of grandchildren, perhaps, than that of her son. "Maurice, who was so happy with me, was afraid he'd be unhappy otherwise."[2] Or, perhaps, for the sake of having another daughter, since both Solange and Augustine had failed her. Solange, after the death of Nini and her complete separation from Clésinger, now whirled about Europe with a succession of wealthy lovers—and George chose not to know the details. Augustine corresponded when there was a favor to be asked for her husband.

What bride for Maurice, what daughter for his mother? In 1860 George Sand had written Maurice's former tutor, Jules Boucoiran, for his aid. She preferred, George said, someone from "a Protestant family . . . charming, serious, shapely and intelligent."[3] Sand found her, two years later, in the daughter of her old friend, Luigi Calamatta, the engraver. Dark-eyed, charming, warm and intelligent, Marcelina Calamatta, known as Lina, was a familiar of Nohant, having been brought up and educated in Paris before finishing her studies in Genoa. Republican as her father, she was as "freethinking" as George and Maurice in reaction to a bigoted, dominating Catholic mother, now living separate from her father; she was nineteen and Maurice almost thirty-nine when they became engaged.

"I feel certain," George wrote Lina Calamatta on March 31, 1862, "that I shall be a true mother to you, for I need a daughter and I can find none better than the child of one of my dearest friends."[4] Marrying Maurice in May—civilly in the mayor's office, not religiously in church—Lina did become that daughter for George Sand, devoted, loving and loyal. "You see," she would say, "it was really George Sand I married rather than Maurice Sand, and I married him because I adored her."[5] And George would remark to Flaubert, "My daughter Lina is my true daughter. The *other* gets along; she is beautiful, which is all I can ask of her."[6]

It was a pleasant summer: Lina gratified George by quickly becoming pregnant; Maurice was showing some signs of fatherhood; Manceau was a pillar of strength—"all heart and all devotion."[7] It was a productive fall: something of Lina went into Mademoiselle La Quintinie, rounding and softening the characterization. The following summer, on July 14, 1863, George became a grandmother again, and the birth of Marc-Antoine Dudevant-Sand, straightway called Cocoton (Little Chick), was celebrated, along with Bastille Day, by the firing of the miniature cannon and the customary Nohant theatricals. Writing had resumed, particularly on the dramatization of *Villemer* with Dumas' help. A frequent visitor, he had introduced Théophile Gautier—poet, novelist, critic, esthete and Romantic par excellence—to Nohant, as he had Charles Marchal.

Gautier's first visit might have been his last. He mistook George's discomfiting silence in the drawing room for a deliberately "glacial reception." He searched out Dumas and told him he was leaving the next morning. Dumas laughed and conducted "dear Théo" to Sand's study. "Didn't you warn him," George exclaimed for Gautier's benefit, "that I am as stupid as can be, that I don't know how to talk to clever people?" Her guest mollified, the three talked until dawn.[8]

When Gautier finally returned to Paris, several days later, he had a somewhat more elaborate tale for his demanding, literary friends who met twice monthly in the Left Bank Magny restaurant. "Was it amusing at Nohant?" he was asked. Théophile Gautier's reply, chronicled by the Goncourt brothers, aimed above all at being itself *amusant*: to be a bore at the Magny dinners was fatal.

Was it amusing, then, at Nohant?

As entertaining as a convent of the Moravian Brothers. I arrived in the evening. It's a long way from the railroad. [One coached from Châteauroux.] I found my trunk mislaid in a bush. I arrived by way of a farmyard, surrounded by dogs that scared the wits out of me! . . . They gave me dinner. The food is quite good, but there is too much game and chicken—for my taste . . . Marchal the painter, Dumas the younger, Madame Calamatta [Lina's mother] were there . . .

What is life like at Nohant?

Breakfast at ten. At the stroke of ten, everyone sits down. Madame Sand arrives, looking like a sleepwalker, and stays asleep all through breakfast. After breakfast, we all go into the garden. We play bowling games, which revive her. She sits down and begins to talk. The conversation at this hour is usually about pronunciation—the pronunciation of *ailleurs* and *meilleur*, for example. Very appetizing chats—water-closet jokes and that sort of thing.

Whew!

But not a single word about sex. I'm convinced you'd be thrown out of the door if you made the slightest allusion to it.

At three, Madame Sand goes back upstairs to turn out copy until six. Then we dine, but rather hurriedly, so that Marie Caillaud will have time to dine. She's the maid of the house, a Petite Fadette whom Madame Sand picked up in the countryside to take part in her theatricals and who joins everyone in the salon in the evening.

After dinner, Madame Sand plays games of patience [solitaire] without uttering a word—until midnight. . . . On the second day, for instance, I began to remark that if no one was going to talk literature, I was going to leave. . . . Ah! literature . . . they all seemed to return from that other world! . . . Now, I must say, there is only one thing that interests people down there: mineralogy. Everyone carries a hammer and no one goes out without one. . . . So I declared that Rousseau was the worst writer in the French language and *that* led to a discussion with Madame Sand until one in the morning . . .

But I must say Manceau has really turned Nohant into a writing factory. She cannot sit down in any room without pens, blue ink, cigarette papers, Turkish tobacco and lined writing paper suddenly materializing for her. And how she runs through them! As you all know, she starts writing again from midnight until four in the morning.

And "monstrously" once finished a novel and started another "the same night."

As for the rest, one is very comfortable down there. The service, for instance, is silent. In the corridor there is a box with two compartments: one for mailing letters, the other for letters to the house. In the latter you put communications saying what you need, indicating your name and bedroom. I needed a comb, so I wrote: "Monsieur Gautier, such and such a bedroom" and what I wanted. The next day at six in the morning I had thirty combs to choose from.[9]

The role of Manceau in George Sand's life emerges in Gautier's "amusing" account. There's scarcely ever a word about the man-child Maurice. How galling it must have become for him, especially now that he was father of a child and head of at least his own household within the domain of Nohant. What remarks he must have heard from his own father Casimir at Guillery, where he went annually for long stays. The mounting hostility Maurice felt for Alexandre Manceau had to surface. The cryptic entries of George Sand in the agenda-book diary of 1863 manifest it. There was also the ominous note on March thirty-first: "Manceau is coughing"; and on April second: "Manceau still coughing." The cough will be a constant background sound.[10]

Three plays were in preparation that fall: *Villemer*, *Datura Fastuosa*, and a verse drama by Manceau, *Une Journée à Dresde*. Maurice, meantime, was "working" on a second novel, but the work was not progressing. Almost every night there were readings from the plays with musical interludes. ("Lina sings divinely. . . . After *Datura*, Manceau reads to us from his drama. . . . Charming . . .") Marie Caillaud, the housemaid taking an active part in the performances, has become a prima donna and a problem. She resents Manceau's direction. George Sand has to "restore peace." September twenty-seventh: "Play [*Datura*] a great success. *Manceau surpasses himself*." George underlined the sentence. Manceau's entry for October 21 indicates general nervousness. Concerning *Villemer*, as it approaches production, George Sand, October twenty-second: "Manceau and I working like two blacks . . . the invincible Manceau." On October 28 they were sufficiently advanced for a special run-through at Nohant for Charles de La Rounat, director of the Odéon theater. "Reading of *Villemer* to La Rounat, Boucoiran, [Luigi] Calamatta, all except Maurice. Manceau reads like an angel." Manceau, November 13: "Maurice does not feel very well. . . ." Sand, November 14: "The play is a pleasure. Manceau reads like a jewel. . . . Maurice is ill." Manceau, November 16: "Madame is ill. . . ."

A week later there was an eruption; Marie Caillaud was its cause—or occasion. Again she objected to Manceau's direction. Maurice took her part. Tempers rose; the quarrel reached an unresolved climax; Maurice took it to his mother, re-enacting the drama with Chopin. It was he or

Manceau, Maurice said. One or the other must leave Nohant. George Sand retreated; a direct assault always made her recoil. Of course Maurice must stay; he was her son, her family. That evening Manceau wrote the entry in their diary. It would be read, he knew, that night by George Sand, as was sometimes their way with each other—a kind of note left on the other's pillow. November 23, 1863:

> After I know not what conversation, I am told that I am free to leave on Saint John's day [midsummer next]. Torrents of tears on my account. It did not take long. So much for all the regret on my leaving after fifteen years of devotion. I want to put it down here, so that I may never again cry over it and may even hope one day to smile about what has happened. Anyway, it's all the same to me. Humanity, on the whole, is a poor thing. So now I am to regain my freedom and should I wish to love someone and again devote myself to that person, since such is my pleasure, I can do it in all freedom. Freedom! There's another pretty thing. . . .

Years later, when Maurice fell heir to the ledgers, he would add in an even smaller, tighter hand: "Re-read *Tartuffe*"—Molière's play about a religious hypocrite. For George Sand, reading Manceau's sad, dignified lines, was deeply moved, and the following morning she told Maurice she had changed her mind. She was leaving Nohant with Manceau. That night she left *her* diary note on her lover's pillow, replying to his own:

> I do not feel sad. And why not? Because, as we have known all along, things have gone badly. I, too, am recovering *my* freedom. After all, *we* are not parting. Are we not content that things should change? Have I not been longing for some change in this life of bitterness and injustice? Let us go, my friend. Let us go without rancor, without ill-feeling, and let us —you and I—never part. Let them have everything, but not our dignity, not the sacrifice of our friendship. That, NEVER.

Maurice penned another comment, bitter and unjust: "Re-read the part of the father in *Tartuffe*. My mother was always a dupe!" There was a well-mannered show of no ill-feelings, however; the decision to leave Nohant, and Nohant to Maurice, was kept secret within its walls. Nevertheless, George was "sick to her stomach" and on December 4 she recorded a recurring Kafkaesque dream: "Again that nightmare. Condemned to death, not knowing why." The evenings were spent with a dripping regularity looking at Maurice's puppet play. Manceau, December 26: "Madame passionately worked on costumes for the puppets this evening. It is not folly; it is a kind of frenzy. And when there are no more puppets?" When they lived away from Nohant and Maurice, alone together? Manceau wondered.

The transition was rendered easier by a stay in Paris during the first months of 1864. On January 13, Manceau's little verse drama had its performance—and success—at the Odéon theater. Prince Jérôme loudly called for the author to come to his box.) There were rehearsals of *Villemer* for performance at the end of February. There was a smaller studio apartment to be found—eventually on the Rue des Feuillantines —replacing Manceau's more expensive one on Rue Racine. And there was the "little house" they sought, not too far from Paris, for their permanent remove from Nohant. Here Manceau's cousin, Louis Maillard, was of greatest help, discovering an isolated cottage in the village of Palaiseau, an hour's drive south of Paris.

How to pay for the Palaiseau house? Again Manceau dipped into his small reserves—the place would be in his name—and George Sand unexpectedly found herself left a small fortune on the death of Delacroix. A sale for the benefit of his heirs displayed a sudden, soaring interest in his work. George wrote Maurice to sell their own Delacroix treasures— *La Chasse au Lion*, two *Lélias*, *Les Fleurs*, *Cléopâtre*, *Les Carrières*, a dozen other paintings, sketches and drawings. "I will keep *Le Centaure* for myself as long as I live. It was his last gift, as *La Confession du Giaour* was his first."[11] The bulk of the money gained, however, went towards assuring Maurice an annuity of three thousand francs a year, a tidy sum.

The reception of *Villemer*, but a few weeks later, may have made George Sand regret having sold her Delacroix canvases, but she was not given to such regrets. Moreover, it allowed her to put the best possible face on the departure from Nohant. "The success of *Villemer*," she wrote Augustine in explanation, March thirty-first, "permits me more freedom than I have had these last few years." The burden of Nohant and half of the Berry, she said, "the friends of friends looking to me for my 'influence' and jobs," were too much for her work, her purse, her peace of mind. "Now I am making a change and I am delighted by the prospect. I find it droll that some people are pitying me . . . saying all sorts of things about it, making me laugh when they ask me, 'Are you really leaving us? How will you manage to live without us?' Ah, those Berry people!"[12]

In truth, the servants at Nohant had kept the countryside informed —"Marie Caillaud has been rummaging in my basket," Sand would note in her agenda, May twentieth, "and takes the liberty of reading my diary. Go to it!"—and it is doubtful that Titine did not know what had really brought about George's decision to leave her beloved Nohant. The actual leaving was painful. Restlessly she arranged and rearranged her papers and affairs in preparation for the move while

Manceau was away getting their Palaiseau house in order. On an impulse she left for Gargilesse, to be absolutely alone for several days. Refreshed, herself again, she returned. Her diary delightfully discloses it. Following the printed date "April 25" in her agenda book was the provocative theme for the day: "Abstinence." George Sand underscored it heavily with her quill:

> *Abstinence!* Abstinence from what, fools? You might well abstain from evil the rest of your lives. But do you believe that God has made what is good so that we should deprive ourselves of it? Abstain then from enjoying the sun, from watching the lilacs grow. . . .[13]

Such was not for George Sand, scarcely more at sixty than at twenty.

Manceau returned early in June: the house at Palaiseau was ready for them. Workers and artisans of La Châtre, who had vainly petitioned George Sand to remain, now sent her a moving testimonial letter, which they each signed. "No one," they wrote, "has ever honored the work and dignity of the poor as Madame." And they referred to *Le Compagnon du Tour de France*. "Today," they continued, "the author of *Mademoiselle La Quintinie*, alone or in the forefront, still fights triumphantly against the retrograde ideas of the past. We align ourselves anew with her in the name of liberty." And they quoted in their farewell from the ballad of *Consuelo*—"The Goddess of the Poor."[14]

Manceau penned his own quiet note for his companion to read. Diary, June 11, 1864:

> Last evening at Nohant. We shall all remember it, I believe. So there is no need to write about it. But despite myself I cannot help thinking that during the fourteen years I have spent here, I have laughed more, cried more, *lived* more than in all the thirty-three preceding them. From now henceforth I shall be alone with Her. What a responsibility! But what an honor, what a joy!

George Sand would never read Maurice's cramped comment: "What a conceited ass and fool!" The leave-taking was more seemly, partly because no one but a few caretakers would be left at Nohant. Ironically, "the dear children," Maurice and obediently Lina, decided they could not manage the burden of the great place without its grand matriarch and so accepted Casimir Dudevant's invitation to stay at Guillery. As they betook themselves there, Manceau and George Sand went to Palaiseau via Paris, arriving at eight in the evening. George to her diary that night, June twelfth: "I am delighted with *everything*: the countryside, the little garden, the view, the house, the dinner, the maid, the silence. It's an enchantment. The good Manceau has thought of everything to *perfection*."

The diamond-like pool on the small Palaiseau estate, the splendid surrounding trees, wheatfields and meadows composed a painter's landscape—"a real Ruysdael," said George.[15] For her there was the special pleasure of beginning anew in a new, clean place, celebrated by a kind of symbolic burning of old manuscripts (for which, too, there was less space)—the ill-fated *Engelwald*, rejected fragments of *Mauprat* and *Cosima*, and lesser things. She watched the cinders whirl up the chimney. There were frequent trips to Paris, it took so little time, to see Buloz or Prince Jérôme, to go to the theater. On July fifth George's sixtieth birthday was fêted in a "May freshness." It was marred only by an earlier note in the diary, June twenty-third: "Manceau has spit some blood. Surely it doesn't mean anything."

Then, on July tenth, in Manceau's hand: "Bad news of the Little Chick." Lina's child had become very ill at Guillery. July fourteenth, George Sand's large, sprawling lines: "Sad anniversary for my poor little one. But this evening the telegram is encouraging. There is hope." Manceau, July eighteenth: "No telegram this evening." July nineteenth: "Before we sat down to dinner, we received the dreadful news that Marc is dying: MUCH WORSE LITTLE HOPE. We pack our trunks and leave." They miss the train from Paris to Bordeaux by five minutes. "We sleep at Rue des Feuillantines." July twentieth in Paris: "Another telegram: IF YOU WANT TO SEE HIM [alive] COME." Accompanied by Manceau's cousin, Louis Maillard, George's doctor, Camille Leclerc, and their maid Lucie, they arrive at Guillery on the twenty-first at two in the afternoon. "A half hour earlier we learned from a postman that we were too late—the child had died this morning. The first person we saw was Maurice, then Monsieur Dudevant and Madame Dalias, then Madame Maurice . . ." Manceau, his cousin and the doctor go to Nérac for the night, "leaving Madame Sand to console the children."

Long after all the participants were to pass away, the good people of Guillery would recall the odd meeting, the strained occasion. Madame Dalias, mentioned in the diary by Manceau (who had arrived as George Sand's intimate companion), was Jeanny Dalias, housekeeper and mistress of Casimir Dudevant (still George Sand's husband) and mother of his grown-up daughter Rose. Casimir, now sixty-nine, intimidated as ever by his wife, had surrounded himself with friends in anticipation of her arrival. He was, however, courtesy itself as he asked Madame Dalias to show "Madame la Baronne" to her room, murmuring to George, "It has been unoccupied since you left." Not to be outdone, George remarked to Madame Dalias somewhat later, "I confide my old husband to you."[16]

The following day Manceau, on Maurice's request, brought a Protestant pastor from Nérac to conduct the morning burial services. During lunch George was speechless and Maurice wept. After the meal, the servants long remembered, she smoked endlessly, a behavior as shocking for them as the red petticoat they descried under a tucked-up skirt. The farewells were brief. By July twenty-fourth, Manceau and George Sand were back in Palaiseau. On the twenty-fifth, George corrected proofs that had followed her since her departure; Buloz came to fetch them. "The weather is gray—as indeed are we! Manceau coughs and goes to bed early." July twenty-sixth: "Manceau is better. With a great effort I finish my novel [*The Lost Child*, begun before Marc-Antoine's illness]. It is bad. God knows it is not my fault!" July twenty-eighth: "Camille [Leclerc] auscultates Manceau, finds him sound and puts him on arsenic." Tuberculosis, rightly called the scourge of the nineteenth century (along with syphilis), had still not found its early diagnosis and cure.

To Maurice and Lina, who were in Nîmes before their eventual return to Nohant, George Sand wrote that life must go on; despite its "terrible mixture" of joys and sorrows, hopes and despair—"we will live again."[17] To Armand Barbès, who was living and would die in exile in Holland, she would write: "What grief! We have not yet recovered from it. But I demand, I *command*, another child. For we must love, we must suffer, we must cry, hope, create, *be*."[18] With this remarkable philosophy, Sand tried to maintain a normal life with normal activity—gardening and long walks as usual, trips to Paris, dinner at Magny's, work on yet another play, *Mademoiselle de Drac*, even sending Manceau on exhausting errands to the capital. But the visits of Camille Leclerc were beginning to occur with alarming regularity. September fourth: "Poor Manceau is impatient and coughing horribly." September sixth: "Manceau coughing and still choking." George herself is suffering from small ills and unusual sleeplessness; the outlook was bleak.

On September 11, 1864, Manceau makes the entry: "Marchal and Maillard come to dinner—long conversation afterwards. . . . Madame in admirably good form." Then, added dryly the same day: "Madame plans to spend a week in Gargilesse with Marchal."

As if to draw a breath before the terrible ordeal she knew lay ahead, on impulse George Sand had proposed to Charles Marchal, the gay "Mastodon" among her younger friends, this interlude, open and uncamouflaged. Marchal had accepted. But what draws one's own admiration is Manceau's reaction: he seems not to have objected. He was devoted; he was generous. What in reality were a few days out of the many years he and George had been closely together? Was he not a sick man and she most likely more nurse than mistress now? George had left Nohant and even Maurice for him; life for a long moment would be dreary for her—and it was George Sand, not Manceau, who seems to have been more disturbed after the initial impulsive gesture.

Manceau, September twelfth: "Madame slept badly. She is tired and ill. . . . She spends the day packing her trunks for the trip to Gargilesse with Marchal. . . . We play bézique [a card game similar to pinochle] in the evening." September thirteenth: "Madame not very well. We leave for Paris at 11 o'clock with Lucie. . . . Dinner with Marchal, Maurice, his wife, Maillard. . . . Maillard and I take Madame Sand to the train. She is charming. She teases Marchal a great deal. We say good-bye exactly as if she were going to the Bois de Boulogne [Paris' park]. It is 10 o'clock. The rest will probably be done by Madame."

The four following pages of the 1864 agenda book, however, two days per page, September fourteenth to the twenty-first, remain blank. The diary resumed on the return from Gargilesse: Manceau met Marchal and George Sand in Paris: they dined at Magny's.

A week was spent in the capital, because of last rehearsals of *Mademoiselle de Drac* before its opening at the Odéon. Manceau, September twenty-ninth: "Madame ill all night with a stomach ache. . . . Odéon. Dinner at Magny's with Maurice and his wife. Second performance of *Drac*. It's going fairly well. I'm convinced it won't make a penny, but honor is saved. Maurice is as insolent as the hangman's valet." George Sand, September thirtieth: "Manceau is quite tired." They returned to Palaiseau, where everything—"sky, countryside, the little house"— seemed "more beautiful than ever." The year ended with George frequently noting "reading and needlework" and "Manceau coughing."

On January 14, 1865, the little Palaiseau house shook in "a tempest . . . the chimneys trembling as if they had *delirium tremens*."[19] Three days later, defying his condition, Manceau went alone to Paris—"to see the Prince, his mother, the Odéon performance." But his courage was terribly shaken by the sudden death of his cousin Maillard. Together with George he went again to Paris, to sit among the mourners. "Madame does not leave my side—the dear woman!" On January twenty-fifth, after Maillard's funeral, which they had followed on foot to the Père Lachaise cemetery, George Sand: "Manceau sleeps—I hope." On returning to Palaiseau, George began writing a novel in collaboration with the sick Manceau, hoping to distract him. The novel was entitled *Le Bonheur* (Happiness). Manceau, March seventeenth: "I am choking fit to die." Sand, May seventh: "The novel of Happiness is finished."

The same month Manceau traveled to Paris to consult a new doctor whose special treatment consisted of repeated inhalations of oxygen, taken at home. May sixteenth: "Tomorrow I begin the treatment." Ten question marks follow, the tenth fills half the entry. Twice a day Manceau inhaled oxygen, each time with sharp pain, each time "No result." May thirtieth: "She is sad, my Lady, seeing me like this. Yet I do what I can to laugh, whenever the fever allows me." June third: "I try to work, but this terrible coughing is killing me. 43rd *gaz*. They are permitting me to skip the treatment tomorrow. I'm as happy as a schoolboy on vacation." The writing grows weaker; on June sixth we read it for the last time: "This evening I cough a great deal. Madame advises me to discontinue the *gaz*. In the evening, lotions . . . compresses . . . tomorrow morning I shall perhaps be better."

Manceau's Calvary, George Sand's devotion, have not come to an end. Night after dreary day, each with hope diminishing, the lotions and compresses, the washings and rubbings and incessant nursing care continued. Now even their diary is no longer one of collaboration, though Manceau followed the course of his illness through George Sand's recording.

June eleventh: "Great bursts of coughing . . . rubbed with camphor, he is quieter. . . . The fever is hard to combat." June eighteenth: "He is cold, even after a rubbing." Friends came: Buloz, the Boutets of Palaiseau, the Lamberts, Marchal. On the twenty-first George was ill. On the twenty-third she decided that quinine was "of no help" and fell back on sulfates. "His throat burns. . . . No rubbings tonight. My hand aches." June twenty-fifth: "Sad day. He is discouraged, irritable, despairing. I can only cry, which doesn't help. He blames me for his not getting well, for the doctors being no good. He has fever all day, coughs for two hours before dinner, is exasperated afterwards, grumbles at Dr. Morin, at his friends, at everybody. . . . And then he feels terrible on my account." June twenty-sixth: "I cry all day." July fifth: "61 years old. What a birthday!" July sixth: "He's being very brave, I can see, but I, instead of giving him courage, cannot hold back my tears. He is my strength, my life! Now that he is the weaker physically, I am the weaker morally."

Reaching for every straw, George Sand had been corresponding with a Professor Fuster of the distant Montpellier medical faculty. He too was reputed to have discovered a miracle cure for tuberculosis. July eighth: "Still weaker, still more irritable. This evening Dr. Fuster arrives with his secretary and Camille. Dr. Morin comes also. Fuster examines and auscultates. Always the same thing: one lung perfectly normal, a small spot on the other. Nothing serious there, but that fever, those nerves, that irritable temper!" George was pleading with Manceau via the diary. "Fuster says he must cure himself *by the effort of his own will* and by submitting rigorously to his treatment. He must have applications of cold water—immediately and without my flinching. He tells me that he has cured much worse cases, but that I must not weaken, that I must be prepared to be hated, if need be. Poor child! He cries during the cold-water treatment. It is heart-rending. I want to kill myself. No! I must care for him and save him, in spite of himself."

August eighteenth: "He coughs all night and all day. 48 hours! It's agonizing to hear him, and yet he is infinitely calmer than he has been." August nineteenth: "Diarrhea again. . . . What a combat!" August twentieth: "Alas! Everything that I have written, *he has been reading*, and sometimes I was afraid to irritate him by making light of his illness, sometimes I was afraid he might realize how hopeless it was. It is more than a month since I have known; what a struggle to keep it from him! Now he is at his worst. He is sleeping, worn out by the fever, hardly able to breathe; he is no longer coughing. Is this the last sleep?"

August twenty-first: "Poor, dear friend! *Dead* this morning at six o'clock, after a night of complete calm—or so it seemed. On waking, he spoke a little, his voice already dead, his words wandering as if in a dream. A few efforts to breathe, then pallor, and then—*nothing!* He wasn't conscious, I hope. At midnight he had spoken to me lucidly by force of will. He had talked of going to Nohant! I have changed him and arranged him on his bed. I have closed his eyes. I have laid flowers on his body. He is handsome and looks quite young. Oh my God! I shall never watch over him again. . . ."

August twenty-second: "I spent the night alone, beside this eternal sleep! He lies on his bed. He has found peace. There is nothing ugly or frightening. No bad odor. I have laid fresh roses on him. . . . Marchal, La Rounat, Borie, Dumas and Fromentin came to see me. . . . Marchal dined with me. . . . Alone now, and he is there, beside me, in this little bedroom. No longer will I listen for his breathing, and tomorrow night, nothing more, still more lonely! Now and forever . . ."

Manceau's sister came the same day, but she did not want to look at her brother's corpse. "She said it would have a bad effect on her." Bier and winding sheet were refused by the Church, since George did not want a religious burial. But the workers of Palaiseau, who had an admiration and reverence for Manceau, carried the body, "wrapped in a white sheet," and the coffin to the village graveyard and covered it "with flowers."[20]

Manceau left all he possessed—Gargilesse, Palaiseau, his engraving tools and his savings, to Maurice, who hesitated to accept them at first, since he might have faced a suit by Manceau's family—father, mother and unmarried sister—and be obliged to provide some income to them from the properties. Assured they would make no claim, Maurice took possession of Manceau's legacy. It was George Sand who assured Maurice that Manceau's family would not trouble him. "So sleep in peace," she wrote Maurice, October 3, 1865, "seigneur of Nohant, Palaiseau and Gargilesse."[21]

36

Conversations with Flaubert at Midnight

For three nights George Sand slept badly or not at all, then packed her trunk and left for Nohant, where she found Lina rosily pregnant, toured the grounds and the tidy barnyard, and that night "slept very well." There was no longer a Manceau—"rest quietly, *your* part of me is imperishable"—but there was the family and a restored tranquillity. "Life is gentle here now. No more heated discussions, no more agitation, no more noise, no more gaiety." Several weeks later George returned to Palaiseau and there found herself. "I have begun to work again."[1]

And once again as part of her cure and recovery, George turned to Charles Marchal, who could love lightly, healthily and well. George had no illusions, nor would she ever mourn morbidly long.[2] The strings, if any, were kept as loose as Marchal, adventurously involved with actresses and models, could wish. If there is some wistfulness in George's notes to the younger painter, it is as much for her own arrival at the threshold of old age as for his frequent unavailability. "*Once and for all*," she wrote on October 6, 1865, underscoring the words, "you have no need for excuses with me." Tactfully she added: "I know what it is like to be hard at work."[3] By November, George was addressing Marchal as her "great big springtime," rather than, say, her "Indian summer."[4] "You take me as I am," she was content to remark.[5] Living her stories before writing them—as Oscar Wilde would observe, comparing her to Goethe—George Sand worked on her novel *Le Dernier*

Amour (The Last Love), but she would dedicate it to Gustave Flaubert—to Flaubert's embarrassment.[6]

For truly the meaningful relationship at this time occurred with Flaubert rather than with Marchal, and its depth and length can be measured by the dimensions of each man. Flaubert was the germinal figure of the age in fiction; his *Madame Bovary* marked the birth of the modern novel. For several years more, George and Marchal would meet for an occasional dinner, go to the theater or have tea and an intimate evening at her apartment, the intimacy fading gently into asexual friendship, but in those years and until her death the filiation of George Sand and Gustave Flaubert remains the marvel.

Theirs may have been a bowing acquaintance since 1859, but the friendship really began in January 1863, quite properly for two writers, with George's article of praise for Flaubert's Carthaginian novel, *Salammbô*—a kind of anti-Bovary romance or, as Flaubert himself offhandedly described it to the Goncourt brothers, a four-hour "revel in historical hashish."[7] Badly received by critics and public alike, the novel's praise by the attention-catching Sand was doubly appreciated. Gratefully Flaubert wrote in thanks, asking for George's portrait. Two would be sent—three years later—the one by Marchal, the other, which Flaubert preferred, as had Delacroix, by Manceau. By this time they knew each other; their friendship had been knit.

Born in 1821, seventeen years later than George Sand, Gustave Flaubert had unreluctantly abandoned law studies and Paris for literature and Croisset, a tiny village near Rouen in Normandy, following a series of sudden epileptic attacks. The house at Croisset, bought by his father, a prosperous surgeon, shortly before his death, as if by destiny had once belonged to a Benedictine abbey of Rouen. Here since his illness, Flaubert, a tall, muscular young man reduced to semi-invalidism (later complicated by syphilis), had lived with his widowed, melancholy mother on an income left by his father, in hermetic seclusion, wrapped in a monkish robe with a cord as his belt. His one great travel adventure had been a tour around the Eastern Mediterranean—Egypt, Syria, Greece, Carthage—with Maxime du Camp, 1849–51. Now his sorties were almost wholly restricted to short stays in Paris to see his publisher and a few friends. Flaubert's devotion was to the *mot juste*, the exact word—and phrase—immaculately conceived in his Croisset monastery. It was a self-sacrificial devotion to the cult, launched by Théophile Gautier, known as Art for Art's sake, since, in Flaubert's almost unique case, it was more accurately, devastatingly, Life for Art's sake. He had both feared and admired his dominating father, his life "riveted"—as he often said[8]—to his mother: hers was the greater tyranny, that of tears exercised on an inviting victim.

Flaubert's philosophy, re-enforced by his physical state, was not one of Romantic, but rather *total*, despair. His hatred for bourgeois mentality, "whether in frock coat or worker's blouse," was matched only by his contempt for socialist utopians, whose doctrine, he believed, was fatally crippled by its debt to religious mysticism. His only hope was for a mandarin, elitist society, whose impossibility, which he recognized, crowned his pessimism. Few writers have been so polarly opposite as Flaubert and George Sand, and so they brought a great deal to each other being wholly different; and completely valuing the difference, they freed it, as Musset could not, from a corrosive friction. They both benefited, but Flaubert—Antaeus to Sand's Mother Earth—benefited the more; he would envy no man as he would Maurice.

The friendship between the two writers burgeoned in February 1864, when the recluse of Croisset came to Paris and unashamedly wept as he shared the success of *Villemer* with George Sand. It deepened after the death of Manceau the following year. Meantime they had seen each other at Magny's, where George Sand in 1866 became the only woman regular of the fortnightly dinners. Her patrons, besides Flaubert, were old friend Sainte-Beuve and the gadabout Goncourt brothers, who had been most impressed by her multivolume *Story of My Life*. Théophile Gautier and Hippolyte Taine, critic and literary historian, weighed in with their support. But second to none in his admiration was Ernest Renan, author of the immensely popular *Life of Christ*. "Madame Sand," he told the Goncourts with his almost saintly flatness, "is the greatest artist, the truest talent of our time."[9] He would call her, in elegiac remembrance, the century's "Aeolian harp," sounding "our hopes, our faults, our plaints, our sighs."[10]

"Their welcome," says Sand (*Diary*, February 12, 1866), "could not have been warmer. They were all very brilliant, except for the great scientist Berthelot, who alone, I think, was sensible." Gautier was "as dazzling and paradoxical as ever." Saint-Victor, a literary critic, was "charming and distinguished." The best talker and most intelligent of them all, thought George, was still "Uncle Beuve." But Gustave Flaubert, "so impassioned when *he* talked, I found more sympathetic than all the others. Why? I do not yet know."[11]

The indefatigable Goncourts had made their own notes (on their shirtcuffs, said Flaubert). They were struck that historic evening at Magny's by George Sand's "lovely, charming face," the complexion that seemed daily to become darker and the "marvelously delicate small hands almost lost in the lace of her sleeves." Looking about with an "intimidated air," she had whispered in Flaubert's ear, " 'You are the only one here who does not make me feel awkward!' " As usual, she had listened, and spoken little.[12]

A kinship had been early felt for the forty-four-year-old Flaubert of the Magny dinner, an affinity for the tall, heavily built monk of literature with the large, dark eyes and fine, sensual lips half-hidden by a huge, down-curving mustache. Before they had even met they had been tangentially joined in Louise Colet's *Lui*, which had been even more vicious vis-à-vis Colet's former, younger lover Flaubert than in its fictional account of the Sand-Musset affair. Flaubert himself, "riveted" as he was to his mother, always had a penchant for older women. He had, moreover, suffered his greatest passion at fourteen, when he met and worshiped Madame Élisa Schlésinger, twenty-five and married. The passion, unrequited, would be diverted, before and after Louise Colet, by an unconcealed passion for prostitutes.

From the very beginning of their friendship, George had invited Flaubert for a stay at Nohant, where she was most at ease and herself. Flaubert, who had a neurotic distaste for any displacement, found various excuses for refusing, but finally countered in the summer of 1866 with an invitation to Croisset. Intensely curious, George accepted.

August 28th: Arrived at Rouen at 1. Found Flaubert at the station with a carriage. He took me on a tour of the city, its fine monuments, cathedral, Hôtel de Ville, St. Maclou, St. Patrice. It's marvelous. An old charnel house and ancient streets; all very odd. We arrive at Croisset at 3:30. Flaubert's mother is an old, charming woman [of seventy-three]. The location of the house [on the banks of the Seine estuary] is delicious—the house comfortable, handsome and well-arranged; good service, spotless housekeeping, all wants *anticipated,* everything one could wish. I am living like a fighting cock—completely spoiled. This evening Flaubert read to me from his *Temptation of Saint Anthony.* Superb. We talk in his study until 2 in the morning. *August 29th:* We leave at 11 on the river steamboat with Mme Flaubert, her niece [Caroline, married two years before], her friend Mme Vaas and the latter's daughter, Mme de la Chausée. We go to La Bouille. Wretched weather: wind and rain. But I stay on deck, looking at the water, superb in the rain. . . . We spend ten minutes at La Bouille and return on the tidal *bore,* or *flood,* or *sweep,* a veritable tidal wave. We get back by 1. A fire is lighted, we dry ourselves, we drink tea. I go out again with Flaubert to walk around his estate: the garden, terraces, orchard, vegetable patch, farm, and the *citadel*—a very curious old wooden house that serves him for storage. *The Path of Moses* [leading to the upper slope]. View of the Seine [and Rouen's spires]. The orchard—beautifully sheltered way up high. Soil dry with a whitish topsoil. Everything charming, very poetic. I dress for dinner. Dinner very good. Play cards with the two old ladies

[George is sixty-two]. Talk later with Flaubert and go to bed at 2 in the morning. Excellent bed; slept well, but my cough came back. My cold is discontented with me. Too bad for my cold. *Paris, August 30th:* Departure from Croisset at noon with Flaubert and his niece. We dropped her off at Rouen. We revisited the city, the bridge—vast and superb. Beautiful baptistery belonging to a Jesuit church. Flaubert packs me off [for Paris].[13]

"We talk of nothing but you at Croisset," Flaubert wrote George Sand almost immediately after her departure, "because you pleased everyone so much." Again he asked for the portrait which would finally be sent, "so that I might always have your dear, lovely face before me."[14] George was intrigued: not all her curiosity had been satisfied, even in their conversations at midnight. Flaubert had been voluble, but reserved. Much of his past, to be sure, was no secret; Louise Colet had seen to that. But had his mistress seen the essential man?

"You are a being very much apart," George wrote Flaubert from Nohant, "very mysterious, yet gentle as a lamb." She had wanted to ask him questions, but had restrained herself; she had her own reserve. Sainte-Beuve, George continued, had told her that Flaubert was "frightfully vicious," but that may have been in the "rather soiled eyes" of Sainte-Beuve. In any case, that sort of thing—debauchery and prostitutes implied but unmentioned—was certainly Flaubert's affair: "the highly intelligent and creative" are permitted to range widely and freely in the search of experience and material. "I have not," says George, "for lack of courage"—or the freedom of a man. Then George extended to Flaubert her great gift of tolerance and understanding: "The artist is an explorer whom nothing should arrest; who does neither good nor evil in going left or right: his goal [which is his work] sanctifies all"—it is for him to choose the conditions for his creativity.[15]

"I, a mysterious being, *chère maître* [dear master]? Come now!" protested Flaubert. "I find myself disgustingly platitudinous, sometimes terribly upset by the bourgeois I have under my skin. . . . I know few men less 'vicious' than myself. I have imagined much and done very little." But in time, Flaubert promised, he would "confess" all.[16]

Lightly George Sand spoke of her own past: "I had a brother who was very droll and who often said, 'Once upon a time, when I was a dog . . .' He thought he became a man late in life. As for myself, I think I was once a plant or a stone." Then, possibly disarmingly, she spoke of her present: "Now that I am no longer a woman, I would, if the good Lord were just, be a man. I would have the physical strength and I would say to you, 'Let's take a trip to Carthage or anywhere else.' But I cannot. One advances towards infancy, which has neither sex nor energy."[17] ("Oh you, of the third sex!" Flaubert would hail George Sand sometime later in their intimacy, the encompassing man-woman he often considered *himself* to be, and others sensed in him.[18])

In this fashion was engaged the dialogue between the younger and older writer, one of the most fascinating in literary history. The letters of a *released* Flaubert—deliberately invisible in his novels—are particularly revealing; but in both cases their correspondence may be their finest work—that is, their letters to their contemporaries, especially, for Flaubert, those written to Louise Colet and George Sand, where artist and man, strictly separated in his work, become a self-examining, remarkable one.

A second visit to Croisset, twice as long as the first, occurred early in November. The hermetic Flaubert could still not be enticed to Nohant—a trip would upset his work; he was too impressionable, he said—whereas George Sand welcomed the diversion. "You do not have my restless foot, ever ready to roam. You live in your dressing gown, that great enemy of freedom and action."[19] Bound so many months to the bedside of the dying Manceau, George was at last free to move about, and she profited from it. The November visit to Flaubert followed the two portraits sent him in October, as well as the shipment of the *seventy-five* volumes of her collected work in its popular edition. This to a writer who could agonize as long over the perfection of a paragraph as George Sand in the writing of an entire novel! Yet Flaubert, if envious in his blackest moods, was never bitter about Sand's fluency; and George was modestly aware of the transience of most of her work, and said as much to Flaubert: they were friends.

Flaubert stirred sufficiently to accompany George by train from Paris to Rouen, where they were met by "Madame Flaubert and her other son, the doctor," and then went on to Croisset, where George "slept like a log." *Diary*, November 4, 1866: "Bewitching weather. Walk in the garden up to the orchard. Work. . . ." *In the evening*: "Gustave read to me from his fairy tale. Full of admirable and charming things. Too long, too rich, too full. We talk again until 2:30 in the morning. I felt hungry. We go down to the kitchen to look for cold chicken. We poke our heads into the courtyard to get water from the pump. Air as mild as spring. We eat. We go back upstairs. We continue our talk. We separate at 4 in the morning." The following day George worked in the afternoon and read to "Gustave" from the new novel she was writing, *Cadio*, with its new accent of disenchantment with revolutionary violence. Trips of research (on the Chouans) in Brittany between visits to Croisset confirmed the feeling and depressed George Sand, but it deeply interested Flaubert, hard at work on his own devastating *Éducation Sentimentale* and the revolutionary "horrors" of 1848, about which he posed many detailed questions to George Sand and through her to her involved socialist friends, especially Armand Barbès.

The week at Croisset passed; George returned to Paris. Flaubert wrote how much he missed her: it seemed to him as if ten years had passed since she had left. He felt, he said, "a *particular* tenderness" for her, which he had never felt for anyone before.[20] George replied, describing her own contentment at Croisset, and said *she* had been particularly touched by his "infinitely kind protectiveness." There had been "something paternal" about him. "One evening when you called your mother *my girl*, tears came to my eyes. It cost me an effort to leave you, but I was keeping you from your work, and then, well, a malady of my old age is not wanting to remain in one place. I am afraid of attaching myself too much and weighing on others. The old should be extremely careful."[21]

George's loneliness surfaces, as well as her restlessness; then there is the eternal recovery of her serenity. To Charles Poncy, November 16, 1866, four days after the letter to Flaubert: "One makes oneself happy when one knows what it takes to be happy—to have simple tastes, a certain courage, a certain self-sacrifice, love of work and, above all, a good conscience. Happiness is no chimera; I am sure of that now. . . . Let us, then, live life as it is, without being ungrateful, fully aware that joy is neither enduring nor assured."[22] Three days later, to Charles Marchal: "It seems to me that I am recommencing my life and reviewing everything for the first time. Why? I have no idea. Why rejuvenate oneself at sixty-three when one is on the point of entering infancy? Oh, pooh! Too bad! Why a sudden cascade of falling stars? No one knows, and *they* are far bigger and more interesting than I am. Are you working? Or are people, I'm afraid, keeping you from it? . . . Best of luck in everything."[23]

From Palaiseau, George sounded a deeper, sadder note to Flaubert, then as usual recovers: "Here I am, *all alone*, in my little house. The gardener and his family live in a pavilion on the grounds. . . . But the place makes me feel sad. This complete solitude, which has ever been vacation and recreation for me, is shared now by one dead, who ended his days here like a lamp that has gone out, but is still here. I do not believe he is unhappy in that region he is inhabiting, but the image he has left behind is a pale reflection which always seems to be complaining that it cannot speak to me. Never mind! There is nothing unhealthy about sadness: it keeps us from drying up. And you, my friend, what are you doing at this hour? Are you plugging away, alone too, since your mother is probably in Rouen? . . . Do you think sometimes of the 'old troubadour in the tavern clock who sings, and will ever sing, of the perfect love'? Well, in spite of everything, so do I! Your Highness, I know, is not one for chastity, but that is your affair. I say:

There is *some good in it*. And with this, a big hug. I'm off to put words, if I can find them, into the mouths of people who love in the old way. . . . I'll be in Paris next week, then again at Palaiseau, then at Nohant."[24]

Flaubert did indeed often think of "the old troubadour in the tavern clock," and their cozy moments together. "They were very nice, our nocturnal talks. (There were times when I had to hold myself back from kissing you like a big child.)" As for chastity, Flaubert sounded more like George Sand than the older George Sand herself: "Condemn the flesh, like the Catholics? God knows where that would lead! . . . Great natures, which are the good natures, are above all prodigal; they do not look too closely at the cost of expending themselves. We must laugh and cry, love, work, enjoy and suffer, vibrate to the maximum the entire length of our frame. That, I believe, is what is truly human."[25]

Out of the accumulation of her years of experience, adjusting her reply to the man addressed—with Musset surely in her mind—the older George Sand immediately responded:

> The great natures are not the most robust natures. . . . Great artists are often infirm and some have been impotent. Others, too potent in their desire, were quickly exhausted. . . . I do not believe in Don Juans who are at the same time Byrons. Don Juan did not write poetry; and Byron, it is said, made love badly. There must have been times—never many in a lifetime—when he knew the complete ecstasy of heart, mind and senses; he knew it sufficiently to be one of the poets of love. We need no more to vibrate completely. The constant winds of petty appetites would wreck our fragile instruments.[26]

There were many vibrations and varying winds moving in their letters to each other. Earlier in his "troubadour" letter, Flaubert had taken up what most preoccupied him: writing. His most intense working, living and suffering, by the time he had met George Sand, were in the confines of his study; and he had been piqued by her query, Why did he suffer so much in his work, in the willful, painful pursuit of exactitude and perfect, translucid style? "Is it a kind of coquetry?" George Sand had asked. She herself let the wind blow as it willed through her "old harp." It was, she said, as if *another* sang through her, freeing her from the tensions of self-conscious style. "Let the wind blow a bit through *your* chords. . . . Let the *other* speak through you more often."[27] So Sand advised Flaubert, simultaneously recognizing and admiring the perfection of a *Madame Bovary*, achieved at such pains.

With an affection and restraint he would show no one else, Flaubert acknowledged the agony. "*You* do not know what is it like to spend the entire day with your head in your hands, squeezing your miserable brain for a single word. For you, the idea flows broadly, incessantly, like a flood. For me, it's a tiny trickle. I must build a great dam to produce a waterfall. Oh, I have known the *pangs of style!*"[28]

Sand went to the extreme in an effort to liberate Flaubert from his self-inhibiting insistence on the water-tight separation of literature and life. After her demolition of the mythical Don Juan-Byron syndrome, she suggested that Flaubert "someday try to write a novel with an artist, a true artist, as hero"—perhaps himself. Flaubert painting Flaubert in *his* "Portrait of the Artist"—George Sand was suggesting no less—a hero equal to himself, rather than the personages he deliberately chose who were middle class and "average," and for whom he felt no tenderness and knew no regard. He might thus have hurdled the wall he erected between his life and his work which ultimately became an impasse. She herself, George remarked, was not the true artist. She was too diversified—a bit of a teacher, of a child's nurse, of a naturalist and "a fool"—"besides, I do not like perfectionism."[29]

The artist as hero, Flaubert rejoined, "would be a monster. Art is not for the painting of the exceptional. Moreover, I have an invincible revulsion for putting the smallest fraction of my heart on paper. I further believe that a novelist *does not have the right to express his opinion.* Has God ever expressed his? . . . Anyone you meet by chance is more interesting than Monsieur G. Flaubert, because he is more *general* and consequently more typical."[30]

"What," exclaimed George Sand, " 'not put one's heart into what one writes'? I do not understand that. Oh, not at all! It seems to me that one cannot put in anything else. . . ." Flaubert, by return mail: "I meant not put one's own person on stage. I believe that great Art"—always capitalized for Flaubert—"is scientific and impersonal."[31]

And such impersonality, George Sand would reply, is inhuman, if not "anti-human." Yet Sand and Flaubert had a great deal more in common than uncommon—their interest as writers in writing, which sustained their disagreements; a shared contempt, lofty for the one, socialist for the other, for the money-grubbing materialism which accompanied the prosperity of the Second Empire; their hatred for clericalism, the Church and the "religious hypocrisy" masking the rapacity of the bourgeoisie.[32] Fondly George urged her "anchorite" to go out into the sun, to breathe fresh air, to take a long walk. Jubilantly Flaubert replied (at least once): "I did!"[33] When George mentioned she wished she could go down to the Riviera, but lacked the funds, Flaubert quickly responded with an offer of a thousand francs.

They were an esthetic, aristocratic, comradely pair, despite their disagreement on socialism. "I am still a troubadour," George wrote Armand Barbès, "who believes in love, in art, in the ideal, and sings his song while the world jeers and jabbers. As Flaubert just wrote me, 'Ah, yes! I would indeed like to follow you to another planet. Money will rapidly make our own uninhabitable. . . . Everyone will have to spend several hours of the day playing with his capital. Charming!' "[34]

With the growth in friendship came the gain in frankness. When Flaubert pitied "poor old Sainte-Beuve" because he could no longer frequent brothels and enjoy prostitutes—"woman, for all men, is the archway to infinity," wrote Flaubert—the dormant feminist was stirred awake and George snapped back:

> The ugly old men who buy young bodies are not making love. It has nothing to do with . . . archways, or infinity, or male, or female. It is a thing against nature; for it is not desire that presses the young body into the arms of the ugly and old. Where there is no freedom and reciprocity, there is an offense against holy nature.[35]

Obviously, Gustave Flaubert as a man and George Sand as a woman could not possibly see prostitution with the same eye, though there was much that was "feminine" in the first and "masculine" in the second. Nor, for that matter, was Flaubert a family man, despite—or because of —his attachment to his mother. Art's hero was, in his hermetic seclusiveness, life's coward—the phrase is his.[36] Life, like love, took a second place to Art and was "tolerable only to the extent that one did not participate in it."[37]

Rejecting once more an invitation to Nohant as 1867 drew to a close, Flaubert pleaded work on his *Éducation Sentimentale*; he would have to deprive himself of the pleasure, he said. "It is always the same old story of the Amazons. They cut off a breast the better to draw their bows."[38] For George Sand, wholeness was all:

> I believe completely the contrary. . . . I believe that the artist should, as much as is possible, live true to his nature. For the one who likes combat, war; for the one who likes women, love; for the old, as myself, who like nature—voyages, flowers, rocks, great landscapes, children and family, too. . . .
>
> I believe that art needs a palette brimming over with both violent and delicate colors to be used as the subject requires; that the artist is an instrument whose every chord must be played before he plays any other.[39]

Colors and chords, like the conception of truth, vary with the perceptions of each age. "In the setting sun of life, when one is old," said George Sand to Flaubert, "that loveliest time of day for tones and reflections, one acquires a new notion of everything, especially affection." One becomes convinced that *"there is only one sex. A man and a* woman are indeed the same thing and one marvels at all the distinctions and subtle rationalizations with which societies feed themselves in that matter. I have observed the childhood and development of my son and daughter; my son was myself and consequently more feminine than my daughter, who was a failed man."[40]

The observation was made earlier the same year, January 15, 1867. After a severe illness, George had been persuaded by Maurice and Lina to abandon Palaiseau permanently for Nohant, where the family had a new granddaughter for George, now exactly one year old. Infant Aurore, soon "Lolo," had the velvety black eyes of her ancestry and bore its well-omened name. She was the fourth Aurore since the Countess of Koenigsmark and would live to be ninety-four. There were, too, at Nohant and La Châtre, the grandchildren of Hippolyte—the Simonnets; and the grandchildren of Sand's friends, who were in and out of the great house at Nohant. There were the inevitable changes as well, such as that of Victor Borie, the proletarian editor who had become a bank director with a salary of twenty-five thousand francs a year. And there were new friends: the American Henry Harrisse, who could be a bore on the subject of Christopher Columbus and George Sand, and Edmond Plauchut, "the castaway of the drawing room." Shipwrecked as a young traveler and cast upon a Portuguese island, Plauchut had impressed the local consul with his album of autographs, including those of George Sand, with whom he had corresponded and whom he eventually met; *his* subject at the dinner table was that tale.

Above all, there was Juliette La Massine, a young writer who represented the new generation of women for George Sand and brought her an especially warm friendship. Born in 1836, thirty-two years younger than George, Juliette had made her entry into the literary world in 1858 and at a remarkably high level: by nothing less than taking on the prestigious Proudhon. Two men largely contributed to it: her father, an intelligent, erudite Fourierist, socialist and doctor, and her husband, La Massine, a libertine, lawyer and misogynist to whom Juliette had been married at sixteen. Proudhon, for Juliette, had committed several crimes in his *La Justice dans la Révolution*, which appeared in the late 1850s: he attacked women in general and two women in particular— George Sand and Daniel Stern, pen name of Marie d'Agoult—both of whom Juliette "most admired." A brash, brilliant twenty-two, she undertook their defense. "For two months," she recounts, "I wrote, copied, rewrote and redid my little book at night, in secret, locking myself in my bedroom with my child, my husband more occupied with one of the servants than with me."[41]

The book that emerged, its publishing financed by her father, was boldly entitled *Idées anti-Proudhoniennes sur l'Amour, la Femme et le Mariage* and signed: Juliette La Massine. Juliette's father: "It is your grandmother's wish realized." Juliette's mother: "The life of work and troubles facing you makes me afraid." Juliette's husband: "Not bad for a beginning. I will be glad to sign it with my own name when the first printing is exhausted." Juliette: "That's an unpleasant joke." Juliette's husband: "For you perhaps, but not for me. The law authorizes it. . . . The work of a wife belongs to her husband." And he did indeed sign the second printing, Juliette continues, "as he said he would, since no French law forbade it. That, moreover, could still happen today.* . . . In the press, the 'joke' was never even mentioned."[42]

Juliette La Massine's book was favorably received, however, by the *Revue des Deux Mondes* and praised by Eugène Pelletan in *La Presse*. The notice in *Le Siècle* was brief: "A book destined to create a great sensation has just been given us. . . . It is said to be by a very young woman, though very virile."[43]

"Monsieur Proudhon," Juliette began her work, "tries to establish the subordination of women as based on nature," which is "the general attitude of men . . . whether progressive or reactionary, republican or monarchist. . . . Monsieur Proudhon asserts, with no hesitation, the physical, intellectual and moral inferiority of women"—which Juliette La Massine refuted one by one. Physical inferiority? What about physical beauty? she asks. And have not the pistol and the machine made all persons physically equal? As for morality, Proudhon spoke almost exclusively in terms of strength, hardly a moral criterion. And as for intellectuality, Juliette La Massine abundantly demonstrated her own.[44] George Sand wrote the young woman a letter of appreciation. So did Countess d'Agoult, who added, "It is astonishing, Monsieur, that you should have taken a woman's name, when we women have chosen a male pseudonym." "I replied," says Juliette, "that I was a woman, and very womanly, it seemed to me."[45]

The young, very attractive Juliette was quickly invited by Countess d'Agoult to join her literary and political circle; as the sensation of the season, she would brighten any salon. Juliette accepted; at the same time she corresponded with George Sand, seeking a meeting. Sand resisted. Her relationship with Marie d'Agoult had chilled into a cold break, and she did not want to be accused of taking Juliette away from her, as she was still accused by Marie of having tried in the case of Liszt. Captain d'Arpentigny was dispatched to explain all this to the young woman, since it was better not to put it in a letter. "She will wait!" the captain assured Juliette La Massine. "The day you quarrel with Madame d'Agoult, you will find a friend in George Sand and can go to her. . . . That day, I am certain, is not far off." Louis de Ronchaud, whom Juliette had met in Marie's salon, also attempted to

---

* Written in 1904. Not until 1970 would the French marital law be appropriately changed.

explain the situation to her. "The affection between two superior people cannot endure, for there is a perpetual struggle for domination."[46]

The sense of rivalry was particularly, if not uniquely, true of Marie d'Agoult, Juliette noted. Incessantly in her conversations with the young writer, Marie engaged in criticisms of George Sand, as much, it seemed, to persuade herself as Juliette. The aggressiveness might account for Juliette's first impression: "There is something virile in Madame d'Agoult," Juliette herself yielding to the received attitude that strength in a woman was "virility." Nor did Marie d'Agoult gainsay it, so pervasive was the attitude. White-haired now, virtually on their first meeting she freely offered to Juliette: "I have reached the age of manhood." Regarding George Sand, she said: "Never get to know her. You will lose all your illusions. As a woman—I mean, a *man*—she is insignificant. She has no conversation. She is the ruminating kind, as she herself realizes. You see it in her look, her eyes, which are very handsome."[47]

Juliette in the meantime continued to correspond with George Sand ("too much Flaubert," she wrote an amused Sand after receiving her novel *Monsieur Sylvestre*). Then the day prophesied by Captain d'Arpentigny finally came in 1867. Juliette's husband, La Massine, died. "Joyfully" she and her daughter embraced on hearing the news—she and her husband had been separated—and she determined to marry the man she loved, Edmond Adam, an astute republican, editor and journalist. The reaction of Marie d'Agoult, on being told, was violent. Sometime before, she had disdainfully remarked to Juliette, "The misfortune of being a widow is that one has the stupid desire to remarry. I cannot imagine you would be so stupid. A woman who thinks should remain free—mistress of her thought." Juliette: "I prefer happiness to freedom." Now, when Marie d'Agoult heard of her intention to remarry, "she flew into rage," says Juliette, "called me a provincial idiot and predicted that in two years I would stop writing in order to keep the family accounts." The scene struck Juliette as an "attack of madness," sadly "confirmed later by Madame d'Agoult's entering Dr. Blanche's clinic." That it was really "madness" raises the entire question of Marie d'Agoult's life—with Liszt; as Daniel Stern; in conflict with society and herself. The odd, disconcerting thing is Juliette's unquestioning acceptance of the "madness." In any case, she continued, "my falling out with Madame d'Agoult let me free to see George Sand. So I wrote to her."[48]

"Come tomorrow at three," Sand responded when in Paris. Heart pounding, stomach-sick with emotion, Juliette went to the Rue des Feuillantines apartment, and almost turned back. She knocked, however, and entered. George Sand looked unexpectedly tiny in the large armchair, wordlessly rolling a cigarette. She beckoned Juliette to a chair beside her. "Her large, gentle eyes enveloped me, drew me." Juliette tried to say something, but choked. George lit her cigarette, smoked, made an effort to speak also, but the words faltered. Juliette burst into tears. George Sand put down her cigarette, rose and opened her arms. "I flung myself into them." Then for two hours they talked. "Oh, if I could only say, and say over and over, how much delicacy of feeling, nobility of heart, elevated thought and understanding of life, serenity wrung from the cruelest of schools and experiences, there is in George Sand!"[49]

It was a "filial tenderness" that endured for Juliette, and George once again found a daughter. Soon she met Edmond Adam and approved Juliette's choice. She took her to a Magny dinner to meet the Goncourts, Gustave Flaubert, Alexandre Dumas *fils*. The occasion of Baudelaire's death and Juliette's provocative presence gave rise to off-color stories. Sand objected, "Flaubert laughed his beautiful laugh," Juliette further remarking "his long, curling hair, his large, blue eyes with their long lashes, his reddish face, his huge Vercingetorix mustache, his tall, proud carriage." Nor would she ever forget the "pitiless, exquisite Flaubert" when it came to her writing. How could she, in one of her stories, he scolded, describe a farm laborer, who had lost an arm earlier in a threshing machine, as "'taking a money box in both hands'? —general laughter. I joined in it . . . and gaily said, 'Thank you, Master!'" Dumas praised Juliette's beauty and hoped it meant she had no talent. "'With that figure and that face, why become a bluestocking . . . a writer?'" She should, he implied, make love, not literature. George Sand riposted, addressing Juliette: with *their* treatment of their women in love, "'their Madame Bovarys, their Madame Aubrays,'" *they* were in no position to give any woman any advice, especially on love.[50]

George Sand's own advice on love in her long conversations with Juliette, which the younger woman recorded *à la* Eckermann with Goethe, rose in reflections on her past. There would be a prolonged silence while George smoked and mused, throwing her cigarettes, after a few puffs, into a vase of water. Then the words came as if from a reverie. For one to possess her utterly, George said one evening, a person had but to arouse her compassion, and often she had thrown herself into "good deeds" for people which turned into "bad actions. As I examine myself, I can see that the only real passions of my life were maternity and friendship. I accepted the love that was offered without seeking or choosing it. As a result, what I brought to love and demanded from it was not what I received. I might have found friends or sons in those who obtained love from me . . . but men are loathe to love as friends." She had not had the moral or intellectual "authority to impose friendship." That, she left unsaid, came later in her life.[51]

George Sand clearly perceived that the grand Romantic illusion was the "great passion," with a consequent depreciation of friendship between men and women, of *tendresse* and respect. Women, as a result, who sought to rise above that regard of them as either the virgin mother-wife or the prostitute-mistress, adopted the attitude of men; that is, they conceived and conducted themselves as did the men of their period, achieving the only equality and fulfillment then possible. This lay unconsciously in the mind of Sand as she made a request to Juliette. Should any man accuse her of dishonesty, she said, Juliette was to reply, "If George Sand can be said to have lost the right to be judged as a woman, she has maintained the right to be judged as a man, and in love she has been more honest than any of you. She has never deceived anyone, has never engaged in two adventures at the same time. Her only guilt, in a lifetime in which art played the greatest role, is to have chosen the society of artists, to have preferred male morality to female morality." In other words, the freedom of the male. George Sand, however, goes on to wonder if it had been worth the candle. "I have experienced complete love, many times, alas," she said to Juliette. "If I had my life to begin again, I would be chaste."[52] This was the older, not the younger, George Sand speaking. Rereading her youthful *Sketches and Hints* in September 1868, she saw this with remarkable clarity: "One changes from day to day and after a few years, one is another person. . . . Here I am, a very old woman, gently embarked on my sixty-fifth year. . . . I enjoy absolute tranquillity, an old age as chaste in my mind as it is in fact."[53]

Together with Juliette, Edmond Adam and Juliette's young daughter, George went on trips to Normandy, to the theater in Paris, to the Great Exhibition of 1867. Here she noted "the superb Chinese giant" and "the ugly Chinese dwarf," but it is doubtful she paid attention to the new giant cannon of Krupp, breech-loading and steel, seen for the first time.[54] That winter George was invited by Juliette to her villa, Les Bruyères, on the Riviera. In need of sun, George accepted, but on the condition, she said, "that I meet neither Mérimée nor Solange," both of whom happened to be in the same Golfe Juan area as Juliette's villa. Thoughtfully, Juliette had contacted Mérimée in advance. "Tell me in time," he had responded, "and I will make myself scarce around Les Bruyères while she is here."[55] Solange, installed at Cannes with a foreign prince, was not so easily to be managed. She was incensed—she let it be known—that her mother planned to stay with Madame La Massine rather than with herself.

With Maurice to cope with Solange, should it be necessary, and Maxime Planet, son of her old friend, and Edmond Plauchut as company, George descended for her winter stay in Juliette's villa. Lina, advanced in pregnancy, was left behind. Visit, villa and weather were delightful, with the kind of side trips and excursions by day, word games and story telling at night that brightened George's spirits. Joined from the beginning by Edmond Adam, they all became a close, intimate little group by the time George returned in March, 1868, to Nohant. Solange had been successfully avoided, and Lina, two days before George's arrival via Paris, had given birth to a second, "lovely, dark-eyed" daughter.

George Sand's own birthday in July brought Juliette and Edmond Adam, just married, to Nohant. They came, to their annoyance, accompanied by the American Henry Harrisse, "who played guide [to the Berry] with insupportable pedantry" from Châteauroux to George's great house. Nohant itself lived up to their expectations: the Louis XIV furniture; the portraits of George's ancestors—the dashing, uniformed Maurice de Saxe, the black-tressed Aurore de Koenigsmark; the Venetian chandeliers; the two pianos, the one, untouched, which had belonged to Chopin, the other played by George. That evening she performed for them, and very well, from memory—Mozart and Gluck, but no Chopin. It was an evening of Nohant enchantment: the sweet smells wafting through the open windows from the garden, the stars studding the sky visible from the drawing room. "Happiness," Juliette decided, "is as blue at Nohant as it is at Les Bruyères."[56]

All that night Maurice hung garlands of flowers for the next day's celebration of his mother's anniversary. At breakfast time, the little cannon was fired, and George descended. Maurice flourished a scroll and read a birthday greeting. His mother embraced him and said, "How adorably stupid you are!"—but her eyes, Juliette observed, were moist. And that evening there was the most elaborate puppet show, with Maurice playing all the roles and ad-libbing with the spectators, Juliette had ever seen. "Maurice would gladly spend twenty nights preparing one hour's entertainment for his adored mother."[57]

George Sand herself was not a "gay person," her Nohant doctor of the last years noted: "She needed to be made gay. When she came down from her study, she wanted to find people, laughter, noise. . . . Serious, saying little, she liked to be surrounded by talkers, even chatterers."[58] The level of the talk, of the entertainment, was less important than its intensity, its verve. There was a camp humor at Nohant which she specially enjoyed—pranks and practical jokes which Edmond Adam, for one, did not appreciate as much, though Juliette immediately swung into the spirit of the house. Such was the time when Maurice, genius of the puerility, put a rooster into the emptied wood chest of the Adams' bedroom, Juliette aware of it, which woke the furious Edmond with its crowing at two in the morning, and kept him looking for it the rest of the night.

It was a humor, along with the puppet shows, which Flaubert, when he finally visited Nohant, would appreciate even less. But that would be the following year. In the meantime, Flaubert's having refused yet again an invitation to Nohant in the spring—"your friend is a veritable man of wax," the impressions would disturb his work for days[59]—George had gone once more to Croisset. But except for these rare visits and a dinner at Magny's, their "conversations" were by letter.

Apropos 1848, for instance, and Flaubert's incessant demands for details, George Sand replied, revealing her drift from radical politics: "You must realize that all those with any intelligence have gone a terribly long way in the past twenty years and it would not be generous to reproach them for what they are now most likely reproaching themselves." In George's case, there has been a further distancing. "I have lost the labyrinthine thread of republican dreams," she remarked to Henry Harrisse, "these past few years."[60] She had talked politics somewhat with Edmond Adam, whose republicanism embraced the rising young leader of the far left, Léon Gambetta. "He is excellent," George noted of Adam in her diary, "and boring."[61]

In truth, George was more interested in her two grandchildren—"who laughed and chattered away from morning to night like little birds"—than in politics. She had not, however, lost her feeling for people. In the fall of 1868, when she was continually in Paris for the rehearsals of her dramatization of *Cadio*, she spent days and nights with the troupe. "You say I like them too much," George wrote the misanthropic Flaubert. "I like them as I like the woods and the fields, all the things I know a bit and study a great deal. I make my life in the middle of all this and since I like my life, I like everything that nurtures and renews it. . . . I have an enormous indulgence for life, for people."[62] Flaubert, in reply: "Dear Master, your letter yesterday was an *edification*. That is the word. What you say about indulgence for the egoists of the world is so beautiful that I wanted to weep."[63]

The compensation for the old, said George Sand on her sixty-fourth birthday, was that "winter days count double" and friendships, rather than fading, are nourished by the very passage of time.[64] As 1869 opened, George cultivated her garden, carefully noted "botanical novelties, sewed dresses for Lina, costumes for the puppets . . . and, above all, spent hours with Aurore." But her own work went on at a slower pace. "I write my little novel of the year," she wrote Flaubert, "whenever I find an hour or two during the day to put my mind on it." The wind of inspiration, now a gentle breeze, still blew through her modest harp. "The old retired troubadour," she said, "sings his little song from time to time to the moon, not much caring whether he sings well or badly, so long as he sings the little tune running through his head, and the rest of the time he takes delicious walks."[65]

She would like to have several more years of greater leisure, George told Dumas *fils,* "to write for myself and a few friends. . . . But I shall most probably die turning the wheel of my winepress."[66] Death was decimating the thin ranks of her contemporaries. In March 1869, it took Lina's father, Luigi Calamatta; in October, Sainte-Beuve, who had been born the same year as herself. George went to Paris for the funeral—"to bury poor Sainte-Beuve."

All Paris was at the Montparnasse cemetery—"*les lettres, les arts, les sciences,* youth and the people. No senators, no priests." It was a civil, nonreligious ceremony, as Sainte-Beuve had requested. Among the mourners George caught sight of Flaubert, "who was greatly affected," but she could not reach him because of the crowd; "Alexandre [Dumas] and his old father, who could barely walk; Adam . . . Borie . . . Taine . . . old Grzymala. . . . Atheists, believers, people of all ages and all opinions." When she left the cemetery on the arms of Plauchut and Adam, the great crowd at the gate "escorted me to the carriage, moving backward to make place for me, lifting their hats in silence." Slowly George's carriage pulled away, people continuing their silent homage as it passed. George was very touched. "Plauchut and Adam almost wept. . . . Dinner at Magny's."[67]

The following month, as Flaubert was correcting proofs for his *Éducation Sentimentale,* George Sand was going through galleys for her novel *Pierre Qui Roule* (A Rolling Pierre, or Stone), which she dedicated to him. There is some irony and more sadness in the coincidence. *Pierre* was based on the puppet-characters of Maurice, which Flaubert would so dislike when he finally came down to Nohant for Christmas. The sadness lies in the reception of his novel, which would be published by then. The reviews were harsh, the public was hostile. Flaubert's anti-hero, Frédéric Moreau, and the unrelenting non-heroics of his story were not to the taste of the time. George Sand was virtually alone in defending it, but even she had difficulty placing her article in its praise. Write to poor Flaubert about his novel, George implored Juliette Adam, he badly needed encouragement. "He is brusque and violent, but infinitely good."[68]

Flaubert was indeed brusque and violent, but not very good at Nohant's festivities. His sorties from Croisset were too few to be frivolous. Like Gautier, when finally at Nohant he wanted to "talk literature" and Life and Art with Sand, not play word games or spend hours watching Maurice play with his puppets. Maurice was quite put out, though Flaubert would become fond of him personally, envying him his mother and his family, especially his little girls. Flaubert, wrote Maurice to Juliette Adam, "was insupportable at the puppet shows, because he criticizes everything and will not allow anything foolish." Yet, "the hermit of Croisset read us part of *The Temptation of Saint An-*

thony, and it was superb, one of the most beautiful things he has ever written."[69]

The gentlest, truest observation was tendered to Flaubert himself by his friend George Sand. They had all liked his *Saint Anthony*, she wrote, January 9, 1870, as indeed they had all liked him. And everybody had come to the conclusion, " 'He does not know whether to be a poet or a realist; and since he is both the one and the other, it bothers him.' "[70]

Thus began the "Terrible Year"—1870–71. Within a few months, even before the Franco-Prussian War began, Flaubert would morbidly tick off the recent dead—Sainte-Beuve, Jules de Goncourt, Armand Barbès, two close friends—and write to George Sand: "Other than you and Turgenev, I do not know a single mortal to whom I can pour out my heart; and you both live so far from me!"[71]

37

War, Peace and the Commune

In February 1870, George Sand went up to Paris for the opening of her new play, *L'Autre* (The Other), in which a young actress, Sarah Bernhardt, played the leading role. "What success!" George exclaimed afterwards in a letter to Maurice. Seats were being set up and sold in the aisles and in the orchestra pit. "A second *Villemer!* . . . I have been receiving students all day. They have been coming by the dozen to thank me . . ."[1] There was a new turbulence in the air; the students, as usual, were the first to sense it, and they had come to thank George Sand for what she represented to them—liberal socialism, militant republicanism, radical change. Sand's speedy return to Nohant, however, was symbolic of her removing herself from Paris, from political events. Having reached the serenity of her approaching seventies, she saw society in terms of slow-moving change, or reconciliation rather than confrontation. Violence had become the absolute horror, and her family, which had always been important, now became almost all.

At Nohant, Sand found Maurice very ill and was terribly affected by it. "When he is down," she wrote Flaubert, "we are dead: mother, wife, daughters. Aurore says she would like to be sick instead of her father. We love each other passionately, we five, and *sacrosanct literature*, as you call it, is secondary in my life. I have always loved someone more, and my family more than that someone."[2]

On her sixty-sixth birthday in July, George went bathing in the Indre with Plauchut and little Aurore. It would be the last peaceful dip for some time.

Prussia's Chancellor Bismarck sought a war with France, the "hereditary enemy," as a way to unite the German states into a nation. Stupidly Napoleon III—"the sleepwalker," George Sand termed him—and his government fell into the trap. The vacant throne of Spain, which Prussia proposed to fill with a Hohenzollern king, was the pretext. France objected. Tactfully Bismarck yielded, dropping the candidacy. France pressed its advantage, determined to "teach" Prussia a lesson; "insultingly" it demanded a written apology from the Prussian king—or so Bismarck make it appear by doctoring the French message. Prussian opinion was aroused; the ultimatum was turned down. Now French opinion pressed for a smart rebuke to the Prussians. The war party of both nations had won. "On to Berlin!" was heard from Paris crowds. "Let us love each other, not war," George Sand noted in her diary, July 12, 1870.[3] On July nineteenth war was declared on Prussia.

Plauchut, now in Paris, wrote George Sand that the capital was "roaring with enthusiasm." George replied that if true, "Paris is mad." To the Adams', who had just left Nohant, George gloomily reported that the feeling in the provinces was entirely different. There, people were "consternated." The war, said George, "is not a question of national honor, but a stupid, hateful testing of guns, the game of princes! . . . To sing the *Marseillaise* to the tune of the Empire is a sacrilege. . . . My patriotism . . . is unstirred. . . . The whole world is going mad."[4] Flaubert foresaw a "horrible butchery without even a decent pretext."[5] George wholeheartedly agreed. She saw no reason why the French and the Germans should slaughter each other. Why not a "fraternal Europe"? she asked.[6]

Late July and early August were hellishly hot at Nohant. Temperatures in the shade rose to 113 degrees Fahrenheit. An unknown "they," George wrote Flaubert, "are burning the forests! . . . Wolves come prowling in our courtyard and we chase them away at night, Maurice with a revolver, I with a lantern. The trees are losing their leaves and perhaps their lives. Water will be lacking; harvests are virtually nil. But we have the war. What luck!"[7] "What, dear master," replied Flaubert, "you, too, demoralized and depressed? What then will happen to the weak?"[8]

Outgunned, outmanned, outmaneuvered, the French Army—with a sick Napoleon III in personal command—was being swept from the field by the Prussians within the first weeks of the war. Alsace was lost, Lorraine invaded. Now patriotism stirred half awake in George Sand. "We must rid ourselves of Prussians and empires with one blow," she wrote Juliette Adam. By mid-August Sand was informing Prince Jérôme Bonaparte, "The Empire is finished. . . . The Republic will be reborn."[9] On the twenty-first she sent "an enormous box to the International." Founded in 1864 by Karl Marx, the First International was headquartered in London and had a small, active branch in France. But even as she was sending her box, presumably of clothes, to the French branch of the international revolutionary organization, George was making clear to her correspondent her differences with it: "I am, as always, socially *red* . . . but one must never impose one's convictions by force . . . for what is born of violence is condemned to die a violent death."[10]

Finally, on September fourth, there was news from the front. "Dismal!" But there was one consolation for George: "The Emperor has been taken prisoner." Pounded and broken by the Prussian cannon, over eighty thousand French troops had surrendered and were about to be taken to Germany, Napoleon III among them. September fifth: "Maurice wakes me, saying the Republic has been proclaimed in Paris *without a shot being fired*—an immense achievement, unique in the history of peoples! God protect France! Once again she has become worthy of His regard."[11]

"Long live the Republic, despite everything!" cried George from Nohant to Juliette Adam.[12] In Paris, revolutionaries raced moderate republicans to the Hôtel de Ville. A compromise Government of National Defense was formed with thirty-two-year-old Léon Gambetta as the Minister of Interior, at the head of the National Guard. Parisians had a holiday: not a single barricade had been raised to bring the Empire down.

But the war with Prussia went on, and Moltke's siege of Paris began. Smallpox struck Nohant. George and Maurice took the family to the Creuse for safety and stayed with friends. Communications with Paris were cut. Then George learned with astonishment of two balloons—the *Armand Barbès* and the *George Sand,* named in her honor—floating out of the besieged capital on October seventh. "Hers" carried a few Americans to safety; the *Barbès* bore a pale, nervous but courageous Gambetta, his hand grazed by a Prussian bullet, towards Tour and the organization of a southern army for the relief of Paris. "They say," Sand noted in her *War Journal,* "Monsieur Gambetta is a remarkable orator, man of action, iron will and perseverance." She had probably heard it from the Adams'. In a very short time she would be calling Gambetta and the officials with him, "our dictators of Tours." Her criticism of the new government was that it had not gone to the people of the nation to have "all France proclaim the Republic, . . . stop the enemy at the gates of Paris and make proposals of peace in the name of a reconstituted France." Lacking the support of universal suffrage, the government risked becoming "insupportably tyrannical in the course of events."[13]

The birth of the Republic had brought Ledru-Rollin, Louis Blanc, Félix Pyat, Pierre Leroux, Victor Hugo hurrying back to Paris from exile. But George Sand, returned to Nohant, had no way, nor great desire, to be in touch with even her old friends. Her *War Journal* became a monologue in the dark. "Locked in our solitude, we are like passengers on a ship struck by contrary winds and incapable of movement." The government at Tours left for Bordeaux to escape the approaching Germans; Gambetta joined the Army of the Loire. Sand had no faith in his military ability. Fifty miles from Nohant, Vierzon fell without resistance to the enemy. "We may be invaded tomorrow." George sought refuge and sanity in work on a new novel. "I continue to work, even with enthusiasm, the closer danger comes. It's like a task I must finish, so that I can die with the satisfaction of having worked to the end."

In Paris, news of the defeats coincided with rumors of negotiations with the enemy. Again patriotic crowds exploded around the Hôtel de Ville, crying, "Down with the government!" and for the first time, "Long live the Commune!" The Communards—those advocating a Paris Commune—were not Communists, though they *were* Reds. Centuries before the *Communist Manifesto*, communes existed in France as a form of self-government. George Sand rejected the reaction's calling the Reds the real enemy. "One can be *red*, that is, socially *advanced*, and be peaceful, too." However, she added, "I do not know the doctrines of the modern Commune. I can find nothing about them. But if they are to be imposed by force, whether or not the social panacea itself, I condemn them in the name of all that is human, patient, tolerant and jealous of freedom. . . . The misfortune and crime of the moment is this contempt for the masses." But immediately George Sand noted with characteristic honesty: "I cannot come to any clear opinion as to what is happening in that closed world called Paris. . . . The absence of communication between Paris and France has made the communication of ideas impossible between us."[14]

Sand was truly cut off from the evolving spirit of Paris and its radical republicans, and would remain so throughout the war. She could not see—nor possibly appreciate—the rapid transformation in process, turning a patriotic military struggle with invading Germans into a political and social struggle at home, in short, the resumption of the 1848 Revolution. Rather, Sand was wholly exposed to the sentiment in the provinces for a quick peace and to the news of Paris events as they were filtered through a conservative press. Her opinions, her *War Journal*, reflect it.

Occasionally there was a one-way communication from the besieged Paris—by balloon. *War Journal*, December twenty-eighth: "Letter of the 22nd. They say they have horse meat for another forty-five days." It was optimistic. Rats, cats, dogs and the Paris zoo's butchered animals soon provided much of the fare. On December twenty-seventh, the first shell from a Krupp siege gun struck the capital; they would average three hundred to four hundred a day. One shell, George heard from Plauchut, hit the building housing her apartment. January 18, 1871: "We cannot accept a peace which dishonors us." The situation worsened. George Sand to her diary, January twenty-fourth: "Sadder still, blacker still. . . . Dear God, dear God—we despair. . . . I write a few pages. Alas, I can write nothing that is worthwhile."[15]

Armistice talks resumed between Bismarck and the Government's foreign minister, Jules Favre, at the Prussian headquarters in Versailles. Bismarck: "You have grown grayer." Favre, discussing terms: "I cannot, at any price, afford to have the National Guard disarmed." Bismarck, cynically: "Provoke an uprising then, while you still have an army with which to suppress it."[16] The armistice was agreed upon. Paris reacted with stupor and rage. George Sand, *Diary*, January twenty-ninth: "Ah, dear God, at last, at last! An armistice has been signed— for 21 days. Convocation of an assembly at Bordeaux. We don't know more. It seems Gambetta is furious. . . . Will Paris receive food, at least for 21 days? Will peace come out of the suspension of hostilities? Will we be able to communicate with Paris? The *sous-préfet* who brought us the dispatch at 2 o'clock thinks Gambetta will resist. Does that mean civil war, then?" To Henry Harrisse, the same day: "I can breathe. My children and I embrace each other, crying. Politics to the rear! To the rear with that ferocious heroism of the Bordeaux party! . . . For three months I have been in revolt against the hateful notion that France must be martyred in order to be awakened."[17] Elections were scheduled during the armistice period. To Edmond Adam, Paris Prefect of Police since October: "I want peace for the sake of Germany almost as much as for ourselves. Now we must elect deputies who want neither peace at any price, nor war at any cost. The dictatorship of that schoolboy [Gambetta] has brought us to this."[18]

As predicted, Gambetta resigned in fury. But the siege was lifted, Paris ate and on February 8, 1871, France went to the polls. Out of 768 elected deputies—Paris was deliberately limited to 43—only 150 favoring the Republic and a continued war were returned to the Assembly, Edmond Adam, Louis Blanc, Gambetta among them. The majority was conservative, even monarchist, and a scorned, and scornful, republican Paris called it the Assembly of Rurals. Diminutive, seventy-three-year-old Adolphe Thiers was made the Assembly's Chief of the Executive Power. To Thiers, the people were "that vile multitude." To Karl Marx, Thiers was "that monstrous gnome."[19] For George Sand, he was the best the moment offered; she was even optimistic about the future, now that peace was at hand.

As head of state, Thiers concluded a peace treaty at the cost of Alsace and Lorraine, a German victory parade in Paris and an indemnity of five billion francs, or one billion dollars. The Assembly ratified the treaty; leftist republican deputies resigned. Paris no longer felt itself represented. Thiers moved swiftly and foolishly. He lifted the wartime moratorium on debts, antagonizing the petty bourgeoisie. He ended the modest pay of National Guardsmen, converting them into angry unemployed. He sentenced key leftist leaders to death, infuriating the revolutionary proletariat. He then adjourned the Assembly and announced it would meet thereafter in Versailles, thus further alienating the Parisians.

On March first, German Uhlans, Saxons and Bavarians paraded on the Champs Élysées, greeted with silence and black-draped streets. After their departure to camps north and east of Paris, pending payment of war claims, National Guardsmen fumigated the area of their parade. On the night of March 17–18, Thiers sought a showdown with the National Guard. Refusing to surrender their heavy cannon—theirs by popular subscription—the Guardsmen had dragged the guns to the heights of Montmartre for safekeeping. Thiers sent twelve to fifteen thousand Regulars to seize the guns.

George Sand's diary, March nineteenth:

> Paris is in an *unknowable* state of delirium. Last night they tried to retake the guns of Montmartre with troops. After surrounding "Mont Aventin," as it is called, the troops themselves were surrounded by armed crowds from Belleville and turned their rifle butts up [in sympathy with the crowds]. They say there was a quick exchange of fire, but it was soon ended, because the soldiers refused to fire on the people.

Down from Montmartre swept citizens, Guardsmen and defecting Regulars to surround the Hôtel de Ville. Thiers fled with his government to Versailles. That night a red flag hung from the bell tower of the Hôtel de Ville. A surprised, unprepared Central Committee, consisting of elected officers of the National Guard, found itself in power in Paris. George Sand's diary resumes:

> During the day [of the nineteenth], the government issued a communiqué saying it was established in Versailles and that all orders other than its own are to be disregarded. This would prove that the Hôtel de Ville has been occupied and the revolution—riot or conspiracy—has control of Paris. Does this mean another June [1848]? I feel sick.

Henceforth the principal source of news—and newspapers—for George Sand would be from Versailles. Within a few weeks Thiers ordered military action against Paris, cutting off virtually all communications, as during the Prussian siege. In Paris itself, the first few days, there was general confusion but little violence. There had not even been a pursuit of demoralized government forces as they withdrew to Versailles. ("A decisive mistake," said Marx in London.) The Central Committee announced elections for Paris on March twenty-sixth—"if the provinces think as we, they will imitate us." Meanwhile the principal ministries were occupied; judges, magistrates and police officials, most of whom had fled to Versailles, were replaced by election; but incredibly, the Bank of France was *not* taken over.* Instead, the Central Committee *borrowed* a million francs from it; and the Versailles government would borrow several millions more.

George Sand at Nohant, however, was hearing differently. *Diary*, March twenty-third: "The horrible adventure continues. They are ransoming, menacing, arresting, sentencing. They are preventing the tribunals from functioning. They have demanded a million from the Bank and five hundred thousand from Rotchild [sic]." But Sand also scores off the Assembly at Versailles as "stupidly reactionary" and "refusing reconciliation."

She had hoped for a peaceful Republic slowly, patiently evolving towards a libertarian socialism, even under Thiers. Instead she foresaw a revolutionary Paris Commune, proclaimed immediately after the elections, imposing its doctrines and rule on a France, which, she insisted, was ultraconservative outside Paris. Overreacting to a "reactionary Assembly, which was actually not very united and consequently not very formidable," she wrote Plauchut on March twenty-fourth, "Paris went to the other extreme. It behaved like a tenant who lets his house burn, and himself with it, in order to spite his landlord. . . . Paris is great, heroic, but mad. It doesn't allow for the provinces, which greatly outnumber it and constitute a *compact* reactionary mass. . . . You and your friends should realize that advanced republicans are in the proportion of 1 to 100 in the land, and you will not save the Republic without showing a great deal of patience and trying to control the extremists."[21]

"Without a civil war," Sand continued two days later, "France can

* "The proletariat stopped halfway . . . instead of annihilating its enemies, it endeavored to exercise moral influence on them." The writer: Lenin. Friedrich Engels, co-founder with Marx of modern communism, would note: "The hardest thing to understand is certainly the holy awe with which they remained standing respectfully outside the gates of the Bank of France." Leon Trotsky: "Brought up on the Marxian criticism of the Paris Commune," the Bolsheviks would seize the State Bank even before they took the Winter Palace at Saint Petersburg.[20]

be converted to republicanism; with it, she will withdraw deeper into a fear of the future and a blind love of the past. It will be the fault of the Commune and also of the Assembly, and somewhat, too, of the advanced ones of our party—Louis Blanc and company. . . . In fact, everyone is guilty. It has happened before in such fatal periods. . . ."[22]

Sand's diary, March thirtieth: "The revolutionary Commune rules in Paris. . . . And the Prussians are there outside, waiting. . . ." April first: "No newspapers, no letters from Paris. . . ." April second: "During the day Bebart [?] brings me yesterday's *Journal Officiel* of Versailles. So Paris is cut off again. This time it is its own fault. It has closed its gates. . . . A bulletin of Monsieur Thiers assures us that all is well, that the Assembly is protected by a superb army, that the Commune is divided, that this rash adventure is coming to its end. He says he is not going to march on Paris. . . ."

On April second, Thiers began his march on Paris. His Versailles force of some one hundred and seventy thousand struck at a western Paris suburb, seizing it and shooting the prisoners taken. In reprisal, the Commune ordered hostages rounded up in Paris, threatening to kill three for every Communard prisoner shot. The hostages were rounded up—among them a number of priests, including the Archbishop of Paris—but the threat was not put into execution. On Palm Sunday, Thiers ordered the shelling of Paris.

The Communards fought back enthusiastically but ineffectively, and in the first month of their two months' existence initiated the reforms which would become part of their legend: Church was separated from State—priests were to be paid by their congregations, not by the government as under the Second Empire; public education was made free, lay and obligatory for children; idle, deserted factories were to be turned over to workers' associations. These events reported by *Le Gaulois*, the newspaper George Sand was receiving from Versailles, were "disproperty," "theft," "dictatorship," etc.[23] However, the Commune's decrees were to remain a dead letter, as the Commune itself died.

Forts to the south and west of Paris—the Prussians were north and east—fell one by one to Thiers' Versailles force. In desperation the Commune turned to an authoritarian, Blanquist Committee of Public Safety, to which Proudhonian socialists and Marxist internationalists at first objected, then yielded. Sometime before, Edmond Adam had had to give way to the fanatical Raoul Rigault. In angry, inept response to the shelling of Paris, Thiers' Paris town house was ordered demolished. Sand's diary, April ninth: "Only one newspaper, *Le Gaulois*. . . . What do we really know?" April nineteenth: "They stole Monsieur Thiers' silver." May seventh: "Another bloody battle. . . . The hatred for Paris is mounting terribly. They [the Communards] are demolishing the [Napoleonic] Vendôme column. They continue to call their defeats victories. Their madness grows." May ninth: "Energetic declaration by Monsieur Thiers to the Parisians. He accuses them of cowardice. A hundred to one, they have allowed themselves to be dominated by bandits." May tenth: "At last, the fort of Issy has been taken and held. . . . We [sic] have done what the Prussians could not." May twelfth: "The climax approaches. . . ." May twenty-first: "Threats against the Archbishop of Paris if Blanqui [prisoner of the Versailles government] is not exchanged. Monsieur Thiers rightly refuses." May twenty-second: "At last! . . . Half the army is in Paris. . . . The newspapers announce the flight or disappearance of Pyat." May twenty-third: "Stifling heat. . . . *Le Gaulois* has details on the entry into Paris. It could have been more bloody."

It would be murderous, but *Le Gaulois* would never report it.

On Sunday May twenty-first, the Versailles forces poured through a strangely unguarded western gate of Paris. The seven days known in history as "Bloody Week" began. The Trocadéro was taken, then the Arc de Triomphe, from which guns could sweep the Champs Elysées. Leaders of the Commune called for a scorched Paris, for the burning of the Seine bridges to hold up "the enemy." Cautiously, methodically, one column of *Versaillais* worked along the Left Bank, another along the Right, outflanking the barricades by way of boulevards expressly designed for that purpose by the Empire's Baron Haussmann. On the north and east they had the passive co-operation of the Prussians. Montmartre was taken; Communards—men, women and children—were executed on the spot where two generals had been killed during the night of March 17–18, in accordance with Thiers' proclamation, "Expiation will be complete!" Now uncontrollable, Rigault had the Commune's hostages dragged out—gendarmes, priests and the Archbishop of Paris—and lingeringly executed. Hearing the news, old Louis Charles Delescluze, the Commune's commander, covered his face with his hands and cried, "What a war!"

George Sand's diary, May twenty-sixth: "The infamous ones are burning Paris!" Paris was indeed burning—the Tuileries Palace, the Palace of Justice, the Prefecture of Police, the Rue de Rivoli, the Hôtel de Ville. The rumor of *pétroleuses*, mythical women with bottles of petroleum, set the soldiers of Versailles on a witch hunt. More than one woman with an empty milk bottle would die. *Diary*, May thirtieth: "Letter from Plauchut in Biarritz. It seems it is official that women poisoned our soldiers in Paris and set fire in rage to buildings with the aid of their children."

On the fifth day, when only eastern, working-class Paris was still holding out, Delescluze, dressed in frock coat and top hat, walked to a deserted barricade, climbed to the top and waited for the bullet ending his life. It may have been the cleanest death of "Bloody Week," which ended on Whitsunday with one hundred and forty-seven Communards lined up against a wall in the Père Lachaise cemetery and finished off. George Sand's diary, May thirty-first: "It is over, over!—they are all taken prisoner, or killed, or in flight, or in hiding. Delescluze was killed by his own men. . . . But what will be done with the 20,000 prisoners?"

The purge, the "expiation," after the fighting was over, was completed: the wounded were dispatched; in prisons, parks, streets and public squares, suspects were shot by rifle squads, except where there were too many, in which case the new machine guns were employed. From twenty to twenty-five thousand died, most of them as prisoners.* A glimmer of the horror began to reach George Sand at Nohant. *Diary,* June seventh: "We do not know much, but the cowardly bourgeoisie, who submitted to everything, now want to kill everyone. Are they still shooting people without trial? I fear so, but they are not saying. Tomorrow the military court opens in Versailles." Forty thousand were marched to Versailles for judgment. Many were executed, more were sent to prison, forced labor, the French islands. Adolphe Thiers had *his* victory parade on a Paris racetrack, June twenty-ninth.

It was a kind of peace.

George Sand did not conceal the fact that the Muse of the Revolution of 1848 had become the Cassandra of the Commune of 1871. "Don't justify me when they accuse me of not being *sufficiently republican,*" she wrote Plauchut, who was back in Paris. "On the contrary! Tell them I am not republican in *their* manner."[24] Nevertheless, there was an uneasiness in George's mind and conscience. "I am entering my sixty-eighth year," she told Harrisse in July, "with a heart flayed alive by the misfortunes of my cruelly torn country." Blame lay on both sides, she felt, but the greater blame was the Commune's. France, she believed, must proceed by moderation: Thiers' Republic was the only "instrument for *cold, slow* progress."[25]

For Flaubert, with whom letters resumed, humanity itself was "despicable," as he had "known since youth." The reply of George Sand became so long she sent it as an article to *Le Temps.* It appeared in August as "*Résponse à Un Ami*"—an open letter not only to Flaubert, but to her friends (there was a cooling off with the Adams' and others), her critics and the public:

> You say that people have always been brutal, priests hypocritical . . . the peasant a fool? You say that you have known

* One tenth as many died in the entire year of the French Revolution's Reign of Terror. The Communards, in contrast, executed less than five hundred of their hostages.

this since your youth? . . . Then you have never been young.
Oh, we do indeed differ, for I have never ceased being young,
if to be young is to love. . . . You cannot despise your own
kind. Humanity is not an empty word. Our life is made of love
and not to love is not to live. The people, you say. This "people" are you and I. . . .

To her critics on the left:

Read what I write in its entirety. Do not judge me by isolated
fragments. . . . By my feeling and reason I am more than
ever opposed to fictitious differences, to the inequality of life's
condition, which is imposed as an inherited right for some and
a deserved fate for others. More than ever I feel the need to
lift up those who are down and raise those who have fallen. . . . If today it is the people who are underfoot, I will ex-
tend them my hand. If tomorrow they are the oppressors and
executioners, I will tell them they are cowardly, odious
brutes. . . .
    I do not need to ask where my friends are and where my en-
emies. They are there where the storm has flung them. . . .
The unthinking accusation of those who have broken with me
does not make me think of them as my enemies. . . . The
heart . . . knows how to await the return of justice and affection. . . .
    I love, therefore I live, let us live, let us love![26]

Gustave Flaubert was "moved," he replied, but "unconvinced."
Again and again they debated democracy itself. "The essential first remedy," said Flaubert, "is to rid ourselves once and for all of universal
suffrage . . . where numbers count for more than intelligence, education, breeding, even money. . . ." He himself, Flaubert liked to say,
was worth "twenty Croisset voters."[27] To this George Sand incessantly
replied that she could see no preferable alternative to democracy, certainly not monarchy or tyranny, or the rule of a Flaubertian élite. But it
was to a young poet that George Sand, still haunted by the bloody days
of the Commune and her fears for future social violence, exploded with
a poetry of her own:

I'll have no more bloodshed, no more evil means to bring
about good ends, no more killing in order to create. No, no!
My age protests against the tolerance of my youth. That
which has just taken place should make us take a great step
forward. We must rid ourselves of the theories of 1793. . . . A
curse on all those who dig charnel houses. No life ever comes

out of them. Let us learn to be stubborn, patient revolutionaries, but never terrorists. We will not be heard for a long time, but what does it matter! The poet should live on a height above his contemporaries and see beyond his own life. Humanity will progress only when it learns to despise the lie in men and respect mankind despite the lie.[28]

38

The Last Chapter:
"Let Green Things..."

To know how to grow old, it has been said, "is the masterwork of wisdom, and one of the most difficult chapters in the great art of living."[1] Fewer still know how to *be* old, as Goethe at Weimar, George Sand at Nohant. On her birthday in July 1872, told by her doctor to nurse her whooping cough, the grand old lady with the gypsy-dark body went for a dip with Plauchut in the cool waters of the Indre. "The doctor says I'm mad," she wrote Flaubert gaily. "I let him talk. While his patients follow his orders, I regain my health, and they die."[2] There was not time —how trite it sounds, but there was no longer writing after midnight for George Sand; age had taken that toll—to lie sick in bed. There were two hours a day with the quick, eager mind of six-year-old Aurore, another hour of instruction for Titite—four-year-old Gabrielle—who was learning how to read, other hours in the garden and the fields collecting rock and plant specimens ("to do nothing but give myself to botany would be paradise on earth for me"[3]), and a few hours for writing the "little novel (or two) of the year."

The people of La Châtre, old and young, even those who remembered the teen-age Aurore Dupin, who woke them at night as she clattered through their streets with their young men astride her horse like one of them, and the young wife and mother, Baronne Dudevant, who went off boldly and scandalously to live with a yet younger man in Paris, now called her *La Bonne Dame*—the Good Lady—of Nohant. Perhaps only old Casimir still held closely to the evergreen image of the young George Sand. The grand old lady contributed to it, though sometimes less than grandly. Spurred by their wary, watchful mother,

Maurice and Solange had brought suit against their father to prevent him from leaving Guillery on his death to his "other" daughter Rose, child of Madame Dalias. They won their suit. Casimir was obliged to sell Guillery during his lifetime. From the sale he was permitted to retain one hundred and forty-nine thousand francs—Maurice and Solange divided the remaining one hundred and thirty thousand francs*— and bought a small house six kilometers from Guillery, where he died in March 1871. Two years before Casimir had sent a petition to Napoleon III, which had been found on the Emperor's desk after his abdication; it had lain there for several months, so curious had the Emperor considered it, showing it, no doubt, to his visitors. Baron Dudevant, "in the evening of my days," formally—and pathetically—requested the red ribbon of the Legion of Honor:

> In asking for this award [his petition read], I base my claim
> not only on my services since 1815 to the nation and its established
> authority, services without great brilliance, insignificant
> perhaps, but also on the eminent services rendered by my father
> from 1792 until the return from Elba. Even more do I
> dare invoke those domestic misfortunes which now belong to
> history. Married to Lucille Dupin, known in the literary world
> by the name of George Sand, I have cruelly suffered in my affections
> as a husband and a father, and I have the conviction
> of having earned the sympathetic interest of all those who have
> followed the lugubrious events of that period of my existence.[4]

* * *

The distant past also returned with Pauline Viardot, who had not visited Nohant for two decades, because her husband, at odds with the imperial regime, refused to live in France. Pauline came with her two grown-up daughters, and all three enchanted George Sand with their singing. "What emotion, what an immersion in music! Day and evening Pauline sang. . . . She is more incomparable than ever, I cry like a calf. . . . Lolo *drank up* the music with her big eyes. The Viardot girls sang deliciously, they are charming. Voices of crystal. But Pauline, Pauline, what a genius . . ." By week's end, George was "drunk" with music.[5] Then, on October third, they were joined by a new acquaintance, the fine Russian writer Ivan Turgenev, an admirer of Pauline Viardot for many years and a close friend of Gustave Flaubert.

Flaubert himself had been invited to come to Nohant with Turgenev and Viardot, to lift himself from the despondency of his mother's death, but he had preferred to suckle at his despair and so declined.

---

* Casimir's illegitimate daughter received nothing, an injustice which would remain unchanged in French law until 1974, and go unremarked even longer. Madame Dalias, too, has been treated with less regard than, say, Manceau.

The death of Théophile Gautier—"dear Théo"—plunged him deeper into his gloom. If only he would see his friends, those who loved him, George wrote compassionately, instead of refusing their comfort. Her own source of strength these days was her grandchildren. "The little girls run about like rabbits in heather taller than themselves. Dear God, how good life is when all one loves is teeming with life! You are the only *dark spot* in the life of my heart, because you are sad and refuse to look at the sun. . . . Well, perhaps in order to be happy, one must have been unhappy. I have been that and I know a great deal about it. But I forget so well!

"We are not literary enough for you at Nohant, I know. But we love and that fills life."⁶

Flaubert was finally coaxed to Nohant for Easter. The festivities were more frenzied than ever, perhaps because everyone strained too much to ease him from his mood, and Flaubert at first tried too hard to join in. On Easter Sunday, when a costumed Spanish dance was the order of the day, he put on a skirt and determinedly danced a fandango. "Very funny," George confided to her diary, "but he was out of breath in five minutes. He is much older than I am! Yet he seems thinner and less tired. He lives too much with his brain at the expense of his body. Our racket deafens him. . . . At midnight he was overwhelmed by Maurice's collection of butterflies." The following day Flaubert read aloud from his completed *Temptation of Saint Anthony*—"from 3 to 6 and from 9 to 12"—overwhelming Maurice to the point of a "blinding headache."

On the third day, Turgenev arrived. On the fourth: "Leaping, dancing, singing, shouting. Flaubert's head bursting, he kept trying to stop everything in order to talk literature. We're too much for him. Turgenev likes noise and gaiety. He's as much of a child as we are. He dances, he waltzes. What a good, jovial man of genius!" Then Maurice read a long poem he had composed, "overwhelming Flaubert." It went on one more day. April 18, 1873: "Flaubert delivered a long talk, very animated, very droll, but no one else had a chance to speak and Turgenev, who is more interesting, could hardly put in a word. In the evening it was a veritable assault, until 1 in the morning. Finally we said good-bye. They leave in the morning."

The day after, George reflected on the visit: "One *lives* with one's character rather than one's intelligence and greatness. I am tired, *worn out*, by my dear Flaubert. Yet I am fond of him, he is an excellent man, but too exuberant in personality. He breaks you down. . . . Tonight we dance, make a lot of noise, act silly with delight. We miss Turgenev, whom we know less, love less, but who has the grace of true simplicity and the charm of genuine good humor."

Despite the long years behind her and the so few ahead, George Sand was rarely inclined to look back, but on one occasion she did, recalling other visitors at Nohant. It was shortly after her sixty-ninth birthday; she was lying full length in the languid waters of the Indre. "Lying there, completely covered with water, I found myself thinking of all those who bathed with us here long ago—Pauline and her mother, Chopin, Delacroix, my brother. We bathed here even at night. We came on foot and returned the same way. All are dead now, except Madame Viardot and I. . . . Tonight we played hide-and-seek with the children."[7]

Solange was not included in Sand's nostalgia. When she sought to purchase Hippolyte's neighboring Château de Montgivray from his indebted daughter, George bent every effort to prevent it. Operating through an intermediary, however, Solange succeeded in acquiring it, settling at Montgivray in 1873. She would appear uninvited at Nohant and sometimes stay for dinner, though her mother avoided her. With a sturdiness lacking in their father, the little grandchildren, who disliked their aunt, would stand guard outside George's study and prevent their grandmother's being disturbed.

George Sand cheered, or tried to cheer, Flaubert with such stories about little Titite and Lolo. "Never," he wrote darkly on February 28, 1874, "have I felt so abandoned, so empty, so battered. What you tell me . . . about your dear little ones has moved me to the bottom of my soul. Why do I not have children? I was born surrounded by affection, myself! But we do not make our destiny, we sustain it. I was a coward in my youth, *I was afraid* of life! Everything receives its due."[8] As a young man, Flaubert had written a friend, "Do not marry, have no child, no attachments, offer the enemy no hold."[9] The life and philosophy of George Sand could not have been more dissimilar. When, on the death of his mother, she had told Flaubert, "Why don't you marry? To be alone is odious," the fifty-one-year-old Flaubert had replied to his sixty-eight-year-old friend, Too late.[10]

Two years later, afflicted with boils, skin trouble, nervous headaches —a second play of his had failed in Paris—Flaubert was in Switzerland on his doctor's orders. "To calm my nerves!" he wrote George Sand. "But I doubt the remedy will work. In any event, my stay has been a deadly bore. I am not a *man of nature* and I have no interest in any country without a past. I would gladly exchange all the glaciers for the Vatican museum. It is there one can dream."[11]

Herself sick with a touch of influenza and a rheumatism almost immobilizing her right arm, George Sand, who had just fêted her seventieth birthday the day before, replied: "I do not have the strength to stay in bed. I spend the evening with the children and forget my little miseries. They will pass; everything passes. . . ."

You say you do not want to be a "man of nature." Too bad
for you! Because you then attach too much importance to petty
things and don't appreciate that natural force in yourself
which waves away the *ifs* and *buts* of idle social chatter. We
are of nature, in nature, by nature and for nature. Talent, genius and will are natural phenomena like volcanoes, lakes,
mountains, wind, stars, clouds. What man dabbles at is ugly
or nice, foolish or ingenious. What he receives from nature is
good or bad, but it *is*; it exists and endures. . . . Enough now,
I can barely hold my pen. You are dear to me. Don't have any
more black thoughts. Resign yourself to boredom, if the air
there is good for you.[12]

There was no resignation for Flaubert, but the exchange of letters
until the end inspired some of their finest writing. "You love literature
too much," said George. "It will kill you and you will not have put an
end to human stupidity. . . . You have too much knowledge and intelligence. You forget that there is something above art—wisdom, of which
art at its apogee is but the expression." Accept life, she pleaded, as it is.
See Victor Hugo, "I think he will calm you. As for me, I am no longer
sufficiently stormy for you to understand me." "Ah!" replied Flaubert,
"how I envy you, how I wish I had your serenity!" He chose his "desolation," said George Sand. He did not, said Flaubert. That was the way
he objectively saw life and objectively portrayed it. He entered his
work no more than "God in nature. Man is nothing, the work is all."
"Supreme impartiality," replied Sand, "is something anti-human and a
novel should be human above all. . . . Hold fast to your cult of form,
but think more about content."[13] Out of this would come—unseen by
George Sand—Flaubert's most moving, perhaps most perfect work, *A
Simple Heart*, the tale of an old servant and her parrot.

As France wavered between restoring the monarchy or settling down,
as it finally did, to a Third Republic, politics, for George Sand, had become a "comedy." "I conscientiously read my paper every morning; but
beyond that, it is impossible for me to think about it or take any interest in it." Everything seemed "empty of any ideal."[14] Three years after
the passions of the Commune, there was absolution for all who had
participated for or against it. "I confess I do not see clearly in that great
tempest. I can only approve or disapprove certain events taken in themselves. The whole affair seems like a case of terrible fever which, to an
extent, makes everyone innocent. I can ascertain no real *party* or *school*.
I perceive nothing but anguish as each blindly plunged on, not knowing
what he was doing, not caring about political rights, or civil rights, or

human rights, alas. Is it in delirium that one can ever consider grave problems?"[15] She well knew, Sand wrote Charles Poncy on the eve of 1875, "that the world is going badly. . . . So I try to *stuff* the children with happiness, so they will have the moral stamina to confront the disappointments inevitably before them."[16]

Most of her days now were spent with the children, teaching them their lessons, writing her *Grandmother's Fairy Tales* for their reading. But the best teaching of George Sand, in her old age as in early womanhood, was by her example. She did not, in her fiery youth, simply 'preach' feminism; she exercised it. She did not write manifestos about what life could be in a better society for women and await that miracle; she lived out her life despite the actual odds—and that was her revolutionary act to the end of her life. Had George Sand really been a "conservative at heart," as concentrating narrowly on her political attitudes in her last years has led some, generally men, to conclude, there would have been no George Sand. These thoughts occur as one sees her at the end of her days at Nohant with the children, with friends, with her scarcely faltering pen: the life is the lesson and the story, as the novels themselves appeared like the seasons—*Ma Soeur Jeanne, Flamarande, La Tour de Percemont, Marianne Chevreuse*. And in her seventy-second year the extraordinary Sand began another—*Albine Fiori*.

Flaubert, as usual, received each volume as it was published and for each he habitually had a kind word. But *Marianne Chevreuse*—"the touching story of the dark-eyed melancholy girl who led her brave life among the uncomprehending gossips of her small village"[17]—truly reached him. "Marianne," he wrote George, February 8, 1876, "has moved me profoundly and two or three times I cried. I saw myself in the person of Pierre. Certain pages seemed almost fragments of my memoirs, if I had the talent to write them in your fashion! How charming it all is, how poetic and *true!* The *Tour de Percemont* pleased me extremely, but *Marianne* has literally enchanted me. . . . So this time I admire you fully and without the *slightest* reservation."[18]

Six weeks later George wrote Flaubert of "atrociously persistent . . . stomach cramps," then stoically recalled her old priest (Abbé de Prémord?). "He used to say, when he had the gout, 'It will pass, or I will.' And he would laugh, contented with his *bon mot*."[19] It may be George Sand's last letter to Flaubert.

On May twentieth, George consulted Dr. Marc Chabenat, who had come from La Châtre to see Maurice about his neuralgia. For a fortnight, she told him, she had been troubled with "obstinate constipation."[20] For a lifetime, in fact, George Sand had been afflicted with a "writer's stomach," and for the past few years likely suffered from a developing, latent cancer which further blocked her bowel movements. "In spite of my age (soon seventy-two)," she wrote her Paris doctor,

Henri Favre, on May twenty-eighth, "I do not feel the effects of senility. . . . I go up the stairs as nimbly as my dog. However, with one part of my vital functions almost completely suppressed, I wonder what is going to happen to me and whether I should not be prepared for a sudden departure one of these mornings."[21]

On May twenty-ninth George Sand left off writing *Albine Fiori* in the middle of a chapter and made the last entry in her diary:

> Delicious weather. Not suffering very much. Took a nice walk
> in the garden. Gave Lolo her lesson. Reread a play by
> Maurice. After dinner, Lina went to the theater in La Châtre.
> Played *bésig* with Sagnier [young visitor from Nimes]. Draw.
> Lina returned at midnight.[22]

George Sand does not mention Dr. Chabenat's arrival, his concern about her greatly distended stomach. The blockage was complete. "I have the devil clawing inside me," she told him. The pain was agonizing and she vomited that evening. Gustave Papet was also sent for. He told Maurice there was no hope. Until four in the morning George's cries of pain could be heard at the far end of the garden. Two more doctors were summoned the following morning. All three suggested to Maurice that he telegraph for a specialist from Paris. Maurice decided to send for Dr. Favre. Knowing him to be a *beau parleur* and an incompetent practitioner, the three doctors insisted he come accompanied by someone "uncontestably qualified," preferably a surgeon. When Favre arrived on June first, he arrived alone. Before even examining his patient, Favre pronounced her illness "dysentery . . . or a hernia," and prescribed a massage. On June second, a surgeon did appear, but too late for any operation other than a puncture of the stomach wall for some relief.[23]

Maurice sent a telegram to Solange at Montgivray, describing the gravity of the situation. She received the message in Paris and arrived the next morning. Maurice took her emotionally in his arms, but Lina was distant. Solange addressed her respectfully as "Madame." She went upstairs to see her mother. George received her impassively, though several times she had asked that no one but the doctors enter her bedroom. She was deeply humiliated by the character of her illness—the soiling of the bed, of herself. She constantly asked to be washed, for the bed linen to be changed. "She would have liked to die as the ermine, from a single stain."[24]

On the morning of June 7, 1876, George Sand sent for her granddaughters, kissed them and said, "Be good." She suffered from an unslakable thirst and had difficulty in speaking. In the evening she said, "Adieu, adieu, I am going to die . . . *Let green things* . . ." During the night she cried out six, seven times, "Let me die, dear God, let me die!"

At three in the morning of the eighth, Maurice appeared at her bedroom door. She waved him away; she did not want him to see her before she had been changed. At six she asked Solange, who never left her side, to move the bed so that she might face the first light. At nine she sent for the grandchildren to join the family. "Adieu, Lina," she murmured, "adieu, Maurice, adieu, Lolo, ad . . ." She lost consciousness and died.[25]

At the table that night at Nohant, Solange sat in her mother's place —imperially. Death did have its small victory after all, and it would claim another. Solange enlisted her cousins—Cazamajou and Simonnet —and a "note" of her mother—never produced—to bear down on an emotionally shocked and disabled Maurice to have her mother buried by the Church in a religious ceremony. Lina objected, then told Solange that while George Sand was alive, she protected her, but her burial was in the hands of her children. After Maurice weakly gave way, she said no more. The Archbishop of Bourges was telegraphed for his authorization. He readily granted it: though she had requested no last rites while she still lived, Mademoiselle La Quintinie would be properly interred.

George Sand's friends came down from Paris by train for the funeral —Flaubert, Dumas *fils*, Renan, Borie, Prince Jérôme; Harrisse, her publisher Calmann Lévy, the actors Édouard Cadol and Paul Meurice. Marchal was not among them; Aucante and Plauchut were already at Nohant. It was raining when they started from Paris; it was still raining when they reached Nohant. Flowers covered the body of George Sand, as she had covered Manceau's. Only her right hand—"small and pretty and smooth as polished ivory"[26]—was visible.

Peasant men carried the coffin in the steadily falling rain to the small family cemetery on the edge of the park. Peasant women, dressed in black, knelt in the mud as the priest intoned the ceremony. Flaubert towered among the mourners and wept like a child: he was burying his mother for the second time. Each of George's friends held a laurel branch given them by Lina to be laid on the grave. Victor Hugo had sent an elegiac message which was read, after Ernest Périgois had spoken, by Paul Meurice: "*Je pleure une morte et je salue une immortelle.* . . . I weep for one dead and I salute an immortal. . . . George Sand was an idea. Liberated from the flesh, she is now free. Dead, she now lives. . . ."[27] Ernest Renan thought the oration banal; Gustave Flaubert thought it sublime, and one does see, perhaps as Flaubert, the younger, essential George Sand rising from the poor, swollen body of the Good Lady of Nohant, the person we see in our mind in all her strength and daring and greatness when we say George Sand.

Flaubert wrote sadly of the funeral to Turgenev, how he had wept twice, the first time when kissing George Sand's granddaughter Aurore —"whose eyes, that day, so resembled hers that it seemed a resurrection"—and the second time, "on seeing the coffin pass by."[28] To a woman whose friendship he had shared with George Sand—Mademoiselle de Chantepie—he wrote:

> One had to know her as I knew her to realize how much of the feminine there was in that great man, the immensity of tenderness there was in that genius. She will remain one of the radiant splendors of France, unequaled in her glory.[29]

But "the moral of George Sand's tale, the beauty of what she does for us"—it is Henry James speaking, after having talked shortly after Sand's death with a "distinguished, intimate friend of her later years," surely Flaubert—"is not the extension she gives to the feminine nature, but the richness that she adds to the masculine"—the lesson of the wholeness of George Sand.[30]

Notes and Bibliography

Chapter 1 Past as Prologue

1. George Sand, *Oeuvres autobiographiques,* Pléiade edition, 2 vols. (Paris, 1970–71); see Vol. I, pp. 461 and 464, for references to George Sand's birth date and the wedding day of her parents.

The Pléiade edition, published by Gallimard, is superbly collated, edited and annotated by Georges Lubin, leading George Sand scholar. It contains: "Histoire de ma vie," Vol. I, pp. 5–1129, Vol. II, pp. 5–465—the most important source, together with Lubin's edition of Sand's *Correspondance* (see Note 5 below), for students of George Sand; it was commenced in 1847, when the author was forty-three and her nine-year attachment to Chopin was coming to an end;

"Voyage en Espagne," II, pp. 467–74—recollections of Sand's travels in Spain when she was three years old and four years old;

"Mon grand-oncle," II, pp. 475–96—concerns Abbé de Beaumont, Sand's granduncle;

"Voyage en Auvergne," II, pp. 497–527—account of a cure at Mont-Dore with husband Casimir Dudevant, Aug. 1827;

"La Blonde Phoebé," "Nuit d'hiver," "Voyage chez M. Blaise," II, pp. 529–69—"interesting sketches of provincial life during the time young Baronne Dudevant [not yet George Sand] had not yet taken flight to Paris" (Lubin);

"Les Couperies," II, pp. 571–81—early piece of fiction, involving Jules Sandeau;

"Sketches and Hints," II, pp. 583–632—original title in English;

"Lettres d'un voyageur," II, pp. 633–943—written between 1834 and 1836, contains pages on Venice and music, Alfred de Musset, Michel de Bourges, Franz Liszt and Marie d'Agoult;

"Journal intime," II, pp. 945–71—fall of 1834 with Musset;

"Entretiens journaliers avec le très docte et très habile docteur Piffoël," II, pp. 973–1018—Sand masquerading as Dr. Piffoël, a self-mocking pseudonym deriving from *pif,* meaning *large-nosed;*

"Fragment d'une lettre écrite de Fontainebleau," II, pp. 1019–25;

"Un hiver à Majorque," II, pp. 1027–1177—winter in Majorca with Chopin, 1838–39;

"Souvenirs de mars-avril 1848," II, pp. 1179–90—apropos the spring time of a revolution;

"Journal de novembre-décembre, 1851," II, pp. 1191–1222; "Après la mort de Jeanne Clésinger," II, pp. 1223–33—on the death of George Sand's granddaughter; "Le théâtre et l'acteur," II, pp. 1235–44; "Le théâtre des marionnettes de Nohant," II, pp. 1245–76—one of the last writings, intended to be added to "Histoire de ma vie."

2. Sand, op. cit., I, p. 1125.

3. Ibid., p. 23.

4. One reason for dwelling on her ancestors was evasion of the revelations expected of George Sand. Another was the colorful substance of her ancestral history. Yet another was simply the professional reason of having been paid by the volume for her memoirs. So impatient were contemporary readers following George Sand's reminiscences serially, one critic thought her story, *Histoire de ma vie*, better retitled, "*Histoire de ma vie avant ma naissance*"—The Story of My Life Before My Birth. Cuvillier-Fleury, in *Journal des Debats*, 28 January 1855.

5. George Sand, *Correspondance*, edited by Georges Lubin, 11 vols. (Paris, 1964–76), VIII, p. 264. More to come.

6. Sand, *Oeuvres autobiographiques*, I, pp. 307–08.

7. Jon Manchip White, *Marshal of France, the Life and Times of Maurice, Comte de Saxe* (London, 1962), p. 8.

8. W. H. Wilkins, *The Love of an Uncrowned Queen*, 2 vols. (London, 1900), II, p. 486.

9. Sand, op. cit., p. 29.

10. White, op. cit., p. 10.

11. ". . . and vivacity, rather than of line and distinction," George Sand had added, then deleted, in the original manuscript. The portrait itself may be seen in Paris' Musée Carnavalet.

12. Voltaire, *Histoire de Charles XII* (Paris, 1846), p. 64.

13. Saint-René Taillandier, *Maurice de Saxe* (Paris, 1865), p. 13.

14. White, op. cit., p. 21.

15. General Camon, *Maurice de Saxe* (Paris, 1934), passim.

16. Taillandier, op. cit., p. 60.

17. Sand, op. cit., I, p. 30.

18. Pierre-Edouard Lémontey, *Histoire de la régence*, 2 vols. (Paris, 1832), II, p. 328.

19. Taillandier, op. cit., p. 110.

20. Maurice de Saxe, *Mes rêveries*, 2 vols. (Amsterdam, 1757), II, pp. 159–60.

21. Sand, op. cit., I, p. 154.

22. Adrienne Lecouvreur, *Lettres* (Paris, 1892). "Mlle. Lecouvreur died in my arms of an inflammation of the entrails," wrote Voltaire, her intermittent lover and faithful friend, in denial.

23. Sanche de Gramont, *Epitaph for Kings* (New York, 1967), p. 187.

24. Gaston Maugras, *Les demoiselles de Verrières* (Paris, 1890), p. 32.

25. Sand, op. cit., I, p. 31.

26. Maugras, op. cit., p. 36.

27. Sand, op. cit., I, p. 31.

28. Jean-Francois Marmontel, *Mémoires*, 4 vols. (Paris, 1804), I, pp. 286–87.

29. Ibid., p. 288.

30. Madame Louise d'Épinay, *Mémoires*, 2 vols. (Paris, 1863), I, pp. 17–18.

31. Baron d'Espagnac, *Histoire de Maurice, Comte de Saxe*, 2 vols. (Paris, 1775), II, p. 492.

32. Sand, op. cit., I, p. 155.

33. Louis Petit de Bachaumont, *Mémoires secrètes*, 36 vols. (Paris, 1777–89), I, p. 247.

34. Edmond and Jules de Goncourt, *La femme au dix-huitième siècle* (Paris, 1887), pp. 224 and 229.
There was a loose, but still largely double, standard of morality and conduct, one for men and the other for women, dependent on the tolerance, indifference or simply fear of ridicule of the husband. He could, however, have an unfaithful wife put away by routinely procuring a *lettre de cachet* (sealed letter). "But what was done to the unfaithful husband?" Marivaux asked. "Where are the husbands who are put under lock and key?" He, unlike his wife, was society's hero, "pointed to with admiration. And what airs he puts on!" Pierre de Marivaux, *Cabinet du philosophe (cinquième feuille)* (Paris, 1734), pp. 110–11.

35. Sand, op. cit., I, p. 36.

36. French Ministry of War. Administrative Archives. *Dossier du Maréchal de Saxe.* 212 MF. The archives and document are in the great Château de Vincennes on the edge of eastern Paris.

37. Ibid.

38. Bibiothèque de l'Arsenal, Paris. Archives de la Bastille. Doc. 10238. See also, Gaston Capon and Robert Yve-Plessis, *Les théâtres clandestins* (Paris, 1905), pp. 194–95.

39. W. H. Lewis, *The Splendid Century.* Anchor Books (New York, 1953), p. 259 and passim. See also, Joseph Barry, *Passions and Politics—a Biography of Versailles* (New York, 1972), pp. 160–61.

40. Charles Gailly de Taurines, *Aventuriers et femmes de qualité. La fille du Maréchal de Saxe* (Paris, 1907), p. 41.

41. Archives Nationales de Paris. Parlement. X i A 4533. May 15, 1766.

42. Sand, op. cit., I, pp. 33–34.

43. French Ministry of War. Administrative Archives. *Ancien Régime.* Trésor Royal 11897. See Note 36, above.

44. Same as Note 36, April 1768.

45. Sand, op. cit., I, pp. 38, 1245 and 1246.

46. Ibid., p. 38.

47. Same as Note 36, November 1772.

48. Sand, op. cit., I, p. 35.

49. Ibid., p. 36.

50. Ibid., p. 37.

51. Gailly de Taurines, op. cit., p. 329.

52. To another suitor Aurore wrote that she preferred friendship to the more "blinding" emotions: "I have always lived with people considerably

older than myself and insensibly I reached their level. I was not young very long and perhaps it was a loss, but I gained much in good sense." Ibid., p. 329.

53. Sand, op. cit., I, pp. 40–41.

54. Ibid., p. 51.

Chapter 2 Sons as Lovers

1. Manuscript in the Sand collection, Bibliothèque Spoelberch de Lovenjoul, Chantilly, E 803. Cf. George Sand, *Oeuvres autobiographiques*, 2 vols. (Paris, 1970–71), I, p. 1344.

2. Charles Gailly de Taurines, *Adventuriers et femmes de qualité. La fille du Maréchal de Saxe* (Paris, 1907), p. 333.

3. Sand, op. cit., I, p. 52. Cf. Roland Derche, *Le Laonnois J.-L.-F. Deschartres, précepteur de George Sand* (1761–1828) (Fontenay-le-Comte, 1954), p. 22.

4. Sand, op. cit., I, p. 55.

5. Ibid., pp. 55–56.

6. Ibid., p. 57.

7. Cf. Paule-Marie Duhet, *Les femmes et la révolution*, 1789–94 (Paris, 1971), passim.

8. Gailly de Taurines, op. cit., p. 333.

9. Sand, op. cit., I, p. 61.

10. Aurore Sand, *Le Berry de George Sand* (Paris, 1927), p. 24.

11. Nohant, château and park, is now a national museum.

12. Aurore Sand, op. cit., p. 24.

13. Archives Nationales. Comité de Sûreté Générale. Dossier Amonnin. Cf. Gailly de Taurines, op. cit., p. 335.

14. Archives Nationales. Comité de Sûreté Générale. Dossier Dupin (Aurore). Cf. Gailly de Taurines, op. cit., p. 336.

15. Sand, op. cit., I, pp. 66–67.

16. Archives Nationales. Comité de Sûreté Générale. Dossier Dupin (Aurore). 21 Frimaire (Dec. 11), 1793. Cf. Gailly de Taurines, op. cit., pp. 338–39.

17. Idem.

18. Sand, op. cit., I, p. 76.

19. Ibid., pp. 113 and 122.

20. Ibid., pp. 122–24.

21. Ibid., p. 157.

22. Ibid., pp. 104 and 175.

23. Ibid., p. 176.

24. Ibid., p. 226.

25. Most of the letters of Maurice are in manuscript at the Bibliothèque Historique de la Ville de Paris (BHVP, Fonds Sand), and the most striking alterations have been noted by the incomparable Georges Lubin in his edition of Sand's *Oeuvres autobiographiques* (see Chap. 1, Note 1).

26. Cf. André Maurois, *Lélia, ou la vie de George Sand* (Paris, 1952), p. 26.

27. Sand, op. cit., I, p. 248.
28. Ibid., p. 341.
29. George Sand, *Correspondance*, 11 vols. (Paris, 1964–76), VI, p. 327. To Charles Poncy, Dec. 23, 1843.
30. Bibliothèque Historique de la Ville de Paris (BHVP Fonds Sand, E 184). Cf. Sand, *Oeuvres autobiographiques*, I, pp. 1323–24.
31. Sand, op. cit., I, pp. 342–44.
32. Ibid., pp. 356–58.
33. BHVP, Fonds Sand, E 191. Cf. Sand, *Oeuvres autobiographiques*, I, pp. 1328–30.
34. Lovenjoul, Chantilly, E 803.
35. Sand, op. cit., I, pp. 361–62.
36. Ibid., p. 370.
37. BHVP, Fonds Sand, E 210. Cf. Sand, *Oeuvres autobiographiques*, I, p. 1338.
38. Since 1802 was the year of the reunion of Maurice and Sophie at Charlesville, and George Sand was born in 1804, there is an insufficiency in the years allowed. Nevertheless the children seem to have existed. Maurice mentions *three*, including a son, in a letter to Sophie, written in 1807 (BHVP, Fonds Sand, E 289). Possibly one is Caroline, and the second George Sand, but of the son there is no further trace.
39. Geneviève Gennari, *Le dossier de la femme* (Paris, 1965), p. 23.
40. BHVP, Fonds Sand, E 5. Cf. Sand, *Oeuvres autobiographiques*, I, pp. 1359–60.
41. A plaque commemorates the event at 46 Rue Meslay in today's Paris.
42. Sand, op. cit., I, p. 464.

Chapter 3 *The Seedling Years*

1. Sigmund Freud, *The Basic Writings* (New York, 1938), p. 581.
2. Alfred de Musset, *La confession d'un enfant du siècle* (Paris, 1880), pp. 2–3.
3. Sand, *Oeuvres autobiographiques*, 2 vols. (Paris, 1970–71), I, p. 479.
4. Ibid., pp. 484 and 486–87.
5. The story which follows was told George Sand by her mother.
6. Ibid., pp. 499–500.
7. Ibid., p. 501.
8. Louise Vincent, *George Sand et le Berry*, 2 vols. (Paris, 1919), p. 21.
9. Sand, op. cit., I, pp. 501–02.
10. See Note 2, above.
11. Sand, op. cit., I, p. 503.
12. Ibid., pp. 519 and 527–28.
13. Bibliothèque Spoelberch de Lovenjoul, E 803, f. 290–91.
14. Sand, op. cit., I, p. 530 and passim.
15. Ibid., pp. 541–42.
16. Ibid., p. 543.
17. Ibid., p. 548 and passim.
18. Frances Winwar, *The Life of the Heart: George Sand and Her Times*

(New York, 1945), pp. 12–13. The emphasis is mine; the insight is that of a woman biographer.

19. Sand, op. cit., I, pp. 573–74.
20. Sand, "Voyage en Auvergne" in op. cit., II, pp. 505–07.
21. Sand, "Voyage en Espagne" in op. cit., II, p. 472.
22. Sand, op. cit., I, p. 575 and passim.

Chapter 4 The Apple of Discord

1. *Encyclopaedia Britannica*, 11th ed., Vol. 24, p. 202.
2. George Sand, *Oeuvres autobiographiques*, 2 vols., (Paris, 1970–71), I, p. 586 and passim.
3. Frances Winwar, *The Life of the Heart: George Sand and Her Times* (New York, 1945), p. 25.
4. Mention of Deschartres' flute reminds George Sand of the "village fool" of La Châtre who often came to hear Deschartres play. When asked what else he might want, he would invariably reply: "I am still looking for *tendresse.*" Sand, op. cit., I, pp. 717–18.
5. *Vallée Noire*, Black Valley, was the name given by George Sand in her pastoral novels to the valley in which Nohant nestles and by which it is known today. *Black* here has the dark, romantic sense of the German Black Forest.
6. Sand, op. cit., I, p. 605 and passim.

Chapter 5 From Deviltry to Piety and Back

1. George Sand, *Oeuvres autobiographiques*, 2 vols., (Paris 1970–71), I, p. 944.
2. Abbé F.-M.-Th. Cédoz, *Un couvent de religieuses anglaises à Paris de 1634 à 1884.* (Paris, 1891).
3. Sand, op. cit., I, p. 870.
4. Ibid., p. 865.
5. George Sand, *Correspondance*, 11 vols. (Paris, 1964–76), I, pp. 15–21.
6. Sand, *Oeuvres autobiographiques*, I, p. 867 and passim.
7. André Maurois, *Lélia* (Paris, 1952), p. 42.
8. Sand, Ibid., p. 900 and passim.
9. A strikingly appropriate comment of Virginia Woolf, author of the long essay on women as writers, *A Room of One's Own*, is quoted by Raymond Mortimer in *The Sunday Times* of London, Oct. 22, 1972. To quote it in full: "A writer is a writer from his cradle; in his dealings with the world, in his affections, in his attitudes to the thousand small things that happen between dawn and sunset, he shows the same point of view as that which he elaborates afterwards with a pen in his hand." *His* would be more properly written *his/her*, if it were not so awkward.
10. Sand, op. cit., I, p. 944.
11. From a notebook of George Sand at the Bibliothèque Nationale, Paris, N.a.fr. 13641. Cf. Sand, op. cit., I, pp. 1425–26.
12. Sand, op. cit., I, p. 946 and passim.

Chapter 6 The View from the Saddle

1. George Sand, *Oeuvres autobiographiques*, 2 vols., (Paris, 1970–71), I, p. 1032.

2. Ibid., p. 1011 and passim.

3. Edmond Plauchut, *Autour de Nohant* (Paris, 1898), p. 14. George Sand's friend Plauchut could still read the penciled lines on the window sill at the century's end, when he revisited Nohant. G.S.'s notebook: Bibliothèque Nationale, Paris. N.a.fr. 13641.

4. George Sand, *Correspondance*, 11 vols. (Paris, 1964–76), I, p. 32.

5. Ibid., p. 54.

6. Sand, *Oeuvres autobiographiques*, I, p. 1043.

7. Sand, *Impressions et souvenirs* (Paris, 1896), p. 132.

8. Sand, *Oeuvres autobiographiques*, I, p. 1056.

9. Sand, *Correspondance*, II, p. 861.

10. Sand, *Oeuvres autobiographiques*, I, pp. 1060–61.

11. Ibid., p. 1026 and passim.

12. Sand, *Correspondance*, I, p. 69.

13. Cf. Ferdinand Denis, *Journal* (Fribourg, Switzerland, 1932), pp. 63–69.

14. Sand, *Correspondance*, I, pp. 212–13.

15. Sand, *Oeuvres autobiographiques*, I, pp. 1072 and 1074.

16. Ibid., p. 1045.

17. Sand, *Correspondance*, I, pp. 74–79.

18. Letter, dated Nov. 23, 1821, in the George Sand Museum, La Châtre.

19. Sand, *Oeuvres autobiographiques*, I, p. 1106 and passim.

Chapter 7 Marriage in Haste

1. George Sand, *Oeuvres autobiographiques*, 2 vols., (Paris, 1970–71) I, p. 1120.

2. Ibid., p. 1122.

3. Ibid., pp. 1123–25. Cf. George Sand, *Correspondance*, 11 vols., (Paris, 1964–76), I, pp. 218–19.

4. Ibid., pp. 1127–29.

5. Letter, Bibliothèque Spoelberch de Lovenjoul, E 936. Cf. George Lubin's note, Sand, *Oeuvres autobiographiques*, II, pp. 1305–06.

6. Sand, *Oeuvres autobiographiques*, II, p. 8 and passim.

7. Sand, *Correspondance*, I, pp. 198–99. Letters to Aurélien de Sèze and Casimir Dudevant at this time (Oct. 11–end Nov. 1825) were collected and incompletely published by Aurore Lauth-Sand, George Sand's granddaughter, as *Le roman d'Aurore Dudevant et d'Aurélien de Sèze* (Paris, 1928). André Maurois has referred to them somewhat loosely in his *Lélia* as Aurore's *Journal*.

8. Sand, *Oeuvres autobiographiques*, II, p. 17.

9. Ibid., p. 13 and passim.

10. Scene and conversation constructed almost word for word from George Sand's memoirs. Cf. Ibid., p. 25.

11. *Revue de l'Agenais*, 1876, pp. 432–33. Cf. Louise Vincent, *George Sand et le Berry*, 2 vols. (Paris, 1919), I, 68–69.

12. Sand, *Correspondance*, I, p. 92.

13. Sand, *Oeuvres autobiographiques*, II, pp. 25–27.

14. Bibliothèque Nationale, N.a.fr. 13641 fol. 8. Aurore to her notebook, Sunday, June 2: "Unbelievabe happiness—days of joy!"

15. Sand, op. cit., II, p. 31.

16. Ibid, p. 31.

Chapter 8 Ennui

1. George Sand, *Correspondance*, 11 vols., (Paris, 1964–76) I, p. 270.

2. Bibliothèque Spoelberch de Lovenjoul, Chantilly, E 869, f. 3. Casimir would spend half his wedding settlement on Aurore's "caprices." Sand, op. cit., I, 269. After deducting 3,000 francs a year for Sophie from Nohant's revenues, another 2,000 for Deschartres and pensioned old servants, there remained about 7,000 francs for the young couple. Cf. Louise Vincent, *George Sand et le Berry*, 2 vols. (Paris, 1919), I, p. 75.

3. Sand, op. cit., I, pp. 103–05.

4. Ibid., VI, p. 43. Citing this letter, André Maurois wrote, "Aurore was seized with horror of physical union"—and he made it central in the story of her life. Maurois, *Lélia, ou la vie de George Sand* (Paris, 1952), p. 79.

5. George Sand, *Oeuvres autobiographiques*, 2 vols., (Paris, 1970–71), II, p. 37.

6. Bibliothèque Historique de la Ville de Paris (Fonds Sand, D 216). Cf. Sand, op. cit., II, pp. 1312–13.

7. Sand, *Correspondance*, I, pp. 108 and 112.

8. See Note 4, above. See also Curtis Cate, *George Sand* (Boston, 1975), p. 97.

9. One must temper George Sand's coolish memoirs of a later date with her letters of that earlier time. If history, in Voltaire's view, is a series of tricks we play on the dead, then George Sand's *Histoire de ma vie* is the conscious gamesmanship of one dealing with a long-dead marriage.

10. Sand, *Correspondance*, I, pp. 115 and 117–18.

11. Ibid., pp. 267–68. From the "confessional letter" to Casimir Dudevant, Nov. 9, 1825 (pp. 262–92).

12. Heinrich Heine, *Gesammelte werke* (Berlin, 1893), 9 vols., VII, p. 162. The fragment is dated 1854. By "pagoda," Heine characteristically meant "Buddha" or "Buddha-like."

13. Sand, op. cit., I, p. 127.

14. Sand, *Oeuvres autobiographiques*, II, p. 39.

15. Sand, *Correspondance*, I, p. 270.

16. Ibid., pp. 137–39, 143–45 and 149.

17. Bibliothèque Lovenjoul, E 868, ff. 195, 197–98.

18. Sand, op. cit., III, p. 135. From letter, dated Nov. 15, 1835.

19. Idem.

20. Sand, *Oeuvres autobiographiques*, II, pp. 42, 48 and 49–50.

21. Sand, *Correspondance*, I, pp. 269–70.

22. Sand, *Oeuvres autobiographiques*, II, pp. 58–59. The journal itself, *Voyage aux Pyrénées*, has disappeared, other than as quoted by Sand in *Histoire de ma vie*. There is little doubt that it had existed. Cf. Letter to Zoé Leroy, dated Sept. 5, 1825, in which Sand refers to Zoé's having read it. Sand, *Correspondance*, I, p. 168.

Chapter 9 Half a Life Plus Half a Life Equals Half a Life

1. From memory.
2. George Sand, *Oeuvres autobiographiques*, 2 vols., (Paris, 1970–71), II, pp. 62, 64–65.
3. Ibid., p. 61.
4. George Sand, *Le roman d'Aurore Dudevant et d'Aurélien de Sèze* (Paris, 1928), p. viii. From the preface by G.S.'s granddaughter, Aurore Lauth-Sand.
5. Bibliothèque Spoelberch de Lovenjoul, Chantilly, E 902, f. 24.
6. George Sand, *Correspondance*, 11 vols., (Paris, 1964–76), I, p. 240.
7. Ibid., p. 244.
8. Ibid., p. 277. From the "confessional letter" to Casimir, Nov. 15, 1825 (pp. 262–92).
9. Ibid., p. 245. From a letter to Aurélien de Sèze, Nov. 11, 1825.
10. Ibid., pp. 278–79.
11. Ibid., pp. 171–72.
12. Ibid., p. 281.
13 Ibid., p. 193. From a letter to Aurélien reminding him of the scene, Oct. 17, 1825.
14. Ibid., pp. 282–85.
15. Ibid., pp. 181 and 183. From a letter to Aurélien, Oct. 13, 1825.
16. Ibid., p. 226.
17. Ibid., p. 183.
18. Ibid., pp. 175–76, 182, 192 and 280.
19. Ibid., p. 231. Letter to Aurélien, Nov. 8, 1825.
20. Henry James in *The North American Review*, Jan.–June 1902, p. 544.
21. Sand, *Le roman d'Aurore Dudevant* . . . , pp. 122–24.
22. Sand, *Correspondance*, I, p. 227 and passim.
23. Bibliothèque Lovenjoul, E 868, ff. 209–10.
24. Ibid., ff. 217–23.
25. Sand, op. cit., I, pp. 294–95.
26. Ibid., pp. 262–92.
27. Louise Vincent, *George Sand et le Berry*, 2 vols. (Paris, 1919), I, p. 97. Told to the author by a Gascon gentleman, Jules Nimes.
28. Bibliothèque Lovenjoul, E 868, f. 227.

Chapter 10 Aurore's Aeolian Web

1. George Sand, *Correspondance*, edited by Maurice Sand, 6 vols. (Paris, 1882–92), V, p. 237.
2. George Sand, *Correspondance*, edited by Georges Lubin, 11 vols.

(Paris, 1964–76), I, p. 329. (Lubin edition hereafter, unless otherwise indicated.)

3. George Sand, *Oeuvres autobiographiques*, 2 vols., (Paris, 1970–71), II, p. 94.

4. George Sand, "Nuit d'hiver" in Ibid., pp. 545–51.

5. George Sand, "Lettres d'un voyageur" in Ibid., pp. 799–800, 802.

6. Sand, *Correspondance*, I, p. 418.

7. Ibid., p. 363. Letter to Zoé Leroy, Oct. 10(?), 1826.

8. Bibliothèque Historique de la Ville de Paris (Fonds Sand, G 447, 448, 452).

9. Sand, op. cit., I, pp. 383–85.

10. Samuel Rocheblave, "George Sand avant George Sand" in *La Revue de Paris*, Paris, Mar 15, 1896, pp. 342–83.

11. Sand, *Oeuvres autobiographiques*, II, p. 99.

12. Sand, "Voyage en Auvergne" in Ibid., pp. 503–11.

13. Ibid., pp. 520–27.

14. Louise Vincent, *George Sand et le Berry*, 2 vols. (Paris, 1919), I, pp. 216–17.

15. Sand, *Correspondance*, I, p. 399.

16. *Le Moniteur Général* (unofficial organ of the *Service des Travaux de la Ville de Paris*), Paris, Jan. 6, 1900, p. 4. Director of this publication was Stéphane de Grandsagne's son, Paul-Émile (1842–1902). In reply to a reader's query, he published the following:

"As we have said, we have in our possession 123 unpublished letters of [George Sand], written between 1820 and 1838. . . . In the Berry, everyone knew, in effect, that from the age of sixteen or seventeen, Aurore Dupin for several years was, how should I say it, the *very intimate* friend [original emphasis] of Stéphane Ajasson de Grandsagne, creator of Public Libraries in France.

"The letters in question are very interesting, but too strange to be published. If known, they would upset all the views generally held of this distinguished woman who was one of the glories of the literature of our century. . . .

"The Director of *Le Moniteur Général* [Stéphane's son, writing this note] often saw George Sand between 1858 and 1876 [when she died] at Nohant, Paris and Palaiseau. Several times she expressed the desire that her correspondence with Stéphane should never be made public.

"And since you do us the honor of asking us our private and personal opinion, we should like to reply that G. Sand was, all in all, a good girl to begin with and a good woman thereafter, always very simple, if too natural, having done a great deal of good and a great deal of evil during the course of her long life (everything depends, of course, on the point of view one takes!) and despite everything, a superior being whom one must generously forgive for her monstrously wild ways, since she succumbed throughout her life with great stoicism, indeed *too stoically*, and with admirable serenity(!) [exclamation in text; one might translate *sérénité* here as complacency] and with a philosophy unknown to our generation at the end of the century, to very *numerous* attacks of that *serious and incurable* physiological affliction to which doctors have given a name beginning with N."

Thus a gentleman of almost sixty at the turn of the century attributed N(ymphomania) to George Sand, an accusation to which there will be more than one occasion to return. Meantime one might academically note that *nymphomanie* was first used in France in 1732 (to describe a behavior normally reserved for men). *Fureur utérine* was more frequently used before the Revolution, as in pamphlets attacking Marie Antoinette.

17. Sand, *Correspondance*, I, pp. 403–04, 411–12, 414–19 and 420–24.

18. Sand, *Oeuvres autobiographiques*, II, p. 90.

19. "Proof" of Stéphane's paternity of the child to be called Solange is necessarily circumstantial. Stéphane's son, in the same issue of *Le Moniteur Général* (see Note 16, above), pointedly remarks that in Aurore's correspondence with his father, "the question of Solange came up more than once." Another descendant asserts the paternity in his history of the Grandsagnes.

In research for her doctoral thesis, Louise Vincent (op. cit., I, p. 122) heard confirming stories in the Berry: "When Stéphane de Grandsagne used to go to Nohant, and his friends teased him about it, he would say: 'Why not? I am going to see my daughter!' Madame Dudevant herself often called her daughter, 'Mademoiselle Stéphane.' " Mlle. Vincent does not conceal her own sympathy for Casimir vis-à-vis George Sand.

20. Sand, *Correspondance*, I, p. 438.

21. Bibliothèque Lovenjoul, Chantilly, E 902, f. 108.

22. BHVP, Fonds Sand, G 5351, ff. 193–95.

23. Sand, *Oeuvres autobiographiques*, II, p. 90.

24. Lovenjoul, E 902, ff. 113 and 115.

25. Sand, *Correspondance*, I, p. 493.

26. Vincent, op. cit., I, p. 218.

27. Sand, op. cit., I, p. 511.

28. Ibid., p. 510. Letter to Charles Meure, Feb. 7, 1829.

29. Vincent, op. cit., I, p. 122.

30. Lovenjoul, E 948, f. 40. Casimir's notes for the separation trial of 1836.

31. Sand, op. cit., I, p. 566.

32. Camille Pitollet, "George Sand et le précepteur de ses enfants, Jules Boucoiran" in *La Grande Revue*, Paris, Jan. 1926, p. 411. Also, Aurore's letter to Boucoiran, Sept. 13, 1830, recalling the period, Sand, op. cit., I, p. 700.

33. Cf. Vincent, op. cit., I, pp. 103–04.

34. Sand, op. cit., I, pp. 582–83.

35. Ibid., p. 483. Letter to Caron, Dec. 4, 1828.

36. From only chapter published, *La Revue de Paris*, Paris, May 15, 1895, p. 226.

37. Sand, *Oeuvres autobiographiques*, II, p. 101.

38. Ibid., pp. 105–06.

39. Sand, *Correspondance*, I, pp. 636–47.

Chapter 11 Closing a Door Opens a Door: Vive la Liberté!

1. George Sand, *Correspondance*, 11 vols. (Paris, 1964–76), I, p. 738. Letter to Jules Boucoiran, Dec. 1 or 3, 1830.

2. Henrik Ibsen, *A Doll's House* (Everyman edition) (New York, 1910), p. 86. On Oct. 11, 1895, Ibsen wrote literary critic George Brandes: "I hereby swear on my honor and conscience that I have never in my whole life, neither in my youth nor later, read a single book by George Sand. I once began *Consuelo* in translation, but put it aside. . . ." His wife, Suzannah, however, read *Consuelo*, a major Sand novel, "almost annually." Cf. Michael Meyer, *Ibsen, a Biography* (New York, 1971), pp. 464 and 741. After the first production of *A Doll's House* in France (Paris, 1894), Réjane performing as Nora, Émile Zola declared, according to the Goncourts, that Ibsen had "sprung from French Romanticism, especially George Sand." Ibid., p. 716.

3. Sand, op. cit., I, pp. 818 and 921.

4. James Joyce, *A Portrait of the Artist as a Young Man* (London, 1932), p. 288. First published in 1916. How mind-teasing to substitute "sex" for "race."

5. Sand, op. cit., I, pp. 683–89.

6. Jules Sandeau, *Marianna*, 2 vols. (Paris, 1839), I, pp. 46–47. Autobiographical novel.

7. From Charles Duvernet's memoirs, still in manuscript, as quoted in Mabel Silver's doctoral thesis, *Jules Sandeau, l'homme et la vie* (Paris, 1936), p. 22.

8. Sand, op. cit., I, p. 683.

9. Cf. Théophile Gautier, *Histoire du romantisme* (Paris, 1874), pp. 1–114.

10. Karl Marx, *Die klassenkampfe in frankreich* (Berlin, 1920), p. 24. "After the July Revolution, when the liberal banker, Lafitte, led his crony, the Duke of Orleans, in triumph to the Hôtel de Ville, he let fall the words: 'From now on the bankers will rule.' Lafitte had betrayed the secret of the revolution."

11. Sand, op. cit., I, p. 691. Letter to Charles Meure, Aug. 15, 1830.

12. Sandeau, op. cit., I, p. 45.

13. Sand, op. cit., I, p. 877. Letter to Émile Regnault, May 25(?), 1831.

14. Idem.

15. Sandeau, op. cit., I, p. 45.

16. Sand, op. cit., I, p. 722.

17. Ibid., p. 721.

18. Ibid., pp. 740–43.

19. Ibid., pp. 736–37. No one other than George Sand has ever referred to Casimir's "testament," and no copy exists as confirmation. It is unmentioned in subsequent correspondence, even between Aurore and Casimir. Yet one tends to believe it existed (Georges Lubin is in agreement with the author), if only because George Sand refers in her letter about it to Casimir's "*réflexions*" about her "*perversité*," scarcely a flattering phrase.

The "testament" is not alluded to in Sand's *Histoire de ma vie,* written for the public.

20. Ibid., p. 738.
21. Ibid., p. 752.
22. Ibid., p. 762. Letter to Félix Pyat, Dec., 1830.
23. George Sand, *Oeuvres autobiographiques,* 2 vols., (Paris, 1970–71), II, p. 108.
24. Sand, *Correspondance,* I, p. 763.

Chapter 12 A Season in Paris

1. Jules Sandeau, *Marianna,* 2 vols. (Paris, 1839), I, pp. 115–16.
2. Cf. Félix Pyat's colorful—and colored—"*souvenirs*" in *La Revue de Paris et de Saint-Pétersbourg,* Paris.
3. The old building at 31 Rue de Seine now houses the Academy of Raymond Duncan, late brother of the more famous Isadora.
4. André Billy, *Vie de Balzac,* 2 vols. (Paris, 1944), I, p. 116.
5. George Sand, *Correspondance,* 11 vols. (Paris, 1964–76), I, p. 887.
6. George Sand, *Oeuvres autobiographiques,* 2 vols., (Paris, 1970–71), II, p. 135.
"The central image of a young man from the provinces going out into the world on a symbolic journey of self-discovery is the dominating image of our literature and it is, of necessity, a male image." Vivian Gornick, "Toward a definition of the female sensibility," *Village Voice,* New York, May 31, 1973.
"One of the provinces . . . is womanhood." Carolyn Heilbrun, "The masculine wilderness of the American novel," *Saturday Review,* New York, Jan. 29, 1972.
7. Bibliothèque Historique de la Ville de Paris (Fonds Sand, G 4404).
8. Today's *Figaro* reassures the bourgeois at his breakfast table that he lives in the best of all possible, if declining, worlds.
9. George Sand, Introduction to Henri de Latouche, *La vallée aux loups* (Paris, 1875), p. iii. Written in 1851.
10. Charles-Augustin Sainte-Beuve, *Causeries du lundi,* 7 vols. (Paris, 1852–54), III, p. 372.
11. Sand, Introduction to Latouche, op. cit., p.v.
12. From Duvernet's memoirs, as quoted in Mabel Silver, *Jules Sandeau, l'homme et la vie* (Paris, 1936), p. 28.
13. Sand, *Correspondance,* I, p. 783.
14. Sand, *Oeuvres autobiographiques,* II, p. 151.
15. Ibid., p. 148.
16. Sand, *Correspondance,* I, p. 826. The "monsters" referred to specifically are characters in two Balzac short stories, "*Sarrasine*" and "*Une passion dans le désert.*"
17. Sand, *Oeuvres autobiographiques,* II, pp. 149–50.
18. Sand, *Correspondance,* I, pp. 800–01. Letter to Boucoiran, Feb. 12, 1831.
19. Duvernet quoting Latouche in his memoirs, Mabel Silver, op. cit., p. 29.

20. Sand, Introduction to Latouche, op. cit., p. vii.

21. Sand, *Oeuvres autobiographiques*, II, p. 152.

22. Frédéric Ségu, *Le premier Figaro* (Paris, 1932), pp. 50–51.

23. Sand, *Correspondance*, I, p. 823. Letter to Duvernet, Mar. 6, 1831.

24. Ibid., p. 825. Letter to Boucoiran, Mar. 7, 1831.

25. Ibid., p. 784. Letter to Duvernet, Jan. 19, 1831.

26. From chapter of *La Marraine*, published in *La Revue de Paris*, Paris, May 15, 1895, p. 230.

27. Sand, *Correspondance*, I, p. 817. Letter to Boucoiran, Mar. 4, 1831.

28. Ibid., p. 888. Letter to Sophie, May 31, 1831. Written after the return to Nohant.

29. Ibid., pp. 829–30.

30. Ibid., p. 824. Hippolyte's letter is quoted by Aurore in her letter to Boucoiran, Mar. 7, 1831.

Chapter 13 Between Identities

1. George Sand, *Correspondance*, 11 vols. (Paris, 1964–76), I, p. 862.

2. Ibid., pp. 837 and 855.

3. Ibid., p. 888. See Chap. 12, Note 28.

4. Honoré de Balzac, *Correspondance*, 5 vols. (Paris, 1960–69), I, pp. 522–23.

5. Sand, op. cit., I, p. 858.

6. Ibid., pp. 875, 878, 881–82, 907 and 912.

7. Bibliothèque Lovenjoul, Chantilly, E 868, f. 236.

8. Sand, op. cit., I, pp. 913, 919 and 921.

9. Lovenjoul, E 868 ff. 238–39.

10. George Sand, *Oeuvres autobiographiques*, 2 vols., (Paris, 1970–71), II, p. 154.

11. Sand, *Correspondance*, I, p. 939.

12. *Histoire de ma vie* hereafter becomes even less reliable, though occasionally quotable for its afterthoughts. We know the story of the night in September, thanks to two letters which Gustave Papet and Émile Regnault failed "to burn"—as Aurore so often adjured them. There is whisper of it in Sand's memoirs.

13. Sand, *Correspondance*, I, pp. 944–46, 953, and 955–63.

14. Ibid., p. 972. Letter to her friend, Laure Decerfz of La Châtre, Oct. 28, 1831.

15. Sand, *Oeuvres autobiographiques*, II, p. 156.

16. Sand, *Correspondance*, I, pp. 980–81.

17. Bibliothèque Historique de la Ville de Paris (Fonds Sand, G 86).

18. Sand, op. cit., I, pp. 990–91.

19. Sand, op. cit., II, pp. 41–42.

20. J(ules) Sand, *Rose et Blanche, ou la comédienne et la religieuse*, 5 vols. (Paris, 1831), V, p. 258. The volumes are small and thin.

Chapter 14 Aurore Becomes George

1. Virginia Woolf, *A Room of One's Own* (London, 1970), p. 52. Penguin edition. First published in 1928.

2. George Sand, *Correspondance*, 11 vols. (Paris, 1964–76), II, pp. 12–13.

3. Ibid., p. 25.

4. Ibid., p. 36.

5. Ibid., p. 42. Letter to Sophie, in which Aurore explains the "shocking" elements of *Rose et Blanche* and announces she is writing her own novel.

6. Ibid., pp. 43–46.

7. Ibid., pp. 47–48. Letter to Regnault, Feb. 27, 1832.

8. Cf. Carolyn G. Heilbrun, *Toward a Recognition of Androgyny* (New York, 1973), p. 49. Ms. Heilbrun, in her admirable study: "The birth of the woman as Hero occurred, insofar as one may date such an event, in 1880, when almost at the same moment Ibsen and James invented her." The study is based (as the author indicates) almost exclusively on English and American literature. Ibsen and James, as we shall very shortly see, were preceded by George Sand.

9. Sand, op. cit., II, p. 50.

10. Marie-Louise Pailleron, *George Sand*, 3 vols. (Paris, 1938–53), II, pp. 58–61.

11. Sand, op. cit., II, p. 65.

12. George Sand, *Oeuvres autobiographiques*, 2 vols. (Paris, 1970–71), II, p. 141.

13. Sand, *Correspondance*, II, pp. 71–73.

14. Sand, *Oeuvres autobiographiques*, II, p. 138.

15. Idem.

16. Ibid., p. 139.

17. Cf. Lubin note, Ibid., p. 1336.

18. When Marian (or Mary Ann) Evans in turn was to choose the pen name, George Eliot, it was in homage to her companion George Henry Lewes, who happened also to be an admirer of George Sand as a writer. But there may well have been a companionly bow to George Sand in Eliot's choice. Jane Carlyle and other English contemporaries often referred to Eliot as "our George." Lawrence and Elisabeth Hanson, *Marian Evans and George Eliot* (London, 1952), p. 234.

19. Sand, op. cit., II, pp. 173–74.

20. Bibliothèque Historique de la Ville de Paris (Fonds Sand, G 4409).

21. Sand, op. cit., II, p. 202.

22. George Sand, *Indiana* (Paris, 1962), p. 9. Edited and annotated by Pierre Salomon, this Garnier edition is the most satisfactory and complete.

23. Sand, *Oeuvres autobiographiques*, II, p. 174. Eminently quotable in this context as well (Heilbrun, op. cit., pp. 73–74) is the British *Economist's* review of George Eliot's *Adam Bede* in 1859 by a gentleman unaware of the fact that George Eliot was a woman:

"Novel-writing has of late years devolved so largely upon women that it is quite rare to meet with a well-matured and carefully executed novel by a man of genius. In novels written by women, the exaltation and predominance of one class of feelings, and the slight and inadequate treatment of all that lies beyond their immediate influence, make even the best of them seem disproportionate and unreal. . . . Novels written by men are nearly always more in keeping with the actual world, have a wider outlook, and embrace a greater personal sort of knowledge to be gained from them; when they are original and clever and artistically constructed, they are more delightful as well as more profitable than the best novels by women. *Adam Bede* is one of the best of this class of novels."

24. André Maurois, *Lélia* (Paris, 1952), p. 148.

25. One aspect of traditional marriage had long been under attack, as in Bernardin de Saint-Pierre's immensely popular *Paul et Virginie*, 1789: "How does one become the tyrant of women? By marrying them without consulting them." One might note that this had not been the case of Casimir and Aurore.

26. Sand, *Indiana*, pp. 23–24.

27. Ibid., p. 136.

28. Planche, *Revue des Deux Mondes*, Dec. 15, 1832; Sainte-Beuve, *Le National*, Oct. 5, 1832.

Chapter 15 Blood, Sand and Partings

1. George Sand, *Correspondance*, 11 vols. (Paris, 1964–76), II, p. 105.

2. Jules Sandeau, *Marianna*, 2 vols. (Paris, 1839), II p. 201.

3. *The New Cambridge Modern History*, 12 vols. (London, 1957–60), IX, p. 358.

4. George Sand, *Oeuvres autobiographiques*, 2 vols., (Paris, 1970–71), II, p. 143 and passim.

5. Sand, *Correspondance*, II, pp. 103–04. Letter to Laure Decerfz, June 13, 1832. Same as Note 1, above

6. Ibid., p. 105.

7. Jules Janin in *Journal des Débats*, Paris, July 9, 1832.

8. Sand, op. cit., II, p. 120.

9. Sandeau, op. cit., II, p. 174.

10. Bibliothèque Lovenjoul, F 1031, ff. 175–76.

11. Lovenjoul, F 1031, f. 176.

12. Sandeau, op. cit., II, p. 177.

13. Sand, "Sketches and hints" in *Oeuvres autobiographiques*, II, pp. 591–92.

14. Ibid., p. 593.

15. Sand, *Correspondance*, II, pp. 170–71.

16. Ibid., pp. 179 and 183.

17. Sandeau, op. cit., II, pp. 191–92.

18. Ibid., p. 182.

19. Sand, *Oeuvres autobiographiques*, II, p. 153.

20. As quoted in Frédéric Ségu, *Un romantique républicain: H. de Latouche, 1785–1851* (Paris, 1931), pp. 446–47.

21. Sand, *Correspondance*, II, p. 193.

22. Lovenjoul, A 316 f. 101.

23. Sandeau, op. cit., II, p. 185 and passim. Sandeau, in his novel, has the grace not to give himself the heroic role and the intelligence to describe both lovers from within.

24. Maurice Regard, *Gustave Planche*, 2 vols. (Paris, 1955), I, p. 9.

25. Bibliothèque Historique de la Ville de Paris (Fonds Sand, G 5 169).
26. As quoted in Regard, op. cit., II, p. 63. Vol. II of this biography is lanche's correspondence.
27. Ibid., p. 69.

Chapter 16 Women in Love

1. George Sand, "Sketches and Hints" in *Oeuvres autobiographiques*, 2 ols. (Paris, 1970–71), II, p. 598. A leather album of G.S. at the ibliothèque Nationale, metal-clasped, bears this English title of a collection of odds and ends, some of which have been published under the misading title *Journal intime (posthume)* (Paris, 1926).
2. Cf. Pierre Reboul's introduction to George Sand, *Lélia* (Paris, 1960), p. xxxix and xl. This scholarly edition contains both complete versions of and's novel.
3. George Sand, *La Marquise, Lavinia*, etc. (Brussels, 1842), pp. 29 and 2. Originally published in *La Revue de Paris*, Dec. 1832.
4. George Sand, *Questions d'art et de littérature* (Paris, 1878), pp. 62–3.
5. Sand, *Oeuvres autobiographiques*, II, p. 228. The last passionate tribte in G.S.'s memoirs is to Marie Dorval, p. 461.
6. Alfred de Vigny, *Le journal d'un poète*, Conard edition, (Paris, 1935), . 223.
7. Ibid., pp. 173–74.
8. George Sand, *Correspondance*, 11 vols. (Paris, 1964–76), II, p. 242.
9. Ibid., pp. 248, 249 and 251.
10. Marie Dorval, *Lettres à Alfred de Vigny* (Paris, 1942), p. 29.
11. Vigny, op. cit., p. 157.
12. As quoted in Simone André-Maurois' introduction to *Correspondance* rédite of George Sand and Marie Dorval (Paris, 1953), p. 31.
13. Vigny, op. cit., pp. 239–40.
14. Sand, *Correspondance*, II, p. 290.
15. Arsène Houssaye, *Les confessions, souvenirs d'un demi-siècle*, 6 vols. Paris, 1885–91), II, pp. 13–14.
16. Ibid., IV, p. 263.
17. Sand, *Oeuvres autobiographiques*, II, pp. 617–18. "Sketches and Iints."
18. Paul de Musset, *Lui et elle* (Paris, 1886). First published in 1860, llowing George Sand's *Elle et lui*.
19. Sand, *Correspondance*, II, pp. 272–73.
20. Honoré de Balzac, *Lettres à Madame Hanska*, 4 vols. (Paris, 967–71), I, pp. 43–44 and 52.
21. Ibid., pp. 256 and 394.
22. Houssaye, op. cit., IV, pp. 330 and 331.
23. *Les belles femmes de Paris et de la province*, 2 vols. (Paris, 1839–40), I, pp. 384 and 388. Collective work by Balzac, Gautier, Nerval, Sandeau, t al.
24. Ibid., p. 186.

Chapter 17 The Existential Spring of George Sand: Lélia Unlocks Her Heart

1. George Sand, *Correspondance*, 11 vols. (Paris, 1964–76), II, p. 374.

2. Ibid., III, p. 403.

3. Letter, Aug. 16, 1833, as quoted in Marie-Louise Pailleron, *George Sand*, 3 vols. (Paris, 1938–53), I, p. 206.

4. Cf. Pierre Reboul's introduction, George Sand, *Lélia* (Paris, 1960), p. xliv.

5. Jane Austen, too, had to reshape the male sentence she had found— "and laughed at"—for her own purpose and use. Virginia Woolf, *A Room of One's Own* (London, 1970), p. 77. "The weight, the pace, the stride of a man's mind," Woolf added, "are too unlike her own for [the woman writer] to lift anything substantial from him successfully. . . . The novel alone was young enough to be soft in her hands—another reason, perhaps, why she wrote novels," pp. 76–77.

6. Charles-Augustin Sainte-Beuve, *Mes poisons* (Paris, 1926), p. 106.

7. Sand, op. cit., II, pp. 274–75.

8. Ibid., p. 277.

9. Sainte-Beuve, *Correspondance générale*, 15 vols. (Paris, 1935–64), I, p. 347.

10. Sand, op. cit., II, pp. 277–78. See Lubin note 2.

11. Prosper Mérimée, *Correspondance générale*, 6 vols. (Paris, 1941–58), I, pp. 228–29.

12. Armand de Pontmartin, *Mes mémoires*, 2 vols. (Paris, 1885–86), II, p. 66.

13. Cf. Maurice Parturier, *Une expérience de Lélia, ou le fiasco du Comte Gazul* (Paris, 1934). A flimsy, 30-page book on the George Sand-Prosper Mérimée ("Comte Gazul") affair.

14. George Sand, "Sketches and Hints" in *Oeuvres autobiographiques*, 2 vols. (Paris, 1970–71), II, p. 609.

15. Sand, *Correspondance*, II, pp. 374–75. Letter, July 24(?), 1833.

16. Henry James, *Notes on Novelists* (New York, 1914), pp. 164–65. Written in 1897.

17. Prosper Mérimée, *La double méprise* (Paris, 1885), pp. 37–38. Originally published in 1833.

18. Sand, op. cit., II, pp. 376–77. Same letter as in Note 15.

19. Sand, *Lélia*. Same edition as in Note 4, above, containing the original version as well as G.S.'s auto-censored revision of 1839. All references are to the original version, particularly pp. 145–204.

20. The unsustainable thesis of Curtis Cate, *George Sand* (Boston, 1975), p. xxvii.

21. For centuries, wrote Virginia Woolf, women have served men "as looking-glasses possessing the magic and delicious power of reflecting the figure of man at twice its natural size." It explained in part the need men often have for women. "And it serves to explain how restless they are under

her criticism. . . . For if she begins to tell the truth, the figure in the looking-glass shrinks; his fitness for life is diminished." It is at this point the man reproaches the woman *her* unfitness for love. Op. cit., p. 37.

22. Capo de Feuillide, *Europe Littéraire*, Aug. 9–22, 1833.
23. Sand, *Correspondance*, II, pp. 369–71. Letter, July 24, 1833.

Chapter 18 *The Cracked Brilliance of Musset*

1. As quoted in Paul Mariéton, *Une histoire d'amour: les amants de Venise: George Sand et Musset* (Paris, 1903), p. 3.
2. Henri Lefebvre, *Musset: essai* (Paris, 1970), pp. 26–27.
3. Charles-Augustin Sainte-Beuve, *Causeries du lundi*, 15 vols. (Paris, 1857–72), p. 298.
4. Alfred de Musset, *La confession d'un enfant du siècle* (Paris, 1968), p. 20. Originally published in 1836.
5. Paul de Musset, *Biographie d'Alfred de Musset* (Paris, 1877), p. 22.
6. Alfred de Musset, *Correspondance* (Paris, 1907), pp. 11–12 and 16. Letters to Paul Foucher, Sept. 23 and Oct. 19, 1827.
7. Alfred de Musset, *Poésies*, 2 vols. (Paris, 1881), I, p. 1.
8. Paul de Musset, op. cit., p. 78.
9. Alfred de Musset, *La confession d'un enfant du siècle*, pp. 86 and 89.
10. Paul de Musset, op. cit., p. 86.
11. Maurice Allem, *Alfred de Musset* (Paris, 1947), p. 27.
12. Ibid., p. 38.

Chapter 19 *The Pen-crossed Lovers*

1. Paul de Musset, *Lui et elle* (Paris, 1886), pp. 79–80. Originally published in 1860.
2. George Sand, *Elle et lui* (Paris, 1859), p. 56. Originally published in 1859.
3. Paul de Musset, op. cit., p. 60.
4. George Sand-Alfred de Musset, *Correspondance*, Evrard edition (Paris, 1956), p. 22.
5. Ibid., p. 19.
6. Alfred de Musset, *Poésies complètes* (Paris, 1957), pp. 512–13.
7. George Sand, *Correspondance*, 11 vols. (Paris, 1964–76), II, pp. 340–41.
8. Paul de Musset, op. cit., pp. 77–78.
9. Sand, op. cit., II, p. 349.
10. Ibid., pp. 351–52.
11. Sand-Musset, op. cit., pp. 77–78.
12. Sand, *Elle et lui*, pp. 30–36 and 58–59.
13. Sand-Musset, op. cit., p. 24.
14. Ibid., pp. 27–28.
15. Ibid., pp. 29–30.
16. Sand, op. cit., p. 87.

17. Alfred de Musset, *La confession d'un enfant du siècle* (Paris, 1968), p. 175.

18. Ibid., p. 34.

19. Sand, op. cit., pp. 109–12. Since childhood, according to his moving poem, *Nuit de Décembre*, Musset had had such hallucinations. A long letter of his mistress in 1849 confirms G.S.'s account in *Elle et lui*, as do the memoirs of the governess-nurse who had cared for Musset the last ten years of his life. Letter, July 17, 1849, of Louise Allan-Despréaux, *Revue de Paris*, 1906, p. 539; see also, p. 546. Adèle Colin Martellet, *Alfred de Musset intime, souvenirs de sa gouvernante* (Paris, 1906), pp. 25, 27 and 127.

20. Sand, op. cit., pp. 115–16.

21. Paul de Musset, *Biographie d'Alfred de Musset* (Paris, 1877), p. 119.

22. Paul Mariéton, *Une histoire d'amour* (Paris, 1903), p. 39.

23. André Maurois, *Lélia, ou la vie de George Sand* (Paris, 1952), p. 191.

24. Capo de Feuillide's reviews of *Lélia* in *Europe Littéraire*, August 9 and 22, 1833.

25. George Sand, *Oeuvres autobiographiques*, 2 vols. (Paris, 1970–71), II, p. 620.

26. Sand, *Correspondance*, II, pp. 406–10.

27. Ibid., pp. 394–96.

28. Paul de Musset, *Lui et elle*, pp. 89–90.

29. George Sand, *Le secrétaire intime* (Paris, 1884), p. 109. Originally published in 1834.

30. Sand, *Oeuvres autobiographiques*, II, pp. 96–97.

31. Sand, *Correspondance*, II, p. 420. Lubin footnote.

32 Ibid., p. 422.

33 Ibid., p. 427.

34. Ibid., p. 447.

35. Paul de Musset, *Biographie d'Alfred de Musset*, pp. 125–26.

36. Maurois, op. cit., p. 194.

Chapter 20 "Is Love of Life a Crime?"

1. Paul de Musset, *Lui et elle* (Paris, 1886), pp. 125–27.

2. George Sand, *Correspondance*, 11 vols. (Paris, 1964–76), II, p. 460.

3. George Sand, *Oeuvres autobiographiques*, 2 vols. (Paris, 1970–71,) II, p. 206.

4. Juliette Adam, *Mes premières armes littéraires et politiques* (Paris, 1904), pp. 292–93.

5. Sand, *Correspondance*, II, p. 730. Letter to Alfred de Musset, end October 1834(?). The handwriting belongs to the period of 1856–60, which is markedly different from that of 1834. Samples are convincingly presented by Georges Lubin in this volume of his edition; see illustrations between pp. 538 and 539. In each of the half-dozen cases involved, Lubin indicates what might be considered authentically original (in view of Musset's responses, for example). In his Introduction to Vol. II, Lubin offers three hypotheses for George Sand's falsification of the incriminating letters: (1) They were damaging to the memory of Musset and third persons (*"version George*

Sand"). (2) They were damaging for G.S. alone. (3) They were damaging for all parties concerned. Lubin strongly supports the third hypothesis as the explanation for G.S.'s rewriting a number of her letters to Pagello and Musset. The author of this biography tends to combine the second and third hypotheses. George at this time was particularly concerned about her public image and the opinion of her two children. In no case is any line or letter of doubtful authenticity quoted in this book without the necessary qualification. The curious might look at Henri Guillemin's *La Liason Musset-Sand* (Paris, 1972) for an example of how far an anti-Sandist might take Lubin's findings, and then read Lubin's refutation in *Revue d'Histoire Littéraire de la France*, Jan.–Feb. 1973, pp. 99–112. The last word is Lubin's.

6. Ibid., p. 495.

7. Pietro Pagello, *Da Parigi a Genova* (Biblioteca Marciana, Venice, Mss. 175 885), as quoted in Paul Mariéton, *Une histoire d'amour: les amants de Venise: George Sand et Musset* (Paris, 1903), p. 83 and passim. See also, Annarosa Poli, *L'Italie dans la vie et dans l'oeuvre de George Sand* (Paris, 1960).

8. Cf. Alfred de Musset, *La confession d'un enfant du siècle* (Paris, 1968), p. 264; and Paul de Musset, op. cit., p. 203.

9. George Sand, "Journal intime," *Oeuvres autobiographiques*, II, p. 955. A fascinating journal of November 1834, sent to Musset and eventually returned to G.S., who most likely destroyed it. A copy, however, was made (1840?) by a Madame Jaubert, to whom Musset had confided it for safe-keeping, and is regarded as sufficiently accurate by Sand scholars, Lubin, et al.

10. Pagello, as quoted in Mariéton, op. cit., p. 92.

11. Sand, *Correspondance*, II, pp. 501–03. For the story of the Sand-Pagello correspondence and its preservation, see Poli, op. cit. (Note 7), pp. 69–73.

12. Pagello, as quoted in Mariéton, op. cit., p. 99.

13. Paul de Musset, op. cit., pp. 215–16.

14. George Sand, *Letters à Alfred de Musset et à Sainte-Beuve* (Paris, 1897). Letter to Sainte-Beuve, Feb. 6, 1861.

15. Sand, "Journal intime," op. cit., p. 957.

16. Idem.

17. George Sand, "Lettres d'un voyageur, I," *Oeuvres autobiographiques*, II, p. 670. Begun in mid-April 1834 and finished May 1, 1834.

18. George Sand-Alfred de Musset, *Correspondance*, Évrard edition (Paris, 1956), pp. 67 and 69.

19. Sand, *Correspondance*, II, p. 522.

20. Ibid., p. 576.

21. Ibid., p. 592.

22. Ibid., p. 626.

23. Sand-Musset, op. cit., pp. 69–71.

24. Sand, op. cit., II, pp. 561–67.

25. Ibid., p. 569.

26. Alfred de Musset, op. cit., pp. 82–83 and 91.

27. Sand, op. cit., II, p. 589.

28. Alfred de Musset, op. cit., pp. 93–94 and 148.
29. George Sand, *Jacques* (Paris, 1887), pp. 36 and 67. Originally written in 1834.
30. Sand, op. cit., II, p. 625.

Chapter 21 Journeys End

1. Pagello, *Da Parigi a Genova*, as quoted in Paul Mariéton, *Une histoire d'amour* . . . (Paris, 1903), p. 183.
2. Ibid., p. 184.
3. George Sand, *Correspondance*, 11 vols. (Paris, 1964–76), II, p. 637.
4. Pagello, as quoted in Mariéton, op. cit., p. 185.
5. Louise Colet, *Lui*, 2nd edition (Paris, 1860), pp. 288–89.
6. Ibid., p. 276.
7. George Sand-Alfred de Musset, *Correspondance*, Évrard edition (Paris, 1956), p. 154.
8. Ibid., p. 159.
9. Sand, op. cit., II, pp. 687 and 690.
10. George Sand, *Oeuvres autobiographiques*, 2 vols. (Paris, 1970–71), II, pp. 737, 752, 1448 and 1453.
11. Sand-Musset op. cit., pp. 61–65.
12. Rather *rewrote*, for we are quoting from another letter recopied and rearranged by G.S. for later publication. Such lines as those at the close in which she "reminds" Musset of his having "joined our hands [in Venice]" —Pagello's and hers—"despite ourselves, saying, 'You love each other, and yet you love me, you have saved me, body and soul!' " thus sanctioning their union, might very well have been added to the original. Sand, *Correspondance*, II, pp. 691–95. Lubin's notes here are invaluable.
13. Sand-Musset, op. cit., pp. 172–73.
14. Pagello, as quoted in Annarosa Poli, *L'Italie dans la vie et dans l'oeuvre de George Sand* (Paris, 1960), p. 147.
15. Alfred de Musset, *La confession d'un enfant du siécle* (Paris, 1968), p. 306.
16. Sand, *Correspondance*, II, pp. 731–32. Another of the rearranged, rewritten letters, the reader is warned.
17. Heinrich Heine, *Sämtliche werke*, 6 vols. (Leipzig, 1887), V, p. 485.
18. Charles-Augustin Sainte-Beuve, *Correspondance générale*, 15 vols. (Paris, 1935–64), I, p. 478.
19. Sand-Musset, op. cit., p. 184.
20. Sand, "Journal intime," *Oeuvres autobiographiques*, II, pp. 954–63. See Chap. 20, Note 9.
21. Ibid., pp. 967–68.
22. Ibid., p. 968.
23. Ibid., p. 969.
24. Sand, *Correspondance*, II, p. 790.
25. Ibid., pp. 800–01.
26. Ibid., p. 815.
27. Henry James, *Notes on Novelists* (New York, 1914), p. 171.
28. Sand-Musset, op. cit., p. 234.

29. Alfred de Musset, *Correspondance* (Paris, 1907), p. 120.
30. Charles-Augustin Sainte-Beuve, *Causeries du lundi*, 15 vols. (Paris, 1857–72), I, p. 302.

Chapter 22 The Republic of Comrades

1. George Sand, *Correspondance*, 11 vols. (Paris, 1964–76), III, p. 326.
2. Sand, op. cit., II, pp. 819–20.
3. Ibid., p. 861.
4. Ibid., p. 784.
5. George Sand, *Oeuvres autobiographiques*, 2 vols. (Paris, 1970–71), II, pp. 293–96.
6. Sand, *Correspondance*, II, p. 825.
7. Sand, *Oeuvres autobiographiques*, II, p. 315.
8. Ibid., pp. 318–21.
9. Sand, *Correspondance*, II, p. 848.
10. Sand, "Lettres d'un voyageur, VI," *Oeuvres autobiographiques*, II, pp. 779–817. All quotations until Note 14 are contained in this "Lettre d'un voyageur" to Michel de Bourges.
11. Sand, *Correspondance*, III, p. 815. Letter to Michel de Bourges, April 28, 1837.
12. Ibid., pp. 659–60.
13. Sand, op. cit., II, p. 855.
14. See Note 10, above.
15. Sand, op. cit., II, p. 876–77.
16. Ibid., p. 887. See footnote 2.
17. Sand, *Oeuvres autobiographiques*, II, p. 324.
18. Jules Janin, "George Sand," in Alfred de Montferrand, *Biographie des femmes auteurs* (Paris, 1836), pp. 451–52. Janin refers to George Sand as "the great writer attracting the greatest public attention today. After only six years of writing [actually five], she is as high in the admiration of Europe as the most renowned . . . she who could have been celebrated for her beauty alone. . . . She might have been anything she wanted, had she not been stopped by an insurmountable wall of bronze: . . . She is a woman!" Minister, bishop, general, member of the French Academy, all is closed to George Sand, capable of them all, because—"She is a woman!"
19. Sand, *Correspondance*, III, pp. 743–44. Letter to Michel de Bourges, March 25, 1837.
20. Sand, *Oeuvres autobiographiques*, II, p. 326.
21. Ibid., p. 364.
22. Ibid., pp. 334, 337–38.
23. Frances Winwar, *The Life of the Heart* (New York, 1945), p. 199.
24. Félicité de Lamennais, Abbé, *De l'art et du beau* (Paris, undated), p. 149.
25. Heinrich Heine, "Lettres confidentielles," in *Revue et Gazette Municipale de Paris*, 1838, V, p. 42.
26. Sand, "Journal intime," *Oeuvres autobiographiques*, II, p. 959.
27. Sand, "Lettres d'un voyageur, VII," op. cit., II, p. 846. This "Lettre d'un voyageur" is addressed to Franz Liszt.

28. As quoted by Samuel Rocheblave "Une amitié romanesque, George Sand et Madame d'Agoult," *Revue de Paris*, Dec. 15, 1894, p. 819.

29. Sand, *Correspondance*, III, pp. 44–45.

30. Ibid., pp. 72–73.

Chapter 23 Trials and Interludes

1. George Sand, *Correspondance*, 11 vols. (Paris, 1964–76), III, p. 501.

2. Ibid., pp. 88–90 and 125. Accounts of the scene vary, but not significantly.

3. George Sand, *Oeuvres autobiographiques*, 2 vols. (Paris, 1970–71), II, p. 371.

4. Sand, *Correspondance*, III, p. 111.

5. Ibid., pp. 228–30.

6. Ibid., pp. 74–90. Letter to Michel de Bourges, Oct. 22, 1835.

7. Sand, *Oeuvres autobiographiques*, II, p. 376.

8. Sand, *Correspondance*, III, pp. 279–90.

9. Bibliothèque Lovenjoul, E 868 ff. 250–51. Cf. Sand, *Correspondance*, III, p. 343, footnote 2.

10. Sand, op. cit., III, p. 290. Letter to Marie d'Agoult, Feb. 26(?), 1836, on Hortense Allart's *La femme et la démocratie de nos temps*, which had just appeared: "There are true, powerful and beautiful things in it. But she is pedantic and doesn't please me a bit."

11. All extracts of Charles Didier's *Journal* (Diary) referring to George Sand are found in the Oct.–Dec. 1959 issue of *Revue des Sciences Humaines*, Lille.

12. Lovenjoul, E 948 f. 63.

13. Lovenjoul, E 948 ff. 40–42. Cf. Sand, op. cit., III, pp. 847–51. Original style largely retained.

14. Idem.

15. Edouard Maynial, "Le procès en séparation de George Sand," in *Mercure de France*, Dec. 1, 1906, p. 335.

16. George Lubin Collection. Cf. Sand, op. cit., III, p. 277, footnote 1.

17. Lubin Collection. Cf. Ibid., pp. 359–61.

18. Ibid., pp. 428–34.

19. See Note 11 above.

20. Sand, op. cit., III, pp. 477–79.

21. Sand, *Oeuvres autobiographiques*, II, p. 385.

22. *Le Droit*, Paris, July 30–31, 1836, p. 1.

23. See Note 15, above. *Mercure de France*, Dec. 1, 1906, p. 337.

24. Michel de Bourges, *Plaidoyers et discours* (Paris, 1909), pp. 135–49.

25. Sand, *Correspondance*, III, p. 501.

Chapter 24 Arrivals and Departures

1. George Sand, *Les sept cordes de la lyre. Lettres à Marcie . . .* (Paris, 1869), p. 230.

2. George Sand, *Correspondance*, 11 vols. (Paris, 1964–76), III, pp. 521 and 530 (also footnotes 2 and 3).

3. Wladimir Karénine, pseud. of Varvara Dmitrievna Komarova, *George Sand: sa vie et ses oeuvres*, 4 vols. (Paris, 1899–1926), II, pp. 329–30.

4. George Sand, "Lettres d'un voyageur, X," *Oeuvres autobiographiques*, 2 vols. (Paris, 1970–71), II, pp. 897–98. Addressed to Didier as "Herbert."

5. Adolphe Pictet, *Une course à Chamonix* (Paris, 1838).

6. Ibid., pp. 20 and 77. Quotations are from 1930 Geneva edition.

7. Ibid., p. 30.

8. Sand, op. cit., II, p. 914.

9. George Sand's rendering, *Le Contrebandier*, has been overpraised by Berlioz, one of her social companions, but she herself had no illusions. "You cannot translate one art by another," she said. It was one of Liszt's composing fallacies to believe he could.

10. Quoted by Samuel Rocheblave, "Une amitié romanesque," in *Revue de Paris*, Dec. 15, 1894, p. 800.

11. Sand, *Correspondance*, III, p. 45.

12. Marie d'Agoult, *Mémoires* (Paris, 1927), p. 90.

13. Sand, op. cit., III, pp. 561–67. "Is this the language of a 'frigid' woman?" asks Georges Lubin.

14. Charles Didier, "Journal," in *Revue des Sciences Humaines*, Lille, Oct.–Dec. 1959, p. 473.

15. Thérèse Marix-Spire, *Les romantiques et la musique. Le cas de George Sand, 1804–1838* (Paris, 1954), p. 526.

16. Didier, op. cit., XXX, pp. 473–74.

17. Sand, op. cit., IV, p. 81.

18. Marix-Spire, op. cit., pp. 508–09.

19. Sand, op. cit., III, p. 642.

20. Ibid., p. 644.

21. Ibid., p. 647.

22. Cf. Ellen Moers, *Literary Women* (New York, 1976), p. 101.

23. George Sand, *Mauprat* (Paris, 1969), pp. 33, 96, 105 and 172.

24. Quoted by Ellen Moers, op. cit.

25. Agoult, op. cit., pp. 89–90.

26. Sand, *Correspondance*, III, p. 699.

27. Ibid., p. 672.

28. Ibid., p. 713.

29. Franz Liszt-Marie d'Agoult, *Correspondance*, 2 vols. (Paris, 1933–34), I, p. 199.

30. George Sand, . . . *Lettres à Marcie* . . . , p. 230.

31. It is further deformed by Curtis Cate in his tendentious rendition, covering two pages. Not once, however, does Mr. Cate quote from the sixth *Lettre à Marcie*, whose feminism might upset his picture of George Sand as "a feminine reactionary, not to say an outright enemy of Women's Liberation. . . ." Curtis Cate, *George Sand* (Boston, 1975), pp. 417–19.

32. Sand, op. cit., pp. 194 and 201.

33. Sand, *Correspondance*, III, p. 716.

34. Marix-Spire, op. cit., p. 555.

35. Sand, op. cit., III, pp. 733–37.

36. Ibid., pp. 741–46 and 753.

37. Ibid., p. 765.

38. Jacques Vier, *La comtesse d'Agoult et son temps*, 6 vols. (Paris, 1955–63), I, p. 258.

39. In this spring of 1837, the first full biography of George Sand appeared. Moralizing and "deploring," it was penned by a Théobald Walsh, pious Catholic of Irish ancestry which had settled in France. For G.S., his criticisms were as inconsequential, she said, as "the autumn leaves falling in my garden," Sand op. cit., IV, p. 225.

40. Ibid., pp. 18–19.

41. Ibid., p. 32.

42. Ibid., p. 38.

43. *Revue Illustrée*, Paris, Jan. 15, 1891, p. 100. Cf. Sand, op. cit. IV, p. 85, footnote.

44. Sand, op. cit., IV, pp. 86–87.

45. Agoult, op. cit., pp. 75–76.

46. Sand op. cit., IV, p. 111.

47. Ibid., pp. 112–13.

48. George Sand, "Entretiens journaliers avec le très docte et très habile docteur Piffoël," *Oeuvres autobiographiques*, II, pp. 987–89.

Chapter 25 The Odds and Ends of Art and Life

1. George Sand, "Entretiens avec le docteur Piffoël," *Oeuvres autobiographiques*, 2 vols. (Paris, 1970–71), II, pp. 980–81.

2. Quoted by S. Rocheblave, "Une amitié romanesque," in *Revue de Paris*, Dec. 15, 1894, p. 819.

3. Thérèse Marix-Spire, "Bataille de dames, George Sand et Madame d'Agoult," in *Revue des Sciences Humaines*, Lille, Apr.–Sept. 1951, p. 229.

4. Sand, op. cit., II, p. 980.

5. Ibid., pp. 989–90.

6. Wladimir Karénine, pseud., *George Sand: sa vie et ses oeuvres*, 4 vols. (Paris, 1899–1926), II, p. 362.

7. Ibid., pp. 362–63.

8. Charles Didier, "Journal," in *Revue des Sciences Humaines*, Lille, Oct.–Dec. 1959, pp. 477–78.

9. Marie d'Agoult, *Mémoires* (Paris, 1927), p. 88.

10. Didier, op. cit., p. 479.

11. George Sand, *Correspondance*, 11 vols. (Paris, 1964–76), IV, pp. 153–55.

12. Agoult, op. cit., p. 97.

13. Ibid., pp. 82–83.

14. A book of our time makes a case for Maurice as having been the "great love" of George Sand's life. (Maurice Toesca, *Le plus grand amour de George Sand: Maurice Sand*, Paris, 1933). If one were, as its author, to center exclusively on the many times Maurice is referred to anxiously, lovingly, despairingly, proudly, preoccupyingly by his mother, it would be quite persuasive, but in the context of so much else, it would be at the least mis-

leading. On the other hand, in the course of pursuing what one considers the more important, determining dramatic moments, one can too easily forget that Maurice—*and* Solange—are often physically present at these moments or disturbingly alive in George Sand's mind. The maternal/paternal aspect of her character, affectively its most puissant, is always there to summon one, as it were, homing to her.

15. Sand, *Oeuvres autobiographiques*, II, pp. 398–401.

16. Sand, *Correspondance*, IV, p. 190.

17. Ibid., pp. 217–19.

18. Sand, "Dr. Piffoël," *Oeuvres autobiographiques*, II, pp. 1003–04.

19. Pierre Leroux, however, was recalled quite recently as the man who "clouded George Sand's common sense for half-a-dozen years"—*Times Literary Supplement*, London, Nov. 30, 1973. To this one must add that Leroux had greatly impressed John Stuart Mill.

20. Sand, *Correspondance*, IV, p. 590.

21. Pierre Leroux and George Sand, *Histoire d'une amitié (d'après une correspondance inédite 1836–1866)*. Edited by Jean-Pierre Lacassagne. (Paris, 1973), p. 29.

22. Ibid., pp. 99 and 101.

23. Sand, op. cit., IV, p. 251.

24. Ibid., p. 293. Letter to Marie d'Agoult, Dec. 26(?), 1837.

25. Ibid., pp. 238 and 340.

26. Ibid., pp. 334–35.

27. Ibid., pp. 364–65. Both the letters of Balzac and George Sand are quoted on these pages.

28. Honoré de Balzac, *Lettres à Madame Hanska*, 5 vols. (Paris 1967–70), I, pp. 584–89.

29. For Henry James, as gifted a writer, subtler in his understanding of women in the gathering consciousness of his own ambivalent sexuality and more generous concerning George Sand, Balzac "puts his finger again and again on the truth," solving the "riddle" of George Sand: "her distinction and her vulgarity." The distinction, for James, was in George Sand's writing, the vulgarity in her life, "that of a nature robust and not too fastidious" in the men—"greasy males"—taken, tasted and cast aside. How differently we would view her, says James, if we were to think of her, as Balzac, as a man. "As a man Madame Sand was admirable. . . . Above all she becomes in a manner comprehensible, as any frank Bohemian"—that is, any man, especially of "genius," but never a woman, unless riddled by "the marks of a man," as George Sand—"is comprehensible." Clearly for James, as for Balzac, not to speak of more ordinary, conventional men, a woman who takes men as men have taken women for millennia is not wholly a woman, for that "active" element in her (the phrase is James') must be called male, and in any case the "frank Bohemian" can scarcely be considered female and most certainly not a lady. However, from "such mixed elements," Henry James concluded with a handsome salute to the "monumental" George Sand, emerged her prodigious "affirmation of an unprecedented intensity of life." Henry James, *Notes on Novelists* (New York, 1914), pp. 210–13.

One would wish that Henry James had taken George Sand as the subject matter of one of his own insightful novels, calling it, if not the portrait of a lady, the complexity of the woman as hero. Without the "active" element he characterized as male, where then would be the heroic "affirmation" he saluted? His own Isabel Archer, very much the *lady*, is not the passive Clarissa of Richardson or even the Gwendolen Harleth of George Eliot, disallowed her creator's own affirmation of what she termed "the larger life." Miss Archer, too, within the limits of Henry James and his time, was the woman as hero. Cf. Carolyn G. Heilbrun, *Toward a Recognition of Androgyny* (New York, 1973), p. 90ff.

30. Karénine, op. cit., II, p. 370.
31. Balzac, *Béatrix*, Maurice Regard edition (Paris, 1962), p. 69.
32. Ibid., pp. 79, 80, 73, 98 and 74 respectively.

Chapter 26 Frédéric Chopin—
Fragile Genius

1. Casimir Wierzynski, *The Life and Death of Chopin* (New York, 1949), p. ix. From Artur Rubinstein's introduction.
2. Frédéric Chopin, *Correspondance*, B. E. Sydow edition, 3 vols. (Paris, 1953–54), II, p. 208.
3. George Sand, "Dr. Piffoël," *Oeuvres autobiographiques*, 2 vols. (Paris, 1970–71), II, p. 999.
4. Chopin, op. cit., I, p. 282.
5. Ibid., pp. 81, 134, 139, 178 and 184.
6. Camille Bourniquel, *Chopin* (Paris, 1970), pp. 71 and 86.
7. Bernard Gavotty, *Frédéric Chopin* (Paris, 1974), p. 246.
8. George Sand, *Correspondance*, 11 vols. (Paris, 1964–76), IV, p. 395.

Chapter 27 The Dominant Note of George Sand

1. Henry James, *Notes on Novelists* (New York, 1914), p. 220.
2. Ibid., p. 224.
3. "*On vous adore*" has been too boldly translated as "I adore you!" Cf. André Maurois, *Lélia* (New York, 1953), p. 262.
4. George Sand, *Correspondance*, 11 vols. (Paris, 1964–76), IV, p. 408.
5. Ibid., p. 429.
6. Ibid., pp. 428–39.
7. Ibid., p. 445.
8. Frédéric Chopic, *Correspondance*, B. E. Sydow edition, 3 vols. (Paris, 1953–54), II, p. 254.
9. Idem.
10. George Sand, *Les sept cordes de la lyre* (Paris, 1973), p. 105 and passim. Originally published in *La Revue des Deux Mondes*, 1839.
11. Ibid., p. 52.
12. Sand, *Correspondance*, IV, pp. 482–83.
13. Ibid., pp. 486–87.
14. Jacques Vier, *La comtesse d'Agoult et son temps*, 6 vols. (Paris, 1955–63), I, p. 308.

Chapter 28 *That Winter in Majorca*

1. George Sand, *Correspondance*, 11 vols. (Paris, 1964–76), IV, p. 512.
2. George Sand, "Un hiver à Majorque," *Oeuvres autobiographiques*, 2 vols. (Paris, 1970–71), II, pp. 1055 and 1129.
3. Frédéric Chopin, *Correspondance*, B. E. Sydow edition, 3 vols. (Paris, 1953–54), II, pp. 265–66.
4. Sand, *Correspondance*, IV, p. 532.
5. Ibid., p. 522.
6. Sand, "Un hiver à Majorque," op. cit., II, p. 1067.
7. Chopin, op. cit., II, pp. 274–75.
8. Sand, op. cit., II, p. 1119.
9. Ibid., p. 1125.
10. Chopin, op. cit., II, pp. 282–83 and 285.
11. Henry James, *Notes on Novelists* (New York, 1914), pp. 222 and 225.
12. Sand, op. cit., II, p. 1149.
13. Sand, *Correspondance*, IV, p. 569.
14. Sand, "Histoire le ma vie," op. cit., II, pp. 420–21.
15. Ibid., p. 423.
16. Sand, *Correspondance*, IV, pp. 577–78.
17. Chopin, op. cit., II, p. 310.
18. Sand, op. cit., IV, p. 590.
19. George Sand, *Spiridion*, following *Un hiver à Majorque* (Paris, 1881), pp. 445–46.
20. Sand, *Correspondance*, IV, p. 607.
21. Ibid., p. 599.
22. Chopin, op. cit., II, p. 325.
23. Cf. Frances Winwar, *The Life of the Heart: George Sand and Her Times* (New York, 1945), p. 239.
24. George Sand, *Gabriel* (Paris, 1840), p. 20 and passim.
25. Ibid., p. 303.
26. Cf. Winwar, op. cit., p. 240.
27. Alfred de Musset, *Histoire d'un merle blanc* (Paris, 1881), pp. 86–87. Originally published in 1842.
28. Chopin, op. cit., II, p. 261, footnote.
29. Sand, *Correspondance*, IV, p. 654.
30. Ibid., p. 655.

Chapter 29 *Beyond Sexuality*

1. Henry James, *French Poets and Novelists* (New York, 1964), p. 166.
2. Cf. Robert Craft, "Chopin's Progress," *The New York Review of Books*, Oct. 18, 1873.
3. Maximilien Rubel, *Karl Marx: essai de biographie intellectuelle* (Paris, 1957), p. 93.
4. Elizabeth Barrett Browning, *Poems*, 2 vols. (London, 1850), I, pp. 346–47.

5. George Sand, *Correspondance*, 11 vols. (Paris, 1964–76), IV, p. 663.

6. Frédéric Chopin, *Correspondance*, B. E. Sydow edition, 3 vols. (Paris, 1953–54), II, pp. 345, 348–49.

7. Craft, op. cit. No admirer of George Sand, Robert Craft also gallantly adds that "the composer probably would not have lived so long as he did without her solicitude." He is joined in both sentiments by Bernard Gavotty, one of Chopin's latest biographers and Sand's non-admirers.

8. Bernard Gavotty, *Frédéric Chopin* (Paris, 1974), p. 296.

9. Honoré de Balzac, *Lettres à Madame Hanska*, 5 vols. (Paris, 1967–70), II, p. 8.

10. Sand, op. cit., V, p. 60.

11. Ibid. pp. 95–96.

12. Ibid., pp. 103–05.

13. Ibid., p. 227.

14. Ibid., p. 283.

15. Ibid., p. 406, footnote 2.

16. Pierre Leroux and George Sand, *Histoire d'une amitié (d'après une correspondance inédite 1836–1866)*. Edited by Jean-Pierre Lacassagne (Paris, 1973), pp. 127–28.

17. Charles-Augustin Sainte-Beuve, *Correspondance générale*, 15 vols. (Paris, 1935–64,) IV, p. 180.

18. As quoted in Frances Winwar, *The Life of the Heart* (New York, 1945), p. 283.

19. Sand, op. cit., V, pp. 537–42.

20. George Lichtheim, as quoted by William Pfaff, *Condemned to Freedom* (New York, 1971), p. 93.

21. Wladimir Karénine, pseud., *George Sand: sa vie et ses oeuvres*, 4 vols. (Paris, 1899–1926), III, p. 129.

22. George Sand, "Dr. Piffoël," *Oeuvres autobiographiques*, 2 vols. (Paris, 1970–71), II, p. 1018.

23. Karénine, op. cit., III, p. 189.

24. Leroux-Sand, op. cit., p. 152.

25. Sand, *Correspondance*, VI, p. 179.

26. Michael Meyer, *Ibsen, a Biography* (New York, 1971), p. 464.

27. George Sand, *Consuelo. La Comtesse de Rudolstadt*, 3 vols. (Paris, 1959), III, p. 547 and passim.

28. Esther Shephard, *Walt Whitman's Pose* (New York, 1938), p. 17 and passim.

Chapter 30 *George and Solange and Chopin*

1. George Sand, *Correspondance*, 11 vols. (Paris, 1964–76), V, p. 683.

2. Frédéric Chopin, *Correspondance*, B. E. Sydow edition, 3 vols. (Paris, 1953–54), III, p. 112.

3. George Sand, *Oeuvres autobiographiques*, 2 vols. (Paris, 1970–71), II, p. 436.

4. Chopin, op. cit., III, p. 113.

5. George Sand *Impressions et souvenirs* (Paris, 1896), p. 81.

6. Ibid., pp. 72–90.

7. Sand, *Oeuvres autobiographiques*, II, pp. 442–43.
8. Sand, *Correspondance*, VI, p. 286.
9. Ibid., pp. 253–54.
10. George Sand, *Lucrezia Floriani* (Paris, 1853). Originally published in 1847. The "splendid" is Henry James'. The quotations which follow are from the 1853 edition.
11. Sand, *Correspondance*, VI, p. 158, footnote.
12. Ibid., p. 887.
13. Ibid., p. 755. See Lubin's note.
14. Ibid., p. 376.
15. Sand, *Correspondance*, VIII, p. 47. Letter to Emmanuel Arago, July 18–26, 1847. The longest letter preserved—71 mss. pages.
16. Chopin, op. cit., III, p. 152.
17. Ibid., p. 245.
18. Cf. Letter to Emmanuel Arago (Note 15, above).
19. Sand, *Correspondance*, VII, pp. 379 and 381.
20. Ibid., p. 430.
21. Matthew Arnold, "George Sand," in *The Fortnightly Review*, June 1, 1877, pp. 767–81.
22. Caroline Jaubert, *Souvenirs, lettres et correspondance* (Paris, 1881), pp. 43–44.
23. Sand, op. cit., VII, p. 575.
24. Chopin, op. cit., III, p. 245.
25. Sand *Oeuvres autobiographiques*, II, p. 448.
26. Margaret Fuller, *Memoirs*, 2 vols. (Boston, 1852), II, pp. 193–99.
27. Sand, *Correspondance*, VII, p. 686.
28. Ibid., p. 660–61.
29. Ibid., p. 689.
30. Ibid., pp. 700–02.
31. Sand, *Correspondance*, VIII, p. 43.
32. Ibid., p. 12.
33. Ibid., pp. 18–49.

Chapter 31 *Muse of the Revolution*

1. Karl Marx, *Misère de la philosophie* (Paris, 1972), p. 178.
2. George Sand, *Correspondance*, 11 vols. (Paris, 1964–76), VIII, pp. 123–24.
3. Joseph Barry, "1848 Again?" in *Horizon*, New York, Spring 1969. Reference source for quotations, unless otherwise indicated.
4. Sand, op. cit., VIII, p. 281.
5. Jacques Droz, *Europe Between Revolutions* (London, 1967), pp. 65–66.
6. Geoffrey Bruun, *Revolution and Reaction* (Princeton, 1958), p. 108.
7. Sand, op. cit., VIII, pp. 232–33.
8. Ibid., p. 299.
9. Ibid., p. 308.
10. Henry James, *Notes on Novelists* (New York, 1914), p. 169.
11. Sand, op. cit., VIII, p. 3.

12. Ibid., p. 319.
13. Frédéric Chopin, *Correspondance*, B. E. Sydow edition, 3 vols. (Paris, 1953–54), III, pp. 331–32.
14. George Sand, *Oeuvres autobiographiques*, 2 vols. (Paris, 1970–71), II, p. 448.
15. Sand, *Correspondance*, VIII, p. 332.
16. *Bulletins de la République émanés du Ministre de l'Intérieur du 13 Mars au 6 Mai 1848. Collection complète.* (Paris, 1848), pp. 23–24.
17. Sand, op. cit., VIII, p. 359.
18. *Bulletins de la République . . . ,* p. 45.
19. Ibid., p. 55.
20. Sand, op. cit., VIII, p. 392.
21. Ibid., pp. 401–07.
22. *La Cause du peuple*, No. 3, Paris, Apr. 23, 1848.
23. *Bulletins de la République . . . ,* p. 68.
24. Sand, op. cit., VIII, pp. 411–20.
25. Ibid., pp. 430–31.
26. Ibid., p. 432.
27. Barry, loc. cit.
28. Sand, *Oeuvres autobiographiques*, II, p. 1187.
29. Alexis de Tocqueville, *Recollections* (New York, 1970), p. 95.
30. Sand, *Correspondance*, VIII, p. 434.
31. Ibid., p. 435.
32. Prosper Mérimée, *Correspondance générale*, 12 vols. (Paris, 1941–58), V, pp. 303–04.
33. Tocqueville, op. cit., pp. 133–35.
34. Barry, loc. cit.
35. Sand, op. cit., VIII, p. 467.
36. Cf. Pierre Salomon, *George Sand* (Paris, 1953), p. 79.
37. Sand, op. cit., VIII, p. 486.
38. Ibid., p. 498.

Chapter 32 Aftermath

1. Cf. Wladimir Karénine, pseud., *George Sand: sa vie et ses oeuvres*, 4 vols. (Paris, 1899–1926), IV, p. 24.
2. George Sand, *Correspondance*, 11 vols. (Paris, 1964–76), VIII, p. 482.
3. Ibid., p. 478.
4. Ibid., p. 495.
5. Ibid., p. 506.
6. Sand, op. cit., VI, pp. 711 and 720.
7. Joseph Barry, "1848 Again?" in *Horizon*, New York, Spring 1969.
8. Alexis de Tocqueville, *Recollections* (New York, 1970), pp. 136–37.
9. Ibid., p. 162.
10. Sand, op. cit., VIII, pp. 544–45.
11. Ibid., p. 538.
12. Joseph Brault, *Une contemporaine: biographie et intrigues de George Sand* (Paris, 1848), p. 8.

13. Frédéric Chopin, *Correspondance*, B. E. Sydow edition, 3 vols. (Paris, 1953–54), III, p. 377.
14. George Sand, *Le petite Fadette* (Paris, 1967), pp. 33 and 38.
15. Sand, *Correspondance*, VIII, p. 550.
16. Ibid., p. 579.
17. Ibid., p. 594.
18. Ibid., p. 637.
19. Ibid., p. 647.
20. Ibid., pp. 707–08.
21. Ibid., pp. 710–11.
22. Ibid., pp. 717–18.
23. André Maurois, *Lélia, ou la vie de George Sand* (Paris, 1952), p. 395.
24. Sand, op. cit., IX, p. 218, footnote.
25. Ibid., p. 220.
26. Ibid., p. 320.
27. Ibid., p. 343.

Chapter 33 Come, Twilight

1. Henry James, *Notes on Novelists* (New York, 1914), p. 181.
2. George Sand, *Oeuvres autobiographiques*, 2 vols. (Paris, 1970–71), I, pp. 1204–05. George Lubin's addendum to *Histoire de ma vie*.
3. George Sand, *Correspondance*, 11 vols. (Paris, 1964–76), IX, p. 488.
4. Ibid., p. 389.
5. Ibid., p. 450.
6. Ibid., p. 500.
7. Ibid., p. 419.
8. Ibid., p. 484.
9. Ibid., pp. 541–45.
10. Ibid., pp. 608–09.
11. Ibid., pp. 708–11.
12. Ibid., pp. 725–26.
13. Ibid., pp. 876–77.
14. Ibid., p. 305.
15. Sand, op. cit., X, pp. 15–17.
16. Ibid., p. 66.
17. Ibid., p. 97.
18. Ibid., p. 36.
19. Wladimir Karénine, pseud., *George Sand: sa vie et ses oeuvres*, 4 vols. (Paris, 1899–1926), III, pp. 627–29.
20. George Sand, "Journal de Novembre-Décembre 1851" in *Oeuvres autobiographiques*, II, pp. 1195–1222. Scenes and quotes for this period derive from this source unless otherwise indicated.
21. Cf. Albert Guérard, *France, a Short History* (London, 1947), p. 193.
22. As quoted in Karl Marx, "The Eighteenth Brumaire of Louis Bonaparte" in Karl Marx and Frederick Engels, *Selected Works* (New York, 1968), p. 158. Originally published in 1852.
23. Sand, op. cit., X, pp. 659–64.

24. Ibid., pp. 672–74.
25. Ibid., p. 682.
26. Idem.
27. Ibid., pp. 687–89.
28. As quoted in Karénine, op. cit., IV, pp. 222 and 233.
29. Elizabeth Barrett Browning, *Letters*, 2 vols. (London, 1897), II, pp. 55–57 and 62–64.

Chapter 34 Last Passions

1. Cf. André Maurois, *Lélia, ou la vie de George Sand* (Paris, 1952), p. 424. The empathy for the last years is unsurpassable.
2. Wladimir Karénine, pseud., *George Sand: sa vie et ses oeuvres*, 4 vols. (Paris, 1899–1926), III, p. 610.
3. Ibid., pp. 611–16.
4. Bibliothèque Nationale, Paris. N.a.f. 24813. Unpublished manuscript.
5. Samuel Rocheblave, *George Sand et sa fille* (Paris, 1905), pp. 175–76.
6. George Sand, *Correspondance, 1812–1876*, edited by Maurice Sand, 6 vols. (Paris, 1882–92), III, p. 362. George Sand's son was not the ideal editor of his mother's correspondence. Deletions, omissions and wrong dates are all too frequent.
7. See Note 4, above.
8. Eugène Delacroix, *Journal*, 3 vols. (Paris, 1893–95), II, pp. 283–84.
9. Sand, op. cit., III, p. 372.
10. Sand, op. cit., IV, p. 2.
11. Ibid., pp. 47–51.
12. Ibid., pp. 97–99.
13. As quoted in Albert Guérard, *France* (London, 1947), p. 196.
14. George Sand, *La Daniella*, 2 vols. (Paris, 1887), I, p. 61. Originally published in 1857.
15. George Sand *Promenades autour d'un village* (Paris, 1866), p. 102.
16. As quoted in Georges and Christiane Smeets-Sand, *George Sand à Gargilesse* (Paris, n.d.), p. 9.
17. Cf. Karénine, op. cit., IV, p. 384.
18. Bibliothèque Nationale, Paris. N.a.f. 24819.
19. See Note 5, Chap. 20, p. 669a.
20. Charles Spoelberch de Lovenjoul, vicomte de, *La vraie histoire de "Elle et lui"* (Paris, 1897), p. 225.
21. George Sand, *Pourquoi les femmes à l'Académie?* (Paris, 1863), p. 16.
22. Bibliothèque Nationale, Paris. N.a.f. 24812.
23. Sand, op. cit., IV, p. 297; and Bibliothèque Nationale, N.a.f. 24823. R 4 P 698 5-19-76
24. Sand, op. cit., IV, p. 322.
25. Ibid., pp. 295–96.
26. Ibid., pp. 314–15.
27. George Sand, *Mademoiselle La Quintinie* (Paris, 1863), p. 48.
28. Ibid., p. viii.

29. Bibliothèque Nationale, Paris, N.a.f. 24826; and Sand, *Correspondance*, Maurice Sand edition, IV, pp. 16–18.

30. Charles-Augustin Sainte-Beuve, *Nouveaux lundis*, 13 vols. (Paris, 1863–70), V, pp. 4041.

31. Charles Baudelaire, "Mon coeur mis à nu" in *Oeuvres complètes* (Paris, 1968), p. 633. Baudelaire's qualified praise of George Sand appears in his essay "Edgar Allan Poe, sa vie et ses ouvrages," *Revue de Paris*, Mar.–Apr. 1852: "Another particular characteristic of his [Poe's] writing is that it is completely anti-feminine. Let me explain. Women write and write with an overflowing rapidity; their heart babbles by the ream. Generally they have no understanding of art, of measure, or of logic, their style drags and billows like their dress. A very great and justly famous writer, George Sand herself, despite her superiority, has not quite escaped that law of the [feminine] temperament; she posts her masterpieces as if they were letters. Is it not said that she writes her books on letter paper?

"In the work of Edgar Poe, the style is tight, *concatenated* . . ." Baudelaire could not be aware of the dense, concatenated verse of Emily Dickinson, another example of the "feminine temperament."

Chapter 35 Son Versus Lover "Let Us Go, My Friend"

1. George Sand, *Oeuvres autobiographiques*, 2 vols. (Paris, 1970–71), I, p. 55.

2. George Sand, *Correspondance*, edited by Maurice Sand, 6 vols. (Paris, 1882–92), V, p. 148.

3. Ibid., IV, p. 214.

4. Ibid., pp. 324–25.

5. Wladimir Karénine, pseud., *George Sand: sa vie et ses oeuvres*, 4 vols. (Paris, 1899–1926), IV, p. 413.

6. George Sand-Gustave Flaubert, *Correspondance* (Paris, 1904), p. 93.

7. Letter to Alexandre Dumas *fils*, as quoted in Karénine, op. cit., IV, p. 408.

8. Edmond Plauchut, *Autour de Nohant* (Paris, 1897), pp. 71–73.

9. Edmond and Jules de Goncourt, *Journal*, 9 vols. (Paris, 1887–1896), II, pp. 144–46.

10. Bibliothèque Nationale, Paris. N.a.f. 24825. Manuscript agenda-diary for 1863. All subsequent quotations for 1863 are from this source.

11. Karénine, op. cit., IV, p. 463.

12. Sand, *Correspondance*, Maurice Sand edition, V, p. 26.

13. Bibliothèque Nationale. N.a.f. 24826. Mss. agenda book for 1864. Subsequent quotations for 1864 are from this source.

14. Karénine, op. cit., IV, pp. 475–76.

15. Letter to Maurice Sand, as quoted in Karénine, ibid., p. 478.

16. Louise Vincent, *George Sand et le Berry*, 2 vols. (Paris, 1919), I, pp. 622–23. Scene and quotations derive from Madame Vincent's research at Guillery.

17. Sand, op. cit., V, p. 50.

18. Ibid., p. 77.

19. Bibliothèque Nationale. N.a.f. 24827. Mss. agenda book for 1865. Subsequent quotations for 1865 are from this source.

20. Letter to Maurice Sand, Aug. 22, 1865, as quoted in Karénine, op. cit., IV, pp. 495–97.

21. Karénine, op. cit., IV, p. 497.

Chapter 36 Conversations with Flaubert at Midnight

1. Bibliothèque Nationale, Paris. N.a.f. 24827. Mss. agenda book for 1865. Subsequent quotations for 1865 are from this source.

2. Cf. George Sand-Gustave Flaubert, *Correspondance* (Paris, 1904), p. 340. "I forget so well," Sand would write Flaubert, Nov. 22, 1872.

3. Bibliothèque Historique de la Ville de Paris. N.a. 13. Unpublished letter.

4. Ibid., N.a. 15.

5. Ibid., N.a. 17. Unpublished letter.

6. Cf. Gustave Flaubert, *Oeuvres. Correspondance*, 16 vols. (Paris, 1960–65), XII, pp. 117–18.

7. Edmond and Jules de Goncourt, *Journal*, 9 vols. (Paris, 1887–96), I, p. 307.

8. Benjamin F. Bart, *Flaubert* (Syracuse, N.Y., 1967), p. 151.

9. Goncourts, op. cit., II, p. 122.

10. Ernest Renan, *Feuilles détachées* (Paris, 1892), p. 289.

11. Bibliothèque Nationale. N.a.f. 24828. Mss. agenda book for 1866. All quotations for 1866 are from this manuscript source.

12. Goncourts, op. cit., III, p. 21.

13. See Note 11, above. Much of this sequence was published, with some inaccuracies, in Maurois' *Lélia*, p. 481.

14. Flaubert, op. cit., XII, pp. 122 and 125.

15. George Sand, *Correspondance*, edited by Maurice Sand, 6 vols. (Paris, 1882–92), V, pp. 135–36.

16. Flaubert, op. cit., XII, p. 129.

17. Sand, op. cit., V, p. 145.

18. Flaubert, op. cit., XII, p. 340; cf. Bart, op. cit., p. 226: "Women, Zola once said, sensed that he was a feminine type, more like them than like a man."

19. Sand, op. cit., V, p. 229.

20. Flaubert, op. cit., XII, p. 142.

21. Sand, op. cit., V, p. 131. Date should be Nov. 12, not Aug. 12, 1866.

22. Ibid., p. 147.

23. As quoted in Casimir Carrère, *George Sand amoureuse* (Paris, 1967), p. 425. Letter dated by Georges Lubin.

24. Sand, op. cit., V, pp. 99–101. Maurice Sand's dating is inaccurate. Georges Lubin, in a private communication, dates the letter to Flaubert, Nov. 22, 1866.

25. Flaubert, op. cit., XII, p. 151.

26. Sand, op. cit., V, pp. 155–56.

27. Ibid., pp. 154–55.

28. Flaubert, op. cit., XII, pp. 150–51.

29. Sand, op. cit., V, pp. 156–57.
30. Flaubert, op. cit., XII, p. 162.
31. Sand, op. cit., IV, p. 338. Correct date: second week of Dec. 1866; Flaubert, op. cit., XII, p. 165.
32. Flaubert, op. cit., XII, p. 235.
33. Ibid., p. 178.
34. Sand, op. cit., V, p. 164.
35. Flaubert, op. cit., XII, p. 254; Sand, op. cit., V, pp. 180–81.
36. Cf. Jean-Paul Sartre, *L'idiot de la famille: Gustave Flaubert de 1821 à 1857*, 3 vols. (Paris, 1971–72).
37. Gustave Flaubert, *Correspondance*, Conard edition, 9 vols. (1926–1933), III, p. 107.
38. Gustave Flaubert, *Oeuvres. Correspondance*, 16 vols. (Paris, 1960–65), XII, p. 271.
39. Sand, op. cit., V, pp. 256–57.
40. Ibid., pp. 167 and 170.
41. Juliette Adam, *Mes premières armes littéraires et politiques* (Paris, 1904), pp. 67–68.
42. Ibid., pp. 80–82.
43. Ibid., p. 81.
44. Juliette La Massine (Adam), *Idées anti-Proudhoniennes sur l'amour, la femme et le mariage* (Paris, 1858), pp. 55–56 and 92.
45. Juliette Adam, *Mes premières armes . . . .*, p. 83.
46. Ibid., pp. 98 and 84.
47. Ibid., pp. 86–87, 202–03.
48. Juliette Adam, *Mes sentiments et nos idées avant 1870* (Paris, 1905), pp. 136–37 and p. 143.
49. Ibid., pp. 144–45.
50. Ibid., pp. 162–65.
51. Ibid., pp. 169–70.
52. Ibid., p. 220.
53. George Sand, *Journal intime (posthume)* (Paris, 1926), pp. 229–30.
54. Bibliothèque Nationale. N.a.f. 24829. Mss. agenda book for 1867. All quotations for 1867 derive from this source.
55. Adam, op. cit., pp. 194 and 185.
56. Ibid., pp. 265–69.
57. Ibid., p. 269.
58. Dr. Pestel, "Notes," quoted in Wladimir Karénine, pseud., *George Sand: sa vie et ses oeuvres*, 4 vols. (Paris, 1899–1926), IV, p. 529.
59. Flaubert, op. cit., XII, p. 292.
60. Sand, *Correspondance*, Maurice Sand edition, V, to Harrisse, Apr. 9, 1868; to Flaubert, July 31, 1868, p. 272.
61. Bibliothèque Nationale. N.a.f. 24830. Mss. ledger for 1868.
62. Sand, op. cit., V, pp. 276 and 282.
63. Flaubert, op. cit., XII, p. 344.
64. Sand, op. cit., V, p. 267.
65. Ibid., pp. 299–300.
66. Ibid., p. 310.
67. Ibid., p. 323.

68. Adam, op. cit., p. 416.
69. Idem.
70. Sand, op. cit., V, p. 353.
71. Flaubert, op. cit., XII, p. 521.

Chapter 37 War, Peace and the Commune

1. George Sand, *Correspondance*, edited by Maurice Sand, 6 vols. (Paris, 1882–92), V, pp. 365 and 368–69.
2. Ibid., p. 371.
3. Bibliothèque Nationale, Paris. N.a.f. 24832. Mss. ledger-diary for 1870, from which all quotations for that year are taken.
4. Sand, op. cit., VI, p. 3.
5. Gustave Flaubert, *Oeuvres. Correspondance*, 16 vols. (Paris, 1960–65), XII, p. 529.
6. Cf. Pierre Salomon, *George Sand* (Paris, 1953), p. 143.
7. Sand, op. cit., VI, p. 4.
8. Flaubert, *op. cit.*, XII, p. 533.
9. Sand, op. cit., VI, pp. 13 and 15.
10. Ibid., p. 23.
11. See Note 3, above.
12. Sand, op. cit., VI, p. 30.
13. George Sand, *Journal d'un voyageur pendant la guerre* (Paris, 1871), pp. 101 and 15–52.
14. Ibid., pp. 156–209.
15. Bibliothèque Nationale. N.a.f. 24833. Mss. agenda book for 1871, from which the year's quotations are taken.
16. Cf. Alistair Horne, *The Fall of Paris: the Siege and the Commune 1870–71* (New York, 1965), pp. 239–40.
17. Sand, *Correspondance*, VI, p. 69.
18. Ibid., p. 80.
19. Cf. Joseph Barry, "Paris Commune: from a Dream to Bloody Nightmare in Ten Weeks," *Smithsonian*, Washington, D.C., March 1971.
20. See Note 19, above.
21. Sand, op. cit., VI, pp. 104–05
22. Ibid., p. 110.
23. April numbers of *Le Gaulois*, Versailles.
24. Sand, op. cit., VI, p. 135.
25. Ibid., p. 142.
26. George Sand, "Réponse à un ami," *Impressions et souvenirs* (Paris, 1896), pp. 53–66.
27. Flaubert, op. cit., XIV, pp. 130 and 147.
28. Sand, op. cit., VI, pp. 172–73. The violence, one might repeat, did not originate from the Paris Commune.

Chapter 38 The Last Chapter: "Let Green Things . . ."

1. Henri-Frédéric Amiel, *Journal*, Sept. 21, 1874.
2. George Sand, *Correspondance*, edited by Maurice Sand, 6 vols. (Paris, 1882–92), VI, p. 215.

3. Ibid., p. 50.
4. As quoted in Wladimir Karénine, pseud., *George Sand: sa vie et ses oeuvres*, 4 vols. (Paris, 1849–1926), IV, pp. 259–60.
5. Bibliothèque Nationale, Paris. N.a.f. 24834. Mss. agenda book for 1872, from which the year's quotations have been taken.
6. Sand, op. cit., VI, p. 258.
7. Bibliothèque Nationale. N.a.f. 24835. Mss. agenda book for 1873, from which the year's quotations have been taken.
8. Gustave Flaubert, *Oeuvres. Correspondance*, 16 vols. (Paris, 1960–65), XV, p. 191.
9. Gustave Flaubert, *Correspondance*, Conard edition, 9 vols. (1926–33), I, p. 200.
10. Sand, op. cit., VI, p. 251.
11. Gustave Flaubert, *Oeuvres. Correspondance*, XV, pp. 240–41.
12. Sand, op. cit., VI, pp. 315–17.
13. Ibid., pp. 327–28, 379–80; Flaubert, op. cit., XV, pp. 319, 421.
14. Sand, op. cit., VI, p. 369.
15. Ibid., pp. 325–26.
16. Ibid., p. 329.
17. Frances Winwar, *The Life of the Heart* (New York, 1945), p. 294.
18. Flaubert, op. cit., XV, p. 145.
19. Sand, op. cit., VI, p. 398.
20. Karénine, op. cit., IV, p. 598.
21. Ibid., p. 599.
22. Bibliothèque Nationale. N.a.f. 24838. Mss. ledger-diary for 1876.
23. Karénine, op. cit., IV, p. 603 and passim.
24. Henry Harrisse, as quoted by Karénine, op. cit., IV, p. 611.
25. Ibid., p. 611 and passim.
26. Alexandre Dumas *fils*, as quoted by Karénine, op. cit., IV, p. 626.
27. Victor Hugo, *Depuis l'exil*, 2 vols. (Paris, 1884), I, pp. 385–86.
28. Flaubert, op. cit., XV, pp. 181–82.
29. Ibid., p. 174.
30. Henry James, *Notes on Novelists* (New York, 1914), pp. 220 and 222.

Index